FOUNDERS AND PATRIOTS OF AMERICA INDEX

Founders And Patriots

Of America

Index

National Society
of
Daughters of Founders and Patriots
of America
Park Lane Bldg., #615
2025 Eye St., N.W.
Washington, D.C. 20006

MRS. HERMAN E. WESTON
National President

REFERENCE

GENEALOGICAL PUBLISHING CO., INC.

Dedication

"The heritage of the past is the seed that brings forth the harvest of the future." This inscription by sculptor James Earle Fraser appears on the exterior of the National Archives on Constitution Avenue, Washington, D.C.

For more than three quarters of a century the National Society of Daughters of Founders and Patriots of America has made a valuable contribution toward preserving this priceless heritage. The objects of this Society are, in part, to teach reverent regard for the names, history, character, deeds and heroism of the founders of this country and of their descendants, to inculcate patriotism in the present and succeeding generations, and to discover and preserve family records and history, otherwise unwritten and unknown, of the first Colonists, their ancestors and descendants.

In the furtherance of these objectives, this index of 9,275 names of founders and patriots has been prepared. It is dedicated to those generations of members who have devoted their time, work and gifts of money to teaching and perpetuating the ideals embodied in our priceless heritage, and to those generations of future members who will continue the work for which this Society was founded.

Frances M. Weston

Mrs. Herman E. Weston
National President

National Officers
1973-1976

President
Mrs. Herman E. Weston
P.O. Box 216, Saxtons River, Vt. 05154

Vice President
Mrs. Harry H. Lane
871 N. Longfellow St., Arlington, Va. 22205

Chaplain
Mrs. H. David Hickey
174 N. Crest Rd., Chattanooga, Tenn. 37404

Recording Secretary
Miss Elizabeth B. Storer
4 Fair Oaks Park, Needham, Mass. 02192

Corresponding Secretary
Mrs. John G. W. Melbin
816 Fifth Ave., San Bruno, Calif. 94066

Organizing Secretary
Mrs. Lynmar Brock
"Hunter's Hill," Valley Rd., Newtown Square, Pa. 19073

Registrar
Miss Margaret McKay
310 Second Ave., Frankfort, N.Y. 13340

Treasurer
Miss Helen J. Malmstead
77 Princeton Ave., Providence, R.I. 02907

Historian
Mrs. Noah W. Wilkins
425 Milledge Circle, Athens, Ga. 30601

Color Bearer
Mrs. Henry B. Wallace
1915 Ashworth Rd., West Des Moines, Iowa 50265

Editorial Committee

Chairman

MRS. HARRY H. LANE
National Vice President

MISS MARGARET McKAY
National Registrar

MRS. FREDERICK N. TOMPKINS
National Assistant Treasurer

MRS. HENRY B. WALLACE
National Color Bearer

MRS. JAMES K. SEARCY
National Genealogist

*   *   *   *   *

Chapters Of The National Society That Participated In The Preparation Of This Index

Connecticut
District of Columbia
Florida
Hawaii
Illinois
Indiana
Iowa
Kansas
Minnesota
Mississippi
Missouri

New Hampshire
New Jersey
New York
North Carolina
Pennsylvania
Rhode Island
Tennessee
Texas
Vermont
Virginia
Washington

Wisconsin

Preface

The Founders and Patriots of America Index is a compilation of Founders and Patriots listed in the thirty-four volumes of lineages of the members of the National Society of Daughters of Founders and Patriots of America. The publication of the lineages was begun in 1909, and has continued to the present time.

In each lineage is a Founder who arrived in one of the Colonies between May 13, 1607, and May 13, 1687, and a Patriot ancestor who gave military, civil service, or other aid in establishing American Independence in the period of 1775 to 1784.

This Index gives the date of birth and death of each Founder and Patriot, his date of marriage and the name of his wife, except in a few instances where this data is unavailable. It also gives the name of the State in which the area is located where the Founder settled. References are given to all lineages, except a few that were later corrected or have been found to be questionable. In those instances where dates of birth and death have varied in the lineages, sometimes because one is the actual birth date and the other is the baptismal date, the generally accepted date has been used.

In some of the early lineages the proof was not retained by the National Society. Unless these lineages were proved by subsequent applicants using the same line, substantiating information to prove satisfactorily the line and service will be required from future applicants.

The Founder and Patriot of a given lineage may be determined by comparing the volume and page. Only a few Patriots changed their names so completely as to warrant being listed under another name. Cross references to all spellings of names have been included to facilitate the work of genealogists and others using this Index. This publication should be especially useful to descendants of these Founders and Patriots who are interested in becoming members of this unique and beloved patriotic society.

The National Society lineage books are in many state and county libraries located throughout the country as well as in a number of historical society libraries. If the lineage books are not available to anyone desiring to see a particular lineage, it is suggested that inquiry be directed to the Society at Park Lane Bldg., #615, 2025 Eye St., N.W. Washington, D.C. 20006.

In the preparation of this Index, all Chapters of the Society were invited to participate. Twenty-three Chapters assigned members to transfer the required information in each volume to cards. The National Society appreciates the work of those members who undertook and completed their assignments so efficiently. From these cards, this volume was compiled. Without the assistance of the Chapters, this book would not have been possible. To all of them the National Society expresses its deepest gratitude.

Imogene Hawks Lane

Mrs. Harry H. Lane
National Vice President

FOUNDERS AND PATRIOTS OF AMERICA INDEX

ADAMS, cont.
Levi, Jr. (Feb. 14, 1754-Dec. 26, 1833) m. Aug. 9, 1771/2 Hannah Pettingall XXIII, 52
Matthew (....-....) m. .... MASS XX, 82
Moses (Apr. 27, 1726-p. 1781) m. 1763 (2) Mary Swan XIV, 98
Moses (Nov. 30, 1748-Aug. 1777) m. .... Ann Willard X, 264
Nathan (May 16, 1736-Jan. 1, 1832) m. .... (1) Hannah Rood; .... (2) Sybil Ward IX, 44; XXV, 149
Nathaniel (Dec. 20, 1747-Mar. 7, 1806) m. .... Anne Bolton XX, 82
Obadiah, Jr. (Dec. 18, 1721-Feb. 2, 1803) m. Dec. 8, 1744 Sarah Partridge XIX, 86
Peter, I (c. 1640-May 3, 1687) m. c. 1660 Anne Nichols VA XXXII, 220
Philip (c. 1650-1696) m. July 9, 1670 Anne Crewe MD XXIX, 283
Reuben (July 9, 1760-Oct. 17, 1848) m. Apr. 26, 1781 Azubah Jones XXXII, 225
Robert (1602-Oct. 12, 1682) m. .... Eleanor ...... MASS XVIII, 144
Samuel (Nov. 7, 1755-July 11, 1840) m. Aug. 14, 1777 Chloe Legge XIX, 86
Stephen (Dec. 27, 1729-Feb. 11, 1795) m. Feb. 10, 1773 Mary Littlefield XXV, 16
Thomas (bpt. Sept. 18, 1757-May 10, 1799) m. .... Mary Bright IV, 102
Timothy (June 14, 1762-May 23, 1841) m. July 15, 1783 Lydia Robbins XXIX, 317
William (Feb. 3, 1594-1661) m. .... MASS XXII, 121
William (Nov. 2, 1752-Feb. 14, 1811) m. .... Rosabella Loomis XXIII, 57

ADDAMS, see ADAMS

ADDISON
Arthur (1763-May 1825) m. Feb. 3, 1812 (3) Rosanna James XXXI, 261
John (....-1706) m. .... Mrs. Rebecca (Dent) Wilkinson MD XVI, 50
John (1655-Jan. 1716/7) m. .... Barthina ...... VA XXXI, 261

John (....-....) m. a. 1794 Eleanor Watkins XVI, 50

ADDOMS, see ADAMS

ADKINS, see ATKINS

AGEE
Mathieu (1670-....) m. .... Ann Godwin VA XXXIII, 203
Matthew (1747-....) m. 1772 Mary Liggen XXXIII, 203

AINSWORTH
Edward (c. 1652-Mar. 5, 1740/1) m. Jan. 11, 1687/8 Johannah Hemmingway CONN XIV, 50
Nathan (c. 1740-1776/7) m. Feb. 2, 1764 Phebe Kinsley XIV, 50

ALBEE
Benjamin (c. 1600-....) m. .... Hannah Chambers MASS XXVII, 51; XXXI, 95, 96; XXXIII, 66, 67
Benjamin (June 28, 1740-1829) m. .... Abigail Clifford XXVII, 50, 51; XXXI, 95, 96; XXXIII, 66, 67

ALDEN
Henry (a. 1667-Feb. 18, 1730) m. .... (1) .... MASS XXIX, 372
Ichabod (Aug. 1, 1739-Nov. 11, 1778) m. .... Mary Wakefield IX, 45
Job (Sept. 24, 1737-p. 1778) m. Oct. 1764 Lucy Spooner XV, 130
John (1599-Sept. 12, 1687) m. 1621 Priscilla Mullens MASS IX, 45; XV, 130; XXIX, 370; XXXIII, 264
Prince (Oct. 28, 1718-May 22, 1804) m. Dec. 18, 1746 Mary Mason Fitch XXXIII, 264
Silas (Oct. 23, 1736-Feb. 22, 1826) m. Apr. 10, 1760 Margaret Capron XXIX, 372
Simeon (May 10, 1740-....) m. May 23, 1763 Mary Packard XXIX, 370

ALDRICH
Abel (Nov. 16, 1749-1790) m. Jan. 7, 1773 Olive Lovell XXIX, 330
Abner (Nov. 17, 1727-Oct. 31, 1815) m. Dec. 10, 1747 Elizabeth Cook XXXII, 120
George (1605-Mar. 1, 1682) m. Sept. 3, 1629 Katherine Seald MASS XXIX, 330; XXXII, 120, 190
Reuben (July 1, 1728-Oct. 19, 1800) m. Nov. 22, **1744** Ruth Verry

XXXII, 190

ALEXANDER
George (....-May 5, 1703) m. Mar.
 18, 1644 Susan Sage CONN
 XXVI, 181, 182
James (a. 1681-....) m. ....
 Jean Wallace MD XXVIII, 119
John (....-p. 1642) m. ....
 ...... CONN XXVI, 181; XXX, 273
John (July 1738-July 8, 1828) m.....
 Rachel ...... XXVI, 181, 182
Seth (1746-Dec. 10, 1780) m. June
 19, 1768 Hannah Oaks XXX, 273
William (Jan. 30, 1745-May 31, 1820)
 m. .... Esther Brown XXVIII, 119

ALFORD
Benedictus (1619-Apr. 23, 1683) m.
 Nov. 26, 1640 Joan Newton CONN
 XXV, 21, 22; XXIX, 268
Elijah (Apr. 13, 1757-Apr. 11, 1832)
 m. Oct. 11, 1779 Olive Adams
 XXIX 268
Pelatiah (Apr. 14, 1739-Oct. 26,
 1804) m. Sept. 22, 1768 Anne Bacon
 XXV, 21, 22

ALLANSON, see ALLISON

ALLEN, includes ALLIN, ALLING, ALLYN
Abel (Aug. 14, 1733-Aug. 18, 1808)
 m. Jan. 11, 1756 Elizabeth Chapin
 XXXIV, 200
Archelaus (Dec. 21, 1748-Aug. 24,
 1828) m. .... Prudence Merriman
 XXVII, 201
Barnabas (Apr. 28, 1741-1811) m.
 Feb. 12, 1761 Amy Camp XIII, 91
David (Oct. 17, 1757-1792) m. 1780
 Lydia Briggs XXXI, 100
Ebenezer (Feb. 5, 1738-1816) m.
 June 1, 1768 Elizabeth Pousley
 XXXII, 149
Ebenezer, Jr. (July 21, 1739-p.
 1793) m. Feb. 16, 1764 Sarah Allen
 XXIV, 72
Ebenezer (Mar. 10, 1741-Nov. 11,
 1800) m. .... Lydia Punderson
 XV, 86
Edward (....-Nov. 21, 1696) m. Nov.
 24, 1658 Sarah Kimball MASS.
 XVIII, 26, 27; XXX, 95; XXXI, 90
Ephraim (June 18, 1747-Dec. 28,
 1816) m. Nov. 15, 1770 Temperance
 Morgan XXV, 188
George (c. 1619-May 2, 1648) m. ....
 Katherine ...... MASS XXIV, 72
Isaac (bpt. Aug. 3, 1740-....) m.
 Nov. 24, 1763 Abigail Burnham
 XXIX, 312

Ithamar (Sept. 25, 1750-c. 1830) m.
 Sept. 23, 1773 Eunice Chloe Nisley
 XVIII, 26
James (c. 1614-Sept. 27, 1676) m.
 Mar. 16, 1638 Ann Guild MASS
 XIX, 56; XXV, 18
James (July 17, 1739-Oct. 13, 1825)
 m. Dec. 14, 1768 Anna Stanton
 XXI, 48, 49
Job (Nov. 24, 1753-Mar. 23, 1828) m.
 .... Abigail Mather XII, 83
John (May 2, 1719-....) m. ....
 Jerusha Hastings XVIII, 26, 27
John (1749-Aug. 1815) m. Aug. 15,
 1781 Jane Tandy XXX, 67, 68
Matthew (1604-Feb. 1, 1670/1) m.
 .... Margaret Wyatt CONN XII, 83
Nehemiah (Dec. 10, 1733-Dec. 28,
 1799) m. Mar. 23, 1758 Abiah
 Thomas XXVII, 91; XXVIII, 149
Parmalee (1746-Feb. 10, 1806) m.
 Dec. 18, 1777 Deborah (Burroughs)
 Carl XXXI, 179
Philo (1754-p. 1785) m. .... Hannah
 Lines XII, 30
Phineas (Apr. 24, 1764-Aug. 13,
 1836) m. Sept. 6, 1787 Ruth Smith
 XIX, 56
Robert (1608-1683) m. .... Sarah
 ...... MASS XXI, 48, 49;
 XXV, 188
Roger (bpt. Dec. 6, 1612-Sept. 27,
 1674) m. 1642 Mary Nash CONN
 XII, 30; XV, 86; XXVII, 201;
 XXXI, 179, 295
Samuel (....-1669) m. .... Ann
 ...... MASS XXVII, 91; XXVIII,
 149
Samuel (c. 1588-Apr. 28, 1648) m.
 a. 1634 Ann ...... CONN XXXII,
 149; XXXIV, 200
Samuel (Jan. 28, 1715/6-Apr. 4,
 1788) m. c. 1737 Kezia Lines
 XXXI, 295
Samuel, Jr. (1757-1830) m. 1776
 Elizabeth Fleming XXX, 95;
 XXXI, 89, 90
Samuel (Jan. 1, 1767-Aug. 6, 1832)
 m. Nov. 30, 1786 Lucy French
 XXV, 18
Stephen (May 14, 1764-May 4, 1852)
 m. Dec. 31, 1788 Weighty Thorp
 XXIV, 72
Thomas (Apr. 15, 1742-May 30,
 1800) m. May 29, 1769 Amy
 Bicknell XXII, 135
William, Sr. (....-June 18, 1686)
 m. 1638/9 Ann Goodale MASS
 XIII, 91; XXXI, 100
William (1602-May 10, 1678) m. ....
 Alice Norman MASS XXIX, 312

ALLEN, cont.
William, I (c. 1630-1677) m. ....
Judith ...... VA XXX, 67, 68
William (c. 1640-1685) m. ....
Elizabeth ...... RI XXII, 135

ALLERTON
Isaac (1583/5-a. Feb. 12, 1659) m.
1626 (2) Fear Brewster MASS
XVIII, 44, 69
Isaac (Aug. 15, 1725-Dec. 26, 1807)
m. c. 1745 Lucy Spaulding
XVIII, 43, 44, 69

ALLEY
Ephraim (1760-Nov. 1841) m. ....
Susanna Day VII, 46
John (1575-Nov. 25, 1653) m. ....
Rebecca Ayres MASS VII, 46

ALLIN, see ALLEN

ALLING, see ALLEN

ALLIS
Stephen (Mar. 4, 1758-Dec. 3, 1848)
m. Dec. 14, 1797 (2) Mary Munn
XIX, 22
William (1613-Sept. 6, 1678) m. 1641
Mary ...... MASS XIX, 22

ALLISON, includes ALLANSON
Richard (a. 1733-1808) m. a. 1760
Sarah Cheshire XXXI, 94;
XXXII, 157
Thomas (1637-p. 1677) m. Aug. 18,
1662 Mary Roberts MD XXXI, 94;
XXXII, 157

ALLYN, see ALLEN

ALVORD
Alexander (bpt. Oct. 15, 1627-Oct.
3, 1687) m. Oct. 29, 1646 Mary
Vore CONN, MASS VI, 17; X, 74, 76
Caleb (Oct. 5, 1751-Dec. 22, 1819)
m. Dec. 26, 1776 Mary Murdock
VI, 17
Elijah (Jan. 17, 1718-May 15, 1788)
m. 1750 Hannah Judd VI, 17
Saul (July 9, 1753-Sept. 23, 1852)
m. Apr. 14, 1778 Eleanor Kellogg
X, 74, 76

ALWARD
Benjamin (1752-Oct. 24, 1813) m.
Sept. 27, 1774 Sarah Ayers
XXX, 289
Henry (a. 1675-1718) m. Jan. 26,
1693 Judith Hendrickson NJ
XXX, 289

AMBROSE
Henry (1613-Nov. 19, 1658) m. ....
Susannah ...... MASS XV, 26
Samuel (Apr. 21, 1753-Dec. 2, 1830)
m. Feb. 20, 1776 Mary Goodhue
XV, 26

AMERMAN
Albert (Feb. 9, 1733-Sept. 1, 1818)
m. .... Apolonia de la Montague
IV, 119; XII, 98
Derick (Sept. 28, 1759-Mar. 4, 1826)
m. .... Mary Belknap IV, 119
Derick Jans (....-c. 1725) m. ....
Althea Vanderbeck NY IV, 119;
XII, 98

AMES
Elijah (Jan. 7, 1742/3-p. 1786) m.
May 30, 1769 Elizabeth Johnson
XV, 34
Joseph (....-a. Apr. 5, 1719) m.
.... Esther Gray VA XXIX, 20,
78, 113, 138; XXXIII, 14, 15
Levin (....-1825) m. a. 1787 (1)
Mary Hutchinson XXIX, 19, 78,
113, 138; XXXIII, 14, 15
Sylvanus (Jan. 20, 1744-1778) m.
Sept. 20, 1768 Huldah Johnson
XXXI, 13; XXXII, 111; XXXIII,
29, 30
William (bpt. Oct. 6, 1605-Jan. 11,
1654) m. Hannah (Alden) Niles
MASS XV, 34; XXXI, 13; XXXII, 111;
XXXIII, 29, 30

AMSDEN
Isaac (....-Apr. 7, 1659) m. June
8, 1654 Frances Perriman MASS
XXXIII, 76, 77
Noah (June 19, 1758-Dec. 11, 1843)
m. Nov. 1780 Prudence Cummings
XXXIII, 76, 77

ANABLE, includes ANNABLE
Anthony (1599-1673) m. Mar. 3, 1645
(2) Ann Clark MASS XXIV, 85;
XXVI, 255, 256
John (Apr. 18, 1744-Oct. 23, 1815)
m. .... Hannah Stewart XXIV, 85;
XXVI, 255, 256

ANDERSON
David (1745-1795) m. c. 1764 Amediah
...... XXXIII, 22
Garland (....-p. 1799) m. ....
Marcia Burbidge XX, 110; XXI, 88
George (Apr. 6, 1751-Nov. 8, 1839)
m. .... Sarah Skirm XXVI, 16
Richard (1743-p. 1790) m. Mar. 4,1761
Jane Foster XXIV, 46; XXXIII, 68,69

Robert (1640-1712) m. .... Cecelia
Massie VA XX, 110; XXI, 88;
XXIV, 46; XXXIII, 22, 68, 69

ANDREWS, includes ANDRUS
Abraham (Sept. 6, 1747-July 13,
    1823) m. Oct. 19, 1773 Esther
    Stearns XIX, 162
Ammi (Apr. 13, 1737-Mar. 30, 1833)
    m. 1758 Mary (Molly) Brown XX, 31
Daniel (May 12, 1720-Dec. 4, 1799)
    m. Feb. 6, 1746 Eunice Kelsey
    XXI, 63
Daniel (1755-Apr. 20, 1818) m. ....
    Susanna Choate XII, 120
Eden (Apr. 28, 1761-Apr. 26, 1839)
    m. May 12, 1784 Deborah Knapp
    Benedict XX, 48
Elijah (Feb. 16, 1723-Sept. 3, 1792)
    m. Feb. 21, 1745 Phebe Hurlbutt
    XXIV, 78
Elijah (Dec. 25, 1758-June 19, 1826)
    m. May 2, 1782 Mabel Fox XIX, 83
Jeremiah (Jan. 16, 1732-June 1782)
    m. .... Sarah Bryant XII, 103
John (....-1681) m. .... Mary ......
    CONN XII, 103; XIX, 83; XX, 48;
    XXI, 63; XXII, 11; XXIV, 78
John (1621-Apr. 20, 1708) m. ....
    Jane Jordan MASS XII, 120;
    XIX, 162; XX, 31
Joseph (Nov. 3, 1752-....) m. May
    17, 1774 Mable Robards XXVI, 90
Laben (Apr. 25, 1728-June 24, 1813)
    m. Apr. 5, 1758 Prudence Stanley
    XI, 39
Seth (1737-Oct. 24, 1823) m. Apr.
    11, 1764 Sarah Baldwin XXII, 11
Thomas (May 17, 1762-a. 1815) m.
    July 14, 1784 Abigail Stork
    XXIII, 75
William (....-a. Aug. 8, 1659) m.
    ...... Mary ...... CONN XXVI, 90
William (....-Mar. 1675/6) m. c.
    1625 .... CONN
    XI, 39; XXIII, 75

ANDRUS, see ANDREWS

ANGEL, see ANGELL

ANGELL, includes ANGEL

Eseck (Sept. 12, 1752-Nov. 14, 1836)
    m. 1777 (1) Martha Brown X, 196,
    197; XXVII, 127
John (July 16, 1740-Jan. 5, 1817) m.
    Mar. 22, 1765 Martha A. Aldrich
    XXIV, 58
Nehemiah, Jr. (Sept. 3, 1752-Aug. 3,
    1828) m. Sept. 25, 1777 (1)

Anna Hill XXXI, 75
Samuel (Oct. 29, 1742-Jan. 24, 1795)
    m. .... Lydia Medbury XIV, 51;
    XX, 17
Thomas (May 1, 1618-Sept. 2, 1694)
    m. Apr. 10, 1643 Alice Ashton RI
    X, 196, 197; XIV, 51; XX, 17;
    XXIV, 58; XXVII, 127; XXXI, 75

ANNABLE, see ANABLE

ANTWERPEN, see VAN ANTWERP

APPLETON
Isaac (May 31, 1731-Feb. 25, 1806)
    m. Apr. 24, 1760 Mary Adams
    XXIII, 18
Samuel (1586-1670) m. Jan. 24, 1616
    Mary Everard MASS XIII, 54;
    XVIII, 13; XXIII, 18; XXX, 26
Thomas (Oct. 5, 1740-Sept. 14, 1830)
    m. Oct. 19, 1773 (2) Lydia Dane
    XIII, 54; XVIII, 13; XXX, 26

ARMISTEAD
John (1751-1798) m. 1773 Elizabeth
    ...... XXX, 189, 239, 270; XXXI,
    87, 88
Ralph (....-....) m. ....
    ...... VA XXX, 189, 239, 270;
    XXXI, 88
Westwood (c. 1735-a. June 22, 1786)
    m. .... Mary Jenkins XXVII, 178;
    XXIX, 366
William (bpt. Aug. 3, 1610-a. 1660)
    m. .... Ann ...... VA XXVII,
    178; XXIX, 366

ARMS
Consider (Oct. 15, 1736-June 19,
    1792) m. Dec. 10, 1765 Mary Catlin
    XIII, 109
William (1654-Aug. 25, 1731) m.
    Nov. 21, 1677 Joanna Hawks MASS
    XIII, 109

ARMSTRONG
Benjamin (....-Jan. 10, 1717/8) m.
    .... Rachel ...... CONN
    XXXIII, 314, 315
Hezekiah (Nov. 2, 1744-Mar. 4, 1816)
    m. Oct. 26, 1767 Miriam Haynes
    XXXIII, 314, 315
Jonathan (a. 1650-p. 1677) m. ....
    .... RI X, 291; XI, 17;
    XV, 15; XVI, 33; XXIX, 48; XXX,
    28; XXXIV, 268
Lebbeus (Sept. 13, 1738-Oct. 17,
    1789) m. Oct. 23, 1765 Rebecca
    Hyde X, 291; XI, 17; XV, 14; XVI,
    33; XXIX, 48; XXX, 28; XXXIV, 268

ARNOLD

Anthony (c. 1635-p. Jan. 12, 1689)
m. .... Johanna ...... VA XXVIII,
192, 193
Jacob (bpt. Nov. 10, 1745-Jan. 10,
1825) m. Jan. 19, 1774 Martha
Anne Norton XXIX, 44
John (....-Dec. 1664) m. .... Sus-
annah ...... CONN XI, 69;
XII, 23; XXI, 131; XXV, 113; XXIX,
44
John (July 5, 1720-....) m. Feb. 5,
1746/7 Mercy Hurlburt XXV, 113
Joseph (....-....) m. Apr. 8, 1648
Rebecca Curtis MASS XXV, 8
Joseph (Aug. 2, 1738-Nov. 10, 1804)
m. .... Mary Crane XI, 69; XII,23
Moses (1751-June 7, 1788) m. Dec.
12, 1773 Sarah Vinton XXV, 8
Nathan (Oct. 18, 1733-Sept. 1778)
m. .... Lucy Gargill VII, 36
Nathan (May 31, 1761-Mar. 31, 1855)
m. Jan. 30, 1791 Irene Hathaway
XXIII, 20
Peleg (Feb. 15, 1749-Nov. 27, 1839)
m. Apr. 26, 1778 Margaret Slocum
XXX, 175, 176, 200
Samuel (1746-Jan. 7, 1829) m. Dec.
25, 1766 Lucy Pratt XXI, 131
Samuel (c. 1750-Dec. 5, 1831) m.
Sept. 5, 1771 Elizabeth Wright
XXVIII, 192, 193
Stephen (June 12, 1749-....) m.
Apr. 1, 1773 Lois Darby XXV, 113
Thomas (bpt. Apr. 18, 1599-Sept.
1674) m. 1640 Phoebe Parkhurst
MASS, RI VII, 36; XXIII, 20
William (June 24, 1587-1675) m.
a. 1610 Christian Peak MASS,
RI XXX, 176, 200

ARRINGTON

Arthur (1709/10-1801) m. .... Mary
West XXXII, 191
William (....-p. 1709) m. ....
Elizabeth Pedden VA XXXII, 191

ARSDALEN, see VAN ARSDALE

ARUNDEL-HOWARD, see HOWARD

ASH

John (....-Jan. 5, 1694/5) m. Aug.
14, 1667 Mary Bartlett MASS
XXVI, 85
Samuel (Jan. 2, 1759-p. 1799) m.
Oct. 5, 1780 Susanna Marshall
XXVI, 85, 86

ASHBROOK

John (1656-1730) m. 1687 (2)

Mary Hamilton NJ XXVIII, 15;
XXIX, 309
Levi (1738-a. Sept. 1, 1794) m. 1768
(2) Mary Chenoweth XXVIII, 15;
XXIX, 309

ASHCRAFT

Jedediah, Sr. (bpt. 1727-Mar. 6,
1813) m. Feb. 28, 1744 Sarah
Monroe XXXIV, 198
John (....-Sept. 16, 1680) m. Sept.
12, 1670 Hannah Osborn CONN
XXX, 169, 242; XXXIV, 199
Samuel (Mar. 1, 1758-Mar. 25, 1813)
m. 1788 Keziah Moffett XXX, 169,
242

ASHLEY

Enoch (Nov. 25, 1750-....) m. Oct.
21, 1773 Phoebe Owens XXXIII,
232, 282
Joseph (c. 1670-c. 1750) m. Aug. 25,
1704 Elizabeth Percival MASS
XXXIII, 232, 282
Moses (July 23, 1731-July 27, 1792)
m. Apr. 4, 1765 Sarah Rowe
XVIII, 92
Robert (a. 1618-Nov. 29, 1682) m. c.
Aug. 7, 1641 Mrs. Mary Horton
MASS XVIII, 92

ATHERTON

James (1626-Aug. 6, 1710) m. ....
Hannah ...... MASS XXX, 12
Peter, Jr. (Dec. 29, 1734-Sept. 20,
1784) m. May 26, 1756 Betty
Atherton XXX, 12

ATKINS, includes ADKINS

Josiah (....-1690) m. a. 1650 (1)
...... Andrews CONN XXXIII, 66
Luther (1718-Aug. 3, 1788) m. Nov.
14, 1743 Eunice Andrews XXXIII,
66
Samuel (Jan. 17, 1750-July 2, 1830)
m. c. 1770 Eunice Wightman
XXVII, 191
Thomas (....-c. 1694) m. 1672 Jane
Williams CONN XXVII, 191

ATWOOD

Caleb (1760-July 14, 1833) m. July
29, 1781 Marion Walton XXVII, 67
David (1747-1809) m. Jan. 2, 1776
Ruth Knight XXX, 62
Ephraim (Mar. 9, 1728-Oct. 29, 1805)
m. Dec. 15, 1755 Bethiah Harding
XXX, 246
Harmon (....-June 2, 1651) m. Aug.
14, 1646 Ann Copp MASS XXX,
62

ATWOOD, cont.
  Isaac (June 28, 1747-Mar. 15, 1836)
    m. .... Hannah Chubbuck IV, 74, 75
  John (....-....) m. .... Sarah
    Masterson MASS IV, 74, 75
  Stephen (c. 1620-Feb. 1694) m.
    Nov. 6, 1644 Abigail Dunham MASS
    XXX, 246
  Thomas (....-Apr. 3, 1694) m. ....
    Elizabeth ...... MASS XXVII, 67

AUDLIN, see ODLIN

AULD
  James (1665-1721) m. .... Sarah
    Elliott MD XXVI, 224
  Thomas (Aug. 24, 1758-a. July 4,
    1798) m. a. 1786 Elizabeth
    Dawson XXVI, 224

AUSTIN
  Aaron (Aug. 27, 1745-July 15, 1829)
    m. 1767 Esther Kellogg XI, 38;
    XIV, 52
  Anthony (1636-Aug. 22, 1708) m. Oct.
    19, 1664 Esther Huggins MASS
    XI, 38; XIV, 88
  Caleb (Feb. 6, 1719-May 9, 1792) m.
    Nov. 1751 Phoebe King XIV, 88
  David (1732-1801) m. .... Mary Mix
    II, 40
  Isaac (Mar. 10, 1737-Nov. 21, 1824)
    m. 1760 Rhodinah Vaughn XXIX,
    57, 210; XXX, 189
  Job (Mar. 31, 1759-Feb. 7, 1847) m.
    .... (1) Mary Nelson XVI, 132
  John (....-1657) m. .... Constance
    ...... CONN II, 40
  Richard (1598-c. 1639) m. ....
    .... MASS XI, 38;
    XIV, 52; XVI, 132
  Robert (c. 1634-a. 1687) m. ....
    .... RI XXIX, 57, 210;
    XXX, 189

AVERILL
  Daniel, Jr. (c. 1763-Aug. 5, 1842)
    m. May 17, 1784 Eunice Calhoun
    XXV, 300
  Joseph (Aug. 29, 1742-c. 1822) m.
    Apr. 11, 1776 Sarah Stone
    XIV, 13, 62, 63
  Paul (1757-....) m. 1781 ......
    ...... XXX, 29
  William (c. 1611-1653) m. c. 1631
    Abigail ...... MASS XIV, 13, 62,
    63; XXV, 300; XXX, 29

AVERY
  Amos (bpt. Apr. 18, 1736-Aug. 11,
    1823) m. p. 1757 (2) Anna

Edgarton XXII, 145, 146; XXX, 41
  Amos (bpt. Mar. 6, 1743-p. 1824) m.
    c. 1768 Prudence Williams XXXII,
    262
  Christopher (c. 1590-Mar. 12, 1679)
    m. Aug. 26, 1616 Margery Stephens
    MASS II, 31, 42; X, 274, 283; XI,
    172; XVII, 7; XIX, 35; XXII, 145,
    146; XXIII, 65, 81; XXV, 209;
    XXVI, 119; XXVII, 61; XXX, 26, 27,
    41; XXXII, 11, 30, 262
  Daniel (Nov. 14, 1740-Sept. 6, 1781)
    m. Nov. 14, 1765 Deborah Avery
    XI, 172; XXIII, 81
  David (Apr. 5, 1746-Feb. 16, 1818)
    m. Oct. 10, 1782 Hannah Chaplin
    XVII, 7
  Gardiner (Sept. 22, 1751-Dec. 28,
    1831) m. 1772 Amy Newell XXIII,
    65; XXXII, 11
  James (Nov. 29, 1758-Mar. 18, 1798)
    m. Dec. 15, 1781 Rebecca Edes
    XXXI, 247, 248
  John (Jan. 24, 1738-Jan. 5, 1826)
    m. .... Sarah Belton XXV, 209;
    XXVII, 61
  Jonathan (Sept. 10, 1755-June 14,
    1847) m. Dec. 11, 1782 Pamela
    Fox XXXII, 29, 30
  Joseph (Apr. 13, 1747-Mar. 3, 1814)
    m. May 31, 1772 Deborah King
    X, 274, 283
  Nathan (c. 1754-May 3, 1821) m.
    Apr. 9, 1776 Aliff Pearson
    XXX, 26, 27
  Nathan (1759-1841) m. .... Anna
    Ayers II, 42
  Parke (1741-1821) m. .... Hannah
    Morgan II, 31
  Solomon (June 17, 1729-Dec. 23,
    1798) m. Feb. 18, 1751 Hannah
    Punderson XIX, 35
  Waightstill (May 10, 1741-Mar. 31,
    1821) m. Oct. 3, 1778 Leah (Pro-
    bart) Franks XXVI, 119, 120
  William (1622-Mar. 18, 1686/7) m.
    1644 Margaret Allright MASS
    XXXI, 247, 248

AXTELL
  Henry (bpt. Oct. 15, 1641-Apr. 18,
    1676) m. June 14, 1665 Hannah
    Merriam MASS XXIII, 30; XXX, 197
  Thomas (1750-July 12, 1808) m. Dec.
    12, 1771 Mary Tuthill XXIII, 30;
    XXX, 197

AYER, includes AYERS, AYRES, EYRE
  Ebenezer (May 20, 1716-Jan. 1785) m.
    Feb. 14, 1739/40 Elizabeth Holly
    X, 244

AYER, cont.
  Ebenezer (Jan. 16, 1755-May 31,
    1832) m. May 7, 1797 Achasa
    Squires XVI, 26, 27; XXIV,
    141; XXVI, 141
  Ezekiel, Jr. (Nov. 25, 1754-Aug.
    20, 1835) m. Dec. 1787 Eleanor
    Pike XXXII, 136
  John (1592-Mar. 31, 1657) m. ....
    Hannah ...... MASS XVI, 26, 27;
    XVIII, 20; XXIV, 141; XXVI, 140,
    141; XXVIII, 173; XXXII, 136
  Jonathan (1750-Dec. 8, 1826) m.
    July 21, 1771 Deborah Scofield
    XVI, 6
  Perley (Sept. 30, 1733-Apr. 11,
    1781) m. Nov. 13, 1754 Sarah
    Mitchell XVIII, 19, 20
  Richard (....-c. 1719) m. ....
    Mary ...... CONN X, 244; XVI, 6
  Stephen (Dec. 4, 1744-1782) m. Apr.
    18, 1769 Sarah Gray XXVIII, 173

AYERS, see AYER

AYMES, see AMES

AYRES, see AYER

BABB
  Joseph (c. 1735-c. 1781) m. Sept. 7,
    1761 Mary ...... XXXIII, 101
  Philip (1651-Mar. 31, 1671) m. ....
    Mary ...... MASS, ME XXV, 157,
    158; XXVI, 241, 242, 249, 250;
    XXXIII, 101
  Samson (....-Oct. 28, 1814) m. 1767
    Annie Way XXV, 157, 158; XXVI,
    241, 242, 249, 250

BABBITT, includes BOBET
  Edward (....-June 1675) m. Sept. 7,
    1654 Sarah Tarne MASS VII, 48
  John (Aug. 2, 1733-Mar. 8, 1816) m.
    .... Elizabeth Dean VII, 48

BABCOCK, includes BADCOCK
  Christopher (Jan. 28, 1758-Nov. 2,
    1780) m. 1778 Polly Benedict
    XXV, 145
  David (Feb. 2, 1745-Nov. 6, 1820) m.
    Mar. 12, 1767 Mary Hinkley XXIX,
    202
  George (July 27, 1749-Mar. 18, 1816)
    m. 1766/7 Susanna Sheldon XXXI, 17
  Gideon (July 2, 1744-p. 1802) m.
    .... Mary Cheseborough VII, 42
  Henry (June 23, 1757-1835/40) m. Aug.
    4, 1778 Prudence Gavitt

XXXI, 132, 133
  Ichabod (Dec. 12, 1731-Aug. 22,
    1801) m. Mar. 17, 1756 Esther
    Stanton XXXIII, 290, 291
  Isaiah (Jan. 29, 1719-Oct. 5, 1814)
    m. Dec. 25, 1738 Elizabeth Plumb
    XIX, 36; XXXI, 17
  James (1612-June 12, 1679) m. ....
    (1) Sarah ...... RI VI, 116;
    VII, 42; IX, 9, 10; XII, 57; XIII,
    52; XIX, 36; XXV, 145; XXIX, 116,
    172, 202; XXX, 239; XXXI, 17, 133;
    XXXIII, 290, 291
  Job (Jan. 20, 1729/30-....) m. ....
    Susanna Champlin XXIX, 172
  Joseph (Oct. 18, 1726-Jan. 24, 1796)
    m. Sept. 6, 1757 Anna Harris
    XXX, 239
  Joseph (Feb. 3, 1735/6-1804) m. ....
    (2) Hannah Ross IX, 9, 10
  Nathaniel, Jr. (Jan. 24, 1735-Apr.
    19, 1813) m. Dec. 1, 1756 Mary
    Larrison VI, 116
  Oliver, Jr. (Sept. 16, 1722-Feb. 24,
    1806) m. 1744 Patience Pendleton
    XIII, 52; XXIX, 116
  William Avery (Mar. 31, 1747-Sept.
    21, 1829) m. .... Lucretia Davis
    XII, 56

BABER, see BABERS

BABERS, includes BABER
  Robert, I (c. 1650-p. 1718) m. ....
    Sarah ...... VA XXXII, 94
  Robert, III (c. 1725-July 6, 1786)
    m. c. 1745 Jane ...... XXXII, 94,
    95

BABSON
  James, Jr. (1620/5-Dec. 21, 1683)
    m. Nov. 16, 1647 Elinor Hill MASS
    XXVII, 52
  Samuel (Mar. 22, 1740/1-Oct. 8,
    1805) m. July 16, 1765 Lydia
    Plummer XXVII, 51, 52

BACHELDER, see BATCHELDER

BACHILER, see BATCHELDER

BACON
  Darius (Aug. 29, 1745-Aug. 11, 1815)
    m. Dec. 21, 1780 Sarah Sheffield
    XXV, 106
  David (Aug. 24, 1754-Nov. 30, 1849)
    m. Oct. 30, 1777 Abigail Sampson
    XXV, 62, 63; XXXI, 102
  David (Nov. 23, 1766-Nov. 12, 1831)
    m. 1793 Hannah Tarbox
    XVIII, 134

BACON, cont.
  Edmund (c. 1641-1705) m. .... Ann
    Lyddall VA XXXIII, 40
  George (1592-May 1642) m. ....
    Margaret ...... MASS XXV, 106
  Isaiah (May 14, 1763-Jan. 14, 1831)
    m. Aug. 30, 1799 Ruth Carpenter
    XXXIV, 181
  John (May 30, 1721-Apr. 19, 1775) m.
    May 24, 1744 (1) Abigail Sawin
    XX, 42
  Jonathan, Sr. (1732-1815) m. ....
    Martha Wood V, 129, 130; IX, 42
  Jonathan (Apr. 4, 1759-Nov. 1845) m.
    .... Mollie Adams V, 129, 130;
    IX, 42
  Lydall (1717-Oct. 12, 1775) m. 1740
    Mary Allen XXXIII, 40
  Michael (....-July 4, 1688) m. Aug.
    31, 1624 (1) Mary......; Oct. 26,
    1655 (2) Mary Richardson; Nov. 28,
    1670 (3) Mary Noyes MASS V, 129,
    130; IX, 42
  Michael (bpt. Dec. 6, 1579-Apr. 18,
    1648) m. .... Alice ...... MASS
    V, 129, 130; IX, 42; XI, 12; XX,
    42; XXV, 63; XXXI, 102; XXXIV, 180
  Nathaniel, I (c. 1630-Jan. 27, 1708)
    m. c. 1652 Ann Miller CONN
    XVIII, 134
  Nehemiah (Sept. 6, 1736-Nov. 6,
    1832) m. Dec. 29, 1756 Ruth Adams
    XXIV, 129
  Samuel (July 21, 1721-a. Apr. 13,
    1786) m. Mar. 30, 1748 Eunice
    Bacon XI, 12
  Thomas (Nov. 27, 1640-Oct. 25, 1701)
    m. May 27, 1663 Mary Gamblin MASS
    XXIV, 129

BADCOCK, see BABCOCK

BADGER
  Edmund (Feb. 25, 1737-Sept. 1825) m.
    Dec. 15, 1765 Lucretia Abbe
    XXVI, 120, 121
  Giles (Glyes) (....-July 17, 1647)
    m. Elizabeth Greenleaf MASS
    XX, 161; XXVI, 120, 121
  Obadiah (Apr. 19, 1727-Dec. 29, 1821)
    m. Jan. 19, 1757 Mary Martin
    XX, 160
  Stephen (Apr. 17, 1758-Apr. 22, 1852)
    m. Jan. 23, 1804 Sarah Sawyer
    XX, 160

BADLAM
  Stephen, IV (May 7, 1751-Aug. 24,
    1815) m. June 1, 1775 Mary Adams
    XXXII, 223
  William (....-....) m. .... (2)

  Mary French MASS XXXII, 223

BAGBY
  John (1619-1670) m. 1640 ......
    ...... VA XXXII, 166; XXXIV, 77
  Robert B. (1740-a. April 21, 1828)
    m. a. 1800 (3) Fannie ......
    XXXII, 166; XXXIV, 77

BAGG
  Aaron (Sept. 23, 1757-Aug. 16, 1839)
    m. Sept. 27, 1775 Sarah Miller
    XXIX, 272
  John (....-Sept. 5, 1683) m. Oct.
    24, 1657 Hannah Burt MASS
    XXIX, 272

BAILDON, see BELDING

BAILEY, includes BAILY, BAYLEY
  Abijah (c. 1722-1785) m. Nov. 20,
    1765 Sarah Grover XXII, 16
  Christopher Sargent (1767-July
    25, 1826) m. Oct. 15, 1803 Abigail
    Marshall XXVI, 8
  Eli (Apr. 6, 1749-....) m. Aug. 17,
    1776 Ruth Taylor XXIX, 344
  James (c. 1612-Aug. 9, 1677) m. a.
    June 1642 Lydia ...... MASS
    XV, 27; XIX, 76
  Jeremiah (Aug. 14, 1718-1791/2) m.
    a. June 29, 1793 Lydia Crook
    XXXIII, 198
  Jethro (Apr. 21, 1741-c. 1815) m.
    Oct. 16, 1766 Hannah Davis XV, 27
  Joel (Jan. 29, 1658-1732) m. Feb.
    11, 1687 Ann Short PA XXI, 94,
    95; XXV, 177; XXIX, 344
  John (....-p. June 17, 1696) m.
    .... Lydia Backus CONN
    XXXIII, 198
  John, Sr. (1596-Nov. 2, 1651) m.
    .... Eleanor Knight MASS
    XXXII, 62
  John (1613-1691) m. 1640 Eleanor
    Emery MASS XXXII, 62
  Joshua (Apr. 20, 1747-Jan. 26, 1826)
    m. May 13, 1778 Ann Jackson XXI,
    94, 95; XXV, 177
  Joshua (May 11, 1757-Mar. 15, 1809)
    m. Mar. 18, 1780 Sarah Chase
    XXXII, 61, 62
  Nathan (1735-1819) m. Feb. 8, 1757
    Sarah Pillsbury XVII, 14
  Richard (....-1647) m. .... Edna
    Holsted MASS XVII, 14
  Samuel (Feb. 20, 1705-Jan. 5, 1784)
    m. Feb. 2, 1727 Mary Rolf
    XIX, 76
  Thomas (....-1681) m. ....
    ...... MASS XXII, 16; XXVI, 8

BAILY, see BAILEY

BAKER

Aaron (1726-1802) m. 1747 Jemima
    Clark XIX, 80
Abraham (Sept. 27, 1748-May 28,
    1822) m. Dec. 3, 1772 Anna
    Baxter XXX, 282, 283
Absolom (Aug. 10, 1747-June 18,
    1820) m. .... Rebecca Ames
    XXXI, 61; XXXII, 236
Alexander, Jr. (1607-1688) m. 1632
    Elizabeth Farrar MASS XXV, 170;
    XXVII, 140; XXXI, 61, 201; XXXII,
    236; XXXIII, 95, 96
Benjamin (Jan. 15, 1753-Nov. 11,
    1830) m. Apr. 29, 1779 Mary
    George XXII, 132; XXXIII, 265
    266
Cornelius (....-Dec. 29, 1716) m.
    Apr. 26, 1652 Hannah Woodbury
    MASS XXII, 132; XXXIII, 265
Daniel (June 3, 1753-June 10, 1814)
    m. Oct. 26, 1778 Margaret Osborn
    XV, 121; XVII, 16
David (Aug. 22, 1733-Oct. 27, 1786)
    m. July 3, 1757 Mary Conklin
    XVI, 7
Edward (c. 1610-Mar. 16, 1687) m. a.
    1640 Joan ...... MASS XVI, 17;
    XIX, 80
Elisha (Oct. 17, 1724-May 22, 1797)
    m. Oct. 28, 1746 Phoebe Nichols
    XXXI, 201
Francis (1611-July 23, 1696) m. June
    17, 1641 Isabel Twining MASS
    XXX, 283; XXIV, 80
Francis (Jan. 1, 1762-Apr. 20, 1846)
    m. Jan. 21, 1790 (1) Ann Davis
    XXXII, 236
Gideon (Nov. 27, 1711-Dec. 19, 1805)
    m. .... Lois Rogers XXXIII, 95,
    96
Jacob (c. 1706-p. 1776) m. 1775
    Deborah Brown XVII, 23; XXIX, 320
Jeremiah (May 9, 1749-Dec. 23, 1825)
    m. .... Anna Stephens X, 59
John (....-....) m. .... Lydia
    Baysey CONN X, 59
John (1589-....) m. .... Elizabeth
    ...... MASS XXVII, 119
John (May 16, 1753-p. 1780) m. June
    28, 1774 Mary Flagg XVI, 17
Jonathan (1724/5-Mar. 9, 1805) m.
    Oct. 22, 1745 Mary Conant XXII,
    132; XXXIII, 265, 266
Joseph (....-....) m. 1778 Jane
    Usher XXV, 170; XXVII, 140
Joseph (Jan. 25, 1704-Dec. 29, 1791)
    m. May 31, 1739 (1) Hannah
    Lovewell X, 133

Joseph, Jr. (Jan. 22, 1721-1776) m.
    1742 Sarah Wheeler XXXI, 73
Lovewell (Sept. 18, 1743-p. 1785) m.
    1766 Mary Worth X, 133
Maurice (....-a. Dec. 28, 1700) m.
    .... Elizabeth Greenif MD
    XXXII, 236
Paul (Feb. 17, 1753-Oct. 14, 1829)
    m. .... Elizabeth Pinkham XXXIV,
    80
Samuel (Jan. 21, 1724-Apr. 9, 1801)
    m. Dec. 13, 1757 (2) Mary Allen
    XXVII, 119
Thomas (....-Jan. 28, 1683) m. ....
    Elizabeth ...... MASS X, 134
Thomas (Sept. 29, 1618-Apr. 30,
    1700) m. June 20, 1643 Alice
    Dayton NY XV, 121; XVI, 7; XVII,
    16, 23; XXIX, 320
William (....-Feb. 8, 1679) m. 1661
    Mary ...... MASS XXXI, 73

BALCH

Benjamin (Feb. 12, 1743-May 4, 1815)
    m. 1764 Joanna O'Brien VI, 50
Hart, Jr. (Nov. 9, 1751-Feb. 15,
    1846) m. Sept. 27, 1779 (2) Dorcas
    Somers XXXI, 180
John (1579-May 1648) m. .... (1)
    Margery ...... MASS VI, 51;
    XXXI, 180

BALCOME

Alexander (....-May 4, 1711) m.
    .... Jane Holbrook RI XX, 143
Samuel (Mar. 10, 1727-Feb. 4, 1783)
    m. Jan. 3, 1745 Susanna Jepson
    XX, 143

BALDWIN

Barnabas, Jr. (Aug. 31, 1726-Dec.
    24, 1804) m. .... Mary Turrell
    XXVI, 199; XXVII, 53, 54; XXXIII,
    177, 178
Benjamin (Apr. 21, 1727-a. July 5,
    1785) m. Sept. 27, 1750 Ruth
    Porter XXXII, 69
Benjamin (Jan. 22, 1761-July 11,
    1838) m. 1783 Isabella Wright
    XXVIII, 81
Caleb (May 2, 1723-Sept. 5, 1827)
    m. Apr. 16, 1761 Jerusha Parmelee
    XXV, 66
Eleazer (Oct. 24, 1764-1859) m. May
    8, 1785 Jane Redfield XXV, 66
Ezra (Sept. 1706-Mar. 26, 1782)
    m. Dec. 2, 1728 Ruth ......
    XVI, 118
George (Sept. 9, 1733-July 18, 1802)
    m. July 2, 1766 Hannah Frisbie
    XXX, 275

BALDWIN, cont.
Henry (....-Feb. 14, 1697/8) m. Nov.
1, 1649 Phebe Richardson MASS
XI, 164
Hezekiah (Sept. 26, 1732-p. 1795) m.
Apr. 5, 1759 Abigail Peet VI, 11;
X, 276
Hezekiah, Jr. (May 25, 1762-May 7,
1831) m. Sept. 22, 1784 Abiel
Curtis VI, 11
Hezikiah (Aug. 24, 1756-Nov. 6,
1831) m. Jan. 1, 1782 Elizabeth
Hine IX, 16; X, 185
Israel (Oct. 31, 1718-July 1, 1797)
m. Oct. 9, 1743 Hannah Chatterton
XXI, 126, 127
Jacob (1760-Oct. 13, 1844) m. ....
᠄ Sarah Turner XVI, 61
James (Jan. 29, 1760-Mar. 3, 1839)
m. 1785 Bethia Goodsell XXII, 18
Jared (Jan. 30, 1731-1817) m. Sept.
18, 1753 Damarus Booth XX, 132;
XXVII, 164
Jared (bpt. Apr. 18, 1740-1830) m.
.... Hannah Plant VI, 117
Jeduthan (Jan. 13, 1730-June 4,
1788) m. .... Lucy Parkman
XI, 164
John (....-Sept. 25, 1687) m.
May 15, 1655 Mary Richardson
MASS V, 45; XVI, 61; XXXIII, 238,
239
John (....-June 21, 1681) m. Aug.
15, 1653 Mary Bruen MASS, CONN
VI, 117; VIII, 5; XX, 132; XXV,
66; XXVII, 164; XXX, 275; XXXI,
190
John (c. 1630-....) m. Apr. 12,
1653 Hannah Birchard CONN
XXXII, 69
Joseph (c. 1609-Nov. 2, 1684) m. a.
1644 (1) Hannah ...... CONN, MASS
XVI, 118; XXI, 126, 127; XXII, 18;
XXVIII, 81
Joseph (Dec. 26, 1758-Sept. 29,
1825) m. June 11, 1781 Rosanna
Meloy XXXI, 190
Joshua (Sept. 14, 1733-Feb. 15,
1807) m. .... Sarah ...... V, 45
Levi (Aug. 19, 1753-a. 1778) m. ....
Sarah Olds VIII, 5
Moses (July 6, 1731-....) m. ....
Elizabeth ...... XXII, 18
Nathaniel (....-Mar. 22, 1658) m.
c. 1649 Mrs. Joanna West Coat
CONN XV, 18
Richard (bpt. Aug. 25, 1622-July 23,
1665) m. Feb. 5, 1642/3 Elizabeth
Alsop CONN VI, 11; IX, 16; X,
185, 276; XI, 113; XXVI, 199;
XXVII, 54; XXXIII, 177

Samuel (May 25, 1755-June 16, 1818)
m. .... Lucina Hill XV, 18
Theophilus (Nov. 27, 1735-Jan. 7,
1826) m. Apr. 24, 1776 (1) Sarah
Strong XI, 113
William (Sept. 15, 1710-Dec. 21,
1762) m. Sept. 23, 1741 Mary
Farmer XXXIII, 238, 239

BALL
Allen (Alling) (....-Nov. 1716)
m. 1646 Dorothy Fujell NH
XXXIII, 341
Benjamin (Feb. 12, 1752-p. 1780) m.
Oct. 18, 1774 Jerusha Woodbury
XXVI, 64
Edward (1644-1722/4) m. .... Abigail
Blatchley NJ XXX, 249
John (1585-Oct. 1, 1655) m. ....
.... MASS XXVI, 64;
XXVII, 17; XXX, 44
John (Oct. 2, 1742-1806) m. 1767
Sarah Ellen Payne VI, 28, 31
John (Aug. 6, 1743-1799) m. c. 1774
Lucretia ...... XXXIII, 341
Jonas (Oct. 16, 1748-Nov. 21, 1803)
m. Oct. 31, 1776 Mehitable Latham
XXVII, 17; XXX, 44
Jonathan (Dec. 31, 1759-July 31,
1834) m. Nov. 1782 Sarah Styles
XXX, 249
William (1615-Nov. 1680) m. July 2,
1638 Hannah Atherold VA VI, 29,
31; XXXI, 173, 184; XXXIII, 335;
XXXIV, 195, 198
William (1738-1807) m. .... Hannah
Smith XXXI, 173, 184; XXXIII,
335; XXXIV, 194, 198

BALLARD
Daniel (May 1, 1728-May 31, 1808)
m. Jan. 26, 1754 Ruth Houlton
XX, 28; XXXI, 203, 204
Josiah (Aug. 14, 1721-Aug. 6, 1799)
m. Mar. 23, 1744 Sarah Carter
VII, 11; XXX, 63, 64, 66
Philip (Mar. 24, 1747-Aug. 25, 1835)
m. Apr. 30, 1778 Mary Ewers XIV,
126
Sherebiah, Jr. (Sept. 24, 1722-1802)
m. .... Keziah Osgood IX, 23
Uriah (Oct. 7, 1758-Dec. 22, 1840)
m. c. 1784 Lois Lovejoy XXX, 104,
105
William (1617-July 10, 1689) m. May
16, 1638 (1) Elizabeth ......;
a. 1653 (2) Grace Berwick
MASS VII, 11; IX, 23; XIV,
126; XX, 28; XXX, 63, 64, 66,
104, 105; XXXI, 203,
204

BALLOU
Ariel (Nov. 18, 1715-Apr. 16, 1791)
m. c. 1740 Jerusha Slack XVIII,
127
James (Dec. 10, 1723-Jan. 21, 1812)
m. June 7, 1744 Tamasin Cook
XXII, 25
*Maturin (1610/20-1661/3) m. 1646/9
Hannah Pike RI XVIII, 127;
XXII, 25*
Seth (Feb. 20, 1749-Sept. 15, 1778)
m. 1766 Margaret Hilton XXII, 25

BANCKER
Adriaan (Apr. 2, 1770-a. 1822) m.
.... Elizabeth Decker XXXIII,
226, 227
*Gerrit (....-1690/1) m. Apr. 10,
1658 Elizabeth Dirkse Van Eps NY
XXXIII, 226, 227*

BANCROFT
Benjamin (May 6, 1701-July 21, 1787)
m. .... Anna Lawrence XXXIII, 274
Ephraim (Mar. 12, 1718/9-1791) m.
Dec. 6, 1739 Esther Gleason
XIV, 43
*John (....-1637) m. .... Jane ......
MASS XIV, 43*
Oliver (July 24, 1757-Aug. 18, 1840)
m. .... Sarah Hawley XIV, 43
Samuel (Apr. 22, 1737-Jan. 2, 1820)
m. June 14, 1759 Elizabeth Spelman
XIV, 59
*Thomas (....-Dec. 14, 1684) m. ....
Hannah ...... MASS XIV, 59
Thomas (c. 1625-Aug. 19, 1691) m.
Jan. 31, 1647 Elizabeth Metcalf
MASS XXXIII, 274*

BANGS
*Edward (Oct. 28, 1591-1678) m. ....
(2) Rebecca ...... XXX, 60, 61;
XXXII, 77*
James, Jr. (1738-....) m. Mar. 16,
1757 Susanna Hallett XXX, 60, 61
Nathan (May 2, 1736-Dec. 26, 1793)
m. Jan. 18, 1759 Abigail Wing
XXXII, 77

BANKESTOK, see BANKSTON

BANKS
*Adam (1645/8-a. 1690) m. ....
...... VA XXVI, 31; XXXIV, 273*
Gerard (c. 1725-June 15, 1787) m. c.
1750 Frances Bruce XXXIV, 273
*John (c. 1608-Dec. 12, 1685) m. ....
Mary Taintor CONN XX, 72*
Nehemiah (Feb. 28, 1722-Nov. 16,
1807) m. .... Abigail Bradley
XX, 72

Nehemiah, Jr. (Oct. 20, 1754-Apr.
19, 1835) m. Jan. 21, 1779
Sarah Sherwood XX, 72
Reuben (1745/50-p. 1810) m. 1783
Ann Hill XXVI, 31

BANKSTON, includes BANKESTOK,
BENKESTOK
*Andrew (Andre) (1640-1706) m. Nov.
22, 1668 Gertrude Rambo PA
XXX, 119, 120; XXXI, 114*
Jacob (1731-1817) m. 1753 Elinor
Cock XXXI, 114
John (June 15, 1754-Sept. 15, 1823)
m. June 10, 1778 Henrietta Coates
XXX, 119; XXXI, 114

BANTA
Albert (Aug. 29, 1728-Sept. 29,
1810) m. Nov. 28, 1756 Magdalena
Van Vorhees XXV, 38
*Epke (1615-1686) m. a. 1655
Tietske Dircksda NY XXV, 38;
XXXI, 225*
Hendrick, Sr. (c. 1718-a. Oct. 14,
1805) m. Aug. 12, 1738 (1)
Rachel Brower XXXI, 225

BANUM, see BYNUM

BARBER
Elijah (Jan. 11, 1745-May 22, 1825)
m. Dec. 29, 1768 Abigail Wood
XVI, 12; XVII, 8
Jacob (Sept. 23, 1738-1817) m. c.
1762 Prentice Lawrence XVII, 97,
98
*James (....-....) m. ....
...... RI XV, 104; XXVI, 201,
202*
Samuel (May 1, 1762-1843) m. Dec.
27, 1782 Thankful Kenyon XXVI,
201, 202
Stephen (Apr. 14, 1724-Aug. 22,
1806) m. Jan. 12, 1748 Alice Case
XIX, 130
*Thomas (1614-Sept. 11, 1662) m.
Oct. 1640 Jane ...... CONN XVI,
12; XVII, 8, 98; XIX, 130*
Thomas (June 5, 1731-Apr. 19, 1796)
m. Oct. 22, 1754 Mary Barney
XV, 104

BARDWELL
Joseph (1713-1791) m. .... Lydia
...... XV, 128
*Robert (....-Jan. 9, 1726) m. Nov.
29, 1676 Mary Gull MASS XV, 129*

BARKER
Benjamin (Sept. 4, 1755-1844) m. May
6, 1780 Lydia Foster XIII, 81

BARNES, cont.
William (c. 1635-Dec. 1, 1700) m.
1665 Elizabeth Mulford NY IV,
112; XXXI, 170

BARNEY
Aaron (Apr. 12, 1734-1817) m. Dec.
13, 1754 Susanna Bosworth
Carpenter XXXII, 123
Jacob (1601-Apr. 23, 1673) m. ....
Elizabeth ...... MASS XXIII;
12; XXXII, 123
John (May 1, 1730-Feb. 9, 1807) m.
Nov. 15, 1748 Rebecca Martin
XXIII, 12

BARNS, see BARNES

BARNUM
Ephraim (Aug. 28, 1733-Apr. 17,
1817) m. Feb. 1, 1775 Rachel
Starr Beebe XX, 46
Stephen (Feb. 17, 1757-Aug.
24, 1834) m. .... Lucy Wolcott
X, 77
Thomas (1625-Dec. 26, 1695) m. 1662
(1) Sarah Hurd CONN X, 77; XX,
46

BARRET
Francis (John) Feb. 22, 1762/3-July
6, 1833) m. 1781 Elizabeth Lowrey
XXVII, 47, 48; XXIX, 40
Robert (1710-1797) m. 1760 (2) Ann
Lee (Leigh) XXVII, 47
William (1590-1640) m. .... Ann
Ferrell VA XXVII, 47
William (Aug. 30, 1623-July 1705)
m. .... Anne Ludwell VA XXVII,
47; XXIX, 40

BARRETT
Alexander (1756-p. 1794) m. Jan. 19,
1779 Eleanor Cecil XXXI, 76, 77
Humphrey, Sr. (1592-Nov. 7, 1662) m.
.... Mary ...... MASS XXXI, 215
John, Sr. (c. 1651-p. May 3, 1722)
m. .... Ann Hill MD XXXI, 76,
77
Jonas (Sept. 24, 1737-July 31, 1803)
m. Feb. 8, 1781 (2) Urania Locke
XXXI, 215
Jonathan (Oct. 27, 1746-Sept. 11,
1818) m. Mar. 28, 1771 Abigail
Raymond VI, 91
Moses (Sept. 3, 1751-Apr. 30, 1830)
m. Jan. 24, 1774 Hannah Fuller
XXIX, 238
Thomas (....-Oct. 6, 1668) m.
.... Margaret ...... MASS VI,
91; XXIX, 238

BARROWS
John (c. 1609-Jan. 12, 1692) m. ....
(1) Ann ...... MASS XIII, 69
Moses (1724/5-Feb. 23, 1795) m. ....
Deborah Totman XIII, 70

BARTHOLOMEW
Abraham, Jr. (Jan. 28, 1732/3-1785)
m. .... Eunice Orvis XVIII, 96
William (1602/3-Jan. 18, 1680) m.
.... Anna Lord MASS XVIII, 96

BARTLETT
Aaron (Mar. 30, 1753-Apr. 22, 1823)
m. Nov. 25, 1775 Joanna Perkins
XXIX, 203
Abner (1755-Oct. 28, 1813) m. 1774/5
Anna Hovey XV, 30
Henry (....-....) m. .... Mary Bush
MASS XXIX, 223
Jeremiah (Aug. 16, 1741-....) m.
Mar. 25, 1762 Rebecca Lapham
XXXII, 124, 125
John (....-Aug. 17, 1684) m. c. 1665
Sarah Aldrich MASS XXXII, 124,
125
Jonathan (May 16, 1757-Feb. 20,
1830) m. June 10, 1779 Dorcas
Bartlett XVIII, 128
Joseph (c. 1630-Dec. 26, 1702) m.
Oct. 27, 1668 Mary Waite MASS
XXIX, 203
Joseph (Jan. 14, 1751-Sept. 20,
1800) m. Dec. 16, 1773 Hannah
Colcord XXX, 153, 154
Matthias (Sept. 26, 1740-p. 1790)
m. July 12, 1779 Tamison Herbert
XXII, 158; XXXIV, 60
Richard (1575-May 25, 1647) m. 1610
.... MASS XXII, 158;
XXX, 153, 154; XXXIV, 61
Robert (1603-Mar. 14, 1675/6) m.
.... Anne ...... MASS, CONN
XVIII, 128
Robert (c. 1606-1676) m. .... Mary
Warren MASS XV, 30
Zadoc (Apr. 10, 1756-Jan. 23, 1837)
m. 1780 Hannah Sever XXIX, 223

BARTON
Benjamin (Apr. 21, 1758-July 9,
1834) m. Dec. 9, 1779 Mehitable
Frye XXIV, 36, 66
Bezaleel (July 26, 1722-June 14,
1775) m. Apr. 30, 1747 Phebe
Carlton XXIV, 36, 66
Edward (....-a. Apr. 1671) m. ....
Elizabeth ...... MASS NH
XXIV, 36, 64; XXV, 15, 16; XXXI,
155
Joshua (Dec. 24, 1697-Feb. 13, 1793)

m. .... (1) Ann ...... XXV,
15, 16
Lewis (1726-1813) m. .... Sarah
Hustis (Husted) XIX, 88
Roger (1620-1688) m. .... Mary
Lounsberry NY XIX, 88
Stephen (June 10, 1740-Oct. 21,
1804) m. May 28, 1765 Dorothy
Moore XXXI, 155
Timothy (Apr. 13, 1732-1796) m.
Oct. 11, 1753 Hepzibah Stow XXV,
15, 16
Timothy Stow (Oct. 1758-June 30,
1844) m. June 20, 1780 Phebe
Stone XXV, 15, 16

BASCOM
Elias (May 8, 1738-Nov. 29, 1833) m.
.... (1) Eunice Allen VII, 14;
XXX, 157
Thomas (....-May 9, 1682) m. ....
Avis ...... CONN, MASS VII, 14,
XXX, 157

BASS
Ebenezer (Oct. 26, 1746-Mar. 6,
1814) m. Dec. 13, 1769 Ruth Waldo
XXIII, 77; XXVIII, 53
Samuel (1601-Dec. 30, 1694) m. ....
Anne ...... MASS XXIII, 77;
XXVIII, 53

BASSETT
Amos (Feb. 13, 1757-Dec. 31, 1826)
m. Oct. 24, 1782 Hannah Goodyear
XXXIII, 138, 139
Elisha (Feb. 11, 1761-Sept. 28,
1814) m. July 14, 1793 Kerurah
West XXXIV, 161
Isaac (1750-Feb. 18, 1841) m. Sept.
16, 1782 Desire Hotchkiss
XXIII, 31
Jeremiah (1751-1817) m. .... Hannah
Woodward II, 47
John (....-Feb. 1653) m. ....
Margery ...... CONN XXX, 34
Joseph (Apr. 26, 1743-Oct. 23, 1826)
m. Apr. 1782 Mary Tilton XXXIII,
52, 53
Nathan (Aug. 13, 1750-Oct. 10, 1841)
m. June 17, 1776 Martha Bassett
XXX, 185
Samuel, Jr. (Nov. 29, 1719-1809) m.
Oct. 26, 1748 Sarah Botsford
XXX, 34
Samuel (1723-Aug. 21, 1806) m. May
17, 1746 Susannah Morris XXIII,
31
Thomas (c. 1597-c. 1670) m. ....
Lydia Allcock CONN XXIII,
31

William (Oct. 21, 1600-Apr. 4, 1667)
m. 1622 (1) Elizabeth ...... MASS
II, 47; XVIII, 105; XXX, 185;
XXXIII, 52, 53; XXXIV, 162
William (1626-Aug. 29, 1684) m. Nov.
7, 1648 Hannah (Dickerman) Ives
CONN XXXIII, 138, 139
William (Dec. 17, 1702-1779) m. ....
Anna Mayhew XXX, 185
William (June 5, 1726-Dec. 15, 1776)
m. Mar. 16, 1748 Lydia Fisher
XVIII, 105

BATCHELDER, includes BACHELDER,
BACHILER, BATCHELLER, BATCHILER
Abraham (June 5, 1722-Jan. 31, 1813)
m. May 15, 1751 (1) Sarah Newton
V, 105, 106; XVI, 132, 133
Abraham, Jr. (Mar. 26, 1752-Aug. 13,
1832) m. .... Rebecca Dwight
V, 105, 106
David (Sept. 1, 1734-Oct. 5, 1816)
m. .... Mary Taylor XVII, 150
David (June 13, 1736-Mar. 11, 1811)
m. Jan. 1, 1771 (2) Mary Emery
XXXII, 54
Jacob (1752-1831) m. .... Lois
Rice IV, 95
Jeremiah (Sept. 19, 1740-Feb. 1,
1818) m. Aug. 22, 1765 Sarah Page
XXXIII, 254, 255
John (Sept. 7, 1741-June 6, 1812) m.
.... Sarah Murray XXI, 16, 17
John (Aug. 16, 1755-Dec. 18, 1848)
m. Mar. 17, 1780 Elizabeth
Batchelder XXI, 43, 44; XXVII,
69; XXIX, 389
Joseph (c. 1600-Mar. 1647) m. ....
Elizabeth ...... MASS IV, 95;
V, 105, 106; XVI, 133; XXI, 43,
44; XXVII, 23, 69; XXIX, 389
Joseph (Dec. 28, 1750-Mar. 25,
1827) m. 1769 Sarah Ferrin XX,
83; XXI, 176, 177; XXV, 295
Josiah (Dec. 19, 1753-May 2, 1827)
m. Dec. 26, 1786 Ruth Fletcher
XXVII, 23
Nathan (Oct. 25, 1734-1801) m. Apr.
8, 1756 (1) Margaret Bean X, 99
Stephen (1561-1660) m. .... (1)
Anna Bate; .... (2) Helen ......
NH X, 99; XVII, 150; XX, 83; XXI,
16, 17, 176, 177; XXV, 295; XXXII,
54; XXXIII, 254, 255

BATCHELLER, see BATCHELDER

BATCHILER, see BATCHELDER

BATEMAN
Eleazer (1662-Dec. 31, 1751) m.

BATEMAN, cont.
Nov. 2, 1686 Elizabeth Wright
MASS XXXIV, 114
Luther (Mar. 11, 1740-p. 1806) m.
c. 1775 Ruth ...... XXXIV, 114

BATES
Abraham, Jr. (Apr. 28, 1751-....)
m. May 20, 1773 Hannah Pratt
XXXIV, 68
Clement (Jan. 22, 1595-Sept. 17,
1671) m. .... Ann Blythe (Bliss)
MASS XXI, 27, 28; XXIV, 164;
XXIX, 182; XXXIV, 165
Edward (c. 1605-Mar. 25, 1686) m.
a. 1639 Susanna ...... MASS
XXXI, 15; XXXII, 208; XXXIV,
68
Joseph (Mar. 18, 1721/3-July 27,
1796) m. Nov. 16, 1749 Eunice
Tinkham XXXI, 15; XXXII, 208
Laban (Oct. 30, 1748-Apr. 17, 1832)
m. Dec. 28, 1768 Olive Wheelock
XXXIV, 165
Moses (Feb. 1754-Mar. 11, 1822
m. (int.) Oct. 9, 1790 Susannah
Mendall XXIV, 164
Nehemiah (June 19, 1740-May 20
1817) m. (int.) Dec. 5, 1761
Mrs. Mehitable Marble XXIX, 182
Samuel (Nov. 14, 1744-Nov. 3, 1801)
m. Oct. 13, 1764 Martha Beal XXI,
27, 28

BATTAILE
John (c. 1658-Feb. 1708) m. c.
1690 (2) Elizabeth Smith VA XXV,
90, 130; XXVI, 38, 39, 40; XXXII,
203, 208
Lawrence (1766-Jan. 1847) m. June
10, 1799 Ann Hay Taliaferro XXV,
90, 130; XXVI, 38, 39, 40; XXXII,
203, 208

BATTLE
Jesse (July 8, 1738-Aug. 25, 1805)
m. 1756 Susanna Fawcette XXXIV,
108
John (....-1690) m. .... Elizabeth
...... VA XXXIV, 108

BAUDOUIN, see BOWDEN

BAYLDON, see BELDING

BAYLES
John (1617-1682) m. .... Rebecca
...... NY XXXII, 138
John (Apr. 26, 1727-1784) m.
Mar. 30, 1747 Susannah Burtis
XXXII, 138

BAYLEY, see BAILEY

BAYNE, see BEAN

BAYNHAM, see BYNUM

BEACH
Augur (Agur) (p. Dec. 1724-Oct. 6,
1794) m. a. Dec. 19, 1751 (2)
Deborah Barnum XXXIII, 303
Eliakim (July 13, 1751-June 16,
1821) m. .... Abiah Summers V, 65
John (1623-June 16, 1677) m. 1650
Mary Staples CONN V, 65; XIX,
149; XXXII, 227; XXXIII, 303
John (May 18, 1718-Mar. 25, 1805) m.
.... Rebecca Berry XIX, 149
John (May 12, 1757-Feb. 16, 1801) m.
.... Jerusha Bonnell XIV, 15
John (Dec. 9, 1757-June 10, 1830)
m. June 13, 1779 Mabel Beers
XXXII, 227
Nathaniel (Feb. 14, 1741/2-Dec. 1,
1812) m. Mar. 14, 1765 Phebe
Potter XXIV, 10
Obil (Dec. 25, 1758-Sept. 1, 1846)
m. June 27, 1782 Elizabeth Kil-
bourne XVII, 44; XXI, 24; XXIX,
343; XXVIII, 77
Richard (c. 1618-c. 1688) m. 1641
Katherine (Cook) Hull CONN XXIV,
10
Thomas (1622-1662) m. Sept. 25,
1654 Sarah Platt CONN XIV, 15;
XVII, 44; XXI, 24; XXVIII, 77;
XXIX, 343

BEAL, see BEALL

BEALE, see BEALL

BEALL, includes BEAL, BEALE, BEALS
Alexander (Oct. 11, 1649-Aug. 1744)
m. .... Elizabeth ...... MD X,
66, 90, 102, 270; XXIX, 302; XXXI,
267
Andrew (1721-July 1781) m. a. 1745
Margaret Beall XIV, 106
Elisha (May 11, 1761-Nov. 1830) m.
Oct. 29, 1780 Lydia Tower
XIII, 122
James (bpt. Feb. 5, 1652-May 10,
1725) m. 1693 Sarah Pearce MD
XXI, 108, 109; XXIV, 127
John (1588-Apr. 1, 1688) m. July 13,
1630 Nazareth Hobart MASS XIII,
122; XXXI, 152
Jonathan, Sr. (May 22, 1737-p. 1810)
m. Oct. 31, 1760 Mary Joy XXX, 57
Joseph (....-....) m. ....
...... NH XXX, 57

Nathan (Oct. 9, 1727-....) m. ....
  Bathsheba ...... XXXI, 152
Ninian (1625-Feb. 28, 1717) m. c.
  1649 (1) Elizabeth Gordon; 1670
  (2) Ruth Moore MD XIV, 106;
  XXIX, 178
Ninian Edmonston (Jan. 27, 1755-
  Apr. 1831) m. Mar. 7, 1780
  Ann Marie Stricker XXIX, 302
Richard (1735-1799) m. ....
  Rebecca Adamson XXIX, 178
Richard (1738-Aug. 1778) m. 1758
  Sarah Brooke X, 66, 90, 102
Richard (1751-a. 1835) m. 1788
  Eleanor Magruder XXXI, 266, 267
Samuel (1714-Jan. 1778) m. May 23,
  1734 Eleanor Brooks X, 66, 90,
  102, 270
Thomas (July 1744-Nov. 30, 1823) m.
  1763 Verlinda Beall X, 269
William (....-1653) m. ....
  ...... ME X, 155, 251
William (bpt. July 13, 1749-p. 1790)
  m. May 17, 1772 Anna Woods X,
  155, 251
Zepheniah, Sr. (1720-July 1801) m.
  1768 Keziah Offutt Pritchett
  XXI, 108, 109; XXIV, 127

BEALS, see BEALL

BEAN, includes BAYNE, BEANE
Ebenezer (Jan. 20, 1737-p. July 18,
  1820) m. 1766 Eliza Thomas XXVII,
  26
Henry (1753/4-1833/40) m. 1775
  Sophia Duvall XXVI, 197, 198
John (c. 1634-1718) m. c. 1660 (2)
  Margaret ...... NH XXI, 15, 16;
  XXXIV, 319
John, Jr. (1756-1832) m. 1787 Betsy
  Moody XXI, 15, 16
Lewis (....-Apr. 4, 1677) m. 1668
  Mary Mills MASS XXVII, 26
Phineas (Sept. 1, 1750-Mar. 2, 1825)
  m. Dec. 11, 1770 Judith Snow
  XXXIV, 319
Walter (....-a. May 28, 1670) m.
  June 1661 (2) Eleanor Weston MD
  XXVI, 197, 198

BEANE, see BEAN

BEARCE
Asa (May 13, 1740-July 15, 1829) m.
  Nov. 27, 1760 Mary Randall
  XXXIII, 205
Austin (1618-a. 1697) m. 1639 Mary
  Hyanna MASS XXXIII, 205

BEARD
Andrew (bpt. Mar. 1, 1751/2-Jan. 3,

1838) m. Nov. 30, 1779 Susan
  Rogers XXXI, 214
David, Jr. (1755-1840) m. .... Mary
  (Polly) Tomlinson I, 44
James (Aug. 28, 1728-1812) m. ....
  Ruth Holbrook XII, 22
John (c. 1630-Sept. 1690) m. 1653
  Anna Hawley CONN I, 44; XII, 22;
  XXXI, 214

BEARDSLEE, see BEARDSLEY

BEARDSLEY, includes BEARDSLEE
Benjamin (Jan. 30, 1754-June 6,
  1837) m. Feb. 9, 1785 Amelia
  Stevens XXVI, 43, 135, 136;
  XXXIV, 215
Charles (May 28, 1739-Nov. 25, 1803)
  m. 1761 Mary Cary XXV, 168, 169;
  XXIX, 171; XXX, 183, 198; XXXII,
  126; XXXIII, 142
David (1728-May 11, 1802) m. a. 1752
  Mary Gregory IV, 123; VI, 62;
  XVII, 54, 55; XXVII, 183; XXVIII,
  71; XXXIII, 333
Elijah (May 27, 1760-Oct. 2, 1826)
  m. 1780 Sarah Hubbell XXX, 260
Gideon (1738-May 28, 1810) m. Apr.
  28, 1762 Mary Bearse XXXIII, 190;
  XXXIV, 137
Obadiah (June 18, 1763-Nov. 15, 1841)
  m. Nov. 10, 1784 (1) Eunice Moore
  V, 98; VIII, 16; X, 96
Phineas (Mar. 5, 1733-Jan. 20, 1812)
  m. 1755 Ruth Fairchild IX, 35, 42;
  XXX, 260; XXXI, 303, 304, 310;
  XXXIV, 255
Samuel (bpt. June 30, 1719-June 20,
  1790) m. Nov. 9, 1741 (1) Ann
  French; ....(2) Thankful Doolittle
  XXVI, 259, 260, 261, 262
Stephen (Mar. 20, 1763-Feb. 8, 1849)
  m. 1791 Catharine Beardsley IV,
  123; VI, 62
William (1605-1661) m. Jan. 26, 1631
  Marie (Mary) Harvie CONN I, 123;
  V, 98; VI, 62; VIII, 16; IX, 35,
  42; X, 96; XVII, 54; XXV, 168,
  169; XXVI, 43, 136, 259, 260, 261,
  262; XXVII, 183; XXVIII, 71; XXIX,
  171; XXX, 183, 198, 260; XXXI,
  303, 304, 310; XXXII, 126; XXXIII,
  142, 190, 333; XXXIV, 137, 215,
  255

BEATTY
John (....-p. Apr. 26, 1720) m. c.
  Nov. 7, 1691 Susanna Asfordby NY
  XXVII, 76
John (bpt. Nov. 15, 1719-p. Dec. 3,
  1799) m. Sept. 10, 1743 (1) Mary
  Brink XXVII, 76

BEAUCHAMP
  Edmund (....-Sept. 26, 1691) m.
    July 11, 1668 Sarah Dixon MD
    XXVII, 65
  Joshua (1731-c. 1817) m. Mar. 28,
    1773 Mary Davis Beauchamp
    XXVII, 65

BEAVEN, includes BEVAN
  Charles (....-1699) m. .... Mary
    Marsham MD XIII, 98; XVI, 22,
    59, 81; XIX, 19
  Charles (Apr. 11, 1756-1827) m.
    1778/9 Anna Jenkins XIII, 98;
    XVI, 22, 59, 81; XIX, 18

BECKER, includes BECKKER
  Abraham (bpt. May 20, 1733-May 3,
    1815) m. .... Elizabeth Becker
    XXIX, 132
  Henricus (Henry) (bpt. Apr. 27,
    1743-1830) m. May 3, 1772 Maria
    Zimmer XXXI, 124
  Jan Jurgerison (....-1697) m. a.
    Sept. 1, 1660 Maria Adriance NY
    XII, 59; XXIX, 132; XXXI, 124
  Johannes H. (bpt. Dec. 27, 1719-
    1794) m. .... Anna Maria Scherg
    XII, 59
  Pieter (bpt. Nov. 2, 1740-Mar.
    19, 1803) m. .... Anna Eckerson
    XII, 59

BECKKER, see BECKER

BECKWITH
  David (Feb. 16, 1754-1834) m. a.
    1793 Abigail Whitney XXIII,
    38
  Jason (c. 1764-Feb. 18, 1821) m.
    May 19, 1785 Elizabeth Crocker
    VIII, 24; X, 301
  Matthew (Sept. 22, 1610-Dec. 13,
    1681) m. 1635 Elizabeth ......
    CONN VIII, 24; X, 301; XXIII,
    38; XXIX, 11; XXXIV, 238
  Roswell (Oct. 21, 1753-Feb. 2, 1836)
    m. Jan. 13, 1780 Lydia Dorr
    XXIX, 11
  Silas (1746-Oct. 13, 1835) m. p.
    1760 (1) Anna Reeves; .... (2)
    Anna Smith XXXIV, 238

BEDFORD
  Thomas, Sr. (1725-Mar. 7, 1785) m.
    Sept. 24, 1750 Mary Ligon Coleman
    XXX, 214; XXXII, 291
  Thomas, Jr. (1751-Apr. 1804) m. 1780
    Anne Robertson XXX, 214
  William (1600-....) m. ....
    ...... VA XXX, 214; XXXII, 291

BEEBE
  Alexander (Oct. 29, 1759-Jan. 30,
    1841) m. July 31, 1780 Sarah
    Bowker XXXII, 294
  John, II (Nov. 4, 1628-Apr. 14,
    1714) m. a. 1660 Abigail Yorke
    CONN XXXII, 122
  Joseph (1748-Mar. 17, 1835) m. Apr.
    15, 1773 Tameson Terrill XXXII,
    122
  Samuel (June 23, 1633-1712) m. a.
    1662 Mary Keeney CONN XX, 76;
    XXXII, 294
  Stewart (1759-June 13, 1825) m.
    Jan. 14, 1779 Huldah Beebe XX,
    76

BEECHER
  David (Apr. 25, 1738-June 12, 1805)
    m. Mar. 1775 (3) Esther Lyman
    XXII, 106; XXIV, 120; XXX, 218,
    219
  John (1590/1600-1637/8) m. ....
    Hannah Potter CONN XXII, 106;
    XXIII, 51; XXIV, 120; XXX, 218,
    219
  Nathaniel (Mar. 7, 1706-Feb. 9,
    1786) m. .... Sarah Sperry XXX,
    218, 219
  Thomas (Apr. 20, 1722-Nov. 22, 1787)
    m. Dec. 15, 1745 Elizabeth Terrell
    XXIII, 51

BEEKMAN
  Christopher (Jan. 1, 1730-Nov. 11,
    1829) m. .... Martha Veghte
    XII, 19
  Wilhelmus (Apr. 28, 1623-Sept. 21,
    1707) m. Sept. 5, 1649 Catalina
    de Boogh NY XII, 19

BEEMAN
  Daniel (Jan. 18, 1756-Apr. 3, 1844)
    m. Feb. 23, 1779 Mary Bliss
    XV, 138; XIX, 149
  Simon (....-1675) m. Oct. 15, 1654
    Alice Young MASS XV, 139; XIX,
    149

BEERS
  Anthony (....-1676) m. .... Elizabeth
    ...... MASS, CONN XVI, 74; XVIII,
    118; XX, 47, 49
  Nathan (Feb. 10, 1718-June 18, 1805)
    m. .... Lydia Hawley XVI, 74,
    75; XVIII, 118; XX, 47, 49

BELCHER
  Adam (June 30, 1756-May 30, 1819)
    m. c. 1780 Elizabeth Bennett
    XXXIII, 125, 126

Andrew, Sr. (1613/4-1673) m. ....
(2) Elizabeth Danforth MASS
XXXIII, 125, 126
Gregory (Mar. 30, 1606-Nov. 25,
1674) m. .... Catherine ......
MASS X, 303; XIII, 6
Jeremiah (c. 1613-Mar. 1692/3) m.
.... Mary Clifford MASS XII
89
Jonathan (Feb. 27, 1717/8-Oct. 17,
1785) m. .... Elizabeth Tuttle
XII, 89
Joseph (May 10, 1751-1816) m. ....
Rachel Shute XII, 89
William (Aug. 29, 1731-June 27,
1801) m. Mar. 23, 1752 Desire
Morgan XIII, 5; X, 303

BELDEN, see BELDING

BELDING, includes BAILDON, BAYLDON,
BELDEN, BELDON
Azor (1749-Nov. 27, 1828) m. ....
Hannah Couch Smith IV, 118
Joab (July 2, 1758-Jan. 12, 1814)
m. Oct. 6, 1782 Betsy Stevens
XXXI, 306
Joseph (Oct. 31, 1735-p. 1796) m.
c. 1770 Lydia Silvey XVIII, 146
Moses (Oct. 25, 1740-July 4, 1811)
m. Feb. 25, 1762 Rachel Hayes
XVII, 97; XXII, 138, 139
Richard (bpt. May 26, 1591-c. Aug.
1655) m. .... CONN
XVII, 97; XVIII, 147; XXII, 138,
139; XXXI, 306
William (c. 1622-1660/5) m. ....
Tomasin ...... CONN IV, 118

BELDON, see BELDING

BELL
Francis (....-Jan. 8, 1689) m. ....
Rebecca ...... CONN XIX, 63;
XXXII, 16, 17
George (Nov. 11, 1760-Apr. 25, 1834)
m. Dec. 25, 1795 Susannah Bell
XII, 14, 15
Robert (....-1624) m. ....
...... VA XII, 15
Thaddeus (Mar. 18, 1758/9-Oct. 31,
1851) m. May 4, 1780 Elizabeth
Howe XIX, 63; XXXII, 16, 17

BELLOWS
Hezekiah (Mar. 16, 1734-....) m.
Aug. 3, 1759 Mary Newell XXX,
147
John (c. 1623-Jan. 10, 1683) m. May
9, 1655 Mary Wood MASS X, 293;
XXVI, 83; XXIX, 279; XXX, 147

John (Oct. 22, 1742-Aug. 19, 1812)
m. 1770 Rebecca Hubbard X, 293
Joseph (May 26, 1744-May 22, 1817)
m. Oct. 3, 1764 Lois Whitney
XXVI, 82, 83; XXIX, 278

BEMIS
Isaac (Mar. 21, 1756-Dec. 28, 1839)
m. Oct. 21, 1784 Mary Esther
Stevens XXIII, 21; XXXI, 98
Joseph (1619-Aug. 7, 1684) m. ....
Sarah ...... MASS XXIII, 21;
XXXI, 98

BENEDICT
Amos (Sept. 17, 1722-July 29, 1809)
m. .... Martha Sturtevant XXX,
64, 65, 187
Isaac Oliver (Aug. 14, 1764-Oct. 24,
1845) m. 1788 Asenath Beach
XXXII, 228
John (1717-Mar. 17, 1792) m. ....
Lydia ...... XI, 121
John (Oct. 3, 1726-July 9, 1814)
m. Jan. 24, 1749/50 Esther
Stebbins XI 40
Jonathan (Apr. 12, 1744-July 20,
1834) m. 1763 (1) ....;
July 11, 1782 (2) Huldah Seelye
XI, 166; XXVI, 78
Nathaniel (....-a. Oct. 26, 1805) m.
.... Hannah ...... XXVI, 78
Solomon (....-Jan. 1777) m. Mar. 7,
1776 Hannah Benedict XXX, 64, 65,
187
Thomas (1617-1690) m. 1640 Mary
Bridgum CONN, NY XI, 40, 121,
166; XXVI, 78; XXX, 64, 65, 187;
XXXII, 228

BENHAM
John (....-1661) m. ....
...... MASS, CONN XXIX, 367;
XXXIV, 174
John (Oct. 4, 1723-May 24, 1811) m.
Sept. 23, 1747 Mary Curtis
XXXIV, 173
Joseph (....-1703) m. Jan. 15, 1657
Winifred King CONN XXXIV, 174
Lyman (May 6, 1759/60-Feb. 16, 1831)
m. Feb. 26, 1784 Lois Hall XXIX,
366

BENJAMIN
John (c. 1598-June 14, 1645) m. 1619
Abigail Eddy MASS XX, 22
Samuel (Feb. 5, 1753-Apr. 14, 1824)
m. Jan. 16, 1782 Tabitha Livermore
XX, 21

BENKESTOK, see BANKSTON

BENNET, see BENNETT

BENNETT, includes BENNET
Benjamin, Jr. (May 22, 1753-Aug.
25, 1832) m. 1774 Martha
Brownell XIX, 136
Ebenezer, III (Jan. 31, 1747-Nov.
19, 1778) m. Oct. 19, 1769
Mrs. Elizabeth Ellis XXXIII, 105
Ephraim (c. 1718-Oct. 7, 1779) m.
June 19, 1745 Ann Baldwin
XXVII, 20
Henry (c. 1629-p. 1707) m. c. 1650
Lydia Perkins MASS XIII, 8
Isaac (1650-May 23, 1720) m. June 2,
1683 Elizabeth Rose CONN X, 305
James (....-....) m. c. 1639 Hannah
Wheeler MASS, CONN XIX, 136;
XXVII, 20
James (1727-p. 1809) m. July 3,
1751 Sarah Dodge XIII, 8
John, Sr. (1641-Mar. 21, 1717) m.
1671 Deborah Grover VA, MASS
XXXIII, 105
Nathan (Feb. 1741-June 11, 1800)
m. .... Elizabeth Lewis X, 304
William Adriance (a. 1636-p. 1654)
m. Mary Ann Badger Thomas NY
XVIII, 56
Winant (Feb. 29, 1740-Mar. 31, 1816)
m. Aug. 1763 Jemima Van Duyn
XVIII, 56

BENT
David (Mar. 30, 1730-Jan. 15, 1798)
m. Apr. 3, 1751 (1) Lucy Moore
XII, 13; XXVII, 104
Francis (Mar. 10, 1754-Oct. 27,
1828) m. Nov. 20, 1794 (2) Abigail
Dexter Bates XXXII, 240, 241
Joel (Feb. 22, 1750-Nov. 25, 1812)
m. July 13, 1768 Mary Mason
XXVIII, 20, 21
John (Nov. 20, 1596-Sept. 27, 1672)
m. c. 1624 Martha ...... MASS
XII, 13; XXVII, 104; XXVIII, 21;
XXXII, 241

BENTLEY
George (1730-Oct. 28, 1814) m.
June 27, 1751 Amy Carter XVII,
100
William (....-c. 1720) m. .... Sarah
Litchfield RI XVII, 100

BENTON
Andrew (bpt. Oct. 15, 1620-July 31,
1683) m. 1649 (1) Hannah Stocking
CONN X, 13; XXXIV, 202
David, Jr. (Dec. 2, 1763-Mar. 7,
1845) m. Mar. 17, 1784 (1)

Sarah Bingham X, 13
Jacob, Jr. (Jan. 2, 1729-Jan. 13,
1807) m. 1755 Hannah Slade XXXIV,
202

BERGEN
Hans Hansen (....-p. July 19, 1653)
m. 1639 Sarah Rapalje NY
XXXII, 24
John B. (Mar. 27, 1739-June 2, 1808)
m. June 8, 1763 Sarah Stryker
XXXII, 24

BERNARD
Thomas (Mar. 1756-June 12, 1834) m.
Dec. 28, 1792 Mary Hicks XXXII,
234; XXXIV, 250
William (....-1704) m. ....
...... VA XXXII, 234; XXXIV, 250

BERRY
Benjamin, Jr. (Aug. 25, 1739-p.
1788) m. .... Phoebe Perkins XII,
104
James (....-c. 1685) m. .... Eliza-
beth ...... VA, MD VI, 96
Samuel (Aug. 6, 1711-....) m. Oct.
14, 1735 Mary Fuller XIV, 100
Thaddeus (....-1718) m. .... Hannah
Farrar MASS XII, 104; XIV, 100
Zachariah, Sr. (July 11, 1749-1845)
m. c. 1778 Mary Williams VI, 95

BERRYMAN
John (....-a. Jan. 28, 1679/80) m.
.... Jane Tucker VA XXX, 56;
XXXII, 101
William (1713-Mar. 11, 1784) m.
Sept. 10, 1743 Rebecca Vowels
XXX, 56; XXXII, 101

BERTHOLF
Guiliaem (1656-1724) m. 1677
Martyntje Vermeulen NY, NJ
XVI, 104; XVII, 42; XVIII, 70
Henry (Aug. 12, 1750-1818) m. Nov.
21, 1773 Anna Vandervoort
XVIII, 70
Samuel (1745-1813) m. 1772 Hannah
Hopper XVI, 104; XVII, 42

BEVAN, see BEAVEN

BEVIER, see BOVIER

BEVILL, see BEVILLE

BEVILLE, includes BEVILL
Essex, Sr. (....-....) m. c. 1699
Amy (Ann) Butler VA XXXI,
95

Robert, III (c. 1753-p. 1838) m.
Dec. 27, 1774 Sarah (Williams)
Hudson XXXI, 95

BIBB
Benjamin (1610-1702) m. .... Mary
...... VA XII, 43, 60; XVI, 11,
12; XIX, 127; XX, 113; XXII, 108;
XXIX, 16
James (1753-Nov. 23, 1846) m. ....
(1) Nancy Fleming; .... (2) Sallie
Nowlin XII, 60; XIX, 127; XX,
113; XXII, 108; XXIX, 15
John (1750-1795) m. .... Susannah
...... XVI, 11, 12
Thomas (1731-c. 1789) m. .... Eliza-
beth ...... XIX, 127; XXII, 108
William (1735-1796) m. .... (2)
Sallie E. Wyatt XII, 43

BIDDLE
Charles (Dec. 24, 1745-Apr. 4, 1821)
m. Nov. 25, 1772 Hanna Shepard
XIII, 114
William (c. 1630-1712) m. Feb. 1665
Sarah Kemp NJ XIII, 114

BIDWELL
Adonijah (Aug. 6, 1761-Feb. 14,
1837) m. Jan. 1, 1789 Melicent
Dench VI, 34
John (c. 1618-1687) m. June 26, 1640
Sarah Wilcox CONN VI, 34;
XXXIII, 216; XXXIV, 97, 98, 131
Stephen (Nov. 1730-May 26, 1806) m.
a. 1760 Rebecca Keeney XXXIII,
216
Thomas (1738/9-Dec. 3, 1802) m. 1759
Esther Orton XXXIV, 97, 98, 131

BIGELOW, includes BIGLO, BIGLOW,
BIGOLOUGH
Asa (Sept. 13, 1738-Sept. 22, 1807)
m. May 19, 1766 Rebecca Richardson
XXV, 199
Charles (Apr. 22, 1729-Nov. 20,
1782) m. Dec. 23, 1760 Lucy Bennett
XXIX, 33; XXX, 22; XXXII, 158
Daniel (July 16, 1732-p. 1799) m.
.... Martha Pratt IV, 158
David (May 7, 1732-Oct. 6, 1820) m.
June 17, 1762 Patience Foote
XXVI, 174; XXXI, 187, 188
Jabez (Dec. 19, 1736-Aug. 13, 1822)
m. Oct. 5, 1760 Deborah Knowlton
XVII, 136
Joel (June 30, 1752-1830) m. c. 1773
Sarah Stowell XXXIII, 339
John (bpt. Feb. 16, 1616-July 14,
1703) m. Aug. 30, 1642 (1) Mary
Warren MASS IV, 158; IX, 5;

XVII, 136; XIX, 89; XXV, 199;
XXVI, 60, 174; XXIX, 33; XXX, 22;
XXXI, 53, 188; XXXII, 158; XXXIII,
339
John (Nov. 20, 1739-June 23, 1780)
m. June 30, 1771 Hannah Wadsworth
XXVI, 60, 61
Jotham, Sr. (Sept. 1, 1717-Apr. 8,
1786) m. May 23, 1750 Mary Richard-
son XIX, 89
Otis (Jan. 24, 1747-Sept. 10, 1832)
m. .... Betsey Bartlett IX, 5
Solomon (July 1, 1742-May 12, 1808)
m. June 10, 1772 (2) Hannah
Sanderson XXXI, 53, 54

BIGGS
John (....-p. 1687) m. .... Mary
Hall NY XXXI, 12
John (1752-June 7, 1782) m. 1770
Abigail ...... XXI, 12

BIGLO, see BIGELOW

BIGLOW, see BIGELOW

BIGOLOUGH, see BIGELOW

BIGSBY, see BIXBY

BILL
Eleazer (Feb. 24, 1758-Apr. 4, 1851)
m. May 27, 1790 Elizabeth Cole
XIV, 16
Philip (c. 1620-July 8, 1689) m.
Hannah ...... MASS, CONN XIV,
16

BILLING, see BILLINGS

BILLINGS, includes BILLING
Jesse (1742-1801) m. Mar. 14, 1770
Sarah Bardwell XXVI, 128, 205,
206
Roger (1620-Nov. 15, 1683) m. 1640
(1) Mary ......; .... (2) Hannah
...... MASS XVIII, 110; XXVI,
128, 205, 206
Samuel (Mar. 26, 1757-Apr. 1842) m.
May 24, 1781 Hannah Whiting
XVIII, 110
Sanford (Apr. 20, 1736-Apr. 25, 1806)
m. Jan. 24, 1760 Lucy Geer X, 52
William (c. 1629-Mar. 16, 1713) m.
Feb. 12, 1657/8 Mary ...... MASS
X, 53

BILLINGSLEY
Charles (1739-a. Jan. 15, 1810) m.
1783/4 (2) Rachel ...... XXVI,
124; XXVIII, 37

BILLINGSLEY, cont.
Francis (1620-June 10, 1695) m. ....
    Ann ...... MD XXVI, 124; XXVIII,37

BILLUPS
George (1630-p. 1684) m. 1655 Sarah
    ...... VA XV, 80
John (Mar. 17, 1755/6-Oct. 23,
    1814) m. 1798 Susannah (Carleton)
    Cox XV, 80

BINGHAM
Elijah (June 1, 1719-Mar. 19, 1798)
    m. July 19, 1752/3 (2) Sarah
    Jackson XIII, 46
Elisha (July 13, 1740-Dec. 21, 1821)
    m. c. 1770 Hannah Slapp XV, 102
Thomas (bpt. June 25, 1642-Jan. 16,
    1729) m. Dec. 12, 1666 Mary Rudd
    CONN XIII, 46; XV, 102

BIRCHARD
Jesse (Sept. 12, 1736-Aug. 3, 1809)
    m. Aug. 13, 1765 Lydia Waterman
    Backus XVIII, 59
Thomas (1595-Oct. 3, 1657) m. ....
    Mary Robinson MASS, CONN
    XVIII, 59

BIRD
Isaac (Jan. 18, 1723/4-Aug. 1804)
    m. Apr. 13, 1748 Elizabeth Searle
    XXIV, 122
Matthew (Jan. 7, 1756-Jan. 11, 1816)
    m. 1778 Mary Cone XXXIV, 99
Thomas (1613-June 8, 1667) m. .....
    Anne ...... MASS XXIV, 122;
    XXXIV, 99

BIRGE
James (Oct. 16, 1758-Feb. 10, 1850)
    m. Oct. 29, 1780 Sally Palmer '
    XXXIV, 47
Richard (....-Sept. 29, 1651) m.
    Oct. 5, 1641 Elizabeth Gaylord
    CONN XXXIV, 47

BISHOP
Edward (....-c. 1715) m. c. 1646
    Hannah More MASS XXI, 18
Elkanah (June 2, 1743-c. 1820) m.
    Aug. 10, 1759 Lydia Leonard Cobb
    Robinson XXI, 18
John (1604-Feb. 1661) m. .... Anne
    ...... CONN XII, 49
Linus (May 10, 1749-Sept. 14, 1830)
    m. June 29, 1785 Mrs. Sarah (Hill)
    Chapman XII, 49
Reuben (Nov. 2, 1740-Sept. 24, 1775)
    m. Feb. 18, 1761 Hannah Bishop
    XVIII, 28, 29

Thomas (....-Feb. 7, 1670) m. ....
    Margaret ...... MASS XVIII, 28

BISSELL
Benjamin (Dec. 12, 1743-Feb. 28,
    1821) m. .... Mabel Griswold XXV,
    214; XXVIII, 104, 166
Hezekiah (May 20, 1737-Nov. 4, 1831)
    m. .... (3) Elizabeth Bartlett
    XXXI, 294, 295
John (1591-Oct. 3, 1677) m. ....
    Mary Drake CONN IV, 132; XXIV,
    112; XXV, 214; XXVIII, 104, 166;
    XXXI, 294, 295
Isaac (Aug. 5, 1747-June 19, 1823)
    m. Dec. 1770 Abiatha Way XXIV,
    111
Zebulon (1724-1777) m. .... Abigail
    Smith IV, 132

BIXBY, includes BIGSBY
Jonathan (c. 1730-Jan. 30, 1812) m.
    July 4, 1752 (1) Martha Hull
    XXXIV, 291
Joseph (bpt. Oct. 28, 1621-Apr. 19,
    1701) m. Oct. 15, 1647 Sarah
    (Wyatt) Heard MASS XXXIV, 291

BLACKFORD
Jeremiah (Oct. 10, 1752-Jan. 1825)
    m. 1780 Mary Kelley XXXIV, 181
Samuel (c. 1640-a. Feb. 12, 1711/2)
    m. .... Anna ...... NJ XXXIV,
    181

BLACKMER, includes BLACKMORE
Joseph (Mar. 21, 1729-Feb. 21, 1795)
    m. 1751 Mary Corbett XXXIV, 178
Salisbury, Sr. (Apr. 2, 1750-1816)
    m. (int.) Dec. 12, 1772 Phoebe
    Reed XXXIV, 274
William (c. 1636-Apr. 21, 1676) m.
    July 17, 1666 Elizabeth Banks
    MASS XXXIV, 178, 274

BLACKMORE, see BLACKMER

BLACKWELL
Jacob (Nov. 20, 1717-Oct. 23, 1780)
    m. Feb. 19, 1755 Lydia Hallett
    XVII, 68, 69
Joseph (1615-p. 1680) m. ....
    ...... VA XI, 176, 177
Joseph (1755-Sept. 8, 1823) m. 1802
    (2) Mary Waddy Brant XI, 176, 177
Robert (May 15, 1650-1717) m. 1676
    Mary Manningham NJ, NY XVII, 68;
    XXIX, 232, 252
Stephen (1756-Dec. 3, 1831) m. ....
    Rachel Hunt XXIX, 231, 232,
    252

BLAISDELL, includes BLASDEL
Isaac (Mar. 27, 1738-Oct. 9, 1791)
m. Mar. 16, 1758 Mary Currier
XXII, 73
Jacob (Apr. 8, 1754-Apr. 25, 1831)
m. Mar. 26, 1778 Ruth Morse XVI,
106, 107; XXV, 283; XXXIV, 73
Jedediah (May 4, 1754-Jan. 13,
1844) m. May 2, 1779 Lydia
Trafton XXVII, 29, 30
Nathaniel (Apr. 6, 1720/1-Dec. 22,
1786) m. Jan. 14, 1744/5 Mary
Blay XX, 6
*Ralph (c. 1600-1649) m. ....
Elizabeth ...... ME XVI, 106,
107; XX, 6; XXII, 74; XXV, 283;
XXVII, 29, 30; XXIX, 69; XXXII,
60; XXXIV, 73*
William (Nov. 30, 1756-p. Mar. 26,
1818) m. Jan. 19, 1782 Lydia
Robbins XXIX, 69; XXXII, 60

BLAKE
Asahel (Oct. 16, 1749-Sept. 7, 1822)
m. Oct. 8, 1780 (2) Sarah Dearborn
XXXI, 311
Benjamin (May 9, 1739-Oct. 12, 1809)
m. Aug. 17, 1763 Elizabeth Harris
XIII, 116; XXIV, 16
Ebenezer (Sept. 28, 1730-Sept. 12,
1819) m. Oct. 11, 1756 (1) Tamar
Thompson XXXIV, 312
George (Oct. 30, 1758-Dec. 17, 1851)
m. Aug. 1, 1782 Huldah Leonard
XIX, 72
*Jasper (Feb. 6, 1647-Jan. 5, 1673/4
m. .... Deborah Dalton NH
XXXI, 311*
*John (c. 1652-Nov. 11, 1690) m. 1673
Sarah Hall CONN XIX, 72*
Seth (Sept. 19, 1752-Mar. 4, 1829)
m. 1772 Rooksby (Ruxbee) Leadbet-
ter XXX, 72
*Thomas, I (....-p. Jan. 30, 1707) m.
.... Alice (Alise) ...... VA
XXXII, 83*
*William (July 10, 1594-Oct. 25,
1663) m. Sept. 23, 1617 Agnes
(Thorn) Bland MASS XIII, 117;
XXIV, 16; XXX, 72; XXXIV, 313*
William (c. 1745-p. Oct. 18, 1796)
m. .... XXXII, 83

BLAKER, includes BLEEKER, BLEIKER
Euchylus (c. 1752-1822) m. 1753
Sarah Buckman XVIII, 38
*Johannes (1660-1741) m. .... Judith
...... PA XVIII, 38*

BLAKESLEE, includes BLAKSLEE
David (Nov. 7, 1722-Feb. 11, 1781)

m. May 18, 1752 (2) Abigail How
XXVII, 123
Jonah (May 3, 1753-1791) m. ....
.... XX, 26
Joseph (Apr. 1, 1732-1804) m. Apr.
1, 1756 Lois Ives XXII, 35
Jotham (July 4, 1736-Feb. 18, 1792)
m. Jan. 18, 1758 (1) Hannah Todd;
June 1, 1781 (3) Mary Gilbert
Wooden XI, 11; XV, 133; XVII, 129
*Samuel (1620/5-May 17, 1672) m. Dec.
3, 1650 Hannah Potter CONN XI,
11; XV, 133; XVII, 129; XX, 26;
XXII, 35; XXVII, 123*

BLAKSLEE, see BLAKESLEE

BLANCHARD
Abel (Feb. 17, 1761-Aug. 12, 1827)
m. c. 1782 Elizabeth Eastman
XXIII, 63
David (Apr. 10, 1740-p. 1780) m.
Nov. 11, 1760 Margaret Dolliver
XXIII, 55
*Thomas (a. 1620-May 21, 1654) m. ....
Agnes Brent MASS XXIII, 55, 63*

BLAND
Richard (1710-Oct. 26, 1776) m. 1729
Anne Poythress XXXIV, 118
*Theodoric (bpt. Jan. 16, 1629-1671)
m. c. 1641 Anne Bennett VA
XXXIV, 118*

BLANDEN, see BLANDING

BLANDING, includes BLANDEN, BLANTINE,
BLANTON
Ebenezer (Feb. 26, 1754-c. 1844) m.
Aug. 29, 1773 Nancy Wheeler XXX,
271; XXXI, 58
*William (....-June 15, 1662) m. ....
Phoebe ...... MASS XXX, 271;
XXXI, 58*

BLANTINE, see BLANDING

BLANTON, see BLANDING

BLASDEL, see BLAISDELL

BLAUVELT
Arie (Sept. 2, 1738-Mar. 8, 1801)
m. Sept. 14, 1763 Altie Smith
XIV, 34, 35
*Gerrit Hendricksen (Apr. 9, 1620-a.
Mar. 4, 1685) m. May 7, 1646 Mar-
retje Lambertse Moel NY VIII,
17; XIV, 34, 35; XXX, 80; XXXIV,
149*
Hendrick (June 26, 1732-Nov. 24,

BOBET, see BABBITT

BOCHOLTE, see BOOKHOUT

BOCKEE, includes BOKEE, BOUCQUET
Jerome (1621-p. 1667) m. 1641(1)
   Anne L'Agache NY XI, 42, 44;
   XII, 25
William (Feb. 25, 1733-1798) m.
   Nov. 6, 1756 Jenette Minthorne
   XI, 41, 44; XII, 25

BODDIE, see BODIE

BODIE, includes BODDIE
John, III (a. 1750-p. 1790) m. 1772
   Hannah ...... XXXI, 297
William (bpt. 1633-p. Dec. 17, 1712)
   m. 1684 Elizabeth ...... VA
   XXXI, 297

BODFISH
Jonathan (Aug. 10, 1727-Jan. 18,
   1818) m. May 3, 1753 Desire How-
   land XXVIII, 182, 183
Robert (....-1651) m. .... Bridget
   ...... MASS XXVIII, 182, 183

BOGAERT, see BOGART

BOGARDUS
Cornelius   (Apr. 26, 1726-....)
   m. Jan. 4, 1753 Catherine Maghtij
   Phillips XXIV, 39
Cornelius, Jr. (Jan. 22, 1758-July
   6, 1811) m. .... Elizabeth Roe
   XXIV, 39
Everardus (1607-Sept. 1647) m.
   Jan. 29, 1638 Annetjen (Webber)
   Jans NY XIII, 84; XXIV, 162;
   XXV, 299
James C. (Oct. 23, 1762-Oct. 13,
   1836) m. 1784 Mary Scutt XXIV,
   162; XXV, 299
Lewis (1753-p. 1783) m. ....
   Annetji Knoxen XIII, 84

BOGART, includes BOGAERT
Jacob (Apr. 7, 1723-p. May 15, 1777)
   m. .... (1) Ann Doremus XXVI,
   270, 271
Tunis Gysberten (c. 1625-1685) m. c.
   1655 (1) Sara (Rapalje) Bergen NY
   XXVI, 270, 271

BOKEE, see BOCKEE

BOLLES
Joseph (Feb. 1608-1678) m. 1640
   Mary Howell ME XXXIII, 48, 49
Lemuel (Aug. 13, 1757-June 16, 1825)

m. Feb. 16, 1785 Lucy Perkins
   XXXIII, 48, 49

BOLLING
Robert (Dec. 26, 1646-July 17, 1709)
   m. 1675 (1) Jane Rolfe; .... (2)
   Anne Smith VA VII, 40; XIII, 94;
   XVII, 75; XXXIV, 19
Robert (1730-Feb. 24, 1775) m. Apr.
   11, 1758 (2) Mary Marshall Tabb
   VII, 40; XIII, 94; XVII, 75
Samuel, Sr. (Sept. 27, 1758-Aug. 14,
   1808) m. Nov. 2, 1772 Abigail
   Choice XXXIV, 18
William (May 5, 1731-1776) m. 1755
   Amelia Randolph XXXIV, 18

BOND
Ephraim (Dec. 3, 1746-Mar. 29, 1819)
   m. May 28, 1772 Eleanor Abbot
   XXX, 292
John (bpt. Feb. 5, 1624-Dec. 3,
   1674) m. Aug. 15, 1649 Hester
   Blakeley MASS XXX, 292
John (Mar. 16, 1724-June 30, 1808)
   m. Nov. 21, 1751 Silence King
   XXXIII, 317, 318
Peter (....-1706) m. ....
   ...... MD XXII, 49
Thomas (1739-1807) m. Feb. 1771
   Rebecca Stansbury XXII, 49
William (bpt. Sept. 3, 1625-Dec. 14,
   1695) m. Feb. 7, 1649/50 Sarah
   Biscoe MASS XXXIII, 317, 318

BONNELL
Abraham (Aug. 4, 1732-Nov. 1,
   1797) m. .... Elizabeth Foster
   XII, 24
William (....-p. Aug. 27, 1669) m.
   .... Anne Wilmot MASS XII, 24

BONSALL
Jonathan (Sept. 3, 1738-Apr. 10,
   1814) m. Mar. 9, 1763 Elizabeth
   Evans XXIX, 153; XXX, 82, 117
Richard (bpt. Mar. 17, 1641-July
   13, 1699) m. .... Mary Wood PA
   XXIX, 153; XXX, 82, 117

BOOKER
Edward (1761-Jan. 1800) m. Oct. 27,
   1783 Edith Cobbs Anderson XXI,
   156
Richard (1652-1704) m. .... (1) Rebecca Leake; .... (2) Hannah Hand
   VA XXI, 156; XXX, 275; XXXII,
   138; XXXIV, 74
Richard Marot (1751-1805) m. Nov. 2,
   1770 Elizabeth Palmer XXX, 275;
   XXXII, 138; XXXIV, 74

BOOKHOUT, includes BOCHOLTE, BUCKHOUT
Jan (....-a. Mar. 23, 1694/5) m.
.... Hannah ...... NY XXXIII,
33, 34
John (Nov. 17, 1777-p. July 25, 1853)
m. .... Nancy Smart XXXIII, 33, 34

BOOMER
Martin (Dec. 25, 1732-June 1802) m.
Oct. 31, 1776 (2) Sarah Stillwell
XXXIV, 28
Matthew (....-....) m. .... Eleanor
...... RI XXXIV, 28

BOOTH, includes BOOTHE
Adam (....-a. Sept. 15, 1703) m. a.
1690 ...... Barret VA XXXII, 46,
47
Daniel (Feb. 6, 1724-May 8, 1801) m.
.... Mary (Polly) Judson V, 61;
XVI, 139
Daniel (c. 1730-Nov. 17, 1812) m.
Apr. 11, 1757 (2) Rose Terry XIV,
72, 73; XXV, 173
James (Oct. 1, 1734-Mar. 19, 1809)
m. .... Abigail Anne Patterson
IV, 116; V, 86
John (....-June 27, 1689/90) m. ....
Mary ...... NY XIV, 72, 73;
XXV, 173
John (1732-1798/1800) m. 1756 Wini-
fred (Sydnor) Routt XXXII, 46, 47
Richard (1607-p. Mar. 1698) m. c.
1640 (1) Elizabeth Hawley CONN
IV, 116; V, 61; 86; XVI, 139, 140

BOOTHE, see BOOTH

BORDMAN, see BOARDMAN

BOREMAN, see BOARDMAN

BOSTWICK
Arthur (bpt. Dec. 22, 1603-p. 1680)
m. Jan. 8, 1627/8 (1) Jane Whittel
CONN, NY VI, 30
John (c. 1754-1802) m. 1777 Sarah
Holmes VI, 30

BOSWORTH
Allen (Nov. 7, 1758-Mar. 18, 1830)
m. Nov. 18, 1802 (2) Sarah Harwood
XVI, 13
Nathaniel (a. 1615-1634) m. ....
Mary ...... MASS XVI, 13
Nathaniel (a. 1634-Aug. 30, 1693) m.
.... Mary ...... MASS XVI, 13

BOTSFORD
Ephraim; Sr. (June 25, 1720-Dec. 5,
1795) m. Nov. 5, 1741 Sarah Hawley

XXIX, 126
Henry (bpt. June 15, 1608-a. Apr.
15, 1686) m. .... Elizabeth ......
CONN XXIX, 126; XXX, 52
Jared (....-May 15, 1828) m. Dec.
15, 1768 Ann Sherman XXX, 52

BOUCQUET, see BOCKEE

BOULDEN
James (Sept. 4, 1712-p. Jan. 4,
1783) m. .... Elizabeth Phillips
XXXI, 223
Nathan (Feb. 22, 1737-p. Sept. 28,
1802) m. .... Sarah ......
XXXI, 223
William (....-p. 1677) m. ....
.... MD XXXI, 223

BOURNE
Benjamin (July 25, 1760-Mar. 14,
1829) m. July 22, 1783 Hannah
Perry XXX, 138
James (1757/9-June 4, 1847) m. 1788
Elizabeth Gore XXV, 138
John, II (....-c. 1720) m. ....
Elizabeth ...... VA XXV, 138
Richard (bpt. 1610-1682) m. 1637
Bathsheba Hallett MASS XXX, 138

BOUTELLE, see BOUTWELL

BOUTON
Daniel (Oct. 24, 1740-Feb. 12, 1821)
m. Dec. 31, 1767 Mary Mead XXXII,
67
Ezra (Nov. 18, 1723-1790) m. June
28, 1749 Mary Bouton X, 6; XIII,
65
John (c. 1580-....) m. .... Alice
...... CONN XXXII, 67
John (1615-p. Dec. 25, 1706) m. Jan.
1, 1656 Abigail Marvin CONN X,
6; XIII, 64; XXXII, 67

BOUTWELL, includes BOUTELLE
James (a. 1625-p. June 22, 1651) m.
.... Alice ...... MASS X, 166;
XIX, 94; XXVII, 172; XXVIII, 106;
XXXII, 234; XXXIII, 100
James (June 26, 1736-Feb. 6, 1804)
m. Nov. 4, 1756 Mary Johnson
X, 166; XXVIII, 106; XXXII, 234;
XXXIII, 100, 101
John (Aug. 8, 1762-Sept. 12, 1847)
m. Jan. 29, 1784 Betsy Eaton
XXVII, 171, 172
Kendall (Aug. 11, 1736-Aug. 12, 1820)
m. 1756 Sarah Boutelle XXVII, 172
Timothy (Jan. 1740-May 25, 1810) m.
Jan. 21, 1768 Rachel Lincoln XIX,94

BOYNTON
John (1614-Feb. 18, 1670) m. c. 1644
  Ellen (Eleanor) Pell MASS IV,
  67; VI, 40; XXI, 127, 128; XXV,
  203; XXIX, 222
John (Sept. 8, 1736-Mar. 21, 1825)
  m. Dec. 16, 1762 (2) Elizabeth
  Beaman; .... (3) Mrs. Phebe (Jew-
  ett) Graves IV, 67; XXIX, 221
Joseph (Jan. 17, 1755-June 24, 1830)
  m. .... Rebecca Thurston XXI,
  127, 128
Richard (Mar. 22, 1741-p. 1780) m.
  Oct. 29, 1761 Rebecca Abbott
  XXV, 205
Thomas (Sept. 2, 1752-Sept. 24, 1823)
  m. Dec. 10, 1776 Elizabeth Keezer
  VI, 40

BRADBURY
Moses (Feb. 4, 1731-p. 1776) m. c.
  Sept. 22, 1759 Mary Page XVIII,
  88
Moses (June 29, 1755-Dec. 22, 1822)
  m. (int.) Aug. 12, 1780 Eunice
  Millett XXXIV, 240
Sanders (Nov. 29, 1737-Nov. 15,
  1779) m. May 26, 1763 Sarah Colby
  I, 31, 40; II, 34
Thomas (Feb. 28, 1610-Mar. 16, 1695)
  m. 1636 Mary Perkins ME, MASS
  I, 31, 40; II, 34; XVII, 143;
  XVIII, 88; XXXIV, 240

BRADFORD
Ebenezer (May 29, 1746-Jan. 3, 1801)
  m. Apr. 8, 1776 Elizabeth Green
  XXIV, 104
John (Dec. 7, 1739-June 5, 1818) m.
  .... Mary Fitch IX, 50
John (1748-1806) m. Dec. 26, 1776
  Eunice Loring XXVIII, 164, 165
Peleg (Mar. 9, 1727-May 13, 1804)
  m. Mar. 19, 1746 Lydia Sturtevant
  XXV, 43
Robert (c. 1627-Jan. 13, 1707) m.
  .... Martha ...... MASS XV, 17
Robert (Oct. 18, 1706-Aug. 12, 1782)
  m. Nov. 4, 1726 Sarah Stetson
  XXXII, 25
Samuel (May 8, 1720-Aug. 1776) m.
  Dec. 29, 1743 Mary Taylor
  XV, 17
William (bpt. Mar. 9, 1589-May 9,
  1657) m. Aug. 14, 1623 Alice Car-
  penter Southworth MASS IX, 50;
  XXV, 43; XXIV, 104; XXVIII, 164;
  XXXII, 25

BRADLEY
Aaron (Aug. 27, 1762-Oct. 25, 1843)

m. .... Loren Abernathy XX, 80
Abraham (1746-Jan. 28, 1825) m. ....
  Mary Prichard XI, 71
Aner (Mar. 5, 1753-Mar. 13, 1824)
  m. May 12, 1778 Anna Guernsey VI,
  25
Daniel, IV (July 15, 1750-May 2,
  1818) m. Dec. 8, 1772 Esther Ives
  XXX, 233, 234; XXXII, 52
Edmund (Sept. 24, 1757-Feb. 10,
  1828) m. .... Lydia Chedsey XII,
  92
Elisha (Nov. 3, 1732-Mar. 5, 1815)
  m. Jan. 24, 1753 Mary Ives XXI,
  91, 92
Francis (....-Oct. 1689) m. ....
  Ruth Barlow CONN XIV, 122; XXVI,
  173
Henry (....-a. July 1, 1679) m. ....
  Mary ...... MD XX, 120
Isaac (1650-Jan. 12, 1712/3) m. ....
  Elizabeth ...... CONN XII, 92
Jesse (May 4, 1736-July 26, 1812)
  m. Jan. 19, 1758 Mamre Ives
  XXVII, 28
John, Jr. (Sept. 1764-May 15, 1840)
  m. May 1795 Hannah Nichols XXVI,
  173
Joseph (June 24, 1720-1809) m. ....
  Sibyl Meigs XXXI, 147
Seth (Apr. 5, 1735-May 29, 1798)
  m. Feb. 18, 1773 (2) Dorothy
  Treadwell XIV, 122
Stephen (1642-June 20, 1702) m. Nov.
  9, 1663 (1) Hannah Smith CONN
  XI, 150; XX, 80; XXXI, 147
Thomas (c. 1750-a. May 31, 1817) m.
  .... Ester ...... XX, 120
Timothy (Apr. 30, 1721-Oct. 10,
  1803) m. Feb. 1744/5 Mercy Baldwin
  XXXII, 19
Timothy (July 25, 1735-Sept. 8, 1806)
  m. Mar. 6, 1765 Esther Shipman
  XI, 150
William (c. 1620-1691) m. Feb. 18,
  1645 Alice Prichard CONN VI, 25;
  XI, 71; XXI, 91, 92; XXVII, 28;
  XXX, 233, 234; XXXII, 19, 52

BRADSTREET
Henry (Nov. 30, 1741-Sept. 2, 1818)
  m. June 15, 1769 Abigail Porter
  XXXIV, 70
Simon (bpt. Mar. 1603/4-Mar. 27,
  1697) m. c. 1628 ....
  MASS XXXIV, 70

BRADT, includes BRATT
Albert Andriessen (1607-June 7, 1689)
  m. 1630 Annetje Barentse Van Rol-
  mers NY XXXI, 224; XXXII, 174

Peter A. (bpt. Oct. 19, 1744- Nov.
22, 1826) m. .... Jane Hunder-
man XXXII, 174
Pieter (Peter) (bpt. May 22, 1754-
a. Mar. 8, 1810) m. 1778 Maria
...... XXXI, 224

BRAGDON
Arthur (c. 1597-p. 1665) m. ....
Mary ...... ME XXXIV, 241
William (July 14, 1754-Feb. 28, 1802)
m. Aug. 3, 1780 Sarah Hagens
XXXIV, 241

BRAINARD, includes BRAINERD
Abijah (Nov. 26, 1705-Sept. 1782)
m. Dec. 28, 1727 Esther Smith
XXI, 86, 87
Ansel (May 4, 1765-June 12, 1855)
m. Mar. 6, 1787 Mary (Polly)
Warren XXXII, 45
Asahel (Jan. 20, 1739/40-Mar. 23,
1822) m. Mar. 30, 1763 Experi-
ence Ackley XXXI, 212
Chiliab (Oct. 21, 1741-c. Mar. 1816)
m. Dec. 14, 1769 Jemima Worcester
X, 290
Daniel (....-Apr. 1, 1715) m. 1663
(1) Hannah Spencer CONN V, 59;
X, 290; XI, 7, 112, 113; XII, 104;
XXI, 57, 58, 86, 87; XXIX, 156;
XXXI, 148, 212, 291; XXXII, 45;
XXXIV, 87, 316
Daniel (Sept. 10, 1734-May 3, 1798)
m. c. 1772 (2) Mrs. Unice (Brooks)
Hubbard XXI, 57, 58
Dudley (Nov. 4, 1732-Aug. 5, 1811)
m. Nov. 13, 1754 Mindwell Ackley
XXIX, 156
Jeptha (Mar. 2, 1746-Jan. 6, 1790)
m. Jan. 10, 1771 Anna Markham
XII, 104; XXXIV, 316
Jesse (Aug. 7, 1757-Sept. 18, 1839)
m. June 28, 1781 Hannah Cook
XXXI, 148; XXXIV, 87
Josiah (Aug. 17, 1739-Nov. 6, 1805)
m. May 24, 1759 Lois Hurlburt
XI, 6, 112, 113
Shubael (Jan. 12, 1751/2-c. June 4,
1782) m. Dec. 7, 1775 Ruth Stock-
ing XXXI, 291
Simon (Oct. 7, 1730-c. Sept. 11,
1806) m. .... Hepizibah Spencer
XXI, 86, 87
William (Aug. 27, 1746-Jan. 26, 1820)
m. .... Lucy Day V, 59

BRAINERD, see BRAINARD

BRANCH
Christopher (1595-1681/2) m. a.

Sept. 2, 1619 Mary Addie VA
XIV, 20; XXVI, 151; XXXIII, 136,
137
Edward (c. 1736-1781) m. 1756/7
Lucy Finney XIV, 20
Henry (c. 1740-1797/8) m. ....
Tabitha ...... XXVI, 151
William Scott (1765-July 22, 1838)
m. Oct. 28, 1791 Dicy Jane Calicut
XXXIII, 136, 137

BRATT, see BRADT

BRAY
John (....-1716) m. .... Susannah
...... NJ XXXIV, 129
John (1755-Oct. 1845) m. Apr. 8,
1779 Rachel Rittenhouse XXXIV,
129

BRAYTON
Francis (1612-1692) m. .... Mary
...... RI XVII, 106; XXV, 44,
182, 281, 282
Francis (....-July 17, 1718) m. Mar.
18, 1671 Mary Fish RI XXIX, 233
James Wheaton (Oct. 1757-Sept. 23,
1832) m. Dec. 12, 1777 Roby Esta-
brooks XXV, 44
John (Apr. 12, 1762-Mar. 12, 1829)
m. Mar. 21, 1782 Sarah Bowers
XVII, 106
Joseph (Mar. 3, 1757-July 27, 1812)
m. July 10, 1780 (2) Elizabeth
Reed XXV, 182, 281, 282; XXIX,
232, 233

BRAZER, includes BRAZIER
Christopher, II (1747-Oct. 12, 1803)
m. Aug. 4, 1773 Margaret Corbett
XXXII, 213, 214, 248
Edward (1602-Dec. 3, 1689) m. ....
Magdelen ...... MASS XXXII, 213,
248

BRAZIER, see BRAZER

BREED
Allen (1600/1-Mar. 17, 1690/1) m.
Nov. 14, 1622 (1) Elizabeth Wheeler;
Mar. 28, 1656 (2) Elizabeth Knight
MASS, NY XX, 75; XXV, 31
Allen (July 14, 1759-Apr. 2, 1842)
m. July 1781 Lucy Taylor XX, 75
Amos (Dec. 23, 1744-Mar. 20, 1785)
m. Jan. 25, 1768 Lucy Randall
XXV, 31

BRETT
Simeon (Jan. 8, 1720-Aug. 18, 1792)
m. Jan. 31, 1749 Mehitable Packard

BRETT, cont.
XVI, 112
William (1618-Dec. 17, 1681) m. ....
Margaret Ford MASS XVI, 112

BREWER, includes BROUWER, BROWER
Adam (....-p. Jan. 22, 1692) m. 1645
Madalena Jacob Verdon NY XXIX,
326; XXXIII, 183
Cornelius (Dec. 1, 1716-Aug. 1808)
m. 1753 Mary Archer XXIX, 326
John (....-....) m. a. 1642 Anne
...... MASS XXXI, 105, 259
John (Oct. 10, 1642-Jan. 1, 1690)
m. .... Elizabeth Rice MASS
XXXI, 21, 22
John (May 27, 1743-July 31, 1825)
m. June 1, 1769 (1) Martha Graves
XXXI, 104, 105, 259
Jonas (Mar. 23, 1726-Oct. 24, 1812)
m. June 27, 1771 (2) Thankful
Brown Whitcomb XXXI, 21, 22
Matthew B. (Aug. 8, 1743-....) m.
Dec. 30, 1763 Sarah West XXXIII,
183

BREWSTER
Asa (Oct. 11, 1739-Mar. 10, 1811) m.
.... Ruth Badger V, 118, 119
Elias (Sept. 11, 1759-Mar. 17, 1834)
m. Jan. 20, 1785 Margery Morgan
XXX, 222
Jedediah (June 7, 1754-July 1827) m.
May 19, 1773 Prudence Robinson
XXVI, 210, 211
Jonah (Sept. 1, 1750-1833) m. ....
Sarah Robinson XXXII, 199
Love (....-p. Mar. 4, 1650/1) m.
.... Sarah Collier MASS V, 118,
119
Martin (Nov. 16, 1758-Aug. 22, 1833)
m. Apr. 23, 1786 Sarah Nye Drew
XI, 116, 152, 153, 154, 156
Nathaniel (....-Dec. 18, 1690) m.
.... Sarah Ludlow NY XVII, 67
Simon (June 10, 1720-June 29, 1801)
m. May 25, 1742 Anne Andrus
XXVI, 37, 38; XXVIII, 148
William (1566/7-Apr. 10, 1644) m.
.... Mary ...... MASS V, 118,
119; XI, 116, 152, 153, 154, 156;
XXVI, 37, 210, 211; XXVIII, 148;
XXX, 222; XXXII, 199
William (1732-May 18, 1793) m.
1770 Temperance Sweezey
XVII, 67
Wrestling (Aug. 29, 1724-Feb. 8,
1810) m. July 12, 1750 Deborah
Seabury XI, 116, 152, 153, 154,156

BREYANDT, see BRYANT

BRIANT, see BRYANT

BRICK
John, Sr. (....-a. 1752/3) m. ....
Hannah Davis NY XXXIII, 151, 152
Joseph, Sr. (Mar. 24, 1735-Apr. 4,
1798) m. Apr. 30, 1783 Martha
Reeve XXXIII, 151, 152

BRICKEY
Garrard (Jared, Jarratt) (Apr. 10,
1760-1841) m. 1780 Amy Compton
XXXII, 105, 106
John (....-....) m. ....
...... SC, MD XXXII, 105, 106

BRIDGE
John (....-Apr. 15, 1665) m. ....
.... MASS XXXIV, 214,
317
Jonathan (Sept. 20, 1758-Feb. 16,
1850) m. Feb. 22, 1781 (1) Phebe
Bowman XXXIV, 317
Joseph (June 18, 1752-1831) m. c.
1822 Sarah Crossett XXXIV, 214

BRIDGES
Edmund (1612-Jan. 13, 1684) m. ....
(1) Alice ......; .... (2) Eliza-
beth ...... MASS XVIII, 22
Moody (Jan. 19, 1723-July 14, 1801)
m. Nov. 5, 1747 Naomalia Frie
XVIII, 22

BRIDGHAM
Henry, Sr. (1573-Jan. 11, 1641) m.
Aug. 2, 1610 Ursula Brett MASS
XXXII, 282
John (Aug. 27, 1729-....) m. Feb.
28, 1754 Joanna Comer XXXII,
282

BRIDGMAN
James (....-Mar. 17, 1676) m. ....
Sarah ...... CONN, MASS XXIX,
325; XXX, 284
Joseph, II (Jan. 4, 1745-Mar. 10,
1826) m. June 21, 1770 Ruth
Wright XXIX, 325; XXX, 284

BRIGGS
Abiezer (Mar. 27, 1753-May 4, 1849)
m. May 16, 1783 Pamelia Palmer
XXVI, 136, 137
Clement (c. 1600-1648) m. 1630/1 (1)
Joanne Allen; .... (2) Elizabeth
...... MASS XXXIV, 36
Ephraim (Oct. 19, 1744-p. Nov. 12
1783) m. July 1, 1765 Lettice Hill
XXVII, 36
Hugh (....-....) m. Mar. 1, 1682/3

BRIGGS, cont.
Martha Everson MASS. XXVII, 36
John (....-1641) m. ....
...... MASS XXVI, 137
Michael (Sept. 16, 1751-Feb. 10,
1828) m. Dec. 28, 1775 Sarah
Greene XXXIV, 35

BRIGHAM
George (Mar. 17, 1730-Mar. 27, 1808)
m. 1754 Mary Bragg X, 192
Joel (Oct. 2, 1714-Apr. 1797) m.
Mar. 17, 1740 Mary Church XXIV,
154
Samuel (Dec. 3, 1760-Mar. 2, 1813)
m. .... Phebe Davis
XXIV, 154; XXXII, 208
Stephen (Mar. 8, 1743/4-Mar. 7, 1816)
m. Nov. 11, 1771 Hannah Field
XXVIII, 204
Stephen (May 13, 1754-Oct. 11, 1849)
m. Feb. 1, 1781 Sarah Harrington
XXX, 82
Thomas (1603-Dec. 8, 1653) m. 1637
Mercy Hurd MASS X, 192; XIX,
105; XXIV, 154; XXVIII, 204; XXX,
82; XXXII, 208
Winslow (Aug. 30, 1736-Aug. 29,
1791) m. July 29, 1760 Elizabeth
Harrington XIX, 105

BRINCKERHOFF
Derick (Apr. 9, 1750-1822) m. Dec.
14, 1771 Catharine VanVlack
XXXII, 55
Joris Derickson (1609-Jan. 16, 1661)
m. .... Susanna Dubbels NY
XXXII, 55

BRINSMADE, includes BRISMADE
Abraham (Feb. 27, 1726-Nov. 17,
1801) m. Jan. 14, 1747/8 Mary
Wheeler VI, 52
John (....-1673) m. a. 1640 Mary
...... MASS, CONN VI, 52

BRINTON
Joseph (July 1, 1754-Feb. 4, 1826)
m. Apr. 7, 1774 Mary Martin
XXXI, 119, 120
William (Dec. 1, 1636-1700) m. 1659
Anne Bagley DE XXXI, 120

BRISCOE
Hanson (1749-Sept. 12, 1817) m.
.... Mary A. Jordan XXXII, 169
John, I (1590-....) m. .... Eliza-
beth DuBois MD XXIX, 31, 230,
353; XXX, 91; XXXI, 138; XXXII,
169
John Hanson (1752-Sept. 26, 1796)

m. c. 1780 Elizabeth Attaway Bond
XXIX, 31, 353, XXX, 91
William 1750-p. Oct. 7, 1829) m.
1772 Elizabeth Wallace XXIX, 230;
XXXI, 138

BRISMADE, see BRINSMADE

BRISTOL
Henry (c. 1625-1695) m. Jan. 26,
1656 (2) Lydia Browne CONN XIV,
27; XVIII, 120
Justus (Dec. 19, 1736-Jan. 13, 1820)
m. Nov. 11, 1761 Sarah Hawkins
XIV, 27
Nathan (Feb. 1751-1825) m. ....
Annie Lambert XVIII, 120

BROCK
John (1751-Dec. 4, 1792) m. 1784
Ann Curtis XXV, 230
Joseph, I (c. 1668-1742) m. c. 1699
Elizabeth ...... VA XXV, 230

BROCKETT
Hezekiah (Dec. 31, 1727-Apr. 17,
1797) m. Feb. 22, 1760 Mary
Beecher X, 164; XXX, 100
John (1609-Mar. 12, 1690) m. 1640/6
.... CONN X, 164; XXX,
100; XXXIII, 257, 344, 345; XXXIV,
257
William (June 26, 1748-May 3, 1821)
m. Oct. 1, 1771 Patsy (Martha)
Ives XXXIII, 257, 344, 345;
XXXIV, 256

BRODHEAD
Daniel (1631-July 14, 1667) m. 1661
Ann Tye NY XII, 27; XXV, 77;
XXVII, 73; XXVIII, 9, 114
Daniel (bpt. Sept. 26, 1756-1836) m.
Mar. 1, 1778 Blondina Elmendorf
XXVII, 73
Garrett (Jan. 21, 1733-Nov. 15,
1804) m. Mar. 15, 1759 Jane Davis
XII, 27; XXV, 77; XXVIII, 9, 114

BROKAW, includes BROUCARD
Bourgon (1645-....) m. Dec. 18, 1666
Catherine LeFebre NY XXX, 246,
247
Evert (Nov. 22, 1740-1784) m. Sept.
19, 1765 Cornelia Stryker XXX,
246, 247

BROME, see BROOME

BRONDIG, see BRUNDAGE

BRONDISH, see BRUNDAGE

BRONSON
Asa (Oct. 25, 1733-p. 1794) m. ....
    Etheldred Parker XII, 115
Asahel (Nov. 28, 1759-Apr. 22, 1850)
    m. Feb. 12, 1784 Esther Upson
    XVII, 145
Eli (June 30, 1743-Sept. 30, 1816)
    m. Mar. 4, 1773 Mehitable Atwater
    XXXII, 78
James (Oct. 22, 1727-....) m. Aug.
    22, 1750 Sarah Brockett XXI, ·
    125, 126, 127
John (....-Nov. 28, 1680) m. ....
    .... MASS, CONN XII,
    115; XVII, 115, 145; XVIII, 80;
    XXI, 125, 126, 127; XXXII, 78;
    XXXIII, 61
John, Sr. (July 6, 1735-Nov. 10,
    1838) m. Mar. 30, 1758 Sarah
    Barnes XXXIII, 61
Roswell (Sept. 9, 1751-Mar. 1836)
    m. Nov. 25, 1773 Susanna Adams
    XXI, 125, 126
Stephen (June 30, 1735-Dec. 15,
    1809) m. May 14, 1764 Sarah
    Humaston XVIII, 80
William (May 30, 1734-Nov. 5, 1801)
    m. 1758 Esther Kelsey XVII, 115

BROOK, see BROOKS

BROOKE, see BROOKS

BROOKINGS
Henry (1641-a. 1712) m. a. 1686 (3)
    Sarah ...... ME XXXI, 248
Samuel (bpt. Aug. 10, 1745-a. 1825)
    m. Apr. 5, 1772 Elizabeth Mighill
    XXXI, 248

BROOKS, includes BROOK, BROOKE
Basil (Dec. 13, 1738-Aug. 22, 1794)
    m. May 1, 1764 Elizabeth Hopkins
    XVIII, 85
Ebenezer (Jan. 23, 1725-....) m.
    May 4, 1757 Mary Glazier XXIX,
    150
James (1758-Dec. 30, 1832) m. 1782
    Lydia King XXVI, 14
John (c. 1623-Sept. 29, 1691) m.
    Nov. 1, 1649 Eunice Mousall MASS
    XXIX, 150
John (1650-1695) m. Mar. 25, 1685
    Sarah Peat CONN XXXI, 242
John (Dec. 17, 1728-1784) m. p. Jan.
    9, 1754 Eunice Darby X, 121
Lemuel (Mar. 23, 1741/2-1815) m.
    Sept. 19, 1764 Hannah Raymond
    XXXI, 242, 243
Luke (Aug. 10, 1731-a. Apr. 1, 1817)
    m. May 16, 1755 Lucy Wheeler VI, 48

Nicholas (a. Feb. 13, 1752-p. Dec.
    14, 1797) m. .... Hill
    XXXI, 220; XXXII, 220
Robert (June 3, 1602-July 20, 1655)
    m. Feb. 25, 1627 (1) Mary Baker;
    .... (2) Mary Mainwaring MD
    XVIII, 85; XXXI, 220; XXXII, 220
Stephen (Dec. 1, 1756-May 1836) m.
    July 7, 1779 Prudence Whitcomb
    VI, 48
Thomas (....-May 21, 1667) m. ....
    Grace ...... MASS VI, 48; X, 121
Thomas (1617-Oct. 1668) m. 1662
    Alice Spencer CONN XXVI, 14

BROOME, includes BROME
John (....-1689) m. .... Margaret
    ...... MD XIX, 140
John (Jan. 14, 1743-1783) m. June
    19, 1775 Sarah Isdall XIX, 140

BROUCARD, see BROKAW

BROUGHTON
John (1615-Mar. 16, 1662) m. Nov.
    15, 1650 Hannah Bascom MASS
    XXXII, 109
John (June 16, 1717-1775) m. 1753
    Anna Ainsworth XXXII, 109

BROUWER, see BREWER

BROWER, see BREWER

BROWN, includes BROWNE
Abraham (....-....) m. .... Lidia
    ...... MASS XXX, 252
Abraham (Jan. 1, 1734-....) m. Mar.
    10, 1756 Abigail Wilbur XXIX,
    322
Adam, Jr. (c. 1750-1840) m. Dec. 3,
    1772 Priscilla Putnam XXXII, 161
Benjamin, Sr. (Jan. 19, 1745-c. 1819)
    m. 1788 (3) Mary Huston XXXII,
    128
Chad (1600-1663) m. Sept. 11, 1626
    Elizabeth Sharparrow RI XX, 97;
    XXIII, 10
Chad (Sept. 1729-Sept. 19, 1814) m.
    June 19, 1749 Zerviah Evans XX,
    97
Charles (....-Dec. 1687) m. Aug. 14,
    1647 Mary Acy MASS XIX, 7;
    XXII, 39
David (Mar. 12, 1730-May 22, 1802)
    m. Apr. 30, 1756 Abigail Monroe
    XI, 62
Ebenezer (Aug. 13, 1752-Apr. 1,
    1834) m. 1787 (2) Lydia Cogswell
    XIV, 95; XXIII, 48
Elias (Mar. 16, 1758-1843) m. c.1778

BROWNELL
Benjamin, Jr. (Feb. 2, 1760-Apr. 14,
1830) m. Mar. 18, 1784 Abigail
Milk XVIII, 12
Elijah (c. 1736-July 29, 1812) m. a.
1759 Sarah Fish XXXIV, 61
Stephen (Dec. 20, 1749-....) m. Dec.
29, 1774 Susanna Sherman XXI, 61,
62
*Thomas (1619-1665) m. 1638 Ann
...... RI XVIII, 12; XXI, 61,
62; XXXIV, 61*

BROWNING
Charles (1754-1821) m. 1770 Frances
Wright XXII, 89; XXIV, 12; XXVI,
41, 42
*John (1588-....) m. 1614 ......
...... VA XXII, 89; XXIV, 13;
XXVI, 42; XXXIV, 190*
John (Apr. 16, 1749-Sept. 25, 1818)
m. 1774 Elizabeth Strother XXXIV,
189

BROWNSON, see BRUNSON

BRUEN
Jabez (July 24, 1750-Nov. 27, 1814)
m. .... Abigail Spining X, 210
*Obadiah (Dec. 25, 1606-p. 1681) m.
1632/3 Sara ...... MASS X, 210*

BRUNDAGE, includes BRONDIG, BRONDISH
*John (c. 1597-a. Oct. 27, 1639) m.
.... Rachel Hubbard CONN XXXIV,
239
John (c. 1632-1697) m. a. 1685
.... NY XXXIV, 123*
Joseph (c. 1748-a. Dec. 14, 1814)
m. .... Catherine ...... XXXIV,
239
William (1741-Nov. 12, 1825) m. a.
1771 Ann Perkins XXXIV, 123

BRUNSON, includes BROWNSON
David (1733-Oct. 24, 1784) m. ....
Elizabeth Cantey, Jr. XXXII, 76
*Richard, I (....-c. 1637) m. ....
.... CONN XXXII, 76*
William, Sr. (Dec. 29, 1756-May 11,
1803) m. Jan. 25, 1785 Elizabeth
Powell XXXII, 76

BRYAN
*Alexander (bpt. Sept. 29, 1602-Nov.
5, 1679) m. a. 1630 Ann Baldwin
CONN XXIX, 134*
Oliver (June 3, 1756-Dec. 15, 1832)
m. June 21, 1777 Esther Bryan
XXIX, 134
Samuel (1756-Mar. 3, 1837) m.

Oct. 5, 1775 Mary Hunt XXX, 190,
191
*William (....-....) m. ....
.... VA XXX, 190, 191*
William (1733-May 7, 1780) m. 1755
Mary Boone XXX, 190, 191

BRYANT, includes BRIANT, BREYANDT
*Abraham (1647-July 6, 1720) m. Feb.
2, 1664 (1) Mary Kendall MASS
XXVIII, 131, 132
Cornelius Aertszen (1607-....) m. a.
1650 Belitje Hendricks NY XXXIV,
43*
David (May 22, 1756-Aug. 1835) m.
1782 Catherine Woodruff Woolley
XXXIV, 43
Job (Sept. 17, 1745-1790) m. May 3,
1764 Mary Turner XXXI, 232
*John (....-Nov. 20, 1674) m. Nov.
14, 1643 Mary Lewis MASS XXXI,
164; XXXIV, 270*
Micah (Apr. 2, 1744-1790) m. Nov.
22, 1770 Margaret Paddock XXXI,
164; XXXIV, 270
*Stephen, Sr. (a. 1632-....) m. ....
Abigail Shaw MASS XXXI, 232*
Thomas (Feb. 25, 1742-Jan. 30, 1796)
m. .... Elizabeth Chandler
XXVIII, 131, 132

BUCK
Benjamin (Oct. 10, 1744-1807) m.
Feb. 10, 1763 Dorcas Sutton
XXXIV, 338
Daniel (1744-Nov. 19, 1828) m. Dec.
3, 1775 Sarah Saltonstall XXV,
69, 70
*Emanuel (1623-1700) m. 1645 (1)
Sarah Ryley; Apr. 17, 1658 (2)
Mary Kirby CONN XV, 94; XXV,
69, 70; XXVII, 206; XXX, 178*
Isaac (Mar. 19, 1729-Jan. 20, 1776)
m. Feb. 10, 1758 Elizabeth Waters
XXX, 178
James (Mar. 24, 1726-Jan. 29, 1793)
m. Feb. 23, 1748 Elizabeth Sherman
XV, 94
*John (....-1688) m. .... Catherine
Acton MD XXXIV, 338*
Lemuel (Sept. 6, 1732-Sept. 6, 1788)
m. Aug. 27, 1755 Bethia MaCuen
XXVII, 206

BUCKHOUT, see BOOKHOUT

BUCKINGHAM
Ebenezer (Nov. 1, 1748-Oct. 24, 1824)
m. Oct. 23, 1770 Esther Bradley
X, 109, 160
Jared (bpt. Oct. 16, 1732-Jan. 1,

1814) m. May 1, 1764 (1)
Eunice Brooks XXV, 117
John (Sept. 27, 1744-Mar. 3, 1788)
m. c. 1768 Susan Green V, 85
*Thomas (c. 1610-p. Sept. 19, 1657)
m. .... (1) Hannah ...... CONN
V, 86; X, 109, 160; XXV, 117*

BUDD
Daniel (July 27, 1722-Dec. 24, 1806)
m. c. 1746 Mary Burdy XXXIV, 252
*John (....-1670) m. .... Kathlene
Browne CONN, NY XXXIV, 252*

BUDDINGTON
*Walter (....-Nov. 20, 1713) m. ....
(2) Mary Haynes CONN XXXIII,
300*
Walter (1731-Apr. 4, 1799) m. ....
Ruth Waterman XXXIII, 300

BUELL
Ebenezer (Mar. 26, 1746/7-May 26,
1823) m. Nov. 24, 1768 Hannah
Plumb XXI, 155, 156; XXII, 137
Samuel (June 22, 1713-Mar. 9, 1790)
m. Jan. 1, 1735 Lydia Wilcox
VI, 10; X, 191
Samuel (1742-Sept. 14, 1819) m. c.
1766 Clarinda Hoadley VI, 10;
X, 191
*William (c. 1610-Nov. 23, 1681) m.
Nov. 18, 1640 Mary ...... CONN
VI, 10; X, 192; XXI, 155, 156;
XXII, 137*

BUFFINGTON, see BUFFINTON

BUFFINTON, includes BUFFINGTON
*Thomas (....-1725/9) m. Dec. 30,
1670 Sarah Southwick MASS
XVI, 60*
Zadoc (c. 1752-June 14, 1799) m.
Aug. 15, 1776 (1) Abigail Proctor
XVI, 60, 61

BUFORD
Abraham (July 31, 1749-June 30, 1833)
m. Oct. 14, 1788 Martha McDowell
XXXIV, 259
*Richard (....-....) m. .... (2)
Margaret ...... VA XXXIV, 259*

BUGBEE
*Edward (c. 1594-Jan. 26, 1669) m.
.... Rebecca ...... CONN XIV,
21, 22; XV, 108*
Hezekiah (Feb. 9, 1746-Aug.
4, 1826) m. Jan. 21, 1773
Bathshua Holmes XIV, 21, 22;
XV, 108

BULFINCH
*Adino (....-June 17, 1746) m. Oct.
10, 1727 (2) Susanna Green MASS
XXXIII, 256, 257*
Thomas, II (1728-1802) m. Aug. 22,
1759 Susan Apthorp XXXIII, 256,
257

BULKELEY
Charles (May 22, 1752-Feb. 12, 1824)
m. Oct. 27, 1771 Betsey Taintor
XVIII, 145; XXXII, 122, 123
Eleazer (Feb. 2, 1763-Feb. 5, 1843)
m. Dec. 22, 1785 Mary Ogden XIX,
98
*Peter (Jan. 31, 1583-Jan. 9, 1659)
m. c. 1633 (2) Grace Chetwode
MASS XVIII, 145; XIX, 98; XXXII,
123*

BULL
Asa (Sept. 4, 1752-1805) m. ....
Tamar Little V, 58
Caleb (Mar. 13, 1717-Feb. 14, 1789)
m. Apr. 11, 1745 Martha Cadwell
X, 132
Crispin (c. 1740-Mar. 24, 1810) m.
c. 1763 Mary Carpenter XXXIV, 164
*Isaac (1654-....) m. .... Mary .....
MASS XXXIV, 164*
*Thomas (1615-1684) m. .... Susan
...... CONN V, 58; X, 133*
Timothy (c. 1720-c. 1810) m. a.
1740 Patience Page XXXIV, 164

BULLARD
Asa (July 15, 1730-June 12, 1803)
m. Nov. 1, 1764 (2) Hannah Cook
VI, 119
*Benjamin (1630-Sept. 21, 1689) m.
1659 (1) Martha Pidge MASS
VI, 119*
*John (1601/2-Oct. 27, 1678) m. ....
Magdalene ...... MASS XXV, 281*
Lemuel (Mar. 5, 1762-Feb. 28, 1828)
m. .... Lucretia Newton XVIII,
60
Nathan (Jan. 15, 1754-Dec. 25,
1836) m. Apr. 10, 1777 Rebecca
Fenton XXV, 281
*Robert (1599-June 24, 1639) m. ....
Anne ...... MASS VI, 119;
XVIII, 60*

BULLEN
Jeduthan (Jan. 30, 1751-Mar. 5,
1832) m. c. 1807 (1) Beulah Clark
XXXII, 256, 257
*Samuel (....-Jan. 16, 1691/2) m.
Aug. 10, 1641 Mary Morse MASS
XXVI, 303, 304; XXXII, 256*

BULLEN, cont.
Samuel (July 29, 1733-1802) m.
July 7, 1773 Elizabeth Legg
XXVI, 303, 304

BULLOCK
James (Feb. 23, 1735-Feb. 21, 1813)
m. 1765 Rebecca Wingfield XXXII,
159
Nathaniel (c. 1741-Feb. 5, 1815)
m. a. 1804 (2) Elizabeth Brantley
XXXI, 36; XXXIV, 337
Richard (1622-Oct. 20, 1667) m. ....
(2) Elizabeth Billington MASS
X, 203
Richard (1641-....) m. a. 1662
Dorothy ...... VA XXXI, 36;
XXXII, 159; XXXIV, 337
Stephen (Oct. 10, 1736-Feb. 2, 1816)
m. Oct. 30, 1760 Mary Horton
X, 203

BUNNELL
Isaac (June 12, 1734-May 1808) m.
.... Ann Collins XVII, 5
William (....-p. 1654) m. .... Ann
Wilmot CONN XVII, 5

BURBANK
Abraham (Feb. 24, 1738/9-Aug. 8,
1808) m. Dec. 26, 1770 (2) Sarah
Pomeroy VI, 35
John (....-Apr. 1681) m. .... (1)
Ann ...... MASS VI, 35

BURDETT, see BURDICK

BURDGE, see BURGESS

BURDICK, includes BURDETT
Abel (1752-1815) m. Dec. 21, 1775
Comfort Palmer XIII, 86; XXV,
263
Elijah (c. 1758-Dec. 17, 1833) m.
c. 1778/9 Avis Robinson XXII, 98
Ichabod (1740-June 16, 1821) m.
Feb. 6, 1764 Bathsheba McKee
XXXIV, 303
Joshua (....-1800) m. Dec. 25, 1734
Abigail Lanphere XXXII, 272
Luke (Apr. 25, 1749-Jan. 5, 1825) m.
Nov. 8, 1772 Sarah Haskell
XXVI, 189
Peter, Jr. (May 12, 1730-Feb. 7,
1828) m. May 24, 1754 Esther
Gavitt XXX, 118
Robert (c. 1630-Oct. 25, 1692)
m. Nov. 2, 1655 Ruth Hubbard
RI XIII, 86; XXII, 98; XXVI, 189;
XXV, 263; XXX, 118; XXXII, 272;
XXXIV, 303

BURGESS, includes BURDGE, BURGIS
Isaac (Feb. 8, 176..-Mar. 22, 1858)
m. July 12, 1793 Elizabeth Layton
XXIII, 23
Jonathan (....-p. 1698) m. ....
Hannah (Sushannah) ...... NY
XXIII, 23
Joseph (Jan. 27, 1727-Feb. 17, 1806)
m. 1750 Elizabeth Dorsey XXVII,
159
Joseph (Mar. 8, 1734-May 20, 1820)
m. Mar. 21, 1756 Mehitable Shepard
XXXIII, 42, 43
Thomas (1603-Feb. 13, 1685) m. ....
Dorothy ...... MASS XXXIII, 42,
43
William (1622-1686) m. c. 1649 (1)
Elizabeth Robins MD XXVII, 159

BURGIS, see BURGESS

BURHANS
Edward (Nov. 28, 1752-Sept. 3, 1832)
m. Nov. 6, 1778 Bretje Blanchant
XXXII, 167
Henry (June 22, 1766-Sept. 18, 1848)
m. Aug. 1, 1798 Lydia Churchill
XXVI, 149
Jacob (....-a. Sept. 27, 1677) m.
.... NY XXVI, 149;
XXXII, 167
Jan (bpt. Jan. 1, 1727-Apr. 25,
1787) m. Dec. 2, 1749 Catherine
Whitaker XXXII, 167

BURLEIGH
Giles (....-1668) m. 1656 Rebecca
...... MASS XIX, 23; XX, 140
Thomas (1736-1782) m. 1755 Mercy
Norris XX, 140
William (1721-June 18, 1801) m.
.... Hannah Smith XIX, 22

BURLINGAME
Jeremiah (Sept. 19, 1752-Apr. 15,·
1826) m. .... Leah Ide XI, 56
Roger (1620-a. Sept. 13, 1718) m.
.... Mary ...... CONN, RI, XI,
56

BURNAP, see BURNETT

BURNETT, includes BURNAP
Aaron, Jr. (1730-1791) m. ....
Sarah Squires XXII, 100
Abraham (Sept. 1, 1730-May 7, 1800)
m. Nov. 8, 1753 Irene Wright
XXXII, 100
Daniel (Sept. 17, 1758-July 12,
1824) m. 1780/1 Mary Parcells
XIX, 49

James (Apr. 5, 1756-Jan. 27, 1840)
m. Feb. 28, 1780 Chloe Martin
XXXI, 219
Matthias (May 13, 1723-Oct. 18,
1783) m. 1744 Mary Lindsley
XXX, 277
Robert (c. 1595-Sept. 27, 1689) m.
c. 1624 Ann (Agnes) Miller MASS
XXXI, 219; XXXII, 100
Thomas (1630-May 26, 1691) m. Dec.
3, 1663 (1) Mary Pierson NY
XIX, 49; XXII, 100; XXX, 277
William (....-1806) m. .... Mary
Miller XXII, 100

BURNHAM
John, I (c. 1618-Nov. 5, 1694) m.
.... Mary ...... MASS XXXIII,
157, 158
John, Sr. (1714-1811) m. May 10,
1736 Bethiah Marshall XVIII, 126
Jonathan (1716-Mar. 26, 1802) m.
Oct. 4, 1737 Elizabeth Proctor
XXXIV, 109
Jonathan (Nov. 30, 1758-Feb. 5,
1839) m. .... Rachel Holt X, 29;
XXI, 34, 35
Samuel (Oct. 5, 1744-Apr. 4, 1811)
m. Nov. 27, 1766 Mary Perkins
XXXIII, 157, 158
Thomas (1623-June 1694) m. 1643/5
Mary Lawrence MASS X, 29; XVIII,
126; XXI, 34, 35; XXXIV, 109

BURPEE
Jeremiah (Feb. 19, 1749-p. 1792) m.
.... Elizabeth Maxfield XII, 114
Nathaniel (Feb. 7, 1721-Dec. 25,
1815) m. .... Esther Rolfe XII,
114
Thomas (c. 1613-June 1, 1701) m.
.... (2) Sarah Kelley MASS
XII, 114

BURR
Benjamin (....-Mar. 31, 1681) m.
.... Anna ...... CONN XXI, 35,
36, 129, 130; XXIII, 62
Ezekiel (Mar. 23, 1750-p. 1792) m. c.
1783 Hulda Merchant XVI, 30, 31
Jehu (c. 1600-1672) m. a. 1624
...... Cable CONN XXII, 92
Jehu (Mar. 15, 1752-Aug. 4, 1833) m.
1777 Mary Hawley XXII, 92
John (c. 1600-p. 1635) m. ....
...... MASS XVI, 30
Jonathan (1728-....) m. c. 1758
Jerusha Williams XXI, 35, 36
Jonathan (Apr. 11, 1756-Feb. 10,1804)
m. .... Lydia Bailey XXI, 129, 130
Noadiah, Jr. (Apr. 29, 1732-June 28,

1793) m. May 17, 1757 Abigail
Pease XXIII, 62

BURRAGE, see BURRIDGE

BURRIDGE, includes BURRAGE
John (Apr. 10, 1616-Oct. 10, 1685)
m. 1654/5 (2) Joanna Stowers MASS
XXXI, 244
John (Aug. 29, 1755-July 2, 1822) m.
May 10, 1781 Lois Barthrick XXXI,
244

BURRITT
Blackleach (1744-Aug. 27, 1794) m.
1765 Martha Wells XXXII, 98, 99
Stephen (Feb. 14, 1737-p. 1792) m.
.... Anna Osborn XI, 120; XII, 53
William (....-a. Jan. 15, 1650/1) m.
.... Elizabeth ...... XI, 120;
XII, 53; XXXII, 99

BURROUGH
Samuel (....-c. 1692/3) m. ....
Hannah ...... NJ XXX, 94
Thomas (c. 1752-Jan. 3, 1825) m.
Sept. 8, 1777 Rebecca Fish XXX,
94

BURROWS
Caleb (Feb. 12, 1765-Nov. 6, 1853)
m. .... Rebecca Madison XII, 20
Hubbard (June 26, 1739-Sept. 6,
1781) m. .... Priscilla Baldwin
V, 74
Robert (....-Aug. 1683) m. ....
Mary Ireland CONN V, 74; XII, 20

BURSON
George, Sr. (....-p. Nov. 26, 1715)
m. .... Hannah Gouda PA XXXI,
268
James (1735-p. Feb. 5, 1814) m. a.
Mar. 28, 1756 Mary ...... XXXI,
268
John (1739-1789) m. .... Jane Whinery
XIII, 59; IX, 24, 25
Joseph (1650-1700) m. .... Gemima
Stroud PA IX, 24, 25; XIII, 59

BURT
Daniel, Sr. (July 8, 1716-Mar. 18,
1805) m. Mar. 12, 1737 Hannah
Benedict XVII, 33
Elijah (Oct. 3, 1742-Apr. 5, 1820)
m. Dec. 1767 Deborah Colton XX,136
Henry (1590/5-Apr. 30, 1662) m. Dec.
23, 1619 Eulalia Marche MASS
XVII, 33; XX, 136; XXVII, 116;
132; XXVIII, 191; XXXII,
263

BURT, cont.
Ithamar (Dec. 16, 1755-Sept. 25,
1841) m. Feb. 14, 1780 Prudence
Dickinson XXXII, 262, 263
Martin (bpt. Nov. 10, 1745-June 6,
1803) m. Jan. 14, 1773 Dorcas
Clark XXVII, 116, 132; XXVIII,
191
Richard (....-a. Oct. 26, 1647) m.
.... MASS XXXI,
24
William (June 28, 1745-Nov. 17,
1832) m. Jan. 11, 1770 Prudence
Lincoln XXXI, 24

BURTON
Benjamin (Jan. 28, 1718-Nov. 5,
1783) m. c. 1765 (2) Hester Cord
XXXIV, 246
Jesse (1750-1795) m. 1774 Anne
Maria Hudson XXIX, 309
John (1632-1689) m. ....
...... VA XXIX, 309
Josiah (June 6, 1732-May 28, 1793)
m. Jan. 25, 1756 Sarah Howes
XXXII, 86
Solomon (c. 1660-c. 1720) m. Aug. 1,
1687 Mercy Judson CONN XXXII, 86
Thomas (....-c. 1686) m. a. 1664
Susannah ...... VA XXXI, 51, 52;
XXXIII, 167, 168
Thomas, Jr. (1760-a. July 7, 1828)
m. 1783 Nancy (Ann) Nunnelee XXXI,
51, 52; XXXIII, 167, 168
William (....-a. Jan. 5, 1695) m.
.... Anne Stratton VA XXIV, 246

BURWELL
John (Oct. 5, 1602-Aug. 17, 1649) m.
...... Alice ...... MASS, CONN
XXV, 132
Lewis (Mar. 5, 1621-Nov. 19, 1658)
m. .... Lucy Higginson VA XII,
122
Nathaniel (Apr. 15, 1750-Mar. 29,
1814) m. .... Susannah Grimes
XII, 122
Samuel (Dec. 12, 1729-1816) m. 1759
Abigail Arnold XXV, 132

BUSH
Abiel, Sr. (Sept. 15, 1759-Dec. 1,
1813) m. .... Barbara Freeman
XXXIV, 155
Benjamin (1744/5-Oct. 11, 1830) m.
c. 1789 Marcellus Skaneateles
XXX, 286, 287
David (Oct. 29, 1762-Nov. 12, 1836)
m. Aug. 13, 1783 Anna Brown XXIV,
6
Eliphalet (c. 1749-June 8, 1846) m.

Nov. 11, 1777 (2) Abigail Dunning
XXXIII, 311, 312
Jan Wouters (1638-....) m. 1654
Arentje Arends NY XXXII, 19
John (1613-1670) m. .... Grace .....
ME XXX, 287
John (Aug. 18, 1736-June 30, 1819)
m. 1763 Sarah Richards XXXII, 19
Jonathan (c. 1650-Feb. 15, 1739) m.
July 22, 1679 Sarah Lamb MASS
XXXI, 146; XXXIV, 155
Richard (c. 1640-a. Nov. 10, 1714)
m. 1668 Joanna Sammis NY
XXXIII, 311, 312
Samuel (1647-May 17, 1733) m. ....
Mary ...... MASS, CONN XXIV, 6
Stephen, Sr. (Aug. 9, 1759-May 16,
1842) m. .... Zilpha Thresher
XXXI, 146

BUSHNELL
Alexander (Dec. 2, 1739-Mar. 18,
1818) m. Feb. 12, 1761 Chloe
Waite XXXIV, 86
Francis (c. 1580-a. July 13, 1646)
m. May 13, 1605 Ferris Quenell
CONN XXXIV, 86

BUSS
Stephen (Mar. 8, 1743/5-Oct. 16,
1816) m. June 8, 1771 Phoebe Keyes
XXVIII, 177
William (c. 1613-Jan. 31, 1698) m.
.... (1) Ann ...... MASS XXVIII,
177

BUTCHER
John (....-1707) m. .... Hannah
...... PA XII, 12
Samuel, Jr. (Mar. 25, 1756-May 3,
1847) m. .... Hannah Drake XII,
12

BUTLER
Daniel (Oct. 23, 1748-Nov. 29, 1831)
m. Aug. 6, 1776 Molly Tenney XIX,
96, 159; XX, 100; XXIV, 36; XXVII,
204
David (Feb. 27, 1764-Apr. 3, 1815)
m. (int.) Nov. 1, 1788 Olive Henry
XXXI, 320
Elijah (May 16, 1713-Apr. 5, 1789)
m. Apr. 14, 1737 Thankful Smith
XVII, 82
Elijah, Jr. (1738-Aug. 30, 1825) m.
1760 Jane Kelley XVIII, 11;
XXVIII, 133
Ezekiel (Nov. 3, 1761-June 15, 1830)
m. .... Lydia Frisbie IX, 41,
42
Henry (Nov. 27, 1754-July 20, 1813)

m. Apr. 11, 1776 Isabella Fisk
XXIV, 151; XXV, 171, 172
Isaac (June 14, 1752-Jan. 6, 1833)
m. May 11, 1775 Hannah Hull
XXXII, 171
Israel (July 14, 1759-Apr. 10,
1846) m. 1792 Mercy Covill XXXII,
147
James, Sr. (c. 1630-Jan. 20, 1681)
m. c. 1670 Mary ...... MASS XIX,
96, 160; XX, 100; XXIV, 36; XXVII,
204
James (Dec. 15, 1736-....) m. Feb.
11, 1762 Puella Luce XXXIII, 77,
78
John (bpt. Jan. 2, 1624-1658) m. c.
1650 Mary Lynde MASS XVIII, 11
John (....-Mar. 26, 1733) m. ....
Katherine Houghton CONN IX, 41,
42
Nicholas (1595/1600-Aug. 13, 1671)
m. Jan. 22, 1623 Joyce Baker MASS
XVII, 82; XVIII, 11; XXIV, 151;
XXV, 171, 172; XXVIII, 133; XXXII,
147; XXXIII, 77, 78
Peter, I (....-a. 1660) m. .... Mary
Alvord MASS XVIII, 59, 60; XXIX,
268; XXXI, 161; XXXIII, 89, 90;
XXXIV, 199, 200, 218
Phineas, II (Apr. 8, 1758-Sept. 25,
1852) m. Oct. 18, 1781 Milea
Robbins XVIII, 59, 60; XXIX, 267;
XXXI, 161; XXXIII, 89; XXXIV, 199,
200, 218
Richard (....-Aug. 6, 1684) m. ....
(2) Elizabeth Biglow MASS XIX,
59; XXXI, 320; XXXII, 171
Stephen Goodwin (Oct. 31, 1759-Mar.
29, 1846) m. June 6, 1780 Thankful
Bishop XIX, 59

BUTT
Beriah (p. July 12, 1755-1792) m. p.
1775 Catherine Nicholas XXXI, 319
Robert, Sr. (....-July 3, 1676) m.
.... Jane ...... VA XXXI, 254,
319
Solomon (1764-p. Sept. 21, 1810) m.
June 7, 1789 Dorcas Williamson
XXXI, 254

BUTTERFIELD
Benjamin (....-Mar. 2, 1687) m. June
2, 1633 (1) Ann ......; June 2,1663
(2) Hannah Whitmore MASS III, 38,
60; IV, 82, 113; XVIII, 127; XXI,
137; XXIV, 90, 109; XXIX, 89
Benjamin (May 15, 1726-Dec. 7, 1804)
m. Sept. 26, 1748 Susanna Spaulding XXIX, 89
Ebenezer (July 13, 1706-....) m.

.... Sarah ...... XXIV, 90, 109
Jonas (Sept. 12, 1742-June 22, 1826)
m. Sept. 1, 1767 Esther Cummings
XVIII, 127; XXIV, 90, 109
Nathaniel (Dec. 22, 1734-Sept. 24,
1809) m. Mar. 23, 1758 Elizabeth
Campbell XXI, 137
Timothy (June 26, 1730-Apr. 10,
1819) m. Feb. 10, 1757 Lucretia
Adams III, 38, 60; IV, 82, 113

BUTTON
Daniel (1746-p. 1783) m. Dec. 20,
1777 Elizabeth Button XI, 60;
XII, 29; XXII, 122
Matthias (bpt. Oct. 11, 1607-Aug.
13, 1672) m. a. 1654 (2) ......
Teagle MASS XI, 60; XII, 29;
XXII, 122

BUTTS
John (c. 1750-1787) m. .... Mary
Anne Claibourne XVI, 14
Thomas (1675-....) m. Apr. 2, 1713
Catherine Maclagalee VA XVI, 14

BUXTON
Anthony (1601-1684) m. .... Eliza-
beth ...... MASS XXV, 112, 205
Enos (July 24, 1752-Dec. 10, 1838)
m. Jan. 3, 1775 Mary Dodge XXV,
112
John (1742-1845) m. .... Betsey
Kelley XXV, 205

BUYS, see BOYCE

BYNUM, includes BANUM, BAYNHAM
Britton (1762-Oct. 8, 1834) m.
Aug. 24, 1803 Virginia (Jincy)
Dupree XV, 62
John (1569-p. 1624) m. .... Eliza-
beth ...... VA XV, 62

CADMUS, includes CUYPER, DE CUYPER
Henry (1751-1809) m. c. 1785 Aeltje
(Letitia) Keen XIX, 47; XX, 125
Peter (June 2, 1739-June 30, 1810)
m. June 17, 1759 Blandina Kif
XIV, 81; XV, 9
Thomas (bpt. Jan. 16, 1736/7-
Nov. 2, 1821) m. June 29, 1760
Peterchie Cadmus XXVII, 112,
113
Thomas Fredericksen (1611-May 19,
1702) m. 1646 Marretje
Adriance NY XV, 9, XIV,
81; XIX, 47; XX, 125; XXVII,
114

CADWELL
Samuel, II (Nov. 1, 1710-Nov. 21,
1788) m. July 15, 1737 Elishaba
Brace XXXIII, 107
Samuel, III (Jan. 6, 1743-Oct. 9,
1776) m. Sept. 2, 1762 Ruth
Woodruff XXXIII, 107
✳ Thomas (....-Oct. 9, 1694) m. 1658
Elizabeth Stebbins CONN XXXIII,
107

CADY
Isaac (Dec. 25, 1739-....) m. Oct.
1, 1760 Sarah Hildreth XXVIII,
178
Jeremiah (July 17, 1752-June 4,
1848) m. Nov. 12, 1772 Hannah War-
ner XIII, 105
John (Apr. 5, 1728-June 30, 1805) m.
Feb. 13, 1752 Deborah Benjamin
XXXIV, 94
Jonathan (June 14, 1748-July 12,
1834) m. Nov. 20, 1766 Rebecca
Cady XXVI, 112, 113
Nicholas (....-1712) m. c. 1648
Judith Knapp MASS XIII, 105;
XXVI, 112; XXVIII, 178; XXXIV, 94
Samuel (Feb. 24, 1724-Apr. 8, 1799)
m. Jan. 1, 1746 Elizabeth Winters
XIII, 105

CAHOON
Daniel (July 1, 1737-Sept. 13, 1811)
m. Oct. 10, 1760 Lillis (Dyer)
Thomas XX, 167
William (....-1675) m. ....
...... RI XX, 167

CALKINS
David (1757-Nov. 1796) m. Dec. 7,
1780 Elizabeth Deming XVIII, 30
Eleazer (1762-Feb. 22, 1836) m. a.
1782 Polly Disbrow XXXIV, 31
Hugh (1600-1690) m. .... Ann ......
CONN XVIII, 30; XXXIV, 31

CAMFIELD, see CANFIELD

CAMP, includes CAMPE

Abel, Jr. (July 11, 1748-May 8, 1825)
m. .... Sabra Marsh V, 116, 117
Edward (1622-1659) m. c. 1645 Mary
Canfield CONN IV, 108; V, 116,
117; XXXI, 28, 219
Ephraim (1734-Jan. 28, 1811) m. ....
Rachel ...... X, 100
Job (Nov. 16, 1747-Jan. 17, 1822) m.
Feb. 22, 1773 Anna Oviatt XXX,
203; XXXI, 28
Moses (Aug. 26, 1747-July 13, 1828)

m. .... Thankful Gaylord IV, 108
Nathan (Apr. 7, 1743-p. Nov. 16,
1802) m. Nov. 11, 1767 Sarah Smith
XXXI, 219
Nicholas (1597-c. 1635) m. ....
Sarah ...... CONN XXX, 203
William (....-....) m. Jan. 29, 1661
Mary Smith NJ X, 100

CAMPE, see CAMP

CAMPFIELD, see CANFIELD

CANDE, see CANDEE

CANDEE, includes CANDE
Caleb, Jr. (1743-Dec. 1, 1828) m.
Apr. 10, 1764/5 Anna Sperry
XVIII, 86; XXXIII, 49, 50
Daniel (Feb. 19, 1762-Aug. 9, 1831)
m. May 3, 1784 Lydia Wilmot XVI,
55
Job (Apr. 20, 1759-Dec. 3, 1845) m.
Oct. 3, 1784 Sarah Benham XIX, 38
Zaccheus (1640-1720) m. Dec. 5,
1670 Rebecca Bristol CONN XVI,
55; XVIII, 86; XIX, 38; XXXIII,
49, 50

CANFIELD, includes CAMFIELD, CAMPFIELD
Daniel (May 19, 1761-Mar. 8, 1841)
m. 1785 Ruth Stevens XXVIII, 60
David (Mar. 17, 1725/6-Jan. 26, 1806)
m. Oct. 3, 1745 Mary Northrop XV,
49
Elijah (Mar. 1758-Apr. 1841) m. 1778
Anna Read XV, 49
Jeremiah (Aug. 20, 1737-Mar. 31,
1791) m. Mar. 7, 1759 Mary Everton
XXXIV, 297
Josiah (Dec. 31, 1739-Feb. 11, 1778)
m. Feb. 28, 1768 (2) Naomi Davis
III, 17
Matthew (bpt. Feb. 27, 1604-June
1673) m. a. 1643 Sarah Treat CONN
XXVIII, 60; XXXIII, 89; XXXIV, 39
Samuel, IV (Dec. 20, 1734-....) m.
Sept. 9, 1760 Mehitabel Stilson
XXVIII, 60
Thomas (....-Aug. 22, 1689) m. ....
Phebe Crane CONN III, 17; XV,
49; XXXIV, 297
Williams (Apr. 13, 1752-Aug. 28,
1824) m. Apr. 27, 1773 Sarah
Squier XXXIII, 89; XXXIV, 39

CANNON
James (....-Feb. 1712) m. ....
Mary ...... MD XXII, 156; XXX,
124
James (1731-Sept. 8, 1784) m. ....

Margaret Alexander XXII, 156;
XXX, 124

CAPEN
Barnard (1562-Nov. 8, 1638) m. 1596
Joan Purchase MASS XXI, 124,
125
Josiah (Nov. 1, 1722-p. 1779) m.
Jan. 1, 1744 Charity Dwelly
XXI, 124, 125

CAPPS
John (c. 1750-1806) m. c. 1770
Martha ...... XXIX, 319
William (c. 1585-p. 1630) m. ....
.... VA XXIX, 319

CAPRON
Banfield, Sr. (1660-Aug. 20, 1752)
m. c. 1681 (1) Elizabeth Cal-
lender MASS, RI XXV, 265; XXIX,
227; XXX, 242; XXXI, 124
Benjamin (Sept. 15, 1724-Aug. 27,
1817) m. Mar. 17, 1754 Rachel
Weathers XXIX, 226; XXX, 242
John (July 28, 1759-July 11, 1836)
m. 1783 Asenath Cargill XXV, 265
Oliver (1754-1815) m. Oct. 29, 1773
Sarah Colvin XXIX, 226
Philip (May 9, 1745-July 21, 1821)
m. Nov. 8, 1772 Priscilla Tillson
XXXI, 124

CARD
Richard (....-a. July 1, 1674) m. a.
1648 Rebecca ...... RI III, 71
William (Aug. 27, 1752-July 29,
1842) m. c. 1778 Abigail Carpenter
III, 71

CAREY, see CARY

CARHART
Cornelius (Sept. 6, 1729-June 3,
1810) m. 1754 Willemptje Coleman
XXXIII, 313, 314
Thomas (c. 1650-Mar. 1696) m. Nov.
22, 1691 Mary Lord NY XXXIII,
313, 314

CARLETON, includes CARLTON
Caleb (June 22, 1757-May 9, 1823) m.
1779 Margaret Day XX, 13; XXVI,
110, 111; XXVII, 100
Edward (bpt. Oct. 20, 1610-a. 1661)
m. Nov. 3, 1636 Ellen Newton MASS
IV, 111; XX, 13; XXVI, 110; XXVII,
100; XXVIII, 75; XXXIV, 24
Edward (July 4, 1715-p. 1790) m.
July 2, 1734 Abiah Clement
XXVIII, 75

Jonathan (1731-1785) m. ....
Mainard IV, 111
Woodman (July 2, 1755-Feb. 13, 1837)
m. May 1778 Rebecca Rogers XXXIV,
23

CARLTON, see CARLETON

CARMAN
John (1606-1653) m. .... Florence
...... MASS, NY XXIV, 112
Silas (Apr. 15, 1709-Jan. 3, 1797)
m. June 15, 1736 Hannah Smith
XXIV, 112

CARPENTER
Cyril (Sept. 7, 1743-Nov. 23, 1811)
m. Nov. 28, 1765 Lucy Lane
XXVII, 223
Ebenezer (May 17, 1764-Aug. 31,
1807) m. Jan. 25, 1798 (2) Hannah
Fisher XXX, 187
Ephraim (July 24, 1735-Aug. 21, 1809)
m. May 14, 1761 Tabitha Chaffee
VI, 21; XI, 190
James (Feb. 16, 1738/9-Nov. 4, 1829)
m. Sept. 3, 1767 Bethiah Hyde
XXXI, 145; XXXIII, 207
James (Apr. 4, 1741-Nov. 4, 1813) m.
Apr. 5, 1761 Irene Ladd XIII,
102; XVIII, 14
John (c. 1725-a. 1787) m. a. 1752
Amy Jennings XXXIII, 95
John (1735-Feb. 25, 1803) m. ....
Susannah Turner XXVII, 141;
XXVIII, 31, 32, 33, 34, 35; XXIX,
92; XXX, 27; XXXIII, 208
John (Feb. 1745-Feb. 1800) m. Jan.
31, 1779 Abigail Moore XXIX, 131
Jonathan (June 19, 1757-Mar. 14,
1837) m. Mar. 20, 1784 Olive
Sessions X, 39
Jotham (c. 1749-p. 1782) m. Aug. 2,
1769 Hannah Gulley XXV, 272, 273
Oliver (Sept. 26, 1756-Feb. 21,
1845) m. Apr. 13, 1780 Prudence
Alexander XXII, 54
Robert (Mar. 5, 1722-....) m. Oct.
26, 1755 (1) Charity Roberts
XXIX, 185
Simeon (Mar. 23, 1740-Oct. 21, 1830)
m. May 11, 1769 Anna Burton VI,
7, 110
Thomas (Nov. 8, 1692/3-May 3, 1799)
m. Jan. 17, 1720/1 Mary Barstow
XVII, 34, 35
Thomas (Oct. 24, 1733-Apr. 26, 1807)
m. Dec. 26, 1754 Elizabeth Moulton
XIV, 5, 6
William (1605-Feb. 7, 1659) m. a.

CARPENTER, cont.
  *1628 Abigail ...... MASS
  VI, 7, 21, 111; X, 39; XI, 190;
  XIII, 102; XIV, 5, 6; XVII, 35;
  XVIII, 14; XXII, 54; XXV, 272,
  273; XXVII, 141, 223; XXVIII,
  31, 32, 33, 34, 35; XXIX, 92,
  131, 185; XXX, 27, 187; XXXI,
  145; XXXIII, 95, 207, 208*

CARR
  *Caleb (Dec. 9, 1616-Dec. 17, 1695)
  m. .... Mercy Vaughan RI
  XXX, 248*
  Caleb (June 19, 1744-1793) m. 1772
  Abigail Very XXXI, 204, 205
  *George (1599-Apr. 4, 1682) m. c.
  1640 (2) Elizabeth Oliver MASS
  XI, 35; XXI, 141, 142*
  John (June 4, 1711-May 2, 1786) m.
  July 28, 1738 (1) Anne Moody
  XI, 35; XXI, 141, 142
  John (Oct. 6, 1738-Mar. 25, 1814)
  m. July 19, 1761 Mary Arnold
  XXX, 248
  John (May 16, 1739-Jan. 12, 1825)
  m. May 5, 1763 Ruth Morse XI,
  35
  *Robert (Oct. 4, 1614-p. Apr. 30,
  1681) m. ....
  RI XXXI, 205*

CARRIER
  Amaziah (Sept. 22, 1754-Dec. 25,
  1832) m. May 25, 1790 Abiah
  Churchill XXIV, 64
  *Thomas (....-Mar. 16, 1735) m.
  May 7, 1664 Martha Allen MASS
  XXIV, 64*

CARRINGTON
  *Peter (....-p. Jan. 30, 1726) m.
  1691 Ann Wilmot Lines CONN
  XXXII, 89*
  Riverius (June 13, 1757-May 29,
  1823) m. 1790 Loly Wheeler
  XXXII, 89

CARTER
  Daniel (Apr. 8, 1718-....) m. ....
  Hannah Fowler XVIII, 54, 55
  *Edward (....-....) m. .... Margaret
  ...... PA XXII, 125*
  George (Dec. 18, 1728-1788) m.
  May 1783 Frances Diana Goodloe
  XXIV, 168
  *Giles (1634-1699/1700) m. ....
  Hannah .... VA XXX, 226*
  James (May 26, 1752-May 14, 1789)
  m. Sept. 24, 1778 Eleanor Knott
  XXII, 125

  Joel (Apr. 28, 1749-p. 1796) m. Dec.
  26, 1771 Sarah Jenkins XVIII, 54
  *John, I ˉ(....-June 10, 1669) m. 1662
  Sarah Ludlow VA XXXII, 87, 88*
  John, III (1727/8-1781/2) m. 1751
  Elizabeth Taylor XXXII, 87, 88
  John (June 10, 1759-....) m. ....
  Lucy Davis Wells XVIII, 54, 55
  Joseph (Sept. 13, 1731-Aug. 26,
  1824) m. Mar. 9, 1758 Ruth Curtis
  X, 297; XXV, 101
  Josiah (Jan. 26, 1726-Feb. 13, 1812)
  m. 1745 Tabitha Hough X, 118
  Peter (Mar. 9, 1743-Jan. 1791) m.
  1763 Mary Anne Ellis XIV, 114;
  XVI, 57
  Richard (....-....) m. .... Susannah
  ...... XXX, 226
  Robert (Aug. 12, 1735-1784) m. ....
  .... XI, 62
  *Thomas (....-Nov. 14, 1676) m. ....
  Mary ...... MASS XVIII, 54, 55*
  *Thomas (1608/10-Sept. 5, 1684) m. a.
  1640 Mary Parkhurst MASS X, 118,
  297; XVIII, 54; XXV, 101*
  *Thomas, Sr. (c. 1630-Oct. 22, 1700)
  m. May 4, 1670 Catharine Dale VA
  XI, 62; XIV, 114; XV, 52; XVI, 57;
  XXIV, 168; XXXII, 187; XXXIII,
  280, 281*
  Thomas (Nov. 27, 1734-July 15, 1817)
  m. July 10, 1764 Winifred Hobson
  XV, 52; XXXII, 187
  Thomas (1754-1817) m. 1776 Susanna
  Gaines XXXIII, 280, 281

CARTWRIGHT
  *Matthew (1634-1688) m. .... Sarah
  ...... MD XXVI, 284, 285; XXIX,
  15, 26, 68*
  Matthew (Feb. 20, 1754-Feb. 2, 1812)
  m. .... Polly Grimmer XXVI, 284,
  285; XXIX, 15, 26, 68

CARVER
  John (Nov. 30, 1738-Aug. 3, 1803) m.
  Oct. 18, 1762 Bathsheba Edson
  XXV, 45, 46; XXXIII, 247
  Joseph (Mar. 23, 1717-Jan. 6, 1787)
  m. Dec. 25, 1746 Sarah Hartwell
  XVI, 65
  *Robert (c. 1594-Apr. 1680) m. ....
  Christian ...... MASS XVI, 65;
  XXV, 45, 46; XXXIII, 247*

CARY, includes CAREY
  Dudley (1756-1803) m. Nov. 11, 1775
  Lucy Tabb XXVIII, 101
  Elihu, I (1740-p. 1790) m. ....
  Catherine North XXXIV, 305
  Jabez (July 30, 1727-p. 1790) m.

CHAMBERLAIN, cont.
Samuel (July 18, 1734-p. Aug. 28,
1792) m. May 13, 1755 Margaret
(Atwood) Ballard XXV, 298
Simon (Sept. 5, 1739-Dec. 21, 1816)
m. Mar. 7, 1756 Elizabeth Dodge
XXXIV, 107, 124
Swift (1764-Nov. 25, 1828) m. Mar.
8, 1795 Mary Tuttle VI, 58, 60
William (1620-May 31, 1706) m. c.
1648 Rebecca ...... MASS IV, 160;
XXV, 298; XXVII, 174; XXXI, 315,
316; XXXIV, 107, 124
William (July 6, 1725-Dec. 13, 1815)
m. .... Eleanor Hòrne IV, 160

CHAMBERLIN, see CHAMBERLAIN

CHAMBERS
Henry (Oct. 1753-July 17, 1822) m.
Dec. 8, 1779 Elizabeth Fox XXX,
276
John, Sr. (....-....) m. ....
.... NJ XXX, 276
John, Jr. (....-p. 1740) m. ....
.... NJ XXX, 276
John (1712-Dec. 4, 1778) m. July
31, 1746 Susannah Carter XXX,
276

CHAMPLIN
Jeffery (....-a. 1695)' m. ....
...... RI XXIX, 399
Jeffery (Mar. 21, 1744/5-1797) m.
Feb. 21, 1768 Mary Gardiner
XXIX, 399

CHANDLER
Benjamin (a. 1721-1777) m. ....
Elizabeth Jeffreys II, 25, 26
Daniel, Sr. (Mar. 21, 1729-Jan. 7,
1790) m. Dec. 24, 1754 Violet
Burnham XIX, 95; XXVI, 107
Daniel, Jr. (Dec. 5, 1764-Jan. 15
1853) m. June 25, 1797 Polly
Ayres XIX, 94; XXVI, 107
Ebenezer (May 14, 1749-Sept. 15,1823)
m. .... Sarah Averill XXXIV, 277
Edmund (....-p. 1684) m. ....
...... MASS II, 25, 26
Isaac (1717-June 5, 1787) m. Feb.
28, 1740/1 Abigail Hale XXXIV, 78
Isaac (June 24, 1743-July 10, 1791)
m. Oct. 3, 1771 Anna Loomis
XXIII, 83
John (Sept. 7, 1725-Jan. 10, 1812)
m. Feb. 14, 1754 Lydia Taylor
XIX, 39
John (Aug. 15, 1730-Mar. 1, 1807)
m. 1751 Mary Carter XXX,
250

John, Jr. (Nov. 27, 1754-Nov. 7,
1837) m. June 10, 1783 Hannah
Streeter XIX, 39
Joseph (Aug. 30, 1745-Oct. 11, 1831)
m. Feb. 4, 1777 Olive Backus XXII,
102
Joseph (1753-1844) m. .... Patient
Mary Andrus II, 25, 26
Moses, Sr. (Aug. 19, 1720-Mar. 16,
1800) m. June 28, 1742 Dorothy
Marble XXX, 250
Moses (Nov. 23, 1765-Sept. 10, 1822)
m. 1792 (1) Sally Goodwin XXX,
249, 250
Samuel, Sr. (Aug. 7, 1745-a. July
14, 1796) m. .... Rebecca Walton
XXX, 250, 251
Thomas (1630-1703) m. .... Hannah
Brewer MASS XIX, 39; XXX, 250,
251
Timothy (Apr. 5, 1738-....) m. ....
Mary Walker XXXII, 202
William (bpt. Oct. 12, 1595-Nov. 26,
1641/2) m. Nov. 6, 1625 (2) Annis
Bayford Parmenter MASS XIX, 95;
XXII, 102; XXIII, 83; XXVI, 107;
XXX, 250; XXXII, 202; XXXIV, 78,
277

CHANEY, see CHENEY

CHAPIN
Abner (May 29, 1749-Apr. 1, 1814)
m. Dec. 7, 1769 Rhoda Kibbe XXIX,
348
Benjamin (May 24, 1736-1778) m. Mar.
4, 1760 Margaret Colton VI, 32,
36
David (Sept. 16, 1745-Feb. 15, 1826)
m. Apr. 7, 1766 Lydia Cook XXIII,
26
Frederick (May 12, 1760-June 12,
1802) m. Sept. 11, 1788 Lucretia
Morton XXVI, 213, 214
Japhet (Aug. 8, 1760-Oct. 6, 1822)
m. p. Oct. 25, 1783 Lovina Wright
XI,' 143
Jesse (Aug. 27, 1761-Mar. 4, 1854/5)
m. Nov. 20, 1783 Eunice Wheelock
XVI, 34
John, Jr. (Oct. 7, 1730-July 17,
1815) m. May 28, 1754 Rhoda Albee
XX, 104
Judah (Apr. 17, 1756-Nov. 4, 1821)
m. Mar. 2, 1786 Lois Stebbins
X, 114, 271
Martin (Oct. 6, 1738-Apr. 24, 1793)
m. Mar. 20, 1769 Bathsheba Cooper
X, 113
Peter (Sept. 23, 1756-Sept. 23, 1839)
m. a. Oct. 2, 1780 Elizabeth Austin

XVIII, 39
Phineas (Mar. 7, 1747-Mar. 2,
1821) m. Jan. 26, 1775
Sabrina Wright XXXIV, 256
Samuel (bpt. Oct. 8, 1598-Nov. 11,
1675) m. Feb. 9, 1623 Cicely Penny
MASS VI, 32, 36; X, 113, 114, 272;
XI, 143; XVI, 34; XVIII, 39; XX,
104; XXIII, 26; XXVI, 213, 214;
XXIX, 349; XXXIV, 256

CHAPLIN, includes CHAPLINE
Hugh (May 22, 1603-a. Mar. 31, 1657)
m. May 18, 1642 Elizabeth ......
MASS XXVII, 134
Isaac (1584-....) m. 1606 Mary Calvert
MD XII, 82
Joseph (Jan. 23, 1741/2-a. 1801) m.
Apr. 5, 1764 Lois Hastings XXVII,
134, 135
Moses Caton (Oct. 20, 1754-Feb. 10,
1812) m. .... Mary Caldwell
XII, 82

CHAPLINE, see CHAPLIN

CHAPMAN
Constant (Dec. 27, 1761-Sept. 24,
1847) m. Jan. 27, 1785 Jemima Kelsey XXXI, 292, 293
Edward (....-Dec. 19, 1675) m. ....
Elizabeth Fox CONN IV, 164; IX,
43; XI, 92
Edward (c. 1620-Apr. 18, 1678) m. c.
1642 (1) Mary Symonds MASS XIX,
84
Levi (Oct. 9, 1740-p. 1805) m. Sept.
18, 1767 Elizabeth Hull XXXIV,
166
Phineas (1716-Nov. 20, 1782) m. Dec.
22, 1742 Sarah Ketchum XI, 144
Robert (1616-Oct. 3, 1687) m. Apr.
29, 1642 Ann Bliss CONN XI, 144;
XXXI, 293; XXXIV, 167
Samuel (Dec. 7, 1706-c. 1795) m. c.
1729 .... XIX, 84
Simon (Dec. 23, 1736-July 26, 1823)
m. Eunice Preston IV, 164; IX,
43; XI, 92

CHASE
Abel, Sr. (Aug. 9, 1750-p. 1799) m.
Nov. 30, 1768 Elizabeth Elliott
XVII, 59; XVIII, 62
Aquila (1618-Dec. 27, 1670) m. June
14, 1646 Anne Wheeler NH, MASS
X, 105, 190; XII, 122; XIII, 13;
XIV, 46; XV, 82; XVII, 59; XVIII,
49, 62, 78, 125; XX, 10, 148; XXVI,
209, 210, 277, 278, 288, 289; XXX
114, 115; XXXI, 84, 97, 98, 116,

131, 153, 192; XXXIV, 228
Caleb (Nov. 29, 1722-Oct. 2, 1808)
m. Apr. 1745 Sarah Prince XVIII,
49; XX, 148
David (p. Aug. 21, 1721-1798) m.
Oct. 11, 1753 Elizabeth Asten
XXXIV, 148
Edmund (June 21, 1748-1822) m. Nov.
30, 1769 Esther Merrill XVIII,
125
Ezekiel (July 9, 1761-Sept. 14, 1843)
m. Aug. 1784 Betsy Goodwin XXXI,
192
James (Mar. 6, 1751-....) m. Oct.
15, 1772 Elizabeth Haseltine XXXI,
83, 84, 97, 98, 116, 131, 153
Jonathan (Aug. 18, 1723-Oct. 6,
1799) m. Jan. 24, 1744/5 Joanna
Morse XXVI, 209, 210
Joseph (Apr. 26, 1753-July 17, 1844)
m. Nov. 24, 1772 Judith Cooper
XXXIV, 228
Josiah (Nov. 30, 1713-Dec. 26, 1778)
m. Apr. 5, 1743 Sarah Tufts XIII,
13
Josiah (Apr. 16, 1746-Sept. 21,
1824) m. .... Hannah Grow XII,
122
Moses (Mar. 16, 1727-Oct. 18, 1799)
m. Apr. 17, 1752 Hannah Brown
XIV, 46; XV, 82; XVIII, 78; XXVI,
277, 278, 288, 289
Rufus (Sept. 29, 1745-1815) m. ....
Sarah Kingsley VIII, 9
Samuel (Sept. 28, 1707-Aug. 12, 1800)
m. May 1728 (1) Mary Dudley X,
105, 190
Solomon (Sept. 8, 1743-June 1828) m.
Jan. 24, 1765 Rebecca Chamberlain
XX, 10; XXX, 114, 115
William (c. 1600-May 1659) m. a.
1627 Mary ...... MASS VIII, 9,
XXXIV, 148

CHATFIELD
George (....-June 9, 1671) m. Mar.
29, 1660 (2) Isabel Nettleton
CONN XIII, 67; XVI, 72; XX, 131
Joel (Feb. 21, 1757-Jan. 14, 1836)
m. Nov. 13, 1785 Ruth Stoddard
XX, 131
Oliver (July 23, 1730-June 30, 1778)
m. a. May 1755 (2) Zerviah ......
XIII, 67; XVI, 72

CHEATHAM
Obediah (....-1776) m. .... Margaret
Rudd XX, 127
Thomas (c. 1640-May 2, 1720) m.
Oct. 1681 .... VA.
XX, 128

CHEESEBROUGH, see CHESEBROUGH

CHEEVER
Aaron (Feb. 9, 1741/2-May 26, 1803)
m. Nov. 30, 1773 Elizabeth Smith
XXXI, 134
Daniel (1621/2-Mar. 4, 1703/4)m.
Esther ...... MASS X, 233; XXXI,
134
Daniel (Apr. 9, 1735-May 21, 1823)
m. Dec. 11, 1766 Abigail Guild
X, 233

CHEINE, see CHENEY

CHENEY, includes CHANEY, CHEINE,
CHEYNEY
Charles, II (Aug. 30, 1703-1781) m.
c. 1725 Mary Powell XXXIV, 36,
126
Eliphatet (Dec. 5, 1756-Sept. 11,
1822) m. Nov. 23, 1780 Mary Ela
XXVII, 77, 78
Ephraim (Aug. 1, 1741-p. 1792) m.
Jan. 15, 1767 (2) Bathsheba Segur
VI, 74
John (c. 1605-July 28, 1666) m. ....
Martha ...... MASS IV, 74;
XVIII, 50; XXVI, 7; XXVII, 78;
XXXII, 25, 26; XXXIV, 282
Moses (Oct. 20, 1715-p. 1782) m.
Apr. 3, 1755 (2) Hannah Woodward
XXXIV, 281
Nathaniel, Jr. (Oct. 7, 1747-Aug.
3, 1833) m. Oct. 5, 1769 Eliza-
beth Ela XXVI, 7; XXXII, 25
Richard (1625-1685/6) m. .... (2)
Eleanor ...... MD XXXIV, 36,
126
Timothy (May 10, 1731-Sept. 27, 1795)
m. Jan. 19, 1758 (1) Mary Olcott
XXXII, 26
Tristram (Oct. 14, 1726-Dec. 1816)
m. Nov. 28, 1745 Margaret Joyner
XVIII, 50

CHESEBOROUGH, see CHESEBROUGH

CHESEBROUGH, includes CHEESEBROUGH,
CHESEBOROUGH
Jabez (Sept. 26, 1756-....) m. Jan.
27, 1780 Rhoda Woodworth XXI, 73,
74
Perez (Mar. 2, 1762-Jan. 10, 1851)
m. June 1785 Priscilla Thompson
XXIX, 216
Samuel (Mar. 25, 1743-Sept. 9, 1811)
m. Jan. 10, 1765 Submit Palmer
VII, 44; XIX, 102
William (1594-June 9, 1667) m. Dec.
15, 1620 Anne Stevenson MASS,

CONN. VII, 44; XIX, 102; XXI, 73,
74; XXIX, 216

CHESLEY
Philip (c. 1606-c. 1674) m. ....
Elizabeth ...... NH XXXII, 225;
XXXIII, 178
Thomas (....-1778) m. .... Mary Hill
XXXII, 224, 225; XXXIII, 178

CHESTER
Samuel (Oct. 5, 1625-1710) m. ....
(1) .... CONN XXI, 45
Thomas (Aug. 18, 1721-Mar. 6, 1804)
m. Sept. 9, 1742 Sarah Eldrege
XXI, 45

CHEW
John (1590-1655) m. .... Sarah
Howard VA XXVI, 232
Samuel (1737-Feb. 20, 1790) m. ....
Sarah Weems XXVI, 232

CHEYNEY, see CHENEY

CHICKERING
John (Aug. 23, 1715-....) m. Dec. 7,
1743 (1) Mary Dewing XXIV, 81
John (Aug. 21, 1744-1802) m. July 2,
1767 Lois Marsh XXIV, 110
Nathaniel (Oct. 8, 1647-Oct. 21,
1694) m. Dec. 5, 1674 (2) Lydia
Fisher MASS XXIV, 81, 99, 110
Timothy (Mar. 10, 1750-Jan. 10, 1829)
m. May 14, 1774 Rhoda Wheelock
XXIV, 81, 99

CHILD, see CHILDS

CHILDS, includes CHILD
Abel (Oct. 13, 1752-Nov. 12, 1807)
m. Mar. 11, 1779 Rebecca Allard
XV, 107
Benjamin (Apr. 8, 1620-Oct. 14,
1678) m. c. 1653 Mary Bowen MASS
XII, 72; XV, 107; XXXIV, 184
David, Jr. (Feb. 7, 1735-....) m.
Apr. 4, 1758 Hannah Davis XXX,
221
Henry (May 28, 1717-Jan. 17, 1795)
m. .... (1) Rebecca Bacon XII, 72
Increase (Dec. 13, 1740-June 20,
1810) m. Nov. 3, 1762 Olive Pease
XXXIV, 184
John (1636-Oct. 15, 1676) m. ....
Mary Warren MASS IV, 89
Moses (Apr. 6, 1731-Feb. 8, 1793) m.
.... Sarah Styles IV, 89
Samuel (....-Mar. 25, 1675)
m. .... MASS
XXX, 221

CHILTON
John (1630-p. Nov. 15, 1706) m.
.... Jane ...... VA XXVIII,
78; XXXI, 89
John (Aug. 22, 1739-Sept. 11, 1777)
m. Apr. 10, 1768 Letetia Blackwell XXVIII, 78; XXXI, 89

CHIPMAN
Benjamin (May 23, 1729-1787) m. May
9, 1751 Hannah Wadsworth XXVI,
238, 239
Jesse (Feb. 28, 1755-June 4, 1841)
m. Dec. 8, 1779 Mary White XV,
34
John (1614-Apr. 7, 1708) m. 1646
Hope Howland MASS XV, 34; XXII,
68; XXVI, 238, 239; XXVIII, 174;
XXX, 178, 179; XXXI, 258
John (1755-1843) m. .... Elizabeth
Hall XXVIII, 174
Joseph (Oct. 26, 1738-May 9, 1817)
m. Feb. 7, 1809 Elizabeth Fowler
XXII, 68
William (May 6, 1731-Mar. 18, 1795)
m. Mar. 3, 1772 (2) Betsy Mayo
XXX, 178, 179; XXXI, 257, 258

CHITTENDEN
Abraham (Feb. 16, 1723-July 19,
1810) m. Mar. 15, 1749 Marcy Burges
XIV, 112
Samuel (Aug. 16, 1704-July 10, 1783)
m. .... Mrs. Phyllis (Burgis)
Johnson XII, 49
William (bpt. Mar. 1594-Feb. 1660/1)
m. .... (1) Joanna Sheaffe CONN
XII, 49; XIV, 113

CHOATE
John (bpt. June 6, 1624-Dec. 4,
1695) m. 1660 Anne ...... MASS
XV, 26; XXXIV, 172
Nehemiah (Dec. 6, 1730-Jan. 24,
1797) m. Mar. 29, 1755 Susanna
Brown XV, 26
William, Sr. (Sept. 5, 1730-Apr.
23, 1785) m. Jan. 16, 1756 Mary
Giddings XXXIV, 171

CHRISTIANCE
Christian (....-....) m. .... Maritie
Ysbrantse Elders NY XXVII, 158
Cornelius (bpt. May 26, 1760-Dec. 2,
1790) m. a. 1784 Elizabeth Bradt
XXVII, 158

CHURCH
John (Aug. 3, 1755-Dec. 6, 1834) m.
Mar. 29, 1780 Deborah Spencer
XI, 194, 196, 197

Richard (Feb. 6, 1610-Dec. 16, 1667)
m. May 18, 1627 Ann March CONN,
MASS XI, 194, 196, 197, 200;
XVIII, 90; XXIV, 139; XXVII, 9,
10; XXVIII, 137; XXXI, 294, 311
Richard (Jan. 23, 1741/2-Nov. 12,
1807) m. Feb. 4, 1767 Rebecca
Warner XXXI, 311
Samuel, Sr. (May 1, 1758-Mar. 13,
1844) m. Mar. 11, 1784 Dorothy
Olmsted XXXI, 294
Timothy (May 12, 1736-Nov. 13, 1823)
m. June 9, 1757 Abigail Church
XVIII, 90; XXVIII, 136, 137
William (Harrison), Sr. (Mar. 3,
1730-p. 1783) m. Nov. 15, 1750
Jane Wood XXVII, 9, 10
William (Jan. 26, 1753-Aug. 20,
1829) m. .... Mollie Pitts XI,
200; XXIV, 139

CHURCHILL
Hezekiah (Feb. 2, 1752-Dec. 19,
1792) m. .... Reliance Byington
VIII, 23
Jesse, Sr. (Aug. 31, 1726-May 7,
1806) m. Nov. 8, 1750 Jerusha Gay-
lord XXXIII, 115, 116
John (June 2, 1744-Nov. 15, 1815)
m. .... Allen XXV, 271
Josiah (....-a. Jan. 1687) m. ....
Elizabeth Foote CONN VIII, 23;
XXXIII, 115, 116
William (....-a. Sept. 25, 1714) m.
Mar. 10, 1672 Susannah Brayser NY
XXV, 271

CILLEY, includes SEALEY
Benjamin (May 12, 1742-Mar. 9, 1823)
m. Oct. 8, 1763 Apphia Keniston
XXXIII, 23
Joseph (Nov. 1734-Aug. 25, 1799) m.
Nov. 4, 1756 Sarah Longfellow VI,
70
Richard (a. 1632-....) m. ....
...... NH VI, 70
Robert (1601-1668) m. Dec. 25, 1626
Mary Mason MASS, CONN XXXIII, 23

CLAFLIN, includes MCCLAFLIN, MACK-
CLOTHAN, MACKCLOTHIAN
Daniel (Sept. 8, 1749-p. 1792) m.
.... Submit Page XXVI, 67; XXXI,
231
John (July 5, 1750-Jan. 28, 1838) m.
Apr. 5, 1770 Mary Sheffeld XXVII,
115
Robert (....-a. Sept. 19, 1690) m.
Oct. 14, 1664 Joanna Warner MASS
XXVI, 67; XXVII, 115; XXXI,
231

CLAGETT
Henry (1728-1777/8) m. 1750 Ann Magruder XXVI, 240, 241; XXXII, 278, 279
Thomas (1635-1703) m. 1674 (1) Mary Nutter (Hooper); m. 1683 (2) Sarah Patterson MD XXVI, 240, 241; XXXII, 278

CLAIBORNE
Augustine (1721-May 3, 1787) m. .... Mary Herbert X, 101
William (c. 1587-1676) m. .... Elizabeth Butler VA X, 101

CLAP, see CLAPP

CLAPP, includes CLAP
Daniel (Aug. 7, 1743-Sept. 22, 1802) m. .... Abigail Root VI, 16
David (Aug. 30, 1744-Sept. 5, 1823) m. Aug. 18, 1767 Hannah King XVIII, 114
Ezekiel (Mar. 14, 1756-Nov. 4, 1823) m. Mar. 26, 1778 Lydia Pratt IV, 168; XV, 116
Jonathan (Sept. 2, 1713-May 10, 1782) m. Jan. 23, 1735 Submit Strong XXXI, 121
Jonathan (Oct. 1, 1714-c. 1794) m. 1743 Sarah Hewes XVIII, 114
Joseph (Nov. 3, 1736-1797) m. .... Hannah Lyman XXXI, 121
Nicholas (1612-Nov. 24, 1679) m. .... Sarah Clapp MASS IV, 168; XV, 116
Norman (1761-May 6, 1830) m. Aug. 3, 1782 Huldah Wright XX, 35
Roger (Apr. 6, 1609-Feb. 2, 1691) m. Nov. 6, 1633 Joanna Ford MASS VI, 16; XV, 140; XVI, 5; XX, 35; XXXI, 121
Roger (Apr. 28, 1721-Aug. 1, 1807) m. Feb. 23, 1748 Susannah Wales IV, 168; XV, 116
Rufus (Dec. 23, 1759-May 10, 1810) m. Aug. 12, 1782 Sybil Hodges XXXIV, 59
Seth (Nov. 4, 1722-Sept. 10, 1788) m. Mar. 30, 1745 (1) Mary Bullard XXXI, 274; XXXIV, 59
Stephen (July 30, 1752-May 3, 1829) m. 1783 Catherine Wheeler XIV, 10; XXXIV, 175
Thomas (1597-Apr. 20, 1684) m. .... Abigail ...... MASS XIV, 10; XVIII, 115; XXXI, 274; XXXII, 118; XXXIV, 59, 176
Timothy (Aug. 16, 1740-p. 1770) m. Dec. 3, 1761 Rachel Bascom XV, 140; XVI, 5

William (Dec. 3, 1733-a. Jan. 14, 1805) m. .... Priscilla Otis XXXII, 118

CLARK, includes CLARKE
Aaron (Sept. 30, 1758-May 7, 1848) m. June 11, 1786 Elizabeth Fowler IV, 114; XVI, 102, 103
Asabel (Sept. 2, 1744-Apr. 23, 1814) m. June 22, 1786 (2) Mary Bugbee XXI, 100
Dan (Aug. 11, 1748-Dec. 9, 1827) m. Jan. 24, 1771 Lucy Stanley XXXIV, 251
Daniel (1622-Aug. 10, 1710) m. June 13, 1644 Mary Newberry CONN XXVII, 107, 108; XXXII, 286
Daniel (c. 1723/4-Mar. 10, 1792) m. 1757 Hannah Dearborn XXII, 107
David (July 31, 1713-Mar. 6, 1800) m. July 15, 1742 Hannah Peck XIV, 121
David (1751-July 17, 1831) m. .... Anna Clark XXIV, 29
Edward (....-1683/1700) m. Dec. 14, 1678 Dorothy Raynell NY XXV, 191
Edward (c. 1622-1695) m. a. 1653 (1) Dorcas Bosworth MASS II, 36; XXII, 107; XXXI, 208; XXXIII, 346
Elisha (May 14, 1734-Sept. 9, 1811) m. Feb. 14, 1760 Hannah Hopkins XIII, 102; XV, 44; XXVI, 68, 69
Elisha (Oct. 19, 1758-May 30, 1840) m. Jan. 14, 1777 Sarah Beach XV, 83
George (1610-Aug. 10, 1690) m. .... Sarah ...... CONN IV, 114; XIV, 122; XV, 83, XVI, 102, 103; XXIV, 29; XXIX, 323; XXXIII, 279, 280
George (June 13, 1752-Nov. 21, 1841) m. Jan. 9, 1783 (2) Lydia Osborn XXXIII, 279, 280
Gideon (Oct. 15, 1738-Apr. 4, 1817) m. .... Eunice Browning XVII, 160
Gideon (Apr. 16, 1759-Jan. 2, 1835) m. Apr. 10, 1787/8 Jemima Newcomb XXV, 156, 157
Henry (Apr. 23, 1717-Feb. 27, 1804) m. July 10, 1766 Katherine Bean XV, 103
Hezekiah (1723-1776) m. 1746 Mary Peck IV, 114
Ira (bpt. Mar. 13, 1757-Jan. 26, 1836) m. Oct. 10, 1779 Bede Barnes XXVII, 107, 108
Jacob (Apr. 16, 1742-Aug. 11, 1793) m. 1767 Elizabeth Depew Dann XXXI, 170; XXXIII, 85, 86
Jacob (Mar. 15, 1749-July 4, 1833 m. Aug. 24, 1775 Mary Ricker XXXI, 208; XXXIII, 346

CLEMENT, cont.
Benjamin (Mar. 19, 1717-Dec. 22,
1786) m. July 10, 1739 Mary
Bartlett XII, 56; XXVII, 25
Jeremiah (....-....) m. .... Edey
...... VA XXVI, 32
Job (Nov. 19, 1722-Nov. 13, 1799) M.
c. 1744 Elizabeth Rollins XXI, 7
John (Jan. 10, 1755-Oct. 14, 1823)
m. Apr. 22, 1778 Susannah Massey
XXVII, 25, 26
Philip (Mar. 15, 1744-Nov. 10,
1817) m. .... Phebe Sawyer XII,
56
Richard (Aug. 5, 1760-Dec. 23,
1815) m. Aug. 21, 1783 Mehetable
Runnels XXIII, 13, 43
Robert (bpt. Dec. 14, 1595-Sept. 29,
1658) m. a. 1615 (1) Lydia ......
MASS XII, 56; XXI, 6, 7; XXIII,
13, 43; XXVII, 25; XXXI, 207
William (Nov. 24, 1757-Aug. 24,
1833) m. c. 1787 (2) Abigail Hill
XXXI, 207

CLEMENTS, see CLEMENT

CLEVELAND, includes CLEAVELAND
Ezra (Apr. 17, 1726-Nov. 7, 1802)
m. a. 1745 Jerusha Newcomb XXXII,
226
Ezra (1746-1822) m. .... Abiah Neal
I, 45
Frederick (Nov. 28, 1756-Mar. 7,
1827) m. 1780 Susannah Hill XI,
26
George (1762-1805) m. 1784 Sarah
Mabee XXXIII, 246
James (July 3, 1730-p. 1775) m.
Nov. 15, 1752 Susanna Hartshorn
XI, 25
Moses (1624-Jan. 9, 1701/2) m. Sept.
26, 1648 Ann Winn MASS I, 45;
XI, 26; XVIII, 71; XXVII, 153;
XXXI, 291; XXXII, 226; XXXIII,
246, 278
Moses (June 26, 1744-....) m. Mar.
24, 1768 Azubah Kendall XVIII,
70, 71
Samuel (June 7, 1730-1806) m. May 7,
1751 Ruth Darbe (Derby) XXXIII,
278
Samuel (July 14, 1753-May 30, 1839)
m. May 22, 1777 Mercy Wilbur
XXVII, 153
William, Sr. (July 7, 1719-1791)
m. 1739 Rachel Warren XXXI, 290,
291
William, Jr. (1747-Dec. 28, 1799) m.
Jan. 5, 1799 Sarah Tozer XXXI,
290, 291

CLIFT
Amos, Sr. (Sept. 20, 1737-July 29,
1806) m. .... Mary Coit V, 97
William (1666-Oct. 17, 1722) m. ....
Lydia Wells MASS V, 97

CLINTON
John (Nov. 8, 1721-p. 1790) m. Nov.
1746 Elizabeth Beecher XXIII, 56
John, Jr. (May 4, 1752-1832) m. c.
1773 Mary Scribner XXIII, 56
Lawrence (1643-p. Oct. 1704) m. p.
1690 Margaret (Painter) Morris
MASS XXIII, 56

CLIZBE
James (c. 1670-a. 1712) m. ....
Elizabeth Burwell NJ XXIX, 327;
XXX, 175
Joseph (June 27, 1756-Jan. 20, 1840)
m. .... Hannah Robards XXIX, 327;
XXX, 175

CLOPTON
John (Feb. 7, 1756-Sept. 11, 1816)
m. May 15, 1784 Sarah Bacon XX,
63; XXXI, 156
William (1655-1733) m. p. Aug. 25,
1673 Ann (Booth) Dennett VA XX,
63; XXXI, 156

CLOSE
Benjamin (Dec. 15, 1743-Apr. 29,
1812) m. .... Theodosia Mead
XXII, 44
John (c. 1600-1653) m. .... Eliza-
beth ...... CONN XXVIII, 184
Odle (Oct. 22, 1738-Apr. 26, 1812)
m. Dec. 16, 1756 Bethia Reynolds
XXVIII, 184
Thomas (1636-1709) m. 1669 Sarah
Hardy CONN XXII, 44

CLOUGH, includes CLUFF
Daniel (Aug. 11, 1763-July 1, 1840)
m. May 15, 1785 Abigail Atwood
XXIV, 107; XXXIII, 174; XXXIV, 180
David (c. 1758-1815) m. Aug. 25,
1783 Hannah Winslow XXXIV, 30
Elisha (May 14, 1717-....) m. Oct.
2, 1740 Mary Welch XXXIV, 30
Isaac (Apr. 23, 1753-p. 1789) m.
Feb. 18, 1779 Hannah Page XIX, 73
John (1613-July 26, 1691) m. c. 1641
(1) Jane Macomber MASS XIX, 73;
XX, 122; XXIV, 107; XXXI, 222;
XXXIII, 70, 174; XXXIV, 30, 180,
188, 189
Samuel (Apr. 29, 1738-Dec. 31, 1811)
m. Feb. 1760 Miriam Satterly XX,
122

Theophilus (Nov. 28, 1703-Feb. 14, 1781) m. Mar. 10, 1739 Sarah French XX, 122
Wyman, Sr. (Oct. 4, 1726-1796) m. 1760 Sarah Hall XXXI, 222
Zacheus (bpt. Jan. 23, 1728-c. 1810) m. Dec. 1752 Love Meader XXXIII, 69, 70; XXXIV, 188, 189

CLUFF, see CLOUGH

CLUTE, includes KLEUT
Gerardus (bpt. Oct. 19, 1735-Dec. 12, 1803) m. c. 1775 (2) Sarah Abel XXIV, 83; XXVI, 17
Johannes (....-Nov. 26, 1725) m. 1672 Baata Van Slichtenhorst NY XXIV, 83; XXVI, 17

COALBORNE, see COLBURN

COATE
John (....-Dec. 29, 1699/1700) m. 1663 Elizabeth Humphreys NJ, PA XXXI, 233
John (1735-1802) m. 1769 Susannah Ennis XXXI, 233

COBB
Ebenezer (Aug. 13, 1731-Aug. 20, 1811) m. May 12, 1754 Lydia Churchill XXIV, 113
Henry (....-1679) m. 1631 Patience Hurst MASS XXIV, 113

COBURN, see COLBURN

COCHRANE
John (....-....) m. .... NH XXII, 51
Joseph (Aug. 17, 1739-Mar. 20, 1816) m. .... Margaret Murray XXII, 51

COCK, see COX

COCKE, see COX

CODDINGTON
Benjamin (c. 1756-Aug. 28, 1836) m. .... Hannah Coon XXVII, 126
Benjamin (Oct. 8, 1761-July 25, 1848) m. Mar. 1, 1787 Mary Denton XIV, 36, 37; XV, 46
John (....-Aug. 18, 1655) m. .... Emma ...... NJ XXVII, 126
William (1601-Nov. 1, 1678) m. 1649 (3) Ann ...... RI XIV, 36; XV, 46

CODMAN
Richard (June 23, 1729-Sept. 12,

1793) m. Feb. 23, 1763 Sarah Smith XV, 106
Robert (....-c. 1687) m. .... MASS XV, 106

COE
Abel (July 20, 1727-Jan. 10, 1798) m. Jan. 23, 1756 Prudence Rossiter VI, 71
Benjamin (Dec. 28, 1738-Oct. 14, 1818) m. c. 1767 Bethia Grummon XXVI, 250, 251; XXXI, 27, 48, 130
Charles (July 12, 1760-Mar. 11, 1823) m. Oct. 20, 1784 Hannah Bates VI, 71
David (Feb. 18, 1716-Jan. 14, 1807) m. .... Hannah Parsons Camp VI, 12; VII, 15, 16, 17
James (Feb. 3, 1741-July 31, 1790) m. Oct. 30, 1766 Huldah Wilcoxson XXXI, 189
John (Sept. 18, 1729-Dec. 10, 1783) m. Sept. 8, 1755 Hannah Chatfield XVII, 143, 144
Joseph (Sept. 5, 1713-June 10, 1784) m. Dec. 1739 Abigail Curtis XVII, 126, 127
Morris (Aug. 30, 1752-July 22, 1799) m. June 15, 1775 Lucy Rossiter XXXIV, 142
Robert, Sr. (Oct. 16, 1596-1689) m. c. 1623 (1) Mary ......; Apr. 29, 1630 (2) Anna Dearslay MASS, CONN, NY VI, 12, 72; VII, 15, 16, 17; XVII, 126, 127, 143, 144; XXVI, 250, 251; XXVII, 21; XXXI, 27, 48, 130, 189; XXXIV, 142
Robert, Jr. (1627-1659) m. .... Hannah Mitchell CONN, NY VII, 15, 16, 17
Seth (Dec. 21, 1756-Nov. 15, 1839) m. c. 1787 (2) Sarah Elmer XXVII, 21
Simeon (Mar. 22, 1720/1-Sept. 23, 1782) m. Jan. 16, 1745/6 Anna Morris XXXIV, 142

COEVERS, see COVERT

COFFIN
Nathaniel, Jr. (July 6, 1711-June 10, 1800) m. .... Mary Sheffield XVII, 29, 30
Tristram (1605-Oct. 2, 1681) m. 1629 Dionis Stevens MASS XVII, 29; XIX, 113, 114; XX, 65; XXXII, 222
William (Nov. 4, 1720-Nov. 10, 1803) m. Oct. 4, 1740 Priscilla Paddock XXXII, 222
William (July 25, 1747-1796) m. .... Esther Hunt XIX, 113, 114; XX, 65

COGGESHALL
John (Dec. 9, 1601-Nov. 27, 1647) m.
.... Mary ...... MASS, RI XXXI,
230; XXXIV, 122
Newby (Aug. 17, 1726-Jan. 8, 1807)
m. Nov. 28, 1751 Mary Mason
XXXI, 230; XXXIV, 122

COIT
Daniel (June 5, 1760-July 4, 1832)
m. Oct. 8, 1788 Ruth Eastman XI,
199
John (a. 1600-Aug. 29, 1659) m. ....
Mary Jenners MASS XI, 199

COLBORNE, see COLBURN

COLBURN, includes COALBORNE, COBURN,
COLBORNE
Alpheus (Dec. 16, 1759-Nov. 25, 1813)
m. May 27, 1780 Joanna Edwards
XXIX, 217
Edward (1618-1712) m. .... Hannah
...... MASS XIII, 6, 21; XXIII,
37; XXIV, 102; XXVI, 95; XXVIII,
111; XXIX, 217
Jacob (Feb. 10, 1729-Feb. 2, 1809)
m. Sept. 24, 1757 Lydia Hall
XXIV, 102
John (Aug. 3, 1738-Feb. 6, 1827)
m. Oct. 7, 1770 Anna Darley XIII,
6
Jonathan (Dec. 19, 1723-....) m.
.... Hannah XXIV, 96
Joseph (July 7, 1718-Mar. 18, 1776)
m. Nov. 23, 1744 Dorothy Draper
XXVII, 34
Joseph, Jr. (Aug. 21, 1745-p. Jan.
2, 1776) m. Jan. 8, 1772 Elizabeth
Clark XXVII, 34
Lemuel (Sept. 12, 1758-June 3, 1839)
m. May 1, 1788 Sarah Russ XIII,
21; XXIII, 37
Nathaniel (....-May 14, 1691) m.
July 25, 1639 Priscilla Clark
MASS XXIV, 96; XXVII, 34; XXX,
283
Peter (Nov. 5, 1737-May 8, 1813) m.
Nov. 26, 1763 (1) Dolly Varnum
XXVIII, 111
Samuel, Sr. (Mar. 6, 1714-Oct. 18,
1804) m. July 2, 1740 Mary Fair-
banks XXX, 283
Samuel, Jr. (Apr. 3, 1743-June 21,
1794) m. Feb. 3, 1770 Mehitable
Lewis XXX, 283
William (Dec. 5, 1726-Feb. 2, 1776)
m. 1757 Abigail Wheeler XXVI, 95

COLBY
Anthony (1590-Feb. 1, 1661) m. 1632

(1) Susanna Sargent MASS XXVIII,
205; XXX, 66; XXXIII, 305
Eliphalet, Sr. (1728-1812) m. Feb.
14, 1750 Mary Rogers XXX, 66
Eliphalet, Jr. (1751-1824) m. 1773
Apphia Flanders XXX, 66
Ezekial, Sr. (July 15, 1739-1791) m.
c. 1759/60 Sarah Fowler XXVIII,
205
Ezekial, Jr. (Sept. 1763-Mar. 24,
1848) m. 1786 Ruth Davis XXVIII,
205
Henry (c. 1742-1808/14) m. May 22,
1766 Mary Herrenden XXXIII, 305

COLE, includes COOL, KOAL, KOHL, KOOL
Abraham (Feb. 19, 1744-p. June 12,
1794) m. c. 1764 Catherine Ber-
ringer XXXII, 182, 183, 293;
XXXIV, 345
Barent Jacobsen (bpt. May 18, 1610-
p. Nov. 4, 1668) m. c. 1636
Marretje Leenderts De Grauw NY
XXXII, 182, 183, 293; XXXIV, 346
Daniel (1614/5-Dec. 21, 1694) m.
.... Ruth Chester MASS X,
117, 260
Daniel (Sept. 19, 1758-June 24,
1842) m. Feb. 23, 1783 Edith
Wilbur VII, 13; XI, 158
Ebenezer (Oct. 28, 1732-1789) m.
1756 (1) Elizabeth Wheeler VII,
13; XI, 158
Ebenezer (1754-Aug. 18, 1815) m.
.... (1) Polly (Mary) Ogden
X, 117
Elisha (1719-p. 1801) m. Dec. 13,
1739 (2) Hannah Smalley X, 117,
260
Elisha (Jan. 26, 1743-Feb. 3, 1826)
m. 1763 Charity Hazen X, 260
James (....-1698) m. 1624 (1) Mary
Lobel MASS VII, 13; XI, 159
James (c. 1580/90-1652) m. ....
(1) .... CONN XXXII,
116
James (June 18, 1761-Mar. 5, 1834)
m. July 25, 1782 Annah Stilson
XXXII, 116
Phineas (Nov. 20, 1744-....) m. Dec.
20, 1765 Abiah Hazeltine XVIII,
106
Solomon (Apr. 1, 1743-1835) m.
Jan. 8, 1766 Mehitable Barker
XXI, 75
Thomas (....-p. Dec. 15, 1678) m.....
.... MASS XVIII,106; XXI,
75

COLEMAN, includes COLMAN
Asaph (Sept. 27, 1747-Nov. 15, 1820)

m. .... Eunice Hollister IX, 37
Benjamin (c. 1720-a. Feb. 1, 1803)
m. .... (1) Hannah Wood XXXII,
84, 85
Henry (....-....) m. ....
...... VA XVI, 53, 54
James (1640/2-1691) m. .... Sarah
...... MASS 'XV, 127; XVI, 48, 64
Job (Oct. 20, 1741-Sept. 2, 1805) m.
Feb. 20, 1765 Elizabeth Martin
XV, 127; XVI, 48, 64
John (1735-May 7, 1811) m. 1761
Sarah Coleman XXIX, 148
John (May 16, 1753-July 15, 1837) m.
Jan. 10, 1791 Lucy Chiles XVI,
53, 54
Phineas, Jr. (Dec. 12, 1739-Aug.
1783) m. Feb. 24, 1774 Sarah
Whidden XXXIII, 172
Robert (1656/7-a. Oct. 1713) m. ....
Anne ...... VA XXVIII, 52
Robert (p. 1710-p. Aug. 3, 1794) m.
a. 1748 Elizabeth Lindsay XXVIII,
52
Thomas (1600-Oct. 1, 1674) m. ....
.... CONN, MASS IX, 37
Thomas (1602-1685) m. .... (2) Sus-
anna ...... MASS, NH XXXIII, 172
William (1619-Apr. 18, 1680) m. ....
(1) .... MASS XXIX, 149
William (c. 1650-p. May 24, 1706) m.
.... Mary Mapes NY XXXII, 85

COLEY
Ebenezer (Oct. 19, 1741-Nov. 2, 1811)
m. Aug. 11, 1763 Abigail Morehouse
XIX, 67
Samuel (....-1684) m. 1640 Ann
Pruden MASS, CONN XIX, 67

COLLIER
Charles (1660-1735) m. .... Mary
...... VA IX, 40; X, 44
Cornelius (1720-1810) m. 1754 Eliza-
beth Wyatt IX, 40, 41; X, 43
James (Oct. 13, 1757-Aug. 3, 1832)
m. June 3, 1788 Elizabeth Bouldin
IX, 40, 41, X 43
John (1742-Apr. 2, 1821) m. ....
Mildred ...... XXXI, 132
Joseph (1749-1819) m. Dec. 5, 1776
Amy Mosley XVI, 43
William (1620-1682) m. 1655 Sallie
Collier VA XVI, 43; XXXI, 132

COLLINS
Amos (July 16, 1749-May 22, 1796) m.
Aug. 10, 1767 Thankful Clark XIV,
120; XXVII, 122, 154, 155
Cyprian (Mar. 4, 1733-Jan. 7, 1809)
m. Jan. 9, 1756 Azuba Gibbs

XXXI, 105
Henry (1606-Feb. 20, 1687) m. c.
1629 Ann ...... MASS XIV, 120;
XXVII, 122, 154, 155
John (1616-Mar. 29, 1670) m. c. 1650
Susannah ...... MASS XXXIV, 258
John (1640-Dec. 10, 1704) m. 1662
Mary Trowbridge MASS XXXI, 105
John (June 1, 1739-Feb. 25, 1792)
m. c. 1765 Lydia Buell XXXIV, 258

COLMAN, see COLEMAN

COLTON
Abijah (Apr. 14, 1731-Aug. 8, 1815)
m. Apr. 24, 1774 Mary Gaylord
XXII, 104
Benjamin, Jr. (Feb. 1, 1722-June 20,
1808) m. .... Abiah Cooley V, 120,
121
George (c. 1610/20-Dec. 17, 1699) m.
c. 1644 (1) Deborah Gardner MASS
V, 120; X, 145; XI, 198; XXII, 104
Isaac (Aug. 9, 1720-Aug. 20, 1800)
m. Nov. 19, 1745 (2) Marcy Colton
XI, 198
John Gunn (Oct. 22, 1747-Jan. 16,
1822) m. Aug. 25, 1770 Martha
Warriner V, 120, 121; X, 145
Jonathan (Feb. 28, 1758-p. 1782) m.
.... Elizabeth Strong XI, 198

COLVER, see CULVER

COMLY
Henry (....-Mar. 14, 1684) m. a.
1682 Joan ...... PA XIX, 34
John (Jan. 13, 1743-1792) m. June
10, 1767 Mary Hellings XIX, 34

COMSTOCK
Abel (1721-1814) m. Sept. 17, 1747
Judith Paine XXXIV, 146
Abijah (Nov. 19, 1721-June 1797) m.
May 30, 1745 Deborah Benedict
XXXIII, 194, 195
David (Sept. 19, 1748-Oct. 15, 1812)
m. Dec. 29, 1774 (1) Sarah Leeds
XXXIII, 195
Ichabod, Jr. (Mar. 17, 1727/8-Oct.
30, 1800) m. Jan. 9, 1777 (2)
Catherine Smith X, 217; XXIX, 211,
213
James (June 18, 1712-Sept. 6, 1781)
m. Apr. 17, 1738 Hannah Allen
XXIX, 385
Noah (Mar. 26, 1757-Feb. 2, 1825) m.
c. 1781 (2) Hannah Lord XXIV, 15,
59; XXIX, 61; XXXIII, 304; XXXIV,
209
Peter (July 11, 1731-Apr. 3, 1803)

COMSTOCK, cont.
  m. May 12, 1774 (2) Sarah Mirick
  IV, 100, 106; XXVII, 192
Stephen (Apr. 13, 1750-Nov. 19,
  1834) m. Dec. 18, 1777 (2) Mary
  Benedict XXXIV, 157
William (c. 1595-c. 1683) m. a.
  1624 (2) Elizabeth Daniel CONN
  IV, 100, 106; X, 218; XXIV, 15,
  59; XXVII, 192; XXIX, 61, 211,
  213, 385; XXXIII, 195, 304; XXXIV,
  147, 157, 209, 210

CONANT
Daniel (c. 1740-July 20, 1808) m.
  Jan. 14, 1772 Martha Cole XXV,
  141
Jonathan (Feb. 3, 1732/3-p. Jan. 4,
  1790) m. Dec. 24, 1763 Eunice
  Farwell XXXIV, 322
Moses (1750-....) m. June 29, 1779
  Mary Wildes XXIX, 28
Roger (bpt. Apr. 15, 1590-Nov. 19,
  1679) m. Nov. 11, 1618 Sarah
  Horton MASS XX, 70; XXV, 141;
  XXIX, 28; XXXIV, 322
Timothy (Nov. 21, 1732-Apr. 15,
  1777) m. Oct. 27, 1754 Hannah
  Blackman XX, 70

CONARD, includes KUNDERS
John (Feb. 20, 1738-Apr. 9, 1803) m.
  Dec. 17, 1762 Elizabeth Potts
  XXXI, 225, 226
Thones (1648-1729) m. .... Eliza
  Streypers PA XXXI, 226

CONE
Daniel (1626-Oct. 24, 1706) m.
  1660/1 Mehitable Spencer CONN
  XI, 20; XIX, 116; XXXII, 150
Daniel Hurlburt (July 16, 1753-Apr.
  17, 1841) m. Aug. 18, 1776 Eliza-
  beth Atkins XI, 20
Rufus (bpt. Oct. 10, 1737-p. Aug.
  27, 1776) m. Dec. 18, 1760 Esther
  Stewart XXXII, 150
Sylvanus (bpt. Jan. 21, 1734-May 5,
  1812) m. Nov. 15, 1755 Hannah
  Ackley XIX, 116

CONGDON
Benjamin (c. 1650-June 19, 1718) m.
  .... Elizabeth Albro RI XXVII,
  89; XXXIII, 324
James (Mar. 28, 1741-Feb. 16, 1829)
  m. Mar. 3, 1768 (2) Lydia Headley
  XXVII, 89; XXXIII, 324

CONGER
James (Jan. 11, 1760-Nov. 11, 1813)

  m. .... Elizabeth McNab XXX, 39;
  XXXII, 196
John (....-Sept. 1712) m. Apr. 12,
  1666 Mary Kelly NJ XXV, 180;
  XXVI, 100; XXVII, 92; XXVIII, 87;
  XXIX, 124; XXX, 39, 255; XXXII,
  196
John (1751-1793) m. Jan. 5, 1769
  (1) Mary Ross XXV, 180; XXVI,
  100; XXVII, 92; XXVIII, 87; XXIX,
  124
Uzziah (Jan. 14, 1758-June 21, 1841)
  m. 1779 Mary Hungerford XXX,
  255

CONKLIN, includes CONKLING
Abraham (bpt. May 15, 1737-p. 1806)
  m. Apr. 17, 1761 Sarah Carpenter
  XXXIV, 132
Ananias (c. 1600-1657) m. Feb. 26,
  1630/1 Mary Lavendar MASS, NY
  XXXIII, 58, 59, 107
Jacob (bpt. Aug. 20, 1732-....) m.
  .... Catherine Schellinger
  XXXIII, 58, 59, 107
Jeremiah (Dec. 14, 1758-Sept. 13,
  1840) m. Apr. 22, 1785 Tamar Tomp-
  kins XXV, 128
John (....-a. 1700) m. .... Helena
  ...... NY XXXIV, 132
John (1600-Feb. 23, 1683) m. Jan.
  24, 1625 Elizabeth Alseabrooke
  MASS XVIII, 138; XIX, 20; XXII,
  150, 154; XXV, 128; XXIX,
  148
John (Nov. 9, 1727-Jan. 24, 1789) m.
  Feb. 6, 1753 Jane Drake XXV,
  128
John (May 8, 1756-Apr. 23, 1846) m.
  1780 Ursula Van Noy XVIII, 137;
  XIX, 20
Joseph, Sr. (bpt. May 2, 1731-p. July
  12, 1782) m. Jan. 15, 1752 Charity
  Rogers XXIX, 148
Joseph, Jr. (Dec. 1759-1792) m. Dec.
  24, 1778 Martha Conklin Ketcham
  XXIX, 148
Platt (Sept. 24, 1711-June 25, 1780)
  m. Dec. 2, 1767 Phebe Smith XXII,
  150, 154

CONKLING, see CONKLIN

CONOVER, includes COUWENHOVEN, COVEN-
  HOVEN, VAN COUWENHOVEN, VAN KOU-
  WENHOVEN
Dominicus (1730-1778) m. .... Mary
  Updike XXXIII, 18, 19
John P. (Jan. 6, 1740-Dec. 24, 1811)
  m. .... Jane McGalliard XXIV, 70;
  XXXII, 275, 276

Micajah (a. 1730-Feb. 3, 1797) m.
Jan. 29, 1750 Deborah Stanton
XXVI, 154, 155; XXIX, 356
Wolfert Gerretsen (1588-1661) m.
1605 Neltje Jans NY XXIV, 70;
XXVI, 154, 155; XXIX, 357; XXXII,
275, 276; XXXIII, 18, 19

CONSTANT, see SMITH, Thomas and
Richard, Sr. XXXIV, 321

CONVERS, see CONVERSE

CONVERSE, includes CONVERS
Asa (Sept. 30, 1730-....) m. Jan. 19,
1755 Ruth Leed XXXII, 233
Benjamin (Sept. 14, 1746-1790) m.
May 17, 1786 (2) Esther Grosvenor
XXXII, 170
Edward (Jan. 30, 1590-Aug. 10, 1663)
m. 1617 (2) Sarah ...... MASS V,43;
XXII, 135; XXXII, 35, 170, 233;
XXXIII, 35, 36
James (1620-May 10, 1715) m. ....
(1) Anna Long MASS V, 43
Jonathan (Jan. 27, 1760-Oct. 25,
1845) m. Nov. 20, 1783 Esther
Whipple XXXII, 35
Joseph (Nov. 13, 1739-Feb. 16, 1828)
m. May 27, 1762 Elizabeth Davis
V, 43; XXXIII, 35, 36
Thomas (Nov. 5, 1738-1809) m. ....
Sabrina Smedly XXII, 135

CONWAY
Dennis (a. 1641-June 1709) m. ....
.... VA XXXI, 227, 228;
XXXII, 70, 88
Edwin (1610-1675) m. 1640 (1) Martha
Eltonhead VA VII, 34; X, 206;
XIII, 73; XXV, 242, 269, 270
Francis (Mar. 7, 1748-Feb. 13, 1794)
m. Mar. 20, 1770 Elizabeth Fitz-
hugh VII, 34; X, 206; XIII, 74
Robert (May 10, 1749-a. July 1, 1806)
m. .... XXXI, 227;
XXXII, 70, 88
William (1742-....) m. a. 1785
Jane ...... XXV, 242, 269, 270

CONWELL
Francis (....-1691) m. c. 1659 Mary
Yeates VA, DE XXI, 77
William (1732-1782) m. Nov. 2, 1752
Rebecca Claypoole' XXI, 77

COOK, includes COOKE
Aaron (c. 1610-Sept. 5, 1690) m.....
...... Ford MASS, CONN V, 121; VI,
20, 26; X, 70, 170; XVIII, 62;
XXIV, 171; XXVI, 141, 142

Aaron (Sept. 4, 1743-May 19, 1804)
m. c. 1767 Lydia ...... XXIV, 171
Andrew (....-....) m. ....
...... MD XXI, 134, 135
Benajah (Dec. 19, 1759-Nov. 8, 1839)
m. Feb. 24, 1793 Cassandra Fanning
XXXIV, 289
Benjamin (Aug. 16, 1742-Dec. 2,
1790) m. .... Lydia Hammond V,
122, 123
David (Oct. 12, 1731-Mar. 16, 1816)
m. June 25, 1775 Alice Bradford
Cooke XXVI, 28
Elisha (Feb. 22, 1715-Mar. 7, 1794)
m. Sept. 8, 1743 Sarah Cook X, 69
Gregory (....-Jan. 1, 1690/1) m. ....
(2) Mary ...... MASS XXIX, 19,
XXX, 160; XXXIV, 289
Henry (....-a. Dec. 1700) m. a. 1633
Judith Birdsall MASS XXIX, 304,
344; XXXIV, 170
Henry (1754-1810) m. .... Margaret
Bennett XXI, 134, 135
Isaac (July 22, 1710-Mar. 16, 1780)
m. Oct. 13, 1733 Jerusha Sexton
XXX, 179
Isaac (July 28, 1739-June 1810) m.
Mar. 5, 1760 Martha Cook XXIX,
304, 344; XXX, 179; XXXIV, 170
John (....-....) m. 1778 (2) Cath-
erine Burton XXXII, 129
John, Jr. (May 16, 1758-Feb. 25,
1847) m. Apr. 7, 1803 Thankfull
Eggleston XXIX, 19; XXX, 160
Joseph (c. 1608-p. 1665) m. ....
Elizabeth ...... MASS V, 122,
123
Joseph (bpt. Feb. 3, 1735-May 5,
1821) m. Nov. 18, 1756 (1)
Lucretia Post V, 121; VI, 19, 26;
X, 170; XVIII, 61, 62; XXVI, 142
Josiah (c. 1610-Oct. 17, 1673) m.
Sept. 16, 1635 Elizabeth (Ring)
Deane MASS XXXI, 72
Josiah (Nov. 26, 1746-Nov. 12, 1817)
m. Oct. 17, 1771 Miriam Shepard
XXXII, 72
Mordecai (....-a. 1667) m. 1648 Sus-
annah Peasley VA XXXII, 94, 129
Samuel (July 30, 1641-Mar. 1703) m.
May 2, 1667 Hope Parker CONN
XXX, 179
Thomas (c. 1603-1677) m. c. 1626
Mary ...... MASS XXVI, 28
William (1740-....) m. Oct. 22,
1779 Ann Nelson XXXII,
94

COOKE, see COOK

COOL, see COLE

COOLEY
Aaron (1743-June 1833) m. Oct. 9,
1783) Persis Cleveland XIV, 67,
85
Abel (Apr. 12, 1717-June 13, 1778)
m. Mar. 21, 1741 Mercy Cooley
XVII, 98, 99
Benjamin (c. 1617-Aug. 17, 1684) m.
.... Sarah Tremaine MASS XIV,
67, 85; XVII, 98; XIX, 75; XXXI,
178
Reuben (Apr. 25, 1752-....) m. c.
1785 Elizabeth Needham XIX, 75
William (Mar. 17, 1736-Apr. 14,
1825) m. Nov. 27, 1759 Sarah Mather
XXXI, 178, 179

COOLIDGE
Elisha (July 9, 1720-Aug. 29, 1807)
m. (int.) Feb. 1, 1754 Sarah
Boutell XXVII, 211, 212
John (bpt. Sept. 16, 1604-May 7,
1691) m. .... Mary ...... MASS
XVI, 82; XX, 121; XXVII, 212
Joseph (June 18, 1730-Apr. 19, 1775)
m. Dec. 11, 1753 Eunice Stratton
XX, 121
Joseph (July 27, 1747-Oct. 6, 1820)
m. June 1, 1772 (1) Elizabeth
Boyer XVI, 82

COOMBS
Anthony (c. 1642-c. 1728) m. Feb. 5,
1688 Dorcas Wooden ME XVI, 46,
47
Joseph (Mar. 10, 1752-Nov. 22, 1817)
m. June 6, 1776 Elizabeth Gamble
XVI, 46, 47

COOPER
Ichabod (1741-Nov. 27, 1809) m. June
21, 1778 Mrs. Hannah (Morris) Lyon
XI, 179
John (....-1662) m. ....
Wilbroe MASS, NY XI, 179;
XXXIII, 131, 132
Zebulon, Sr. (Jan. 25, 1752-Dec. 22,
1835) m. Apr. 27, 1775 Mary White
XXXIII, 131, 132

COPELAND
Elijah (June 10, 1739-Sept. 8, 1817)
m. .... Rhoda Snell XII, 67; XIII,
63
Lawrence (1589-Dec. 31, 1699) m. Oct.
12, 1651 Lydia Townsend MASS XII,
67; XIII, 63

CORBIN
Clement (1626-Aug. 1, 1696) m. Mar.
7, 1655 Dorcas Buckmaster MASS

XVII, 140
Clement (May 1, 1733-1825) m. July
12, 1770 (2) Mary Phillybrown
XVII, 140

COREY, includes CORY
Abner (June 3, 1748-Dec. 10, 1786)
m. Sept. 11, 1770 Naomi Freeman
XXII, 70
Ebenezer (Nov. 15, 1754-July 2,
1833) m. Jan. 14, 1774 Joanna
Fletcher XII, 40; XVI, 93
Ephraim (Mar. 13, 1736-1820) m. Nov.
10, 1764 Susanna Stevens XXIX,
387
John (1611-Mar. 1685) m. ....
Margaret ...... NY XXII, 70;
XXV, 229; XXXII, 237
Joseph (Oct. 9, 1737-June 23, 1780)
m. Sept. 10, 1765 Phoebe Simpson
XXV, 229; XXXII, 236, 237
Thomas (....-p. 1667) m. ....
...... MASS V, 84
Thomas (c. 1618-1706) m. Sept. 19,
1665 Abigail Gould MASS XII,
40; XVI, 93; XXIX, 387
Timothy (Oct. 27, 1741-Sept. 19,
1811) m. 1766 Elizabeth Greggs
V, 84

CORLISS
Bliss (May 10, 1754-Mar. 13, 1839)
m. Oct. 26, 1775 Phoebe Wright
XXV, 99, 100
George (c. 1617-Oct. 19, 1686) m.
Oct. 26, 1645 Joana Davis MASS
IV, 169; XII, 58; XXV, 99, 100;
XXIX, 20; XXXI, 196
Joshua (Jan. 19, 1733-Jan. 29, 1819)
m. 1759 (2) Molly (Wells) Colby
IV, 169; XII, 58; XXIX, 20; XXXI,
196

CORNELISE, see CORNELL

CORNELL, includes CORNELISE
Edward (Feb. 22, 1737-Apr. 30, 1784)
m. c. 1758 Sarah Burt XXVII, 41,
42
Gideon (Feb. 5, 1746-June 22, 1825)
m. Jan. 4, 1771 Elizabeth Tucker
XXV, 293
Guilliame (....-a. July 1666) m. ....
.... NY XXXI, 128
Jan (John) Nov. 7, 1745-p. July 1803)
m. Nov. 20, 1768 Catrina Suydam
XXXI, 128
Thomas (c. 1595-c. 1655) m. 1620 Re-
becca Briggs MASS XXV, 293;
XXVII, 42; XXXIV, 106
Thomas (1742-May 29, 1807) m. June 5,

1772 Ann Gale XXXIV, 106

CORNING
Bliss (Oct. 30, 1763-Feb. 10, 1846)
m. 1787 Lucinda Smith XXVIII, 99
John (Oct. 20, 1729-Mar. 30, 1807)
m. Aug. 2, 1753 Mariam Crowell
XXVIII, 141
Samuel, Sr. (c. 1616-a. Mar. 11,
1694/5) m. .... Elizabeth ......
MASS XXVIII, 99, 141

CORNISH
James (c. 1612/5-Oct. 29, 1698) m.
1662 (2) Mrs. Phoebe Larabee CONN
XXIX, 207
Elisha (June 5, 1722-Apr. 27, 1794)
m. Sept. 25, 1740 (1) Hepsibah
Humphrey XXIX, 206

CORSA, see CORSON

CORSEN, see CORSON

CORSON, includes CORSA, CORSEN, COURSEN
See also JANSEN
Abner, Sr. (June 25, 1729-1799) m.
.... (1) Jane Cresse XXIX, 275;
XXX, 216
Andrew (Jan. 24, 1762-Nov. 21, 1852)
m. Oct. 12, 1792 Mary Poole XV,10
Benjamin (Mar. 6, 1743-Oct. 2, 1811)
m Apr. 12 1761 Sarah Dungan
XXI, 60, 61; XXIV, 124
Peter (....-....) m. ....
...... NY XV, 10; XXI, 60, 61;
XXIV, 125

CORTELYOU
Jaques (c. 1625-1693) m. c. 1655/6
Neeltje Van Duyn NY XXXIII, 273,
274; XXXIV, 56, 57
Simon (Mar. 11, 1746-Aug. 15, 1828)
m. May 1763 (1) Sarah Van Wyck
XXXIII, 273, 274; XXXIV, 56, 57

CORTRIGHT, see COURTRIGHT

CORWIN, includes CURWEN
David (Oct. 30, 1733-1794) m. Jan.
1750 (1) Mary Wells; .... (2) Abi-
gail Davis XXI, 78, 79; XXIX,
247; XXXI, 88, 108; XXXII, 53
Joshua (Mar. 25, 1735-July 6, 1812)
m. May 1, 1755 Anna Paine XXIV,111
Matthias (1599/1600-Sept. 1658) m.
.... Margaret Morton MASS, NY
XXI, 78, 79; XXIV, 111; XXIX, 247;
XXXI, 88, 108; XXXII, 53

CORY, see COREY

COSBY
Charles, II (1728-p. 1800) m. 1744
Elizabeth Wingfield XIV, 7
Charles, III (1745-Dec. 1795) m.
1764 Rebecca Wood XIV, 7
John (1630-1695) m. c. 1660 Sarah
...... VA XIV, 7

COSSART, see COZAD

COTTON
John (Dec. 4, 1585-Dec. 23, 1652) m.
Apr. 25, 1632 Sarah Story MASS
XIV, 41, 42; XXIV, 140; XXIX, 297,
XXXII, 111
John (Apr. 5, 1712-Nov. 4, 1789) m.
Dec. 9, 1746/7 Hannah Sturtevant
XIV, 41, 42; XXIV, 139
Josiah (Aug. 14, 1747-Apr. 19, 1819)
m. Nov. 19, 1789 (2) Rachel Barnes
XIV, 41, 42; XXIV, 139
Willard (Feb. 4, 1757-Nov. 19, 1828)
m. Nov. 28, 1781 Mercy Gallup
XXIX, 296; XXXII, 111
William (c. 1614-1678) m. c. 1650
Elizabeth Ham NH XXIV, 158;
XXVI, 18, 63, 82; XXVIII, 13;
XXXI, 76
William (Feb. 24, 1738-Mar. 17,
1798) m. Oct. 30, 1761 Mary Clark
XXXI, 76
William (Oct. 5, 1751-Mar. 29, 1813)
m. 1783 Ruth Cram XXIV, 158;
XXVI, 18, 63, 82; XXVIII, 13

COUCH
Ebenezer, Jr. (Jan. 20, 1733-Oct.
26, 1800) m. Nov. 4, 1777 Sarah
(Kenney) Bostwick XX, 99
Gideon (Sept. 12, 1757-Sept. 21,
1817) m. Dec. 26, 1781 Eleanor
Wakeman XIII, 17
Simon (c. 1633-a. Mar. 15, 1687/8)
m. .... Mary Andrews CONN VI,
82; XIII, 17; XX, 99
Simon (Apr. 5, 1729-Apr. 25, 1809)
m. Jan. 27, 1753 Rebecca Nash
VI, 82
Thomas Nash (Apr. 18, 1758-Jan. 3,
1821) m. Dec. 13, 1787 Abigail
Stebbins VI, 82

COUNCILL
Hodges (....-1699) m. c. 1665
Lucy Hardy VA XXIX, 281;
282
Joshua (c. 1712-1793) m. ....
.... XXIX, 281,
282

COURSEN, see CORSON

COURTRIGHT, includes CORTRIGHT, VAN
   KORTRIGHT, VAN KORTRYK
   Abraham (July 8, 1748-Jan. 12, 1825)
   m. 1776/8 Effie Drake XIX, 158;
   XXII, 37; XXXI, 107
   Jan Bastiansen (1618-....) m. ....
   .... NY XIX, 158; XXII,
   37; XXXI, 107
   John (Aug. 15, 1714-p. May 14, 1783)
   m. Jan. 24, 1735 Margaret Denne-
   merken XIX, 158; XXII, 37

COUWENHOVEN, see CONOVER

COVELL
   Ezra (Sept. 21, 1746-c. 1793) m.
   Jan. 12, 1767 Hannah Hollister
   XXXII, 215
   James, I (....-c. 1690) m. ....
   .... MASS XXXII, 215

COVENHOVEN, see CONOVER

COVERT, includes COEVERS
   Teunis Jansz (c. 1625-1690/1700) m.
   .... Barbara Lucas NY XIV, 117;
   XV, 77
   Tunis, Sr. (Mar. 25, 1745-Jun. 17,
   1798) m. 1765 Magdeline Van
   Hauglar XIV, 117; XV, 77

COVINGTON
   Robert (Jan. 3, 1760-Aug. 10, 1847)
   m. 1782 Mary Duncan XXVI, 137,
   138; XXXI, 134
   William, I (....-a. 1697) m. ....
   Dorothy ...... VA XXVI, 137, 138;
   XXXI, 134

COWDREY
   Nathaniel, Jr. (Apr. 19, 1737-June
   30, 1807) m. Apr. 13, 1758 Sarah
   Parker XXXI, 234
   William (1602-Nov. 10, 1687) m. ....
   Joanna ...... MASS XXXI, 234

COWING
   James (May 16, 1740-Apr. 8, 1829)
   m. Dec. 31, 1780 (2) Sarah Randall
   XII, 31; XIII, 86
   John (....-....) m. Mar. 8, 1656
   Mrs. Rebecca Man MASS XII, 31;
   XIII, 86

COWLES
   Ebenezer (Feb. 26, 1718-Aug. 12,
   1800) m. July 13, 1749 (2) Mercy
   (Mary) Johnson XXXIV, 294
   Eleazer (Oct. 18, 1746-July 19, 1795)
   m. Dec. 5, 1771 Hannah Dickinson
   XV, 38

John (c. 1600-a. Sept. 15, 1675) m.
   .... Hannah ...... MASS XV, 38,
   74; XXXIV, 294
   John (July 28, 1731-1811) m. 1757
   Hannah Bardwell XV, 75

COX, includes COCK, COCKE
   James (....-1690) m. .... Sarah
   Clarke NY XII, 27
   James (Oct. 16, 1753-Sept. 12, 1810)
   m. Feb. 29, 1776 Anne Potts XII,
   94; XV, 137, XVI, 49, 115
   John (....-1702/3) m. c. 1672 Marg-
   aret ...... MD XXII, 49, 92;
   XXVIII, 89
   John (Oct. 3, 1713-1785) m. 1736
   Rebecca ...... XXII, 48, 92;
   XXVIII, 89
   John (a. 1740-1798) m. .... Anne
   Starke IX, 29, 40; XXV, 237
   John (1750-1798) m. Sept. 21, 1776
   Lucy Herbert Claiborne XXXII, 15
   Moses (Oct. 20, 1742-1808) m. ....
   Hannah Eavenson XII, 27
   Richard (1600-p. Oct. 4, 1665) m. a.
   1639 Temperance Baley VA XXXII,
   15
   Thomas (....-Aug. 1681) m. Apr. 22,
   1665 Elizabeth Blashford NJ XII,
   95; XV, 137; XVI, 49, 115
   Walter (....-1738) m. .... Anna
   Hamlin VA IX, 29, 40; XXV, 237

COZAD, includes COSSART
   Jacques (May 29, 1639-c. 1685) m.
   Aug. 14, 1656 Lea (Lydia)
   Willemyns NY XXXIV, 64
   Samuel, Jr. (June 12, 1756-Mar. 28,
   1822) m. Mar. 28, 1785 Jane
   McIlrath XXXIV, 64

CRAMPTON
   Demetrius (Feb. 25, 1745-....) m.
   Apr. 9, 1764 Abigail Parmelee
   XXIV, 103
   Dennis (1638-Jan. 31, 1689) m. Dec.
   17, 1668 Sarah Munger   CONN
   XXIV, 103

CRANDALL
   Benajah (1729/30-1809) m. Mar. 18,
   1754 (1) Elizabeth Slack XXXI,
   112
   John (1612-1676) m. .... Mary Opp
   RI XXXI, 112

CRANE
   Benjamin (1630-May 31, 1691) m. Apr.
   23, 1655 Mary Backus CONN XXV,
   154, 155
   Bernice (Jan. 9, 1742-Nov. 10, 1828)

m. Mar. 10, 1763 Joan Axtell XV,
17, 106
David (c. 1721-Mar. 6, 1794) m. ....
(1) Sarah A. Dodd XI, 117, 136,
155; XII, 76; XIX, 131
David D. (Sept. 19, 1763-Sept. 11,
1838) m. Nov. 30, 1784 Martha
Banks XI, 117, 136, 155; XII, 76;
XIX, 131
Eliakim (c. 1727-c. 1811) m. ....
Joanna ...... XXV, 102
Ezekiel (Oct. 29, 1747-Mar. 15,
1813) m. .... Eunice Hayward
V, 114, 115
Henry (1621-Mar. 21, 1709) m. ....
(1) Tabitha Kingsley; 1655 (2)
Elizabeth Kingsley MASS VI, 98;
XV, 17, 106; XXXII, 155
Jasper (c. 1605-1681) m. .... Alice
...... CONN, NJ III, 52; V, 114,
115; XI, 117, 136, 155; XII, 70,
76; XIX, 131; XXV, 102
John (a. 1630-Jan. 8, 1637) m. ....
.... MASS XXXII, 139
John (June 17, 1755-May 14, 1837)
m. c. 1778 Phebe Ross XIX, 28
Joseph (Sept. 11, 1737-1810) m.
Dec. 20, 1757 Mary Savel XXXII,
154, 155
Joseph, Jr. (Jan. 9, 1756-June 30,
1841) m. c. 1780 Deliverance
Mills VI, 97
Josiah (June 25, 1745-July 14, 1822)
m. Mar. 28, 1768 Abigail Hathaway
III, 52
Rufus (1755-Nov. 30, 1820) m. ....
Rachel Grant XXV, 154, 155
Samuel (May 29, 1752-July 28, 1818)
m. Nov. 7, 1776 Charity Higley
XXXII, 139
Stephen (1635-c. 1709) m. 1663 ......
...... NJ XIX, 28
William (....-....) m. .... Mercy
...... NJ XII, 70

CRANNELL
William (....-....) m. ....
...... NY XXXIV, 270
William Winslow (Sept. 26, 1749-Dec.
27, 1828) m. Jan. 9, 1780 Marie
Eman XXXIV, 270

CRANSTON
Caleb (p. 1730-Oct. 12, 1800) m.
.... Mary Gould XXVII, 181
James (June 1, 1764-June 21, 1832)
m. Mar. 1, 1786/7 Ruth Austin
XXXI, 237
John (1625-Mar. 12, 1679/80) m. June
3, 1658 Mary Clarke RI XXVII,
181; XXXI, 237, 238; XXXIV, 175

John (Nov. 3, 1755-Aug. 29, 1825) m.
Apr. 4, 1790 (1) Phoebe Ann
Edwards XXXI, 238; XXXIV, 175

CRARY
Nathan (Mar. 9, 1762-Mar. 21, 1852)
m. May 8, 1783 Lydia Arnold XXXIII,
327, 328
Peter (c. 1645-Oct. 24, 1708) m.
Dec. 31, 1677 (1) Christobel
Gallup MASS, CONN XXXIII, 327,
328

CRAWFORD
Joel, Sr. (Oct. 16, 1736-Oct. 1788)
m. 1760 Fanny Harris XXXIII, 229,
230; XXXIV, 246
John (1600-1676) m. ....
...... VA XI, 183; XXXIII, 229,
230; XXXIV, 246
Nathan (Oct. 16, 1744-Mar. 4, 1833)
m. .... Judith Anderson XI, 182

CREHORE
Teague (1640-Jan. 3, 1695) m. 1665
Mary Spurr MASS XXXII, 100, 101
William (Jan. 1, 1730-July 9, 1803)
m. Jan. 2, 1752 Ann Bowen XXXII,
100, 101

CRISPIN
Jacob, Sr. (1755-Mar. 19, 1848) m.
July 18, 1781 Ann Chubb XXX, 280;
XXXI, 111, 112, 113
Silas (1655-May 31, 1711) m. 1697
(2) Mary (Stockton) Shinn PA
XXX, 280; XXXI, 112, 113

CRITTENDEN, includes CRITTENTON
Abraham (c. 1610-Jan. 21, 1683) m. c.
1630 (1) Mary ...... CONN
V, 127, 128; VI, 95; XI, 21; XV,
64; XXXI, 270
Amos (Sept. 26, 1754-Jan. 27, 1838)
m. Jan. 23, 1777 Phebe McIntire
XV, 64
Jason (Mar. 30, 1761-Apr. 17, 1813)
m. June 24, 1792 Keziah Brown
XXXI, 270
Levi (Nov. 28, 1757-Apr. 25, 1845)
m. 1780 Clarina Fanning VI, 94
Samuel (Sept. 11, 1712-Jan. 4, 1802)
m. .... Sarah Eaton V, 127, 128
Samuel (Feb. 20, 1734-May 31, 1816)
m. .... Rebecca Mason XI, 21

CRITTENTON, see CRITTENDEN

CROCKER
Daniel (Mar. 1, 1725/6-Nov. 12, 1788)
m. May 19, 1748 Elizabeth Childs

CROCKER, cont.
XXXIV, 164
Job (Mar. 29, 1724-Jan. 3, 1809) m.
Nov. 25, 1747 Mrs. Mercy Freeman
Knowles XVIII, 64
Job (May 6, 1749-May 7, 1831) m.
Nov. 26, 1778 Elizabeth Huckins
XIX, 161; XXXIV, 164
Nathaniel (May 7, 1736-Nov. 11,
1824) m. Jan. 25, 1766 Catharine
Bridgham XXVI, 97, 98
William (1612-Sept. 1692) m. 1636
(1) Alice ...... MASS XVIII, 64;
XIX, 161; XXVI, 97, 98; XXXIV,
164

CROCKETT
Nathaniel (Apr. 25, 1750-....) m.
July 5, 1771 Eunice Cooper XXXIV,
67
Thomas (bpt. Jan. 13, 1610/1-1679)
m. a. 1642 Anne ...... ME XXXIV,
68

CROESEN, see CRUSER

CROESON, see CRUSER

CROM, see CRUM

CROMWELL
Stephen (Nov. 30, 1747-Apr. 10, 1783)
m. .... Elizabeth Murray XXX, 46,
47; XXXI, 16
William (....-a. June 19, 1680) m.
a. 1677 (2) Elizabeth Trahearne
MD XXX, 46, 47; XXXI, 16

CROSBY
Anthony (Oct. 5, 1635-Jan. 16, 1672/3)
m. Dec. 28, 1659 Prudence Wade
MASS XV, 109
John (Aug. 24, 1735-Aug. 20, 1820)
m. Nov. 26, 1766 Martha Goodspeed
XXIV, 70, 137
Simon (c. 1609-1639) m. .... Anne
Brigham MASS XXIV, 71, 137
Stephen (Jan. 5, 1734-Sept. 15,
1776) m. Feb. 16, 1755 Hannah
Carroll XV, 109

CROSMAN, see CROSSMAN

CROSSMAN, includes CROSMAN
Robert (....-1692) m. Mar. 25, 1652
Sarah Kingsbury MASS IV, 122;
XXXIII, 121, 122
Robert (1707-July 6, 1799) m. ....
Martha Gaskett IV, 122
William (Apr. 29, 1751-Nov. 8, 1837)
m. Jan. 16, 1786 Susanna Gates

XXXIII, 121, 122

CROWELL
Aaron(c. 1750-Apr. 12, 1814) m. c.
1778 Abigail Brown XXIV, 153;
XXIX, 129, 130
Edward (Apr. 3, 1761-Nov. 1, 1800)
m. c. 1780 Sarah Martin XXXI, 144;
XXXIV, 40
Lot (Apr. 8, 1730-Mar. 20, 1809) m.
Dec. 1, 1747 Hannah Hamblin
XVIII, 91
Yelverton (c. 1620-Oct. 24, 1683) m.
c. 1640 Elizabeth ...... MASS
XVIII, 91; XXIV, 153; XXIX, 129,
130; XXXI, 144; XXXIV, 40

CRUM, includes CROM
Flotis Willmse (....-a. June 29,
1706) m. Mar. 29, 1670 Catalyntze
Ariens NY XXXII, 204
Richard D. (Feb. 3, 1763-Sept. 10,
1847) m. c. 1785 Elizabeth Gardner
XXXII, 204

CRUMB
Daniel (....-1713) m. Nov. 6, 1676
Rachel Roberts RI XXX, 281
Joseph, Sr. (Sept. 20, 1738-....)
m. Mar. 17, 1765 Hannah Brand
XXX, 281

CRUSEN, see CRUSER

CRUSER, includes CROESEN, CROESON,
CRUSEN, KROSEN
Abram (June 1, 1733-Apr. 12, 1819)
m. Apr. 5, 1758 Martha Doolhagen
XXXIII, 111, 112
Garret (1640-Mar. 7, 1680) m. Oct.
30, 1661 Neeltie Jans NY XVI, 6;
XXXIII, 111, 112
John (1740-Oct. 4, 1796) m. 1767
Jane Corsen XVI, 6

CULVER, includes COLVER
Christopher (1753-....) m. Dec. 14,
1779 Phoebe Holt XVIII, 61
Ebenezer (June 13, 1722-Dec. 12,
1783) m. Oct. 24, 1745 Mary Stone
XXXIII, 118, 119, 182; XXXIV, 333
Edward (1600-1685) m. Sept. 19, 1638
Ann Ellis MASS IV, 164, 165; VI,
101, 104; XI, 102; XVI, 29, 105;
XVII, 86, 87; XVIII, 61; XIX, 113;
XXIV, 128; XXXIII, 118, 119, 182;
XXXIV, 333
Enoch (Jan. 30, 1725-Sept. 22, 1812)
m. Feb. 8, 1749 Lois Benham XVI,
29, 105; XVII, 86, 87
Jonathan (Mar. 15, 1726-June 1808)

m. Nov. 16, 1749 Sarah Hinman
VI, 101, 103; XXIV, 128
Joshua (1729-Nov. 8, 1817) m. 1752
Jerusha Holcomb XI, 102
Moses (Apr. 11, 1747-1795) m. ....
Lucy Turner IV, 164, 165
Nathaniel (June 29, 1728-Feb. 19,
1809) m. Oct. 23, 1752 Ruth
Kilbourn XIX, 113
Solomon (Aug. 18, 1760-Apr. 2, 1835)
m. 1782 Lodamia Burr VI, 101,
103; XXIV, 128

CUMMINGS
David (Mar. 26, 1729-May 9, 1799)
m. July 16, 1748 Joanna Jones
XIV, 89
Ebenezer (Jan. 29, 1730-1804) m.
.... Sarah Stevens VIII, 30
Ebenezer (Sept. 21, 1749-June 4,
1821) m. June 22, 1774 Jemima
Hartwell XIV, 89
Isaac (1601-May 1677) m. ....
.... MASS VIII, 30; XI,
191; XIV, 89; XIX, 155; XXIX, 347;
XXX, 43; XXXII, 103, 104
Jesse (Nov. 6, 1745-Oct. 9, 1835)
m. Aug. 29, 1771 Mary Fitz XI,
191
Oliver (Apr. 10, 1728-Aug. 15, 1810)
m. c. 1754 Sybil Bailey XXX, 43
Samuel (Sept. 16, 1718-June 9, 1723)
m. Dec. 1, 1741 Abigail Sarah
Spaulding XIX, 155
Simeon (1739-Jan. 18, 1810) m. June
18, 1763 Hannah Bowers XXIX, 347
Thaddeus (June 16, 1746-Mar. 10,
1815) m. July 8, 1773 Katharine
Goodrich XXXII, 103, 104

CURREY, see CURRY

CURRIER
Gideon (Aug. 13, 1754-Oct. 1, 1835)
m. (2) Anna Richardson XXXI, 47,
48, 211
Jonathan (c. 1757-Nov. 6, 1829) m.
Sept. 7, 1779 Nancy Sargent XXXI,
69, 70
Richard (May 3, 1616-Feb. 22, 1686/7)
m. a. 1643 Ann ...... MASS XVIII,
12; XXV, 110; XXXI, 48, 69, 211
Richard (Sept. 10, 1755-1838) m.
June 18, 1778 Mary Currier XVIII,
12, 13
Seth (June 8, 1743-Mar. 1792) m.
Jan. 16, 1766 Ellice Sargent XXV,
110

CURRY, includes CURREY
Richard (....-1720) m. 1680 ......

...... NY XXX, 102
Stephen (Nov. 1742-June 6, 1830) m.
1768 Frances Moore XXX, 102

CURTICE, see CURTIS

CURTIS, includes CURTICE, CURTISS
Deodatus (....-....) m. ....
...... MASS XXX, 140
Ebenezer (Jan. 17, 1749-Feb. 24,
1803) m. c. 1773 Rhoda ......
XXVIII, 141, 142
Eleazer, II (Sept. 23, 1736-Oct. 1,
1788) m. Feb. 7, 1759 Mary Carter
XXX, 140
Eleazer, III (Oct. 20, 1759-Sept. 7,
1801) m. Nov. 7, 1782 Eunice Starr
XXX, 140
Ephraim (Mar. 27, 1739-Aug. 30,
1794) m. Dec. 23, 1764 Ann Curtiss
XV, 133
Jacob (bpt. Mar. 10, 1730-Feb. 22,
1797) m. May 26, 1752 Mary Stiles
XXV, 262
John (1611-Dec. 6, 1707) m. 1641
Elizabeth Welles CONN XV, 33,
133; XVI, 70; XXVIII, 142; XXXI,
43
John (Sept. 29, 1745-Aug. 31, 1825)
m. Apr. 17, 1769 Mary Shelton
XXXI, 43
Nathaniel (Aug. 6, 1738-Aug. 1806)
m. Dec. 5, 1770 Elizabeth Curtis
XXIV, 145
Nehemiah (1740-May 13, 1810) m. Apr.
4, 1763 (1) Phebe Welles XVI, 69,
70
Peter Burr (Apr. 30, 1755-Mar. 1837)
m. .... Phebe Sherman XV, 33
Stephen, Sr. (Aug. 18, 1754/5-Feb.
20, 1832) m. c. 1776/7 (1) Abigail
Small XXV, 262
William (Nov. 12, 1592-Dec. 8, 1672)
m. Aug. 6, 1618 Sarah Eliot MASS
XXIV, 145
Zaccheus (1619-1682) m. .... Joanne
...... MASS XXV, 262

CURTISS, see CURTIS

CURWEN, see CORWIN

CUSHING
Benjamin, Jr. (Sept. 28, 1735-June
5, 1786) m. Nov. 5, 1767 Hannah
Cooke XXX, 292, 293; XXXII, 278
Benjamin (July 16, 1739-Dec. 4, 1792)
m. July 26, 1770 (2) Mary Coles-
worthy XXXI, 52
Frederick (Feb. 1, 1729-July 23, 1824)
m. Oct. 18, 1747 Grace Bates XXXI, 210

CUSHING, cont.
John (1627-Mar. 31, 1708) m. Jan.
20, 1658 Sarah Hawkes MASS
XXXI, 52
John (Jan. 23, 1743-Feb. 19, 1822)
  m. Aug. 15, 1773 Olive Wallingford
  XXIII, 54
Matthew (Mar. 2, 1589-Sept. 30, 1660)
  m. Aug. 5, 1613 Nazareth Pitcher
  MASS XXIII, 54; XXX, 293; XXXI,
  210; XXXII, 278; XXXIV, 302
Theophilus (Dec. 5, 1740-Mar. 11,
  1820) m. Apr. 6, 1768 Patience
  Dunbar XXXIV, 302

CUSHMAN
Cephas (bpt. 1746-1815) m. Dec. 1766)
  Judith Clark X, 146
Eleazer (Jan. 17, 1758-1815) m. 1790
  Elizabeth Plumly XXXI, 260, 261
Ichabod, Sr. (May 12, 1725-...) m.
  Mar. 4, 1751 Patience Macfern
  XVII, 63, 64
Ichabod, Jr. (Mar. 28, 1757-Oct. 14,
  1805) m. Nov. 28, 1782 Molly Morton
  XVII, 63, 64
Isaac (Aug. 12, 1730-Aug. 1, 1820) m.
  1756 Sarah Miller XX, 51
James (Dec. 22, 1756-Nov. 15, 1832)
  m. .... Mercy Morton IV, 167, 168
Joseph (Oct. 6, 1733-Oct. 3, 1822)
  m. .... Elizabeth Sampson XXXI,
  279
Noah (May 14, 1745-Mar. 29, 1818)
  m. May 25, 1769 (1) Mercy Soule
  XIX, 74
Robert (May 1580-a. Apr. 1625) m.
  July 3, 1606 (1) Sarah Rider MASS
  IV, 167; X, 146; XVII, 64; XIX, 74;
  XX, 52; XXV, 137; XXXI, 28, 260,
  261; 279; XXXII, 64
Solomon (Feb. 17, 1734-Feb. 1814) m.
  May 26, 1768 ...... Cross XXV,
  137; XXXI, 27, 28
Thomas (1608-Dec. 11, 1691) m. ....
  Mary Allerton MASS IV, 167
Thomas (Dec. 19, 1739-p. Apr. 11,
  1787) m. June 5, 1764 Mary Frazee
  XXXII, 64

CUSTER, includes KUSTER
Paul (c. 1737-July 31, 1800) m. c.
  1763 Elizabeth ...... XXV, 36
Paulus (c. 1640-Feb. 23, 1707/8) m.
  c. 1670 Gertrude Streipers PA
  XXV, 36

CUTLER
James (1606-May 17, 1694) m. Mar. 9,
  1645 Mary King MASS XXII,
  31

William (Mar. 24, 1726/7-Feb. 21,
  1802) m. Nov. 7, 1750 Susannah
  Shepard XXII, 31

CUTT, see CUTTS

CUTTER
John (Sept. 26, 1737-Oct. 16, 1788)
  m. Jan. 24, 1765 Rebecca Hill
  XXXII, 65, 66
Richard (c. 1621-June 16, 1693) m.
  a. 1644 Elizabeth ...... MASS
  XXXII, 66

CUTTING
Benjamin (Aug. 19, 1760-Feb. 15,
  1848) m. Mar. 15, 1779 Anna Bemis
  XXXIV, 160
Jonas (Jan. 24, 1765-Apr. 5, 1834)
  m. Apr. 25, 1785 Sarah Baker
  XXIV, 160
Richard (1623-Mar. 21, 1696) m. c.
  1644 Sarah ...... MASS XXII,
  83; XXIV, 160; XXXII, 107; XXXIV,
  160
Samuel (Nov. 20, 1720-...) m. Aug.
  9, 1763 (2) Lois Willis XXXII,
  107
Zebedee (Oct. 18, 1759-Apr. 30,
  1833) m. .... Phebe Strong XXII,
  83

CUTTS, includes CUTT
Joseph (Aug. 2, 1736-1808) m. Nov.
  2, 1758 Mary Stevenson XXXII,
  162
Robert (1619-June 18, 1674) m. ....
  Mary Hoel ME XXXII, 162

CUYPER, see CADMUS

DAGGETT, includes DOGGET, DOGGETT
Ichabod (Dec. 7, 1736-Sept. 3, 1781)
  m. June 15, 1769 Lucy Hadden XI,
  74
John (1602-Mar. 1673) m. .... (1)
  .... MASS XI, 75; XV,
  125
John (Feb. 2, 1724-Jan. 20, 1803)
  m. Nov. 19, 1751 Mercy Shepard
  XV, 124

DAKIN
Joshua (Apr. 22, 1744-Oct. 24,
  1813) m. 1769 Ruth Craw XXXI,
  178
Thomas (1624-Oct. 21, 1708) m. June
  11, 1660 Susanna Stratton MASS
  XXXI, 178

DAMON
Isaac (July 10, 1739-Mar. 1, 1829)
m. .... Lucy Cutting IV, 73
Jabez (Nov. 16, 1722-Sept. 5, 1775)
m. Apr. 3, 1755 Lucy Wyman
XXVIII, 23
John (1620-Apr. 8, 1708) m. 1645
Abigail Sherman MASS XXXIII,
233
Samuel (Feb. 2, 1715/6-....) m. Mar.
27, 1738 Annie Gowing XXXIII,
233
Thomas (....-p. 1712) m. ....
...... MASS IV, 73, 77; XXVIII,
23
Thomas, III (Dec. 25, 1703-Mar. 6,
1796) m. .... Abigail Rice IV,
73, 77

DANA
Francis (Feb. 6, 1737-Feb. 6, 1813)
m. Jan. 14, 1768 Eleanor Foster
XXVI, 268, 269
George (Jan. 1, 1742-Apr. 11, 1787)
m. Jan. 19, 1771 Elizabeth Park
XXX, 238; XXXI, 65
John Winchester (1740-1813) m. ....
Hannah Pope Putnam I, 42, 43
Richard Henry (1612/20-Apr. 2, 1690)
m. 1648 Anne Bullard MASS I, 42,
43; X, 200, 201; XXVI, 268, 269;
XXX, 238; XXXI, 65
William (Aug. 9, 1736-Dec. 11, 1805)
m. .... Joanna Sessions X, 200,
201

DANFORTH
Benjamin (Dec. 8, 1724-Oct. 10,
1816) m. Apr. 7, 1750 Mary Frost
XXII, 113
Nicholas (bpt. Mar. 1, 1589-Apr.
1638) m. c. 1617/8 Elizabeth .....
MASS XXII, 113; XXXI, 18; XXXIV,
232
Thomas (Feb. 20, 1745-Apr. 23, 1794)
m. May 26, 1771 Lydia Abbott
XXXI, 18; XXXIV, 232

DANIEL, see DANIELS

DANIELL, see DANIELS

DANIELS, includes DANIEL, DANIELL
Jeremiah (Oct. 17, 1744-Apr. 21,
1784) m. Dec. 24,'1772 Abigail
Fisher XXVII, 33; XXXI, 216, 217
Peter Mickelborough (Sept. 22, 1763-
Dec. 1856) m. Oct. 9, 1810 Ann
Pemberton Gooch XXII, 43; XXXI,
133
Robert (a.1595-July 6, 1655) m.....

(1) Elizabeth Morse MASS XXVII,
33; XXXI, 217
Robert (1646-May 17, 1718) m. 1701
(2) Martha Wainwright SC XXIX,
72, 270; XXXI, 77, 162
Verin (Feb. 15, 1737-Feb. 1, 1776)
m. 1760 Ruth Billings XXX, 28
William (....-Aug. 26, 1678) m. ....
Catherine Greenway MASS XXX, 28
William (....-a. May 13, 1687) m.
.... VA XXII, 44;
XXXI, 133
William (Nov. 25, 1743-Sept. 5, 1840)
m. June 11, 1787 (2) Mary (Polly)
Melton XXIX, 72, 270; XXXI, 77,
162

DANIELSON
James (....-Jan. 22, 1728) m. ....
(1) Abigail ......; Jan. 22, 1700
(2) Mrs. Mary Tosh RI, CONN
X, 199; XXIV, 123
John (Dec. 8, 1727-Feb. 10, 1815)
m. Aug. 30, 1750 Ruth Blodgett
XXIV, 123
William (Aug. 11, 1729-Aug. 19, 1798)
m. Dec. 29, 1757/8 Sarah Williams
X, 199

DARBY
Caleb, Sr. (Mar. 17, 1762-Mar. 1802)
m. Mar. 24, 1792 Sarah Gartell
XXI, 152
Samuel (....-....) m. ....
...... MD XXI, 152

DARCEY, see DORSEY

DARCY, see DORSEY

D'ARCY, see DORSEY

DARE
Daniel (Sept. 2, 1728-a. Dec. 13,
1782) m. May 9, 1757 Ruth Pierson
XXXIV, 301
William (....-Mar. 15, 1719/20) m....
.... PA, NJ XXXIV, 301

DARROW
George (....-....) m. .... Mary
Sharswood CONN XXXII, 119
Jonathan, Jr. (Mar. 30, 1746-1780)
m. Feb. 8, 1778 Mollie Thorp
XXXII, 119

DART
Ebenezer (Oct. 26, 1736-p. 1782) m.
May 14, 1759 (1) Elizabeth Miner
XIII, 53, 54
Richard (....-Sept. 24, 1724) m.

DART, cont.
  *1664 Bethia ...... CONN XIII,
  53, 54*

DASHIELL
  George (Aug. 28, 1743-....) m. Aug.
  6, 1760 Rose Fisher XVIII, 44;
  XIX, 21; XXXII, 118
  *James (1634-Aug. 1697) m. 1659 Ann
  Cannon VA, MD XIII, 26; XVIII,
  44; XIX, 20; XXIV, 54; XXXII, 118*
  James (Aug. 20, 1740-1795) m. ....
  Sarah Evans XIII, 26
  John (Apr. 17, 1751-Dec. 15, 1816)
  m. Nov. 24, 1780 Sarah (Killam)
  Handy XXIV, 53

DAUGE, see DOZIER

DAVENPORT
  Benjamin (June 16, 1743-Dec. 28,
  1833) m. Jan. 26, 1769 Sarah Wil-
  son XXXII, 60, 61, 287
  Ephraim (May 22, 1762-Sept. 23,
  1838) m. 1790 Sarah Pierce XX, 12
  Hezekiah (Jan. 14, 1738-1777) m.
  Dec. 7, 1763 Ruth Ketchams XX,
  50
  James Madison (1742-1824) m. 1778
  Elizabeth Gilliam XXX, 135, 136
  *John (....-1684) m. .... Margaret
  ...... VA XXXIII, 173, 174*
  *John (1597-Sept. 15, 1676) m. ....
  .... MASS XX, 50*
  *Joseph, Sr. (....-1720) m. ....
  .... VA XXX, 135, 136*
  Joseph Pope (Aug. 7, 1759-1834) m.
  Aug. 5, 1782 Caty Frances Dobyns
  XXXIII, 173, 174
  *Thomas (1605-Nov. 9, 1685) m. ....
  Mary ...... MASS XX, 12; XXXII,
  60, 287*

DAVIDSON, includes DAVISON
  Asa (Sept. 1, 1736-Jan. 29, 1824)
  m. .... Sarah Pride XIII, 71;
  XXVII, 208
  John (Nov. 1, 1734-Dec. 28, 1815) m.
  Jan. 6, 1757 Mehitable Sabin XXX,
  110, 111
  *Nicholas (1611-1664) m. .... Joanna
  Hodges MASS XIII, 71; XXVII,
  208; XXX, 110, 111; XXXIII, 130*
  Peter (May 15, 1739-May 4, 1800) m.
  Apr. 28, 1768 (1) Abigail Woodard
  XXXIII, 130

DAVIS
  *Aaron (....-....) m. .....Mary .....
  RI, MASS XXI, 145*
  Barnabas (1599-Nov. 28, 1685) m.

*.... (2) Patience ...... MASS
XX, 87*
Benajah (June 27, 1734-....) m. Mar.
31, 1754 Elizabeth Snow XXVI, 131,
132
Benjamin (July 17, 1719-Sept. 27,
1797) m. Feb. 21, 1748/9 Rachel
Port XXX, 253
Benjamin (c. 1720-....) m. .... (1)
Sarah ...... XX, 87
Daniel (Sept. 28, 1713-Apr. 22,
1799) m. Aug. 2, 1739 Mehitable
Lothrop III, 12
Daniel (a. 1726-p. May 15, 1775) m.
c. 1765 (2) Abigail Overton
XXXI, 243, 244
Daniel (Sept. 9, 1736-June 23, 1817)
m. Apr. 29, 1756 Patience Barney
XXX, 176
David (June 1740-Feb. 11, 1824) m.
1769 Abigail Brown XXXIII, 169
*Dolor (1593-June 1673) m. Mar. 29,
1624 (1) Margery Willard MASS
XXIII, 66; XXVI, 15, 16, 131, 132;
XXVIII, 206; XXXIII, 169*
Edward, Sr. (Jan. 23, 1714-Aug. 30,
1784) m. Dec. 25, 1735 Abigail
Learned V, 55, 95; VI, 78, 79
*Foulk (c. 1615-1687) m. 1639 (1)
....; Mar. 11, 1660 (2)
Mary ...... NY XXII, 14, 15;
XXXI, 244; XXXII, 227*
*Francis (....-Apr. 12, 1710) m. Jan.
20, 1673/4 Mary Taylor MASS XXII,
9*
*George (....-July 14, 1667) m. ....
.... MASS XX, 90*
Isaac (1724-1796) m. 1757 Sarah
...... XXI, 145, 146
Isaac (Oct. 4, 1741-Apr. 20, 1814)
m. 1770 Hannah Roe XXII, 14, 15
Israel, Jr. (June 1743-Feb. 4, 1811)
m. Jan. 16, 1766 Rebecca Hubbard
XXIII, 66
*James (1583-Jan. 29, 1678/9) m. June
11, 1618 Cicely Thayer MASS XXX,
176; XXXIV, 183*
James (Feb. 11, 1733-Oct. 19, 1802)
m. Apr. 22, 1762 Joanna Roe XXXII,
227, 228
*John (1599-1646) m. .... Mary ......
VA XV, 132*
John (Mar. 5, 1749-....) m. Feb. 27,
1777 (1) Esther Austin XXVIII,
206
*Jonathan (....-....) m. .... Martha
Drayton Vernon VA XIV, 113;
XV, 37*
Joseph (Aug. 4, 1745-Sept. 6, 1795)
m. Apr. 7, 1767 Jean Hamilton
XXXIV, 117

Joshua, II (Oct. 25, 1743-Feb. 15, 1792) m. Sept. 19, 1776 (2) Mrs. Harteine Simpkins XX, 89
Morgan (1622/3-Dec. 17, 1694) m. .... Catherine ...... PA XXX, 253
Nathaniel (....-....) m. 1680 Elizabeth Hughes VA XXXIV, 117
Nathaniel, Jr. (1754-June 10, 1835) m. Aug. 14, 1780 Lydia Harwood XXVI, 15, 16
Nehemiah, Sr. (1709-a. Apr. 13, 1789) m. 1729 (1) Mary Manlove; 1729 (2) Susannah ...... XXX, 149, 181, 234; XXXI, 283, 284
Reuben (June 5, 1748-1826) m. .... Sarah ...... XXII, 9
Richard (1746-Oct. 8, 1812) m. 1773 Ann (Nancy) Chiles XV, 132
Robert (1608-1693) m. c. 1657 Anne ...... MASS III, 12
Thomas (1632-a. Jan. 13, 1698) m. Nov. 8, 1670 Judith Bost VA XXX, 149, 181, 234; XXXI, 283
Thomas (Aug. 19, 1726-Sept. 19, 1805) m. Jan. 13, 1750 Martha Squire XXIII, 49
William (1617-Dec. 9, 1683) m. a. 1643 (1) Elizabeth ...... MASS V, 55, 95; VI, 78, 79; XXIII, 49
William (Mar. 31, 1746-1826) m. 1772 Martha Taylor Winston XIV, 113; XV, 37
William (Mar. 1750-p. Apr. 5, 1824) m. 1768 Susan Mary Dunham XXX, 253
Winthrop (1767-Aug. 8, 1842) m. Nov. 1785 Sarah Evans XXXIV, 183

DAVISON, see DAVIDSON

DAWSON
John (c. 1740-c. May 1, 1792) m. c. 1720 Sarah ...... XXIV, 149
Nicholas (....-1727) m. a. 1706 Mary Doyne MD XIX, 68
Nicholas (June 11, 1750-Mar. 18, 1806) m. Aug. 27, 1781 Elizabeth Bayne XIX, 68
Ralph (c. 1635-July 1, 1706) m. c. 1660 Mary Archer MD XXIV, 149

DAY
Anthony (c. 1616-Apr. 23, 1707) m. 1650 Susanna Matchet MASS XIX, 104; XXVI, 103; XXXI, 240, 241
Benjamin (Oct. 27, 1710-May 10, 1808) m. Oct. 9, 1742 Eunice Morgan III, 45
Benjamin (Sept. 13, 1731-Jan. 26, 1811) m. May 9, 1764 (2) Eunice (Rood) Young XIII, 64

Daniel (July 8, 1749-Aug. 19, 1825) m, Mar. 3, 1773 Anna Vanhorne XXX, 24
Elijah (Dec. 1, 1754-Apr. 22, 1798) m. Mar. 10, 1776 Dorothy Olmstead XVI, 23, 70, 71
Eliphaz (Mar. 2, 1744-Feb. 19, 1820) m. Mar. 2, 1769 Anna Peck XIX, 104
Ezra (Apr. 22, 1743-Nov. 21, 1823) m. Oct. 3, 1767 Hannah Kendall XIII, 26
Heman (Jan. 27, 1755-Jan. 9, 1837) m. c. 1779 Lois Ely III, 45
John (Dec. 30, 1751-Dec. 1840) m. .... Rebecca George XXXI, 260, 279
Joseph (Dec. 8, 1750-Mar. 1832) m. Nov. 18, 1773 Elizabeth Gay XXX, 50, 51
Manuel (Emanuel) (....-....) m. .... Hannah ...... MASS XXXI, 260, 279
Ralph (....-Nov. 28, 1677) m. Oct. 12, 1647 Susan Fairbanks MASS XXX, 50; XXXIV, 179
Ralph (June 19, 1717-Mar. 25, 1795) m. 1762 Mercy (Leland) Winship XXXIV, 179
Robert (c. 1604-1648) m. .... (1) Mary ......; a. 1640 (2) Editha Stebbins MASS, CONN III, 45; XIII, 26, 64; XVI, 23, 70, 71; XXX, 24
Robert, Sr. (bpt. Dec. 21, 1718-p. 1786) m. Sept. 8, 1744 Elizabeth Andrews XXVI, 103
Samuel (1758-Oct. 19, 1812) m. Jan. 1, 1794 Sally Bates XXXI, 240, 241

DAYTON
Abraham (a. 1684-p. 1696) m. .... NY XVII, 134
Caleb (Jan. 19, 1735-Mar. 31, 1813) m. Apr. 19, 1759 Sarah Taylor XVII, 134; XXXIII, 248, 249
Michael (June 4, 1722-Sept. 22, 1776) m. Jan. 29, 1746 Mehitable Doolittle XIV, 110; XXIX, 194; XXXI, 283
Ralph (c. 1588-p. July 25, 1658) m. June 16, 1617 (1) Alice (Goldhatch) Tritton; 1629 (2) Agnes Pool CONN, NY XIV, 111; XXIX, 194; XXXIII, 248, 249; XXXI, 283

DEAKINS
John (c. 1647-Mar. 1744) m. 1718 (2) Priscilla ...... MD XVIII, 136

DEAKINS, cont.
Leonard Marbury (Mar. 9, 1746-June
28, 1824) m. 1796 (2) Deborah
Manduit Duke XVIII, 136
William, Sr. (1720-Dec. 1800) m.
Feb. 9, 1738 (1) Tabitha (Mar-
bury) Hoye XVIII, 136

DEAN, includes DEANE
Ebenezer (May 31, 1741-Feb. 24,
1808) m. May 11, 1769 Hannah
Whitman XXVI, 278, 279, 280, 281,
282
Edward (1717-Apr. 9, 1791) m. ....
Mercy Pratt V, 62
Elijah (1747-1782) m. Apr. 28, 1768
Susannah Bass XXI, 149, 150.
Isaac (c. 1735-Jan. 15, 1824) m.
Feb. 20, 1766 Rachel Staples
XIII, 110
James (1647-May 29, 1726) m. 1693
Sarah Tisdale MASS XXI, 82
John (c. 1600-p. Apr. 25, 1660) m.
Alice ...... MASS XXI, 149, 150;
XXVI, 278, 279, 280, 281, 282
John (Apr. 14, 1707-Mar. 3, 1788)
m. Oct. 17, 1750 Martha Black
XXI, 82
Jonathan (1743-Aug. 17, 1825) m. ....
1770 Eunice Lee XIX, 29
Sylvester (Feb. 1757-Dec. 1817) m.
.... Abigail Holley X, 230
Walter (1612-p. Aug. 1693) m. a.
1643 Eleanor ...... MASS V, 62;
X, 230; XIII, 111; XIX, 29

DEANE, see DEAN

DEARBORN
Benjamin (Aug. 1, 1713-a. 1779) m.
Oct. 31, 1735 Susanna Colcord
XXIII, 23
Godfrey (....-Feb. 4, 1686) m. ....
(1) .... NH XVIII, 7;
XXIII, 23; XXIX, 274
Phineas (Apr. 24, 1749-....) m.
Sept. 19, 1771 Anna Neal XVIII, 7
Thomas (Mar. 11, 1745-Aug. 28, 1778)
m. 1768 Mary Morrison XXIX, 274

DEAVER
Richard (c. 1627-Feb. 5, 1701) m. c.
1657 Grace Fitzmorris MD XXXIV,
293
William, Sr. (c.1724-c.1800) m. Dec.
1754 Susannah Birchfield XXXIV,293

DEBOIS, see DUBOIS

DECKER
Daniel (Apr. 22, 1737-Mar. 1, 1813)

m. Dec. 4, 1756 Blandina Vreden-
burgh XXXII, 26
Jan Gerretsen (....-....) m. Mar. 23,
1664 Grietje Hendricks Westercamp
NY XXXII, 26
Thomas (Sept. 3, 1704-1780) m. June
21, 1727 Jenneke Van Nimwegen
XXXII, 26

DE CUYPER, see CADMUS

DE DUYTSCHER, see DUTCHER

DE GRAAF
Andries (....-....) m. ....
...... NY XXIII, 33, 34
Emanuel (Feb. 10, 1751-Nov. 10, 1824)
m. Feb. 25, 1776 Rebecca Gonzalous
XXIII, 33, 34

DE GROOT
Willem Pieterszen (Oct. 24, 1659-
....) m. .... Lysje Gerrits NY
XXVIII, 95; XXX, 263
William (July 6, 1742-Aug. 28, 1841)
m. Dec. 30, 1780 Anne La Tourette
XXVIII, 94; XXX, 263

DE LA CHAIRE, see CHAIRES

DE LA GRANGE
Johannes (1630-....) m. ....
...... NY XXI, 37
Omie (1660-....) m. .... Ametie De
Vries NY XXI, 36, 37
Omie (Apr. 10, 1726-1809) m. May 26,
1763 Eytie De La Grange XXI, 36,
37

DELAMATER, includes LE MAITRE
Claude (....-c. 1683) m. Apr. 24,
1652 Hester DuBois NJ XIX, 52
John (1754-Dec. 28, 1819) m. ....
Catherine Van Aken XIX, 52

DELANO, includes DE LA NOYE
Alisha (1746-Aug. 25, 1802) m.
.... Hannah Howey XII, 80
Philip (1602-Dec. 19, 1681) m. ....
Mrs. Mary Pontus MASS XII, 80;
XXXIV, 251
Zebedee (Feb. 27, 1727-Dec. 3, 1804)
m. Jan. 3, 1750 Sarah Worthy
XXXIV, 251

DE LA NOYE, see DELANO

DE LA PLAINE
John (1741-June 25, 1804) m. Sophia
Shelar Miller XXVIII,
18

Nicholas (....-....) m. Sept. 1,
1658 Susanna Cresson NY
XXVIII, 18

DE LOACH
Michael (1649-1727) m. 1671 Jane
Griffith VA XXVI, 193
Samuel (c. 1762-1845) m. c. 1785
...... Burton XXVI, 193

DE MANDEVILLE, see MANDEVILLE

DEMAREE, see DEMAREST

DEMAREST, includes DEMAREE, DES MAREST,
DES MARETS
Daniel J. (Sept. 11, 1738-July 26,
1820) m. Aug. 26, 1762 Effie
Westervelt XXXIII, 11, 12, 167,
185, 236, 237
David (1620-Oct. 16, 1695) m. July
24, 1643 Marie Sohier NY, NJ
XIII, 81; XXX, 73; XXXIII, 11, 12,
167, 185, 236, 237; XXXIV, 261
Jacobus (Jan. 23, 1732-Jan. 29, 1808)
m. Nov. 16, 1751 Tryntji (Cath-
erine) Lozier XIII, 81
Petrus (bpt. Nov. 20, 1737-c. 1818)
m. Sept. 30, 1759 Mary Allen
XXXIV, 261
Pieter (Peter) (Jan. 2, 1761-Apr.
30, 1828) m. Jan. 4, 1787 Marie G.
Demarest XXX, 73; XXXIII, 166,
167, 185

DE MERRITT
Eli (....-1747) m. 1695 Hopestill
Runnells NH XIX, 24
John (Dec. 29, 1728-Jan. 7, 1826)
m. May 5, 1756 Betsey Cate
XIX, 24

DEMING
Aaron (Mar. 29, 1744-Mar. 12, 1837)
m. Nov. 14, 1771 Lydia Stoddard
XXII, 94
John (1616-Nov. 21, 1705) m. ....
Honor Treat CONN XXII, 90, 94
Selah (Nov. 15, 1762-May 26, 1805)
m. Jan. 13, 1788 Lovina Curtiss
XXII, 90

DENISE, includes NYSSEN
Denise (Dec. 22, 1745-1798) m. p.
1770 (2) Catherine (Jane) Schenck
XXX, 35
Teunis (1610-c. 1685) m. 1640 Phoebe
(Femmetje Jans) Feliz NY XXX, 35

DENISON
Daniel (Dec. 16, 1730-1793) m.

July 1, 1756 Katherine Avery
XIII, 103; XX, 150
George (1618-Oct. 23, 1694) m. 164..
Ann Barodel CONN XII, 42; XVI,
32
George (Oct. 8, 1751-Jan. 19, 1829)
m. Jan. 9, 1772 (1) Theoda Brown
XVI, 32
Henry (Nov. 26, 1751-1836) m. 1778
Mary Gallup III, 30
James (Aug. 25, 1745-Apr. 26, 1813)
m. Sept. 29, 1773 Eunice Stanton
XIX, 136
Joseph (Sept. 21, 1707-Feb. 15,
1795) m. .... Mrs. Bridget (Noyes)
Wheeler XII, 42
Robert (1749-1820) m. .... Deborah
Dewey II, 28, 29
William (Feb. 3, 1571-Jan. 25, 1653)
m. Nov. 7, 1603 Mrs. Margaret
(Chandler) Monck MASS II, 28,
29; III, 30; XIII, 103; XVI, 32;
XIX, 136; XX, 150

DENNEN, see DENNING

DENNING, includes DENNEN
Nicholas (1645-June 9, 1725) m. ....
(1) Eme Brown ME, MASS XXXI, 203
Samuel (Nov. 5, 1733-1798) m. Mar.
14, 1754 Keziah Bray XXXI, 203

DENT
John (....-a. May 5, 1712) m. a.1678
(2) Mary Hatch MD XXXIV, 271
John Brewer (May 9, 1759-Apr. 24,
1838) m. c. 1785 Priscilla Eliza-
beth Dent XXXIV, 271
Thomas (....-p. Mar. 28, 1676) m.
.... Rebecca Wilkinson MD
XXXIV, 60
Walter (1744-....) m. .... Eliza-
beth ...... XXXIV, 60

DENTON
Jonas (1743-1786) m. Nov. 1, 1765
Eleanor Jackson XIV, 7, 8
Richard (c. 1586-c. 1662) m. c. 1623
Mary ...... NY XIV, 7, 8; XXX,
98
Solomon (Aug. 4, 1754-Feb. 11, 1828)
m. 1786 Clarissa Fowler XXX, 97,
98

DE POLLOK, see POLK

DEPUY, includes DUPUIS, DU PUY
Benjamin (Mar. 3, 1728-1806) m.
1746 Elizabeth Swartwout XXXII,
214, 215
Ephraim (Jan. 15, 1755-....) m.

DEPUY, cont.
    Dec. 21, 1782 Cornelia Snyder
    XI, 163; XII, 119
    Nicolaes (....-1691) m. ....
    Catrina deVaux NY XI, 163;
    XII, 119, XXXII, 214, 215

DE RAPALIE, see RAPELYEA

DE RAPALJE, see RAPELYEA

DERBY
    John (....-....) m. .... Alice
    ...... MASS XXV, 124
    Samuel (Sept. 6, 1757-Mar. 13, 1839)
    m. Aug. 18, 1785 Hannah Minot
    XXV, 124

DES MAREST, see DEMAREST

DES MARETS, see DEMAREST

DEVOL
    Gilbert (May 11, 1740-June 9, 1824)
    m. May 18, 1760 Ruth (Brown) How-
    land XXV, 37
    William (....-p. 1680) m. ....
    .... MASS, RI XXV, 37

DE WANDELAER, see WANDEL

DEWEY
    Aaron (Jan. 1751-Feb. 17, 1824) m.
    Mar. 12, 1777 Sibyl Cadwell XIV,
    90
    Daniel (June 19, 1731-Mar. 9, 1816)
    m. Feb. 22, 1753 Temperance
    Bailey VI, 68
    John (Dec. 12, 1735-June 11, 1830)
    m. Nov. 18, 1756 Rhoda Gillett
    XIII, 96
    Simeon (Feb. 22, 1744-Sept. 2, 1830)
    m. 1733 (2) Mrs. Elizabeth Turner
    XXVIII, 128
    Solomon (Mar. 1, 1743-Dec. 22, 1818)
    m. .... Olive Otis IV, 121
    Thomas (1597-Apr. 26, 1648) m. Mar.
    22, 1639 Mrs. Frances Clark MASS
    IV, 121; VI, 69; XIII, 96; XIV,
    90; XXVIII, 128, 171; XXIX, 173,
    324; XXX, 241
    William (Jan. 11, 1746-June 10,
    1830) m. 1768 Rebecca Carrier
    XXVIII, 171; XXIX, 173, 324; XXX,
    241

DE WITT
    Andries (bpt. Nov. 10, 1728-June 26,
    1813) m. 1753 Blandina Ten Eyck
    XXXII, 194
    John (Feb. 24, 1752-Apr. 28, 1808)

    m. Apr. 1773 Catherine van Vliet
    XXIX, 391
    Tjerck Claeszen (c. 1630-Feb. 17,
    1700) m. Apr. 24, 1656 Barbara
    Andrieszen NY XXIX, 391; XXXII,
    194

DE WOLF, includes DOLPH
    Abda (Oct. 25, 1743-Oct. 26, 1833)
    m. Mar. 17, 1766 Mary Coleman
    VI, 46
    Balthazer (1620-p. 1695) m. a.
    1646 Alice ...... CONN VI, 46

DEXTER
    Gregory (1610-1700) m. .... Abigail
    Fuller RI VI, 64; X, 213, 214;
    XI, 53; XXVI, 212, 213
    Nathan (1759-c. 1806) m. Sept. 30,
    1781 (1) Elsey Warner VI, 64;
    XI, 53
    Nathaniel Balch (July 16, 1759-
    1832) m. July 26, 1781 Lucy Wil-
    lard XXVI, 212, 213
    Samuel (1757-1831) m. .... Candace
    Windsor X, 213, 214

DEYO
    Abraham (1710-1777) m. Sept. 14,
    1740 Elizabeth Du Bois XIII, 22
    Christian (1620-Dec. 18, 1693) m.
    1643) .... NY XIII,
    22
    Jonathan (1745-1833) m. Feb. 16,
    1780 Maria (Mary) La Fever
    XIII, 22

DICKERMAN
    Isaac (Sept. 16, 1740-Apr. 3. 1801)
    m. Aug. 21, 1765 Sibyl Sperry
    XVI, 113
    Jonathan (July 4, 1719-July 28,
    1795) m. Jan. 27, 1742 Rebecca
    Bassett XIV, 79
    Jonathan (Jan. 13, 1747-May 27,
    1821) m. Nov. 16, 1770 Miriam
    Bradley XIII, 77
    Thomas (....-1657) m. .... Ellen
    ...... MASS XIII, 77; XIV, 79;
    XVI, 113

DICKINSON
    Abijah (bpt. Jan. 13, 1739/40-
    Feb. 9, 1815) m. Mar. 8, 1764
    Hannah Sevey XXXII, 155
    Asahel (Jan. 9, 1762-July 26, 1836)
    m. c. June 1782 Lucy Russell
    XXIV, 156
    Ebenezer (1722-Sept. 12, 1798) m.
    May 4, 1757 Chloe Holton XXVI,
    91; XXVII, 14

Ebenezer (Feb. 6, 1761-Aug. 15, 1818)
m. Nov. 17, 1782 Abigail Belding
XXVII, 14, 15
Gideon (bpt. Dec. 1, 1745-p. 1787) m.
Abigail Field IV, 128; V, 128, 129
John (....-....) m. 1651 Elizabeth
(Howland) Hicks NY XVII, 67
Nathaniel (1600-June 16, 1676) m.
1630 Anna Gull CONN, MASS IV,
128; V, 128, 129; XX, 73; XXIV,
156; XXVI, 91; XXVII, 14; XXXII,
111
Nathaniel (1718-20-Jan. 28, 1794) m.
.... Thankful Beckley XX, 73
Nathaniel (Sept. 1, 1750-Nov. 10,
1802) m. Dec. 9, 1779 Sarah Marsh
XXXII, 111
Thomas (....-Jan. 29, 1662) m. ....
Jennet ...... MASS XXXII, 155
Zebulon (c. 1761-....) m. July 22,
1782 Elizabeth Brush XVII, 67

DIGGES
Edward (1620-Mar. 15, 1675/6) m. ....
Elizabeth Page MASS XXXIII, 168,
169
Edward (Jan. 22, 1746-Oct. 29, 1818)
m. June 11, 1775 Elizabeth Gaskins
XXXIII, 168, 169

DILLE, see DILLEY

DILLEY, includes DILLE
Caleb (1759-1839) m. .... Rebecca
Martin XXI, 74
Ephraim, Sr. (Nov. 6, 1755-July 26,
1844) m. .... Lucy Ayers XXII,
96; XXVI, 244, 245
John, Sr. (1649-Mar. 12, 1683/4) m.
.... Sarah ...... NJ XXI, 74;
XXII, 96; XXVI, 244, 245; XXVIII,
40, 41
Price (1754-a. May 29, 1826) m. ....
Sera (Sarah) ...... XXVIII, 40, 41

DILLON, includes DILLWYN
William (....-....) m. .... Sarah
Fuller PA XXX, 259, 260
William (1743-1824) m. .... Sarah
Smith XXX, 259, 260

DILLWYN, see DILLON

DIMAN, includes DYMONT
Joseph (1748-Oct. 19, 1821) m. Nov.
26, 1767 Margaret DeWolf XXV, 7
Thomas (....-1682) m. July 24, 1645
.... NY XXV, 7

DIMICK, includes DIMMOCK, DIMOCK
Shubel (Oct. 4, 1757-1828) m. ....

Elizabeth Wright IV, 97
Solomon (Apr. 29, 1745-June 29,
1797) m. June 18, 1781 Electa Bird
Hull XXXIII, 144
Thomas (....-1658/9) m. .... Ann
Hammond MASS IV, 97; XXXIII, 144

DIMMOCK, see DIMICK

DIMOCK, see DIMICK

DINGEE
Daniel (....-Feb. 8, 1786) m. ....
Macada Hazzard VIII, 10
Robert (....-....) m. .... Rebecca
...... NY VIII, 10

DINGLEY
Jacob, Jr. (Feb. 23, 1727-Mar. 3,
1782) m. Feb. 2, 1748 Desire
Phillips XXIV, 34; XXXII, 243
John (1608-1658) m. ....
...... MASS XXIV, 34; XXXII, 243

DISBROW
John D. (Sept. 9, 1757-Apr. 15, 1835)
m. 1782 Susan Morgan XXII, 48
Peter (1631-May 21, 1688) m. Sept. 6,
1667 Sarah Knapp CONN XXII, 48

DIX
Anthony (....-Dec. 15, 1636) m. ....
Tabitha ...... MASS XIII, 24
Edward (c. 1615-July 9, 1660) m.
1635/6 (1) Jane Wilkinson MASS
XXI, 13
James (Oct. 13, 1716-Apr. 19, 1801)
m. 1742/3 (1) Sarah Bond XXI,
13, 14
Timothy (Dec. 7, 1743-June 27, 1824)
m. .... Rachel Burbank XIII, 24

DOANE
John (c. 1590-Feb. 21, 1685) m. ....
Abigail ...... MASS XXX, 21
Nehemiah (Mar. 17, 1737-a. Mar. 3,
1790) m. Jan. 25, 1766 Lydia Hig-
gins XXX, 21

DOD, see DODD

DODD, includes DOD
Caleb (May 26, 1740-1780) m. c. 1760
Mary Harrison XXVII, 221
Daniel (bpt. Oct. 15, 1615-1665/6)
m. .... Mary Wheeler CONN XIII,
62; XVI, 79; XXVII, 221; XXX,
40
Isaac (July 8, 1728-Aug. 19, 1804)
m. 1750 Jemima Williams XXX,
40

DODD, cont.
  Matthias (Apr. 29, 1757-July 23,
    1801) m. .... Sarah Munn XIII,
    62
  Parmenas (1748-Apr. 28, 1811) m.
    1769/70 Patience Wright XVI,
    78, 79

DODGE
  Andrew (Apr. 20, 1745-c. 1828) m.
    May 8, 1777 Jane Carriel XVIII,
    15
  Caleb (Dec. 14, 1726-1798) m. Apr.
    4, 1757 Miriam Gilbert XXX, 118,
    119
  Israel (Sept. 3, 1760-1806) m. 1780
    (1) Nancy Hunter XXXIV, 136
  Jeremiah, Jr. (Jan. 19, 1744-1824)
    m. Mar. 25, 1770 Judith Follans-
    bee Spofford XX, 145
  John (Jan. 7, 1739-p. 1800) m.
    Mar. 12, 1760 Mary Mastin XXXII,
    160, 161
  John (July 12, 1751-c. 1800) m.
    1782/3 Nancy N. Patterson XXXII,
    231
  Jonathan (Aug. 3, 1721-Jan. 19,
    1794) m. Nov. 7, 1744 Mercy
    Williams XIII, 90
  Nathaniel (bpt. Mar. 28, 1762-Nov.
    8, 1850) m. .... Polly Hover XXX,
    118, 119
  Nicholas (Nov. 19, 1752-Dec. 10,
    1827) m. .... Elizabeth Fly
    XVIII, 68, 69
  Oliver (Sept. 2, 1745-Jan. 1, 1802)
    m. Nov. 1, 1773 (2) Abigail Harris
    XIII, 90
  Phineas (Sept. 9, 1745-Sept. 15,
    1824) m. Feb. 15, 1768 Lucy Nelson
    X, 187
  Richard (c. 1602-June 15, 1671) m.
    a. 1631 Edith ...... MASS X, 187;
    XVIII, 15; XX, 52, 145; XXX, 119;
    XXXII, 160
  Samuel (Mar. 27, 1730-Oct. 4, 1807)
    m. .... Helen Amerman IX, 27
  Simon (Aug. 26, 1751-Dec. 8, 1838) m.
    Oct. 8, 1775 Abigail Cook XX, 52
  Tristram (1628-1718) m. ....
    ...... MASS, RI IX, 27; XIII,
    90; XXXII, 231; XXXIV, 136
  William (1604-c. 1685/92) m. ....
    .... MASS XVIII, 68, 69

DODSON
  Caleb (1752-1836) m. c. 1772 Eliza-
    beth Petty XXXII, 144; XXXIII, 219
  Charles (c. 1649-a. Feb. 6, 1705) m.
    a. 1680 Ann ...... VA XXXII,
    144; XXXIII, 219

DOGGET, see DAGGETT

DOGGETT, see DAGGETT

DOLLIVER
  Peter (May 3, 1726-Feb. 5, 1806) m.
    Sept. 24, 1748 Abigail Ingersoll
    XIX, 117
  Samuel (bpt. 1608-July 22, 1683) m.
    Aug. 1, 1654 (2) Mary Elwell MASS
    XIX, 117
  William (Feb. 3, 1759-Oct. 10, 1841)
    m. Nov. 25, 1789 Elizabeth Foster
    XIX, 117

DOLPH, see DE WOLF

DOODES, see also GARRETT MINER
  Meindort (....-Jan. 1678) m. ....
    Mary ...... VA XXIX, 271

DOOLITTLE
  Abraham (1619/20-Aug. 11, 1690) m.
    1639 (1) Joan Allen; July 2, 1663
    (2) Abigail Moss CONN XI,9; XV,45;
    XVII, 112; XIX, 121; XXIV, 67;
    XXVI, 57, 58; XXVIII, 57
  Ambrose (Nov. 23, 1719-Sept. 25,
    1793) m. .... Martha Munson XI,
    9
  Amzi (Nov. 15, 1737-Apr. 9, 1830)
    m. Dec. 6, 1757 Jerusha Smith
    XV, 45
  Hopkins (Feb. 22, 1764-Jan. 28, 1827)
    m. Apr. 15, 1804 Mary Cronk XXIV,
    67
  Joseph (Jan. 21, 1738-1808) m. Aug.
    10, 1757 Abigail Rockwell XVII,
    112; XXIV, 67; XXVI, 57, 58, 59;
    XXVIII, 57
  Thomas (Mar. 5, 1736-May 28, 1805)
    m. Apr. 14, 1763 Sarah Gitteau
    XIX, 121

DORMAN
  Jesse (1718-June 1802) m. 1748
    Eunice Averill XXXII, 205
  Thomas (1592/1600-Apr. 25, 1670) m.
    .... Ellen Bradley MASS XXXII,
    205

DORSEY, includes DARCY, D'ARCY
  Edward (....-a. Aug. 1659) m. ....
    Ann ...... VA, MD V, 106, 107;
    XII, 96; XXII, 116; XXV, 152;
    XXVI, 104; XXIX, 256; XXXI, 319
  John (1641-a. Mar. 22, 1715) m. ....
    Pleasance Ely MD V, 106,
    107
  John (1726-Jan. 1, 1810) m. ....
    Mary Hammond V, 106, 107

DOWNS, includes DOWNES
Ebenezer, II (Mar. 28, 1707-Oct. 1,
1790) m. Sept. 14, 1727 Dinah
Bristol XIII, 107; XV, 113; XIX,
37; XXIX, 158
John (....-....) m. ....
...... CONN XIII, 107; XV, 113;
XIX, 37; XXIX, 158

DOZIER, includes DAUGE, D'OZIER
James Smith (c. 1740-c. 1803) m.
c. 1783 Molly (Mary) Hutt
XXXIII, 138
John (Dec. 2, 1741-Dec. 22, 1807) m.
Jan. 22, 1771 (1) Elizabeth Giles
XXXIV, 281
Leonard (....-July 20, 1693) m. a.
1683 Elizabeth ...... VA XXXIII,
138; XXXIV, 281

D'OZIER see DOZIER

DRAKE
Hezekiah (July 19, 1736-Feb. 24,
1799) m. Nov. 21, 1758 Elizabeth
Packard XXXI, 151
John (....-Aug. 17, 1659) m. ....
Elizabeth Rogers MASS, CONN
VII, 34; IX, 30, 31; XIII, 66
Samuel (Apr. 30, 1730-Sept. 1, 1794)
m. .... Rebecca ...... VII, 34;
IX, 30, 31; XIII, 66
Thomas (bpt. Sept. 13, 1635-1691)
m. c. 1656 Jane Holbrook MASS
XXXI, 151

DRESSER
John (c. 1605-Apr. 19, 1672) m. ....
Mary ...... MASS XXIV, 51
Moses (Apr. 17, 1755-Nov. 29, 1813)
m. (int.) Nov. 23, 1776 Abigail
Blood XXIV, 51

DRIESSEN, see also JOHN AND PETER
JOHNSON
Barent (....-1656) m. .... Aeltie
...... NY XXIII, 46

DUBOIS, includes DEBOIS
Benjamin (Aug. 18, 1716-May 18, 1787)
m. June 20, 1745 Maria Bevier
XXI, 79, 80
Dominie Benjamin (Mar. 30, 1739-
Aug. 21, 1827) m. 1766 Phem-
pertje Denice XX, 86
Jaques (Oct. 25, 1625-1676/7) m.
Apr. 25, 1663 Pierronne Bentyn NY
XXVI, 46
Koert (Jan. 25, 1763-Apr. 25, 1831)
m. Feb. 5, 1786 Elizabeth Bur-
roughs XXVI, 46

Lewis (Sept. 14, 1728-Nov. 19, 1802)
m. 1770 (2) Rachel Jansen XXXIV,
237
Louis (Oct. 27, 1626-Mar. 27, 1696)
m. Oct. 10, 1655 Catharine Blan-
shan NY XX, 86; XXI, 79, 80;
XXXIV, 237

DUBOSE
Andrew (c. 1749-1803) m. 1769
Rebecca DuBose XXXII, 190, 191
Elias, Sr. (Oct. 19, 1737-Mar. 16,
1789) m. Jan. 20, 1763 Lydia Cas-
sels XXVIII, 150
Isaac (1665-1743) m. a. 1689 Susanne
Couillandeau SC XXVIII, 150;
XXXII, 190, 191

DUDLEY
Ambrose (1750-Jan. 27, 1825/6) m.
Feb. 2, 1773 Anne Parker XXX,
211
Benjamin (1730-1814) m. Dec. 14,
1752 Mary Walker XX, 40
Edward (....-a. Feb. 6, 1655) m.
.... Elizabeth Pritchard VA
XXX, 211; XXXIII, 116
Francis (c. 1640-1703) m. Oct. 26,
1665 Sarah Wheeler MASS XX, 40
Gilman (May 3, 1727-June 12, 1803)
m. .... Sarah Connor IX, 21
John (....-May 30, 1690) m. 1673
Martha French CONN XIX, 65
John (Apr. 9, 1725-May 21, 1805)
m. c. 1750 Elizabeth Gilman VI,
24
John (Feb. 25, 1758-Jan. 2, 1846)
m. .... Lydia S. Booth XXIX, 145
Moses (1745-1776) m. .... Anna Stow
II, 39
Nathaniel (Feb. 21, 1721-Sept. 17,
1806) m. Jan. 7, 1748 Sibble
Munger XIX, 64
Nathaniel (Oct. 3, 1745-Feb. 21,
1826) m. Mar. 12, 1777 Mary Hart
XXXIII, 137
Phineas (Nov. 28, 1752-Aug. 20,
1793) m. .... Ruth Dowd XIX, 64
Samuel (Feb. 24, 1763-July 28, 1851)
m. 1801 Margaret McDougal XXIX,
53
Thomas (1576-July 31, 1653) m. a.
1610 (1) Dorothy York MASS VI,
24; IX, 21
William (....-Mar. 16, 1684)
m. Aug. 24, 1636 Jane Lutman
CONN II, 39; XXIX, 53, 145;
XXXIII, 137
William (1731-p. Nov. 7, 1794) m.
Feb. 13, 1773 Anne Pinceback
XXXIII, 116

DUKE
John (c. 1755-p. Apr. 3, 1803) m.
.... Patsey ...... XXXIII, 79, 80
*William (....-1678) m. .... Hannah
Grendon VA XXXIII, 79, 80*

DUMONT
John (Jan. 16, 1759-Nov. 1823) m.
Dec. 25, 1788 Elizabeth Smalley
XXIX, 168, 323
*Wallerand (....-1713) m. Jan. 13,
1664 Grietje Hendricks NY XXIX,
168, 323*

DUNBAR
*Robert (c. 1630-Sept. 19, 1693) m.
.... Rose ...... MASS XXIII, 8*
Simeon (May 10, 1758-Sept. 15, 1792)
m. c. 1781 Phoebe Howard XXIII,
8

DUNCKLEE, includes DUNKLEY
David, Sr. (Aug. 16, 1746-Aug. 13,
1826) m. c. 1765 Phebe Odell XXV,
139
*Elnathan (....-Feb. 17, 1669) m.
Dec. 14, 1656 Silence Bowers MASS
XXV, 139*

DUNGAN
Joseph (Apr. 13, 1736-p. 1791) m.
Sept. 5, 1764 Elizabeth Carrell
XXIX, 122
*Thomas (1634-1687) m. c. 1663 Eliza-
beth Weaver RI XXIX, 122*

DUNHAM
Ebenezer (bpt. Sept. 3, 1759-1846)
m. c. 1782 Anne Denne XXXIII,
283, 284; XXXIV, 63
George (1753-Dec. 6, 1800) m. Oct.
15, 1778 Phebe Lucas XIII, 37
Israel (Oct. 30, 1741-May 31, 1828)
m. Dec. 13, 1764 Hannah Whiting
XXVIII, 16
*John (1588/9-Mar. 2, 1668) m. Oct.
17, 1619 (1) Abigail Wood; Oct. 22,
1622 (2) Abigail Bailliou MASS
XIII, 37; XVIII, 111; XXVIII, 16;
XXXIII, 178, 179, 283; XXIV, 63*
John (1731-Nov. 12, 1811) m. ....
Keziah Marsh XVIII, 111
Jonathan (Apr. 6, 1758-Jan. 4, 1840)
m. .... Betty Babcock XXXIII,
178, 179
Joseph (c. 1763-....) m. .... Abigail
Bates XXVIII, 16
Sylvanus (June 7, 1714-May 8,
1796) m. February 22,
1738 Rebecca Crocker
XXVIII, 16

DUNKLEY, see DUNCKLEE

DUNN
*Hugh,Sr. (c. 1640-Nov. 16, 1694) m.
Dec. 19, 1670/1 Elizabeth Drake
NH, NJ XVIII, 7; XXXIV, 92*
James (1745-Sept. 16, 1820) m. 1772
Priscilla Langstaff XVIII, 7
James (Dec. 10, 1759-June 5, 1846)
m. .... Sarah Harvey XXV, 178
*John (a. 1654-p. 1682) m. 1677
Obedience Burgess VA XXV, 178*
John (Oct. 10, 1719-1792) m. c. 1758
Ann Martin XXV, 178
Philip (June 14, 1754-Apr. 29, 1835)
m. .... Jane Martin XXXIV, 92 ·

DUNNELL, see DWINNELL

DUNNING
Elias (1738-1783) m. .... Sarah
...... XVIII, 39, 40
Silas (May 6, 1755-Sept. 25, 1830)
m. c. 1779 Jerusha Bristol XXXII,
41, 42
*Theophilus (1611-a. Mar. 13, 1642)
m. .... Hannah Lindell MASS
XVIII, 40; XXXII, 41*

DUPUIS, see DEPUY

DU PUY, see DEPUY

DURANT
*John (....-1692) m. .... Susanna
Dutton MASS II, 53*
Levi (1756-1805) m. .... Mary Wright
II, 53

DURDEN
John (1710-1783) m. 1728 Mary
Coleman XXII, 125; XXXII, 172,
173
John (1734-1800) m. 1753 Sarah Newton
Durden XXII, 125
*Stephen (1611-1681) m. .... Mary
...... VA XXII, 125; XXXII, 172,
173*

DURIE, see DURYEE

DURKEE
Sabin (1733-1808/9) m. Nov. 9, 1756
Ruth Crocker XI, 5
*William (1630-p. 1684) m. Dec. 20,
1664 Martha Cross MASS XI, 5*

DURYEA, see DURYEE

DURYEE, includes DURIE, DURYEA
Frederick (Apr. 8, 1755-Dec. 5, 1832)

DURYEE, cont.
    m. 1774 Charity (Geertje) Sutphen
    XXX, 197; XXXIV, 177
Gabriel (bpt. June 23, 1750-p. Feb.
    20, 1782) m. Nov. 30, 1770 Phebe
    Hoogland XI, 77
Joost (c. 1635-a. June 9, 1727) m.
    a. 1660 Magdalena LaFebre NY
    XI, 77; XXX, 197; XXXIV, 177

DUSTIN
Nathaniel (Sept. 12, 1756-Mar. 3,
    1815) m. Mar. 6, 1781 Judith Knight
    XXXI, 23, 24
Thomas (1605-a. July 1, 1662) m.
    .... Elizabeth Wheeler NH, ME
    XXXI, 24

DUTCHER, includes YE DUITCHER,
    DE DUYTSCHER
Christopher (bpt. Jan. 3, 1748-July
    13, 1832) m. June 10, 1768 Mary
    Belden XXVI, 279, 280
Jan Willemszen (....-....) m. a.
    1662 Grietje Cornelisse NY
    XXVI, 279, 280

DU TRIEUX, see TRUAX

DUTTON
David (Apr. 17, 1729-June 9, 1794)
    m. Nov. 13, 1760 Hannah Whittaker
    XXXI, 53
James Smith (1743-1839) m. Sept. 23,
    1775 Lydia Martha Kimler XXIX,
    23; XXXI, 290
John (....-....) m. ....
    ...... MASS XXXI, 53
John (1647-May 5, 1693) m. 1674
    Mary Darlington PA XXIX, 23;
    XXXI, 290

DUVALL
Mareen (....-Aug. 5, 1694) m. 1673/4
    Susannah ...... MD XXXII, 93
William (c. 1723-1810) m. Oct. 20,
    1745 Priscilla Prewitt XXXII, 93

DWIGHT
John (c. 1600-Feb. 3, 1660) m. ....
    (1) Hannah ...... MASS X, 14;
    XXXIII, 152, 153
Joseph, Jr. (Jan. 23, 1744/5-July
    1826) m. c. 1767 Lydia Dewey X, 14
Simeon (Feb. 18, 1719-Feb. 21, 1778)
    m. Dec. 14, 1743 Sybil Dwight
    XXXIII, 152, 153

DWINEL, see DWINNELL

DWINNELL, includes DUNNELL, DWINEL
Henry, II (Feb. 22, 1762-Oct. 17,

1805) m. .... Tamer Gale VIII,
    11
Michael (c. 1620/5-1713/7) m. ....
    Mary ...... MASS VIII, 11; XIX,
    109
Solomon (Oct. 1, 1757-July 26, 1830)
    m. Apr. 1, 1783 Hannah Singletary
    Gould XIX, 109

DYCKMAN, see DYKEMAN

DYE
Peter (1737-Apr. 21, 1811) m. ....
    .... V, 79
William (1654-Mar. 3, 1720/30) m.
    1681 Sarah ...... RI V, 80

DYER
Elkanah, Sr. (1758-July 23, 1820)
    m. Oct. 17, 1784 Catherine Brooks
    XXXIV, 88
Henry (July 12, 1759-Jan. 2, 1855)
    m. Mar. 19, 1787 (1) Sarah Coy
    X, 17
James (Apr. 23, 1756-Mar. 3, 1835)
    m. Dec. 15, 1776 Mary (Molly)
    Marcy XXXI, 175
John (May 9, 1722-a. Apr. 4, 1784)
    m. Mar. 29, 1753 Anna Payson
    XXXI, 175
Thomas (1612-Nov. 6, 1676) m. 1640
    Agnes Reed MASS XXXI, 175
William (1587-1677) m. .... (1)
    Mary Dyer RI X, 17
William (1653-July 27, 1738) m.
    Dec. 1686 Mary Taylor MASS
    XXXIV, 88

DYKEMAN, includes DYCKMAN
Johannes (c. 1619-1672) m. ....
    Marritje Cornelis (Bosyn) NY
    XXXI, 252
Joseph (1737-1822) m. May 25, 1757
    (1) Eunice Darling XXXI, 252

DYMONT, see DIMAN

EAMES
John (Dec. 15, 1742-Apr. 18, 1806)
    m. May 1809 Ruth Stone X, 159
Thomas (c. 1618-Jan. 25, 1680) m.
    1640 (1) Margaret ...... MASS
    X, 159

EARLE
Baylis (Aug. 8, 1734-Jan. 6, 1825)
    m. Apr. 16, 1757 Mary Prince XXV,
    163; XXIX, 39, 371, 372; XXX, 29,
    83; XXXI, 239; XXXIV, 269
Elias (June 19, 1762-May 19, 1823)

m. Sept. 17, 1782 Frances Wilton
Robinson XIII, 78; XVIII, 20;
XXVIII, 157, 158
John (1614-1660) m. 1637 Mary Symons
VA XI, 61; XIII, 78; XXI, 39; XXV,
163; XXVIII, 158; XXIX, 39, 289,
371, 372; XXX, 29, 83; XXXI, 239;
XXXIV, 269
John (1737-1815) m. 1765 (1) Thoma-
sine Prince XI, 61; XXI, 39, 40;
XXIX, 289
Newhall (Mar. 15, 1735-....) m.
Feb. 21, 1759 Rachel Stoddard
XVII, 153
Ralph (a. 1634-1678) m. .... Joan
...... RI XVII, 153
Richard (....-....) m. ....
...... VA XVIII, 20

EASTMAN
Abiather (Apr. 29, 1745-Jan. 10,
1815) m. .... Phebe Merrill XII,
48
Benjamin (Jan. 1719-Apr. 1, 1814)
m. June 16, 1756 Mary Hitchcock
XXIX, 80
Cyprian (Jan. 29, 1749-May 23, 1798)
m. .... Rosmond Nelson IX, 25;
XVII, 92; XXII, 59
Enoch (1748-June 23, 1829) m. ....
Sarah Rising IX, 35, 36
John (May 7, 1751-May 6, 1829) m.
1779 Hepzibah Keyes XV, 115;
XXXIII, 252
Joseph (Feb. 1, 1714-Oct. 23, 1790)
m. 1743 Sarah Ingram XV, 115
Moses (Feb. 28, 1732-Apr. 4, 1812)
m. 1756 Elizabeth Kimball XIII,
19
Oliver (1762-....) m. June 12, 1790
Sophy ...... XXI, 87
Roger (1611-Dec. 16, 1694) m. ....
Sarah Smith MASS IX, 25, 35, 36;
XII, 48; XIII, 20; XV, 115; XVII,
92; XXI, 87; XXII, 60; XXIX, 80;
XXXI, 79; XXXIII, 46, 47, 252
Timothy (1733-1820) m. .... Hannah
Richardson XXXI, 78, 79; XXXIII,
46, 47

EASTON
Ahimaz (Sept. 19, 1739-May 20, 1795)
m. 1764 Mary Phelps XI, 67; XXI,
115, 116
Joseph (c. 1602-Aug. 19, 1688) m.
.... MASS, CONN
XI, 68; XV, 58; XXI, 114, 115,
116; XXV, 107
Samuel (May 1, 1761-May 22, 1800)
m. 1783 Ann Dennison XV, 58;
XXV, 107

EATON
Eliab (1763-1843) m. 1789 Lucretia
Flint XXXII, 102
John (c. 1595-Oct. 29, 1668) m. 1617
Anne ...... MASS XVIII, 143;
XXVII, 219; XXX, 144
John (July 14, 1765-Jan. 19, 1844)
m. Dec. 1788 Phebe Brockway XVIII,
143
William (c. 1604-May 16, 1673) m.
.... Martha Jenkins MASS XXXII,
102
William (c. 1720-1800) m. Nov. 20,
1742 Meribah Ruth Wardwell XXX,
144
William (Mar. 8, 1760-Sept. 3, 1835)
m. Oct. 30, 1777 Betsey Swain
XXVII, 219

EDDY
Charles (Apr. 22, 1748-a. Apr. 22,
1819) m. Apr. 25, 1770 Hannah
Kelsey XXII, 95
Ibrook (Jan. 9, 1754-Jan. 6, 1833/4)
m. Nov. 2, 1780 Lona Pratt XXII,
69
John (....-Nov. 27, 1695) m. May 1,
1672 Deliverance Owen MASS XXII,
69
John (bpt. Mar. 1597-Oct. 12, 1684)
m. p. May 22, 1619 Amie Doget
MASS XXVIII, 61, 62
Jonathan (c. 1726-Aug. 1804) m. May
4, 1749 Mary Ware XXII, 69
Joshua (May 5, 1748-May 1, 1833) m.
Apr. 10, 1778 Lydia Paddock
XVII, 58, 59; XXXII, 162
Nathan (Sept. 8, 1733-Feb. 28, 1804)
m. Nov. 17, 1757 Eunice Sampson
XXII, 81
Olney (Nov. 16, 1750-Feb. 4, 1835)
m. .... Sarah Smith XXX, 133
Parley (Aug. 14, 1763-Dec. 13, 1831)
m. Dec. 18, 1786 Amity Parker
XXVIII, 61, 62
Samuel (bpt. May 15, 1608-Nov. 12,
1687) m. .... Elizabeth Savery
MASS XVII, 58; XXII, 81, 95;
XXIV, 116; XXX, 133; XXXII, 162
Samuel (Nov. 8, 1736-Aug. 23, 1811)
m. Mar. 7, 1754 Rachel Smith
XXIV, 116
William (Feb. 5, 1725-Mar. 16, 1805)
m. Jan. 21, 1747 Sarah Bellows
XXVIII, 61, 62
Zachariah (1639-Sept. 4, 1718) m.
.... Alice Paddock MASS XXX, 133

EDES
Isaiah (Dec. 11, 1730-Nov. 7, 1803) m.
Dec. 6, 1753 Agnes Screech XXV, 147

EDES, cont.
John (1575-Apr. 12, 1658) m. ....
.... MASS XXV, 147
Peter (Sept. 15, 1705-Jan. 25, 1787)
m. Dec. 18, 1729 Esther Hall XXV,
147

EDGCOMBE, see EDGECOMBE

EDGECOMB, see EDGECOMBE

EDGECOMBE, includes EDGCOMBE, EDGECOMB
James (July 25, 1757-May 19, 1835)
m. May 30, 1783 Anna Burnham
XXXIII, 91, 92
John (a. 1640-Apr. 11, 1721) m. Feb.
9, 1673 (1) Sarah Stallion CONN
X, 304
Nicholas (....-p. Apr. 6, 1681) m.
1642/3 Wilmot Randall ME XXXIII,
91, 92
Samuel (Feb. 22, 1760-Feb. 25, 1843)
m. Dec. 11, 1791 (2) Rachel Davison Copp X, 304

EDGERLY
Thomas (....-p. 1715) m. Sept. 28,
1665 Rebecca (Ault) Hallowell NH
XXIX, 317
Thomas (Jan. 6, 1745-1815) m. 1767
Agnes Phillips XXIX, 317

EDGERTON
Jedediah (Aug. 28, 1759-1848) m.
1780 Lucy Curtis XXV, 39, 40
Joseph (Nov. 18, 1738-Apr. 7, 1809)
m. Feb. 4, 1762 Lucy Lyon X, 252;
XX, 98
Nathan (Jan. 8, 1733/4-....) m. Nov.
17, 1756 Lucy Smith XXI, 5
Richard (....-Mar. 1692) m. Apr. 7,
1653 Mary Sylvester CONN X, 252;
XX, 98; XXI, 5; XXV, 40

EDSON
Josiah (1758-Oct. 27, 1819) m. ....
Sarah Pinney XIII, 101
Samuel (1612-1692) m. .... Susanna
Orcutt MASS XIII, 101

EDWARDS
William, Sr. (....-1624) m. ....
.... VA XXXII, 263
William, Jr. (May 1740-Mar. 28, 1783)
m. Jan. 28, 1767 Liddy Wood XXXII,
263

EELIE, see ELY

EELIS
Edward (Apr. 11, 1741-Dec. 7, 1787)

m. Apr. 26, 1770 (2) Abigail (Dunham) Brandegee XXXI, 197
Samuel (May 3, 1640-Apr. 21, 1709)
m. Aug. 5, 1663 Anna Lenthall MASS
XXXI, 197

EGGLESTON
Benjamin (Jan. 2, 1747/8-June 1,
1832) m. Oct. 9, 1774 Mary Gordon
XXVII, 40, 41
Bygod (Begat) (Feb. 20, 1586/7-
Sept. 1, 1674) m. c. 1611 ......
......; .... (2) Mary Talcott MASS
XXVII, 40, 41; XXXIII, 180, 181
Daniel, Sr. (Oct. 29, 1737-a. July
18, 1810) m. a. Oct. 2, 1763 Sarah
Manley XXXIII, 180, 181

ELDER
Ephraim (1735-1800) m. July 9, 1787
Patsy Matthews XXVIII, 95, 120;
XXIX, 16; XXXI, 102; XXXII, 253;
XXXIV, 328
Peter (....-1674) m. ....
...... VA XXVIII, 95, 120; XXIX,
16; XXXI, 102; XXXII, 253; XXXIV,
328

ELDRED, see ELDREDGE

ELDREDGE, includes ELDRED
Christopher (May 29, 1756-Dec. 2,
1785) m. June 24, 1779 Sarah Sat-
terlee XXXIII, 120
Daniel (Sept. 1, 1749-May 20, 1820)
m. 1768 Amy Vaughn XXX, 138
Elnathan (May 16, 1684-1735) m.·....
Hannah Chase MASS XXX, 201
Jesse (Aug. 9, 1715-Dec. 17, 1794)
m. Nov. 7, 1734 Abigail Smith
XXI, 37, 38
Phineas (Nov. 29, 1755-Apr. 7, 1826)
m. May 3, 1770 Jane Ham XXX, 201
Samuel (Nov. 27, 1620-1699) m. ....
Elizabeth Miller MASS, RI XXX,
138; XXXIII, 120
William (....-c. 1679) m. .... Anne
Lumpkin MASS XV, 84; XXI, 37, 38
Zoeth (c. 1757-Mar. 18, 1828) m.
Oct. 16, 1779 (2) Bethiah Hinckley
XV, 84

ELIOT, see ELLIOTT

ELKIN, see ELKINS

ELKINS, includes ELKIN
James, Sr. (Apr. 16, 1755-June 6,
1836) m. Sept. 23, 1782 Martha
Jackson XXI, 160; XXXIII, 349,
350; XXXIV, 26

Ralph (c. 1610-1690) m. ....
...... VA XXI, 160; XXXIII,
349; XXXIV, 26

ELLENWOOD, includes ELLINWOOD, ELWOOD
Benjamin Tuck (Nov. 20, 1748-Mar.
17, 1826/7) m. .... Abigail Lamson
XXXII, 101, 102
Ralph, I (1607-1673/4) m. Mar. 14,
1655 (2) Eleanor (Ellen) Lynn
MASS XXXII, 101, 102

ELLICE, see ELLIS

ELLINWOOD, see ELLENWOOD

ELLIOTT, includes ELIOT
Edmund (c. 1629-a. Mar. 17, 1684) m.
c. 1659 Sarah Haddon MASS XXIII,
39; XXIV, 134
Edmund (Nov. 28, 1716-Oct. 8, 1789)
m. .... Mehitable Worthen XXIV,
134
Jonathan (Dec. 8, 1748-Apr. 30, 1819)
m. 1775 Mary Connor XXIII, 39

ELLIS, includes ELLICE
Benjamin (1729-1784) m. 1758 Sarah
Bate XXI, 98
Henry (Feb. 15, 1747/8-Aug. 3, 1838)
m. Nov. 21, 1771 Malatiah Thayer
XVIII, 68
Joel (Nov. 14, 1724-1785) m. May 2,
1754 Elizabeth Clap XXXII, 48,
49
John (....-Apr. 12, 1697) m. June
16, 1655 (2) Mrs. Joan Clapp MASS
XVIII, 68
John (c. 1619-a. May 23, 1677) m.
June 4, 1645 Elizabeth Freeman
MASS XVIII, 105; XIX, 16, 34;
XXV, 104; XXXII, 48, 49
John (Sept. 1735-Mar. 6, 1803) m.
Dec. 11, 1760 Elizabeth Sawyer
XVIII, 105; XIX, 33
Simeon (....-a. May 12, 1715) m.
Apr. 16, 1692 Sarah Bate NJ
XXI, 98
Stephen (Oct. 14, 1748-Mar. 5, 1824)
m. Nov. 14, 1771 Susanna Thompson
XIX, 16; XXV, 104

ELSTON
Abraham (c. 1745-1823) m. Sept. 28,
1768 Mary Jewell XXXIV, 263
William (a. 1660-a. Mar. 29, 1689)
m. May 12, 1682 Elizabeth Cole NY
XXXIV, 264

ELTON
Bradley (Apr. 11, 1742-Jan. 3, 1830)

m. June 8, 1778 Grace Wilcox
XXXII, 66
John (....-Jan. 1687) m. 1671 Jane
Hall CONN XXXII, 66

ELWOOD, see ELLENWOOD

ELY, includes EELIE
Cullick (Jan. 1732-Aug. 29, 1821)
m. Jan. 5, 1758 Sarah Foote XXIX,
50
Darius (Sept. 29, 1761-Sept. 23,
1844) m. Dec. 21, 1786 Margaret
Ashley XIX, 107; XX, 107
Eley (a. 1750-1813) m. .... Prudence
Phillips XXVI, 9
James (Feb. 9, 1744-1809) m. June
30, 1760 (1) Catherine Hayes
XXIV, 77
John (Oct. 10, 1707-Mar. 11, 1795)
m. May 3, 1731 Phoebe Allison
XXXIII, 146, 147
John P. (1737-Oct. 1800) m. July 12,
1759 Sarah Worthington XXX, 108,
109
Joshua (1649-June 16, 1702) m. Aug.
29, 1673 Mary Seinerd NJ XXXIII,
146, 147
Lewis (Dec. 9, 1756-Sept. 5, 1826)
m. Oct. 23, 1777 Anna Granger VI,
41
Nathaniel (1605-Dec. 25, 1675) m.
.... Martha ...... CONN, MASS
IV, 41; XIX, 107; XX, 107, 111
Nathaniel, Jr. (Mar. 1737-Jan. 14,
1823) m. Mar. 22, 1759 Esther
Leonard XX, 111
Richard (1610-Nov. 24, 1684) m. ....
Joan Phipps MASS, CONN XII, 99;
XXIV, 78; XXIX, 50; XXX, 108, 109
Robert (....-....) m. .... Anne
...... VA XXVI, 10
Zebulon (Feb. 6, 1759-Nov. 18, 1824)
m. .... Sarah Apama Mills XII, 99

EMERSON
Daniel (1716-1801) m. .... Hannah
Emerson I, 32, 41
Daniel, Jr. (1746-1820)m. .... Anna
Fletcher I, 32
John (Sept. 6, 1722-July 7, 1816)
m. Feb. 27, 1745 Mary Wood XIII,
60
John (Apr. 5, 1739-Nov. 14, 1809)
m. Dec. 20, 1764 Catherine Eaton
XXXII, 212; XXXIV, 263
Thomas (July 26, 1584-May 1,
1666) m. July 1, 1611 Elizabeth
Brewster MASS I, 32, 41;
XIII, 60; XXXII, 212; XXXIV,
263

EMERY
Ambrose (Feb. 25, 1738/9-1824)
  m. 1770 Rebecca Yocum XXIV, 163
Anthony (c. 1600-p. 1680) m. ....
  Frances ...... ME, RI V, 107,
  108; XV, 23; XXV, 143
James (c. 1630-p. 1713) m. ....
  Elizabeth ..... MASS V,107, 108
James (Nov. 1738-....) m. 1763
  (1) Mary Scammon XXV, 143
John, Sr. (Sept. 29, 1598-Nov. 3,
  1683) m. Oct. 29, 1650 (1) Mary
  Sh tswell Webster MASS VII, 19,
  20; XX, 37, 108; XXI, 138; XXIV,
  163
John, Jr. (1628/9-p. Aug. 3, 1693)
  m. Oct. 2, 1648 Mary Webster MASS
  VII, 19, 20
John (Sept. 9, 1750-Mar. 26, 1839)
  m. .... Elizabeth Perkins XXI,
  138
John (Sept. 21, 1753-Mar. 13, 1828)
  m. .... Ruth Sanders V, 107
Joseph (June 3, 1739-Nov. 4, 1821)
  m. June 2, 1763 Hannah Stickney
  VII, 19, 20; XX, 37, 108
Stephen (Dec. 1753-1830) m. Sept. 8,
  1775 Sarah Emery XV, 23
Zachariah (Aug. 26, 1716-May 3,
  1804) m. .... Esther Stephens V,
  107, 108

EMMONS
Noadiah (Mar. 1755-Mar. 6, 1808) m.
  May 1, 1777 Elizabeth Brainard
  XVIII, 67
Thomas (....-c. 1667) m. .... Martha
  ...... RI XVIII, 67

ENDECOTT, see ENDICOTT

ENDICOTT, includes ENDECOTT
John (1588-Mar. 15, 1665) m. Aug.
  17, 1630 (2) Elizabeth Gibson
  MASS XXV, 93
Joseph (Feb. 1731-Dec. 19, 1806) m.
  Oct. 6, 1768 (2) Sarah Hathorne
  XXV, 93

ENNES
Alexander (....-....) m. ....
  ...... NY XXIV, 41
Cornelius (Nov. 5, 1761-Mar. 27,
  1836) m. Sept. 22, 1781 Eleanor
  Decker XXIV, 41

ENO
James (bpt. Aug. 21, 1625-June 11,
  1682) m. Aug. 18, 1648 Anna Bidwell
  CONN XIX, 8
Jonathan (Mar. 15, 1738/9-Dec. 5,

1813) m. Jan. 7, 1764/5 Mary Hart
  XIX, 8

ESSELSTYN, see also VAN ESSELSTYN
Richard (Oct. 2, 1731-Jan. 30, 1783)
  m. .... (1) Majika Blom XXIX, 299

ESSEX
Banajah (Benjamin (Feb. 27, 1762-
  July 22, 1843) m. Mar. 24, 1786
  Penelope Fones XXII, 143; XXIV,
  101
Hugh (....-....) m. ....
  ...... RI XXII, 143; XXIV, 101

EVANS
Andrew, Jr. (Nov. 20, 1734-Jan. 20,
  1799) m. Nov. 25, 1760 Sarah
  Centre XXV, 267
David (....-July 27, 1663) m. ....
  Mary ...... MASS XXIV, 45
Elisha (July 11, 1765-Jan. 13, 1853)
  m. Dec. 5, 1783 Mary Mac Donald
  XXIV, 45
Henry (....-c. Mar. 1, 1666/7) m.
  .... MASS XXV,
  267
John (Jan. 5, 1742-Jan. 31, 1816)
  m. .... Martha Foster XIV, 114;
  XVII, 137
Thomas, Sr. (c. 1662-Dec. 1756)
  m. c. 1730 Sarah Martha Elizabeth
  Roberts PA XXXIV, 339
Thomas, Jr. (1739-1825) m. 1762
  Sarah Evans XXXIV, 339
William (....-a. June 1688) m. ....
  Jane Hodges NJ XIV, 114; XVII,
  137

EVARTS, see EVERTS

EVELETH
Isaac (Sept. 13, 1738-....) m.
  Sept. 1, 1762 Emma Bucklin XIII,
  108
Sylvester (....-1689) m. ....
  Susanna ...... MASS XIII, 108

EVEREST
Andrew (....-....) m. .... Barbery
  (Barbara) ...... ME III, 37
Daniel (Apr. 16, 1752-July 25, 1825)
  m. Nov. 27, 1774 Eunice Patterson
  III, 37

EVERETT, includes EVERITT
Abner (May 12, 1760-Nov. 25, 1852)
  m. Sept. 27, 1786 (1) Jedidah
  Bronson X, 276; XIV, 123
Edward (Dec. 9, 1739-c. 1815) m. 1762
  Ruth Field XXVI, 179, 180

Eleazur (Aug. 10, 1712-Jan. 28,
1787) m. Nov. 29, 1759 (2)
Mrs. Bethiah (Lewis) Morse
XXXIV, 265
George (c. 1635-a. June 18, 1712) m.
.... Mary Taylor VA XXXIV, 206
George (Oct. 26, 1763-....) m. ....
...... Raymond XXVI, 179, 180
Jeremiah (Feb. 6, 1737-p. 1789) m.
.... Lydia ...... XIV, 103
John, Sr. (Feb. 28, 1753-Feb. 13,
1845) m. .... (2) Sarah Dedman
XXXIV, 206
Moses (July 15, 1750-Mar. 25, 1813)
m. Dec. 28, 1784 (3) Hannah (Clapp)
Gardner XXIV, 79
Richard (c. 1600-July 3, 1682) m.
.... (1) ....; .... (2)
Mary Winch MASS X, 277; XIV,
103, 123; XXIV, 79; XXVI, 179;
XXXIV, 266

EVERITT, see EVERETT

EVERTS, includes EVARTS
Daniel (Jan. 12, 1749-Dec. 18, 1833)
m. Nov. 8, 1780 Molly Redfield
XXV, 143, 144
John (c. 1600-May 9, 1669) m. ....
Elizabeth ...... MASS, CONN
X, 128, 147; XIII, 83; XXV, 143,
144
John (Sept. 21, 1708-Sept. 25, 1786)
m. Oct. 2, 1734 Submit Stone X,
128, 147; XIII, 83

EVERTSZEN, see also WESSELL
Wessel (....-....) m. Mar. 15, 1643
Goertie Bouwkens NY XXXII, 34

EWER
Peleg (Apr. 2, 1752-Mar. 31, 1836)
m. Oct. 22, 1802 Mehitable Fuller
XXXIII, 39, 40
Thomas (c. 1585-1638) m. ....
Sarah ...... MASS XXXIII, 39, 40

EYAMS, see IJAMS

EYRE, see AYER

FAIRBANKS
Ebenezer (June 1, 1734-June 6, 1812)
m. July 2, 1761 Elizabeth Dearth
XXXIII, 99
Jonathan (c. 1595-Dec. 5, 1668) m.
May 20, 1617 Grace ......
MASS VIII, 26; X, 207; XXXI, 211;
XXXII, 164; XXXIII, 99

Josiah (May 22, 1734-May 9, 1798) m.
.... Abigail Carter VIII, 26
Oliver (bpt. Oct. 8, 1757-July 1839)
m. Nov. 9, 1777 Elizabeth Clark
XXXII, 164
Samuel (Sept. 14, 1728-Mar. 28, 1812)
m. May 15, 1752 Mary Draper X, 207
Samuel (c. 1731/2-May 25, 1794) m.
1755 Mehitable Heine XXXI, 211

FAIRCHILD
Aaron (Aug. 11, 1759-Oct. 18, 1838)
m. Nov. 5, 1781 Elizabeth Smith
XXX, 215, 216
Andrew (bpt. 1729-1806) m. ....
Abigail Hill VII, 29
John Curtis (Feb. 1746-Feb. 22, 1825)
m. Nov. 6, 1768 Elizabeth Burch
XI, 68; XXIII, 27
Lewis (Mar. 14, 1746-May 10, 1817) m.
Sept. 22, 1768 Mary Uffoodt XXIX,
308
Thomas (c. 1610-Dec. 14, 1670) m.
1639 (1)...... Seabrook; .... (2)
.... CONN VII, 29; XI,
69; XXIII, 27; XXIX, 308; XXX, 215,
216

FAIRFIELD
Daniel, Jr. (May 16, 1725-c. 1797)
m. Nov. 27, 1746 Mary Moore XXVII,
129, 130
John (....-Dec. 22, 1646) m. ....
Elizabeth ...... MASS XXV, 155,
156; XXVII, 129, 130
John (Jan. 9, 1757-Oct. 17, 1828) m.
1801/2 Elizabeth Howland XXV, 155,
156
Nathaniel (Oct. 4, 1730-Sept. 17,
1817) m. May 6, 1752 Judith Perce
XXV, 155, 156

FALES
James (Mar. 1635-July 1708) m. July
25, 1655 Ann Brock MASS XIX, 58
Nathaniel (July 4, 1720-Dec. 3,
1801) m. 1740 Sarah Little XIX,
58

FANNING
Edmund (c. 1620-Dec. 1683) m. c.
1649 Ellen ...... CONN XIII,
123
James (c. 1737-......) m. Sept.
26, 1762 Sarah Gillet XIII,
123

FARLEY
Ebenezer (Sept. 19, 1747-Jan. 28,
1827) m. Nov. 6, 1766 Betty
Wheeler XXXIV, 19, 32

FARLEY, cont.
George (1615-Dec. 27, 1693) m. Apr.
9, 1641 Christian Births MASS
XXXIV, 19, 32
Stephen (June 18, 1762-July 5, 1838)
m. Jan. 2, 1788 Mary Mitchell
XXXIV, 191
Thomas (1602-....) m. .... Jane
Sefton VA XXXIV, 192

FARMAN, includes FOREMAN
John (Sept. 16, 1739-Apr. 1792) m.
1764 Rebecca Chamberlin
XXXIII, 33
William (c. 1658-a. Dec. 15, 1730)
m. .... Elizabeth ...... MD
XXXIII, 33

FARNHAM, see FARNUM

FARNSWORTH
Abel (May 19, 1734-Jan. 17, 1801) m.
Dec. 6, 1763 Elizabeth McFarling
XV, 74
Asa (May 2, 1754-June 22, 1830) m.
Aug. 6, 1777 Damaris Gates XIII,
37
Jonas (Aug. 18, 1748-July 16, 1805)
m. 1774 Jane Delap XXIV, 47
Mathias (1612-Jan. 21, 1688) m. a.
1647 (1) Mary Farr MASS IV, 125;
VI, 109; X, 58, 103; XI, 29;
XIII, 37; XV, 74; XX, 106; XXIV,
47
Moses (Jan. 17, 1750-Oct. 23, 1837)
m. 1793 (2) Ruhannah Beckwith
X, 58, 103
Oliver (Nov. 9, 1727-Apr. 30, 1803)
m. Dec. 15, 1749 Sarah Tarball
XI, 29
Reuben, Jr. (June 4, 1751-1813) m.
.... (2) Anna Kellogg XX, 106
Samuel (1750-Nov. 20, 1831) m. a.
1783 Anna Wasson VI, 109
Thomas (Oct. 23, 1752-1839) m. ....
Anna Estabrook IV, 125

FARNUM, includes FARNHAM
John (Apr. 21, 1711-Oct. 21, 1786)
m. Dec. 26, 1738 Sarah Frye
XXIII, 25
Ralph (1603-....) m. .... Alice
...... MASS XXIII, 25

FARR
Ebenezer (Aug. 18, 1750-Feb. 15,
1833) m. Feb. 6, 1777 Mary Titus
XXIII, 51
Salmon (1757-Jan. 13, 1834)
m. .... Mary Swinnerton XIV,
40

Samuel (July 1716-....) m. c. 1735
Rebecca ...... XXIII, 51
Stephen (....-....) m. May 26, 1674
Mary Taylor MASS XIV, 40;
XXIII, 51

FARRAR, includes FARROW
Daniel (Mar. 25, 1755-Nov. 13, 1837)
m. Aug. 1, 1775 Lucy Bruce XIV,
51
Jacob (1620-Aug. 14, 1677) m. c.
1640 Ann ...... MASS XIV, 51
John (....-July 7, 1687) m. ....
Frances ...... MASS XXXI, 277
Thomas (1726-1810) m. .... Elizabeth
Howard XII, 117; XIII, 19
Timothy (Sept. 17, 1751-1819) m.
Oct. 12, 1773 Ruth Gall XXXI, 277
William (1587/94-a. June 11, 1637)
m. .... Mrs. Cicely Jordan VA
XII, 117, XIII, 19

FARRINGTON
Edward (1588-Jan. 2, 1671) m. ....
Eliza (Elizabeth) ...... NY
XXVII, 103
John (Apr. 11, 1754-Oct. 8, 1802)
m. Nov. 4, 1777 Phoebe Poor XXVII,
103

FARROW, see FARRAR

FARWELL
Henry (1605-Aug. 1, 1670) m. May 16,
1629 Olive Welby MASS XXXII,
159
William (Dec. 28, 1712-Dec. 11, 1801)
m. Nov. 7, 1744 Bethiah Eldridge
XXXII, 159

FASSETT
Josiah (Mar. 2, 1725-a. Mar. 26,
1802) m. Aug. 31, 1752 Hannah
Thayer XXXIV, 314
Patrick (1628-Nov. 7, 1713) m. ....
Sarah ...... MASS XXXIV, 314

FAULKNER
Edmond (1625-Jan. 18, 1686/7) m.
Feb. 4, 1647 Dorothy Robinson
MASS XXIX, 88; XXXI, 106
Francis, Sr. (Sept. 16, 1728-Aug.
5, 1805) m. Feb. 24, 1759 Rebecca
Keyes XXIX, 87; XXXI, 106

FAUNTLEROY
Joseph (May 30, 1754-1815) m. 1787
Elizabeth Fouche Fauntleroy XXIV,
115
Moore(....-a. 1665) m. c. 1648 Mary
Hill VA. XXIV, 115

FAXON
Allen (Sept. 1, 1761-Feb. 20, 1838)
m. Oct. 1791 Margaret Smith XXIX,
292
Thomas (1601-Nov. 23, 1680) m. ....
Joane ...... MASS XXIX, 292

FAY
Aaron (Aug. 1, 1759-Oct. 16, 1815)
m. Jan. 1785 Rebecca Winslow XX,
62
Daniel (Oct. 21, 1728-Feb. 28, 1815)
m. Mar. 10, 1757 Mary Crosby XX,
62
Francis (Oct. 3, 1760-1830) m. Feb.
22, 1781 Lovica Ball XXIX, 189
John (1648-Dec. 5, 1690) m. 1669
(1) Mary Brigham MASS XX, 62;
XXIX, 189

FAYERWEATHER
Samuel (Mar. 26, 1761-Apr. 29, 1848)
m. Apr. 28, 1791 Charity Burton
V, 115, 116; XXVII, 184
Thomas (....-1638) m. .... Mary
...... MASS V, 115, 116;
XXVII, 184

FEARN
John (Jan. 17, 1717-1784) m. Dec. 31,
1744 Leeanna Lee XXX, 252
Thomas (....-....) m. ....
...... VA XXX, 252

FEARSON
John (....-1683) m. .... Grace .....
MD XIV, 94
Joseph (1759-Sept. 7, 1832) m. Apr.
11, 1791 Elizabeth Shaw XIV, 94

FEE
George (a. 1670-....) m. ....
Margaret Purnell MD XXX, 192
Thomas (1734-1816) m. 1762 (2) Sarah
Leath XXX, 192

FELCH
Henry, Jr. (1610-Nov. 11, 1699) m.
1650 Hannah Sargent MASS XXVI,
122
John, III (Oct. 5, 1739-1821) m.
Oct. 29, 1761 Sarah Adams XXVI,
122

FELLOWS
Abiel, Jr. (Oct. 29, 1764-Aug. 18,
1833) m. .... (2) Catherine Mann
XII, 77, 78
Isaac (Aug. 29, 1732-Feb. 18, 1814)
m. Jan. 21, 1768 Mary Merrill
XXXII, 273, 274

John (Apr. 27, 1720-1812) m. Mar. 6,
1746 Elizabeth Blaisdell XXII,
123; XXV, 164; XXX, 49
Jonathan (Oct. 18, 1764-p. 1812) m.
1785 Eleanor Weeks XIV, 118
Joseph (Feb. 27, 1714-1796) m. Jan.
1, 1737 Elizabeth Young XXXII,
248
Moses (Aug. 9, 1755-Jan. 30, 1846)
m. May 20, 1782 Sarah Stevens
XXII, 123; XXV, 164; XXX, 49
Samuel (1619-Mar. 6, 1697) m. 1641
Anne ...... MASS XIV, 118; XXII,
123; XXV, 164; XXX, 49; XXXII,
218, 235, 248
Samuel (June 15, 1712-Oct. 27, 1781)
m. July 16, 1735 Eunice Heald
XXXII, 217, 218, 235
William (1609-Nov. 29, 1676) m. ....
Mary Ayers MASS XII, 77, 78;
XXXII, 274
Willis (Oct. 5, 1758-Jan. 18, 1840)
m. May 10, 1781 Sarah Hart XXXII,
217, 218, 235

FELT
George (1601-1693) m. .... Elizabeth
Wilkinson MASS XIII, 85; XIV,
28; XV, 6, 30; XVI, 67; XXVI, 106
Peter (Nov. 3, 1745-Jan. 2, 1817) m.
Nov. 8, 1769 Lucy Andrews XIV,
28; XV, 6
Samuel, III (Apr. 13, 1735-July 31,
1803) m. Nov. 22, 1761 Mehitabel
Buell XIII, 85; XV, 30; XVI, 67;
XXVI, 106

FELTON
Joel (May 14, 1762-Jan. 2, 1829) m.
Nov. 19, 1787 Susanna Hunt XXXI,
111
Nathaniel (bpt. May 10, 1615-July 30,
1705) m. a. 1645 Mary Skelton
MASS XXXI, 111

FENNER
Arthur (1622-Oct. 20, 1703) m. ....
(1) Mehitable Waterman RI IX, 55,
56; XXV, 21
John (c. 1736-1823) m. .... Lydia
Carpenter XXV, 21
Stephen (....-Oct. 22, 1823) m. ....
Mary Fenner IX, 55, 56

FENTON
Eleazer (1655-1704) m. ....
(1) Judith ...... NJ XVIII,
35, 36
Elijah (Aug. 8, 1754-Apr. 17, 1790)
m. Nov. 22, 1774 Ruby Anderson
XXV, 171

FENTON, cont.
 John (1760-1815/6) m. .... Sarah
  Preston XVIII, 35, 36
 Robert (....-p. 1730) m. a. 1668
  Dorothy ...... MASS, CONN
  XXV, 171

FERNALD
 Diamond (Dimon) (Apr. 2, 1750-Dec.
  28, 1805) m. c. 1776 Margaret
  Fernald XXXIV, 147
 Renald (July 6, 1595-Oct. 6, 1656)
  m. .... Joanna Warburton NH
  XX, 147, 148; XXII, 114; XXXIV,
  147
 Thomas (May 1, 1747-....) m. ....
  Anna Kenniston XX, 147, 148
 William (Feb. 22, 1732-1803) m. Dec.
  10, 1761 Mary Staples XXII, 114

FERRIS
 James, Jr. (1740/2-a. Mar. 21, 1780)
  m. c. 1760 Mary Mackay XXXI, 171
 Jeffrey (c. 1610-May 31, 1666) m.
  .... (1) .... CONN XXXI,
  22, 171, 236; XXXIII, 25
 Pack (Pach) (c. 1730-p. 1795) m.
  1760 .... XXXI, 22
 Stephen (Jan. 8, 1742-Feb. 12, 1824)
  m. .... Sarah Hanford Lockwood
  XXXI, 236
 Timothy (Nov. 3, 1722-Mar. 1791) m.
  .... XXXIII, 25

FESSENDEN
 Benjamin (1758-Aug. 17, 1827) m.
  June 27, 1805 (2) Anna Bucknam
  X, 177
 Nathan (Apr. 10, 1749-Apr. 24, 1797)
  m. Oct. 17, 1771 Sarah Winship
  XV, 122
 Nicholas (1650-Feb. 24, 1718/9) m.
  1673 Margaret Cheney MASS X,
  177; XV, 122

FIELD
 Abner (c. 1760-Nov. 7, 1831) m. Dec.
  13, 1793 Jane Pope XXXIII, 151
 Abraham (c. 1636-c. Aug. 26, 1674)
  m. p. 1651 Mary Ironmonger VA
  XXXIII, 151; XXXIV, 38
 David (July 31, 1728-Nov. 25, 1778)
  m. July 10, 1755 Anna Stone
  XXIX, 346, 364
 Eliakim (Nov. 27, 1711-Feb. 8, 1786)
  m. Jan. 11, 1753 Esther Graves
  XIV, 70
 Ezekiel Henry (1750-Aug. 1782)
  m. 1778 Elizabeth Field XXV,
  123; XXX, 116, 117
 Francis (Nov. 29, 1757-Dec. 18,

1812) m. 1780 Naomi Wakelee XXIX,
 286
Henry (1611-....) m. ....
 ...... VA XXV, 123; XXX, 116,
 117; XXXII, 181
Henry (Sept. 2, 1759-Jan. 4, 1813)
 m. Feb. 3, 1783 Rhoda Stratton
 XIV, 77, 78
John, Sr. (1720-....) m. 1757 Anna
 Rogers Clark XXXII, 181
John, Jr. (1747-1810) m. 1769 Dianna
 Field XXXIV, 38
Jonathan (Aug. 15, 1750-Nov. 22,
 1833) m. Sept. 6, 1773 Sarah
 Kellogg XXVIII, 36
Joseph (Nov. 29, 1749-June 10, 1836)
 m. May 3, 1791 (2) Relief Baxter
 XVIII, 83
Robert (1613-1675) m. a. 1635 Mary
 Stanley MASS XVIII, 83
Thomas (c. 1648-Aug. 10, 1717) m.
 .... Martha Harris RI XVIII, 16
Thomas (1741-....) m. Sept. 8, 1761/5
 Deliverance Hammon XVIII, 16
Zachariah (1596-June 30, 1666) m. c.
 1641 Mary Stanley MASS XIV, 70,
 71, 77, 78; XXVIII, 36; XXIX, 286,
 347, 364

FILKINS
 Henry, Sr. (May 26, 1651-a. Apr.
  1714) m. .... Katherine Vonck
  Ruard NY XX, 128, 138
 Isaac (June 1, 1755-Feb. 5, 1834)
  m. 1775/6 ...... Langdon XX,
  128, 138

FILLEBROWN
 James (Apr. 7, 1728-1796) m. Nov.
  19, 1753 (1) Susannah White
  XXVII, 22
 Thomas (1631-June 7, 1713) m. ....
  Anna ...... MASS XXVII, 72

FINCH
 Abraham (c. 1585-1638) m. ....
  .... MASS, CONN XXIX,
  278
 Ezekiel, Sr. (June 11, 1712-Mar. 15,
  1801) m. .... Mrs. Esther Suther-
  land XXIX, 278
 Ezekiel, Jr. (Nov. 2, 1737-
  Feb. 13, 1836) m. ....
  Phebe Sutherland XXIX,
  277

FINNEY, see PHINNEY

FIRMAN, see FURMAN

FIRMIN, see FURMAN

FISH
  Joshua (Jan. 13, 1743-....) m. ....
    Phebe Wright XIX, 54
  Thomas (Jan. 1, 1618/9-1687) m. ....
    Mary ...... RI XIX, 54

FISHER
  Aaron (Jan. 16, 1758-Oct. 10, 1843)
    m. .... Rebecca Moore XXXI, 187
  Anthony (bpt. Apr. 23, 1591-Apr. 18,
    1671) m. .... Mary Anne Fiske
    MASS XI, 79; XIX, 85; XXVI, 169;
    XXX, 146; XXXI, 187; XXXII, 13;
    XXXIV, 207
  David (Jan. 22, 1733-a. Sept. 1,
    1812) m. Sept. 21, 1758 Abigail
    Lewis XXVI, 169
  David (June 26, 1759-Nov. 8, 1829)
    m. Nov. 20, 1781 Mehitable Hewins
    XIX, 85; XXVI, 169, 170
  Jabez (Nov. 19, 1717-Oct. 15, 1806)
    m. Mar. 5, 1740 Mary Adams XXVII,
    7
  John (....-1685/6) m. .... Margaret
    ...... PA, DE V, 83
  Jonathan (Nov. 25, 1743-Mar. 10,
    1777) m. Oct. 26, 1766 Catherine
    Avery XI, 79; XXXI, 207
  Joseph (Oct. 6, 1741-Jan. 26, 1819)
    m. Jan. 7, 1773 Susan Fisher
    XXX, 146
  Joseph (1753-Nov. 21, 1829) m. 1785
    (2) Submit Lewis XXXII, 13
  Joshua (bpt. Feb. 24, 1585-p. 1656)
    m. .... MASS XII,
    93
  Nathan (Sept. 14, 1750-Sept. 26,
    1828) m. Sept. 15, 1772 Mehitable
    Forbes XXVII, 7, 8
  Samuel (Nov. 25, 1709-1799) m. ....
    Ruth Wiglet XII, 93
  Samuel (Feb. 23, 1750-....) m. ....
    (1) Mrs. Lydia Haskell XII, 93
  Thomas (....-1637/8) m. .... Eliza-
    beth ...... MASS XXVII, 7
  Thomas (June 14, 1763-Dec. 2, 1835)
    m. .... (3) Nancy (Owens) Ricards
    V, 83

FISK, includes FISKE
  Abraham (1762-1832) m. 1787 Betsey
    Arnold XXXIII, 93
  David (....-1660) m. .... Sarah
    Smith MASS X, 246; XXII,
    115
  David (Nov. 23, 1760-Nov. 20, 1803)
    m. .... Abigail Harrington XXII,
    115
  Ebenezer (1748-Oct. 7, 1816)
    m. .... (1) Betsey ......
    X, 246

James (Oct. 4, 1763-Nov. 17, 1844)
    m. Apr. 27, 1786 Priscilla West
    XXVI, 29, 30; XXXIV, 197
  Moses (1746-Nov. 22, 1816) m. ....
    Hulda W. ...... XXVIII, 199;
    XXIX, 82
  Moses (July 12, 1755-Mar. 1, 1828)
    m. Apr. 13, 1780 Betsy Bullard
    XXII, 47
  Nathan (c. 1615-June 21, 1676) m.
    .... Susanna ...... MASS XV, 84;
    XXII, 47; XXV, 47; XXVI, 30; XXXII,
    217; XXXIV, 197
  Peleg (Jan. 24, 1739/40-May 30,
    1808) m. May 1, 1763 Lydia Sheldon
    XXXI, 245
  Phineas (....-June 7, 1673) m. 1638
    (1) Sarah ......; .... (2) Eliza-
    beth Esterick MASS XIX, 133;
    XXVIII, 199; XXIX, 82; XXXI, 245;
    XXXIII, 93
  Rufus (Mar. 28, 1752-Dec. 2, 1813)
    m. .... Dorcas Gleason XV, 84;
    XXV, 47
  Samuel (Apr. 14, 1759-May 14, 1828)
    m. Jan. 23, 1784 Rebecca Fiske
    XVI, 38
  Solomon (Dec. 26, 1757-....) m. Mar.
    2, 1791 Mary Harris XIX, 133
  William (c. 1613-Sept. 1654) m. 1643
    Bridgett Muskett MASS XVI, 38
  William (Apr. 26, 1732-p. 1800) m.
    .... XXXII, 217

FISKE, see FISK

FITCH
  Augustus (1733-May 21, 1815) m.
    June 22, 1760 Editha Field XXIX,
    48; XXXIII, 275, 276
  Elisha (May 8, 1749-Aug. 19, 1829)
    m. Oct. 24, 1772 Rachel Kellum
    XXXI, 280
  James (Dec. 24, 1622-Nov. 18, 1702)
    m. Oct. 1648 (1) Abigail Whitfield
    CONN XIV, 99, 105; XXXI, 280
  Jonathan (Apr. 12, 1727-Sept. 22
    1793) m. Sept. 1, 1751 Sarah
    Saltonstall XXX, 217
  Joseph, I (....-p. 1713) m. a. 1663
    Mary Stone CONN XXIX, 49; XXXIII,
    275, 276
  Joseph (Aug. 5, 1746-1830) m. ....
    Mary Andrus XIV, 99
  Matthew, Jr. (June 17, 1744-c. 1790)
    m. Dec. 27, 1770 Sarah Reed VI, 73
  Pelatiah (May 6, 1722-Apr. 6, 1803)
    m. 1746 Elizabeth Barrows XIV, 105
  Thomas (Oct. 24, 1612-1704) m. Nov.
    1, 1632 Anna Stracyor (Stacie)
    CONN VI, 73; XXX, 217

FITTS
  Richard (Aug. 8, 1758-Dec. 9, 1826)
    m. .... Dorothy Kimball XVII, 148
  Robert (....-May 9, 1665) m. ....
    Grace D. ...... MASS XVII, 148

FITZHUGH
  Henry (Sept. 10, 1723-Feb. 7,
    1783) m. Oct. 23, 1746 Sarah
    Battaile XXXI, 92, 93
  John (Feb. 3, 1751-1803) m. c. 1780
    Lucy Redd XXXIII, 256
  William (Jan. 10, 1651-Oct. 1701)
    m. May 1, 1674 Sarah Tucker VA
    XVII, 122; XXXI, 92; XXXIII, 256
  William (Jan. 16, 1721-Feb. 11,
    1798) m. 1752 (2) Anne (Frisby)
    Rousby XVII, 122

FITZ RANDOLPH
  Edward (c. 1614-1675) m. May 10,
    1637 Elizabeth Blossom MASS XIII,
    58, 105; XXVI, 211, 212; XXXIII,
    330, 331
  Ezekiel (Dec. 1, 1718-1813) m. ....
    Mary Robinson XIII, 58, 105
  John (Apr. 4, 1749-p. Apr. 5, 1814)
    m. Feb. 9, 1775 Elizabeth Vance
    XXXIII, 331
  Joseph (Jan. 16, 1750-p. 1808) m.
    .... (1) Mary Laying; .... (2)
    Filia Turman XXVI, 211, 212

FLAGG, includes FLEGG
  Abijah, Jr. (May 6, 1755-Nov. 22,
    1842) m. Feb. 7, 1782 (1) Thankful
    Seymour XIV, 9; XVII, 101, 102
  Henry Collins (Aug. 21, 1742-Apr. 1,
    1801) m. Dec. 5, 1784 Rachel '
    (Moore) Allston XIII, 47; XXV,
    244, 245
  Thomas (bpt. 1615-Feb. 6, 1697/8) m.
    1640 Mary ...... MASS XIII, 47;
    XIV, 9; XVII, 102; XXV, 244, 245;
    XXX, 267
  Timothy (Mar. 10, 1740-Sept. 1801)
    m. Dec. 17, 1761 Elizabeth Pierce
    XXX, 267

FLANDERS
  Enoch (Oct. 23, 1739-June 6, 1810)
    m. a. 1766 Anna Crocker XXX, 184
  Stephen, Sr. (c. 1620-June 27, 1684)
    m. c. 1640 Jane ...... MASS
    XXX, 184

FLEGG, see FLAGG

FLEHARTY
  John (....-p. June 14, 1729) m. ....
    Frances ..... MD XXXIV, 102

Stephen (Oct. 28, 1743-Apr. 21, 1825)
    m. Apr. 4, 1764 Sarah Ann Morgan
    XXXIV, 102

FLEMING
  John (1731-Sept. 2, 1814) m. ....
    Abigail Cowan XVI, 47
  William (1662-1726) m. 1691 Mary
    Moore MD XVI, 47

FLETCHER
  Asa (c. 1735-Dec. 12, 1822) m. Apr.
    6, 1762 Thankful Staples XIV,
    101; XV, 57; XIX, 168
  Ezekiel (Apr. 3, 1741-July 7, 1806)
    m. .... Bridget Parker IV, 147
  Gideon (Dec. 19, 1765-June 13, 1813)
    m. 1790 Phoebe Emerson XXVII, 101
  Jesse (Nov. 9, 1762-Feb. 10, 1831)
    m. Aug. 8, 1782 Lucy Keyes X,
    220; XIV, 108; XVIII, 116; XXIV,
    167
  John (bpt. May 12, 1762-Aug. 8,
    1847) m. Jan. 27, 1785 Silence
    Curtis XXXIII, 135, 136, 177
  Joshua (c. 1732-1785) m. c. 1755
    Sallie ...... XXVIII, 155
  Ralph (1632-1698) m. Mar. 11, 167..
    Elizabeth Sutton VA XXVIII, 155
  Robert (c. 1592-Apr. 3, 1677) m.
    .... Sarah ...... MASS IV, 147;
    X, 221; XIV, 101, 108; XV, 58;
    XVIII, 116; XIX, 168; XXIV, 168;
    XXVII, 101; XXXIII, 135, 136, 177
  Samuel (a. 1630-Dec. 9, 1697) m.
    .... Margaret Hailstone MASS
    IV, 147

FLINT
  Joseph, Sr. (Apr. 21, 1759-July 19,
    1787) m. July 1780 Elizabeth Whit-
    ridge XIX, 118
  Luke (Dec. 20, 1752-p. 1837) m.
    June 6, 1776 Mary Slate XXIII,
    47
  Nathaniel (Sept. 5, 1720-Jan. 1795)
    m. July 3, 1751 (2) Mary Jennings
    Hovey XVIII, 77, 78; XXIII, 47;
    XXV, 205, 206
  Thomas (1603-Apr. 15, 1663) m. 1633
    Ann ...... MASS XVIII, 78; XIX,
    118; XXIII, 47; XXV, 205, 206

FOBES
  John (1610-1662) m. 1645 Constant
    Mitchell MASS XXX, 35, 36
  John (Mar.12, 1758-Oct.13, 1839) m.
    Mar.12, 1783 Rosinda Alden XXX,35,36

FOGG
  Samuel (Feb. 20, 1600-Apr. 16, 1672)

m. *Dec. 28, 1665 (2) Mary Page NH*
XXVII, 185
Seth (Mar. 25, 1739-p. 1790) m. ....
Mary Godfrey XXVII, 185

FOLSOM
Benjamin (c. 1730-1815) m. ....
Mercy Taylor XVIII, 94; XXIV,
135
David (....-1791) m. .... Sarah
Gilman XI, 167
Jacob (....-Oct. 22, 1826) m. June
4, 1787 Elizabeth Smart XXV, 11
James (July 22, 1756-Aug. 17, 1835)
m. Dec. 2, 1784 Mary Folsom XXX,
110
Jeremiah (July 25, 1719-1802) m. Mar.
28, 1742 Mary Hersey XVII, 111
John (bpt. 1615-Dec. 27, 1681) m.
Oct. 4, 1636 Mary Gilman MASS
XI, 168; XVII, 111; XVIII, 94;
XXIV, 135; XXV, 11; XXX, 110;
XXXIII, 342
Josiah (Nov. 5, 1735-Feb. 7, 1816)
m. May 22, 1762 Elizabeth Gilman
XXXIII, 342
William (c. 1723-Feb. 1809) m. ....
Mary Low XXV, 11

FONDA
Cornelius (bpt. Nov. 28, 1754-p.
1787) m. Mar. 26, 1779 Elizabeth
Miller XVI, 113, 114
Isaac (bpt. July 4, 1723-p. 1784)
m. Feb. 4, 1747/8 Cornelia DeForest
XXIII, 9
Isaac, Jr. (Apr. 6, 1753-Sept. 15,
1826) m. Apr. 11, 1779 Anna Van
Santvoordt XXIII, 9
Jellis Douwess (c. 1616-1662) m.
Feb. 10, 1641 Hester Jansz NY
XVI, 114; XXIII, 9; XXXII, 284
John Peter (Oct. 12, 1735/6-....)
m. Mar. 18, 1757 Dirkje Winne
XXXII, 283, 284

FONTEYNE, see VAN TINE

FOOTE
Abraham (June 16, 1725-Dec. 6, 1823)
m. Apr. 15, 1745 Abigail Rogers
XII, 21, 44; XIII, 34
Charles (Nov. 10, 1723-Aug. 25, 1795)
m. Oct. 1750 Jerusha Chamberlain
XXXI, 200; XXXII, 141
David (Jan. 24, 1753-Sept. 27, 1821)
m. 1777 Mary Scovel XIV, 112;
XXXI, 176, 177
Elihu (Aug. 15, 1757-Nov. 27, 1849)
m. Nov. 11, 1789 Lucy Williams
XIII, 16

Elijah (1740-Oct. 15, 1813) m. Mar.
23, 1761 Eunice Peck XXXII, 62
Elijah (Mar. 14, 1755-1828) m.
Dec. 12, 1771 (1) Mary Lattimer
X, 183; XIII, 38
Ephraim (Sept. 1, 1725-Mar. 24,
1791) m. July 31, 1760 Lucy
Barker XXIV, 169
George (Oct. 30, 1749-May 12, 1830)
m. 1776 Weltha Ann Woodward III,
59
Jared (Aug. 28, 1728-Jan. 28, 1806)
m. .... (1) Hannah Buel; .... (3)
Mrs. Joanna Jennings X, 237; XII,
34; XIII, 78; XXIV, 167
Nathaniel (Apr. 1593-1644) m. c.
1615 (1) Elizabeth Deming MASS,
CONN III, 59; X, 183, 237; XII,
21, 34, 44; XIII, 16, 34, 38, 79;
XIV, 112; XXIV, 167, 169; XXXI,
177, 200; XXXII, 62, 141

FORBES
James (....-Nov. 27, 1692) m. ....
Catherine ...... CONN XVIII, 52
Timothy (June 14, 1743-Sept. 14,
1800) m. .... Mary Roberts XVIII,
52

FORD
Andrew (1632-Mar. 4, 1693) m. 1656
Eleanor Lovell MASS X, 205; XII,
111; XIII, 11
Hezekiah (1734-Feb. 8, 1826) m. ....
Sarah Fisher XII, 111
Jacob (Aug. 15, 1738-June 9, 1794)
m. May 14, 1761 Rachel Agur X,
205
Luke (Aug. 18, 1742-p. 1781) m. May
1766 Hannah Reed XIII, 11
Mordacai, Sr. (Dec. 19, 1727-Dec.
1795) m. 1752 Ruth Barney XXXII,
96; XXXIII, 72
Nathan (Dec. 29, 1733-p. 1800) m.
Oct. 18, 1756 Sarah Hine X, 40
Noah (Mar. 19, 1762-Nov. 15, 1817)
m. Dec. 11, 1783 Abigail Whitman
X, 205
Thomas (c. 1631-p. Sept. 1681) m. a.
1670 Elizabeth ...... MD XXXII,
96; XXXIII, 72
Timothy (....-Aug. 28, 1684) m. ....
Gordy ...... MASS, CONN X, 40

FOREMAN, see FARMAN

FORMAN
David (Oct. 1, 1733-Mar. 30, 1812) m.
.... Ann Denise IV, 79
Robert (1605-1671) m. .... Johanna
Pore NY IV, 79; XIX, 62

FORMAN, cont.
Thomas (Dec. 1740-c. 1825) m. Oct.
  1769 Jane Throckmorton XIX, 61

FORT
  Elias, Sr. (a. 1646-1679) m. ....
    Phillis Champion VA XXX, 274;
    XXXI, 85, 109, 118, 125, 129;
    XXXII, 163
  Elias, III (July 14, 1730-Jan. 14,
    1819) m. 1758 Sarah Sugg XXXI,
    125; XXXII, 163
  Frederick (1734-1819) m. c. 1760
    Mary Knight XXX, 274; XXXI, 85,
    109, 118, 129

FORTESCUE, see FOSCUE

FOSCUE, includes FORTESCUE
  Simon, I (1604-1680) m. 1630 Eliza-
    beth ...... VA XXXIV, 339
  Simon, V (1734-1814) m. 1755 Dina
    Sanderson XXXIV, 339

FOSTER
  Asa (June 3, 1765-Aug. 21, 1861) m.
    Nov. 10, 1794 Sarah Morrell
    XIII, 75
  Christopher (1603-Oct. 1687) m. ....
    Frances .....NY XIX, 11; XX, 151
  Daniel (Mar. 12, 1762-Aug. 29, 1833)
    m. Dec. 18, 1783 Dorothy Pingree
    XXVI, 175, 176
  Edward (1610-Nov. 1643) m. Apr. 8,
    1635 Lettice Hanford MASS XII, 79
    XXXIII, 23
  Elisha (Apr. 28, 1745-July 29, 1827)
    m. .... Mrs. Grace Barstow XII,
    79
  Ephraim (Aug. 30, 1731-Nov. 12,
    1803) m. a. 1770 Hannah Moore
    XVI, 107, 108
  Ezekiel, Jr. (Apr. 9, 1759-Oct. 8,
    1821) m. Jan. 1, 1782 Hannah Pres-
    ton XX, 151
  Isaac, Sr. (Aug. 21, 1720-Mar. 12,
    1783) m. Nov. 8, 1744 Sarah Brown
    XXXI, 259
  Isaac (Mar. 8, 1745-....) m. Nov. 9,
    1767 Lydia Bacon XXVIII, 137, 138
  John, Sr. (c. 1628-a. Mar. 14, 1688)
    m. 1648/9 Martha Tompkins MASS XXV,
    161; XXIX, 377; XXXI, 269
  Jonathan (Oct. 11, 1727-July 28,
    1813) m. 1765 Rebecca Dorman
    XXXIII, 266
  Jonathan, Jr. (1745-Oct. 10, 1781) m.
    .... (2) Sarah Billings XXV, 161
  Joseph (Mar. 24, 1732-Dec. 11, 1804)
    m. July 20, 1759 (1) Sarah Jones
    XXIX, 377

Joseph (Dec. 25, 1739-Dec. 15, 1802)
  m. Mar. 26, 1765 Elizabeth Hilton
  XXXII, 248
Obadiah (May 25, 1747-July 25, 1780)
  m. .... Hannah Ballard IX, 48
Paul (July 14, 1750-p. Nov. 8, 1813)
  m. Nov. 17, 1774 Martha Trask
  XXXI, 269
Reginald (1595-June 4, 1681) m.
  1617/8 Judith ...... MASS IX,
  47, 48; XIII, 75; XVI, 107; XXVI,
  175; XXVIII, 138; XXX, 104; XXXI,
  259; XXXII, 248; XXXIII, 266
Richard (Nov. 24, 1744-May 5, 1814)
  m. Dec. 6, 1770 Lydia Titus
  XXXIII, 23
Thomas (Aug. 11, 1724-Aug. 22, 1789)
  m. Apr. 5, 1748 Mehitable Peabody
  XXVI, 175
Thomas (July 25, 1737-June 11, 1826)
  m. Dec. 24, 1761 Martha Elmore
  XIX, 11
Woodin (1730-Feb. 2, 1810) m. May
  28, 1753 Frances Scott XXX, 104

FOWLER
  Abner (Mar. 17, 1753-Apr. 30, 1833)
    m. Dec. 8, 1774 Mary Mason XXV,
    215
  Adijah (June 10, 1717-Dec. 14, 1804)
    m. Dec. 18, 1745 Abigail Bigelow
    XXXIV, 264
  Ambrose (c. 1620-Oct. 18, 1704) m.
    May 6, 1646 Jane Alvord CONN,
    MASS XIX, 91; XXXIII, 16, 17
  David (1715-May 26, 1800) m. June
    17, 1747 Elizabeth Smith XXXIII,
    16, 17
  Ebenezer (Jan. 11, 1718/9-Feb. 9,
    1800) m. Oct. 19, 1743 Desire
    Bristol XXVI, 84, 85
  Henry (....-p. Sept. 19, 1687) m.
    a. June 4, 1655 Rebecca Newell
    MASS, RI XXIX, 135
  Jacob (1760-p. 1786) m. .... Eliza-
    beth Ford III, 26; IX, 34
  James (c. 1748-Mar. 31, 1809) m.
    1769 Susannah Purdy XXIX, 135
  John (1635-Sept. 14, 1676) m. 1647
    Mary Hubbard CONN XVI, 27
  Mark (May 9, 1756-Apr. 27, 1813)
    m. Sept. 11, 1777 Miriam (Sterling)
    Warner XXXIV, 264
  Medad (Aug. 16, 1760-Apr. 26, 1849)
    m. .... Louisa Falley XIX, 91
  Philip (c. 1590-June 24, 1679) m. a.
    1615 Mary Winsley (Winslow) MASS
    III, 26; IX, 34; XXV, 215; XXXIII,
    336; XXXIV, 311
  Reuben (June 11, 1760-Sept. 5, 1832)
    m. .... Ada Willard XVI, 27

Samuel (Jan. 9, 1748/9-Apr. 20, 1813)
m. Mar. 4, 1773 Sarah Putman
XXXIII, 336; XXXIV, 311
*William (1572-Jan. 25, 1660/1) m.
.... (2) Sarah ...... CONN XVI,
27; XXVI, 84, 85; XXXIV, 264*

FOX
David (July 14, 1720-Mar. 1804) m.
1747 Mary Chapman XXVI, 291,
292
Stephen (1760-Feb. 25, 1842) m. ....
Mary Bates XI, 101
*Thomas (1622-Apr. 14, 1658) m.
Dec. 13, 1647 (2) Hannah Brooks
MASS XI, 101; XXVI, 291, 292*

FRANCIS
Amos (Nov. 23, 1757-Nov. 25, 1806)
m. .... Sarah Curtis XXXIII, 19,
232, 233
Asa (Nov. 8, 1757-July 31, 1836) m.
Mar. 8, 1781 Prudence May Warner
XII, 84; XV, 68; XXII, 87; XXVII,
163
James (Dec. 4, 1755-Apr. 7, 1831) m.
1780 Sarah Coe XXXIV, 203
Justus (Nov. 8, 1750-Jan. 8, 1827)
m. Nov. 9, 1786 (3) Lois Andrews
(Andrus) X, 25
*Robert (1629-Jan. 2, 1712) m. c.
1650 Joan ...... CONN X, 25;
XII, 84; XV, 68; XXII, 87; XXVII,
163; XXXII, 146; XXXIII, 19, 232,
233; XXXIV, 203*
Titus (Aug. 22, 1760-Dec. 21, 1837)
m. .... Chloe ...... XXXII, 146

FRANKLIN
*Henry (....-a. Apr. 1, 1710) m. Dec.
26, 1697 (2) Sarah Cox NY XX,
39; XXIX, 45*
John (Apr. 27, 1732-Aug. 29, 1801)
m. July 8, 1756 Deborah Morris
XX, 39; XXIX, 45

FRAZEE, see FRAZER

FRAZER, includes FRAZEE
John (1753-1845) m. 1772 Elizabeth
Saunders XXI, 147, 148
*Joseph (....-a. Feb. 12, 1714) m.
.... Mary Osborn NJ XXI, 147,
148*

FREDERICKSE, see also MYNDERSE
*Myndert (....-1706) m. .... (1)
Cataryna Burger NY II, 48*

FREEMAN
Edmund (c. 1590-1682) m. ....

*Elizabeth Beauchamp MASS X, 73,
143; XI, 134, 192; XVI, 136; XX,
21; XXI, 136; XXIX, 42; XXXII, 199*
Edmund (Sept. 30, 1711-Feb. 11, 1800)
m. Aug. 7, 1736 Martha Otis XI,
134, 192
Edmund, II (Apr. 29, 1737-Feb. 11,
1813) m. .... (1) Sarah Porter
XI, 134
Edmund (Mar. 2, 1757-June 1, 1831)
m. Apr. 3, 1777 Ruth Wiley X, 73,
143
Edmund, III (Aug. 29, 1764-Sept. 26,
1854) m. 1789 Zilpah Poole XI,
134
*Henry (Aug. 7, 1670/2-Oct. 10, 1763)
m. May 16, 1695 Elizabeth Bowne
PA, NJ XXVII, 37, 94, 137*
Isaac (1733-Aug. 6, 1807) m. Nov. 25,
1756 Thankful Higgins XXIX, 42;
XXXII, 199
Israel (Apr. 23, 1742-....) m. ....
Louisa Miller XXI, 59, 60
*John (1627-Oct. 28, 1719) m. Feb.
13, 1649 Mercy Prence MASS XVI,
136*
Jonathan, Jr. (May 18, 1734-....) m.
Nov. 28, 1759 Sarah Parker XXXII,
140
Jonathan (Mar. 21, 1745-Aug. 20,
1808) m. Feb. 2, 1775 Sarah Hunt-
ington XX, 21
*Joseph (Oct. 2, 1639-1682) m. Mar.
14, 1666 Elizabeth Gosse NJ
XXI, 60*
*Samuel (....-1639) m. .... Apphia
...... MASS XXXII, 140*
Samuel (Mar. 31, 1708-Jan. 1, 1778)
m. 1729 Mary Stone XXVII, 37, 94,
137
Silas (Oct. 11, 1746-Sept. 8, 1837)
m. Dec. 6, 1768 Elizabeth Kasson
XXI, 136

FREER, includes FRERE
Elisha (bpt. Aug. 5, 1739-p. 1800)
m. Nov. 25, 1768/9 Martha Everitt
XI, 18, XXXIII, 319, 320
*Hugo (a. 1647-p. Sept. 4, 1697) m.
.... (1) Maria Haye NY XI, 18;
XXXIII, 319, 320; XXXIV, 149*
Jacob (bpt. May 17, 1719-a. Dec. 2,
1795) m. Sept. 20, 1754 Annitje
Van Aken XXXIV, 149

FRENCH
Daniel (Feb. 2, 1752-p. 1780) m. Apr.
19, 1775 Desire Williams XXII, 119
*Edward (Aug. 13, 1598-Dec. 28, 1674)
m. .... Anne Goodale MASS XXV,
218; XXIX, 157; XXX, 144*

FRENCH, cont.
  Haynes (May 15, 1759/60-Nov. 21,
    1814) m. 1804 (2) Sally Hughes
    X, 176
  Jacob (Sept. 19, 1739-p. Dec. 25,
    1792) m. .... Olive ......
    XXXIV, 236
  James (c. 1752-Jan. 14, 1835) m.
    Jan. 19, 1774 Mary Brindsmade
    XXX, 41, 42
  John (c. 1612-Aug. 6, 1692) m. 1640
    Grace ...... MASS X, 176;
    XXVII, 210; XXXIV, 236
  John (Sept. 8, 1755-Apr. 22, 1831)
    m. Sept. 10, 1783 Nancy Cronkhite
    XXXIV, 235
  Jonathan (Apr. 29, 1760-July 18,
    1841) m. Feb. 15, 1801 (2) Mary
    (Mills) Crawford XXV, 218; XXX,
    143, 144
  Joshua (1734-Sept. 11, 1791) m. 1755
    Esther Wales XXVII, 210
  Nicholas (Nov. 28, 1747-Jan. 7, 1826)
    m. June 6, 1769 Anne Pike XXIX,
    157
  Thomas (....-....) m. .... (2)
    Deborah ...... CONN XXX, 42
  Thomas (....-a. Nov. 5, 1639) m.
    .... Mary ...... MASS XXII, 119
  William (Mar. 15, 1603-Nov. 26, 1681)
    m. .... Elizabeth ...... MASS
    XXXIII, 235
  William, Jr. (1713-1793) m. 1736
    Tabitha Pierce XXXIII, 235

FRERE, see FREER

FRINK
  John (a. 1618-a. Sept. 29, 1675)· m.
    .... Mary ...... MASS,CONN VII, 37;
    X, 80; XIV, 58, 59
  John (Oct. 26, 1732-1821) m. Nov. 22,
    1750 Anna Wilcox Pendleton VII,
    36; X, 80; XIV, 58, 59

FRISBEE, see FRISBIE

FRISBIE, includes FRISBEE, FRISBYE
  Edward (1620-May 10, 1690) m. ....
    Abigail Culpepper CONN XXXIII,
    171, 172; XXXIV, 229
  Levi (Jan. 31, 1759-Oct. 5, 1842) m.
    Dec. 20, 1786 Phoebe Gaylord
    XXXIII, 171, 172
  Philip (1740-Mar. 12, 1813) m. ....
    Phoebe Hendricks XXXIV, 229

FRISBYE, see FRISBIE

FROST
  David, I (Feb. 1, 1750-Jan. 22,

  1832) m. .... Esther Bixby XXX,
    85, 86
  Edmund (c. 1600-a. July 12, 1672) m.
    1633 (1) Thomasine ...... MASS
    X, 9; XXIV, 77; XXX, 85, 86; XXXI,
    255; XXXIII, 90; XXXIV, 65
  Jesse (Mar. 9, 1735/6-p. Dec. 9. 1810) m.
    May 6, 1760 Joanna Spaulding
    XXXIV, 65
  John (June 23, 1754-Nov. 1, 1818) m.
    July 6, 1775 (1) Betty Bemis X,
    9
  Jonathan (Feb. 27, 1738-Sept. 25,
    1776) m. 1760 Martha Leland
    XXXIII, 90
  Noah (Apr. 8, 1755-May 9, 1814) m.
    Jan. 7, 1798 Erene Edson XXIV, 77
  Stephen (June 18, 1747-Oct. 31, 1810)
    m. Dec. 20, 1772 Susanna Brown
    XXXI, 255

FROTHINGHAM
  Thomas (Apr. 7, 1743-Oct. 16, 1790)
    m. Nov. 5, 1776 Sarah Pecker
    XXVIII, 170
  William (....-Oct. 10, 1651) m. ....
    Anna ...... MASS XXVIII, 170

FRYE
  Ebenezer (Sept. 17, 1745-Mar. 10,
    1828) m. Dec. 20, 1763 Hannah Bak-
    er XXXI, 234, 235
  John (Apr. 1601-Nov. 9, 1693) m. c.
    1630/1 Ann ...... MASS XXV, 55,
    56; XXXI, 235
  Joseph (Mar. 19, 1711-July 25, 1796)
    m. Mar. 28, 1732 Mehitable Poor
    XXV, 55, 56
  Joseph (July 10, 1743-Jan. 13, 1828)
    m. Feb. 12, 1774 Mary Robinson
    XXV, 55, 56

FULLER
  Abner (1737-Aug. 1776) m. July 16,
    1767 Mary Hilliard Crowfoot XXXII,
    55, 56
  Abraham (Oct. 1735-Sept. 20, 1807)
    m. Nov. 4, 1762 Lydia Gillett X,
    268
  Amos (1717-July 14, 1778) m. May 8,
    1746 Hannah Putnam XXX, 136
  Benjamin (June 16, 1758-Mar. 26,
    1840) m. Sept. 28, 1780 Joanna
    Trowbridge XXIV, 121
  Edward (bpt. Sept. 4, 1575-1621) m.
    .... Ann ...... MASS X, 268;
    XXXII, 55, 56
  Eleazer (Mar. 17, 1752-Sept. 5, 1819)
    m. 1776 Rachel Bartlett XXXI, 273
  John (bpt. c. 1620-June 4, 1666) m.
    .... Elizabeth Emmerson MASS

XXIV, 121
Robert (....-May 10, 1706) m. ....
Sarah Bowen MASS XXXI, 273
Stephen (Nov. 4, 1730-May 24, 1813)
m. Oct. 17, 1751 Mary Abbot
XXIX, 209
*Thomas (bpt. Jan. 20, 1619-June
1698) m. June 13, 1643 Elizabeth
Tidd MASS XXIX, 209; XXX, 136*

FUNTINE, see VAN TINE

FURMAN, includes FIRMAN, FIRMIN
*John (1588-....) m. ....
...... MASS XXVI, 88*
Richard (Oct. 9, 1755-Aug. 25, 1825)
m. May 5, 1789 (2) Dorethea Maria
Burn XXVI, 88, 89
Wood (Oct. 13, 1712-Feb. 11, 1783)
m. Apr. 20, 1742 Rachel Broadhead
XXVI, 88

GAGE
George (July 9, 1740-May 4, 1806)
m. Sept. 7, 1763 Sarah Adams XX,
161
James (Aug. 21, 1736-Aug. 30, 1815)
m. Sept. 29, 1781 Sarah Lamson
XVIII, 87
*John (1601-Mar. 24, 1673) m. ....
(1) Anna ...... MASS XIV, 126;
XVIII, 87; XIX, 153*
Jonathan (Apr. 24, 1747-Aug. 27,
1824) m. May 26, 1773 Dorcas Swan
XIV, 125
Thaddeus (Apr. 1754-May 11, 1845) m.
Nov. 30, 1775 Abigail Merrill
XIX, 153
*Thomas (....-c. 1685) m. a. 1648
Joanna Knight MASS XX, 161*

GAILLARD, see GAYLORD

GAINES
*Henry (....-1642/4) m. .... Jane
...... MASS XXVII, 189*
Moses (1735-Jan. 12, 1821) m. c.1761
Lucy Barbour XXVII, 188, 189
*Thomas (....-....) m. ....
...... VA XXIV, 22*
Thomas (1738-Jan. 30, 1811) m. 1768
Susannah Dabney Strothers XXIV,
22

GAITHER
Daniel (c. 1753-....) m. .... Henri-
etta Riggs XIX, 138
*John (c. 1600-....) m. .... Joan
...... VA XIX, 138*

GALE
*Richard (c. 1613-p. Feb. 25, 1679)
m. 1640 Mary Castle MASS XXII,
152*
Samuel (May 6, 1726-May 6, 1793) m.
July 17, 1755 Anna Fiske XXII,
152

GALLUP
Benadam (Oct. 26, 1716-May 29, 1800)
m. Aug. 11, 1740 Hannah Avery
XVIII, 133
Benadam (Nov. 17, 1761-Mar. 30,
1850) m. Mar. 31, 1785 Elizabeth
Dorrance XXVI, 55; XXX, 43
Isaac (Feb. 24, 1712-Aug. 3, 1799)
m. Mar. 29, 1749 Margaret Gallup
XXVI, 55; XXX, 43
*John (....-Jan. 11, 1650) m. ....
Christobal ...... MASS XVIII,
133
John (....-Dec. 19, 1675) m. 1643
Hannah Lake CONN XXVI, 55; XXX,
43*

GAMBRILL
Augustine (Aug. 27, 1732-1790) m.
1761 Sarah Sappington XXXIV, 125
*William (a. 1660-....) m. ....
...... MD XXXIV, 125*

GANNETT
Joseph (Mar. 29, 1722-Mar. 27, 1789)
m. June 7, 1744 Bettie Latham
XXXI, 302
*Mathew (Feb. 16, 1617-1695) m. ....
Hannah Andrews MASS XXXI, 302*

GANONG, see GENUNG

GANTT
*Thomas (bpt. 1616-....) m. .... Mary
Graham MD XXI, 12, 13; XXIX, 218*
Thomas (1710-....) m. 1735/6 Rachel
Smith XXIX, 218
Thomas, Jr. (1736-....) m. ....
Susanna Mackall XXI, 12, 13;
XXIX, 218

GARDINER, see GARDNER

GARDNER, includes GARDINER
Clarke (Aug. 3, 1737-1787) m. Nov.
1, 1759 Amey Lillibridge XXII,
41
Ezekiel (Sept. 29, 1712-Aug. 13,
1780) m. Aug. 29, 1734 Dorcas Watson XXVI, 21; XXXIII, 35
Ezekiel, Jr. (Aug. 25, 1738-Aug. 9,
1814) m. .... Susannah Congdon
XIII, 99

GEER, includes GEAR
David (Jan. 18, 1755-Aug. 31, 1835)
m. May 17, 1781 Mary Stanton
XXXIV, 74
George (c. 1621-1726) m. Feb. 17,
1658 Sarah Allyn MASS, CONN
IX, 14; XXXIV, 74
Hezekiah (Apr. 26, 1761-Aug. 4, 1822)
m. .... Sarah Gilbert IX, 14

GENTRY
Martin (Sept. 11, 1747-Apr. 22,
1827) m. Jan. 23, 1766 Mary Timber-
lake XXXIV, 162
Nicholas, I (....-p. 1743) m. a.
1687 .... VA VIII,
8; XII, 10; XIV, 31; XXXIII, 260;
XXXIV, 162
Richard (Sept. 26, 1763-Feb. 12,
1843) m. 1784 (1) Jane Harris;
Oct. 12, 1821 (2) Nancy Guthrie
VIII, 8; XII, 10; XIV, 31; XXXIII,
260

GENUNG, includes GANONG, GUENON
Benjamin (May 10, 1758-Mar. 9, 1832)
m. May 9, 1780 Hannah Whitehead
Beach XXI, 120; XXXII, 144
Jacob (1748-Dec. 22, 1834) m. Mar.
16, 1753 Hannah Wilson XVI, 31,
32
Jean (1640-a. May 21, 1714) m. Aug.
13, 1662 Margreta Sneden NY XVI,
31; XXI, 120; XXIX, 191, 219, 220,
221; XXXII, 144
Jeremiah (1743-Oct. 13, 1823) m. ....
Abigail Parrott XXIX, 191
John (....-1795) m. .... (1) ......
...... XXIX, 219, 220, 221

GEORGE
John (1604-1678) m. 1632 Jane ......
VA XXXII, 152
Joseph (p. 1758-Mar. 27, 1815) m.
June 1, 1786 Lydia Shumate XXXIV,
129
Nicholas (....-1661) m. .... Margaret
...... VA XXXIV, 129
Reuben (Nov. 25, 1749-Jan. 16, 1832)
m. .... Mildred Rogers XXXII,
151, 152

GIBBES, includes GIBBS
Darius (Feb. 9, 1759-Jan. 9, 1811)
m. .... Sibbel XIII, 31
Giles (....-May 21, 1641) m. ....
Katherine ...... MASS, CONN
XIII, 31
Robert (Jan. 9, 1644-Jan. 24, 1715)
m. Jan. 12, 1688 (2) Mary ......
SC XII, 74, 75; XXX, 257, 258

Wareham (May 4, 1734-....) m. ....
Eunice Spencer XIII, 31
William (Jan. 8, 1722-Feb. 20, 1789)
m. Feb. 18, 1748 Elizabeth Hasell
XII, 74, 75; XXX, 257, 258
William Hasell (Mar. 16, 1754-Feb.
13, 1834) m. .... (1) Betsy Fort-
son; Jan. 21, 1808 (2) Mary Philip
Wilson XXX, 257, 258

GIBBS, see GIBBES

GIBSON
Abraham (Aug. 15, 1752-Apr. 10,
1829) m. Oct. 13, 1778 Mary Brown
XIX, 61
John, Sr. (c. 1601-1694) m. ....
Rebecca ...... MASS XVIII, 94;
XIX, 61
Reuben (Feb. 14, 1725-July 27,
1800) m. Nov. 13, 1746 Lois Smith
XVIII, 94; XIX, 61

GIDDINGS
George (1608-June 1, 1676) m. ....
Jane Lawrence MASS X, 252; XV,
57
Joshua (Nov. 9, 1756-Oct. 21, 1833)
m. Oct. 28, 1779 (1) Submit Jones;
1787 (2) Elizabeth Pease X, 251;
XV, 57

GIFFORD
Enos (Mar. 23, 1740-Nov. 20, 1820)
m. Mar. 13, 1760 Mary Wilbor
XXXIII, 114
William (1620-Dec. 31, 1687) m.
July 16, 1683 (2) Mary Mills MASS
XXXIII, 114

GILBERT
Abraham (Apr. 15, 1754-1804) m. Jan.
18, 1776 Abigail Cooper XXVII,
105, 106
Isaac (Nov. 8, 1756-Aug. 12, 1835)
m. 1801 (2) Esther Alling X, 56
John (Feb. 12, 1749-1817) m. Mar. 18,
1769 Millicent Goodrich XVII, 73,
74
Jonathan (1618-Dec. 10, 1682) m.
1650 (2) Mary White CONN XVII,
74
Josiah (Jan. 1, 1750-July 29, 1805)
m. June 30, 1772 Lois Brooks XXX,
190
Matthew (1599-1680) m. .... Jane
Baker CONN X, 56; XXVII,
105
Thomas (....-June 5, 1662) m. July
31, 1655 Catherine Chapin Bliss
MASS XXX, 190

GILDERSLEEVE
Nathaniel (1753-1840) m. 1780 Jerusha
Powell XXVII, 148, 149
Richard (1601-1681) m. .... Joanna
Appleton CONN, NY XXVII, 148,
149

GILL
John (....-Dec. 1, 1690) m. May 2,
1645 Phoebe Bushnell MASS XVII,
12, 117, 137
Samuel (1722-1790) m. 1779 Ruth Van-
Meter XVII, 12, 116, 117, 137,
138
Stephen (1634-1673) m. 1669 Alice
...... MD XXX, 173
Stephen (Jan. 1, 1741-Nov. 29, 1811)
m. 1772 Cassandra Cole XXX, 173

GILLET, see GILLETT

GILLETT, includes GILLET, GILLETTE
Aaron (May 23, 1732-June 14, 1786)
m. Mar. 31, 1757 Anna Pratt X, 75
Amos (Oct. 19, 1743-Apr. 4, 1839)
m. Feb. 23, 1764 (1) Susannah
Webster XXXIII, 201
Asahel (Nov. 26, 1751-Mar. 26, 1826)
m. .... (1) Rhoda Avery XXV, 81
Israel (bpt. Sept. 17, 1738-July 8,
1829) m. Nov. 15, 1764 (2) Susanne
Durkee XI, 171, 173
John (Feb. 9, 1733/4-....) m. Nov.
14, 1754 Abigail Hough XXXII, 107,
108; XXXIV, 224
Jonathan (....-Aug. 23, 1677) m.
Mar. 29, 1634 Mary Dolbere
(Dolbiar) MASS, CONN X, 75; XI,
171, 173; XVI, 130; XVII, 60; XXV,
81; XXXII, 107, 108; XXXIII, 202;
XXXIV, 225
Jonathan (Mar. 22, 1720-1779) m.
Jan. 11, 1747 Phoebe Marvin XVI,
130; XVII, 60

GILLETTE, see GILLETT

GILMAN
Edward (c. 1587-June 22, 1681) m.
June 3, 1614 .... MASS
XXIV, 147
Tristram (Nov. 24, 1735-Apr. 1,
1809) m. May 1771 Elizabeth Sayer
XXIV, 147

GILSON
John (Mar. 8, 1762-Jan. 4, 1847) m.
.... (1) Lucy Darby XII, 61
Joseph (c. 1640-Apr. 1676) m. ....
Mary Cooper (Caper) MASS XII,
61

Samuel (Jan. 7, 1728-Oct. 18, 1776)
m. .... Elizabeth Shedd XII, 61

GIRARDEAU
Jean (1665-Feb. 28, 1720) m. ....
Anne LeSade SC XXXIV, 275
William (1752-Jan. 21, 1822) m. 1785
Patience Harris XXXIV, 275

GLAZIER
John (....-Oct. 1688) m. c. 1662
Eliza George MASS XIX, 99
John (1746/7-Aug. 20, 1820) m. Sept.
2, 1764 Freelove Sherman XIX, 99

GLEASON
Henry (Feb. 26, 1749-July 11, 1795)
m. Feb. 15, 1776 Hannah ......
XXXII, 152, 153
Isaac (Aug. 6, 1724-Jan. 7, 1776) m.
1744 Eunice Smith XXXIII, 148
Jonathan (Oct. 30, 1745-June 21,
1827) m. 1771 May Fiske XXIX, 103
Thomas (1607-1686) m. .... Susanna
Page MASS XXIX, 104; XXXII, 153;
XXXIII, 148

GLIDDEN
Charles (c. 1632-p. June 6, 1707) m.
Apr. 7, 1658 Eunice Shore NH
XXIII, 72; XXXII, 255
Charles (c. 1725-Apr. 25, 1776) m.
.... Abigail Weathern XXXII, 255
John (c. 1754-1818) m. Jan. 15, 1779
Abigail Murdough XXIII, 72

GLOVER
Alexander, Jr. (Feb. 1, 1740-July 13,
1813) m. Dec. 28, 1769 Hannah Pope
XIV, 27, 28
John (bpt. Aug. 12, 1600-Aug. 12,
1654) m. 1625 Anna ...... MASS XIV,
27, 28; XXX, 226
John (May 3, 1753-July 21, 1830) m.
Aug. 29, 1778 Mercy Colton XXX,
225, 226
Joseph (June 8, 1720-Apr. 8, 1783)
m. 1751 Anne Wilson Daughty XXX,
224, 253
Richard (1611-1696) m. 1636 Mary
Booker VA XXX, 224, 253

GOBLE
George (May 26, 1750-Aug. 22, 1831)
m. Feb. 18, 1779 Juliana Wisner
XXXIII, 311
Thomas (....-p. Nov. 30, 1657) m. a.
1629 Alice ...... MASS XXXIII, 311

GODFREY
Benjamin (....-p. 1705) m. ....

Mary ...... NJ XV, 101; XVI, 10, 39

Christopher, I (....-1715) m. .... Anne ...... CONN XVI, 100

George (Mar. 19, 1720-June 30, 1793) m. .... Bethiah Hodges VIII, 14

James (Feb. 16, 1752-1835) m. 1781 Abigail Weaver XV, 101; XVI, 10, 40

John (....-p. Mar. 12, 1689/90) m. .... Mary ...... SC XXXIII, 153, 154

John (Feb. 26, 1754-Aug. 1, 1829) m. .... Jerusha Hodges VIII, 14; XII, 96

Nathan (Sept. 25, 1719-....) m. Jan. 24, 1764 (2) Mrs. Sarah Andrews Nash XVI, 100

Richard (....-p. Oct. 4, 1691) m. .... (1) Jane Turner MASS VIII, 14; XII, 96

William, Sr. (Mar. 4, 1754-June 4, 1787) m. June 17, 1771 Sarah Britton XXXIII, 154, 153

GOLD, see GOULD

GOLDEN
William (....-p. 1686) m. .... NY, NJ XXXI, 135
William (Oct. 7, 1743-Feb. 10, 1816) m. June 28, 1777 Christiana Hortman XXXI, 135, 136

GOLDSBOROUGH
John (Oct. 12, 1711-Jan. 18, 1778) m. Oct. 31, 1733 Ann Turbutt XVII, 85
Nicholas (bpt. Dec. 21, 1609-Oct. 31, 1642) m. Feb. 20, 1632/3 Mary Gilbert MD XVII, 85

GOLDTHWAITE
Jacob (1739-Apr. 7, 1817) m. Jan. 1, 1761 Elizabeth Nightingale XXVIII, 60, 61; XXXII, 125
Stephen (Apr. 7, 1734-June 19, 1812) m. (int.) Nov. 16, 1788 Chloe Aldrich XXIV, 125
Thomas (c. 1610-Mar. 1683) m. 1636 Elizabeth ...... MASS XXII, 58; XXIV, 126; XXVIII, 60, 61; XXXII, 125
Thomas (1738-1781) m. Sept. 5, 1765 Lois Stebbins XXII, 58
Timothy (1762-1859) m. Jan. 24, 1788 Mary (Polly) Briggs XXVIII, 60, 61; XXXII, 125

GONSALUS, see GUNSAUL

GOODALE, includes GOODELL
Edward (Apr. 3, 1715-Aug. 30, 1784) m. .... Lydia Eaton IX, 22, 23
Enos (Mar. 28, 1746-1837) m. .... Hannah Dinsmore XVII, 149
Isaac (Aug. 9, 1730-Jan. 14, 1808) m. Dec. 10, 1753 Huldah Burt XX, 160
Robert (1604-June 27, 1683) m. .... Catherine ...... MASS IX, 22, 23; XVII, 149; XX, 160

GOODE
John (1620/30-c. 1709) m. c. 1650 Frances Mackarness VA XII, 68; XIV, 75; XV, 116; XXXIV, 133
John Samuel (....-....) m. a. 1768 Miss Watkins XII, 68
Samuel (Mar. 30, 1749-1792) m. 1770 Mary Collier XIV, 75; XV, 115
Samuel (Mar. 21, 1756-Nov. 14, 1822) m. Oct. 5, 1786 Mary Armistead Burwell XXXIV, 133

GOODELL, see GOODALE

GOODHUE
Samuel (1719-Apr. 1808) m. .... Deborah Wadleigh XI, 36
William (1612/3-1699/1700) m. .... (1) Margery Watson MASS XI, 36

GOODLOE
George, Sr. (c. 1639-Dec. 1710) m. .... Mary ...... VA XIX, 117; XXV, 17; XXXI, 154; XXXIII, 210, 211
Robert (1711-Nov. 5, 1790) m. .... Elizabeth Guinea XXXIII, 210, 211
Robert (Apr. 4, 1741-Jan. 25, 1797) m. .... Sarah Short XIX, 117; XXV, 17; XXXI, 154

GOODMAN
Moses (June 20, 1750-Aug. 17, 1831) m. Oct. 21, 1780 Amy Seymour X, 18
Richard (c. 1609-Apr. 3, 1676) m. Dec. 8, 1659 Mary Terry CONN, MASS X, 18

GOODRICH, includes GOODRIDGE
Abijah (Feb. 21, 1754-Apr. 12, 1842) m. Sept. 21, 1776 (1) Eunice Martin XV, 119
Benjamin (July 7, 1740-June 30, 1834) m. Sept. 5, 1768 Lydia Wilder XXVII, 138
David (July 14, 1749-Oct. 12, 1781) m. Jan. 5, 1769 Anna Strong XXXII, 271

GOODRICH, cont.
Elisha (Jan. 13, 1748-1825) m.
Sept. 17, 1768 Deborah Allen X,
153; XII, 12, 115; XIII, 33; XIV,
23, 24
Elizur (Oct. 18, 1734-Nov. 21, 1797)
m. .... Katherine Chauncey XII,
85
Josiah (Aug. 22, 1717-Jan. 26, 1806)
m. June 30, 1756 (2) Mrs. Mary
Porter XXIX, 305
Josiah, Jr. (Dec. 12, 1761-Jan. 28,
1840) m. 1804 (2) Lucy ......
XXIX, 305
Simeon (Dec. 7, 1762-Aug. 17, 1817)
m. Jan. 10, 1788 Hannah Welles
XVII, 73
Stephen (Mar. 29, 1757-Aug. 18,
1825) m. Dec. 25, 1781 Lydia Terry
XVIII, 119; XIX, 9
William (May 8, 1605-Mar. 21, 1646/7)
m. 1632 Margaret ...... MASS
XV, 120; XXVII, 138
William (c. 1620-1676) m. Oct. 4,
1648 Sarah Marvin CONN X, 153;
XII, 12, 85, 116; XIII, 33; XIV,
23, 24; XVII, 73; XVIII, 119;
XIX, 9; XXIX, 305; XXXII, 271

GOODRIDGE, see GOODRICH

GOODSELL
John (1749-Jan. 29, 1816) m. ....
Abigail Chidsey X, 68
Lewis (Oct. 23, 1744-Aug. 22, 1829)
m. Mar. 2, 1767 Eunice Wakeman
XVI, 26
Thomas (1646-May 16, 1713) m. June
4, 1684 Sarah Hemenway CONN X,
68; XVI, 26

GOODSPEED
Anthony (Apr. 18, 1746-c. 1825)
m. c. 1766 Abigail Lothrop XXIX,
394
Roger (....-Apr. 1685) m. Dec. 1641
Alice Layton MASS XXIX, 394

GOODWIN
Charles (May 5, 1731-Nov. 17, 1787)
m. Mar. 7, 1754 Thankful Russell
X, 263
Edward (a. 1648-p. 1668) m. June 5,
1668 (2) Susanna Stowers MASS
XI, 147; XXI, 20, 21
Eleazer (June 27, 1741-Feb. 1813) m.
c. 1763 Mehitable Cadwell XXVII,
52, 53
James (c. 1628-a. 1678/9) m. 1655
(1) Rachel Porter VA XVIII,
79

James (Dec. 15, 1754-June 24, 1822)
m. Mar. 10, 1783 Hannah Mather
XII, 73; XXVI, 256
Levi (bpt. May 8, 1757-Apr. 24, 1836)
m. .... Jerusha Drake XVIII, 33,
34
Moses (1745-Jan. 1837) m. Aug. 19,
1773 (1) Abigail Blaisdell XXIX,
328, 403
Ozias (1596-a. Apr. 4, 1683) m. ....
Mary Woodward CONN X, 263; XII,
73; XVIII, 33; XXVI, 256; XXVII,
53; XXXI, 199
Richard (....-Mar. 5, 1709) m. Nov.
20, 1666 Hannah Jones MASS
XXIX, 328, 403
Robert (1739-May 12, 1789) m. Dec.
11, 1766 Jane Tulloch XVIII, 79
Samuel (Oct. 7, 1752-Apr. 6, 1807)
m. Jan. 18, 1781 Abigail Butler
XXXI, 199, 200
Simeon (c. 1737/8-Aug. 17, 1823) m.
1759 Susanna Heath XI, 147; XXI,
20, 21

GOOLD, see GOULD

GORDON
Alexander (c. 1635-1697) m. 1663
Mary Lysson NH VI, 90; XXX, 101
Amos (Aug. 7, 1743-....) m. Dec. 15,
1766 Mary Smith XXX, 101
Charles (....-1739) m. 1697/8 Lydia
Hampton NJ XX, 9
William (Apr. 3, 1748-1798) m. ....
Lydia ...... XX, 9
William (Mar. 13, 1753-Oct. 14, 1818)
m. Mar. 25, 1784 Hannah Ladd VI,
90

GORHAM
Daniel (Sept. 10, 1750-Jan. 25,
1836) m. a. 1782 Mary Lyon XXXIV,
119
Isaac, Sr. (Oct. 14, 1730-July 4,'
1798) m. .... Ann Wakeman V, 100,
101
John (Jan. 28, 1621-Feb. 5, 1676) m.
1643 Desire Howland MASS V, 100,
101; XXXIV, 120

GORTON
Joseph (1741/2-Aug. 31, 1821) m. Jan.
1, 1762 Mary Barton XXXIV, 299
Samuel (1592-Dec. 10, 1677) m. c.
1628 Mary Mayplett MASS, RI
XXXI, 223; XXXIV, 299
Samuel (July 5, 1745-Mar. 20,
1834) m. Feb. 10, 1765 Eunice
Austin XXXI, 223,
224

GOSS
John (Feb. 5, 1748-July 5, 1820) m.
Oct. 5, 1772 Hannah Scott XXXIV,
217
*Philip (1654-a. May 1698) m. Mar.
29, 1680 Mary Prescott MASS
XXXIV, 217*
Philip (c. 1720-Apr. 17, 1804) m.
May 12, 1748 Hannah Ball XXXIV,
217

GOULD, includes GOLD, GOOLD
Abraham (May 10, 1732-Apr. 27, 1777)
m. Jan. 1, 1754 Elizabeth Burr
XIX, 101
Amos, Jr. (Dec. 12, 1761-Dec. 28,
1853) m. June 14, 1786 Rebecca
Perley XXXIV, 107
Bezeleel (July 4, 1756-Mar. 18,
1818) m. Apr. 9, 1778 Bathsheba
Robinson XIX, 150
Daniel (Apr. 30, 1737-p. 1820) m.
c. 1765 Dolly ...... XXIII, 78
*Jarvis (Jervice) (1605-May 27, 1656)
m. c. 1644 Mary ...... MASS
XXXI, 185*
Jesse (1750/6-a. 1805) m. Feb. 19,
1778 Sarah Gold XXVIII, 10, 11
*Nathan (....-Mar. 4, 1693/4) m.
.... CONN XIX,
101; XXVIII, 10*
*Nathan (c. 1614-p. Dec. 12, 1692)
m. .... Elizabeth ...... MASS
XXIII, 78*
Nathaniel (July 16, 1753-July 3,
1842) m. Nov. 20, 1777 Hannah Kil-
lam XIX, 18
Tobias (Dec. 2, 1756-Feb. 28, 1815)
m. Nov. 7, 1779 Rhoda Hammond
XXXI, 185
*Zaccheus (1589-1668) m. c. 1630
Phebe Deacon MASS XIX, 18, 149;
XXXIV, 107*

GOVE
*Edward (1630-July 29, 1691) m. 1660
Hannah Partridge MASS VIII, 31;
XXXIV, 51*
Elijah (May 18, 1751-Oct. 23, 1816)
m. July 12, 1773 (2) Sarah Mills
VIII, 31; XXXIV, 50
*John (1604-Feb. 28, 1647/8) m. 1627
Mary Sale MASS XXXIV, 51, 254*
Nathan, Sr. (Nov. 10, 1737-Dec. 31,
1818) m. Oct. 4, 1762 Hannah Trask
XXXIV, 254

GRANGER
Elisha (July 3, 1743-Apr. 12, 1821)
m. .... (1) Sarah Pierce XXIX,
294

John (Dec. 12, 1764-Aug. 1812) m.
.... Sally Morse XXXII, 277
Justin (Feb. 9, 1756-Mar. 19, 1832)
m. May 25, 1780 Hannah Shaler
XXXIII, 159
*Launcelot (1624-Sept. 3, 1689) m.
Jan. 4, 1653/4 Joanna Adams MASS,
CONN XXIX, 294; XXXII, 277;
XXXIII, 159*

GRANNIS
*Edward (c. 1630-Dec. 10, 1719) m.
1662 (2) Hannah Wakefield CONN,
MASS X, 106; XII, 45, 46*
Simeon (a. 1756-1821) m. Apr. 18,
1776 Priscilla Brockett X, 106;
XII, 45

GRANT
Aaron, Sr. (Dec. 12, 1724-Jan. 31,
1804) m. Dec. 22, 1767 Theodosia
(Bull) Pitkin XXVI, 182, 183
George (1750-Oct. 10, 1820) m. c.
1767 Mary ...... XXIX, 264
*Matthew (Oct. 27, 1601-Dec. 16,
1681) m. Nov. 1, 1625 Priscilla
Gray MASS, CONN XXIV, 89; XXVI,
182, 183; XXIX, 265; XXXII, 17*
Noah (June 20, 1748-Feb. 4, 1820)
m. Mar. 4, 1792 Rachel Kelly
XXIV, 88
Reuben (1754-1840) m. Jan. 1779 (2)
Martha Skinner XXXII, 17

GRAVES
Ansel (Feb. 18, 1767-Jan. 3, 1810)
m. .... Caroline Otis IX, 11, 12
Benjamin (Aug. 25, 1734-Sept. 1781)
m. 1756 Mary Ransom XVIII, 74,
75
Eliphalet (c. 1748-1836) m. 1770
Anna Jones XXXIII, 321
Isaac (Sept. 2, 1741-Nov. 29, 1817)
m. c. 1772 (2) Elizabeth Cowherd
XXV, 207; XXVIII, 176; XXXII, 69
*John (....-p. 1645) m. a. 1635 .....
...... MASS IX, 11, 12; XV, 118;
XVIII, 74, 75; XXXIII, 321*
*John (....-Sept. 19, 1677) m. ....
Mary Smith CONN XXVII, 161*
Jonah (June 28, 1728-1825) m. 1749
.... XV, 118
Joseph (c. 1725-May 12, 1785) m.
.... Frances Coleman XXIX, 65
Richard Croshaw (....-1798) m. 1736
Elizabeth Valentine XXXI, 293;
XXXIII, 108
*Thomas (c. 1580-c. 1635) m. ....
Katherine ...... VA XXV, 207;
XXVIII, 176; XXIX, 65; XXXI, 293;
XXXII, 69; XXXIII, 108*

GRAVES, cont.
Thomas (a. 1585-Nov. 1662) m. ....
  Sarah ...... CONN XXVII, 161
Zebadiah (June 15, 1741-June 6,
  1823) m. Sept. 30, 1784 (2) Lydia
  Graves XXVII, 161

GRAY
Daniel (June 4, 1756-May 23, 1830)
  m. a. 1802 (2) Jemima Rix XXV,
  296
Edward (c. 1629-June 1681) m. Jan.
  16, 1650 (1) Mary Winslow MASS
  XXXIII, 245
James (Aug. 3, 1759-1847) m. Mar.
  26, 1786 Parthenia White XXIV, 76
John (....-....) m. ....
  ...... CONN XXIV, 76; XXV, 296
John (Dec. 3, 1729-Apr. 26, 1810)
  m. Jan. 26, 1775 Desire Cushman
  XXXIII, 245

GREELE, see GREELEY

GREELEY, includes GREELE
Andrew (c. 1617-June 30, 1697) m.
  1643 Mary Moyse MASS VIII, 15;
  X, 242; XVIII, 93
Benjamin (Sept. 26, 1708-1792) m.
  Feb. 2, 1736/7 Ruth Eastman X,
  241
Ezekiel (Oct. 11, 1725-Jan. 21, 1793)
  m. 1744/5 Esther Lovewell XVIII,
  93
Joseph (Sept. 9, 1756-May 13, 1840)
  m. .... Sarah Greeley VIII, 15
Reuben (June 26, 1742-Apr. 1, 1778)
  m. Jan. 7, 1773 Rachel Meloon
  X, 241

GREEN, includes GREENE
Benjamin, Sr. (Feb. 21, 1723/4-1796)
  m. 1759 Mary Douglas XII, 20, 36,
  63
Benjamin (Apr. 7, 1752-Aug. 14,
  1839) m. Jan. 11, 1776 Abigail
  Dodge IV, 101; XVIII, 109
Caleb (Sept. 2, 1744-c. June 1790)
  m. 1773 (2) Welthian Ellis XIX,
  46
Charles (June 19, 1749-1810) m. Nov.
  24, 1768 Waite Bailey XI, 80
Elisha, Jr. (July 7, 1726-1802) m.
  Dec. 4, 1748 Isabel Budlong XXX,
  39, 40
George, Sr. (Nov. 14, 1763-Oct. 9,
  1844) m. a. Oct. 5, 1787 (1)
  Priscilla Smedley XXXIV, 212
John (1590-1657) m. Nov. 4, 1619
  (1) Joanna Tattershall RI IV,
  101; XIII, 110; XVIII, 109; XX,

  67; XXV, 276, 277; XXIX, 251; XXX,
  39, 40; XXXI, 91, 92; XXXIV, 27
John (1606-c. 1695) m. c. 1645 Joan
  Beggerly RI XI, 80; XIX, 46;
  XXIX, 220
John (May 12, 1736-Apr. 19, 1803) m.
  Mar. 10, 1759 Abilene Guild XXX,
  124, 125
John (Aug. 14, 1736-Oct. 29, 1799)
  m. Mar. 19, 1762 Mary Ruggles
  XXVI, 193, 194, 195
Joseph (Mar. 20, 1745-Mar. 25, 1825)
  m. Sept. 9, 1770 Patience Sheffield
  XIII, 110
Peleg (July 24, 1747-Nov. 12, 1835)
  m. c. 1772 Lucy Green XXIX, 220
Peter, Jr. (1725-Oct. 20, 1807) m.
  1750 Judith Love XXV, 276, 277;
  XXIX, 251
Thomas, Sr. (....-....) m. ....
  Margaret ...... PA XXXIV, 212
Thomas (1606-Dec. 19, 1667) m. a.
  1628 Elizabeth ...... MASS XII,
  21, 36, 63; XXVI, 193, 194, 195;
  XXX, 125
Thomas (Mar. 21, 1733/4-Jan. 20,
  1816) m. Mar. 24, 1757 Amy Whipple
  XX, 67
William (1754-p. July 10, 1786) m.
  Dec. 23, 1778 Patience Speight
  XXXI, 91, 92; XXXIV, 26, 27
William (Oct. 8, 1757-Nov. 6, 1818)
  m. .... Mary Tibits XXX, 39, 40

GREENE, see GREEN

GREENLEAF
Edmund (c. Jan. 2, 1574-Mar. 24,
  1671) m. .... (1) Sarah Dole MASS
  XX, 24; XXVIII, 203
Enoch (1751-1836) m. June 2, 1787
  Sarah Quent XX, 24
Joseph (c. 1748-....) m. Nov. 5,
  1782 Margaret Nason XXVIII, 203

GREENWOOD
John (Sept. 2, 1750-Apr. 6, 1807) m.
  a. Jan. 2, 1775 Lucy Whittemore
  XVIII, 73
Thomas (1643-Sept. 1, 1693) m. June
  8, 1670 Hannah Ward MASS XVIII,
  73

GREER
Aquilla (1716-Oct. 30, 1790) m. 1740
  Elizabeth ...... XXIX, 274
James (1650-....) m. 1680 Ann Taylor
  MD XXIX, 274
William (Jan. 29, 1748-Sept. 24,
  1812) m. 1774 Jane ...... XXIX,
  274

GRENELL
Daniel (1729-1801) m. 1758 Ann Chapman XI, 114
Matthew (....-c. 1643) m. .... Rose ...... RI XI, 115

GRIDLEY
Hezekiah, II (Jan. 30, 1732-Feb. 18, 1816) m. Dec. 12, 1754 Abigail Peck XXXIV, 127
Thomas (....-1655) m. Sept. 29, 1644 Mary Seymour CONN XXXIV, 127

GRIFFIN
Cyrus (1748-Dec. 14, 1810) m. c. 1768 Christina Stuart VI, 29
George, Sr. (July 10, 1734-Aug. 6, 1814) m. .... Eve Dorr VII, 31
Jasper (1648-Apr. 17, 1718) m. .... Hannah ...... MASS, NY VII, 31
Thomas (....-a. 1660) m. c. 1645 Sarah ...... VA VI, 29

GRISWOLD
Alexander (1745-June 2, 1815) m. .... Abigail Barnard VII, 24; X, 43; XVII, 28, 29
Benjamin (July 12, 1756-Aug. 14, 1831) m. .... Elizabeth Eastman XXV, 153, 154
Ebenezer (July 29, 1725-p. 1773) m. Nov. 7, 1748 Hannah Merrill XII, 114
Edward (c. 1607-1691) m. Oct. 3, 1630 Margaret ...... CONN IV, 141; VI, 59; VII, 24; IX, 38, 39; X, 30, 32, 33, 43; XVII, 28, 29; XXV, 153, 154, 243; XXXIII, 202; XXXIV, 23
Francis (1635-Oct. 1671) m. .... Mary Tracy CONN XII, 114
George (Jan. 4, 1730-Apr. 26, 1813) m. July 26, 1759 (1) Sarah Jones XXXIII, 202
Isaac, II (Aug. 8, 1749-Sept. 21, 1839) m. .... Mindwell Phelps XXV, 243
Jabez, Jr. (May 12, 1764-Nov. 4, 1827) m. .... Ann Spencer XXXI, 121, 122
John, Sr. (Mar. 6, 1725/6-c. Oct. 27, 1776) m. .... Mary Ward IX, 39
John, Jr. (Aug. 4, 1749-a. 1801) m. .... Abigail Williams IX, 38, 39
Josiah (c. 1752-Jan. 1, 1821) m. .... (2) Susannah Simonds IV, 141; X, 30
Matthew (1620-Sept. 27, 1698) m. Oct. 16, 1646 Anna Wolcott CONN XVIII, 132
Matthew (Mar. 25, 1714-Apr. 28, 1799)

m. Nov. 11, 1743 Ursula Wolcott XVIII, 132
Michael (....-Sept. 26, 1684) m. a. 1646 Ann ...... CONN XXXI, 122
Shubael (Dec. 18, 1724-Feb. 23, 1807) m. June 8, 1754 Abigail Stanley X, 32, 33
Sylvanus (Aug. 5, 1733-July 6, 1811) m. p. 1772 (2) Hannah Webb VI, 59
White (Oct. 22, 1727-1778) m. Feb. 14, 1751 Elizabeth Cheney XXXIV, 23

GROCE, see GROSS

GROESBOECK
John D. (July 12, 1741-1795) m. c. 1773 Cathalyna Van Schaick XXIX, 26
William Claas (c. 1660-Dec. 23, 1722) m. 1684 Gertrury Schuyler NY XXIX, 27

GROOT
Abraham Cornelius (1741-July 1818) m. 1780 (2) Elsie McKinney XVI, 106; XXX, 180
Simon Symonse (....-p. 1696) m. .... Rebecca Du Trieux NY XVI, 106; XXX, 180, 181

GROSS, includes GROCE
Elisha (Mar. 16, 1749-Sept. 20, 1829) m. Oct. 14, 1789 Deborah Sylvester XXVI, 176, 177
Isaac (....-....) m. .... MASS XXVI, 176

GROUT
Elijah (Oct. 29, 1732-Mar. 1807) m. July 17, 1757 Mary (Molly) Willard XXXI, 154, 186
Hilkiah (July 23, 1728-1785) m. .... Submit Hawkes XXI, 130
John (1619-1697) m. c. 1642 (2) Sarah (Busby) Cakebread MASS XXI, 130; XXXI, 154, 186

GROW
John (c. 1636-Jan. 9, 1727) m. Dec. 15, 1669 Hannah Lord MASS XIX, 112
Thomas (Apr. 4, 1743-June 5, 1824) m. June 2, 1767 Experience Goodell XIX, 112

GRYMES
Benjamin (1748-Feb. 12, 1804) m. 1767 (1) Molly ...... XXI, 105; XXII, 71
Charles (1612-....) m. .... VA XXI, 105; XXII, 71

GUENON, see GENUNG

GUERNSEY, includes GARNSEY

Amos (Sept. 2, 1743-Feb. 12, 1813)
m. Nov. 15, 1763 Miriam Pike
XXX, 131
David (May 30, 1764-Mar. 1841) m.
May 23, 1784 Esther Fassett   XXXII,
247
Henry (....-Aug. 13, 1692) m. ..:..
Hannah Munnings   MASS   XXX, 131;
XXXII, 247

GUILD

Jesse (Apr. 11, 1765-June 5, 1848)
m. c. 1787 Zelpha Smith   XIII, 97
John (1612-Oct. 4, 1682) m. Apr. 24,
1645 Elizabeth Crooks   MASS
XIII, 98; XXVIII, 26, 27
Samuel (Oct. 23, 1727-....) m. Oct.
30, 1764 Mehitable Clapp   XXVIII,
26, 27

GUILE

Joseph (1735-Aug. 5, 1785) m. 1758
(2) Mary Franklin   XV, 11, 100
Samuel (c. 1620-Feb. 21, 1683) m.
.... Judith Davis   MASS   XV, 12,
100

GUIMARD, see GUMAER

GULICK

Ferdinand (Nov. 15, 1756-June 4,
1836) m. 1780 Hannah Lee   XXX, 31
Hendrick (....-p. May 11, 1653) m.
.... Geertruyt Willekins   NY XXX, 31
Jochem (a. 1653-a. Aug. 26, 1723) m.
c. 1676 Jacomyntie Van Pelt   NY
XXX, 31

GUMAER, includes GUIMARD

Elias (Jan. 22, 1748-Nov. 7, 1820)
m. Apr. 13, 1769 Gretye Du Pui
XII, 106; XIII, 43
Peter (Nov. 15, 1708-1779) m. ....
Charity De Witt   XII, 106
Pierre (1665-1726/32) m. .... Ester
Hasbrouck   NY XII, 106; XIII, 43

GUNN

Jasper (1606-Jan. 12, 1670/1) m.
.... MASS, CONN VII, 12
Nathaniel (Jan. 24, 1726-Apr. 22,
1807) m. .... Dorothy Marsh   VII,
11

GUNSAUL, includes GONSALUS

Joseph (Dec. 4, 1715-Apr. 1782) m.
1757 Margaret Dutcher   XXXI, 262

Manuel (Emanuel) (....-Apr. 18, 1752)
m. 1707/8 (2) Rebecca Westvaal   NY
XXXI, 262

GURNEY

John (....-a. 1662/3) m. .... (1)
.... MASS XXXII, 164,
165
Joseph Pool (May 9, 1761-July 1,
1851) m. (int.) Dec. 18, 1783
Sarah Reed   XXXII, 164, 165

GUSTIN

Amos (Oct. 7, 1753-Aug. 9, 1823) m.
1798 Susan Jones   XXIX, 175, 233
John (Jan. 9, 1647-July 3, 1719) m.
Jan. 10, 1677/8 Elizabeth Brown
MASS XVI, 49; XXIX, 175, 233
Thomas (July 19, 1725-May 14, 1791)
m. Dec. 11, 1746 Hannah Griswold
XVI, 49

HACKETT

Jabez (c. 1627-Nov. 4, 1686) m. a.
1654 Frances ...... MASS XXIX,
34, 143; XXX, 139
Samuel (1748-1785) m. Jan. 10, 1771
Mary Randall   XXIX, 34, 143; XXX,
139

HACKLEY

Francis (May 16, 1740-July 17, 1817)
m. 1768/9 Fanny Lightfoot   XXIX,
64; XXX, 161
John (....-a. 1698) m. .... Eliza-
beth Andrews   VA XXIX, 64; XXX,
161

HAGAR

Nathan (Jan. 26, 1743/4-1802) m.
Jan. 3, 1771 Anna Bigelow   XXVIII,
46, 47; XXIX, 217, 240
William (....-Jan. 10, 1683/4) m.
Mar. 20, 1644/5 Mary Bemis   MASS
XXVIII, 46, 47; XXIX, 218, 240

HAIGHT, see HOYT

HAILE, see HALE

HAINES, includes HAYNE, HAYNES

Cotton (Oct. 28, 1746-Apr. 23, 1823)
m. c. 1764 Martha Nudd   XXIX, 180
Israel (Dec. 11, 1728-p. 1775) m.
.... Sarah Derby   VIII, 31
John (1740-July 5, 1790) m. 1768
Rachel Austin XIII, 119; XXXI, 64
Jonas (Apr. 26, 1759-Dec. 21, 1835)
m. .... Hannah Cutler   VIII, 31

HALL, cont.
XXII, 84; XXVIII, 14, 185; XXXIV,
34, 76
John (c. 1609-July 23, 1696) m.
.... (2) Elizabeth Learned MASS
XI, 178; XII, 68; XIX, 30
John (Sept. 3, 1617-Mar. 4, 1692)
m. .... Elizabeth Leighton NH
XV, 76
Jonathan (July 19, 1745-Mar. 26,
1811) m. Oct. 14, 1767 Lucy Mil-
drum XXII, 84
Joseph (Nov. 5, 1738-p. 1785) m.
Mar. 3, 1763 Mary Cox XV, 76
Luke (July 4, 1744-Sept. 19, 1826)
m. Aug. 5, 1772 (2) Molly (Martha)
Davis XXVIII, 55, 56; XXIX, 97,
257
Miles (Oct. 23, 1740-Oct. 26, 1801)
m. Feb. 3, 1762 Sarah Bishop
XXXI, 235
Nathaniel (Feb. 8, 1724-July 27,
1816) m. Nov. 7, 1745 Martha
Storrs XI, 178; XII, 68; XIX, 30
Reuben (Mar. 14, 1729/30-p. 1800)
m. a. 1755 Sarah Gray XXXIII,
287, 288
Richard (....-June 23, 1691) m. ....
Elizabeth Collicott MASS XXIX,
299
Richard (1600-1688) m. .... Eliza-
beth Wingfield MD III, 18
Samuel (Oct. 4, 1695-Feb. 26, 1776)
m. Jan. 25, 1727 Eunice Ann Law
XXII, 84
Samuel (May 5, 1731-Feb. 13, 1810)
m. Aug. 28, 1755 Mamie Ives
XXXIV, 34
Stephen (June 22, 1760-Apr. 15,
1838) m. Aug. 1785 Elizabeth
Benjamin XXXIII, 287, 288
Timothy (Feb. 18, 1752-1800) m. Aug.
15, 1775 Sarah Keyes XXIX, 299
William (....-Mar. 8, 1668/9) m.
.... Hester ...... CONN XXXI,
235
William (1613-1675) m. .... Mary
Stephenson RI XXXII, 175

HALLAM
Amos (Aug. 26, 1738-Jan. 3, 1816) m.
Oct. 18, 1758 Desire Stanton
III, 24
John (1662-Nov. 20, 1700) m. Mar.
15, 1683 Prudence Richardson CONN
III, 24

HALLENBECK, includes HALENBEEK
Casper Jacobse (c. 1635-Aug. 1703)
m. 1660 .... NY XXVIII,
22

Isaac (1767-1855) m. 1790 Magdalena
Slingerland XXVIII, 22

HALLETT
Andrew, Sr. (....-1647/8) m. ....
Mary ...... MASS XXXI, 81;
XXXIV, 284
Isaac (Aug. 24, 1742-Oct. 5, 1814)
m. Feb. 4, 1762 Elizabeth Eldridge
XXXIV, 284
James (Sept. 11, 1752-Nov. 18, 1824)
m. Dec. 24, 1778 Susannah Taylor
XXXI, 81

HALLEY
James (June 14, 1707-July 6, 1792)
m. .... Elizabeth Simpson XXXI, 86;
XXXIV, 182
Thomas (1662-1750) m. .... Sara Haw-
ley VA XXXI, 86; XXXIV, 182

HALLOCK
Noah, II (1728-1805) m. 1756 Nancy
Hendrikson XXV, 279, 280
Peter (1600-....) m. .... (Widow)
Howell NY XXV, 279, 280

HALLOWELL
John (1650-Oct. 27, 1706) m. 1675
Mary Holland PA XXXIII, 74, 75
John (Dec. 15, 1753-Jan. 6, 1829) m.
Sept. 18, 1775 (1) Martha ......
XXXIII, 74, 75

HALSEY
Abraham (Feb. 19, 1764-May 7, 1822)
m. Oct. 20, 1791 Nancy Beach
XXVII, 66
Elias (Feb. 3, 1730-Feb. 24, 1792) m.
c. 1769 Hannah Howell XXXII, 235
Jabez (Feb. 13, 1762-1820) m. ....
Effie Brower XII, 29
Jesse (May 18, 1739-1815/8) m. Jan.
14, 1761 Charity White XVI, 137
Stephen (Mar. 19, 1760-Apr. 18, 1818)
m. June 2, 1798 Elizabeth Carmichael
XIII, 122
Thomas (bpt. Jan. 2, 1592-1678) m. a.
1627 (1) Phoebe ......; .... (2)
Ann Johnes MASS, NY XII, 29, 30;
XIII, 122; XVI, 137; XXVII, 66;
XXXII, 235

HALSTEAD
Caleb, Jr. (May 8, 1721-June 4, 1784)
m. July 16, 1744 Rebecca Ogden
XXIX, 101
John (1757/8-Jan. 2, 1826/7) m. c.
1783 Rachel Knapp XXVIII, 179
Jonas (Feb. 23, 1611-c. 1682) m.
c. 1632 Sarah ...... NY XXVIII,

179; XXIX, 101

HAM, includes HAMM
  John (1649-1727) m. May 6, 1668 Mary
    Heard NH V, 124; X, 254
  Moses (July 19, 1733-May 11, 1817)
    m. 1756 Anna Grafton V, 124; X,
    254

HAMERSLEY, see HAMMERSLEY

HAMILTON
  David (1620/30-Sept. 28, 1691) m.
    July 14, 1662/3 Annah Jaxson ME,
    NH XXI, 104
  Edward (June 4, 1759-May 27, 1854)
    m. Jan. 19, 1796 Eleanor Hawkins
    XXI, 34
  Ignatius (1760-1806) m. 1787 Anne
    Catherine Bush XX, 102
  James (bpt. Apr. 5, 1731-....) m.
    Dec. 29, 1757 Charity Keay XXI,
    104
  John (....-1682) m. .... Elizabeth
    Burdit MD XX, 102; XXI, 34
  John (1635-....) m. .... Christian
    ...... MASS XXVIII, 158, 159;
    XXIX, 345
  Nathan (1713-Feb. 14, 1795) m. June
    23, 1732 Ruth Wheeler XXVIII,
    158, 159
  Silas (Feb. 10, 1735/6-1816) m. July
    22, 1763 Hannah Hoyt XXIX, 345

HAMLIN
  David (May 23, 1752-1839) m. Jan. 5,
    1780 Rebecca Beals XXX, 159
  James (1614/5-1690) m. .... Anne
    ...... MASS XXX, 159

HAMM, see HAM

HAMMERSLEY, includes HAMERSLEY
  Andrew (1725-1819) m. July 6, 1761
    Margaret Stelle XVI, 111
  Hugh (1565-....) m. .... Mary Derham
    VA XVI, 40, 111
  William (c. 1761-p. 1800) m. ....
    Sarah Sankey XVI, 40

HAMMOND
  Barzillai (Mar. 9, 1706-a. Jan. 25,
    1779) m. Aug. 16, 1750 Anna Tobey
    XXV, 264
  Benjamin (1621-Apr. 27, 1703) m. 1650
    Mary Vincent MASS X, 16; XXV,
    264; XXXI, 14
  Charles (Jan. 4, 1729-1777) m. ....
    Rebecca Wright XXV, 32
  Ebenezer (May 9, 1743-1815) m. Jan.
    18, 1767 Deborah Terry XXXI,14, 15

Elisha (Feb. 4, 1752-Feb. 25, 1839)
    m. .... Catherine Gardenier XXV,
    264
Faunce (May 20, 1737-Feb. 8, 1813)
    m. Dec. 3, 1761 Mary Holmes X, 16
Isaac (1748-1795) m. Feb. 16, 1773
    Mehitable Prime X, 22
John (1643-Nov. 29, 1707) m. 1667
    Mary Howard MD XXV, 32; XXXIII,
    47, 48; XXXIV, 100
John (June 20, 1741-Aug. 20, 1820) m.
    Nov. 27, 1765 Anna Fiske XV, 88
John, Jr. (Apr. 21, 1754-....) m.
    Apr. 21, 1776 (Thomasin) Tomsey
    Simpson XXXIV, 100
Joseph, Sr. (Feb. 3, 1722/3-1804) m.
    Nov. 2, 1752 Mrs. Esther Pierce
    Gould XXVIII, 17
Joseph, Jr. (June 30, 1753-....) m.
    .... Mary Pierce XXVIII, 17
Josiah (Jan. 31, 1723/4-Aug. 21,
    1802) m. .... Abigail Durkee X,
    202
Paul (Dec. 27, 1757-Aug. 8, 1838) m.
    1780 Mary Fuller XXXIV, 307
Philip (May 23, 1744-1799) m. 1769
    Barbara Arianna Wright XXXIII,
    47, 48
Samuel (1621-Apr. 27, 1703) m. 1650
    Mary Vincent MASS XXXIV, 307
Thomas (bpt. Sept. 2, 1603-Sept. 30,
    1675) m. Mar. 12, 1623 Elizabeth
    Cason MASS X, 202
Thomas (Oct. 31, 1719-1782) m. Aug.
    21, 1741 Martha Olmstead XIX, 135
William (Oct. 30, 1575-Oct. 8, 1662)
    m. June 9, 1605 Elizabeth Paine
    MASS X, 23; XIX, 135; XXVIII, 16,
    17
William (....-Jan. 1729) m. July 9,
    1672 Elizabeth Battlecome MASS
    XV, 88

HANCHETT
  Luke (Feb. 3, 1738-Sept. 23, 1821)
    m. Oct. 16, 1766 Sarah Harmon
    XXIV, 21
  Thomas (1610/20-June 11, 1686) m.
    .... Deliverance Laughton MASS
    XXIV, 21

HANDY, includes HENDY
  George (Oct. 30, 1727-Apr. 6, 1782)
    m. Feb. 9, 1755 Nelly Gilliss
    XXXIII, 175, 176
  Jabez (July 14, 1728-Mar. 11, 1809)
    m. Apr. 22, 1760 Mehitable Pope
    Fish XXXI, 25
  John (1714-....) m. 1745 (1) Keziah
    Eldred VII, 25
  Paul (July 14, 1758-1812) m. ....

HANDY, cont.
.... VII, 25
Richard (1611-Aug. 4, 1670) m. ....
Hannah Elderkin CONN XXIII, 40
Richard (c. 1620-a. June 23, 1719)
m. .... Hannah ...... MASS
VII, 25; XXXI, 25
Samuel (....-c. May 15, 1721) m.
Mar. 31, 1675 Mary Sewall MD
XXXIII, 175, 176
William (Mar. 31, 1760-Dec. 22,
1823) m. July 12, 1786 Martha
Parker XXIII, 40

HANFORD
Phineas (1713-Aug. 17, 1787) m. ....
Hannah Comstock XXIX, 249
Stephen (1748-Nov. 20, 1838) m. Jan.
1, 1771 Phoebe Fitch XXIX, 249
Thomas (1621-Dec. 1693) m. Oct. 22,
1661 (2) Mary (Miles) Ince MASS,
CONN XXIX, 249

HANSCOM
Aaron (bpt. Jan. 7, 1739-Nov. 4,
1826) m. Jan. 10, 1764 Sarah
Seavey XXII, 52
Moses (Mar. 2, 1717-Feb. 26, 1793)
m. Aug. 2, 1740 (1) Mary Field
XXXIV, 212
Thomas (c. 1623-a. 1697) m. May 16,
1664 Ann ...... ME, MASS XXII,
52; XXXIV, 212

HANSFORD
John (....-1661) m. .... Elizabeth
...... VA XXVII, 188
William, Jr. (1732-p. Aug. 6, 1777)
m. 1753 Mary Hyde XXVII, 187, 188

HANSON
Ichabod (Sept. 22, 1741-July 5, 1818)
m. c. 1762 Abigail Hayes XXXI, 96
John (1630-p. Dec. 12, 1713) m. ....
.... DE, MD XX, 159
Nathaniel (Nov. 1, 1761-1836) m.
Jan. 3, 1813 Sally Hodgdon Lougee
XXX, 21, 22, 25
Peter Contee, Sr. (Dec. 9, 1748-Nov.
1776) m. 1767 Mary Hanson XX,
159
Thomas (c. 1586-1666) m. c. 1641
Mary Paul NH XXX, 22, 25; XXXI,
96

HARBER, includes HARBOUR
Noah (Oct. 23, 1757-c. 1847) m. c.
1774 (1) Judith Strange XXXIII,
72, 73, 193
Thomas (1675/1680-....) m. ....
...... VA XXXIII, 72, 73, 193

HARBOUR, see HARBER

HARDENBERGH
Gerrit Jans (1647-1696) m. 1666
Jeapie Schepmoes NY XXVI, 27
Johannes (John A.) (1743-p. 1784)
m. 1770 Rachel DuBois XXVI, 27

HARDIN
Martin (....-....) m. 1671 Madeline
DuSauchoy NY XXXIV, 331
William (Apr. 25, 1741-Mar. 4
1810) m. 1763 Sarah Bledsoe XXXIV,
331

HARDING
Abiel (Aug. 1760-1849) m. Mar. 30,
1786 Olive Smith XXVI, 230, 258,
259; XXVIII, 62, 63
Abraham (1615/7-....) m. c. 1639
Elizabeth Harding MASS XIV, 53;
XXVI, 230, 258, 259; XXVIII, 62,
63
Abraham (June 14, 1720-1806) m. 1741
Anna Dolson XVI, 94; XXV, 69
John (1567-1637) m. ....
...... MASS XXV, 69
Joseph (....-1630) m. 1624 Martha
Doane MASS XXI, 161; XXII, 57;
XXV, 286
Perry (1748-Jan. 21, 1825) m. July
25, 1779 Molly Swan Keen XXI, 161;
XXV, 286
Richard (c. 1580-....) m. ....
...... MASS XVI, 94
Samuel, Sr. (Mar. 29, 1736-....)
m. May 10, 1759 Sarah Harding
XXII, 57
Samuel, Jr. (Sept. 25, 1766-Apr. 16,
1850) m. Nov. 25, 1789 Love May-
hew XXII, 57
Stephen (Oct. 21, 1754-Feb. 4, 1807)
m. Nov. 17, 1779 Martha Marsh
XIV, 53

HARDWICK
James (c. 1647-p. Feb. 7, 1698) m.
.... Ann Armsby VA XXXI, 167
William, Sr. (June 6, 1727-p. Mar.
13, 1802) m. .... Cynthia Parker
XXXI, 167
William, Jr. (Mar. 17, 1760-Mar. 1,
1828) m. Apr. 22, 1790 Nancy Shipp
XXXI, 167

HARDY
Ephraim (Sept. 16, 1745-Mar. 6,
1793) m. Nov. 17, 1767 Susanna
Cheney XXXIV, 40
George (....-a. 1665) m. ....
...... VA X, 63, 64

George (1633-1693) m. .... Mary
  Jackson VA IX, 31, 32, 41
Jesse (Dec. 19, 1760-Dec. 29, 1816)
  m. .... (2) Rhoda Wood XXX, 93
John (1613-1670) m. 1632 Olive
  Council VA XXXI, 115, 210, 250;
  XXXII, 117, 254; XXXIII, 308, 309,
  330; XXXIV, 125
John (c. 1740-1810/2) m. 1773 Ann
  Williams XXXI, 115
Joseph (Feb. 22, 1751-May 22, 1831)
  m. 1788 (1) Margaret Mackenzie
  IX, 31, 32, 41; X, 63, 64
Phineas (July 11, 1726-Mar. 7, 1813)
  m. May 19, 1749 Abigail Gage XXX,
  93; XXXI, 84
Phineas, Jr. (June 4, 1753-Nov. 10,
  1810) m. June 3, 1779 Sarah Wyman
  XXXIV, 161
Stephen (Oct. 10, 1743-Nov. 7, 1808)
  m. July 12, 1768 Hannah Thurston
  XXIX, 244
Thomas (1605-Jan. 4, 1677) m. 1630
  (1) Lydia ...... MASS II, 49;
  XXVIII, 195; XXIX, 245; XXX, 93;
  XXXI, 84; XXXIV, 41, 161
Thomas (June 11, 1756-July 25, 1816)
  m. Jan. 1, 1784 Lucy Colburn
  XXVIII, 195; XXXI, 84
William (....-p. Oct. 21, 1790) m.
  .... Mary ...... XXXI, 210, 250;
  XXXII, 117, 254; XXXIII, 308, 309,
  330; XXXIV, 125
William (1757-1832) m. .... Hannah
  Hyde II, 49

HARLAN
George (Nov. 1, 1650-July 1714) m.
  Sept. 17, 1678 Elizabeth Duck
  DE, PA XXXIV, 35
Isaac (July 22, 1743-Dec. 30, 1830)
  m. Jan. 4, 1775 (2) Margaret Talbot
  XXXIV, 205
Joshua (Apr. 17, 1726-Sept. 11, 1804)
  m. Sept. 28, 1748 Abigail Green
  XXXIV, 35
Michael (c. 1660-June 1729) m. c.
  1690 Dinah Dixon PA XXXIV, 205

HARMENSEN, see HENDRICKSON

HARMON
John (1617-Aug. 28, 1683) m. 1640
  Elizabeth ...... MASS XIV, 43,
  44, 119
Joseph (Jan. 14, 1754-Apr.
  1838) m. Nov. 26, 1778 Eleanor
  King XIV, 43, 44
  119

HARRINDEEN, see HARRINGTON

HARRINGTON, includes HEARNDEN,
  HARRINDEEN
Antipas (Sept. 30, 1753-Jan. 27,
  1803) m. July 14, 1774 Levinah
  Brigham XXX, 177; XXXII, 65
Benjamin (....-1687) m. .... Elizabeth White RI XXVI, 87
Ephraim (....-July 6, 1821) m. Jan.
  19, 1772 Sarah Harrindeen XXVI,
  87
John (Feb. 28, 1742-....) m. Dec. 3,
  1760 Mary Wooten XXVI, 206, 207
Peter (May 4, 1752-July 29, 1813)
  m. Feb. 9, 1775 Anna Hammond XIV,
  69
Robert (1616-May 11, 1707) m. Oct.
  1, 1649 Susanna George MASS XIV,
  69; XXVI, 206, 207; XXX, 177;
  XXXII, 65

HARRIS
Abiel (Dec. 20, 1754-Sept. 21, 1831)
  m. Nov. 17, 1774 Susanna Snell
  XXV, 54, 55
Arthur (....-p. 1673) m. .... Martha
  ...... MASS XXV, 54, 55
Christopher (Feb. 5, 1725-1794) m.
  Mar. 8, 1764 (2) Agnes McCord
  XIV, 30; XVI, 57, 58
Daniel (July 24, 1759-Apr. 14, 1842)
  m. Mar. 9, 1780 Lucy Fox XXVI,
  254, 255; XXXII, 24
Ebenezer (Feb. 16, 1756-p. 1836)
  m. .... Lydia ...... XXXII, 143
Ephraim (June 14, 1732-Nov. 2, 1794)
  m. Jan. 30, 1755 (1) Jane Pierson
  XXXI, 48, 49
Gyles (Nov. 1, 1724-Apr. 26, 1797)
  m. Nov. 26, 1747 Mary March XX,
  53
James (1640-1716) m. 1666 Sarah
  Dennison CONN XIII, 50; XVII,
  107; XVIII, 36; XXV, 95
Nathaniel (Apr. 2, 1743-Mar. 12,
  1812) m. Feb. 1, 1764 Mary Tozer
  XIII, 50; XVII, 107; XVIII, 36;
  XXV, 95
Robert (1630-1700) m. 1650 Mary
  Claiborne Rice VA XIV, 30, 53;
  XVI, 57, 58; XXX, 46
Robert (Mar. 8, 1741-a. July 10,
  1806) m. 1762 Lucretia Brown XIV,
  53; XXX, 46
Stephen (Apr. 23, 1761-Sept. 4,
  1843) m. .... Lydia Beverly XXVII,
  190, 191
Thomas (....-a. Nov. 26, 1681) m.
  .... RI, MASS, NY
  XXXI, 48, 49
Thomas (....-June 7, 1686) m. ....
  Elizabeth ...... MASS XXVI, 254,

HARRIS, cont.
    255; XXVII, 190; XXXII, 24, 143
    Thomas (c. 1651-Aug. 2, 1687) m.
    Nov. 15, 1647 Martha Lake   MASS
    XX, 53

HARRISON
    Benjamin, I (1600-1648) m. ....
    Mary Stringer   VA   I, 39;   XXVIII,
    38, 39; XXXII, 252
    Benjamin (1726-1791) m. .... Eliza-
    beth Bassett   I, 39
    Carter Henry (Aug. 22, 1732-1793/4)
    m. 1760 Susannah Randolph XXXII,
    251, 252
    James (Mar. 23, 1720-Dec. 1794) m.
    .... (2) Abigail Foot   VIII, 25;
    XII, 22
    Noah (Nov. 19, 1737-Mar. 7, 1823) m.
    June 30, 1767 Hannah Rogers   VIII,
    20; IX, 17, 26, 50; XI, 125
    Richard (....-Oct. 20, 1653) m. ....
    Sarah ...... CONN VIII, 20, 25;
    IX, 17, 26, 50; XI, 125; XII, 22
    Robert (Feb. 11, 1755-July 8, 1797)
    m. Apr. 12, 1777 Henrietta Maria
    Hardamon XXVIII, 38, 39

HART
    Amasa (June 19, 1754-p. 1794) m.
    .... Phoebe Roberts   VIII, 8
    Benjamin (Oct. 1732-Jan. 2, 1802)
    m. .... Nancy Morgan XXXII, 192
    Daniel, Sr. (Jan. 22, 1747/8-May 9,
    1812) m. Feb. 5, 1771 Bethiah
    Mackentire XXXI, 116, 117
    David (c. 1730-Aug. 25, 1802) m.
    .... Susannah Nunn   XXX, 97
    Edward (....-....) m. ....
    ...... NY XVII, 71
    Elijah (Sept. 26, 1735-Dec. 10,
    1800) m. .... Sarah Gilbert   XIII,
    47
    Isaac (c. 1614-Feb. 10, 1699/1700)
    m. c. 1650 Elizabeth Hutchins
    MASS XXXI, 117
    John (....-1671) m. ....
    ...... NY XXIX, 362
    John (Nov. 16, 1651-Sept. 1714) m.
    1683 Susannah Rush   PA   XXV, 120,
    121
    John (....-p. 1779) m. ....
    Turner XXX, 97
    John (July 8, 1706-Oct. 30, 1777) m.
    c. 1738 (2) Sarah (Savell) Cutt
    XXX, 163
    John (1711-1779) m. c. 1741 Deborah
    Scudder XXIX, 362
    Jonathan (....-Oct. 18, 1785) m. ....
    Elizabeth Bloomer XVII, 71, 72
    Joseph (Sept. 1, 1715-Feb. 25, 1788)

    m. Oct. 9, 1740 Elizabeth Collett
    XXV, 120, 121
    Luke (Jan. 8, 1738/9-1826) m. Mar.
    1764 Deborah Barnes XXXIV, 209
    Phineas (1758-Nov. 7, 1828) m. ....
    Betsy Wickwire XXI, 65, 66
    Stephen (c. 1605-Mar. 1682/3) m.
    .... (2) Margaret Smith MASS,
    CONN VIII, 8; XII, 45; XIII, 47;
    XXI, 65, 66; XXXIV, 209
    Thomas, Sr. (....-....) m. ....
    .... VA XXX, 97; XXXII,
    192
    Thomas (1606-Mar. 8, 1673) m. ....
    Alice ...... MASS XXX, 163
    Thomas (Sept. 29, 1714-July 12,
    1801) m. .... Hannah Coe VIII,
    8; XII, 45

HARTSHORN
    Beriah (Jan. 1, 1757-p. 1789) m.
    Sept. 7, 1782 Lydia Hunt   XII,
    43; XXII, 74
    Oliver (Nov. 1, 1761-Dec. 18, 1810)
    m. Feb. 26, 1786 Hannah Pettingill
    XXXIII, 288, 289
    Rufus (Sept. 17, 1728-p. 1785) m.
    Dec. 24, 1747 Lucy Avery   XXII,
    74
    Thomas (1614-May 18, 1683) m. 1647
    Susanna Buck MASS XII, 44; XXII,
    74; XXXIII, 288, 289

HARTWELL
    Samuel (June 25, 1742-Aug. 12, 1829)
    m. Sept. 12, 1769 Mary Flint   XXVI,
    142, 143
    Thomas (1759-July 15, 1835) m. Aug.
    16, 1784 Hannah Ashe   XXII, 60
    William (1613-Mar. 12, 1690) m. ....
    Susan ...... MASS XXII, 60;
    XXVI, 142, 143

HARVEY
    Isaiah (Dec. 21, 1749-....) m. ....
    Mary Sargent XXXIV, 227
    John (Feb. 5, 1654-Mar. 8, 1706) m.
    1685/6 Sarah (Barnes) Rowell MASS
    XXXIV, 227
    Josiah (Oct. 19, 1745-1807) m. ....
    Elizabeth Bates   V, 113
    Levi (July 1745-1807) m. c. 1780
    Elizabeth Randlett   III, 32, 33,
    34
    Rufus (Oct. 7, 1758-Sept. 9, 1807)
    m. 1790 Sarah Jones   X, 184
    Thomas (1617-1651) m. .... Elizabeth
    Andrews MASS V, 113
    William (c. 1614-Aug. 15, 1658) m.
    Apr. 2, 1639 (1) Joanne Hucker; c.
    1650 (2) Mrs. Martha Slocum Copp

MASS III, 32, 33, 34; X, 184

HARWOOD
Benjamin (Nov. 13, 1766-p. Nov. 24, 1852) m. July 1789 Elizabeth Cutler XXVI, 101, 102
Nathan (Feb. 22, 1737-Feb. 3, 1790) m. Feb. 16, 1760 Hulda Bannister XXXI, 183
Nathaniel (1626-Feb. 7, 1716) m. .... Elizabeth ...... MASS XIV, 90; XV, 19; XXI, 81, 82, 163, 164; XXVI, 102; XXXI, 183
Thomas (....-c. 1652) m. p. 1620 (2) Ann ...... VA XXVIII, 122
William (1710-a. 1782) m. .... Mary ...... XXVIII, 122
Zachariah (Mar. 11, 1742-June 6, 1821) m. .... Lovina Rice XIV, 90; XV, 19; XXI, 81, 82, 164

HASBROUCK
Abraham (1650-Mar. 17, 1717) m. Nov. 17, 1676 Maria Deyo NY XXV, 240; XXXIII, 272, 273
Isaac (Mar. 21, 1712-Apr. 6, 1778) m. July 14, 1766 Antje Low XXXIII, 272, 273
Jacob J. (Apr. 5, 1727-June 6, 1806) m. Apr. 14, 1751 Jannetje DuBois XXXIII, 173; XXXIV, 205
Jean (John) (1642/3-p. Aug. 14, 1714) m. a. 1664 Anna Deyo NY XXXIII, 172, 173; XXXIV, 205
Petrus (Aug. 20, 1738-p. 1783) m. Oct. 26, 1765 Sarah Bevier XXV, 240

HASCALL, see HASKELL

HASELTINE, see HAZELTINE

HASKELL, includes HASCALL
Elias (July 31, 1752-Mar. 27, 1812) m. Jan. 20, 1774 Sarah Roberts XXX, 195
Jeremiah (1740-1838) m. Mar. 22, 1773 Hannah Nichols XXXIII, 114, 115; XXXIV, 99
Roger (bpt. Mar. 6, 1613-June 1667) m. a. 1639 Elizabeth Hardy MASS XXXIII, 114, 115; XXXIV, 100, 178
Samuel (Feb. 17, 1733/4-Nov. 15, 1820) m. June 20, 1765 Elizabeth Macomber XXXIV, 178
William, I (Nov. 8, 1617-Aug. 20, 1693) m. Nov. 6, 1643 Mary Tybbot MASS XXX, 195

HASKINS, includes HOSKINE, HOSKINS
Bartholomew (1601-....) m. ....

.... *VA XVII, 36*
Eli (Nov. 21, 1759-Nov. 12, 1846) m. 1789 Rhoda Drake XII, 11; XXX, 265; XXXII, 245; XXXIV, 213
George, Sr. (....-p. 1781) m. .... Mary ...... XXXIV, 169
John (Mar. 22, 1751-Dec. 19, 1813) m. 1778 Elizabeth Chaney XVII, 36
William (c. 1604/5-Sept. 7, 1695) m. Dec. 21, 1638 Ann Hinde MASS XII, 11; XXX, 265; XXXII, 245; XXXIV, 170, 213
William (Mar. 7, 1717-1812) m. .... Rebekah Lincoln XII, 11

HASSELTINE, see HAZELTINE

HASSEN, see HAZEN

HASTINGS
Amos (Feb. 3, 1757-July 28, 1829) m. Sept. 10, 1778 Elizabeth Wiley XXXIV, 53
Eliphalet (Oct. 10, 1734-1824) m. Aug. 20, 1761 Susan Fisk XV, 5
Robert (May 11, 1653/4-a. 1721) m. Oct. 31, 1676 Elizabeth Davis MASS XXXIV, 53
Samuel (Mar. 30, 1721-Feb. 8, 1820) m. .... Lydia Tidd V, 80
Samuel (July 11, 1757-Jan. 8, 1834) m. .... Lydia Nelson V, 80
Thomas (1605-1685) m. Apr. 1651 (2) Margaret Cheney MASS V, 80; XV, 5

HATCH
Anthony (....-a. Jan. 1688/9) m. .... Elizabeth ...... VA XXXI, 29
David, Jr. (May 2, 1735-....) m. Jan. 16, 1755 Desire Standish XXXIV, 41
Elisha (bpt. Mar. 27, 1743-Sept. 15, 1843) m. Aug. 7, 1766 Betsy Howland XV, 98, 99
John (Dec. 8, 1760-June 16, 1849) m. Oct. 6, 1785 Anna Wadhams XXII, 105
Joseph (May 28, 1754-1795) m. May 26, 1774 Mrs. Phebe (Tilden) Lewis XIV, 110
Lemuel (....-a. Feb. 3, 1777) m. .... Mary Fonville XXXI, 29
Oliver (Feb. 5, 1755-Feb. 20, 1839) m. Oct. 16, 1788 (3) Phoebe Perry XXVIII, 146
Samuel (June 6, 1719/20-Apr. 30, 1797) m. May 7, 1758 Hannah Sweet XX, 57
Simeon (1757-Oct. 14, 1802) m. .... Jemima Pease XXV, 131

HATCH, cont.
  Thomas (c. 1596-a. June 14, 1646) m.
  1622 Lydia ...... MASS XXXIV, 41
  Thomas (c. 1603-1661) m. c. 1624
  Grace ...... MASS XXII, 105;
  XXV, 131; XXVIII, 146
  William (c. 1598-Nov. 6, 1651) m.
  July 9, 1624 Jane Young MASS
  XIV, 110; XVI, 99; XX, 57

HATHAWAY
  Isaac (July 29, 1729-Dec. 25, 1798)
  m. Aug. 13, 1752 Phebe Bailey
  XXXI, 120
  John (c. 1629/30-1704/5) m. c. 1649
  Martha Shepard MASS VII, 35;
  XXXIII, 39
  Joshua (Jan. 19, 1728-May 4, 1807)
  m. Aug. 23, 1749 Mary (Reed) Evans
  XXXIII, 39
  Nicholas (....-....) m. ....
  ...... MASS XXVIII, 54, 55;
  XXXI, 120
  Simeon (June 25, 1719-1804) m. Nov.
  11, 1742 Deborah Austin XXVIII,
  54, 55
  Stephen (Sept. 4, 1745-Apr. 29, 1815)
  m. .... Hope Pierce VII, 35

HAUGHTON
  Jonathan (Oct. 19, 1741-Dec. 1817)
  m. Jan. 11, 1766 Deborah Pratt
  XXIX, 27, 28, 120
  Thomas (....-a. July 29, 1707) m.
  .... Sarah ...... NC XXIX, 27,
  28, 120

HAUKSIE, see HOXIE

HAULEY, see HOLLEY

HAVEN
  Elias (June 18, 1742-Apr. 19, 1775)
  m. 1764 Jemina Whiting XVII, 156
  Jedediah (bpt. Dec. 11, 1743-Sept.
  18, 1811) m. Feb. 20, 1765 Susannah Vaile XIII, 7
  Richard (....-1703) m. .... Susan-
  nah ...... MASS XIII, 7; XVII,
  156; XXXIII, 53, 296
  Samuel (Jan. 4, 1762-Sept. 22, 1840)
  m. Aug. 19, 1784 Desire Cloyes
  XXXIII, 53, 54, 296

HAWARD, see HAYWOOD

HAWES
  Edward (....-June 28, 1687) m. Apr.
  15, 1648 Eliony Lombard MASS
  XXXII, 239
  James (Jan. 21, 1761-Jan. 18, 1826)

  m. Feb. 12, 1788 Jemima Farrington
  XXXII, 239

HAWKINS
  Alexander (June 17, 1713-May 2, 1787)
  m. Apr. 19, 1740 Tabitha Satterly
  XVIII, 51
  Benjamin, Jr. (May 8, 1759-Jan. 10,
  1838) m. July 28, 1816 Elizabeth
  Arnold Colby XXV, 294
  Robert (1610-July 7, 1704) m. ....
  Mary ...... MASS, NY XVIII, 51;
  XXI, 10, 11; XXXII, 241; XXXIII,
  319; XXXIV, 266
  William (1609-1699) m. .... Margaret
  Harwood RI XXV, 294
  Zachariah (c. 1710-1800) m. ....
  Abigail Jayne XXI, 10, 11; XXXII,
  241; XXXIII, 319; XXXIV, 266

HAWKS
  Eleazer (Aug. 25, 1747-Jan. 1, 1827)
  m. .... (1) Rhoda Kingsley X, 257
  John (....-June 30, 1662) m. ....
  Elizabeth ...... CONN, MASS X,
  257; XXXIV, 45
  Paul (Nov. 7, 1736-Oct. 15, 1814) m.
  a. 1766 Lois Wait XXXIV, 45

HAWLEY
  Aaron (1739-July 31, 1803) m. Nov.
  24, 1759 (1) Elizabeth Hawley
  V, 60; XIV, 102; XVI, 63; XIX, 60
  Joseph, I (1603-May 20, 1690) m.
  1646 Catherine Birdsey CONN V,
  60; VI, 112; XIV, 102; XVI, 63;
  XIX, 60; XXVIII, 42
  Joseph Chrysostom (Oct. 10, 1757-
  Apr. 1845) m. .... Amey Bradley
  VI, 111
  Thomas (Sept. 8, 1734-Aug. 28, 1817)
  m. Nov. 16, 1760 Sarah Olcott
  XXVIII, 42, 43

HAYDEN, includes HEYDON
  Aaron (Mar. 4, 1750-Aug. 11, 1804)
  m. .... Sara Rice XII, 16
  Augustine (Aug. 24, 1740-Feb. 24,
  1823) m. Dec. 7, 1769 Cynthia
  Filer XIV, 88
  David (Oct. 8, 1738-Feb. 3, 1813)
  m. Mar. 11, 1761 Jemima Ellsworth
  XXXI, 30
  Francis (1628-1694) m. .... Thoma-
  sine Butler VA, MD XXIX, 165
  George (c. 1750-p. 1801) m. ....
  Mary ...... XXIX, 165
  John (....-1678) m. .... Susanna
  ...... MASS XVI. 98
  Levi (May 28, 1747-Aug. 24, 1821) m.
  1772 Margaret Strong XVII, 141

Richard (Nov. 7, 1741-1829) m. ....
Mary ...... XVI, 98
William (1600-Sept. 27, 1669) m.
.... (1) .... MASS
XII, 16; XIV, 88; XVII, 141;
XXXI, 30

HAYES, includes HAYS
Daniel (Aug. 26, 1723-Feb. 26, 1807)
m. Mar. 22, 1749 Sarah Plumer
XXV, 57
George, Sr. (1655-Sept. 2, 1725) m.
Aug. 29, 1683 Abigail Dibble CONN
XXIX, 359
Jacob (Aug. 5, 1757-Dec. 21, 1848)
m. Mar. 15, 1781 Jane Gray XXXIV,
76
John (....-Oct. 25, 1708) m. June 28,
1686 Mary Horne NH XXV, 57;
XXXIV, 76
Jonathan, Jr. (1744-Mar. 9, 1790) m.
1767 Anna Noble XXIX, 359
Richard (May 12, 1753-Oct. 6, 1826)
m. July 17, 1777 Lydia Watson
XXV, 57

HAYNE, see HAINES

HAYNES, see HAINES

HAYS, see HAYES

HAYWARD, includes HAWARD, HAYWOOD, HEY-
WARD, HEYWOOD. See also HOWARD
Amos (Oct. 3, 1719-Feb. 7, 1792) m.
Aug. 30, 1743 Mary Buttrick X,
266
Charles (Dec. 24, 1723-....) m. July
14, 1748 Abigail Hubbard XVIII,
42
Daniel (Feb. 2, 1752-Jan. 8, 1842)
m. Apr. 22, 1777 Bethiah Howard
XXV, 59
Edmund (May 12, 1720-Feb. 12, 1781)
m. Aug. 12, 1751 Anna Snell XIX,
165
John (c. 1615-Jan. 11, 1707) m. Aug.
17, 1656 Rebecca Atkinson MASS X,
266; XII, 57; XVII, 77 XVIII, 42;
XXXII, 282; XXXIII, 314
Jonas (Aug. 21, 1721-July 28, 1808)
m. Sept. 13, 1753 Ann Prescott
XII, 57; XVII, 76, 77; XXXIII,
314
Nathaniel (Nov. 5, 1748-Nov. 18,
1834) m. July 1, 1793 Mary Chamber-
lain XXXII, 281, 282
Thomas (....-1681) m. .... Susannah
...... MASS XIX, 165; XXV, 59
Waldo (Mar. 20, 1758-Nov. 18, 1834) m.
Dec. 5, 1781 Lucy Bartlett XIX, 165

HAZELTINE, includes HASELTINE,
HASSELTINE
James (July 20, 1729-Nov. 3, 1803)
m. .... (2) Hannah Kimball VII,
19, 20
John (c. 1620-Dec. 23, 1690) m. ....
Jane Auter MASS XXVIII, 8
Joseph (Dec. 27, 1731-May 30, 1798)
m. .... Elizabeth Abbott XI, 105
Nathaniel (Sept. 20, 1656-Jan. 14,
1723/4) m. July 20, 1688 (2) Ruth
(Plumer) Jacques MASS XXVIII, 8
Peter (May 19, 1751-Apr. 1, 1823) m.
May 7, 1774 Sarah Jones XXVIII, 8
Robert (1615/8-Aug. 27, 1674) m. Oct.
23, 1639 Ann ...... MASS VII, 19,
20; XI, 105

HAZEN, includes HASSEN
Caleb (Nov. 7, 1749-Mar. 31, 1806)
m. .... Ruth Wright XXX, 116
Edward (bpt. Dec. 14, 1614-July 22,
1683) m. Mar. 1650 (2) Hannah Grant
MASS XIV, 115; XXX, 116; XXXII,
105; XXXIII, 27, 84
Edward (May 2, 1738-1796) m. Jan.
10, 1758 (1) Sarah Willard XXXII,
105; XXXIII, 27
Moses (Feb. 1758-Jan. 20, 1835) m.
.... Mary Caldwell XXXIII, 84
Thomas (Sept. 30, 1719-Aug. 19,
1782) m. Mar. 7, 1742 Ann Terry
XIV, 115

HEAD
Arthur (a. 1671-a. May 7, 1718) m.
.... Sarah ...... NH XVII, 80,
107
Benjamin (1731-Aug. 19, 1803) m.
1754 Martha Sherman (Marshall)
XXXIV, 308
James (....-c. 1748) m. .... Betty
...... VA XXXIV, 308
James (Nov. 16, 1727-Aug. 31, 1777)
m. Dec. 14, 1748 Sarah Thurston
XVII, 80, 107

HEALD, see HALE

HEALE, see HALE

HEARNDEN, see HARRINGTON

HEARNE
William (1627-Oct. 1691) m. Sept. 2,
1683 Mary Cuthbert MD XXX, 285
William (1746-Sept. 21, 1832) m. ....
Tabitha Hearne XXX, 284, 285

HEATH
Abraham (....-Aug. 22, 1688) m. ....

HEATH, cont.
    Ursula ...... *VA XXXI, 313*
    Bartholomew (c. 1615-Jan. 15, 1681)
    m. a. 1643 Hannah Moyce MASS
    XXII, 82
    Bartholomew (1735-p. 1790) m. ....
    Ann Millard XXII, 82
    Peleg (Apr. 8, 1747-July 4, 1786)
    m. .... Annie Kent V, 92, 93
    William (....-May 29, 1652) m. ....
    Mary Spear MASS V, 92, 93
    William (Nov. 7, 1725-Oct. 20, 1791)
    m. Aug. 24, 1749 Mary Bannister
    XXXI, 313

HEATON
    Isaac (June 20, 1731-Apr. 1, 1814)
    m. 1760 Hannah Bowen XI, 186
    Nathaniel (a. 1619-1643/9) m. ....
    Elizabeth ...... MASS XI, 186

HEDGE, see HEDGES

HEDGES, includes HEDGE
    Joseph (1740-Sept. 1828) m. 1774
    Elizabeth Rawlings XXIII, 29
    Joseph (1743-1804) m. .... Sarah
    Biggs XXIV, 108
    Samuel (c. 1650-a. June 18, 1714)
    m. Feb. 1676 Anne Fenwick NJ
    XXIII, 29; XXIV, 109
    William (....-1678) m. ....
    ...... DE XXXIV, 79
    William (c. Sept. 1742-c. Apr. 1777)
    m. c. 1763 Elizabeth ......
    XXXIV, 79

HEMENWAY
    Daniel, Sr. (Feb. 2, 1719-Nov. 15,
    1794) m. June 7, 1743 Ruth Bige-
    low XXIX, 192
    Ralph (....-June 1678) m. July 5,
    1634 Elizabeth Hewes MASS XXIX,
    192

HENDERSON
    Nathaniel, Sr. (1736-1803) m. 1725
    Rebecca Nallie Holliday XXVIII,
    49, 50
    Nathaniel, Jr. (1756-1821) m. 1784
    Rebecca Jamina Branson XXVIII,
    49, 50
    Thomas (....-....) m. ....
    ...... VA XXVIII, 49, 50

HENDRICK
    Daniel (c. 1610-1700) m. 1642
    Dorothy Pike NH XVII, 39
    Jabez, IV (Dec. 19, 1720-Jan. 18,
    1808) m. Jan. 4, 1749 Lois Marcy
    XVII, 39

HENDRICKSEN, includes HARMENSEN
    Hendrick (....-a. 1677) m. Feb. 13,
    1658 Egbertie Jans NY XXV, 173,
    174
    Jan (John) (Nov. 9, 1733-Sept. 12,
    1815) m. c. 1753 Mary ...... XXV,
    173, 174

HENDY, see HANDY

HENNION
    John (Johannis) (c. 1740-....) m.
    .... Sara ...... XXX, 209
    Nathaniel Pietersen (....-....) m.
    June 28, 1664 Anneken Ackerman
    NY XXX, 209

HENSHAW
    Joshua (1644-a. Mar. 3, 1723) m.
    .... Elizabeth Sumner MASS XXVI,
    271, 272, 273, 274
    William (Mar. 16, 1736-July 8, 1799)
    m. .... Agnes Anderson XXVI, 271,
    272, 273, 274

HERBERT
    Walter (....-....) m. .... Bridget
    ...... NJ XXX, 146
    William Henry, Sr. (Aug. 2, 1762-
    ....) m. Aug. 24, 1784 Elizabeth
    Tallman XXX, 145, 146

HERICKE, see HERRICK

HERNDON
    Edward (July 16, 1738-May 11, 1831)
    m. Nov. 30, 1762 Mary Ann Gaines
    XXXI, 49
    John (1748-a. July 6, 1821) m. Dec.
    21, 1773 Mary Ann Clarkson XXVIII,
    97; XXXIII, 69
    William (1649-1722) m. 1677 Catherine
    Digges VA XXVIII, 97; XXXI, 49;
    XXXIII, 69

HERRICK, includes HERICKE
    Daniel (May 18, 1742-p. 1795) m. c.
    1774 Mary Guile XXV, 87
    Ebenezer (Mar. 12, 1759-Jan. 7, 1842)
    m. Sept. 26, 1782 Lydia Eaton
    XXVI, 96; XXIX, 258
    Elijah (1758-1808) m. 1788 Hannah
    Russell XXII, 97; XXXI, 278
    Henry (Aug. 16, 1604-1671) m. a.
    1629 Edythe Laskin MASS XXII,
    97; XXV, 87; XXVI, 36, 95, 96;
    XXIX, 258; XXXI, 278; XXXII, 80,
    81
    Stephen (Mar. 1760-Nov. 2, 1841) m.
    1783 Rebecca McCray XXVI, 36,
    37

Zebulon (c. 1733-....) m. .... Maria Brown XXXII, 80, 81

HERSEY
Jeremiah, Jr. (Oct. 18, 1741-Oct. 7, 1796) m. Dec. 31, 1772 Mary Hersey XXII, 148
William (....-Mar. 22, 1657/8)m. .... Elizabeth ...... MASS XXII, 148

HEWINS
Jacob (a. 1650-Nov. 19, 1711) m. .... Mary ...... MASS XVII, 18, 19; XXVIII, 112, 113
William (Dec. 16, 1735-Mar. 4, 1802) m. Nov. 27, 1759 Ruth Cummings XVII, 18, 19; XXVIII, 112, 113

HEWIT, see HEWITT

HEWITT, includes HEWIT, HUGHITT
Asa (bpt. May 2, 1762-July 5, 1824) m. .... Mary Newton XXVI, 79
Thomas (....-c. 1662) m. Apr. 26, 1659 Hannah Palmer CONN XXVI, 79, 228; XXVII, 128
William (June 3, 1749-....) m. Mar. 1, 1772 Sarah Coye XXVI, 228; XXVII, 128

HEYDON, see HAYDEN

HEYWARD, see HAYWARD or HOWARD

HEYWOOD, see HAYWARD

HIBBARD
Elihu (Jan. 14, 1759-Mar. 1, 1812) m. 1796 Mary Haley XXXII, 253
Robert (Mar. 13, 1613-May 7, 1684) m. .... Joanna Fairfield MASS XXXII, 253

HICHBORN
David (a. 1621-1650) m. .... Catherine ...... MASS XI, 33
Robert (Mar. 28, 1742-Oct. 18, 1800) m. July 17, 1765 Susan Ellenwood XI, 33
Thomas (June 30, 1708-June 16, 1776) m. Feb. 6, 1730 (1) Hannah Fadree XI, 33

HICKES, see HICKS

HICKOX
Samuel (a. Feb. 28, 1638-a. Feb. 28, 1694) m. .... Hannah Upson CONN XXVI, 163
Stephen (June 30, 1749-Sept. 9, 1836)
m. .... Rebecca Robinson XXVI, 163

HICKS
David (c. 1749-p. 1827) m. Nov. 4, 1772 Mary Sprague XXXIV, 249
John (Oct. 6, 1761-Oct. 11, 1834) m. Mar. 4, 1780 Elizabeth Doty XXXII, 39
Joseph (Aug. 12, 1714-Apr. 22, 1803) m. Jan. 21, 1753 (2) Catharin Filkin XXXIV, 320
Robert (1580-Mar. 24, 1647) m. 1596 (1) Elizabeth Morgan MASS XXV, 109, 110, 111; XXXII, 39; XXXIV, 320
Thomas (....-p. Jan. 10, 1653) m. .... Margaret ...... MASS XXXIV, 249
Thomas (1732-1776) m. 1770 Phebe Pearsell XXV, 109, 110, 111

HIGBEE, see HIGBY

HIGBY, includes HIGBEE
Edward (Feb. 2, 1615/6-Sept. 1699) m. c. 1647 Jedidah Skidmore MASS, CONN, NY XXI, 46; XXIX, 384, 390
Elihu (Aug. 5, 1749-Dec. 30, 1777) m. Dec. 22, 1771 Martha Green XXIX, 390
Peter (1760-1845) m. .... XXI, 46
Richard (1753-a. Apr. 26, 1825) m. 1780 Abigail Steelman XXIX, 384

HIGDON
John (1757-Sept. 16, 1816) m. 1792 Mary ...... XXIX, 208, 290, 304, 335
Richard (c. 1625-c. 1665) m. c. 1651 Jane Brookes VA XXIX, 208, 290, 304, 335

HIGGINS
Abisha (June 12, 1753-Jan. 17, 1812) m. Apr. 13, 1780 (2) Hannah Harding XX, 141, 142
Cornelius (July 22, 1721-Oct. 14, 1803) m. Sept. 29, 1743 Sarah Hawes XXXIV, 145
Israel (Oct. 3, 1728-a. Apr. 1, 1793) m. Feb. 15, 1753 (2) Elizabeth Aiken XV, 19
Israel (c. 1742-Nov. 11, 1818) m. Nov. 26, 1767 Mary Snow XX, 142
Moses (1742/3-Feb. 12, 1818) m. Dec. 10, 1767 Dorcas Brainard XXX, 44
Nathaniel (1738-....) m. Oct. 4, 1760 Elizabeth Haviland XXXII, 75

HIGGINS, cont.
Reuben (May 18, 1739-Sept. 2, 1823)
m. Nov. 15, 1761 Mercy Dyer XXIX,
246; XXXII, 50
Richard (bpt. Aug. 1, 1603-a. 1675)
m. Dec. 11, 1634 Lydia Chandler
MASS, NJ XV, 19; XX, 141, 142;
XXIX, 246; XXX, 44; XXXII, 50, 75;
XXXIV, 145

HIGH
John (1655-1740) m. 1676 Sallie .....
VA XV, 91
John (1750-a. May 5, 1782) m. 1781
Martha Madison XV, 91

HIGLEY
Asa (Jan. 31, 1745-Feb. 28, 1805)
m. c. 1770 Eunice Colton XXX,
151, 152
John (July 22, 1649-Aug. 25, 1714)
m. Nov. 9, 1671 Hannah Drake CONN
XXX, 151, 152

HILDRETH
Jonathan (Apr. 9, 1753-Dec. 24, 1818)
m. Aug. 14, 1779 Eunice Warren
XXXIV, 152
Oliver (July 11, 1723-Feb. 1, 1793)
m. Oct. 26, 1744 Ann Blaisdell
XXXIV, 152
Richard (1605-Feb. 23, 1693) m. May
1645 Elizabeth ...... MASS XXXIV,
152

HILL
Abraham (1734-Dec. 16, 1812) m. Feb.
16, 1757/8 Susanna Wellington
XXXII, 108
Daniel (July 16, 1761-Oct. 28, 1826)
m. Aug. 22, 1784 Elizabeth Burleigh XVII, 113
David (Mar. 29, 1762-Nov. 4, 1813)
m. .... Mercy Holbrook XI, 54
Ebenezer (Feb. 26, 1742-Mar. 27,
1798) m. Jan. 17, 1765 Mabel Sherwood II, 27, 30; XXV, 71; XXXIII,
185, 186, 303
Ira (July 17, 1755-Oct. 13, 1841)
m. Feb. 2, 1786 Esther Post XXVII,
97
Jabez (June 17, 1744-Oct. 19, 1779)
m. Nov. 12, 1771 Sarah Read XI,
46, 48, 51; XXV, 90, 91, 231, 232;
XXX, 16
James (Dec. 20, 1734-Aug. 22, 1811)
m. Jan. 31, 1761 Sarah Coffin
XVII, 113; XX, 60
James (Apr. 1, 1754-Dec. 29, 1811)
m. Sept. 30, 1776 (1) Eunice
Gronerd XXV, 211

John (c. 1602-May 31, 1664) m. c.
1629 Frances ...... MASS XI, 54;
XXXI, 45; XXXII, 230; XXXIV, 272
John (c. 1625-p. 1683) m. Jan. 16,
1656 Elizabeth Strong NH XVII,
113; XX, 60
John (Mar. 2, 1749/50-Oct. 12, 1834)
m. Aug. 19, 1772 Priscilla Wilbur
XXXI, 45; XXXII, 230
Luke (....-....) m. May 6, 1651
Mary Hart CONN XXVII, 97
Moses (Apr. 26, 1728-1780) m. Aug.
10, 1749 Abigail Maverick XXXII,
230
Noah (Oct. 6, 1763-p. 1793) m. Nov.
26, 1780 Hannah Beal XXXIV, 272
Peter (....-Aug. 29, 1667) m. ....
.... ME XXV, 211
Robert (....-p. 1670) m. a. 1642
Mary ...... VA XIX, 124; XXI,
117, 118
William, Sr. (....-c. Sept. 9, 1649)
m. Oct. 28, 1619 Sarah Jourdain
MASS, CONN II, 27, 30; XI, 47,
48, 51; XXV, 71, 90, 91, 231, 232;
XXX, 16; XXXIII, 185, 186, 303
William, Sr. (1710-a. Feb. 1787) m.
1736 Susannah Smithers XIX, 125;
XXI, 117, 118
William, Jr. (1737-1792) m. 1758
Elizabeth Halbert XIX, 125
Zachary (....-....) m. Sept. 24,
1668 Deborah Norton MASS XXXII,
108

HILLER, see HILLYER

HILLIARD
Hugh (....-1640) m. .... Margaret
...... MASS I, 36
Joseph (1736-1820) m. .... Sarah
Griswold I, 36

HILLS
Amos (Jan. 1745-Apr. 9, 1813) m.
1773 Rachel Lewis XXIII, 69
Ebenezer (Feb. 7, 1756-Apr. 14, 1826)
m. Nov. 16, 1775 Ruth Deming XX,
133
John (Sept. 20, 1735-Jan. 21, 1782)
m. c. 1757 Mindwell Wright XXX,16
Jonathan (1731-Oct. 13, 1776) m. a.
1757 Mabel Stanley XXVII, 186
William (Dec. 27, 1608-July 1683) m.
1632 (1) Phillis Lyman; ....(2) Mrs.
...... Risley; .... (3) Mary War-
ner Steele CONN XX, 133; XXIII,
69; XXVII, 186; XXX, 16

HILLYER
Asa (Aug. 21, 1738-Dec. 11, 1820) m.

June 1, 1761 Rhoda Smith XIV, 9,
10; XV, 36; XX, 169; XXI, 116,
117
John (....-July 16, 1655) m. .... Ann
...... CONN XIV, 9, 10; XV, 36;
XX, 169; XXI, 116, 117

HILTON
David (Apr. 12, 1755-Oct. 9, 1822)
m. July 18, 1781 Mary Hammond
XXII, 149; XXXII, 14
John (....-....) m. ....
...... MD XXXII, 216; XXXIII,
78
John (c. 1720-1790) m. ....
...... XXXII, 216; XXXIII, 78
Richard (June 30, 1753-Aug. 14, 1842)
m. July 13, 1777 Anna Storm XXXII,
276
Thomas (June 14, 1752-p. 1799) m.
Oct. 1, 1785 (2) Sarah Stratton
XXVIII, 102
William (1585-1655/6) m. a. 1650
(2) Frances ...... MASS, NH, ME
XXII, 149; XXVIII, 102; XXXII, 14
William (1665-Feb. 12, 1749) m. Apr.
6, 1693 (2) Ann Brouwer (Berkhoven)
NY XXXII, 276

HINCKLEY
Enoch (Mar. 27, 1751-Nov. 29, 1842)
m. .... Mercy Crocker XIII, 11
Ira (Mar. 16, 1756-Aug. 21, 1825) m.
Apr. 1779 Elizabeth Hyde XXXI,
183, 184
Philip (Dec. 16, 1755-June 14, 1843)
m. July 10, 1788 Mary (Polly) Covil
XXXIV, 141
Samuel (bpt. May 25, 1589-Oct. 31,
1662) m. May 16, 1617 Sarah Soule
MASS XIII, 11; XXXI, 184
Thomas (1618-Apr. 5, 1706) m. Dec.
4, 1641 Mary Richards MASS
XXXIV, 141

HINE
Joel (bpt. Sept. 26, 1736-July 19,
1819) m. .... Martha Rogers XXII,
127
Joel (Jan. 30, 1752-June 20, 1826) m.
Jan. 1, 1777 (1) Mary Perkins
XXXII, 37
John (bpt. Sept. 8, 1750-May 13,
1837) m. Jan. 13, 1785 (2) Susan
Johnson X, 131, 132
Samuel (Nov. 15, 1743-July 1, 1833)
m. .... Patience Hotchkiss X, 91
Thadeus (Aug. 18, 1739-Nov. 1816) m.
1768/70 Mary Humphries XX, 11,
137; XXVI, 298, 299
Thomas (....-1696) m. a. 1652

Elizabeth .... CONN X,91,131, 132;
XX, 11, 137; XXII, 127; XXVI, 298;
XXXII, 37

HINMAN
Aaron (Jan. 18, 1747-May 20, 1820)
m. Oct. 21, 1772 Ruth Hinman XXV,
271, 272, 275
Abijah (Mar. 12, 1733-Mar. 23, 1807)
m. Mar. 8, 1757 Rebecca Minor
XVIII, 47; XIX, 43, 149; XXXII, 42
Adomiram (Feb. 11, 1757-Mar. 23,
1830) m. 1780 Martha Barber XIX,
43
Asher (Mar. 13, 1742-1809) m. ....
Mary Harris IX, 14, 15
Benjamin (Jan. 22, 1720-Mar. 20,
1810) m. 1745 Mary Stiles XXV,
271, 272, 275
Bethuel (June 27, 1742-p. 1790) m.
Nov. 8, 1770 Hannah Hicock XVII,
20
Edward (1609-Nov. 26, 1681) m. 1651
Hannah Stiles CONN IX, 14, 15;
XVII, 20; XVIII, 47; XIX, 43, 149;
XXV, 272, 275; XXVIII, 201; XXXII,
42
Phineas (Mar. 31, 1740-Mar. 8, 1829)
m. .... Rhoda Hubbel XXVIII, 201

HINSDALE
Barnabas (Feb. 23, 1738-Apr. 29,
1790) m. c. 1761 Magdalen Seymour
III, 13, 39, 65
Robert (....-Sept. 18, 1675) m. a.
1637 (1) Ann Woodward MASS III,
13, 39, 65

HITCHCOCK
Benjamin (Feb. 23, 1724-Oct. 4, 1792)
m. Feb. 27, 1745 Rhoda Cook XIX,
38; XX, 116; XXI, 116
John (Sept. 28, 1716-June 27, 1796)
m. .... (3) Rebecca Buel XIII, 60
Joseph (Feb. 13, 1716/7-Feb. 18,
1790) m. Dec. 14, 1749 Hannah Ball
XXIII, 76
Luke (....-Nov. 28, 1659) m. ....
Elizabeth Gibbons CONN XIII, 60;
XXVI, 167
Matthias (July 5, 1609-Nov. 16, 1669)
m. .... Elizabeth Rogers CONN
IV, 92; XI, 143; XIX, 38; XX, 116;
XXI, 101; XXIII, 76
Samuel (Feb. 28, 1731-1801) m. 1766
Elizabeth ...... XXVI, 167, 168
Samuel (Feb. 27, 1757-Oct. 25, 1841)
m. .... Mary Munson IV, 92
Timothy (Nov. 8, 1748-Aug. 6, 1820)
m. Feb. 4, 1773 Abigail Clark XI,
142

HOADLEY
Daniel (Oct. 21, 1736-a. Aug. 13, 1806) m. Apr. 26, 1759 Mary Barker X, 15
William (c. 1630-1709) m. .... (1)
Mary ...... CONN X, 15

HOAGLAND, includes HOAGLIN, HOGELAND, HOOGLAND
Abraham (Apr. 29, 1759-1840) m. 1782 Anna Bennett XXX, 182, 183, 257; XXXII, 63
Dirck Jansen (c. 1635-c. 1733) m. Oct. 8, 1662 (1) Annetje Hansen Bergen NY XXIX, 401; XXX, 182, 257; XXXII, 63
William (bpt. Oct. 9, 1720-p. Nov. 25, 1799) m. .... Rachel ...... XXIX, 401

HOAR, includes HORR
John (c. 1614-Apr. 2, 1704) m. .... Alice Lisle MASS XXXIV, 221
Jonathan (Dec. 28, 1747-Feb. 13, 1813) m. Apr. 1, 1773 Sarah Heard XXXIV, 221

HOBART
Aaron (June 8, 1729-Mar. 11, 1808) m. Nov. 1, 1753 Elizabeth Pillsbury XVI, 16, 17
Caleb, Sr. (Feb. 9, 1704-....) m. 1724 Elizabeth Hollis XXXII, 218
Edmund (c. 1570-Mar. 8, 1646) m. Sept. 7, 1600 Margaret Dewey MASS XV, 59; XVI, 16, 17; XXX, 290, 291; XXXII, 218; XXXIV, 169
Israel (July 2, 1722-Aug. 31, 1796) m. July 7, 1748 Anna Lawrence XXXIV, 169
John (Apr. 26, 1755-Feb. 18, 1834) m. Sept. 17, 1777 Deborah White XXXII, 218
William (May 23, 1751-Jan. 1, 1801) m. Nov. 16, 1777 (1) Patience Flagg; June 5, 1787 (2) Dolly Smith XV, 59; XXX, 290, 291; XXXIV, 169

HOBBIE, see HOBBY

HOBBS
Elisha (Feb. 8, 1742/3-Sept. 22, 1807) m. May 17, 1764 Lois Hastings XIV, 8
Josiah (1649-May 30, 1741) m. 1683 Mary ...... MASS XIV, 8
Morris (c. 1615-Jan. 4, 1706) m. .... Sarah Eastow MASS, NH XXVII, 121; XXIX, 402
Morris (Apr. 1, 1747-Mar. 25, 1830)

m. .... Deborah Leavitt XXVII, 121; XXIX, 402

HOBBY, includes HOBBIE, HUBBY
Caleb (Mar. 12, 1746-....) m. .... Elizabeth Knapp XXIX, 277
John, Sr. (c. 1630-1707) m. .... CONN XXIX, 277

HOBSON, see HOPSON

HOCKER
John (c. 1635-1696) m. a. 1659 Mary Green MD XXX, 229
William (1749-1810) m. 1771 Elizabeth Lee Parkerson XXX, 229

HODGDON
Benjamin (May 20, 1749/50-Mar. 1, 1823) m. Apr. 8, 1776 Rosamond Coleman XXXI, 68
Nicholas (1610/2-....) m. c. 1639 Esther Wines MASS XXXI, 68

HODGES
Job (1721-Aug. 5, 1808) m. .... (2) Bertha Andrews XVI, 45; XXI, 144, 145
Job (c. 1747/8-Aug. 15, 1822) m. Apr. 15, 1771 Margaret White XV, 111
John (....-c. Feb. 16, 1622/3) m. .... Mary ...... VA XXXIV, 290
John (c. 1650-1719) m. May 15, 1672 Elizabeth Macey MASS XXXIII, 183, 184
John, II (....-c. 1778) m. 1747 Sarah Rebecca Cherry XXXIV, 290
Silas (Feb. 11, 1741/2-Jan. 9, 1804) m. .... Mary Gould IX, 15, 52
William (....-Apr. 2, 1654) m. May 1628/9 Mary Andrews MASS IX, 51, 52; XV, 111; XVI, 45; XXI, 144
William (1755-Aug. 11, 1840) m. Aug. 30, 1784 Sarah Willard XXXIII, 183, 184

HODGKINS, see HOTCHKISS

HODGMAN
Amos (Aug. 21, 1755-May 18, 1822) m. Oct. 9, 1784 Jemima Stone XIII, 120
Benjamin (Dec. 18, 1722-1823) m. .... Lydia ...... XXXIII, 240, 241
Josiah Webber (May 31, 1668-Mar. 24, 1749) m. May 18, 1691 (1) Elizabet. ......MASS XIII, 120; XXXIII, 240, 2

HODGSON
Abel (1742-1817) m. .... Margaret

Frier XIV, 65
Robert (1626-May 19, 1696) m. July
3, 1665 Rachel Shotten NY XIV,
65

HODSDON
Joshua (Oct. 1, 1727-Dec. 1776) m.
c. 1745 Tamsen Twombly XXXI, 296
Nicholas (....-p. Feb. 20, 1679) m.
1639 (1) Esther Wines MASS, ME
XXXI, 296

HOGELAND, see HOAGLAND

HOLBROOK, includes HOLBROOKE
Aaron (Aug. 31, 1730-Apr. 4, 1818)
m. .... Hannah Partridge IX, 30
Abel (Dec. 4, 1762-July 15, 1842)
m. .... Hannah Clark X, 93
Amos (Mar. 4, 1764-Apr. 5, 1813) m.
.... (1) Betsey Badger VII, 26
David (May 17, 1758-July 21, 1828)
m. .... Judith Bullard X, 270
David (July 28, 1760-Nov. 29, 1832)
m. .... Mehitable Wells XV, 15
Ebenezer (Apr. 24, 1796-May 21,
1838) m. Jan. 23, 1783 Diadama
Durkee XIX, 159
John (1617-Nov. 23, 1699) m. ....
Elizabeth Stream MASS XVIII, 65;
XIX, 159
John (Aug. 12, 1726-Jan. 28, 1801)
m. Nov. 4, 1750 Esther Nichols
IX, 18; XIII, 32
Jonathan (June 30, 1743-Nov. 2, 1776)
m. May 9, 1776 Sarah Bedlow XXV,
268
Micah (Mar. 11, 1744-p. 1807) m.
Nov. 27, 1766 Thoda Theyer XV,
8
Nathaniel (Oct. 1, 1758-May 28, 1828)
m. .... Allis Davis XXIX, 35, 36
Nehemiah (May 6, 1745-....) m. May
25, 1765 Elizabeth Hobart XVIII,
65
Richard (....-1670) m. .... Agnes
...... NY IX, 18; XIII, 32;
XXIX, 35, 36
Seth (Nov. 24, 1751-Nov. 13, 1839)
m. .... Dinah Holbrook XII, 25
Thomas, Sr. (1601-1674) m. 1623
Jane Kingman MASS IX, 30; XII,
26; XV, 8, 15; XXV, 268
Thomas (c. 1624-Apr. 11, 1705) m.
Jan. 26, 1668/9 (3) Margaret Bou-
ker MASS VII, 26; X, 271

HOLBROOKE, see HOLBROOK

HOLCOMB, includes HOLCOMBE
Abner (Sept. 16, 1752-1840) m. c.

1773 Mindwell Bull VII, 12
Nathaniel (Nov. 10, 1740-Sept. 11,
1812) m. Dec. 1780 (2) Jemima
(Adkins) Smith XXXI, 198
Thomas (1601-Sept. 7, 1657) m. ....
Elizabeth Ferguson MASS, CONN
VII, 13; XXXI, 198

HOLCOMBE, see HOLCOMB

HOLDEN
Charles (....-....) m. Nov. 3, 1771
Sarah Remington XXII, 65
Jabez (May 12, 1735-Aug. 11, 1787)
m. June 11, 1761 Rachel Farnsworth
XXVIII, 179, 180
Randall (c. 1612-July 23, 1692) m.
.... Frances Dungan RI XXII, 65
Richard (1609-Mar. 1, 1695/6) m.
1640/1 Martha Fosdick MASS
XXVIII, 179, 180

HOLLAND
Ivory (Dec. 27, 1739-July 3, 1820)
m. 1762 Martha Rogers XXIV, 156
Nathaniel (....-p. 1709) m. c. 1661
Sarah Streeter MASS XXIV, 156

HOLLEY, includes HOLLY, HAULEY
Closson (May 1756-Aug. 1, 1832) m.
Nov. 5, 1777 Sarah Waller XXVII,
215
Samuel (....-a. Dec. 5, 1643) m.
.... Elizabeth ...... MASS
XXVII, 215

HOLLIS
John (c. 1640-....) m. .... Eliza-
beth Priest MASS XXV, 125
Thomas (1741-....) m. .... Lydia
Holbrook XXV, 125

HOLLISTER
Ashbel (Mar. 4, 1759-May 4, 1840)
m. Jan. 10, 1790 Mary Pepper
XXXIII, 75, 76
John (1612-Apr. 1665) m. 1640 Joanna
Treat CONN XI, 109, 181; XIII,
71; XVII, 88, 131; XXX, 150;
XXXIII, 75, 102
Josiah (Feb. 21, 1756-Sept. 8, 1849)
m. c. 1787 (2) Asenath Sweetland
XI, 109, 181; XXX, 149, 150;
XXXIII, 102, 103
Nathaniel (1731-June 10, 1810)
m. Oct. 29, 1754 Mehitable Mat-
tison XIII, 71; XVII, 131,
132
Thomas, III (Sept. 23, 1738-Jan. 27,
1813) m. Feb. 19, 1767 Jemima
Goodrich XVII, 88

HOLLOWAY
Peter (Mar. 19, 1751-Mar. 11, 1832)
m. May 4, 1775 Abigail Gooding
XXXI, 249
William (c. 1586-p. May 9, 1664) m.
.... MASS XXXI,
249

HOLLOWELL
Silas Thomas (1754-1789) m. 1774
Miriam Riddick X, 180, 181
Thomas (c. 1628-....) m. ....
Elizabeth ...... VA X, 181

HOLLY, see HOLLEY

HOLME
John (....-1702/3) m. c. 1686
Mrs. Nicholas More PA XXXII, 58
Thomas (Jan. 16, 1749-May 26, 1826)
m. .... Rebecca Jones XXXII, 58

HOLMES
Asa (Mar. 22, 1754-p. 1834) m.
.... (2) Elizabeth Painter Carver
XIII, 40
Ebenezer (Feb. 27, 1761-Feb. 3, 1848)
m. Oct. 25, 1787 Hannah Paul XXXII,
71
Francis (....-p. Sept. 6, 1671) m.
.... Ann ...... CONN XVII, 56;
XXXII, 31
George (1594-Dec. 18, 1645) m. ....
Deborah ...... MASS XIII, 40;
XX, 101; XXIX, 55; XXXII, 71
James (Apr. 22, 1755-p. 1792) m.
.... Esther Babcock VII, 43
Jeremiah (1745-Nov. 15, 1832) m.
1773 Betsey Lewis XXIX, 313
Job (1728-Oct. 4, 1800) m. 1752 (1)
Mehitable Stewart XX, 68
John (....-Oct. 15, 1667) m. ....
Sarah ...... MASS XX, 68
John (c. 1641-1712/3) m. a. Nov.
15, 1666 Mary Peverly NH XXIX,
313
John (c. 1729-p. 1783) m. ....
Rachel Elizabeth Fellows XIII, 40
John (Mar. 9, 1749-Dec. 7, 1809) m.
Dec. 22, 1774 Martha Stanton
XXIX, 253, 348; XXXIII, 187
Jonathan (July 5, 1709-Aug. 5,
1787) m. Jan. 3, 1734 Mary Water-
man XXXII, 223, 224
Joseph (1758-Sept. 1, 1826) m. Sept.
9, 1778 Lydia Curtis XVII, 56
Nathaniel (1715-....) m. Dec. 16,
1740 Sarah Pettee XX, 101
Robert (....-p. 1670) m. ....
...... CONN VII, 44; XXIX, 253,
348; XXXIII, 187

Samuel (June 10, 1733-Feb. 5, 1803)
m. Dec. 2, 1761 Susanna Comings
XXIX, '55
William (....-Nov. 9, 1678) m. ....
Elizabeth ...... MASS XXXII, 223
William (Sept. 22, 1755-Feb. 16,
1819) m. Jan. 10, 1779 Phebe Crom-
well XXXII, 30, 31
Zephaniah (Dec. 8, 1743-Feb. 1800)
m. 1773 Barbara McLucas XX, 101

HOLT, includes HOLTE
Asa (Dec. 13, 1758-July 23, 1847) m.
Apr. 7, 1785 Mary Smith XXX, 266
Benjamin (July 23, 1709-1784) m.
Apr. 7, 1737 Mrs. Sarah (Bridges)
Frye XV, 35
Daniel (Sept. 14, 1744-Dec. 5, 1813)
m. Apr. 7, 1737 Abigail Lovejoy
XV, 35
John, Sr. (Jan. 11, 1719-May 15,
1786) m. Feb. 20, 1746 Sarah
Strickland X, 57, 224; XII, 33
John, Jr. (Dec. 6, 1746-Sept. 6,
1781) m. Nov. 21, 1771 Martha Coit
X, 57, 224; XII, 33
Jonathan, Jr. (May 16, 1756-Dec. 12,
1832) m. Dec. 12, 1782 Molly (Mary)
Bailey XXX, 162
Joshua (June 30, 1730-July 24, 1810)
m. .... Phebe Farnum XXI, 20
Mastin (Aug. 13, 1747-c. 1785) m.
Feb. 13, 1772 Abigail Wheeler
XXX, 120, 121; XXXIII, 270
Nicholas (1602-Jan. 30, 1685) m.
.... Elizabeth Short MASS XV,
36; XVII, 47; XVIII, 89; XXI, 19,
20; XXIX, 375; XXX, 121, 162;
XXXIII, 270
Nicholas (1756-1833) m. Nov. 26,
1782 Phoebe Bacheler XVII, 47
Silas (....-....) m. a. 1776
Sarah Harrington XXIX, 375
Valentine (1763-Dec. 6, 1840) m.
1802 (2) Hannah Day XVIII, 89
William (1610-Sept. 1, 1683) m. ....
Sarah ...... CONN X, 57, 224;
XII, 33; XXX, 266
William (Apr. 4, 1729-Dec. 17, 1811)
m. Apr. 20, 1756 Phebe Lay XXX,
266

HOLTE, see HOLT

HOLTON
Arad (Nov. 3, 1752-Oct. 8, 1841) m.
May 13, 1787 (2) Rebecca Houghton
XI, 188; XXXII, 131
Thomas, Jr. (1705-Dec. 22, 1800
m. .... Sarah ...... XI,
188

William (Oct. 20, 1610-Aug. 8, 1691)
m. .... Mary Pierce MASS, CONN
XI, 188; XXXII, 131

HONEYWELL
Enoch (Apr. 9, 1725-Sept. 11, 1813)
m. a. 1757 Elethear Searles XXVI,
22, 23, 116, 117; XXX, 210
Israel (1660-1720) m. a. 1687 Mary
Spofford NY XXVI, 22, 23, 116;
XXX, 210

HOOD
Amos (Aug. 12, 1757-c. 1796/7) m.
Apr. 16, 1779 Phebe Perkins XXIV,
62
Benjamin (....-....) m. ....
...... MD XXXIII, 338
John, Jr. (c. 1600-....) m. ....
Elizabeth ...... MASS XXIV, 61;
XXXIII, 267, 268
John, Jr. (c. 1740-Dec. 15, 1794) m.
Feb. 10, 1774 (2) Rachel Howard
XXXIII, 338
Nathan (....-May 4, 1792) m. Mar. 6,
1731 (1) Elizabeth Palmer XXXIII,
267, 268

HOOGLAND, see HOAGLAND

HOOK, includes HOOKE
James (1749-Jan. 23, 1824) m. ....
Mary Lyeth XXIX, 199
Thomas (c. 1645-1697/8) m. c. 1679
Annaple ...... MD XXIX, 199

HOOKE, see HOOK

HOOKER
Asahel (Dec. 13, 1736-Nov. 10, 1810)
m. Feb. 15, 1760 Anne Parmalee
XXX, 255, 256
Hezekiah, Jr. (Oct. 30, 1717-1796)
m. .... Elizabeth Stone IV, 70,
71
Jesse (Apr. 23, 1752-1791) m. ....
Sabrina Smith IV, 70, 71
Thomas (1586-July 7, 1647) m. ....
Susan Garbrand CONN IV, 70, 71;
XXX, 255, 256

HOPKINS
David (Dec. 2, 1753-Mar. 7, 1824) m.
Mar. 5, 1801 (3) Isabella Ford
XVII, 116
Ehud (....-Nov. 27, 1809) m. ....
Chloe King XXIX, 46
Gerard, I (....-1691) m. 1658 Mrs.
Thomsin Welsh MD XXV, 40; XXXII,
156, 260; XXXIII, 307, 340
Hezekiah, Jr. (Feb. 20, 1758-May 18,

1834) m. June 12, 1783 Eunice
Hubbell XI, 119
John (c. 1613-a. Apr. 14, 1654) m.
1633 Jane Strong MASS XI, 119;
XV, 71; XVII, 116; XXVII, 180;
XXIX, 46
Samuel (Jan. 16, 1713-May 15, 1795)
m. Sept. 2, 1740 Sarah Giles XXV,
40, 41; XXXII, 156, 260; XXXIII,
307, 340
Samuel (Sept. 17, 1721-Dec. 20,
1808) m. Jan. 13, 1748 (1) Joanna
Ingersoll XV, 71
Timothy (Nov. 25, 1750-Oct. 10, 1803)
m. Jan. 15, 1780 (2) Mrs. Phoebe
(Nesbit) Marvin XXVII, 180

HOPPIN, includes HOPPING
John (c. 1642-Oct. 17, 1722) m. ....
Rebecca Hand NY XXIX, 252
Samuel Rossiter (1755-Feb. 6, 1800)
m. 1781 Elizabeth Curtis XXIX, 252

HOPPING, see HOPPIN

HOPSON, includes HOBSON
John (c. 1610-May 3, 1701) m. c.
1673 (3) Elizabeth Alling CONN
XXXI, 263; XXXIII, 128, 129
Simeon, Sr. (Oct. 14, 1747-p. July
4, 1837) m. Feb. 22, 1776 Naomi
Moss XXXI, 263; XXXIII, 128, 129

HORNE
Peter (c. 1735-1795) m. .... Mercy
Pyrley XIX, 119
William (....-June 28, 1689) m. ....
Elizabeth Clough NH XIX, 119

HORNEY
Jeffery (....-1738) m. .... Margaret
...... MD XXIX, 360; XXXII, 261
John (Jan. 1, 1749-July 22, 1821) m.
Apr. 17, 1774 Mary Chipman XXXII,
261
William (1750-a. 1829) m. 1772 Han-
nah Chipman XXIX, 360

HORNOR
John (....-Feb. 25, 1699) m. ....
Mary Robinson NJ XVIII, 129
John (Oct. 27, 1750-Mar. 19, 1819)
m. July 27, 1777 Patty Richards
XVIII, 129

HORR, see HOAR

HORTON
Barnabas (1600-July 13, 1680) m. 1622
(1) Anne Smith; .... (2) Mary .....
CONN V, 44; XXX, 131, 132; XXXI,

HORTON, cont.
176; XXXII, 132; XXXIII, 97, 122
Caleb Paulding (Sept. 21, 1739-Apr.
18, 1831) m. .... Jane Martine
XXXIII, 97, 122
Daniel (Sept. 13, 1744-Dec. 9, 1807)
m. .... Anna French Gedney
XXX, 131, 132
John (Sept. 28, 1735-May 14, 1799)
m. Dec. 1, 1762 Mary Beecher XXV,
42; XXVII, 75
John (Feb. 26, 1752-Apr. 20, 1810)
m. 1780 Mary De La Montaigne
XXXII, 132, 133
*Joseph (1625-a. June 13, 1696) m. c.
1654 Jane Budd NH, NY V, 44*
Joseph (1738-p. Oct. 7, 1820) m. ....
Keziah ...... XXXI, 176
Nehemiah (1759-1819) m. Apr. 27, 1780
Philadelphia Marsh XI, 66; XII, 8
*Thomas (1602-1641) m. .... Mary Eddy
CONN, MASS XXV, 42; XXVII, 75*
*Thomas (....-c. 1700) m. .... (1)
Rachel ...... MASS XI, 66; XII,
8*
William (Jan. 10, 1743-Jan. 19, 1831)
m. .... Elizabeth Covert V, 44

HOSFORD
Aaron (Dec. 25, 1740-July 19, 1818)
m. Feb. 2, 1769 Lucy Strong XVIII,
102; XX, 19
*William (....-c. 1660) m. .... Mrs.
Jane Fowkes CONN, MASS XVIII,
102; XX, 19*

HOSKINE, see HASKINS

HOSKINS, see HASKINS

HOSMER
Daniel (1749-Apr. 28, 1800) m. June
5, 1774 Mary Belding XXXI, 317
Ephraim (Nov. 22, 1722-Mar. 16, 1811)
m. (int.) Apr. 28, 1753 Sarah Jones
XXVII, 117, 118, 149, 150; XXX,
119
Ephraim, II (June 22, 1756-....) m.
Nov. 6, 1783 Mercy Whitney XXVII,
117, 118, 149, 150; XXX, 119
*James (bpt. Dec. 6, 1605-Feb. 7,
1685) m. p. Nov. 3, 1641 (3) Alice
...... MASS XXVII, 117, 118, 150;
XXX, 119; XXXI, 103*
Josiah, Jr. (Nov. 28, 1740-1837) m.
Apr. 28, 1766 (1) Eunice Whitcomb
XXXI, 103
*Thomas (bpt. Jan. 2, 1603-
Apr. 12, 1687) m. ....
Frances ...... MASS, CONN
XXXI, 317*

HOTALING, includes HOUGHTAILING
*Matthias (1644-1706) m. .... Marie
Hendricksee NY XVIII, 146*
Thomas B. (Dec. 23, 1731-Feb. 1,
1824) m. 1757 Elizabeth Whitbeck
XVIII, 146

HOTCHKISS, includes HODGKINS
Gideon (Dec. 5, 1716-Sept. 3, 1807)
m. June 18, 1737 Anne Brockett
XXXIII, 28; XXXIV, 140
Israel (May 30, 1767-Feb. 23, 1840)
m. .... Martha Royce XV, 88
Joseph (July 31, 1756-1825) m.
.... Temperance Andrews IV, 68
Joshua (Feb. 12, 1733/4-June 3, 1795)
m. .... Mary Panderson XXV, 49
Josiah, III (Dec. 26, 1742-1812)
m. c. 1764/5 Sarah Perkins XV,
88; XVII, 11
Lent (Sept. 2, 1753-Dec. 2, 1805)
m. Sept. 25, 1788 Sarah Bell XI,
47; XII, 35
Levi (May 2, 1754-Sept. 11, 1831) m.
.... (1) Phebe Hitchcock XXXIV,
172, 345
*Samuel (c. 1622-Dec. 28, 1663) m.
Sept. 16, 1648 Elizabeth Cloverly
CONN IV, 68; XI, 48; XII, 35;
XV, 88; XVII, 11; XXV, 49; XXXIII,
28; XXXIV, 140, 172, 345*

HOUGHTAILING, see HOTALING

HOUGHTON
Abijah, Jr. (Sept. 23, 1723-June 23,
1802) m. Mar. 1746 Alice Joslyn
XX, 117
Edward (Dec. 25, 1730-July 30, 1782)
m. Oct. 16, 1760 Lucretia Richard-
son XXV, 265, 266
Elisha (July 20, 1746-p. 1780) m.
Nov. 30, 1768 Mariah Pierce XXVII,
146, 147
*John (Dec. 24, 1624-Apr. 29, 1684)
m. 1648 Beatrix ...... MASS XVI,
9; XX, 117; XXX, 74*
Jonathan (Feb. 21, 1761-p. 1807) m.
June 26, 1783 Rachel Hale XXX, 74
*Ralph (Apr. 21, 1623-Apr. 15, 1705)
m. c. 1647 Jane Stowe MASS XXV,
265, 266; XXVII, 146, 147; XXXIV,
220*
Ralph (Feb. 28, 1729-Nov. 16, 1803)
m. Feb. 15, 1759 Ruth Wadsworth
XXXIV, 220
Rufus (May 8, 1763-p. 1790) m. ....
Mary Gleason XVI, 9, 10

HOUSTON
Alfred (Dec. 6, 1572-....) m. Jan.

13, 1607 Ruth Scence VA XXXII,
267
Samuel (Feb. 6, 1709-1830) m. June
2, 1759 Sarah Henderson XXXII,
267

HOVEY
Daniel (Aug. 9, 1618-Apr. 24, 1692)
m. 1641 Abigail Andrews MASS
XXIX, 167; XXX, 69
Josiah, Sr. (Aug. 24, 1743-Apr. 24,
1820) m. 1770 Theadora Downer
XXIX, 167
Moses (Oct. 28, 1748-Oct. 29, 1813)
m. Aug. 14, 1777 Phoebe Tenny
XXX, 68, 69

HOW, see HOWE

HOWARD, includes ARUNDEL-HOWARD,
HEYWARD
Benjamin (Feb. 17, 1742-June 4, 1828)
m. Sept. 21, 1762 Prudence Sater
XXIX, 279
Ebenezer (Aug. 31, 1752-Apr. 22,
1818) m. Dec. 22, 1772 Silence
Snell XXXII, 216
Elijah (Sept. 6, 1744-July 10, 1831)
m. Mar. 31, 1768 Keziah Hayward
XXX, 278
Ephraim (Jan. 25, 1731-p. 1790) m.
July 12, 1753 Hannah Brett X, 240
Groves (Nov. 5, 1733-Jan. 7, 1806)
m. Mar. 17, 1760 Hannah Allen
XXXIV, 309
Henry (....-Mar. 1708/9) m. Sept. 28,
1648 Sarah Stone CONN XXII, 21
John (....-a. Apr. 24, 1661) m. c.
1650 Margaret Clarke VA XXXIV,
309
John (c. 1620-1700) m. 1645 Martha
Hayward MASS X, 240; XXVIII,
144; XXX, 278; XXXII, 216
John (Mar. 26, 1748-Mar. 1788) m.
Nov. 3, 1770 Eleanor Cobb XXVIII,
144
John Beale (Nov. 30, 1748-Apr. 1,
1788) m. Dec. 20, 1770 Rebecca
Boone XXXIII, 213, 214
Matthew (1609-a. 1659) m. 1630 Ann
...... VA XXIX, 279; XXXIII, 213,
214
Samuel (c. 1613-....) m. c. 1645
Sarah Stowers MASS XXIX, 177
Samuel (Oct. 5, 1739-Feb. 11, 1815)
m. Dec. 10, 1762 Elizabeth Bar-
rett XXIX, 177
Samuel (Nov. 3, 1752-1816) m. Dec.
3, 1788 Rachel Talcott XXII, 21
Solomon (Dec. 6, 1756-June 23, 1840)
m. .... Cynthia Peters XXX, 155

William (....-Mar. 10, 1659) m. 1636
Margery ...... MASS XXX, 155

HOWE, includes HOW
Abraham (....-1676) m. ....
...... MASS XV, 126; XXXI, 83
Abraham, Jr. (Sept. 18, 1754-Jan. 8,
1795) m. Feb. 4, 1784 Eleanor
Spofford XXXII, 232
Antipas (Aug. 19, 1746-Mar. 1833) m.
Jan. 20, 1782 Joanna Lawrence
XXII, 34; XXX, 22, 23
Edward (1585-Apr. 1639) m. 1613/4
Elizabeth ...... MASS XXX, 191
Isaac Cady (Feb. 27, 1741-1800) m.
Sept. 12, 1765 Damaris Burch
XXVI, 275; XXXIV, 280
Ishabod (Jan. 9, 1731-Jan. 16, 1810)
m. 1759 Sarah ...... XV, 126
James (a. 1605-May 17, 1702) m.
June 27, 1628 Elizabeth Dane MASS
XXVI, 275; XXXI, 262; XXXII, 232;
XXXIV, 280
Jesse (1758-June 30, 1827) m. Oct.
4, 1782 Mary Wood XXX, 191
John (1602-May 28, 1680) m. ....
Mary ...... MASS IX, 13, 14;
XIII, 66; XVII, 10; XVIII, 37, 38;
XX, 144; XXII, 34, 120; XXX, 22,
23
Jonathan (Sept. 24, 1746-Oct. 7,
1787) m. Apr. 19, 1778 Lucy Read
XVIII, 37, 38; XX, 144; XXII, 120
Joseph, Sr. (Mar. 6, 1724-Aug. 17,
1794) m. Nov. 1, 1750 Sarah Stone
XIII, 66; XVII, 10
Mark (Dec. 31, 1737-May 28, 1818) m.
Mar. 6, 1760 Mary Payson XXXI,
262
Micajah, Jr. (1726-Jan. 9, 1799) m.
.... (2) Sarah Field IX, 13, 14
Moses, Sr. (c. 1747-Sept. 22, 1822)
m. c. 1780 (1) Mary ...... XXXI,
83

HOWELL
Edward (bpt. July 22, 1584-c. 1655)
m. .... (1) Frances......; c. 1617
(2) Eleanor ...... NY X, 82; XII,
72; XIII, 85; XX, 5
Ezekiel (Oct. 30, 1755-1831) m. ....
Charity Lott X, 82
Hezekiah (Sept. 13, 1741-Apr. 2,
1815) m. .... Juliana Woodhull
XII, 72
Jeremiah (1748-1846) m. ....
...... XIII, 85
John (bpt. Nov. 22, 1624-Nov.
3, 1696) m. c. 1647 Susannah
Townsend MASS, NY XXIX,
162

HOWELL, cont.
  John (June 14, 1727-1779) m. ....
    Naomi Hart X, 82
  Mathew (Feb. 12, 1726-Mar. 5, 1786)
    m. 1758 (2) Margaret Carr XX, 5
  Samuel (bpt. Nov. 15, 1757-p. 1817)
    m. Oct. 10, 1782 Rachel Drake
    XXIX, 162

HOWES
  Joseph (Nov. 25, 1752-Feb. 4, 1831)
    m. Jan. 1, 1777 Martha Howard
    XXXIII, 163
  Thomas (c. 1590-1665) m. c. 1630
    Mary Burr MASS XXXIII, 163

HOWLAND
  Henry (....-Jan. 17, 1661) m. ....
    Mary Newland MASS XXX, 159, 160
  Israel (June 13, 1713-c. 1781) m.
    .... Drusilla Wood XXX, 159, 160
  John (1592-Feb. 23, 1672/3) m. 1623
    Elizabeth Tilley MASS XXXII, 56
  Lemuel (Nov. 28, 1742-Jan. 1802) m.
    Dec. 11, 1765 Abigail Hamlin
    XXXII, 56

HOXIE, includes HAUKSIE
  Benjamin, Jr. (Mar. 14, 1742-p. 1783)
    m. .... Mercy Wells IV, 162
  Gideon (Dec. 4, 1729-June 13, 1805)
    m. .... Dorcas Congdon X, 10;
    XV, 41
  Lodowick (....-1702) m. Oct. 1664
    Mary Presbery MASS IV, 162; X,
    10; XV, 41
  Peleg (Sept. 15, 1756-1818) m. July
    1, 1777 Lucy Babcock X, 10

HOYT, includes HAIGHT, HAIT, HOYTE
  Aaron (Jan. 11, 1750-Sept. 3, 1816)
    m. 1769 Jemima Waters XIII, 68
  Comfort (Feb. 20, 1723/4-May 19,
    1812) m. 1750 Anna Beach XII,
    91; XV, 21, 90; XVI, 35
  Daniel (Aug. 1706-a. May 1, 1797)
    m. Apr. 29, 1731 Jemima Lounsbury
    XXVI, 143, 144
  David (Mar. 20, 1743-Mar. 27, 1822)
    m. Jan. 11, 1775 (2) Lucy Dudley
    XXXIV, 88
  Israel (Nov. 18, 1733-Nov. 2, 1809)
    m. .... Joanna Holmes XXVI, 143,
    144
  Jared (May 20, 1762-Apr. 17, 1826)
    m. June 11, 1780 Mary June XXIX,
    201
  John (1610/5-Feb. 28, 1687/8) m.
    c. 1635 (1) Frances ...... MASS
    IX, 45, 46; XVI, 95; XXI, 151;
    XXIX, 102, 146

John (Sept. 10, 1732-Feb. 1804/5)m.
    Jan. 2, 1755 Abigail Carter IX,
    45, 46; XVI, 94, 95
John (Nov. 24, 1740-Mar. 1, 1825)
    m. Dec. 31, 1761 (1) Abigail Hait
    XXVI, 245, 246, 247, 248, 249;
    XXIX, 250, 378, 379
Matthew (May 6, 1741/2-Apr. 14, 1821)
    m. Jan. 2, 1761 (1) Mary Lockwood
    X, 116
Neazer (Nov. 8, 1751-Feb. 15, 1811)
    m. Dec. 3, 1778 Prudence Weed
    XXII, 157
Noah (Nov. 3, 1753-Dec. 23, 1827) m.
    Dec. 10, 1783 (2) Mary Seeley X,
    198
Samuel (Oct. 19, 1754-Sept. 18, 1819)
    m. Jan. 8, 1778 Elizabeth Olmstead
    XXIX, 73
Simeon (1595-Sept. 1, 1657) m. 1612
    (1) Deborah Stowers; a. 1618 (2)
    Susanna Smith MASS X, 116, 198;
    XII, 91; XIII, 68; XV, 21, 90; XVI,
    35; XXII, 157; XXVI, 143, 144, 245,
    246, 247, 248, 249; XXIX, 73, 201,
    250, 378, 379; XXXIV, 88
Stephen (Sept. 23, 1746-May 17, 1824)
    m. 1768 Sarah Straw XXI, 151
Thomas (May 17, 1731-Sept. 1, 1778)
    m. Sept. 5, 1754 Miriam Kimball
    XXIX, 102, 146

HOYTE, see HOYT

HUBBARD
  Caleb (Apr. 23, 1754-Apr. 7, 1850)
    m. Apr. 2, 1792 (2) Lucretia Ash-
    ley XX, 20, 123
  Daniel (Mar. 1, 1729-1822) m. ....
    Eunice Clark V, 126
  Ebenezer (Mar. 1, 1725-Oct. 7, 1807)
    m. May 7, 1752 Hannah Estabrook
    X, 296
  Ebenezer (Sept. 16, 1747-July 11,
    1819) m. Feb. 23, 1790 (2) Mrs.
    Hannah (Parker) Hall X, 38
  Elisha (Dec. 20, 1744-July 17, 1814)
    m. Dec. 3, 1767 Mercy Hubbard
    XXVIII, 118, 119
  George (c. 1594-Jan. 1683) m. a. 1625
    (1) Mary Bishop; 1640 (2) Elizabeth
    Watts CONN V, 126; X, 296; XV,
    68, 82; XX, 20, 123; XXII, 45; XXV,
    50, 51; XXVIII, 118; XXIX, 127;
    XXX, 20; XXXII, 194; XXXIII, 221;
    XXXIV, 240
  George (Nov. 30, 1739-Apr. 16, 1818)
    m. June 10, 1760 Thankful Hatch
    XXXII, 194
  George (Aug. 17, 1758-Nov. 29, 1838)
    m. .... Mehitable Miller XXXIV,239

Henry (Jan. 1751-July 11, 1825) m.
1771 (1) Lydia Dickinson; June
27, 1785 (2) Hannah Smith XXII,
45; XXV, 50, 51
Israel (Jan. 18, 1725-Apr. 21, 1817)
m. Feb. 19, 1747 Abigail Smith
XX, 20, 123
Jeremiah (Oct. 27, 1732-Mar. 7, 1814)
m. c. 1783 Elizabeth Meigs XV, 68
Jeremiah, Jr. (Jan. 29, 1746-Aug.
23, 1808) m. Feb. 11, 1768 Flora
Hazelton XXX, 20, 21
John (Jan. 24, 1727-Nov. 18, 1786)
m. .... (1) Rebecca Dickerman
IX, 34, 42
John (Mar. 14, 1761-Jan. 5, 1850) m.
c. 1789 Eunice Moore XXIX, 126
Josiah (Aug. 10, 1752-Aug. 7, 1829)
m. Nov. 24, 1796 (3) Susanna Marks
XV, 82
Samuel (1733-1813) m. 1759 Sarah
Smith XXXIII, 221
William (....-Apr. 17, 1694) m. ....
(2) Mrs. Ann Allen MASS, CONN
X, 38
William (1594-p. June 1670) m. ....
Judith Knapp MASS IX, 34, 42

HUBBELL
Gershom (July 17, 1729-Apr. 14, 1802)
m. Nov. 12, 1756 (2) Sarah Wakeman
III, 47; XXIII, 36
John (1709-May 7, 1782) m. .... Han-
nah Wheeler XV, 53; XXIX, 22
John, Jr. (1751-Sept. 22, 1822) m.
June 28, 1773 Sarah Curtis XXXIII,
59, 60
Nehemiah (Apr. 7, 1764-June 21, 1835)
m. .... Jemima (Hayden) Patterson
V, 88
Richard (a. 1626-Oct. 23, 1699) m.
1650 (1) Elizabeth Meigs; .... (2)
Elizabeth ...... CONN III, 47;
V, 88; XV, 53; XXIII, 36; XXIV, 52;
XXVIII, 82; XXIX, 22; XXXIII, 59
Seth (bpt. May 30, 1736-p. 1790) m.
Sept. 28, 1758 (1) Jane Rockwell
XXVIII, 82
Shadrach (July 22, 1740-....) m.
Dec. 11, 1765 Hannah Mosher XXIV,
52

HUBBY, see HOBBY

HUCKINS
James (1730-1818) m. .... Lydia
Scudder II, 50
Thomas (1617-1679) m. .... (2)
Mrs. Rose Hyllier MASS II,
50

HUDSON
Benjamin (July 1, 1735-....) m. Dec.
1757 Ann Sweet XXIX, 193
Daniel (1617-Sept. 11, 1697) m. ....
Joanna ...... MASS XXIX, 79
Eli (Sept. 20, 1751-Dec. 10, 1828)
m. Jan. 7, 1776 Sarah Perkins
XXIX, 78
Thomas (a. 1595-....) m. ....
...... MASS XXIX, 194

HUESTED, see HUSTED

HUGHITT, see HEWITT

HULBERT, see HURLBURT

HULIN, includes HULING
James (1620-Mar. 6, 1697) m. a.
1646 Margaret ...... RI XXIV,
142
Walton (Feb. 8, 1745-Oct. 5, 1823)
m. .... Abiah Mosher XXIV, 142

HULING, see HULIN

HULL
Eli (Mar. 26, 1764-Apr. 31, 1828) m.
Nov. 25, 1790 Sally Beckwith
XVI, 46
Elias (Apr. 13, 1748-June 11, 1834)
m. 1795 Cynthia Carpenter XXXIII,
126, 127
Eliphalet, Sr. (1749-1813) m. 1768
Huldah Patchen XXX, 109
George (1590-1659) m. Aug. 17, 1614
Thomasene Mitchell MASS XVI, 46;
XXIX, 245; XXX, 109; XXXI, 110
Gideon (Mar. 6, 1744-July 29, 1836)
m. 1762 Bathsheba Hoxie XVIII,
43
Isaac (Nov. 17, 1731-p. 1808) m.
Nov. 25, 1751 Anne Dunham X, 216;
XV, 51
Jehiel (Feb. 28, 1728-Feb. 3, 1822)
m. Nov. 8, 1750 Ruth Phelps XXIX,
245
John, III (Aug. 11, 1762-1853) m.
Nov. 23, 1803 (2) Amy Cornell
XXXIII, 244
Joseph (1595-Nov. 19, 1665) m. ....
(1) Joanna ......; a. 1635 (2)
Agnes ...... MASS X, 217; XV,
51; XVIII, 43; XXXIII, 126, 127,
244; XXXIV, 21
Oliver (1731-1803) m. May 1751 Pene-
lope Ffones XXXIII, 244
Richard (1590-1662) m. ....
.... MASS, CONN
I, 29

HULL, cont.
  Samuel (1735-1814) m. 1764 Martha
    Glover XXXIV, 21
  Samuel, Sr. (June 15, 1755-1840) m.
    June 20, 1781 Freelove Kelsey
    XXXI, 110
  Titus (1751-1817) m. .... (2) Olive
    (Lewis) Parmelee I, 29
  Uriah (c. 1765-1830) m. .... Isabella
    ...... XXXIV, 21

HUMISTON
  Ephraim (Dec. 5, 1730-May 3, 1806)
    m. Dec. 1, 1757 Susanna Bassett
    XXVI, 10
  Henry (a. 1629-....) m. ....
    ...... CONN XXVI, 10

HUMPHREY
  Daniel (Aug. 17, 1737-Aug. 27, 1813)
    m. Apr. 10, 1760 Rachel Phelps
    XVIII, 112
  Isaac (Nov. 21, 1748-Sept. 3, 1829)
    m. Oct. 5, 1775 (2) Mary Chapman
    XXVIII, 105
  John (1595-1661) m. .... (3) Susan
    Fiennes MASS XXX, 208, 209
  Jonas (c. 1587-Mar. 19, 1661/2) m.
    June 11, 1607 Frances Cooley MASS
    XXVIII, 105
  Jonathan Davis (July 29, 1764-Aug.
    3, 1836) m. Dec. 20, 1787 Rebecca
    Vinal XXX, 208, 209
  Lot (1764-Jan. 8, 1835) m. Dec. 1,
    1784 Chloe Moses XXVI, 231
  Michael (c. 1620-a. 1697) m. Oct.
    14, 1647 Priscilla Grant CONN
    XVIII, 112; XXVI, 231

HUNGERFORD
  John (c. 1755-p. 1790) m. ....
    ...... XIV, 61
  Thomas (....-1663) m. ....
    ...... CONN XIV, 61

HUNN
  Enos (Mar. 12, 1745-June 21, 1805)
    m. Feb. 28, 1774 Esther Smith X,
    60
  Ephriam Tiffany (May 4, 1766-June 13,
    1862) m. Nov. 5, 1788 Mitty Lath-
    rop XX, 134
  George (....-p. May 25, 1640) m. ....
    Ann Hunn MASS X, 60
  Gideon (Mar. 12, 1709/10-Aug. 29,
    1785) m. 1731 Rebecca Baldin X, 60
  Jonathan (....-1735) m. ....
    ...... CONN XX, 134

HUNT
  Edward (1734-1786) m. 1759 Mary Shuel

  XXII, 157; XXVIII, 7
  Enoch (....-Nov. 18, 1652) m. ....
    .... RI, MASS XXIII,
    67; XXVII, 88; XXX, 43
  Ephraim (c. 1610-Feb. 24, 1687) m.
    .... Anna Richards MASS XII, 14
  John (Nov. 19, 1716-Jan. 19, 1777)
    m. 1738/9 Ruth Fessenden XXVII,
    87, 88; XXX, 43
  Jonathan (1637-Sept. 29, 1691) m.
    .... Clemence Hosmer MASS X, 46
  Jonathan (1707-p. 1782) m. .... (3)
    Margaret Lorrance XVIII, 46
  Jonathan (Feb. 12, 1726-Mar. 25,
    1796) m. .... (2) Hanna Herick
    Pomeroy X, 46
  Moses Willard (Oct. 28, 1756-July
    10, 1822) m. Dec. 10, 1778 Esther
    Jenney XXIX, 47
  Ralph (c. 1613-p. Jan. 12, 1677) m.
    .... Elizabeth Jessup NY XIX,
    91; XXII, 157; XXVIII, 7
  Richard (Mar. 23, 1720-Aug. 27, 1819)
    m. .... Mercy Hull XIX, 91
  Samuel (Oct. 25, 1745-Oct. 8, 1816)
    m. May 3, 1790 Mrs. Elizabeth
    (Gibbes) Shepheard XXIII, 67;
    XXVII, 87, 88; XXX, 43
  Thomas (c. 1588-....) m. ....
    ...... NY XVIII, 46
  Thomas (Sept. 17, 1754-Aug. 18, 1808)
    m. .... Eunice Wellington XII, 14
  William (1605-Oct. 1667) m. a. 1635
    Elizabeth Best MASS XXIX, 47;
    XXX, 141
  William (Apr. 3, 1726-Aug. 4, 1802)
    m. Jan. 1, 1749/50 Mary Wheeler
    XXX, 141
  William (May 7, 1753-Sept. 18, 1845)
    m. May 1771 Mary Plympton XXX,
    141

HUNTER
  Jacob (a. 1750-1780) m. 1766
    Mrs. Elizabeth (Boush) Nimmo XIV,
    83
  William (....-1718) m. 1678 ......
    ...... VA XIV, 83

HUNTINGTON
  Amos (Sept. 4, 1739-July 2, 1822) m.
    Feb. 4, 1767 Peace Clark XXXI, 71
  Andrew (May 9, 1747-July 16, 1811) m.
    Apr. 17, 1768 Ruth Hyde XXI, 157
  Christopher, Sr. (1628-1691) m. Oct.
    7, 1652 Ruth Rockwell CONN XXXI,
    71
  Eliphalet (Apr. 24, 1737-June 15,
    1799) m. Nov. 11, 1762 Dinah Rudd
    XXXI, 156
  Enoch (Dec. 15, 1739-June 12, 1809)

m. June 17, 1764 Mary Gray XVII,
124

Jabez (Aug. 7, 1719-Oct. 5, 1786) m.
Jan. 20, 1741/2 (1) Elizabeth
Backus; July 10, 1746 (2) Hannah
Williams XXV, 26; XXX, 231, 232,
233

Jacob (June 16, 1741-p. 1790) m.
June 13, 1765 Elizabeth Goodman
XXXII, 27, 28

James (Feb. 2, 1706/7-May 12, 1785)
m. Dec. 3, 1735 Elizabeth Derby
XIII, 116; XXIV, 25; XXV, 74

James, III (Oct. 1, 1743-Mar. 22,
1808) m. May 24, 1767 Hannah Curtis
XXV, 74; XXVI, 226, 227; XXXII, 68,
211; XXXIV, 16, 282

Simon (July 6, 1629-June 28, 1706)
m. Oct. 1653 Sarah Clark CONN
XIII, 116; XVII, 124; XXI, 157;
XXIV, 25; XXV, 26, 74; XXVI,
226,227; XXX, 232, 233; XXXI, 156;
XXXII, 68, 211; XXXIV, 16, 282

William (a. 1625-c. 1689) m. a. 1643
Joanna Bayley MASS XXXII, 27

HUNTLEY

Elisha (Dec. 15, 1760-Jan. 17, 1835)
m. .... Clarisa Gustin XV, 44, 53

John (....-Nov. 16, 1676) m. ....
Jane ...... MASS XV, 44, 53

HURD

Abraham (1724-p. 1790) m. 1753 Mrs.
Mary (Stevens) Wilcox XI, 81;
XVI, 68

Adam (c. 1611-....) m. .... Hannah
Barbraum (Bartram) CONN XI, 81;
XVI, 68; XXXI, 169; XXXIII, 148,
149

Ebenezer (Apr. 10, 1756-Oct. 28,
1824) m. July 5, 1781 Abigail
Kempton XXXI, 169

Justus (Apr. 2, 1721/2-Mar. 31, 1804)
m. May 20, 1746 Rachel Love Fuller
XXXI, 169; XXXIII, 148, 149

HURLBURT, includes HULBERT, HURLBUT

Amos (Dec. 3, 1752-Nov. 15, 1835) m.
Dec. 11, 1777 Esther Geer XV, 70

John, Jr. (Mar. 11, 1729/30-Mar. 10,
1782) m. .... Abigail Avery
XXVII, 83

Samuel (Apr. 21, 1748-Aug. 12, 1816)
m. 1766 Jerusha Higgins XV, 50

Thomas (1610-p. Oct. 12, 1671) m.
.... Sarah ...... CONN XV, 50, 70;
XXII, 7, 8; XVII, 83; XXVIII, 74

Thomas (1754-1814) m. Dec.
1775 Eunice Grant XXII, 7, 8;
XXVIII, 74

HURLBUT, see HURLBURT

HUSSEY

Christopher (1595/6-1686) m. c. 1630
Theodate Bacheler MASS, NH
XXXIII, 64

Christopher, Sr. (June 3, 1724-
June 28, 1785) m. Aug. 11, 1743
Mary Coffin XXXIII, 64

HUSTAD, see HUSTED

HUSTED, includes HUESTED, HUSTAD, HUSTIS

Abraham (1760-1820) m. a. 1781 Sarah
Palmer XXXIII, 147; XXXIV, 120

Angell (1620-Apr. 1706) m. ....
Rebecca Sherwood CONN XII, 66;
XX, 14

Jonathan (1747-Jan. 26, 1835) m.
Apr. 6, 1769 Hannah Waterbury
XII, 66; XX, 13

Joseph (Nov. 10, 1719-June 1805) m.
Apr. 5, 1756 Mary Hunt XXIX, 161

Nathaniel (Mar. 29, 1748-....) m.
Apr. 14, 1768 Hannah Webb X, 228

Peter (May 1742-Mar. 24, 1821) m.
Feb. 11, 1768 Eunice Lyon XXII,
141; XXV, 115, 116; XXIX, 321

Robert (1579-1652) m. a. 1635 Eliza-
beth Miller CONN X, 228; XII, 66;
XX, 14; XXII, 141; XXV, 115, 116;
XXIX, 161, 321; XXXIII, 147; XXXIV,
120

Robert (June 7, 1759-Feb. 15, 1833)
m. c. 1802/3 Tamer Budd XXIX, 161

HUSTIS, see HUSTED

HUTCHING, see HUTCHINS

HUTCHINS, includes HUTCHING

Benjamin (July 25, 1756-Sept. 4,
1810) m. a. 1789 Nancy ......
XXV, 165

Enoch (....-May 9, 1698) m. Apr. 5,
1667 Mary Stevenson ME XXV, 165

Jeremiah (Jan. 15, 1736-Nov. 11,
1816) m. a. 1760 (1) Mehitable
Corliss XXVII, 193; XXIX, 212,
292; XXXI, 162, 296; XXXII, 246

John (1604-Feb. 6, 1685) m. ....
Frances ...... MASS XXVII, 193;
XXIX, 212, 292; XXXI, 162, 296;
XXXII, 246

Jonathan, Jr. (bpt. Sept. 22, 1728-
p. 1790) m. May 3, 1746 Elizabeth
Higgins XXV, 165

Nicholas (1637/8-c. Sept. 1693) m.
Apr. 4, 1666 Elizabeth Farr MASS
XXXIII, 263

HUTCHINS, cont.
  Noah, Sr. (Mar. 27, 1758-Aug. 27,
    1836) m. c. 1803 (2) Lydia (Cof-
    fin) Jay XXXIII, 263

HUYCK
  Jans Hanse (c. 1600-1654) m. ....
    Lizabeth Pieters NY XXXIV, 321
  Johannas Andries (bpt. June 27, 1730-
    a. 1797) m. Mar. 8, 1762 Fitje Van
    Derkarr XXXIV, 321

HYATT
  Charles (....-1726) m. .... Sarah
    ...... MD XXX, 219
  Meshach (c. 1723-Nov. 2, 1807) m.
    .... Sarah ...... XXX, 219

HYDE
  Asa (July 21, 1741-Mar. 26, 1797) m.
    May 21, 1763 Lucy French XV, 66
  Elijah (Jan. 17, 1735-Dec. 31, 1800)
    m. Feb. 24, 1757 Mary Clark XXIV,
    49
  Elijah Clark (June 14, 1758-1835) m.
    .... (1) Sarah Taylor XXIV, 49
  James (Apr. 6, 1741-Jan. 25, 1785)
    m. May 14, 1767 Eunice Backus
    XXVIII, 58
  James (1752-1809) m. .... Martha
    Nevins IV, 109
  Jedadiah (Aug. 24, 1735-May 29, 1822)
    m. Jan. 24, 1761 Mary Waterman
    XVI, 21; XXIX, 37
  Matthew (Apr. 28, 1711-Mar. 18,
    1792) m. Apr. 19, 1733 (1) Eliza-
    beth Huntington; Aug. 26, 1776
    (2) Hannah Pember XVII, 146;
    XXXI, 276, 277
  Moses (Sept. 11, 1751-1828) m. Dec.
    6, 1787 Sarah Dana XIV, 59, 60
    71
  Phineas (Nov. 15, 1749-Sept. 5,
    1820) m. Sept. 1782 Esther Hold-
    ridge XXV, 67
  William (c. 1600-Jan. 6, 1681) m.
    .... CONN IV, 109;
    XIV, 59, 60, 71; XV, 66; XVI, 21;
    XVII, 146; XXIV, 49; XXV, 67;
    XXVIII, 58; XXIX, 37; XXXI, 276

IJAMS, includes EYAMS
  Thomas (c. 1740-1806) m. c. 1774
    Mary Ijams XXV, 29
  William (c. 1650-July 28, 1703) m.
    1669 Elizabeth Cheney MD XXV, 29

INGALLS
  Edmund (1598-p. Sept. 16, 1648) m.

  .... Ann ...... MASS X, 156;
    XXVI, 305
  John, Sr. (June 1, 1723-Feb. 11,
    1815) m. Dec. 5, 1748 (1) Sarah
    Hazeltine XXVI, 304, 305
  John, Jr. (Apr. 3, 1751-....) m.
    May 12, 1774 Hannah Massey XXVI,
    304, 305
  Joseph, Jr. (Aug. 22, 1723-Oct. 18,
    1790) m. May 24, 1749 Sarah Abbott
    X, 156

INGERSOLL
  John (1615-Sept. 3, 1684) m. 1667
    (3) Mary Hunt CONN, MASS X, 71;
    XIV, 63; XXXIII, 227
  Peter (May 11, 1733-1785) m. July
    30, 1752 Anna Severill XXXIII,
    227
  William (Apr. 1, 1724-Aug. 10, 1815)
    m. Dec. 11, 1746 Lydia Ingersoll
    X, 71; XIV, 63

INNIS
  James (....-a. Dec. 1710/1) m. ....
    .... VA XXXIII, 316
  James (....-a. Nov. 2, 1778) m. ....
    Mary ...... XXXIII, 316

IRELAN, see IRELAND

IRELAND, includes IRELAN
  Japhet (Nov. 22, 1744-Feb. 20, 1810)
    m. Apr. 21, 1767 Mary Townsend
    X, 250, 268; XX, 163
  Joseph (c. 1713-June 21, 1793) m.
    1735 Elizabeth Losee XXI, 68, 69;
    XXV, 221, 222
  Thomas (....-p. Sept. 30, 1668) m.
    .... Joan ...... NY X, 250, 269;
    XX, 164; XXI, 68, 69; XXV, 221,
    222

IRONMONGER
  Cornelius (1730-1811) m. a. 1762
    Esther Dunton XXXII, 179
  Thomas (c. 1650-1724) m. .... Mary
    Scale VA XXXII, 179

ISHAM
  Daniel (June 22, 1751-June 27, 1841)
    m. Nov. 25, 1773 Rhoda Lord XXXI,
    172
  John (Mar. 31, 1654-Sept. 3, 1713)
    m. Dec. 16, 1687 Jane Parker MASS
    XXXI, 172

IVES
  Charles, Jr. (Apr. 14, 1760-Aug. 16,
    1837) m. Dec. 19, 1783 Mary Francis
    XXXIII, 204

Elam (Dec. 16, 1761-Jan. 24, 1846)
m. May 9, 1790 Sarah Hitchcock
XXX, 80, 81
James, Jr. (Aug. 11, 1751-Aug. 15,
1826) m. June 16, 1779 Mary Brockett XXII, 23
Lazarus (1762-p. 1823) m. Jan. 15,
1781 Esther Thorp XXIV, 73, 115
Lent (Nov. 28, 1758-June 30, 1838)
m. Sept. 26, 1782 Mary Mighill
XXIX, 52; XXXI, 301, 302
William (1607-p. Apr. 3, 1648) m. a.
1639 Hannah ...... CONN XXII,
23; XXIV, 73, 115; XXIX, 52;
XXX, 81; XXXI, 301; XXXIII, 204

JACKMAN
James (c. 1618-Dec. 30, 1694) m. ....
(1) Joanna ...... MASS XVII, 151;
XVIII, 17, 112; XXX, 11
Samuel (Mar. 17, 1749-Aug. 20, 1845)
m. 1770 Submit Brown XVII, 151;
XVIII, 17, 112; XXX, 11

JACKSON
Abraham, Sr. (....-Oct. 4, 1714) m.
Nov. 18, 1657 Remember Morton
MASS XIII, 14; XXXI, 44
Barnabas (Apr. 25, 1753-Jan. 2, 1819)
m. Oct. 19, 1775 Lydia Oldham
XIII, 14; XXXI, 44
Caleb (Apr. 16, 1760-Dec. 15, 1815)
m. Jan. 31, 1782 Rhoda Pratt
XXIX, 21; XXXI, 165
Edward (Jan. 1602-June 17, 1681) m.
.... (1) Frances ...... MASS
XXIX, 21; XXXI, 165
Isaac (May 29, 1732-May 10, 1795) m.
May 11, 1758 Jemima Jones XXXI,
165
Robert (c. 1620-1684) m. 1671 Agnes
Washburn NY XXX, 223
Samuel (....-Oct. 30, 1688) m. Oct.
20, 1672 Ann Clark MD XXX, 182
Samuel (....-May 9, 1791) m. May 27,
1762 Patience Wright XXX, 181
182
Stephen (Sept. 8, 1744-Mar. 24, 1812)
m. Dec. 19, 1763 Mary Burwell
XXX, 223

JACOB, see JACOBS

JACOBISSEN, see JACOBUS

JACOBS, includes JACOB
Asa (Apr. 18, 1758-Nov. 27, 1844) m.
Sept. 11, 1791 Sarah Emerson XV,
110

John (May 29, 1725-Mar. 3, 1820) m.
Jan. 24, 1751 Sarah Plank XXVII,
8, 9
Nicholas (1608-June 5, 1657) m. ....
Mary Gilman MASS XV, 110; XXVII,
8, 9

JACOBUS, includes JACOBISSEN, JANSE,
JANSZ
Cornelius (June 7, 1746-Jan. 8,
1832) m. .... Catherine Garrison
XXVII, 226
Jacobus (....-....) m. .... Judik
Franse NY XXVII, 226; XXVIII,
212
James (c. 1716-p. Aug. 22, 1794
m. June 3, 1743 Maritje Kip
XXVII, 226; XXVIII, 212

JANES, includes JEANES
Eliphalet (Feb. 23, 1743-June 5,
1833) m. 1768 Elfleda Lyon XXVIII,
93
Samuel, III (Sept. 13, 1724-Jan.
1788) m. Jan. 1752 Hannah Brown
XXV, 29
Solomon (June 20, 1748-Apr. 4, 1812)
m. Jan. 27, 1780 Beulah Fiske
XIV, 29, 30
William (1610-Sept. 20, 1690) m.
1637 (1) Mary ...... CONN, MASS
XIV, 29, 30; XXV, 29; XXVIII, 94

JANSE, see JACOBUS

JANSEN, see also CORSON
Carsten (....-....) m. .... Barbara
...... NY XXIX, 275; XXX, 216

JANSZ, see JACOBUS

JANZ, see WESTBROOK

JAQUETT
Jean Paul (1615/20-a. Feb. 18, 1685)
m. .... Maria de Carpentier DE
XI, 13
Peter (Oct. 12, 1760-Nov. 4, 1816)
m. Mar. 9, 1784 Catherine Longhead
XI, 13

JAQUITH
Abraham, I (1643-Sept. 17, 1676) m.
1643 Ann Jordan MASS XXX, 186;
XXXIV, 333
Benjamin, Sr. (Feb. 28, 1737/8-Feb.
11, 1810) m. June 27, 1765 Phoebe
Heacock Marshall XXX, 186
Jonathan, I (Sept. 13, 1749-1778
m. Jan. 14, 1773 Lydia Johnson
XXXIV, 332

JAYNE
John (Dec. 25, 1748-Apr. 25, 1838)
m. Sept. 15, 1775 Cornelia Decker
XIV, 94
William (Jan. 25, 1618-Mar. 24, 1714)
m. June 10, 1675 (2) Mrs. Anna
(Jennings) Briggs NY XIV, 94

JEANES, see JANES

JEFFERIS, see JEFFRIES

JEFFRIES, includes JEFFERIS
Richard (Feb. 24, 1730-Mar. 27, 1817)
m. 1786 (2) Nancy Ann Davis XXVI,
233
Robert (1656-Apr. 4, 1739) m. 1729
(2) Anne Archer PA XXVI, 233

JENCKS, see JENKS

JENKINS
App (....-....) m. ....
MD XVI, 122, 123
Benjamin (June 30, 1707-June 1, 1787)
m. Oct. 29, 1730 Mehitable Blush
XIV, 48
Edward (....-1699) m. p. 1643 (1)
Lettice (Hanford) Foster MASS
XXXIV, 182
Edward (Dec. 4, 1741-....) m. June
14, 1764 Jerusha Neal XXXIV, 182
Henry (Feb. 21, 1768-Nov. 8, 1854)
m. Dec. 10, 1791 Martha Stapp XVI,
122, 123
Joel (....-p. Nov. 2, 1688) m. ....
Sarah ...... MASS XXIX, 175
John (1609-1684) m. Feb. 2, 1653
Mrs. Nancy Ewer MASS XIV, 48
Lemuel (July 31, 1758-Mar. 16, 1844)
m. Oct. 24, 1787 Hannah Lewis
XXIX, 175
Samuel (Aug. 13, 1710-1805) m. Mar.
2, 1740 Rebecca White XXXIV, 182
Southworth (Nov. 29, 1742-Dec. 13,
1820) m. Nov. 15, 1770 Huldah
Wright XIV, 48

JENKS, includes JENCKS
Boomer (Feb'. 19, 1761-June 8, 1797)
m. Aug. 4, 1781 Anna King XXX,
113
Jeremiah (Nov. 29, 1739-Jan. 4,
1811) m. Feb. 26, 1776 Lucy Whipple
XII, 47; XIII, 80
John (1743-p. 1775) m. Aug. 16,
1764 Sarah Seymour XX, 167
John Seymour (1768-Oct. 19, 1843) m.
1794/5 Penelope Webb XX, 167
Jonathan (1718-1787) m. .... Harriet
Pullen XII, 47; XIII, 80

Joseph (1602-Mar. 16, 1683) m. Sept.
16, 1630 Mary Tervyn MASS XII,
47; XIII, 80; XX, 168; XXIV, 131;
XXX, 113; XXXI, 301
Joseph (1714-1789) m. Dec. 18, 1735
Sarah King XXIV, 131
Joseph (Dec. 18, 1740-Feb. 17, 1821)
m. .... Sarah Tingley XXXI, 301

JENNINGS
Baylor (1756-1797) m. July 26, 1779
Susannah Bradford XXI, 168
Isaac (May 18, 1743-Jan. 6, 1819) m.
Nov. 15, 1770 Abigail Gold XXII,
53
Jacob (Dec. 25, 1739-....) m. 1762
Grace Parker XXIX, 367; XXXI, 258,
259
John (....-Feb. 11, 1669) m. a. 1652
Margaret ...... VA XXI, 168
Joshua (1620-a. Feb. 25, 1674) m.
Dec. 23, 1647 Mary Williams CONN
XXII, 53; XXIX, 368; XXXI, 258,
259

JENNISON
Israel (1713-Sept. 19, 1782) m. Feb.
17, 1739 Mary Heywood XXXIV, 104,
128
Robert (1605-July 4, 1690) m. a.
1637 (2) Grace ...... MASS
XXXIV, 104, 128

JERAULD
James (c. 1660-....) m. .... Martha
Dupee MASS IV, 156
James (Feb. 2, 1746-1813) m. ....
Mary Rice IV, 156

JEWELL, includes JUEL
Henry (Mar. 5, 1753-July 7, 1827) m.
.... Sarah Greeley XXIX, 54
Joseph (June 18, 1744-Dec. 13, 1822)
m. Feb. 22, 1775 (1) Mary Crane
XXV, 64
Thomas (1608-Feb. 2, 1654) m. ....
Grisell ...... MASS XXV, 64;
XXIX, 54

JEWETT
Jacob (Sept. 17, 1735-Apr. 25, 1813)
m. July 1, 1762 Mehitable Mitchell
XXXIII, 37, 38; XXXIV, 138
John Cole (bpt. Jan. 29, 1739-Jan.
6, 1811) m. May 18, 1769 Elizabeth
Smith XVIII, 150
Joseph (bpt. Dec. 31, 1609-Feb. 26,
1660) m. Oct. 1, 1634 Mary Mallison
MASS XVIII, 150; XXI, 177, 178
Joseph (June 15, 1740-Aug. 25, 1814)
m. .... (1) Rebecca Abbott IX, 46

Maximilian (bpt. Oct. 4, 1607-Oct.
19, 1684) m. c. 1638 Ann Cole
MASS IX, 46; XVIII, 58; XXXIII,
37, 38; XXXIV, 138
Maximillian (Jan. 27, 1741-Oct. 16,
1823) m. Aug. 16, 1766 Rebecca
Burpee XVIII, 58
Oliver (Feb. 24, 1747-Aug. 22, 1829)
m. Jan. 23, 1772 Betsy Houghton
XXI, 177, 178

JOBE
Andrew, Sr. (....-Nov. 29, 1699) m.
.... PA XXXIV, 268
Samuel (c. 1735-p. 1823) m. c. 1758
Dorcas McKay XXXIV, 267

JOCHEMSEN, see also GEORGE ANDERSON
Andries (....-c. 1663) m. ....
Seletje Arens NY XXVI, 16

JOHNSON
Abel (Mar. 26, 1748-May 21, 1815) m.
.... Mary ...... XXII, 42
David (a. 1735-a. Feb. 11, 1788) m.
.... Nancy Berryman XXVI, 86
Ebenezer (1645-Sept. 18, 1726) m.
.... Hannah Tomlinson CONN
XII, 117
Ebenezer (Aug. 29, 1741-Aug. 26,
1823) m. Dec. 16, 1766 Elizabeth
Rice XVI, 87; XXIX, 56, 281
Edmund (1612-Mar. 1, 1650) m. ....
Mary ...... NH XXXII, 231
Edward (bpt. Sept. 16, 1598-Apr. 23,
1672) m. c. 1620 Susan Munnter
MASS XI, 94; XXVII, 13, 112; XXX,
52; XXXII, 43; XXXIV, 139
Edward (Oct. 23, 1743-1779) m. Oct.
31, 1765 Mary Godfrey XXVII, 111,
112; XXXIV, 138
Elisha (July 1, 1753-Nov. 28, 1832)
m. June 9, 1778 (2) Sarah Perry
XXVII, 139; XXVIII, 140, 209
Haynes (Aug. 28, 1749-Sept. 2, 1775)
m. 1770 Elizabeth Elliot XXVII,
39
Hezekiah (Mar. 12, 1732-Feb. 21,
1810) m. Nov. 1, 1758 Ruth Merri-
man X, 165
Isaac (....-Dec. 19, 1673) m. Jan.
20, 1637 Elizabeth Porter MASS
XXVIII, 169
Jeremiah (....-....) m. .... Sarah
Hotchkiss CONN XXII, 42
John (c. 1600-Sept. 29, 1659) m.
.... Margery Heath MASS XIX, 77;
XXIII, 68; XXVIII, 125, 169; XXXII,
284
John (July 28, 1748-Oct. 3, 1833) m.
Oct. 10, 1786 Abigail Abbot

XXIII, 43
John (bpt. Oct. 12, 1760-a. Feb. 10,
1824) m. c. 1791 Sarah McDonald
XXIII, 46
Joseph (bpt. Feb. 12, 1636/7-Nov. 18,
1714) m. 1666 Hannah Tenney MASS
XXVII, 39
Lemuel (Mar. 14, 1750-p. 1801) m.
.... Jerusha Norton XIX, 76;
XXIII, 68
Nathan (1720-1805) m. 1769 Elizabeth
Hutchings XXV, 255; XXVIII, 187
Nathaniel, Jr. (Mar. 6, 1731/2-1777)
m. Apr. 1, 1756 Anna Child XXVIII,
169
Nathaniel (1756-Sept. 30, 1845) m.
.... Rebecca Pierson XI, 107,
108; XII, 117
Obadiah (Feb. 18, 1735/6-Oct. 27,
1801) m. July 6, 1765 (2) Lucy
(Cady) Spaulding XXVII, 12, 13;
XXX, 52
Obadiah (Feb. 2, 1757-1827) m. Mar.
6, 1777 Lois Winchell XXXII, 42,
43
Peter (....-a. 1654) m. .... Eliza-
beth ...... CONN XI, 107, 108
Peter (c. 1730-a. 1816) m. c. 1755
Rebecca ...... XXIII, 46
Richard (....-1699) m. .... Susana
Dunscomb VA XXVI, 86
Richard (1649-June 18, 1719) m. June
25, 1682 Mary Grover NJ III, 47;
IV, 80
Robert, Jr. (Jan. 26, 1727-Dec. 28,
1796) m. Nov. 3, 1767 Jane Gibbon
III, 47; IV, 80
Samuel (Sept. 12, 1739-Mar. 30, 1822)
m. Mar. 1, 1762 Lydia Roberts
XXXII, 231, 232
Samuel (Apr. 25, 1756-....) m. ....
Phebe Hall XXX, 167; XXXII, 290
Simeon (June 22, 1733-....) m. c.
1777 (2) Elizabeth (Russell) Stone
XXVIII, 125
Solomon (....-Oct. 5, 1687) m. ....
Elinor ...... MASS XVI, 87; XXIX,
57, 281
Stephen (1640-Nov. 30, 1690) m.
Nov. 5, 1661 Elizabeth Dane MASS
XXX, 167; XXXII, 290
Stephen (July 8, 1740-Nov. 12, 1790)
m. Apr. 30, 1761 Elizabeth Pelton
XXXII, 284
Thomas (1621-Feb. 10, 1704) m. Apr.
1688 Mary Baker VA XXV, 255;
XXVIII, 187
Timothy (....-Mar. 15, 1688) m. Dec.
15, 1674 Rebecca Aslett MASS
XXIII, 43
William (....-1716) m. Dec. 1664

JOHNSON, cont.
  Sarah Hall CONN X, 165
  William (c. 1601-Dec. 9, 1677) m.
  1630 Elizabeth ...... MASS
  XXVII, 39, 139; XXVIII, 140, 209
  William, Jr. (Aug. 2, 1725- Sept. 12,
    1804) m. Jan. 25, 1750 Dorcas
    Chamberlain XI, 94

JONES
  Aaron (Dec. 4, 1754-June 11, 1836)
    m. Apr. 8, 1779 Abigail Billings
    XXIV, 14
  Benjamin (1748-p. 1799) m. ....
    Mercy Wilder IV, 146
  Benjamin (Feb. 5, 1757-June 29, 1821)
    m. .... Esther Woodruff V, 62
  David (July 27, 1716-Jan. 20, 1795)
    m. Nov. 10, 1738 Hannah Fox XXVI,
    96, 97
  David (Feb. 12, 1740/1-1827) m. June
    27, 1765 Molly Bailey XXVI, 97
  Ebenezer (bpt. Feb. 3, 1740-....)
    m. Jan. 2, 1770 Rebecca Stirke
    XXI, 153, 154
  Enos (May 31, 1734-Aug. 15, 1803) m.
    1758 Amplias Wadsworth XXXII, 186
  Hardy (c. 1747-June 21, 1819) m. c.
    1777 (1) Sarah Phillips XXXI,
    11, 12
  Henry (Aug. 14, 1733-1786) m. Oct.
    4, 1777 Rebecca Knighton XXIX,
    96
  Hugh (bpt. Jan. 3, 1636/7-c. 1688)
    m. Dec. 31, 1672 Mary Foster MASS
    XII, 55; XXVI, 96, 97; XXXIII, 31
  Israel (Mar. 18, 1716-Dec. 28, 1798)
    m. Nov. 29, 1744 Jemima Clark
    XXVII, 179
  Joel (July 7, 1764-Aug. 11, 1845) m.
    July 16, 1795 Rhoda Sprague
    XXXII, 186
  John (....-....) m. a. 1681 ......
    ...... NJ XVI, 30
  John (c. 1615-June 22, 1673) m. ....
    Dorcas ...... MASS XXIV, 14
  John (Feb. 11, 1757-Feb. 5, 1834) m.
    Sept. 20, 1780 Elizabeth Dashiell
    XXXI, 108, 109
  Joseph (c. 1652-Jan. 16, 1708) m. a.
    1670 Elizabeth Clark MD XXIX, 96
  Joseph (Nov. 17, 1739-May 1816) m.
    .... Phoebe Harrison XVI, 30
  Lewis (c. 1600-Apr. 11, 1684) m. ....
    Ann Stone MASS IV, 146; XXXII, 186
  Malachi (1651-Mar. 26, 1729) m. ....
    Mary ...... PA XXI, 153, 154
  Matthew, I (1640-Mar. 1, 1712) m.
    .... Elizabeth Albrighton VA
    XIX, 54; XX, 103, 110; XXVII, 80;
    XXXII, 20

Matthew (Nov. 25, 1748-Dec. 1793) m.
  1770 Elizabeth Hill XXVII, 79, 80
Nathan (Apr. 13, 1721-Sept. 1799) m.
  Elizabeth Coburn XII, 55
Nathan (Feb. 25, 1748-Nov. 6, 1813)
  m. .... Mrs. Mary Bradford XII,
  55
Nathaniel (c. 1654-Aug. 21, 1691) m.
  Oct. 7, 1684 Abigail Atwater CONN
  V, 62
Paul (Oct. 4, 1737-Sept. 16, 1821)
  m. Sept. 24, 1764 Phebe Roberts
  XXVI, 14
Robert (....-1746) m. Nov. 3, 1693
  Ellen Jones PA XXVI, 15
Roger (1625-Jan. 6, 1701) m. ....
  Dorothy Walker VA XXV, 121, 122
Samuel (June 15, 1740-....) m. July
  2, 1761 Hannah Adams XXII, 112;
  XXXIV, 303
Seth (Mar. 21, 1748-Apr. 14, 1827)
  m. Feb. 23, 1773 Mary Dagget
  XXVII, 48, 49
Thomas (1598-1667) m. .... Ann .....
  MASS XXVII, 48, 49
Thomas (1598-Aug. 26, 1671) m. ....
  Mary North MASS XXVII, 179
Thomas (c. 1635-a. 1675) m. c. 1655
  Mary ...... VA XXXI, 12
Thomas (....-1800/1) m. .... (2)
  Frances Carter XXV, 121, 122
Thomas (June 6, 1751-June 13, 1832)
  m. Nov. 23, 1773 Susanna Adams
  XXVII, 179
Tignal (1720-1807) m. .... Penelope
  Cain XIX, 54; XX, 103, 110
Tignal, Jr. (1746-p. June 21, 1793)
  m. 1770 Martha Anderson XXXII, 20
William (c. 1587-Mar. 8, 1677) m.
  .... MASS XXII,
  112; XXXIV, 303
William (1608-Aug. 30, 1669) m. a.
  1639 Elizabeth ...... VA XXXI,
  108, 109
William (1624-Oct. 17, 1706) m. ....
  .... CONN V, 62
Zebediah (Mar. 12, 1753-Aug. 2, 1823)
  m. (int.) Oct. 19, 1776 Mrs. Jo-
  hannah Goodhue XXXIII, 31

JORDAN
  Benjamin (1738-1814) m. May 12, 1763
    (1) Hannah Wieman VI, 108
  Edward (....-p. 1791) m. .... Eliza-
    beth ...... XXXIII, 347
  John (c. 1650-Mar. 9, 1728) m. c.
    1672 (1) .... MASS
    XXXII, 71
  Joshua (1736-....) m. Mar. 24, 1763
    Catherine Jordan XXXII, 16
  Josiah (Aug. 1, 1760-Aug. 9, 1840)

m. Mar. 11, 1784 Abigail Farrar
XXXII, 71
Robert (1612-p. Jan. 28, 1679) m.
1643/4 Sarah Winter ME VI, 108;
XXXII, 16
Samuel (1575-Mar. 1623) m. .... (2)
Cicely Reynolds VA XXX, 202;
XXXIII, 347
William (Oct. 5, 1748-July 1822) m.
1769 Sarah Wood XXX, 202

JOSLIN, includes JOSSELYN
Abijah (Jan. 24, 1745-Sept. 1, 1811)
m. Jan. 5, 1768/9 Kezia Farrar
XVIII, 23
John, Sr. (Dec. 1710-Aug. 1788) m.
July 4, 1733 Lucy Wilder XVIII,
23
John (Sept. 9, 1734-Oct. 25, 1811)
m. Dec. 18, 1754 Joanna Andrews
XXVIII, 198
Nathaniel (July 6, 1722-May 2, 1790)
m. June 13, 1751 Sarah Low XXIX,
229
Thomas (1592-Nov. 3, 1660) m. 1614
Rebecca Marlow MASS XVIII, 23;
XXVIII, 198; XXIX, 229

JOSSELYN, see JOSLIN

JOY
David (Dec. 6, 1724-1809) m. Dec. 1,
1747 Elizabeth Allen XXXI, 249
Jacob (Sept. 6, 1734-Apr. 1812) m.
Sept. 4, 1758 Jerusha Ripley
XXXIV, 51
Jacob (Feb. 17, 1749-Mar. 12, 1805)
m. Feb. 19, 1775 Hannah Cram
XXIII, 74; XXIX, 191, 193, 202
Thomas (1611-Oct. 21, 1678) m. 1637
Joan Gallup MASS XXIII, 74;
XXIX, 192, 193, 202; XXXI, 249;
XXXIV, 51

JOYNER
Thomas (1619-1694) m. 1646/7 Eliza-
beth Robbins VA XXX, 248
Thomas (....-Dec. 1811) m. ....
Margaret ...... XXX, 248

JUDSON
Benjamin (Feb. 17, 1735-Sept. 11,
1811) m. .... Anna Camp XIII, 107
Daniel (Apr. 26, 1728-Nov. 14, 1813)
m. Jan. 1, 1752 (1) Sarah Curtiss
XVII, 159; XXVI, 157
Isaac (July 5, 1731-Dec. 7, 1787) m.
1750 Mary Stoddard XIX, 79
Joseph (c. 1619-Oct. 9, 1690) m.
.... Sarah Porter CONN XIII,
107

William (....-July 29, 1662) m. ....
(1) Grace ...... CONN XVII, 159;
XIX, 80; XXVI, 157

JUEL, see JEWELL

KEELER
Josiah (Feb. 18, 1768-June 23, 1824)
m. .... Betsey Bradley X, 144
Phineas (Jan. 11, 1744-June 26,
1833) m. May 16, 1769 (1) Mary
Camp XIX, 162; XX, 158
Ralph (1613-Aug. 20, 1672) m. p.
1651 Mrs. Sarah Whelpley CONN X,
144; XIX, 162; XX, 158

KEEN, includes KYN
Joran (1620-a. May 1693) m. ....
.... PA XXXI, 94
Matthias (Dec. 21, 1721-July 28,
1797) m. Nov. 23, 1752 (2) Margaret
Thomas XXXI, 94

KEENE
Isaac, Jr. (Apr. 27, 1736-Mar. 22,
1830) m. Aug. 26, 1764 Bethiah
Tobey XXIX, 67
John (1578-Nov. 14, 1649) m. ....
Martha ...... MASS XXIX, 67

KEENER, see KENNER

KEEP
John (1639-Mar. 26, 1676) m. Dec.
31, 1663 Sarah Leonard MASS XVI,
62
Samuel (May 26, 1739-Oct. 20, 1822)
m. June 4, 1767 Sabina Cooley
XVI, 62

KEESE
John (....-Dec. 10, 1700) m. Sept.
18, 1682 Ann Manton RI XXVI,
269, 270
John (c. 1755-1809) m. c. 1779 Rhoda
Appleby XXVI, 269, 270

KEITH
Comfort (Mar. 6, 1742-Sept. 8, 1823)
m. Oct. 31, 1765 Deborah Nelson
XXXIV, 287
James, Sr. (1643-July 23, 1719) m.
May 3, 1668 (1) Susannah Edson MASS
XXXIV, 287

KELLOGG
Benjamin (Feb. 18, 1761-Dec. 16,
1850) m. .... Lauranah Spalding
XXII, 103

KELLOGG, cont.

*Daniel (bpt. Feb. 6, 1630-Dec. 1688)
m. 1655 (2) Bridget Bouton CONN
VIII, 26; XIV, 96; XVI, 44, 74;
XVIII, 104; XXIII, 41; XXVIII,
139; XXXI, 206; XXXII, 285; XXXIII,
87, 88*

Ebenezer (c. 1722-Nov. 1, 1776) m.
Jan. 13, 1751 Sarah Clapp XXXIII,
194, 322

Ebenezer (Apr. 5, 1737-Sept. 9, 1817)
m. Oct. 20, 1763 Hannah Wright
XXIII, 41

Elijah (June 3, 1754-Mar. 27, 1845)
m. Jan. 4, 1781 Sarah Jones
XXVIII, 139

Isaac (Jan. 17, 1697-July 3, 1787)
m. Dec. 26, 1717 Mary Webster XIV,
87; XXIX, 141

Isaac (Jan. 14, 1745-Apr. 5, 1829)
m. Oct. 10, 1766 (1) Hannah Fitch
XIV, 96; XVI, 44, 45; XVIII, 104

John (Sept. 4, 1726-Apr. 23, 1789)
m. Jan. 11, 1753 Union Stoddard
XIV, 108; XXII, 103

Jonathan (bpt. Oct. 24, 1760-Feb. 28,
1823) m. June 5, 1783 Mary Holland
XXXIII, 194, 298, 322

*Joseph (bpt. Apr. 1, 1626-a. Feb. 4,
1708) m. .... (1) Joanna ......;
May 9, 1667 (2) Abigail Terry
MASS XIV, 42, 53, 54, 87, 108;
XVI, 128; XVII, 90; XXI, 58, 59;
XXII, 103; XXIX, 141; XXXII, 12;
XXXIII, 194, 298, 322; XXXIV, 222*

Martin, II (Oct. 10, 1740-Sept. 1,
1824) m. May 13, 1762 Mercy Benedict VIII, 25; XVI, 74; XXXII,
285

Martin (Mar. 29, 1741-Nov. 28, 1789)
m. Feb. 4, 1762 (1) Sarah Treadway
XXI, 58, 59

Nathan Fairchild (1752-Mar. 1823) m.
Mar. 29, 1779 Hannah (Wasson)
Moorehouse XXXI, 206; XXXIII, 87,
88

Phineas (June 7, 1756-Dec. 2, 1835)
m. Jan. 22, 1778 (1) Olive Frazer
XIV, 87; XVI, 127, 128; XVII, 90;
XXXII, 12

Silas (Apr. 7, 1714-Jan. 24, 1792)
m. May 10, 1739 Ruth Root XXXIV,
222

Solomon (Dec. 10, 1751-Sept. 13,
1795) m. Nov. 16, 1773 Ruth Kellogg XIV, 42

William (May 6, 1759-Oct. 20, 1824) m.
.... Urama Bishop XIV, 53, 54

KELLY

John (....-Dec. 28, 1644) m. ....

.... *MASS XXXI, 189*

John (Oct. 22, 1736-Mar. 29, 1821)
m. June 5, 1758 Elizabeth Hoyt
XXXI, 189

KELSEY

Daniel (Sept. 23, 1734-Oct. 20,
1810) m. c. 1757 Jemima Bronson
XXXIII, 67

George (Feb. 6, 1757-1827) m. c.
1782 Mrs. Susan (Smith) Brooks
XXVII, 174, 175

Stephen (Jan. 8, 1732-June 15, 1812)
m. Mar. 31, 1752 Anne Platt XIV,
36; XVII, 15, 16

Stephen (Jan. 6, 1757-Mar. 22, 1833)
m. Mar. 27, 1783 Lois Griffin
XXII, 12

*William (c. 1600-c. 1680) m. 1625/8
Bethia Hopkins MASS, CONN XIV,
35, 36; XVII, 15; XXII, 12; XXVII,
175; XXXIII, 67*

KEMBALL, see KIMBALL

KEMBLE, see KIMBALL and KIMBLE

KEMP

Benjamin (June 20, 1731-July 12,
1809) m. May 5, 1761 Judith Reed
XXII, 118

John (May 30, 1737-June 7, 1790) m.
.... Mary Wrightson VII, 7, 10

*Robert (c. 1650-1702) m. Mar. 1678
Elizabeth Webb MD VII, 7, 10*

*Samuel (....-....) m. May 23, 1662
Sarah Foster MASS XXII, 118*

KEMPTON

*Ephraim (....-May 5, 1645) m. ....
.... MASS XXVIII, 76*

Stephen (Feb. 23, 1743-....) m. Apr.
15, 1762 Mrs. Catherine Boise
XXVIII, 76

KENDALL

*John (1617-July 9, 1679) m. June 4,
1667 Susanna Savage VA XXXIII,
341, 342; XXXIV, 343*

Samuel (Aug. 30, 1749-1821) m. Mar.
15, 1780 Mary Smith XXXIII, 341,
342; XXXIV, 343

William (July 24, 1717-Aug. 18, 1790)
m. May 10, 1738 Jemima Kirk XXXIII,
341, 342

KENERSON, includes KENNISTON

Aaron (Sept. 14, 1746-Aug. 26, 1823)
m. a. 1774 Phebe Kennison XXXII,
64, 65

John (c. 1620-Apr. 16, 1677) m. a.

1646 Agnes ......   NH XXXII, 65

KENNE, see KINNEY

KENNER, includes KEENER
Francis (1734-1784) m. 1756 Eliza-
beth Howard XXX, 220
Richard, Sr. (1599/1600-1649) m.
.... VA XXXIV, 248
Richard (1640-1692) m. 1671 Eliza-
beth Rodham VA XXX, 220: XXXII,
163, 170
Rodham (c. 1739-Apr. 1802) m. Aug.
3, 1763 Elizabeth Plater XXXIV,
248
Rodham (1759-Oct. 18, 1814) m. 1786
Malinda Paine XXX, 220; XXXII,
163, 170

KENNEY, see KINNEY

KENNICOTT, see KINNICUTT

KENNISTON, see KENERSON

KENT
Abel (Sept. 20, 1753-a. Apr. 8, 1808)
m. .... Thankful ...... XXV, 210
Thomas (....-May 11, 1656/8) m. ....
.... MASS XXV, 210

KENYON, includes KINYON
John (Apr. 26, 1655-c. June 12, 1732)
m. .... Anne Mumford RI XXXI,
303
Samuel (1759-c. Nov. 27, 1822) m.
1787 Hannah ...... XXXI, 303

KERBY
Francis (1758-Oct. 14, 1831) m. Jan.
11, 1783 (1) Elizabeth Collard;
Mar. 17, 1809 (2) Christina Spaulding XXXIII, 21, 145, 155, 156,
344
Walter (....-a. Feb. 4, 1702) m. ....
(1) Jane ......; .... (2) Eliza-
beth ...... MD XXXIII, 21, 145,
155, 156, 344, 345

KETCHUM
Jonathan (Mar. 17, 1751/2-p. 1790)
m. .... Betsy Bristol XXXIV, 114
Joseph (....-a. 1730) m. Apr. 3,
1679 Mercy Lindall CONN XXXIV,
115
Joseph (Mar. 9, 1725-p. 1793) m.
Mar. 8, 1749/50 Elizabeth Hurlbutt
XXXIV, 114

KEYES, includes KEYS
Abner, Sr. (Dec. 11, 1738-Dec. 17,

1819) m. Dec. 20, 1763 Mary Shedd
VI, 89
Robert (....-July 16, 1647) m. ....
.... MASS VI, 89

KEYS, see KEYES

KIBBE
Edward (....-....) m. .... Deborah
...... MASS XXXIII, 217, 218
Israel (Dec. 17, 1727-Mar. 1818) m.
June 7, 1756 Ruth Needham XXXIII,
217

KIDDER
James (1626-Apr. 16, 1676) m. a.
1650 Anna Moore MASS XXVI, 61
Solomon (Aug. 3, 1732-Nov. 20, 1776)
m. Nov. 18, 1762 Lydia White
XXVI, 61

KILBORNE, see KILBOURN

KILBOURN, includes KILBORNE, KILBOURNE,
KILBURN
Ebenezer (Apr. 19, 1744-Aug. 3, 1810)
m. Feb. 2, 1767 Sarah Bill XX, 36
John (Sept. 29, 1624-Apr. 9, 1703)
m. c. 1650 (1) Naomi ......; ....
(2) Sarah Bronson CONN XX, 36;
XXVIII, 160
John (1704-Apr. 8, 1789) m. Oct. 26,
1732 Mehitable Bacon XXXIII, 28
Robert (May 12, 1764-Dec. 1857) m.
a. 1794 Sarah Hubbard XXVIII, 160
Thomas (June 8, 1578-a. 1639) m.
Sept. 5, 1604 Frances Moody CONN
XXVIII, 160; XXXIII, 28

KILBOURNE, see KILBOURN

KILBURN, see KILBOURN

KILBY
Ebenezer, Jr. (bpt. Jan. 25, 1736-
Nov. 30, 1776) m. Nov. 5, 1761
Jerusha Dix (Fox) XXXII, 270
John (c. 1632-Dec. 6, 1710) m. May
9, 1662 Elizabeth (Joslin) Yoemans
MASS XXXII, 270

KIMBALL, includes KEMBALL, KEMBLE
See also KIMBLE
Aaron (Sept. 12, 1747-Dec. 2, 1837)
m. Oct. 6, 1789 Judith Lendall
XXXIV, 55
Abraham (Apr. 18, 1742-May 1828) m.
.... Phoebe Runnels XXXI, 214,
215; XXXIII, 223, 224
Amos (Sept. 8, 1707-Jan. 26, 1788) m.
Mar. 1, 1736 Margaret Hale XXII, 15

KIMBALL, cont.
  Daniel (May 2, 1733/4-Feb. 22, 1814)
    m. May 26, 1757 Abigail Wood
    XXXIII, 112, 113
  David (Dec. 10, 1739-c. Sept. 1804)
    m. .... Abigail Buswell XVII, 139
  John (Feb. 5, 1738/9-Dec. 31, 1819)
    m. Nov. 23, 1765 Anna Ayers XXXIV,
    309
  John (c. 1740-p. 1790) m. .... Sarah
    Burnham XI, 23
  Joseph (Jan. 29, 1730/1-Nov. 6, 1814)
    m. July 12, 1756 (1) Mary Sanborn;
    c. 1762 (2) Sarah Smith XV, 125;
    XXIX, 170
  Moses (Nov. 8, 1747-Nov. 9, 1828) m.
    Oct. 16, 1771 Jemima Clement XXV,
    192; XXXIII, 20
  Phineas (Jan. 7, 1747-Nov. 8, 1842)
    m. .... Molly ...... XXVI, 195,
    196, 197
  Richard (1595-June 22, 1675) m. a.
    1615 (1) Ursula Scott MASS XI,
    23; XV, 125; XVII, 139; XXII, 16;
    XXV, 192; XXVI, 195, 196, 197;
    XXIX, 170; XXXI, 215; XXXII, 210;
    XXXIII, 20, 112, 113, 223, 224;
    XXXIV, 55, 310
  Thomas (Feb. 12, 1730-Feb. 17, 1789)
    m. Feb. 17, 1757 Hannah Kimball
    XXXII, 210

KIMBERLY
  Nathaniel (May 21, 1743-Aug. 18,
    1806) m. a. 1774 Mirabele (Mabel)
    Thompson VI, 21, 69, 75, 76, 80,
    81; VII, 8, 9, 10; X, 8, 84, 85;
    XIII, 121; XXXIV, 141
  Silas (c. Nov. 1743-Jan. 18, 1803)
    m. .... (1) Sarah Smith XXXII,
    153
  Thomas (June 24, 1604-c. Jan. 1672)
    m. Aug. 28, 1628 (1) Alice Aywood
    MASS, CONN VI, 21, 69, 75, 76, 80,
    81; VII, 8, 9, 10; X, 8, 84, 85;
    XIII, 121; XXXII, 153; XXXIV, 142

KIMBLE, includes KEMBLE
  James (June 24, 1729-p. 1803) m.
    .... Frances ...... XVI, 136, 137;
    XVII, 43, 44
  Robert (....-1691) m. ....
    ...... MD XVI, 136, 137; XVII,
    43, 44

KING, includes KINGE
  Clement (c. 1641-c. 1694) m. a. 1674
    Elizabeth ...... MASS, RI VI, 85
  Dan (Oct. 11, 1741-Sept. 1, 1833)
    m. Sept. 13, 1767 (1) Thankful
    Bronson XVI, 117

  Elijah (Dec. 14, 1747-1794) m. Apr.
    21, 1763 Maria Cook XV, 92; XXII,
    131; XXV, 193; XXVI, 243, 244
  James (bpt. Nov. 7, 1647-May 13,
    1722) m. Mar. 23, 1674 Elizabeth
    Fuller MASS, CONN XVI, 117; XXI,
    85; XXII, 30
  Jeremiah (1738-Sept. 28, 1786) m.
    .... Hannah Young XXIX, 223
  John (1600-p. 1669) m. .... Mary
    Blucks MASS XXX, 106; XXXII, 104
  John (1629-Dec. 3, 1703) m. Nov. 18,
    1656 Sarah Holton CONN, MASS
    XXXIV, 98
  John (Aug. 26, 1730-Feb. 6, 1814) m.
    1775 Catharine Leonard XXXII, 104
  John (Sept. 11, 1730-May 1, 1808)
    m. Dec. 15, 1752 Elizabeth Fenner
    XXX, 106
  John (Dec. 1, 1740-1795) m. Oct. 14,
    1772 Mary Hampton XXXIII, 158
  John Edwards (Dec. 21, 1757-May 13,
    1828) m. May 11, 1791 Sarah Clif-
    ton XXII, 17, 100
  Joseph, III (Apr. 15, 1741-Mar. 19,
    1814) m. Sept. 12, 1769 Tryphena
    Kendall Bowker XXI, 85; XXII, 30
  Robert (1636-p. 1680) m. .... Han-
    nah Scarborough VA XXII, 17,
    100; XXXIII, 158
  Samuel (Apr. 5, 1737-Feb. 1, 1804)
    m. Dec. 2, 1759 Freelove Phillips
    VI, 85
  Simeon, Sr. (1743/4-p. 1813) m. July
    1765 Mary Carver XXXIV, 98
  Thomas (bpt. Feb. 24, 1613-Sept. 24,
    1691) m. 1637/8 Sarah ...... MASS
    XV, 92; XXII, 131; XXV, 193; XXVI,
    243, 244
  William (1595-1650) m. Feb. 17,
    1616/7 Dorothy Hayne MASS XXIX,
    223
  William (Feb. 14, 1715-Jan. 10, 1778)
    m. May 21, 1738 Elizabeth Edwards
    XXII; 17, 100

KINGE, see KING

KINGMAN
  Henry (Jan. 2, 1595-Oct. 8, 1667 m.
    1614 Joanna ...... MASS XIX, 57,
    151
  Isaac (Oct. 11, 1747-June 5, 1814)
    m. Dec. 4, 1769 Contene Packard
    XIX, 151
  Mitchell (1744-Oct. 22, 1819) m.
    1770 Keturah Latimer XIX, 57

KINGSBURY
  Daniel (Mar. 11, 1715-Mar. 25, 1783)
    m. Nov. 3, 1737 Beriah Mann

XXXIII, 307
Henry (1615-Oct. 1, 1687) m. ....
  Susanna ...... MASS VIII, 13;
  XXII, 155
Jeremiah (Apr. 20, 1735-Apr. 23,
  1816) m. May 31, 1758 Ruth Ballard
  XXXI, 256, 257
Joseph (....-May 1676) m. ....
  Milicent Ames MASS XXXI, 256,
  257; XXXIII, 307
Lemuel (Sept. 14, 1752-Sept. 14,
  1846) m. .... Alice Terry VIII,
  13
Nathaniel (Feb. 18, 1739-Jan. 26,
  1803) m. Jan. 20, 1791 (3) Re-
  becca Bigelow XXXIII, 307
Sanford (Apr. 7, 1743-Nov. 12, 1833)
  m. Jan. 9, 1766 Elizabeth Fitch
  XXII, 155

KINGSLAND
  Isaac (1648-1698) m. .... Elizabeth
  ...... NJ IX, 18, 19, 20
  Isaac (July 10, 1710-July 28, 1803)
  m. .... Johanna Schuler IX, 18,
  19, 20

KINGSLEY
  John (....-1679) m. .... Elizabeth
  ...... MASS XX, 43
  Moses (Aug. 29, 1744-Apr. 29, 1829)
  m. Jan. 19, 1768 Abigail Lyman
  XX, 42

KINICOTT, see KINNICUTT

KINNE, see KINNEY

KINNEY, includes KINNE, KENNE, KENNEY
  Asa (Sept. 26, 1723-Jan. 12, 1810)
  m. Nov. 12, 1743 Bethiah Kimball
  XXXII, 23, 255
  Elijah (Aug. 7, 1741-Feb. 6, 1830)
  m. .... Jerusha Burton XXX, 126
  Henry (July 8, 1623-June 19, 1696)
  m. .... Ann Putnam MASS XXX,
  126; XXXI, 101; XXXII, 23, 230,
  255; XXXIII, 286
  Jeremiah (Aug. 30, 1702-June 24,
  1798) m. Sept. 30, 1726 Mary Starkweather XXXII, 230
  Robert (Apr. 1738-Oct. 24, 1831) m.
  May 6, 1766 Anne Abigail Brown
  XXXI, 101
  William (Nov. 4, 1753-Jan. 12, 1819)
  m. Aug. 31, 1780 Mary Snow XXXIII,
  286

KINNICUTT, includes KINICOTT, KENNICOTT
  Roger (....-....) m. Nov. 1661 Jo-
  anna Sheperson MASS XXXIV, 42,

44, 118
Shubael (Mar. 28, 1738-1810) m. July
  3, 1766 Elizabeth ...... XXXIV,
  42, 44, 118

KINYON, see KENYON

KIP, see KIPP

KIPP, includes KIP
  Benjamin (bpt. Mar. 21, 1703-May 24,
  1782/3) m. c. 1733 Dorothy Davenport XXXII, 110
  Hendrick (1600-....) m. p. Apr. 20,
  1624 Tryntie Lubbers NY XXXII,
  110
  Hendrick Hendrickson, Jr. (Aug. 14,
  1633-....) m. Feb. 29, 1660 Anna
  de Sille NY XXI, 148, 149
  Peter (Dec. 26, 1743-Mar. 8, 1813)
  m. c. 1768 Willemtje Van Winkle
  XXI, 148, 149

KIRBE, see KIRBY

KIRBY, includes KIRBE
  Isaac (Sept. 23, 1756-Feb. 1, 1833)
  m. Sept. 15, 1799 (2) Phoebe Haines
  XXXI, 146, 208
  Richard (a. 1627-a. July 21, 1688)
  m. .... Jane ...... MASS XXXI,
  146, 208

KIRTLAND
  Nathaniel (1616-Dec. 27, 1686) m.
  .... Parnell ...... MASS, NY
  XXXIV, 250
  Samuel (Aug. 31, 1760-Oct. 4, 1825)
  m. 1781 Statira Cone XXXIV, 250

KITCHELL
  Abraham (Aug. 26, 1736-Jan. 11, 1807)
  m. 1777 (2) Rebecca Farrand XXV,
  135, 136
  Robert (1604-1672) m. July 1632
  Margaret Sheaffe CONN XXV, 135,
  136

KITTREDGE
  Francis (July 1, 1728-Apr. 17, 1808)
  m. Feb. 20, 1752 Abigail Richardson V, 51; XX, 112; XXV, 70
  John (1630-Oct. 18, 1676) m. Nov. 2,
  1664/5 Mary Littlefield MASS V,
  52; XX, 112; XXV, 70; XXVII,
  111
  Solomon (June 9, 1736-Aug. 24, 1792)
  m. May 14, 1755 Tabitha Ingalls
  XXVII, 111

KLEUT, see CLUTE

KNAPP

Benjamin (July 18, 1751-1783) m.
Mar. 2, 1776 Lucy Wheeler XXX,
128
Eben (Feb. 20, 1746-p. 1800) m.
1795 Ruth Hobby XVII, 103
Elnathan (1735-Feb. 20, 1818) m.
Mar. 10, 1752 Ann Kellogg XXIX,
333; XXXI, 36, 37
Jonathan (1756-Jan. 12, 1817) m. ....
Abigail Palmer XII, 5
Joshua (1729-Oct. 15, 1798) m. ....
Eunice Peck XXII, 50
Joshua (Jan. 6, 1761-Feb. 10, 1831)
m. 1788 Charity Mead XVIII, 18
Nathaniel, Jr. (July 6, 1753-1787)
m. .... Sarah Sutton XV, 31;
XXIII, 15
Nicholas (....-Sept. 16, 1670) m.
1630 Eleanor ...... MASS, CONN
XII, 5, 6; XV, 31; XVII, 103;
XVIII, 18; XX, 92, 93; XXII, 50;
XXIII, 15; XXIX, 333; XXXI, 36,
37
William (1578-Aug. 30, 1658) m. ....
.... MASS XXII, 88; XXX,
128
William (bpt. Dec. 17, 1738-June 4,
1780) m. July 2, 1761 Lydia Coombs
XXII, 88
Zephaniah (May 6, 1736-Jan. 20, 1816)
m. 1756 Millah Roe XX, 92, 93

KNEELAND

Edward (c. 1580-....) m. ....
...... MASS II, 37, 43, 46; IV,
98
Hezekiah (June 26, 1722-1799) m. ....
Mercy Pepoon IV, 98
Isaac (1716-....) m. .... Content
Rowley II, 37, 43, 46

KNICKERBACKER, see KNICKERBOCKER

KINCKERBOCKER, includes KNICKERBACKER
Harman Jansen (Mar. 18, 1643-Apr.
2, 1721) m. Jan. 3, 1675 Elizabeth
Van de Bogaart NY XXV, 251, 257,
258
Johannis (Mar. 24, 1723-Aug. 20,
1802) m. 1750 Rebecca Fonda XXV,
257, 258
John (Mar. 24, 1751-Nov. 10, 1827)
m. Mar. 1, 1769 Elizabeth Winne
XXV, 257, 258
Phillipp (Feb. 24, 1745-1819) m. July
1, 1766 Anna Maria Dings XXV, 251

KNIGHT

Amos, Jr. (Mar. 6, 1748-c. 1788) m.
Mar. 26, 1771 (1) Susannah Maynard

XXIX, 340
Ashur (June 26, 1761-July 31, 1825)
m. Jan. 25, 1786 Martha Clark XVI,
52
Enos (Dec. 29, 1729/30-1804) m. June
26, 1750 Lois Gould XXX, 230
John (bpt. Jan. 30, 1595-May 1670) m.
Jan. 27, 1615 (1) Sarah Hawkins;
.... (2) Mary ...... MASS XXIX,
340; XXXI, 281; XXXIV, 244
Mark (July 1, 1731-Dec. 6, 1813) m.
Dec. 31, 1757 Margaret Johnson
XXXIV, 244
Philip (1614-1666) m. .... Margery
...... MASS XXX, 230
Richard (....-1680) m. 1648 Sarah
Rogers MASS XVI, 52
Samuel (Feb. 10, 1730/1-July 23,
1804) m. 1757 Mary Covill XXXI,
281, 282
William (c. 1596-Mar. 1, 1655) m.
.... MASS XXX, 261
William, Jr. (Jan. 2, 1731-Jan. 19,
1797) m. (int.) Apr. 3, 1756 Han-
nah Knight XXX, 261

KNOWLES

Amos (Nov. 4, 1722-1809) m. Oct. 11,
1744 Elizabeth Libby XXIII, 21,
30, 35
David, Jr. (Aug. 23, 1751-p. 1790)
m. Sept. 5, 1776 Mary Hobbs XXI,
140
Freeman (Nov. 24, 1745-p. 1777) m.
Nov. 23, 1769 Esther Myrick XV,
123
John (....-Dec. 5, 1705) m. July 10,
1660 Jemima Astin (Austin) NH
XIX, 25; XXIII, 21, 30, 35
John (Jan. 25, 1732-Mar. 26, 1777)
m. Mar. 20, 1754 Lydia Philbrick
XIX, 25
John (Apr. 25, 1759-May 26, 1832)
m. May 13, 1781 Lydia Chaplin
XXIII, 20, 30, 35
Richard (....-....) m. .... Ruth
Bomer MASS XV, 123
Richard (a. 1620-Feb. 1, 1682) m.
.... Ruth ...... MASS, NH XXI,
140
Seth (Jan. 20, 1721-1789) m. Feb.
21, 1744/5 Ruth Freeman XV, 123

KNOWLTON

Abraham (Apr. 3, 1740-June 14, 1821)
m. Mar. 21, 1763 Molly Knox XVIII, 97
Benjamin (Dec. 10, 1728-July 21,
1809) m. 1750 Phoebe Wright XI,
11
William (1615-1655) m..... Elizabeth
...... MASS XI, 11; XVIII, 98

KOAL, see COLE

KOHL, see COLE

KOOL, see COLE

KROSEN, see CRUSER

KUNDERS, see CONARD

KUSTER, see CUSTER

KYN, see KEEN

LACHARN, see LANGHORNE

LAIGHTON, see LEIGHTON

LAKE

Abraham (1720-1796) m. 1741 Elizabeth ...... XXIX, 291; XXXIII,
269

Daniel (June 22, 1726-Sept. 26,
1810) m. Nov. 30, 1749 Sarah Bixby
XXIV, 148; XXVI, 172, 173, 242,
243

*David (c. 1646-p. June 15, 1709) m.
c. 1678 Sarah Earl Cornell   RI
XXXII, 126*

Garret Striker (Mar. 8, 1753-Nov.
21, 1838) m. .... Charity Sutphen
XXXII, 53, 54

George Bixby, Sr. (Nov. 7, 1750-Apr.
16, 1816) m. Nov. 3, 1772 Sarah
Lovejoy XXVI, 172, 173, 242, 243

*Henry (....-....) m. a. 1634 ......
...... MASS XXIV, 149; XXVI, 172,
242, 243*

Henry (Apr. 11, 1761-Sept. 24, 1851)
m. Aug. 2, 1784 Jemima Waldo XVII,
32, 114, 115; XXX, 271, 272;
XXXIII, 121

*John, Sr. (....-a. Aug. 14, 1696) m.
.... Anne Spicer NY XVII, 32,
114; XXV, 223; XXIX, 291; XXX, 272;
XXXII, 53; XXXIII, 121, 269*

Noah (Jan. 20, 1745-p. Apr. 1, 1803)
m. Oct. 16, 1767 Mrs. Wealthy Chase
(Grinman) XXXII, 126

William (Jan. 7, 1750-Mar. 21, 1783)
m. June 21, 1775 Elizabeth Poillon
XXV, 223

LAMAR, includes LEMAR, LEMORE

John, Jr. (1740-Oct. 12, 1799) m.
1773 (2) Priscilla Bugg XXVIII,
21; XXX, 158

*Thomas, Sr. (c. 1640-a. May 29, 1714)
m. 1661 Mary Pottinger VA, MD*

XXVIII, 21; XXX, 158

LAMB

David (Feb. 24, 1755-July 16, 1838)
m. Mar. 5, 1781 Amy Wightman XXXI,
304

*John, Sr. (c. 1625-p. 1674) m. ....
Ann ...... ME, CONN XXXI, 304*

*Pierce (a. 1662-a. June 7, 1709) m.
.... Mary ...... MD XXV, 238*

Samuel (1735-1802) m. Apr. 5, 1753
Sarah Dana XXVIII, 130; XXXII, 140

*Thomas (....-Mar. 28, 1646) m. July
16, 1640 Dorothy Harbittle MASS
XXVIII, 130; XXXII, 140*

Thomas (Aug. 5, 1756-Dec. 1801) m.
June 29, 1788 Margaret Price Buckingham XXV, 238

LAMDIN

*Robert (1663-c. 1685) m. ....
...... MD XXVII, 56*

William (July 24, 1755-June 25,
1822) m. Mar. 1782 Dorcas Morsell
XXVII, 56

LAMPHERE, includes LANFEAR

*George (....-Oct. 6, 1731) m. ....
.... RI XIV, 111*

Isaiah (....-Mar. 1, 1826) m. Oct.
16, 1763 Thankful Allen XIV, 111

LAMPREY

Daniel (Mar. 4, 1759-Dec. 12, 1840)
m. c. 1775 (1) Sarah Lane XX,
149; XXI, 163

*Henry (c. 1616-Aug. 7, 1700) m. ....
Julian Norris NH XX, 149; XXI,
163*

John (Aug. 17, 1710-1788) m. Sept.
19, 1754 (2) Hannah Johnson XX,
149

LANDON

David (Oct. 30, 1743-Sept. 14, 1796)
m. .... Rebekah Ruggles VII, 6

*Nathan (1664-Mar. 9, 1718) m. 1692
Hannah ...... NY VII, 6*

LANE

Aquilla (May 18, 1753-Nov. 24, 1819)
m. Feb. 1, 1780 Agnes Fitzgerald
XVI, 135; XIX, 71

Benjamin (Mar. 17, 1754-Dec. 20,
1835) m. Dec. 9, 1779 Anna Page
XVII, 89

Ebenezer (Sept. 28, 1733-May 20,
1796) m. Nov. 16, 1757 Huldah
Fogg XXIX, 307

*Edward (Aug. 19, 1664-Mar. 1710) m.
Jan. 26, 1694 (2) Ann Richardson*

LANE, cont.
    PA XXX, 227, 228; XXXI, 11, 74;
    XXXIII, 47
    Francis (Aug. 31, 1750-May 1, 1823)
    m. Sept. 30, 1779 Hepsibah Coolidge
    XXX, 139, 140, 148
    Isaac (bpt. Nov. 4, 1750-c. 1802) m.
    Dec. 20, 1771 Dorcas Bennett
    XXXIV, 291
    James (1620-1676) m. .... Sarah
    White MASS XXXIV, 291
    Job (c. 1620-Aug. 23, 1697) m. Sept.
    1660 (2) Hannah Reyner MASS XVII,
    89; XXX, 139, 140, 148
    John (Apr. 14, 1733-Aug. 26, 1796)
    m. Oct. 26, 1755 Joannah Stevens
    XXV, 126
    Robert (....-Apr. 10, 1718) m. Dec.
    19, 1665 Sarah Pickett CONN
    XXV, 126
    Samuel (1628-1682) m. .... Margaret
    Burrage MD XVI, 135; XIX, 72
    William (....-....) m. Aug. 21, 1656
    Mary Brewer MASS XXIX, 307
    William (Dec. 3, 1757-Apr. 27, 1838)
    m. c. 1778 Mary Bean XXX, 227,
    228; XXXI, 11, 74; XXXIII, 47

LANFEAR, see LAMPHERE

LANG, see also LONG
    Lowell, Sr. (Sept. 17, 1754-Oct. 25,
    1822) m. Apr. 4, 1776 Susanna
    Prescott XXVI, 9
    Robert (a. 1650-Feb. 16, 1716) m.
    .... Anne Williams NH XXVI, 9

LANGDON, includes LANKTON
    George (....-Dec. 29, 1676) m. ....
    .... MASS XIV, 29;
    XV, 94, 103; XXV, 85, 86
    Noah (Aug. 10, 1728-Sept. 20, 1819)
    m. .... Rebecca Porter XIV, 29;
    XV, 94, 103; XXV, 85, 86

LANGHORNE, includes LACHARN
    John (....-....) m. ....
    ...... VA XXX, 68
    William (1730-1798) m. .... Eliza-
    beth Scarsbrook XXX, 68

LANGLEY
    James, Sr. (1754-1808) m. Oct. 1,
    1771 Elizabeth Snayle XXXI, 119,
    125
    William (c. 1620-c. 1676) m. ....
    Joyce ...... VA XXXI, 119, 125

LANIER
    Benjamin (Dec. 14, 1732-Aug. 2,
    1817) m. Jan. 1, 1759 Susannah

    Green XXXII, 20, 21
    Burwell (Aug. 1741-a. Jan. 7, 1812)
    m. Oct: 1761 Elizabeth Hill
    XXXIII, 140
    James (Nov. 4, 1726-1786) m. c. 1745
    Mary Cooke XXXII, 112
    James (Feb. 2, 1750-Apr. 27, 1806)
    m. c. 1774 Sarah Chalmers XIV,
    25, 97
    John, I (bpt. June 10, 1633-p. Jan.
    5, 1717) m. 1677 (1) Lucreace
    ...... VA XXXII, 21, 112; XXXIII,
    140
    John, II (c. 1655-1719) m. ....
    Sarah ...... VA XIV, 25, 97

LANKTON, see LANGDON

LARCOM
    Jonathan (Apr. 30, 1742-1777/8) m.
    May 12, 1763 Abigail Ober XXIII,
    42
    Mordecai (c. 1629-Jan. 4, 1712/3) m.
    .... Elizabeth Clark MASS XXIII,
    41

LARKIN
    Abel (1749-1826) m. .... Sarah Fos-
    ter IX, 19
    Edward (1630-1716) m. ....
    ...... RI IX, 19

LARNED, see LEARNED

LAROE, see LA RUE

LA RUE, includes LAROE, LARUE
    Henry (Oct. 7, 1755-Mar. 1, 1850) m.
    Feb. 24, 1780 (1) Marretje (Mary)
    Mandeville XVII, 144; XVIII, 29,
    82
    Jacques (1657-a. Sept. 2, 1730) m.
    Jan. 25, 1681 Wybrecht Hendricks
    NY, NJ XVII, 144; XVIII, 29, 82

LARUE, see LA RUE

LATHAM
    Eliab (June 11, 1764-Mar. 18, 1818)
    m. Sept. 2, 1787 Lucy Latham
    XXXI, 267
    Robert (....-1688) m. c. 1649 Sus-
    anna Winslow MASS XXXI, 267
    Woodward (Dec. 24, 1729-Dec. 13,
    1802) m. p. June 13, 1763 Rebecca
    Dean XXXI, 267

LATHROP
    Elisha (July 13, 1713-July 2, 1787)
    m. Jan. 31, 1732 Margaret Sluman
    XXVIII, 126, 127; XXX, 206; XXXI, 19

John (....-....) m. ....
...... *MASS XXI, 122, 123*
Samuel (c. 1615-Feb. 29, 1700) m.
Nov. 28, 1644 Elizabeth Scudder
MASS, CONN XXVIII, 126, 127; XXX,
206; XXXI, 19
Simeon (Feb. 11, 1746/7-Dec. 30,
1826) m. Apr. 13, 1760 Esther
Branch XXI, 122, 123

LATIMER
Jonathan (May 27, 1724-1794) m. Jan.
28, 1746 Lucretia Griswold XV,
114; XXV, 75; XXIX, 269; XXX, 129;
XXXIII, 181, 293, 294
Robert (....-c. 1671) m. Sept. 1,
1662 Mrs. Ann (Griggs) Jones MASS
XV, 114; XXV, 75; XXIX, 269; XXX,
129; XXXIII, 181, 292, 293, 294
Wetherell (Mar. 18, 1757-p. 1837) m.
Mar. 21, 1793 (2) Margaret Anderson XV, 114; XXIX, 269; XXX,
129

LAURENCE, see LAWRENCE

LAW, includes LAWES
Benedict Arnold (Dec. 20, 1740-Nov.
19, 1819) m. Dec. 24, 1787 (2)
Henrietta Gibbs X, 215; XVII, 27
Richard (c. 1600-1686/7) m. 1636
Margaret Kilborn CONN X, 216;
XVII, 27

LAWES, see LAW

LAWRENCE, includes LAURENCE
Benjamin (c. 1755-....) m. May 25,
1779 Euphan Barton XXV, 144;
XXIX, 382
David (Jan. 26, 1743-Feb. 18, 1836)
m. 1768 (1) Elizabeth Eastman
XVII, 95
David (Jan. 1, 1748-May 13, 1834) m.
Jan. 2, 1777 Abigail Birch XXX,
133, 134
George (1636/7-Mar. 21, 1708/9) m.
Sept. 29, 1657 Elizabeth Crispe
MASS XXXIV, 307
Henry (....-a. 1647) m. .... Chris-
tiana ...... MASS XXX, 133, 134
Isaac (Feb. 25, 1704/5-Dec. 2, 1793)
m. Dec. 19, 1727 Lydia Hewitt
XXX, 264
Jeremiah (bpt. Oct. 5, 1707-July 9,
1781) m. July 6, 1773 Elizabeth
Clark Higby XXXIV, 15
John (bpt. Oct. 8, 1609-July 11,1667)
m. a. 1635 (1) Elizabeth ......
MASS VI, 87; X, 282; XVII, 95; XX,
59; XXX, 264; XXXI, 218; XXXIV, 15

Jonas (Dec. 1, 1728-May 22, 1793) m.
Sept. 3, 1754 Tryphena Lawrence
XX, 59; XXX, 264
Jonathan (Oct. 4, 1737-Sept. 4, 1812)
m. Aug. 7, 1768 Ruth Riker XIX,
132
Peter (Oct. 12, 1742-Oct. 21, 1798)
m. c. 1765 Persis Robbins XXXI,
218
Phineas (Feb. 19, 1749-1826) m. Nov.
1770 Elizabeth Stearns XXXIV, 307
Samuel (May 2, 1714-1789) m. May 5,
1737 Mary Hildreth VI, 87
Thomas (bpt. Mar. 8, 1619/20-July 5,
1703) m. .... (1) Mary ...... NY
I, 34, 35; X, 219, 220; XII, 9;
XIX, 132
Thomas (Dec. 25, 1757-July 28, 1822)
m. Aug. 10, 1779 Anne Shattuck X,
282
Uriah (Dec. 25, 1720-Nov. 30, 1803)
m. Apr. 13, 1743 Mary Clark XXX,
133, 134
William (a. 1637-a. May 22, 1704) m.
a. 1666 Hannah Townsend NY, NJ
XXV, 144; XXIX, 382
William (July 27, 1729-Jan. 13, 1794)
m. .... Anna Brinckerhoff I, 34,
35; X, 218, 219, 220; XII, 9

LAWTON, includes LOWTON
George (....-Oct. 5, 1693) m. ....
Elizabeth Hazard RI XVII, 126
George (Apr. 12, 1744-....) m. Apr.
10, 1766 Ruth Brownell XVII, 125,
126
John (1630-Dec. 17, 1690) m. ....
Benedicta ...... MASS, CONN IX,
31, XI, 130
William (Apr. 9, 1759-1800) m. 1784
Abigail Farrington IX, 31; XI,
130

LAYTON, see LEIGHTON

LEACH
Benjamin (1744-p. 1825) m. Oct. 2,
1764 Mary Keith XXI, 154, 155
Ephraim (Dec. 1761-Feb. 28, 1840) m.
Nov. 17, 1785 Chloe Shattuck XVI,
19, 20
Hezekiah (1737-Aug. 25, 1823) m.
Sept. 14, 1769 Sarah Bartholomew
XXI, 89
Lawrence (1580-June 24, 1662) m. a.
1605 Elizabeth ...... MASS XVI,
19, 20; XXI, 89, 154, 155; XXIX,
127
Richard (bpt. Sept. 29, 1754-July
6, 1827) m. Mar. 23, 1775 Mary
Strong XXIX, 127

LEAMING
   Christopher (c. 1649-May 3, 1695) m.
   1674 Esther Burnet NY XI, 84;
   XII, 52; XX, 99: XXII, 91
   Judah (1753-June 7, 1829) m. Oct. 4,
   1774 Thankful Tuttle XI, 84; XII,
   52; XX, 98; XXII, 91

LEARNED, includes LARNED
   John (Oct. 30, 1741-Feb. 23, 1830)
   m. Sept. 29, 1768 Abigail Davis
   XXIX, 303
   Jonas (bpt. Aug. 30, 1748-Aug. 1821)
   m. Aug. 16, 1787 Hannah Titterton
   XIII, 5; XVII, 121
   Simon (Aug. 13, 1753-Nov. 16, 1817)
   m. Oct. 28, 1784 Ruth Bull IV,
   166; V, 52; VI, 42
   William (1590-Mar. 1, 1646) m. ....
   Goodith (Judith) ...... MASS IV,
   166; V, 52; VI, 42; XIII, 5; XVII,
   121; XXIX, 303

LEAVENS, includes LEVINS
   Charles (Aug. 26, 1746-Aug. 4, 1822)
   m. June 27, 1773 Lydia Grover XV,
   40, 41
   John (c. 1581-Nov. 15, 1647) m. July
   5, 1639 (2) Rachel Wright MASS
   XV, 40, 41

LEAVENWORTH
   David (1738-1820) m. .... Mary Dunn
   IX, 55
   Thomas (....-1643) m. .... Graye
   ...... CONN IX, 55

LEAVITT
   John (1608-Nov. 20, 1691) m. 1637
   Mary Lovit MASS XXX, 55
   Jonathan (c. 1716-....) m. Sept. 30,
   1744/5 Hannah Leavitt XXX, 55
   Samuel (Dec. 4, 1706-Mar. 17, 1790)
   m. Oct. 29, 1730 Ruth Johnson
   XVIII, 72
   Thomas (c. 1616-Nov. 28, 1696) m. a.
   1644 Isabella Bland Asten NH
   XVIII, 72

LECOMPTE
   Anthony (a. 1635-1673) m. July 11,
   1661 Esther Dottando MD XVI, 123
   Charles (1749-1822) m. 1786 Mrs. Elizabeth (Coons) Waits XVI, 123

LEE
   Benjamin (Feb. 27, 1740-July 2, 1826)
   m. Aug. 23, 1760 Mary Dorr XIII,
   88
   Charles (1723-1792) m. May 7, 1753
   Johanna Morgan VII, 28

Daniel (Sept. 29, 1732-Sept. 12,
1792) m. Apr. 30, 1762 Agnes Camp-
bell XXIII, 5; XXIV, 38
Daniel (Jan. 21, 1753-July 1, 1806)
m. Jan. 8, 1777 Sarah Whittaker
XXX, 25
Daniel, Jr. (Sept. 20, 1762-Sept. 15,
1841) m. 1785 Jerusha Page XIX,
120; XXIII, 5; XXIV, 38
Elijah (1751-June 23, 1829) m. ....
(2) Mary Brown X, 168
Henry (1729-Oct. 1, 1787) m. c. 1750
(1) Lucy Goynes X, 295
John (1620-Aug. 8, 1690) m. 1658
Mary Hart CONN XXX, 25
Joseph (1713-May 10, 1790) m. ....
(1) Sarah ...... X, 168
Peter Perrine (Mar. 10, 1756-Nov.
10, 1848) m. May 11, 1785 Ruth
Huntington Gard XXIX, 190
Richard (1597-Oct. 1663/4) m. ....
(2) Anna Fittsworth VA VII, 28;
X, 295
Solomon (Mar. 29, 1747-Sept. 30,
1811) m. a. Apr. 17, 1775 Anne
Brewster XXIX, 329
Thomas (....-Dec. 5, 1740) m. ....
Sarah Kirtland CONN XIII, 88
Thomas (bpt. July 21, 1728-Jan. 7,
1805) m. 1750 Dinah Perrine XXIX,
190
Walter (....-Feb. 9, 1718) m. 1708
Mary ...... CONN XIX, 120; XXIII,
5; XXIV, 38; XXIX, 329
William (....-1724) m. .... Mary
Marvin NY X, 168; XXIX, 190

LEEDS
   Jeremiah (Mar. 4, 1754-Oct. 1838) m.
   Dec. 8, 1776 Judith Steelman XXXII,
   281; XXXIII, 285, 286
   Thomas (1620-1687) m. .... (2)
   Margaret Collier NJ XXXII, 281;
   XXXIII, 285, 286

LEETE
   Solomon (Dec. 3, 1746-1822) m. Nov.
   3, 1772 Hannah Norton XXVIII, 36,
   37
   William (1613-1683) m. Aug. 1, 1636
   Anna Payne CONN XXVIII, 36, 37

LEFFINGWELL
   Benajah (Jan. 11, 1737/8-Sept. 26,
   1804) m. 1764 Lucy Backus X, 42
   Thomas (bpt. 1622-p. 1714) m. ....
   Mary White CONN X, 42

LE GROW
   Elias (Mar. 1, 1741-Oct. 24, 1815) m.
   Sept. 18,1761 Elizabeth Dodd XXII,24

John (....-p.1716) m.Apr. 13, 1699
Martha Dutch MASS XXII, 24

LEIGHTON, includes LAIGHTON, LAYTON
Hatevil (bpt. Aug. 18, 1751-c. 1796)
  m. a. Dec. 25, 1772 Martha Denbow
  XXVIII, 155, 156
Thomas (c. 1604-Jan. 22, 1672) m.
  .... Joanna ...... NH XXVIII, 156

LE MAITRE, see DELAMATER

LEMAR, see LAMAR

LEMORE, see LAMAR

LEONARD
  Caleb, Sr. (Sept. 23, 1726-1814) m.
    Jan. 27, 1748 Jemima Minthorn XXIX,
    248
  Caleb, Jr. (1750-July 17, 1845) m.
    1773 Sarah Burt XXIX, 248
  Edmund (1722-Dec. 31, 1803) m. Feb.
    9, 1748 Mary Jones XXXIII, 222,
    223
  James (c. 1620-1691) m. .... Mary
    Martin MASS XV, 39; XXXIII, 222,
    223
  Nathan (Aug. 22, 1717-1783) m. Nov.
    12, 1739 Abigail Herrick X, 248
  Simeon (Nov. 24, 1737-Sept. 20,
    1793) m. Apr. 10, 1764 Anna Smith
    V, 50; VI, 38; XIX, 93
  Solomon (1610-1686) m. a. 1640 Mary
    ...... MASS V, 50; VI, 38; X,
    248; XIX, 93; XXIX, 249
  Solomon (May 30, 1759-July 1, 1834)
    m. 1801 Sarah Tucker Sears XXXIII,
    222, 223
  Timothy (July 3, 1757-July 10, 1830)
    m. Mar. 11, 1784 Susan Presbery
    XV, 39

LESTER
  Andrew (....-June 7, 1669) m. Feb.
    2, 1651 (1) Barbara ...... MASS
    XII, 38; XVIII, 32
  Christopher (Sept. 10, 1763-1827) m.
    Apr. 10, 1791 Mary Fish XVIII, 32
  Ebenezer (Dec. 2, 1766-Apr. 8, 1842)
    m. .... Cynthia Avery XII, 35
  John (Jan. 31, 1738-June 14, 1801)
    m. Oct. 7, 1762 Jane Antrim
    XXXI, 38, 39, 116
  Peter (....-c. 1742) m. Apr. 6, 1685
    (1) Mary Duncalf PA XXXI, 38, 116

LEVERING
  Anthony, Jr. (Jan. 11, 1759-Mar. 24
    1826) m. 1784 Sarah Howell XIII,
    69; XXIX, 117

John (Apr. 25, 1750-July 28, 1832)
  m. Jan. 8, 1778 Hannah Howell IV,
  87; X, 209
Wigard (1648-Feb. 2, 1745) m. Apr.
  1674 Magdelena Boker PA IV, 87;
  X, 209; XIII, 68; XXIX, 117

LEVINS, see LEAVENS

LEWAS, see LEWIS

LEWES, see LEWIS

LEWIS, includes LEWAS, LEWES
  Abel (1730-Sept. 22, 1795) m. Aug.
    2, 1751 Thankful Maccoone XXX, 51
  Amos (Sept. 26, 1746-July 23, 1812)
    m. .... Lydia Newhall IX, 22
  Asa (Jan. 2, 1762-Aug. 17, 1843) m.
    Nov. 17, 1791 Bridget Rix XXX, 51
  Barnabas (Aug. 17, 1733-July 3, 1811)
    m. Feb. 24, 1762 Rachel Curtis
    XXXIII, 45, 46
  Benjamin (1648-....) m. c. 1671
    Hannah Curtis CONN XX, 44, 51
  Benjamin (Oct. 16, 1743-May 4, 1829)
    m. Jan. 22, 1792 (2) Desire Bacon
    XXXI, 256
  Benoni (Sept. 28, 1752-....) m. a.
    July 1775 Mary Walton XXX, 165;
    XXXII, 151
  David, Jr. (1720-1787) m. 1761 (2)
    Elizabeth Lockhart XXV, 183, 184,
    185
  Edmund (1601-Jan. 1650) m. .... Mary
    ...... MASS IX, 22
  Eldad (Feb. 15, 1711-Jan. 29, 1784)
    m. .... Sarah Wiard IV, 145
  Elias (Nov. 25, 1746-a. June 14,
    1802) m. Aug. 25, 1765 Prudence
    Hewitt XXXII, 286, 287
  Ephraim (1718-Feb. 29, 1788) m. ....
    Sarah Everitt XX, 44, 51
  George (c. 1600-a. Mar. 3, 1662/3)
    m. c. 1626 Sarah Jenkins MASS XXX,
    165; XXXI, 256; XXXII, 151
  John (1630-1690) m. 1655 (1) Dorcas
    ......; ....(2) Mary ...... RI
    XXVI, 80; XXX, 51, 242; XXXI, 255;
    XXXII, 287
  John (1635/40-1726) m. 1670 Mary W.
    Brent VA XXV, 183, 184, 185
  John (Aug. 31, 1753-p. Aug. 29, 1817)
    m. Feb. 8, 1776 Elizabeth Kennon
    XIV, 96; XV, 80; XXXIII, 103, 104
  Nathan, Sr. (1731-Jan. 30, 1792) m.
    Dec. 16, 1756 Mary Adams XXXI,
    255
  Robert (....-1645) m. a. 1635 Eliza-
    beth ...... VA XIV, 96; XV, 80;
    XXXIII, 103, 104

LEWIS, cont.
  William, Sr. (Jan. 3, 1594-Aug. 2,
    1683) m. Feb. 7, 1618 Felix Col-
    lins CONN, MASS IV, 145; XXXIII,
    45, 46
  William (1605-Dec. 3, 1671) m. a.
    1635 Amy Weld MASS XIX, 103;
    XXI, 31, 32
  William (bpt. Dec. 1, 1737-Apr. 9,
    1822) m. .... Elizabeth Scott
    IV, 145
  William (Oct. 14, 1756-Mar. 16, 1834)
    m. 1780 Sarah Pinkham XIX, 103;
    XXI, 31, 32
  Zebulon (Sept. 3, 1734-c. 1828) m.
    .... Mary York XXVI, 80; XXX, 242

LIBBEY, see LIBBY

LIBBY, includes LIBBEY
  Isaac (1695/8-p. 1780) m. 1718 Mary
    Bennett XX, 55
  Jeremiah (Nov. 5, 1746-Nov. 15, 1816)
    m. Nov. 16, 1770 Anna Libby XXXII,
    224; XXXIII, 15, 16
  Jethro (1759-1843) m. .... Abigail
    Libbey XX, 55
  John (1602-p. Feb. 1682) m. ....
    .... ME XVIII, 24, 25;
    XIX, 148; XX, 55; XXXII, 224;
    XXXIII, 15, 16
  Reuben (Aug. 11, 1734-c. 1820) m.
    July 1, 1754 Sarah Goss
    XVIII, 24, 25; XX, 55
  Solomon (Aug. 26, 1759-Mar. 3, 1832)
    m. Jan. 31, 1782 Sarah Seavey
    XIX, 148

LIGAN, see LIGON

LIGON, includes LIGAN
  Blackman (1757-May 3, 1831) m. 1780
    Elizabeth Townes XVI, 139
  Joseph (c. 1725-1780) m. c. 1754
    Judith ...... XXXIV, 91
  Thomas (1586-1675) m. c. 1648 Mary
    Harris VA XVI, 139; XXXI, 54;
    XXXIV, 91
  William (1738-1787) m. Nov. 14, 1759
    Edith Turner XXXI, 54

LILLIE
  David (Oct. 27, 1742-Sept. 1, 1827)
    m. Sept. 19, 1771 Huldah Blodgett
    XI, 52; XXV, 79
  George (May 18, 1638-Feb. 14, 1690/1)
    m. Nov. 15, 1659 (1) Hannah Smith
    MASS X, 140; XI, 52; XXV, 79;
    XXVIII, 123
  Jonathan (Mar. 19,1731/2-....)m.Dec.
    12, 1743 Hannah Tilden XXVIII, 123

Nathan (May 26, 1755-Apr. 16, 1827)
  m. Jan. 17, 1791 Lydia Robinson
  X, 140
Turner (Oct. 8, 1755-....) m. 1782/3
  Eleanor Churchill XXVIII, 123

LINCOLN
  Benjamin (1754-Nov. 29, 1822) m.
    July 28, 1776 Zilpha Lincoln
    XXI, 56, 57
  Joseph (Dec. 28, 1753-Apr. 13, 1816)
    m. July 11, 1784 Susannah Marsh
    XXXII, 92
  Obadiah (June 1731-Apr. 1802) m.
    Aug. 19, 1755 Jael Curtis XXI,
    152, 153
  Samuel (1619-May 26, 1690) m. c.
    1649 Martha ...... MASS XV, 158,
    159; XXI, 152, 153; XXIV, 97;
    XXXIII, 176
  Seth, Jr. (Mar. 23, 1754-Dec. 1,
    1826) m. Aug. 15, 1779 Jemima
    Miller XVI, 34, 35
  Stephen (Dec. 3, 1751-Mar. 16, 1840)
    m. Apr. 29, 1779 Lydia Foster
    XIII, 115
  Thomas (1603-1684) m. c. 1630 Anis
    (Avith) Lane MASS XIII, 115;
    XVI, 35; XXI, 56, 57; XXXII, 92
  Thomas (Nov. 1758-July 18, 1819) m.
    a. 1780 Priscilla Dickinson XV,
    158, 159; XXIV, 97
  Zenas (Sept. 8, 1757-Dec. 19, 1820)
    m. June 10, 1781 Mary Lincoln
    XXXIII, 176

LINDLY, see LINDSLEY

LINDSAY, see LINDSLEY

LINDSLEY, includes LINDLY, LINDSAY,
    LINSLAY, LINSLEY
  Aaron (1748-1797) m. .... Abigail
    Halsey XVII, 91; XXVII, 49, 50;
    XXX, 23
  Abiel, II (1730-May 7, 1800) m. Oct.
    5, 1752 Thankful Pond V, 130,
    131; XXVI, 50
  David (Jan. 2, 1603-Apr. 3, 1667) m.
    .... Susanna ...... VA XXIV, 68
  Eleazer (Dec. 7, 1737-June 1, 1794)
    m. .... Mary Miller IX, 6, 26
  Francis (c. 1610-1704) m. June 24,
    1655 (2) Susanna Culpeper CONN,
    NJ V, 130, 131; IX, 6, 26; XV,
    107; XVI, 131; XVII, 91; XXVI, 50;
    XXVII, 50; XXX, 23
  Levi (Apr. 27, 1731-Feb. 4, 1801) m.
    .... Anna Davison XVI, 131
  Philip (Sept. 10, 1736-June 20, 1820)
    m. Feb. 8, 1763 Mary McFeran XV,107

William (1742-c. 1792/3) m. c.
1776/7 Anne Calvert XXIV, 68

LINNELL
Joseph (Dec. 3, 1754-Jan. 21, 1834)
m. p. Nov. 20, 1779 Zeruiah Knowles
XXXI, 181
Robert (c. 1584-Feb. 27, 1662/3) m.
.... House MASS XXXI, 181

LINSLAY, see LINDSLEY

LINSLEY, see LINDSLEY

LINTHICUM
John (1751/5-1810) m. a. 1776 Ann
Edwards XXIX, 115
Thomas (1640-Nov. 1701) m. c. 1668
Jane ...... MD XXIX, 115

LIPPETT
Christopher (Oct. 28, 1744-June 17,
1824) m. Mar. 23, 1777 Waite Harris
XXV, 133, 134
John (....-1669) m. ....
...... RI XXV, 133, 134

LIPPINCOTT
Amaziah (Jan. 17, 1745-Feb. 16, 1826)
m. Oct. 29, 1768 Hannah Prickett
XXIX, 112, 137
Jonathan (p. 1743-1777) m. Dec. 6,
1770 Naomi Tyler XXXIII, 62
Richard (c. 1613-a. Nov. 16, 1683)
m. 1640 Abigail ...... NJ XXIX,
112, 137; XXXIII, 62

LITCHFIELD
Elisha, Sr. (June 3, 1733-Oct. 20,
1813) m. Feb. 6, 1755 Ruth Cole
XXVI, 299, 300
Elisha, Jr. (1754-May 14, 1787) m.
June 13, 1777 Delight Beals
XXVI, 299, 300
Isaac (Sept. 4, 1720-Dec. 11, 1800)
m. Sept. 18, 1743 (1) Lydia Cowing
XX, 89
Lawrence (a. 1620-1649) m. c. 1640
Judith Dennis MASS XX, 89; XXVI,
299, 300

LITTLE
Benjamin (Nov. 4, 1732-Apr. 18, 1777)
m. c. 1761 Mary Hazen XXXIV, 12
Enoch (May 21, 1728-Oct. 21, 1816)
m. June 5, 1759 (2) Hannah Hovey
XXX, 18
George (....-p. Mar. 15, 1693) m.
.... Alice Poor MASS XIX, 144;
XXX, 18; XXXIV, 12
Moses (May 8, 1724-May 27, 1798) m.

June 5, 1743 Abigail Bailey XIX,
144

LITTLEHALE
Abraham (Jan. 23, 1725-1810) m. June
7, 1744 Mary Stearns XVI, 92, 93
Richard (....-Feb. 18, 1663) m. Nov.
15, 1647 Mary Lancton MASS XVI,
92

LITTLEJOHN
Oliver (....-1704) m. ....
...... VA XXIX, 30
Samuel (....-1813) m. .... Sarah
Coffer XXIX, 30

LITTLEPAGE
Richard (....-Apr. 20, 1688) m. ....
.... VA XXXIII, 93, 94
Thomas (c. 1735-1786/7) m. a. 1768
Ann Burnley XXXIII, 93, 94

LIVERMORE
Daniel (Jan. 26, 1746-Dec. 14, 1804)
m. Nov. 17, 1768 Elizabeth Hitchcock XVII, 65, 66; XX, 32; XXI,
41, 42
Jason (Dec. 1, 1726-Oct. 14, 1797)
m. Mar. 30, 1749 Abigail Hager
XIX, 122
John (c. 1606-Apr. 14, 1684) m. ....
Grace Sherman CONN, MASS XVII,
65; XIX, 122; XX, 32, 95; XXI, 41,
42
Moses (July 14, 1729-Oct. 18, 1797)
m. Jan. 31, 1750 Hannah Allen XX,
95

LIVINGSTON
Gilbert Robert (bpt. Sept. 27, 1758-
June 5, 1816) m. .... Martha Kane
III, 63; IV, 129
Peter Robert (Apr. 27, 1737-Nov. 15,
1794) m. June 6, 1758 Margaret
Livingston XXV, 10
Robert (Dec. 13, 1654-Oct. 1, 1728)
m. July 9, 1679 Aida Schuyler NY
III, 63; IV, 129; XXV, 10

LOBDELL
Jacob (1732-....) m. Aug. 28, 1757
Ruth Boughton XXVIII, 73
Simon (....-....) m. ....
...... CONN XXVIII, 73

LOCKE
Benjamin (Aug. 6, 1738-Dec. 7, 1791)
m. Aug. 2, 1757 Mary Pierce XIII,
74; XVIII, 5; XXVIII, 90, 91, 116
William (....-....) m. .... Eliza-
beth ...... MASS XVIII, 5

Jonathan (Oct. 14, 1725-May 8, 1805)
m. Nov. 20, 1746 Ruth Rogers XXIX,
74

Nathan (c. 1603-1690/1) m. 1653/4
(1) Judith Conley ME XXX, 88;
XXXIV, 197

Philip, Jr. (Feb. 14, 1723/4-Mar. 22
1816) m. Dec. 13, 1748 Sarah Brown
XXXII, 202

Robert, Sr. (1603-Aug. 12, 1683) m.
Nov. 11, 1630 Mary Wait MASS
XXXII, 202

Thomas (1585-p. Jan. 29, 1643/4) m.
Feb. 23, 1610/1 Dorothy Bird CONN
XXIX, 74; XXXI, 126, 147

LORE, see LOREE

LOREE, includes LORE, LORIAN, LORING
John (....-Apr. 2, 1727) m. ....
.... NY XXXII, 18
Samuel, Jr. (bpt. Nov. 25, 1759-
Aug. 17, 1803) m. Jan. 29, 1781
Sarah Price XXXII, 18

LORIAN, see LOREE

LORING, also see LOREE
Thomas (c. 1600-Apr. 4, 1661) m.
.... Jane Newton MASS XXXII, 182
William (Sept. 15, 1756-June 10
1791) m. Apr. 19, 1776 Jane Brown
XXXII, 182

LOTHROP
John (Dec. 20, 1584-Nov. 8, 1653) m.
.... Hannah House MASS XII, 17
Joseph (Oct. 20, 1731-Dec. 31, 1820)
m. .... Elizabeth Dwight XII, 17

LOTT
Abraham (May 22, 1753-....) m. Dec.
14, 1774 Mary Van Arsdalen XXXI,
32
Henry (1707-Dec. 21, 1784) m. ....
Mercy ...... XXXIII, 210
Johannes (Dec. 31, 1721-Jan. 25,
1782) m. .... Jannetje Probasco
XII, 16
Peter (May 9, 1621-p. 1687) m. ....
Gertrude Lamberts NY XII, 16;
XXXI, 32; XXXIII, 210

LOUD
Francis, Sr. (....-....) m. ....
.... ME XXXII, 90, 91
Jacob (May 24, 1723-Nov. 15, 1779 m.
July 3, 1746 Mary Smith XXXII,
90, 91

LOUGHLAND, see LOFLAND

LOUNSBERRY
Michael (Sept. 12, 1744-p. 1790) m.
Apr. 27, 1769 Abigail Hillman
XXXIII, 282, 283
Richard (....-a. Dec. 7, 1694) m.
Aug. 1, 1670 Elizabeth Penoyer NY
XXXIII, 282, 283

LOVEJOY
Isaac (Feb. 9, 1724-May 25, 1813) m.
.... Deborah Sheldon XV, 138
Jeremiah (Mar. 15, 1738/9-Oct. 1,
1806) m. Dec. 11, 1760 Dorothy
Ballard XXXIII, 250, 251
John (Apr. 11, 1622-Nov. 7, 1690) m.
June 1, 1651 (1) Mary Osgood MASS
XV, 138; XXXIII, 68, 250, 251
William (July 6, 1759-Sept. 24, 1830)
m. Jan. 15, 1800 Mary (Polly) Bar-
ker XXXIII, 68

LOVELAND
John (Dec. 25, 1740-Oct. 30, 1809)
m. Nov. 1795 (2) Mrs. Esther (Buck)
Seward XXI, 128, 129
Samuel (Feb. 28, 1763-Oct. 11, 1788)
m. Sept. 30, 1784 Dorcas Jones
XXI, 26; XXXIII, 243
Thomas (1649-1720) m. 1674 ......
...... CONN XXI, 26, 128, 129;
XXXIII, 243

LOVELL
James (Oct. 23, 1662-....) m. ....
Mary Lumbert MASS IV, 96
James (Oct. 31, 1732-July 14, 1814)
m. .... Mary Middleton IV, 96
Josiah (Oct. 26, 1757-....) m. June
25, 1778 Lydia Vining XXVI, 71,
72
Obadiah (Feb. 17, 1729-Sept. 27,
1810) m. Sept. 11, 1755 Ruth Beal
XXVI, 71
Robert (1595-a. June 25, 1672) m. a.
1619 Elizabeth ...... MASS XXVI,
71

LOVERING
Jesse (Mar. 27, 1745/6-Sept. 28,
1820) m. Apr. 30, 1772 Mercy Jen-
nings VII, 32; XVIII, 65, 66
John (....-July 27, 1668) m. ....
Esther ...... NH XI, 148
John (Aug. 21, 1715-c. 1778) m. 1733
Anna Sanborn XI, 148
Simeon (Jan. 14, 1752-June 7, 1837
m. Dec. 7, 1773 Sarah Sanborn XI,
148
William (....-a. 1690/1) m. a.
1676 Margaret Gutch ME VII, 32;
XVIII, 66

LOW, includes LOWE
John (c. 1642/5-June 1701) m. ....
.... *MD XXII, 142*
Samuel (Oct. 23, 1758-Sept. 14,
1839) m. July 25, 1780 Abigail
Bacon XVII, 84; XXXI, 279, 280;
XXXIV, 313
*Thomas (1605-Sept. 8, 1677) m. June
22, 1630 Margaret Tod MASS XVII,
84; XXXI, 280; XXXIV, 313*
Thomas (1759-1821) m. 1787 Martha
Alexander XXII, 142

LOWE, see LOW

LOWELL
David (Jan. 12, 1716-....) m. 1748
Mary Blood XXIX, 388
*Percival (1571-Jan. 8, 1664) m. 1593
Rebecca ...... MASS XXIX, 388*

LOWTON, see LAWTON

LUCAS
Abijah (Feb. 5, 1759-Sept. 11, 1838)
m. Oct. 25, 1781 Mary Robbins
XXV, 285
Joseph (Oct. 3, 1742-Oct. 22, 1806)
m. Sept. 24, 1767 Ruby Fuller
XXII, 146, 147
*Thomas (....-1675) m. ....
...... MASS XXII, 146, 147; XXV,
285*

LUCE
Benjamin, Jr. (Feb. 5, 1761-Feb. 12,
1806) m. Nov. 9, 1785 Jane Hines
XX, 96
*Henry Jun, Sr. (c. 1645-May 1687) m.
c. 1666 Remember ...... MASS
XVII, 147; XX, 96*
Malachi (Aug. 26, 1755-Mar. 20, 1838)
m. Sept. 23, 1779 Ann Luce XVII,
147

LUDDEN
Ezra (Oct. 3, 1748-Nov. 24, 1833) m.
.... Hannah Wolcott XIII, 30
*James (....-Feb. 7, 1692) m. ....
Alice ...... MASS XIII, 30*

LUDINGTON
Henry (May 25, 1739-Jan. 24, 1817)
m. May 12, 1760 Abigail Ludington
III, 8
Jesse, Jr. (1757-Jan. 1, 1841) m.
Aug. 10, 1779 Thankful Chidsey
XXVI, 152, 300, 301
*William (1607-June 13, 1662) m. a.
1637 Ellen Moulthrop MASS, CONN
III, 8; XXVI, 152, 301*

LUFF
Hugh (1662-1709) m. June 26, 1688
Sarah Hunn DE XXX, 254
Nathaniel (Jan. 4, 1736-Jan. 2, 1806)
m. .... XXX, 254

LUM
Andrew (Feb. 25, 1742/3-1810) m.
1765 Hannah Walker XXIII, 42
*John (1620-c. 1673) m. 1642 Hannah
Strickland NY XIV, 72; XXIII,
42; XXX, 157, 158, 221; XXXII, 36*
Joseph (Jan. 14, 1715-Feb. 24, 1796)
m. Apr. 29, 1741 Sarah Washburn
XXX, 157, 158, 221; XXXII, 36
Stephen (Jan. 26, 1754-1806) m. ....
Abigail Thompson XIV, 72

LUMBARD
Elijah (Jan. 20, 1750-1775/9) m. c.
1774 Eunice ...... XV, 101
*John (....-May 15, 1672) m. Sept. 1,
1646 Joanna Pritchard MASS XV,
101*
Joseph (July 16, 1720-May 25, 1805)
m. .... (1) Ruth ...... XV, 101

LUND
John (Feb. 22, 1749-Mar. 11, 1822)
m. Mar. 26, 1772 Hannah Phelps
XXX, 130
*Thomas (c. 1660-p. 1721) m. c.
1680/1 Eleanor ...... NH XXX,
130*

LUNT
*Henry (....-....) m. .... Ann ......
MASS XXVI, 257, 258*
Joseph (Jan. 20, 1730-Mar. 30, 1776)
m. May 28, 1750 Sarah Stickney
XXVI, 257, 258

LURVEY
Jacob (Oct. 24, 1761-Sept. 11, 1853)
m. Feb. 26, 1782 Hannah Boynton
XXXIII, 123, 124
*Peter (a. 1678-....) m. .... Mary
...... MASS XXXIII, 123, 124*

LUTHER
Frederick (Feb. 15, 1730-May 13,
1822) m. Feb. 16, 1750 Joanna
Luther XXIV, 18; XXXIII, 88
*John (c. 1600-1644/5) m. 1635 Eliza-
beth Turner MASS XXIV, 18;
XXXIII, 88*

LYFORD
Biley (Mar. 10, 1716-Feb. 10, 1792)
m. Aug. 25, 1743 Judith Wilson
XV, 61, 62; X, 212

Biley (Oct. 19, 1755-Apr. 16, 1830)
m. Dec. 2, 1792 Dorothy Blake
XXIII, 45, 53
Francis (a. 1647-1724) m. Nov. 21,
1681 Rebecca Dudley MASS X, 11,
212; XV, 61, 62; XXIII, 45, 53
Oliver Smith (Aug. 24, 1753-1788) m.
May 26, 1780 Elizabeth Johnson
X, 11

LYMAN
Azariah (Dec. 1747-Feb. 28, 1833) m.
Mar. 17, 1774 Jemima Kingsley
XVIII, 108
David (May 20, 1747-July 29, 1813)
m. Oct. 29, 1773 Mary Brown XXV,
148; XXXII, 98
Elias (Sept. 30, 1715-Feb. 18, 1803)
m. .... Anna Phelps X, 272
Isaac (Aug. 18, 1759-May 10, 1827)
m. c. Feb. 1792 (2) Laura Prince
XVIII, 131
James (Jan. 9, 1747-Jan. 25, 1804) m.
1780 Abigail Wright XXXIII, 29
Joseph (July 6, 1744-Feb. 12, 1820)
m. Apr. 9, 1767 Sarah Edwards
XXX, 86
Justus (Dec. 1, 1768-Dec. 4, 1846) m.
Mar. 8, 1798 Nancy Carey XXIV,
108
Lemuel (Aug. 28, 1735-July 16, 1810)
m. .... Lydia Clark XXX, 268, 269
Richard (bpt. Oct. 30, 1580-Aug.
1640) m. 1610 Sarah Osborne MASS,
CONN X, 273; XVIII, 108, 131;
XXIV, 108; XXV, 148; XXX, 86, 268,
269; XXXII, 98; XXXIII, 29
Stephen (Sept. 8, 1742-Dec. 11, 1810)
m. Oct. 23, 1770 (1) Anna Blair
X, 273

LYNDE
John (Mar. 29, 1745-Sept. 26, 1816)
m. .... Sarah Warner VII, 43
Thomas (Jan. 1593/4-Dec. 30, 1671)
m. .... (1) .... MASS
VII, 43
Thomas (c. 1616-Oct. 1693) m. ....
Elizabeth ...... MASS VII, 43

LYON
Aaron (July 28, 1758-Nov. 9, 1819)
m. Mar. 6, 1796 Elizabeth Nelson
XXIX, 226
Caleb, Sr. (Oct. 30, 1718-Aug.
30, 1809) m. .... Eunice Mead
XXVI, 66
David (1747-Mar. 30, 1802) m.
.... Prudence ...... XXXII,
59

Henry (c. 1625-Mar. 23, 1707) m.
1652 Elizabeth Bateman CONN, NJ
VIII, 21; XXX, 262; XXXII, 59
John (Jan. 12, 1748-Apr. 24, 1807)
m. 1774 Elizabeth Moore XXXI, 141
John, Sr. (Aug. 26, 1753-Feb. 1834)
m. 1782 (2) Martha Babbitt XXX,
262
Joseph (Oct. 1, 1733-Nov. 27, 1817)
m. Dec. 22, 1756 Lois Thorp XVII,
74, 75
Moses (1731-Mar. 27, 1813) m. :....
Mary Harris VIII, 21
Nehemiah Webb (Aug. 16, 1759-Apr.
19, 1860) m. Aug. 26, 1778 Sarah
Treadwell XII, 77; XXVI, 140
Noah (Mar. 16, 1756-Sept. 20, 1820)
m. Mar. 29, 1781 Mary Mead XXVI,
66
Richard (....-Oct. 1678) m. ....
Margaret ...... CONN XII, 77;
XVII, 74; XXVI, 140
Roger (Dec. 1715-May 13, 1797) m.
.... Mary Willson XXXIV, 131
Thomas (c. 1620-1690) m. c. 1654 (2)
Mary Hoyt CONN XXVI, 66; XXIX,
226; XXXIV, 131
William (Dec. 23, 1620-May 21, 1692)
m. June 17, 1646 Sarah Ruggles MASS
XXXI, 141

MAC DONALD, see MC DONALD

MACK
John (Mar. 6, 1653-Feb. 24, 1721) m.
Apr. 5, 1681 Sarah Bagley MASS,
CONN V, 126, 127; XXII, 38; XXVI,
200
Nathan (....-p. Nov. 30, 1821) m.
Apr. 22, 1774 Mary (Molly) Diggens
XXII, 38
Orlando (Oct. 10, 1747-c. 1813) m.
.... (2) Lucy Baldwin V, 126, 127
Ralph (June 13, 1760-June 25, 1836)
m. Feb. 6, 1783 Lydia Post Gilbert
XXVI, 200

MACKALL
Benjamin (Feb. 16, 1723-1795) m.
Apr. 24, 1757 Rebecca Covington
XXIX, 200, 352
James (c. 1630-1693) m. c.
1659 Mary Grahame MD XXIX,
200, 352

MACKCLOTHAN, see CLAFLIN

MACKCLOTHIAN, see CLAFLIN

MAC KENNEY, see MC KENNEY

MACKINTOSH
John (....-....) m. Apr. 5, 1650
  Rebecca Metcalf MASS XXXII, 272
  William (June 16, 1722-Jan. 3, 1813)
  m. Aug. 15, 1745 Abigail Whiting
  XXXII, 272

MACOMBER
  David (Sept. 2, 1752-May 13, 1819)
  m. Sept. 6, 1781 Katherine Little-
  field XXXIII, 101, 102
  George (July 7, 1740-July 1820) m.
  Jan. 27, 1767 Susannah Paul XIX,
  15
  John (....-1687/90) m. .... (1)....
  ...... MASS VI, 114; XIX, 15
  John (May 18, 1760-Oct. 11, 1841) m.
  Aug. 25, 1785 (1) Mary Dean VI,
  114
  William (1610-a. May 27, 1670) m.
  .... Ursilla ...... MASS XXXIII,
  101, 102

MACON
  Gideon (c. 1637-1702) m. c. 1680
  Martha Woodward VA XXXIII, 200
  John (Mar. 10, 1755-Feb. 9, 1828) m.
  c. 1776 (1) Joanna Tabb XXXIII,
  200

MACY
  John (Dec. 11, 1721-July 18, 1795)
  m. Nov. 1761 Eunice Coleman XXXII,
  145
  Thomas (1608-1682) m. 1633 Sarah
  Hopcot MASS XXXII, 145

MADDUX
  Alexander (1613-a. Feb. 28, 1659) m.
  Mar. 11, 1651 Eleanor White VA
  XXVI, 115, 116, 296
  Thomas, III (c. 1747-May 29, 1801)
  m. ....Elizabeth Boggess XXVI,
  115, 116, 296, 297

MAGGSON, see MAXSON

MAGRUDER
  Alexander (1610-a. July 25, 1677) m.
  .... (1) Sarah Braithwaite MD
  VI, 53; XXXIV, 111
  Joseph (Oct. 16, 1742-Aug. 1793) m.
  1778 (2) Katherine Fleming VI, 52
  Samuel (Feb. 24, 1708-June 1786) m.
  1729 Margaret Jackson VI, 52
  Zadok (1729-1811) m. 1754 Rachel Pot-
  tenger (Bowie) XXXIV, 111

MAIES, see MAYS

MAIN
  John (1614-....) m. ....
  ...... ME XII, 82, 86
  Nathaniel (July 12, 1754-1823) m.
  .... Nabby (Abigail) Thurston XII,
  82, 86

MAISE, see MAYS

MALLERY, see MALLORY

MALLORY, includes MALLERY
  John (May 1739-Mar. 28, 1824) m.
  .... Esther Barnes XXXIII, 85
  Moses (Mar. 10, 1724-Dec. 7, 1794)
  m. Aug. 19, 1744 Francis Oviatt
  XIII, 31, 32
  Peter (....-1698/9) m. .... Mary
  Preston MASS, CONN XIII, 32;
  XXXIII, 85

MALTBIE, includes MALTBY
  Benjamin (May 12, 1750-Jan. 1, 1847)
  m. July 5, 1771 Abigail Munger
  XVIII, 147
  David (Apr. 4, 1759-Nov. 24, 1807)
  m. Nov. 19, 1786 Nancy Davenport
  XXVI, 76
  William (Mar. 16, 1644/5-Sept. 1,
  1710) m. .... Abigail Bishop;
  1675/8 (2) Hannah Hosmer (Willard)
  CONN XVIII, 147; XXVI, 76

MALTBY, see MALTBIE

MAN, see MANN

MANDEVILLE, includes DE MANDEVILLE
  Gyles Jansen (1620-p. 1700) m. 1648
  Elsie Hendricks NY XXX, 224
  Henry, Sr. (Hendricks) (May 24, 1704-
  Sept. 19, 1790) m. 1729 Elizabeth
  Vreeland XXX, 224
  Henry, Jr. (Oct. 21, 1729-Sept. 7,
  1793) m. 1763 (2) Margaret Johns
  XXX, 223, 224

MANN, includes MAN
  Denton (c. 1765-a. 1812) m. c. 1788
  Sarah Wheeless XXXII, 175, 176
  Joseph (Apr. 5, 1713/4-Apr. 25,
  1798/9) m. Nov. 27, 1740 (2) Han-
  nah Gilbert XXXIV, 121
  Richard (....-Feb. 1655) m. ....
  Rebecca ...... (Cowen) MASS IV,
  161; XXX, 183; XXXIV, 122
  Rufus (Aug. 26, 1755-Aug. 26, 1837)
  m. Jan. 25, 1781 Sybil Allen
  XXIX, 376; XXX, 75
  Seth (Dec. 3, 1747-July 20, 1822) m.
  .... (2) Deborah Dyer IV, 161;

XXX, 183

Thomas, I (c. 1626-1689) m. c.
1659/60 Elizabeth ...... VA
XXXII, 176

William (1607-Mar. 7, 1662) m. 1643
(1) Mary Jarred MASS XXIX, 377;
XXX, 75

MANNING

Hezekiah (Aug. 8, 1721-Apr. 20, 1802)
m. Sept. 22, 1745 Mary Webb XXV,
277, 278

Nathaniel (bpt. Mar. 16, 1760-Mar.
9, 1814) m. 1783 Matilda Morgan
XXV, 277, 278

William (c. 1592-p. Feb. 17, 1665) m.
.... MASS XXV, 277,
278

William (c. 1614-Mar. 14, 1690) m.
.... Dorothy ...... MASS XV, 112

William (Nov. 28, 1733-Sept. 18,
1807) m. June 4, 1759 Mrs. Mary
(Johnson) Payson XV, 112

MANSFIELD

David (1604-1672) m. 1630 Katherine
Clyfton VA XXXII, 79

Ebenezer (July 16, 1757-Oct. 8, 1819)
m. Sept. 23, 1784 Mary Lewis XI,
90

Nathan (Nov. 15, 1718-Mar. 13, 1783)
m. Dec. 5, 1745 Deborah (Todd)
Dayton XXI, 41

Nathan (Nov. 30, 1748-Nov. 5, 1835)
m. Mar. 5, 1775 Anna (Tomlinson)
Tomlinson XXI, 40, 41

Richard (....-Jan. 10, 1655) m. Aug.
10, 1636 Gillian Drake CONN XI,
90; XXI, 40, 41; XXIX, 393

Richard (May 24, 1763-....) m. ....
Mary Stiles XXIX, 393

Robert (Dec. 19, 1762-Oct. 28, 1833)
m. May 4, 1785 Mourning Clark
XXXII, 79

MANSUR

Robert (....-a. 1680) m. June 6,
1670 Elizabeth Brooks MASS XV,
55; XXIII, 32, 39

William (Jan. 1, 1737-c. 1814) m.
Oct. 30, 1762 (1) Isabella Harvey
XV, 55; XXIII, 32, 39

MAPES

Daniel (c. 1734-p. 1781) m. ....
.... XVI, 71; XX, 49

Thomas (1628-1687) m. 1650 Sarah
Purrier. NY XVI, 71; XX, 49

MAPP

John (....-p. 1694) m. .... Ann .....

VA. XXVI, 20

John (a. 1740-a. 1785) m. Feb. 24,
1765 Elizabeth (Jacobs) Haggaman
XXVI, 20

MARCH

Clement (1707-1777) m. 1729 Eleanor
Veazey XXXI, 59, 60

Hugh (1618-Dec. 12, 1693) m. ....
(1) Judith ...... MASS XXXI, 60

MARCY

John (c. 1662-Dec. 23, 1724) m. ....
Sarah Hadlock CONN XII, 42;
XVIII, 9

Reuben (Nov. 28, 1732-Jan. 15, 1806)
m. Nov. 18, 1756 Rachel Watson
XII, 42; XVIII, 9

MARION, see MERION

MARIS

George (1632-Dec. 15, 1705) m. ....
Alice ...... PA X, 98, 108, 148;
XV, 51; XVI, 116; XVII, 65

George (Feb. 28, 1744-Dec. 1783) m.
Apr. 14, 1770 Eleanor Lindley X,
98, 108, 148; XV, 51; XVI, 116;
XVII, 64, 65

MARKHAM

Daniel (1648-Dec. 4, 1736) m. Nov.
3, 1669 Elizabeth Wetmore MASS,
CONN XXX, 17

Jeremiah (Jan. 25, 1735-Nov. 17,
1827) m. Apr. 20, 1769 Amy Deming
XXX, 16, 17

MARSELLUS

Ahasuerus (June 26, 1726-....) m.
Jan. 1750 Maria Vrooman XIX, 106

Janse von Bommel (....-c. 1700) m.
.... Anatie Gerritse NY XIX, 106

MARSH

Ebenezer (Oct. 15, 1735-June 1791)
m. Feb. 3, 1757 Achsah Stearns
XXXII, 268

Isaac (Oct. 18, 1747-Aug. 27, 1792)
m. Sept. 8, 1774/5 Lucy Smith
XXIX, 318; XXXII, 245; XXXIII, 13,
14, 37

John (c. 1610-Nov. 16, 1674) m. 1635
Susannah Skelton MASS XXV, 140;
XXXIII, 92

John (1618-Sept. 1688) m. 1640 Ann
Webster CONN XXIX, 318; XXXII,
245; XXXIII, 14, 37

John (1647/9-....) m. ....
Sarah ...... MASS XXXII,
268

MARSH, cont.
  John, Sr. (Oct. 18, 1718-1802) m.
    c. 1743 Elizabeth Carroll XXV,
    140
  John, IV (July 24, 1751-1814) m.
    1778 Sarah Colburn XXV, 140
  Nathaniel (Sept. 6, 1745-Mar. 26,
    1827) m. .... (3) Elizabeth Grin-
    man XXVI, 160
  Nathaniel (Jan. 22, 1746-Mar. 29,
    1795) m. .... Delight Wilson
    XII, 38, 60
  Reuben (Aug. 18, 1758-Mar. 9, 1843)
    m. Aug. 11, 1791 Lydia Rathbun
    XXXII, 268
  Samuel, Sr. (1738-Mar. 31, 1832) m.
    1762 Rebeckah Wilder XXXIII, 92
  Samuel (Oct. 8, 1751-May 14, 1822)
    m. Nov. 15, 1771 Miriam Leach
    XXVII, 45, 46
  William (c. 1659-1724) m. Oct. 18,
    168?/2 Elizabeth Yoemans CONN
    XII, 38, 60; XXVI, 160; XXVII, 46

MARSHALL
  David (Oct. 21, 1728-Mar. 13, 1776)
    m. .... Naomi Griswold XXXIII, 65
  Gilbert (1758-1795) m. .... Sarah
    Brown XIII, 77
  Isaac (Jan. 31, 1737-May 14, 1813) m.
    .... Abigail Brown VII, 27
  John (....-1672) m. a. Sept. 29,
    1659 Ruth Hawkins MASS XXXII,
    295
  John (1596-p. 1660) m. ....
    ...... VA VI, 37; X, 45
  John (1632-Nov. 5, 1702) m. .... (2)
    Mary Burrage MASS VII, 27
  John, Jr. (Aug. 29, 1747-....) m.
    Nov. 16, 1770 Elizabeth Hayward
    XXXII, 294, 295
  John (Sept. 24, 1755-July 6, 1835)
    m. Jan. 3, 1783 Mary Willis Ambler
    VI, 37
  Richard (c. 1756-Jan. 18, 1816) m.
    Mar. 5, 1782 Margaret Hardy XXXI,
    126, 127
  Samuel (1615-Dec. 19, 1675) m. May
    6, 1652 Mary Wilton CONN XXXIII,
    65
  Thomas (c. 1610-1671) m. ....
    ...... CONN XIII, 77
  Thomas (Apr. 2, 1730-June 22,
    1802) m. c. 1754 Mary
    Randolph Keith VI, 37; X,
    45
  William (c. 1607-p. Apr. 1673)
    m. c. 1656 Katherine Hebden MD
    XXXI, 126, 127

MARSHAND, see MERSHON

MARSTON
  Brackett (c. 1747-c. 1781) m. ....
    Mary Gerrish IX, 10; XII, 53
  David, Jr. (Feb. 5, 1756-Jan. 29,
    1835) m. Apr. 4, 1782 Mary Page
    XXXI, 71, 72
  William (c. 1592-June 30, 1672) m.
    .... NH IX, 10;
    XII, 54; XXXI, 72

MARTIN
  Aaron (July 29, 1742-Mar. 12, 1819)
    m. Nov. 13, 1766 Eunice Flint
    XXIX, 351
  George (....-c. 1686) m. Aug. 11,
    1646 (2) Susan North MASS XXIX,
    351
  John (c. 1615/8-1666) m. .... (3)
    Ann ...... VA XXXII, 87, 88
  John (1628-July 5, 1687) m. 1652
    Esther Roberts NH, NJ XXIV, 105;
    XXXIV, 260
  Joshua, I (Mar. 20, 1725-Jan. 1803)
    m. .... Mary ...... XXXII, 87, 88
  Reuben (bpt. June 22, 1746-Sept. 30,
    1838) m. 1775 Sarah Williams XXV,
    127
  Robert (p. 1720-c. 1800) m. Nov. 30,
    1758 Mary Bloomfield XXIV, 105
  Samuel (....-1683) m. 1646 Phebe
    Bracey CONN XXV, 127
  William (Dec. 28, 1757-Aug. 6, 1824)
    m. Mar. 28, 1780 Margaret Brown
    XXXIV, 260

MARVIN
  Elisha (Mar. 8, 1717-Dec. 31, 1801)
    m. Dec. 31, 1801) m. May 17, 1739
    Catherine Mather XV, 99, 123
  Giles (Dec. 23, 1751-Nov. 5, 1801)
    m. c. 1774 Lucy Barron XII, 110
  Isaiah (c. 1760-....) m. c. 1782
    Sarah Keeler XXVII, 169
  Matthew (bpt. Mar. 26, 1600-1678/80)
    m. c. 1622 Elizabeth ...... CONN
    XXVII, 169
  Reinold (bpt. Oct. 25, 1594-1662) m.
    1617 Marie ...... CONN XII, 110;
    XV, 99, 123

MARYON, see MERION

MASON
  Barachias (1723-1795) m. .... Love
    (Whitney) Battelle I, 27; XIII, 18
  Elijah (Sept. 26, 1756-June 27,
    1833) m. 1778 Mary Marsh XXII,
    129
  Elisha (Apr. 24, 1759-June 1, 1858)
    m. Jan. 8, 1785 Lucretia Webster
    XXIV, 31

George (c. 1629-1686) m. c. 1651
  (1) Mary ...... VA XXXII, 73,
  74
Henry (Apr. 3, 1758-Apr. 24, 1836)
  m. Apr. 21, 1782 Amey Williams
  III, 54; IV, 105; XIII, 50
Hobart (Oct. 6, 1722-1790) m. ....
  Margaret Copp IV, 105
Hugh (1605-Oct. 10, 1678) m. Jan.
  13, 1632 Esther Wells MASS X,
  203
Jesse (Mar. 21, 1737-Oct. 17, 1823)
  m. Mar. 22, 1758 Lois Mason XXXIV,
  344
John (c. 1600-Jan. 30, 1672) m. July
  2, 1640 (2) Anna Peck CONN III,
  54; IV, 105; XI, 170; XIII, 51;
  XXII, 129
John (1652-Feb. 19, 1698) m. Nov. 5,
  1676 Hannah Haws CONN XXIV, 31
Josiah (Oct. 3, 1734-Sept. 9, 1814)
  m. June 21, 1757 Anna Livermore
  X, 202
Peter (Aug. 1, 1752-Dec. 28, 1831)
  m. Mar. 24, 1774 Elishaba Farnam
  XI, 170
Philip (Jan. 29, 1744-July 21, 1813)
  m. .... Mercy Scott XXV, 204
Richard (c. 1740-1797) m. c. 1762/4
  Margaret ...... XXXII, 73, 74
Robert (1590-1667) m. ....
  ...... MASS I, 27; XIII, 18
Sampson (....-Sept. 15, 1676) m.
  1650/1 Mary Butterworth MASS X̀XV,
  204; XXXIV, 344

MATHER
  Charles (Mar. 20, 1734/5-June 14,
    1825) m. c. 1758 Ruth Kelsey
    XXVIII, 18, 19
  Eleazer (June 22, 1753-1837) m. May
    29, 1775 Irene Starlin X, 119
  Joseph (July 21, 1753-Feb. 29, 1840)
    m. May 29, 1777 Sarah Scott
    XXXIII, 104, 105
  Richard (1596-Apr. 22, 1669) m. Sept.
    29, 1624 Catherine Holt MASS X,
    119; XXVIII, 18, 19; XXX, 30, 31;
    XXXIII, 104, 105
  Timothy, Jr. (Mar. 2, 1757-Mar. 8,
    1818) m. Sept. 16, 1779 Hannah
    Church XXX, 30, 31

MATHEWS, see MATTHEWS

MATLACK, includes MATLOCK
  George (July 16, 1753-1782) m. Apr.
    6, 1775 Sarah Matson XXI, 171;
    XXIV, 5
  Timothy (Mar. 26, 1736-Apr. 14, 1829)
    m. Oct. 5, 1758 Ellen Yarnall

XXIX, 12
William (1648-p. Dec. 10, 1720) m.
  1682 Mary Hancock NJ XXI, 171;
  XXIV, 5; XXIX, 12

MATLOCK, see MATLACK

MATTESON
  Henry (Aug. 7, 1646-Oct. 27, 1684)
    m. 1670 Hannah Parsons RI XXXIII,
    98, 99; XXXIV, 196, 215
  Peter (Mar. 31, 1753-Feb. 13, 1825)
    m. .... Phebe ...... XXXIV, 196,
    215
  Thomas (Aug. 23, 1762-July 7, 1833)
    m. .... Thankful Sweet XXXIII,
    98, 99

MATTHEWS, includes MATHEWS
  Aaron (Nov. 19, 1721-Apr. 24, 1806)
    m. Jan. 14, 1742 Huldah Frisbie
    III, 51
  Abel (Feb. 25, 1746/7-May 1, 1822)
    m. July 24, 1777 (1) Eunice Pardee
    XXIX, 341
  Caleb (Dec. 16, 1743-Oct. 20, 1814)
    m. Jan. 1, 1766 (1) Anna Carrington
    XXXI, 316
  Edward (....-Feb. 25, 1678) m. ....
    .... VA XXVIII, 121
  Edward (1660-1712) m. 1688 Sarah
    Bishop VA XXV, 92
  John (Apr. 24, 1750-1840) m. Nov.
    30, 1769 Olive Roys XVII, 15
  William (....-Apr. 1684) m. c. 1671
    Jane (Joanna) ...... CONN III,
    51; XVII, 15; XXIX, 342; XXXI, 316
  William (Apr. 11, 1758-Mar. 31, 1825)
    m. Oct. 7, 1799 Jane Dunbar Hall
    XXV, 92; XXVIII, 121

MAXCY
  Alexander (....-Sept. 20, 1723) m.
    .... Abigale ...... MASS XXXII,
    201
  Benjamin, Sr. (May 11, 1740-July 26,
    1791) m. Oct. 1, 1763 Sarah Fuller
    XXXII, 201

MAXON, see MAXSON

MAXSON, includes MAGGSON, MAXON
  John (Apr. 21, 1701-1786) m. Sept.
    26, 1724 Thankful Randall XXXIII,
    242, 243
  John (Nov. 7, 1725-Aug. 28, 1791)
    m. June 7, 1749 Sarah Burdick
    XXVI, 35, 36
  Richard (....-Dec. 1639) m. ....
    Rebecca ...... MASS, RI XXVI,
    36; XXXIII, 242, 243

MAY, see MAYS

MAYNADIER
Daniel, I (....-Feb. 23, 1745) m.
Jan. 12, 1720 Hannah Haskins MD
XXXII, 219
William Murray (Apr. 28, 1747-p.
1774) m. c. 1770 Margaret Ennalls
XXXII, 219

MAYNARD
Hezekiah, Jr. (June 17, 1708-Oct.
28, 1781) m. .... Tabitha Howe
XXI, 62
John (1610-Dec. 10, 1672) m. June
14, 1646 Mary Axtell MASS XXI,
62; XXXII, 106
Joseph (May 17, 1750-1817) m. May
5, 1775 Deborah Twitchell XXXII,
106

MAYO
John (a. 1617-May 26, 1676) m. ....
Thomasine ...... MASS X, 265
Thomas (Apr. 1, 1725-1778) m. Oct.
5, 1752 (1) Elizabeth Wing X, 265

MAYS, includes MAIES, MAISE, MAY, MEASE
Ezra (Dec. 16, 1731-Jan. 11, 1778) m.
.... Margaret Lyon XIV, 109
Hezekiah (Dec. 14, 1696-Sept. 5,
1783) m. .... Anna Stillman XII,
105
John (c. 1590-Apr. 28, 1670) m. ....
(1) .... MASS XII, 105;
XIV, 109
John (1631-Sept. 11, 1671) m. Nov.
19, 1656 Mrs. Sarah (Brewer)
Bruce MASS XII, 105; XIV, 109
Joseph (1732-1829) m. c. 1766 ......
Baker XXXIV, 146
Joseph (July 12, 1740-Dec. 29, 1822)
m. Feb. 21, 1764 Rebecca Gardiner
XXVI, 221, 287, 288
Samuel (Dec. 25, 1724-Sept. 5, 1783)
m. .... Mary Peirce XII, 105
Samuel (July 23, 1762-Jan. 25, 1816)
m. 1793 Nancy Grigsby XXX, 103;
XXXI, 127
William (1574-p. 1650) m. .... Eliza-
beth ...... VA XXVI, 221, 287,
288; XXX, 103; XXXI, 127; XXXIV,
146

MC CALL
James (....-May 9, 1693) m. ....
Anna ;..... MASS V, 76
Ozias (1758-July 6, 1826) m. ....
Elizabeth Williams V, 76

MC CLAFLIN, see CLAFLIN

MC DONALD, includes MAC DONALD
Brian (1645-Feb. 23, 1707) m. 1678
Mary Doyle Combs PA XXIV, 8;
XXVIII, 25, 28; XXXI, 41
Joseph (Apr. 1, 1722-1809) m. Feb.
17, 1754 Elizabeth Ogle XXIV, 8;
XXVIII, 25; XXXI, 40, 41
William (1766-1849) m. .... Ursula
Hough XXIV, 7; XXVIII, 25, 28

MC INTIRE
Ebenezer (c. 1746-c. June 14, 1814)
m. May 5, 1771 Hannah Linscott
XXXI, 251, 252
Eleazer, Jr. (....-p. Mar. 25, 1782)
m. May 3, 1759 Elizabeth McIntire
XXIX, 405
Micum (1625/30-1700/5) m. .... Dor-
othy Pearce Mackaneer ME XXXI,
251, 252
Philip (....-p. Apr. 14, 1719) m.
Sept. 6, 1666 Mary ...... MASS
XXIX, 405

MC KENNEY, includes MAC KENNEY
John (....-....) m. ....
...... ME XXIV, 24
John (Feb. 9, 1737-Nov. 18, 1818)
m. Apr. 23, 1761 Mary Rand XXIV,
24

MEACHAM
Abraham (June 24, 1753-Dec. 24, 1822)
m. Oct. 15, 1778 Lydia Standish
XIV, 55, 56; XV, 45
Jeremiah (1613-Nov. 11, 1696) m.
1642 (1) Margaret ......; ....
(2) Alice Dorne MASS X, 123;
XIV, 55, 56; XV, 46; XXIX, 242
John (May 31, 1754-Oct. 19, 1839) m.
1780 Tabitha Daniels X, 122
Samuel, Jr. (Nov. 15, 1739-Jan. 22,
1811) m. Mar. 31, 1763 Phoebe Main
XXIX, 242

MEAD
Calvin (Aug. 1, 1760-June 18, 1847)
m. c. 1786 Deborah Mead XXIII, 44
Israel (Mar. 18, 1760-Mar. 26, 1851)
m. May 7, 1786 Mary Ferris XXXIV,
58
James (Sept. 6, 1730-Jan. 17, 1805)
m. Aug. 7, 1752 Mercy Holmes
XXXIV, 150
John, IV (1725-Dec. 3, 1790) m.
1750/2 Mary Brush XXVI, 190, 191
Nathan (May 27, 1757-Feb. 9, 1812) m.
.... Mary King IX, 20
Peter, Sr. (Oct. 2, 1716-1780)
m. July 29, 1744 Hannah Mead XXI,
175

Peter, Jr. (Jan. 4, 1755-Dec. 26, 1832) m. Nov. 19, 1777 Hannah Close XXI, 175
Sylvanus (Jan. 19, 1739-1780) m. June 2, 1763 Sybil Wood XXXI, 82
Titus (Sept. 15, 1729-Sept. 12, 1812) m. June 13, 1754 (1) Rachel Rundel X, 221
William (c. 1600-c. 1663) m. c. 1625 .... CONN IX, 20; X, 222; XXI, 175; XXIII, 44; XXVI, 191; XXXI, 82; XXXIV, 58, 151

MEADOR
Jesse (....-a. 1813) m. .... Martha ...... XXX, 67
Thomas (....-....) m. .... Sarah ...... VA XXX, 67

MEARES, see MEARS

MEARS, includes MEARES
James (Oct. 22, 1731-June 6, 1804) m. May 19, 1757 Ann (Nancy) Greaton XXVII, 124
Robert (c. 1592-p. Feb. 20, 1666) m. .... Elizabeth Johnson MASS XXVII, 124

MEASE, see MAYS

MEDBURY
Benjamin (Dec. 31, 1718-c. 1795) m. .... Sarah ...... XVIII, 21
John (....-....) m. .... Sarah ..... MASS XVIII, 21

MEIGS
Elihu (Sept. 21, 1749-Sept. 9, 1827) m. 1771 Elizabeth Rich XXXI, 236, 237
Vincent (1563-Dec. 1, 1658) m. .... Churchill MASS, CONN XXXI, 236, 237

MERCER, see MESSER

MERCEREAU
Joshua (Dec. 1657-May 23, 1756) m. July 16, 1693 Marie Chadreyne NY XXXII, 257
Joshua (Sept. 26, 1728-June 10, 1804) m. c. 1772 (2) Anne Roome XXXII, 257

MERION, includes MARION, MERYON, MARYON
John (1620-Jan. 7, 1705/6) m. 1640 Sarah Eddy MASS XVIII, 15; XXVI, 129, 130; XXXIV, 37
Nathaniel (Sept. 8, 1749-Jan. 11, 1797) m. Dec. 10, 1776 Lydia Gay

XVIII, 14, 15; XXVI, 130; XXXIV, 37

MERIWETHER
James (1756-Oct. 24, 1801) m. .... Sarah Meriwether VI, 9
Nicholas (....-Dec. 19, 1678) m. .... Elizabeth Wodenhouse VA I, 33; V, 133; VI, 9, 18; X, 179
Nicholas (Oct. 26, 1647-Dec. 1744) m. a. 1688/9 Elizabeth Crawford VA VI, 9, 18
Nicholas (June 4, 1749-Apr. 28, 1828) m. .... Elizabeth Thornton X, 179
William (1760-Feb. 10, 1842) m. .... Elizabeth Winslow I, 33; V, 133; VI, 18

MERRELL, see MERRILL

MERRIAM
David (Jan. 28, 1760-Feb. 15, 1849) m. Feb. 10, 1795 (2) Elizabeth Conant XXIX, 260; XXX, 34
Joseph (c. 1600-Jan. 1, 1640/1) m. c. 1623 Sarah Goldstone MASS XXIX, 260; XXX, 34

MERRICK
Benjamin (Feb. 3, 1754-Oct. 25, 1811) m. .... Levina Ewing XXXII, 53
Jonathan (Mar. 21, 1746/7-Mar. 31, 1812) m. Jan. 1, 1774 Mary Merrick XXXI, 174
Joseph (Oct. 1733-Apr. 1787) m. Jan. 1755 Ann Holt XXX, 48, 49
Thomas (1620-Sept. 7, 1704) m. 1653 Elizabeth Tilley MASS XXX, 49; XXXI, 174; XXXII, 53

MERRILL, includes MERRELL, MERRILLS
Annis (June 13, 1751-1847) m. June 10, 1784 Lydia Merrill XIV, 84
Bildad (bpt. Jan. 28, 1749/50-Nov. 21, 1815) m. Jan. 16, 1774 (1) Damaris Mix XXXI, 205
Ford (Sept. 2, 1753-Nov. 12, 1826) m. .... Elizabeth Merrill V, 111, 112
Gideon (1749-June 27, 1803) m. Aug. 1, 1776 Abigail Merrill XXVIII, 45, 46
James (July 10, 1729-Mar. 2, 1784) m. 1752/3 Sarah Ford V, 111, 112; XIII, 20; XXXII, 90
James (Sept. 21, 1751-Mar. 16, 1807) m. Nov. 24, 1774 Jerusha Seymour XXV, 58
Jeptha (1756-1838) m. .... Mary Royce XV, 131; XXV, 201; XXVII, 209

MERRILL, cont.
  Jerijah (July 25, 1749-June 3, 1791)
    m. Oct. 20, 1789 Tryphrena Merrill
    XXXIV, 52
  Nathaniel (bpt. May 4, 1610-Mar. 16,
    1655) m. c. 1633/4 Susanna Wilter-
    ton MASS V, 111, 112; XIII, 20;
    XIV, 84; XV, 131; XXI, 67, 68;
    XXIV, 74; XXV, 58, 201; XXVII, 209,
    XXVIII, 45, 46; XXXI, 205; XXXII,
    90; XXXIV, 52
  Nathaniel (Feb. 7, 1742-Mar. 1, 1820)
    m. 1761 Hannah Belden XXI, 67, 68
  Stephen (Jan. 29, 1713-Nov. 24, 1793)
    m. May 21, 1740 Joanna French
    XXIV, 74

MERRIMAN
  Nathaniel (June 2, 1613-Feb. 23,
    1693) m. 1649 .... CONN
    XIII, 101; XV, 24; XXIX, 297; XXX,
    272
  Samuel (Sept. 11, 1749-May 27, 1824)
    m. 1768 Eunice Hall XIII, 100; XV,
    24; XXIX, 297; XXX, 272

MERRITT
  Ezekiel (May 24, 1767-Apr. 23, 1847)
    m. Apr. 20, 1788 Sarah Snow XXXII,
    51
  Henry (1570-Nov. 1653) m. .... Judith
    ...... MASS XXXII, 52

MERSHON, includes MARSHAND
  Aaron (1745/6-Aug. 27, 1776) m. 1769
    Mary Gaspen XXXIII, 109
  Henri (....-....) m. ....
    ...... NY, NJ XXXIII, 109

MERWIN
  Daniel (May 30, 1746-Apr. 18, 1820)
    m. Dec. 14, 1769 Rebecca Seward
    XXXIII, 170, 171
  David (Jan. 30, 1743-Apr. 13, 1816)
    m. .... Eunice Perry V, 67; XIV,
    38, 39; XXII, 12
  John (Apr. 3, 1707-Feb. 19, 1792) m.
    Dec. 2, 1730 Elizabeth Nettleton
    V, 67; XVII, 83; XXII, 13
  Miles (Apr. 1623-Apr. 23, 1697) m.
    .... Elizabeth Baldwin Canfield
    MASS, CONN V, 67; XIV, 38, 39;
    XVII, 83; XXII, 13; XXXIII, 170,
    171
  Miles (Mar. 29, 1720-Dec. 12, 1786)
    m. June 30, 1743 Mary Talcott
    XXXIII, 170, 171

MERYON, see MERION

MESLER, see MESSLER

MESSENGER
  Andrew (....-....) m. ....
    ...... CONN XXI, 106; XXV, 220,
    221
  Roderick (Mar. 11, 1741/2-Aug. 28,
    1823) m. Apr. 14, 1763 (1) Tamesia
    Stephens XXI, 106; XXV, 220, 221

MESSER, includes MERCER
  Nathaniel Smith (Oct. 13, 1756-Jan.
    20, 1832) m. Feb. 14, 1785 Sarah
    Clough XXIII, 73
  Richard (....-Mar. 29, 1671) m. Mar.
    18, 1669 Hannah Shatswell MASS
    XXIII, 73

MESSLER, includes MESLER, METSELAER
  Cornelius (Feb. 9, 1759-Nov. 28,
    1843) m. Nov. 15, 1781 Maria Stry-
    ker XXII, 43
  James (Jacobus) (bpt. c. 1730-p. Mar.
    9, 1803) m. Jannetje (Jane) Bergen
    XXXI, 289
  Jan Adamsen (c. 1626-p. Jan. 20,
    1695) m. c. 1657 Geertje Dircksen
    NY XXII, 43; XXXI, 289

METCALF
  Isaac (....-a. Sept. 17, 1689) m.
    .... Anne Bagwell VA XXXII, 188,
    189
  John (c. 1751-Aug. 15, 1820) m. c.
    1790 Anne Penniston XXXII, 188,
    189

METSELAER, see MESSLER

MIDDLEBROOK
  John (1726-1817) m. c. 1754 ......
    Sims XXX, 258
  Joseph (1610-1686) m. c. 1644 Mary
    Bateman CONN XXV, 259; XXX, 258
  Oliver (Oct. 19, 1746-p. Apr. 15,
    1820) m. .... Mary Odell XXV, 259

MILES
  Benjamin (Nov. 26, 1724-Jan. 28,
    1776) m. May 16, 1751 Mary Hubbard
    XIII, 100
  John (c. 1618-Aug. 26, 1693) m. Apr.
    10, 1679 Susanna Rediat MASS
    XIII, 100

MILLER, includes MILLERD
  Abner Isaac (May 3, 1760-Sept. 18,
    1822) m. 1788 Sarah Phillips XXV,
    297
  James (Jan. 17, 1734/5-p. 1800) m.
    Mar. 15, 1756 Mary Clark XXIII, 28
  John (....-June 5, 1685) m. ....
    .... MASS XXX, 287, 288

John (a. 1619-1664) m. .... Mary
Pierson NY XXV, 291, 297; XXVI,
29
Jonathan (1729-1810) m. June 24,
1761 Sarah Woodruff XXIX, 213
Joseph (Aug. 5, 1723-Jan. 31, 1785)
m. Dec. 6, 1752 Lydia Stowe XIII,
23
Joseph (June 24, 1724-Apr. 3, 1803)
m. (int.) Jan. 19, 1744 Catherine
Ferry XXVII, 214; XXXII,150, 291,
292; XXXIV, 90, 155
Joseph (Aug. 26, 1741-Apr. 30, 1832)
m. Apr. 8, 1762 Thankful Gilmore
XIX, 25
Josiah (1749-1817) m. Jan. 1769
Pauline Titus XXV, 291; XXVI, 29
Leonard (Mar. 28, 1752-Oct. 18, 1820)
m. .... (1) Mary Sikes XXVII, 214;
XXXII, 150, 291, 292; XXXIII, 26
Philip (May 6, 1750-Feb. 11, 1824)
m. c. 1770 Rhoda Mason XXX, 287,
288
Robert (1632-Mar. 16, 1699) m. Oct.
24, 1662 Elizabeth Sabin MASS
XIX, 26; XXVI, 186
Samuel (Feb. 17, 1742/3-Feb. 26,
1817) m. 1780 (2) Anne Hill XXVI,
186
Thomas (1609/10-Aug. 14, 1680) m.
June 6, 1666 Sarah Nettleton CONN
XIII, 23; XXIII, 28
Thomas (c. 1624-Oct. 5, 1675) m.
Oct. 12, 1649 Sarah Marshfield
MASS XXVII, 214; XXXI, 150, 291;
XXXIII, 26; XXXIV, 90, 155
William (c. 1620-July 15, 1690) m.
Mar. 3, 1641 Patience Bacon MASS
XXIX, 213

MILLERD, see MILLER

MILLIKEN
Hugh (....-....) m. .... Eleanor
Elleson MASS XXXIII, 62, 63, 281
Joshua (Apr. 10, 1756-Nov. 27, 1832)
m. May 27, 1778 Margaret Lord
XXXIII, 62, 63
Thomas (May 31, 1724-a. Nov. 14,
1793) m. 1777 (2) Mary McKenney
XXXIII, 281

MILLS
Amasa (Feb. 27, 1736-Feb. 24, 1827)
m. May 7, 1756 Lucy Curtis XI,
138, 139, 140, 141
Benjamin, Sr. (May 21, 1720-p. 1780)
m. June 12, 1755 Elizabeth Fellows
XXXI, 42
Benjamin, Jr. (Mar. 8, 1756-p. 1792)
m. Jan. 16, 1778 Sarah Loker

XXXI, 42
Elijah, Jr. (Sept. 6, 1761-Nov. 8,
1831) m. Nov. 6, 1783 Huldah Drake
XXII, 52
Peter (Van der Meulen) (1622-Apr. 17,
1710) m. .... Dorcas Messenger
CONN XXII, 53
Samuel (....-Jan. 7, 1694/5) m. Mar.
11, 1645 Frances Pimbroke MASS
XXXI, 42
Simon (a. 1637-....) m. .... Joan
...... CONN XI, 138, 139, 140,
141
William (1606-a. 1698) m. ....
...... VA XX, 119
William (Oct. 1743-a. July 1823) m.
.... (2) Elizabeth Cottingham XX,
119

MINER, includes MINOR, MYNARD
Christopher (1733-Mar. 10, 1832) m.
May 28, 1758 (2) Abigail Way XII,
88; XXIII, 71
Christopher (Mar. 17, 1745-Jan. 22,
1803) m. Aug. 11, 1765 Mary Randall
IV, 104; XXX, 273, 274
Daniel (July 1735-July 15, 1791) m.
.... Abigail ...... XXV, 194
David (Oct. 15, 1760-July 19, 1826)
m. Apr. 1788 Eunice Warner XXX,
112, 113
Garrett (Mar. 14, 1744-June 25, 1799)
m. May 8, 1769 Mary Overton Terrell
XXIX, 270
John (Jan. 31, 1743-1833) m. Feb. 22,
1776 Cassandra Williams XXIV, 130
Joshua (Aug. 6, 1747-1776) m. 1767
Rebecca Cotterell XXIX, 335; XXX,
269
Manasseh (1647-1728) m. .... Lydia
Moore MASS, CONN II, 28
Manasseh (1755-1837) m. ....
...... II, 28
Seth (Nov. 23, 1733-Nov. 4, 1820) m.
Mar. 8, 1757 Eunice Root XX, 71
Thomas (Aug. 23, 1608-Oct. 23, 1690)
m. Apr. 23, 1634 Grace Palmer CONN
II, 28; IV, 104; VI, 77; IX, 7;
XII, 88; XX, 71; XXIII, 71; XXIV,
130; XXV, 194; XXIX, 335; XXX, 112,
113, 269, 273, 274
William (....-c. 1709) m. Nov. 15,
1678 Lydia Richards CONN XIX, 86
William (Dec. 18, 1751-Feb. 25, 1833)
m. May 10, 1770 Abigail Haley VI,
77; IX, 7
Zebediah (1760-July 27, 1825)
m. Nov. 1783 Ann Atwell
XIX, 85

MINNE, see MINNERLY

MINNERLAY, see MINNERLY

MINNERLY, includes MINNE, MINNERLAY
James (Jacobus) (Oct. 8, 1744-Apr.
26, 1823) m. 1762 Catherine Mart-
ling XXVIII, 196
Johannis (....-a. 1693) m. (1)
Rensie Feddes NY XXVIII, 196

MINOR, see MINER

MINTER
Edward (1612-c. 1684) m. 1633 Grace
...... VA XXVIII, 159
J. Morgan (1750-Nov. 9, 1806) m.
1772 Joanna Rutherford XXVIII,
159, 160

MITCHELL
Andrew (....-Nov. 25, 1736) m. Nov.
12, 1686 Abigail Atwood MASS
XXIV, 136; XXVI, 235, 236
Asahel (Oct. 6, 1723-May 1, 1797) m.
Jan. 21, 1747 Olive Root XXX, 81,
90
Christopher (....-Apr. 1688) m. a.
1665 Sarah Andrews ME XXIX, 14,
179
Dominicus (Apr. 19, 1744-Sept. 6,
1822) m. Aug. 1, 1765 Anna Small
XXIX, 14, 179
Eleazer (Nov. 27, 1732-Feb. 3, 1819)
m. Oct. 5, 1758 (1) Olive Hickox
X, 94; XI, 184, 185; XVI, 119;
XVIII, 98, 109; XXVII, 11, 54, 55,
168
Experience (1609-1689) m. 1628 Jane
Cook MASS XXX, 206, 207
Matthew (1590-1645) m. Aug. 21, ʾ1616
Susan Wood CONN X, 94; XI, 184,
185; XVI, 119; XVIII, 98, 109;
XXVII, 12, 54, 55, 168; XXX, 81, 90
Nathaniel (Aug. 15, 1757-Aug. 31,
1838) m. June 21, 1787 Alice Parker
XXIV, 135; XXVI, 235, 236
William (Apr. 18, 1750-June 9, 1837)
m. Sept. 5, 1776 Elizabeth Ward
XXX, 206, 207

MIX
Eldad (Oct. 4, 1733-Oct. 3, 1806) m.
June 25, 1756 Lydia Beach XXIX,
293
Joseph (Mar. 18, 1740-Feb. 5, 1813)
m. Oct. 15, 1764 Patience Sperry
XXVI, 178, 179
Thomas (c. 1626-p. Apr. 25, 1691) m.
1649 Rebecca Turner CONN XXVI;
178, 233, 234; XXIX, 293
Timothy (Dec. 28, 1727-Jan. 23, 1800)
m. .... Elizabeth ..... XXVI,

233, 234

MIXER, includes MIXTER
Isaac, Sr. (Oct. 3, 1602-p. May 8,
1655) m. May 11, 1629 Sarah Thurs-
ton MASS XXXIII, 199
Timothy (July 17, 1748-....) m. Oct.
7, 1769 Molly (Mary) Eames XXXIII,
199

MIXTER, see MIXER

MONROE, includes MUNRO
Nathan (Aug. 9, 1747-May 26, 1829)
m. Oct. 3, 1769 Elizabeth Harrington XXXIII, 272
William (1625-Jan. 27, 1717/8) m.
.... Martha George MASS XXXIII,
272

MONTAGUE
Caleb (July 27, 1731-Nov. 9, 1782)
m. Oct. 30, 1751 Eunice Root XXX,
142
Moses (Nov. 17, 1724-Dec. 18, 1792)
m. Sept. 22, 1748 Sarah Graves
XVII, 133
Peter (1603-May 1, 1659) m. 1633 (1)
.... VA XXIX, 52;
XXXII, 132
Richard (1614-Dec. 14, 1681) m. c.
1636 Abigail Downing CONN, MASS
XVII, 133; XXX, 142
Thomas (Feb. 20, 1719/20-1778) m.
1753 Jane Daniel XXIX, 52; XXXII,
132

MOOAR, see MOORE

MOODY
Ebenezer (Jan. 9, 1743/4-p. Dec. 21,
1783) m. Nov. 17, 1768 Zerviah
Seymour XXX, 53, 54
John (Apr. 8, 1593-1655) m. Sept. 8,
1617 Sarah Doe CONN XIV, 31, 32;
XXX, 53, 54
Paul (Jan. 20, 1742/3-Dec. 30, 1822)
m. Oct. 25, 1762 Mary Jewett X,
169
Seth (Sept. 28, 1752-Oct. 14, 1837)
m. 1778 Mary Pomeroy XIV, 31, 32
William (....-Oct. 25, 1673) m. ....
Sarah Pierce MASS X, 169

MOORE, includes MOOAR, MORE
Abijah (1749-Apr. 26, 1826) m. ....
Abigail Drake IV, 107
Abraham(....-Apr. 12, 1706) m. Dec.
14, 1687 Priscilla Poore MASS
X, 56
Andrew (....-Nov. 29, 1719) m.

Feb. 15, 1671 Sarah Phelps CONN
XIX, 78; XXXI, 246
Benjamin, Sr. (Feb. 18, 1715-Nov. 8,
1777) m. Sept. 16, 1740 Abiah Hill
X, 55
Benjamin, Jr. (Oct. 28, 1743-Aug.
1828) m. Sept. 29, 1767 Hannah
Phelps X, 55
Daniel, Jr. (Apr. 2, 1716-....) m.
June 1743 Elizabeth White XVI, 25
David (Nov. 25, 1713-June 18, 1789)
m. Jan. 31, 1734 Hepzibah Wilmott
XIII, 112
David (Jan. 21, 1722-....) m. Dec.
22, 1743 Hannah Parker XVII, 158
Henry, Jr. (Nov. 5, 1753-Apr. 17,
1829) m. Feb. 9, 1777 Keturah Petty
XXXII, 113
James (1641-Apr. 9, 1729) m. 1666
Margaret Yeamans SC XV, 135; XX,
163
James (1741-Apr. 19, 1777) m. ....
Ann Ivey XV, 135
John (....-Sept. 18, 1677) m. 1639
Abigail ...... MASS, CONN IV,
107; XXI, 29, 30
John (1610-Jan. 6, 1673) m. ....
Elizabeth Whaley MASS XVI, 25;
XVII, 158
John (1620-Sept. 17, 1657) m. 1641
Margaret Howell MASS, NY VI, 86;
XXX, 170
John (1746-a. Aug. 9, 1808) m. July
22, 1772 Hannah Wortman XXX, 169,
170
John (1758-1810) m. 1783 (1) Drusilla
Sullivan XX, 163
Joseph (July 21, 1720-Nov. 3, 1776)
m. .... Mary Stevens XIX, 77
Roswell (May 17, 1728-Dec. 13, 1794)
m. June 30, 1755 Desire Dunham
XXI, 29, 30
Samuel (Oct. 21, 1761-Aug. 23, 1838)
m. Oct. 23, 1783 Olive Bent XVI,
25
Shadrach, Jr. (May 10, 1757-Sept. 11,
1806) m. 1788 (1) Lovice Selden
Nott XXXI, 246
Stephen (1759-Feb. 18, 1813) m. ....
Parthenia Young VI, 86
Thomas (....-1645) m. ....
...... MASS IV, 107
Thomas (c. 1615-June 25, 1691) m. a.
May 11, 1636 Martha Youngs MASS
XIII, 112; XXXII, 113

MORE, see MOORE

MORGAN
Elisha (Mar. 7, 1762-Apr. 1, 1796) m.
Oct. 1790 Abigail Morgan XVI, 42,55

James (1607-1685) m. Aug. 6, 1640
Margery Hill MASS, CONN IV, 133;
X, 26; XVI, 42, 55; XXII, 19
James (1730-May 16, 1792) m. 1758
Catherine Street IV, 133; XXII,
19
James, Jr. (Apr. 20, 1759-Sept. 14,
1824) m. Apr. 10, 1788 Eunice Turn-
er XXII, 19
John (Dec. 3, 1719-Sept. 25, 1790) m.
June 24, 1761 Margaret Morgan Mig-
hill XX, 155
John, Jr. (Oct. 3, 1762-Dec. 26,
1826) m. Mar. 3, 1808 Mary Pierce
XX, 155
Lucas (Feb. 22, 1743-Nov. 12, 1817)
m. Dec. 21, 1768 (1) Tryphenia
Smith X, 225
Miles (a. 1615-May 28, 1699) m. 1643
(1) Prudence Gilbert; Feb. 15,
1670 (2) Elizabeth Bliss MASS X,
225; XX, 155
William (June 1, 1746-Jan. 17, 1824)
m. Nov. 23, 1769 Miriam Murdock
X, 26

MORICE, see MORRIS

MORLEY
Dimick (Sept. 23, 1750-Apr. 1, 1834)
m. Dec. 15, 1774 Ruth Weston XVII,
70
Thomas, Sr. (....-....) m. ....
Katherine Burnell MASS XVII, 70

MORRILL
John (1640-p. Sept. 6, 1723) m. a.
1667 Sarah Hodsdon ME XXXI, 285
Peter (Sept. 16, 1709-Nov. 11, 1801)
m. Oct. 27, 1731 (1) Sarah Peasley
XXXI, 285

MORRIS, includes MORICE
Anthony (Aug. 23, 1654-Aug. 23, 1721)
m. Jan. 30, 1675 (1) Mary Jones
NJ, PA III, 22
Anthony (Nov. 14, 1705-Oct. 2, 1780)
m. Dec. 1, 1730 (1) Sarah Powell
III, 22
Edward (Aug. 8, 1630-Sept. 14, 1689)
m. Sept. 20, 1655 Grace Bett MASS
V, 104, 105, 109; XXXI, 152
Isaac (Mar. 26, 1725-Jan. 10, 1778)
m. Oct. 18, 1748 Sarah Chaffee
XXXI, 151, 152
Isaac (Sept. 10, 1753-June 26, 1805)
m. .... Irene Johnson V, 104, 105,
109
Lewis (Apr. 8, 1726-Jan. 22, 1798) m.
Sept. 24, 1749 Mary Beekman Walton
XXIV, 150

MORRIS, cont.
  Major (Oct. 16, 1751-Sept. 5, 1811)
    m. .... Elizabeth Hine XXVI, 262,
    263, 264
  Richard (....-1674) m. Nov. 28,
    1628 Leonora Pawley RI XXXII,
    181
  Richard (1636-1672) m. Aug. 17,
    1669 Sarah Poole NY XXIV, 150
  Solomon, Sr. (Sept. 5, 1755-Oct. 26,
    1840) m. Oct. 1, 1779 Keziah Moss
    XXXII, 180
  Thomas (....-July 21, 1673) m. ....
    Elizabeth ...... CONN XXVI, 262,
    263, 264

MORSE
  Amos (Nov. 20, 1762-Jan. 16, 1854)
    m. May 28, 1784 Susannah Sawyer
    XVII, 157
  Anthony (May 9, 1606-Oct. 12, 1686)
    m. .... (1) Mary ......; 1626 (2)
    Ann ...... MASS IV, 90; VI, 92;
    XVII, 157; XXI, 25; XXIX, 237,
    380, 381; XXXIII, 51, 52; XXXIV,
    325
  Anthony (Dec. 22, 1753-Mar. 22, 1803)
    m. .... Huldah Taylor IV, 90
  Asa (Dec. 30, 1748-Mar. 1, 1815) m.
    June 9, 1772 (1) Eunice Parker
    XXI, 93, 94
  David (Feb. 15, 1740-1820) m. ....
    Anna Newman XXIX, 379, 380, 381
  Eli (Sept. 16, 1722-July 1814) m.
    .... Sarah Chenery XXI, 139
  Eliphalet (May 11, 1734-....) m.
    June 27, 1756 Martha Mayo XXIV,
    17
  Jacob (Sept. 21, 1717-Mar. 30, 1800)
    m. 1753 Mary Merrifield XIV, 77;
    XV, 54; XXV, 30
  James (Sept. 22, 1746-1809) m. Nov.
    23, 1769 Hannah Lee XXV, 247, 248
  Jonathan (Aug. 7, 1755-July 1836) m.
    Apr. 1779 Sarah Wyman XXXIII, 51,
    52
  Jonathan (Mar. 3, 1757-Mar. 3, 1840)
    m. June 8, 1786 (1) Abiah Worth
    XXXIV, 325
  Joseph (Jan. 4, 1730/1-Feb. 7, 1802)
    m. Jan. 1757 Sarah Ellice XXIX,
    374
  Joshua (Mar. 8, 1752-Oct. 1, 1828)
    m. Apr. 29, 1773 Levina Holland
    VI, 57
  Nathaniel (Oct. 20, 1728-June 9,
    1781) m. Oct. 11, 1749 Mary
    Morgan VI, 92
  Obediah (Jan. 22, 1697/8-July 21,
    1776) m. Jan. 29, 1728 Bethiah Rug-
    gles XXI, 93, 94, 164

Obadiah (Mar. 20, 1732/3-Jan. 7,
  1800) m. July 10, 1755 Grace Fairbanks XX, 43; XXXIII, 96, 97
Samuel (bpt. July 25, 1587-Apr. 5,
  1654) m. 1610 Elizabeth Jasper
  MASS VI, 57; XIII, 36; XIV, 77;
  XV, 54; XX, 43; XXI, 93, 94, 139,
  164; XXV, 30, 247, 248; XXIX, 142,
  374; XXXIII, 96, 97
Samuel, Sr. (Sept. 30, 1718-Apr. 20,
  1789) m. Feb. 1, 1759 Catherine
  Clark XIII, 36; XXIX, 142
Samuel, Jr. (Sept. 30, 1759-Apr. 4,
  1853) m. Apr. 14, 1785 Esther Wood-
  ward XIII, 36
Thomas (June 30, 1726-Oct. 23, 1799)
  m. May 30, 1747 Elizabeth Bartlett
  XXI, 25; XXIX, 237
William (1614-Nov. 29, 1683) m. 1635
  Elizabeth Titscomb MASS XXIV, 17

MORSMAN, see MOSMAN

MORTENSEN, see MORTON

MORTON, includes MORTENSEN
  Alexander, Sr. (1759-Apr. 13, 1822) m.
    Dec. 2, 1784 Ruth Strong XXVIII,
    189, 190
  Ebenezer (1764-Feb. 3, 1839) m. ....
    Hannah Ingram VII, 21
  Ephraim (1623-Sept. 7, 1693) m. Nov.
    1644 Ann Cooper MASS XXVII, 152
  George (....-June 1624) m. Aug. 2,
    1612 Juliana Carpenter MASS XXII,
    40; XXVII, 152
  Isaac (Apr. 18, 1754-Sept. 24, 1824)
    m. 1774 Anna Barber XXII, 40
  John (c. 1650-1721) m. July 25, 1682
    (2) Joane (Hughes) Anes VA
    XXXII, 68, 137
  John (p. Feb. 1724/5-Apr. 1, 1777) m.
    .... Ann Justis XII, 64
  John (Nov. 20, 1733-1795) m. Sept.
    27, 1777 (2) Lucy Blakely (Bleak-
    ley) XXXII, 68, 137
  Morton (....-1712) m. .... Margaret
    ...... PA XII, 65
  Richard (a. 1649-Apr. 3, 1710) m.
    .... Ruth ...... CONN, MASS
    VII, 21
  Seth (Jan. 20, 1721/2-p. 1789) m.
    Dec. 4, 1746 Elizabeth Allen
    XXVII, 152
  Sketchley (1750-June 19, 1795) m.
    .... Rebecca Taylor XII, 64
  William (....-a.Jan. 7, 1711) m.1670
    Mary Burnham CONN XXVIII, 189,190

MOSELEY, includes MOSLEY
  David, II (Mar. 7, 1735-Nov. 5, 1798)

m. .... Lydia Gay XXVI, 93

John, I (....-Oct. 27, 1661) m. ....
Cicely ...... MASS IV, 84, 86;
XXVI, 93; XXXI, 213

Jonathan (June 10, 1749-July 16,
1831) m. July 17, 1775 Esther
Clark XXXI, 213

Nathaniel (Dec. 22, 1743-1815) m.
.... Roxanna Allworth IV, 84, 86

Robert (Feb. 14, 1732-Jan. 30, 1804)
m. 1758 Magdalene Guerrant XVIII,
135; XXVI, 127; XXXII, 212

Robert Joel, Sr. (Sept. 13, 1755-p.
1803) m. 1774 Mary Ann Stewart
XXXIII, 229

William (bpt. Dec. 10, 1606-p. June
29, 1655) m. .... Susannah Cock-
roft VA XVIII, 135; XXVI, 127;
XXXII, 212; XXXIII, 229

MOSLEY, see MOSELEY

MOSMAN, includes MORSMAN, MOSSMAN

Aaron (Oct. 22, 1787-Nov. 27, 1840)
m. May 28, 1782 Hepzibah Hosmer
XXI, 30, 31

James (July 9, 1626-Oct. 25, 1722)
m. .... (2) Anna ...... MASS XXV,
72; XXI, 30, 31; XXVIII, 147;
XXXIII, 347, 348

Oliver (Jan. 19, 1760-Apr. 30, 1835)
m. 1783 (1) Dolly Trowbridge
XXVIII, 147

Silas (May 27, 1757-Jan. 20, 1829) m.
Feb. 24, 1779 Beulah Hemenway XXV,
72; XXXIII, 347, 348

MOSS

Edward (....-1646) m. .... Ann Belt
VA XXX, 161, 162

Isaac (Mar. 29, 1754-Dec. 15, 1839)
m. June 15, 1774 Sarah Tuttle X,
171

Joel (July 7, 1757/8-Aug. 1794) m.
Mar. 19, 1778 Hannah Hall X, 23,
24; XIII, 113

John (1603-1707) m. ....
...... CONN X, 23, 24, 83, 171;
XIII, 113

John, Sr. (1705/8-a. Dec. 19, 1785)
m. .... Elizabeth Massie XXX, 161,
162

Joseph (Dec. 17, 1742-1819) m. May
21, 1761/2 Esther Lewis X, 83

Moses (1758-1838) m. .... Lucretia
Williams XV, 16

Nathaniel (Dec. 25, 1752-Nov. 23,
1824) m. Dec. 30, 1780 Joanna Johnson XXX, 161, 162

Obed (Sept. 13, 1763-Oct. 26, 1832)
m. Jan. 22, 1786 Sarah Bunnell

X, 83

William (1630-1680) m. .... Jane
North VA XV, 16

MOSSMAN, see MOSMAN

MOULTON

Robert (May 20, 1733-Mar. 4, 1817)
m. c. 1760 Sarah Philbrick XXXIII,
240

Samuel (June 14, 1753-Dec. 25, 1837)
m. Oct. 13, 1774 Hannah Noyes
XVII, 49, 50

Stephen, Jr. (July 11, 1735-Jan. 4,
1776) m. Nov. 24, 1757 Hannah Bliss
XXXII, 83

William (1617-Apr. 18, 1664) m. 1651
Margaret Page NH XVII, 49; XXXII,
83; XXXIII, 240

MOWRY

Ananias (May 2, 1705-Oct. 8, 1789) m.
Mar. 2, 1745 Zerviah Angell XXXII,
148

Roger (a. 1610-Jan. 5, 1666) m. ....
Mary Johnson MASS, RI XXXII, 148

MUDD

Francis (1746-1779) m. .... Sarah
Mitchell XXXI, 149, 150

Thomas (1647-1697) m. 1677 Sarah
Boarman MD XXXI, 150

MUDGE

Simon (Apr. 8, 1748-Aug. 27, 1799)
m. May 19, 1773 Elizabeth Whit-
tredge XXXII, 163

Thomas (c. 1624-....) m. .... Mary
...... MASS XXXII, 163

MULFORD

Jonathan (June 24, 1747-c. 1784) m.
June 24, 1767 Lucy Smith XXXII,
221; XXXIII, 131

Thomas (Nov. 10, 1750-Dec. 31, 1830)
m. .... Phoebe Smith VIII, 23

William, I (c. 1620-Mar. 8, 1687) m.
.... Sarah Akers NY VIII, 24;
XXXII, 221; XXXIII, 131

MULKEY, includes MULLCAY

Eric Pallson (1636-1726) m. 1656
Inglebord Helm DE XXI, 172

Jonathan (1752-1837) m. Nov. 1771
Nancy Howard XXI,
172

Philip (May 14, 1732-1801)
m. 1750 Ann Ellis XXI,
172

MULLCAY, see MULKEY

MUNGER
  Cyrus (Mar. 8, 1751-May 31, 1839) m.
  Sept. 12, 1776 Prudence Rogers
  XXIX, 285
  Elnathan (July 23, 1714-Oct. 5, 1777)
  m. July 23, 1744 Deborah Thompson
  XXIX, 285
  Nicholas (c. 1630-Oct. 17, 1668) m.
  June 2, 1659 Sarah Hall CONN
  XXXIV, 342
  Reuben (Mar. 28, 1725-May 1808) m.
  June 8, 1748 Elizabeth Dudley
  XXXIV, 342

MUNN
  Benjamin (c. 1600-Nov. 1675) m. 1649
  Abigail (Bond) Ball CONN, MASS
  XVIII, 26; XX, 152
  David (Dec. 11, 1760-Apr. 22, 1843)
  m. Mar. 5, 1781 Abigail Baldwin
  XVIII, 26
  Joseph (May 1, 1734-1830) m. 1771
  Sarah Williams XX, 152

MUNRO, see MONROE

MUNSON
  Medad (May 9, 1757-Nov. 29, 1846) m.
  Nov. 20, 1777 Sybil Carrington
  XXXI, 284
  Peter (Nov. 22, 1735-Feb. 3, 1830)
  m. Oct. 6, 1762 Elizabeth Hall
  XXXIII, 297, 298
  Stephen (c. 1733-Nov. 8, 1805) m.
  Feb. 8, 1755 (1) Letitia Ludlam
  XXV, 117, 118
  Thaddeus (Nov. 22, 1748-Aug. 23,
  1814) m. c. 1778 Miriam Dibble
  XXV, 14
  Thomas (bpt. Sept. 13, 1612-May 7,
  1685/6) m. .... Joanna ......
  CONN XXV, 14, 117, 118; XXXI, 284;
  XXXIII, 298, 299

MURDOCK
  John (c. 1660-Mar. 2, 1756) m. Dec.
  10, 1686 (1) Lydia Young MASS
  V, 51; XXXIII, 277
  John (June 6, 1742-Sept. 17, 1817)
  m. Mar. 29, 1764 Sarah Sampson
  V, 51; XXXIII, 277

MURPHEY
  Mark (Mar. 8, 1763-Mar. 1830) m.
  Dec. 25, 1785 Holly Duke XXXI,
  67, 143
  Richard (c. 1670-....) m. c.
  1700 Mary Byrd VA XXXI, 67,
  143

MYNARD, see MINER

MYNDERSE, see also FREDERICKSE
  Barent (1747-1815) m. .... Jannetje
  Van Vranken II, 48

NASH
  Enos (Feb. 12, 1747-Mar. 30, 1796)
  m. Nov. 27, 1771 (1) Martha Gaylord XVIII, 130
  Thomas (a. 1620-May 12, 1658) m.
  .... Margery Baker CONN XVIII,
  130

NASON
  Caleb (bpt. Nov. 16, 1760-....) m.
  Feb. 17, 1780 Olive Andros XXXII,
  99
  Richard (bpt. Aug. 3, 1606-a. Mar.
  15, 1696/7) m. .... Sarah ......
  ME XXXII, 99

NEALE
  Daniel (....-1670) m. .... Elenor
  ...... VA XXI, 96, 97
  John (Feb. 28, 1739-1782) m. ....
  Martha Anne Lewis XXI, 96, 97

NEEDHAM
  Anthony (1628-c. 1705) m. Jan. 10,
  1655 Ann Potter MASS XV, 96;
  XXXIV, 58
  Anthony, Sr. (May 18, 1723-1783) m.
  Sept. 3, 1740 Rebecca Munger XV,
  96
  Christopher (....-a. 1693) m. ....
  .... VA XXXIV, 335
  David (Apr. 22, 1755-Nov. 22, 1815)
  m. Aug. 26, 1779 Marcilvia Ains-
  worth XXXIV, 58
  John (July 3, 1745-1830) m. c. 1790
  (3) Mary ...... XXXIV, 335

NEEDLES
  Edward (May 2, 1756-Dec. 17, 1798)
  m. Feb. 4, 1789 (2) Sarah Berry
  XXXI, 195
  John (1638-Jan. 5, 1704) m. ....
  Frances ...... VA, MD XXXI,
  195

NELMS
  Presley, Sr. (Oct. 5, 1730-a. Feb.
  3, 1797) m. a. 1752 Elizabeth
  Routt XXIX, 76; XXXI, 153
  Presley, Jr. (1767-May 5, 1841) m.
  a. 1814 Ann (Nancy) Montgomery
  Ingram XXIX, 76; XXXI, 153
  Richard, Sr. (a. 1631-a. Oct. 17,
  1688) m. p. 1652 Ann ...... VA
  XXIX, 76; XXXI, 153

NELSON
  Gershom (July 29, 1729-....) m. July
  5, 1753 Mercy Puffer XXVI, 19
  Samuel, Sr. (Sept. 21, 1760-1828) m.
  1783 Sally Tarrey XXVI, 19
  Seth (June 22, 1735-Sept. 10, 1811)
  m. Oct. 28, 1756 Silence Cheney
  IX, 28; X, 104
  Thomas (....-c. 1648) m. .... (2)
  Joan Drummer MASS IX, 28; X,
  104; XXVI, 19

NETTLETON
  John (Oct. 9, 1765-Aug. 8, 1842) m.
  .... Comfort Hine VIII, 15
  Samuel (....-1655) m. .... Maria
  ...... CONN VIII, 16; XV, 69
  Thaddeus (Oct. 24, 1734-Apr. 20,
  1809) m. .... Hannah Camp XV, 69

NEWBERRY
  Amasa (Oct. 27, 1752-Jan. 25, 1835)
  m. Mar. 16, 1784 Ruth Warner V,
  64; XI, 31; XXIX, 75, 99
  Benjamin (....-Sept. 11, 1689) m.
  1646 Mary Allyn CONN V, 64
  Dyer (June 18, 1765-June 10, 1846)
  m. Dec. 12, 1790 (1) Ruth Biege
  XXXII, 145, 146
  Thomas (Nov. 10, 1594-Dec. 1635) m.
  .... Jane Dabinott MASS, CONN
  V, 64; XI, 31; XXIX, 75, 99; XXXII,
  146

NEWCOMB
  Andrew (1618-Nov. 1686) m. ....
  ...... MASS XX, 23; XXIV, 60;
  XXV, 227; XXX, 158, 222, 223;
  XXXII, 180; XXXIII, 49
  Andrew (c. 1640-p. Aug. 20, 1706) m.
  c. 1661 Sarah ...... ME, MASS
  XXVII, 93, 199, 200
  Charles (Dec. 19, 1754-Mar. 14, 1821)
  m. Jan. 15, 1786 Jerusha Adams
  XXIX, 386
  David (Jan. 15, 1739-1824) m. July
  10, 1759 Elizabeth Gross XXV, 227;
  XXX, 158, 222, 223; XXXII, 180;
  XXXIII, 49
  Francis (1605-May 27, 1692) m. ....
  Rachel ...... MASS XXIX, 386
  John (1751-Sept. 1834) m. 1776 Anna
  Chase XX, 23; XXIV, 60
  Simon (Dec. 28, 1745-Dec. 1776) m.
  1769 Mercy Gore XXVII, 93, 199,
  200, 201

NEWELL
  Abraham (1581-June 1672) m.
  .... Frances ...... MASS XV,
  104

Elihu (July 14, 1730-Feb. 14, 1814)
  m. Mar. 1776 (2) Lucy Paine
  XXXII, 46
Jacob (1732-Jan. 1818) m. June 26,
  1775 Hepsibah Hart XV, 104
Josiah (May 18, 1749-Jan. 26, 1828)
  m. Jan. 26, 1772 Ruth Root XXVII,
  76, 77
Thomas (....-Sept. 13, 1689) m. c.
  1648 Rebekah Olmstead CONN XXVII,
  77; XXXII, 46

NEWHALL
  Asa (Aug. 5, 1732-May 1, 1815) m.
  Nov. 21, 1769 Sarah Tarbell VI,
  28
  Joseph (1725-Mar. 9, 1775) m. c.
  Sept. 20, 1741 Abigail Hanson
  XVIII, 55
  Thomas, Sr. (....-May 25, 1674) m.
  .... Mary ...... MASS VI, 28;
  XVIII, 55

NEWKIRK, includes NIEUKIRK, VAN
  NIEUWKIRK
  Cornelius (Sept. 2, 1733-Nov. 8,
  1795) m. Oct. 19, 1758 Mary Miller
  XXVII, 57
  Cornelius (Nov. 24, 1756-Nov. 16,
  1823) m. Mar. 16, 1776 Abigail
  Hanna XXVI, 222, 223; XXVIII, 167
  Garret (Mar. 23, 1726-Sept. 9, 1786)
  m. May 16, 1753 Elizabeth DuBois
  XXVI, 222, 223; XXVIII, 91, 167
  Gerrett Cornelisse (....-a. Mar. 4,
  1695/6) m. .... Chieltje Cornelis-
  sen Slecht NY XXV, 83; XXVI, 222,
  223; XXVII, 57; XXVIII, 92, 167
  John (Jan. 17, 1752/3-June 2, 1840)
  m. May 1, 1776 Sarah Van Kuren
  XXV, 83

NEWMAN
  John (1611-1677) m. 1655 Mary Wood-
  bridge VA XXV, 196; XXVI, 24, 25
  Peter (Jan. 9, 1750-Feb. 23, 1813)
  m. Apr. 22, 1777 Sarah Seymour
  XXII, 99; XXX, 90
  Samuel (c. 1740/5-a. Feb. 24, 1795)
  m. c. 1766 Eve Castleberry XXXIV,
  102
  Thomas (1584-1660) m. Sept. 28, 1607
  Mary Moorton NY XXII, 99; XXX,
  90
  Walter (c. 1659-1729) m. c.
  1687 Mary ...... NJ XXXIV,
  102
  Walter (1742-July 29, 1815)
  m. 1766 Catherine Lair
  XXV, 196; XXVI, 24,
  25

NEWTON
Abner (Dec. 29, 1764-Sept. 9, 1852)
m. Mar. 4, 1788 (1) Abigail Fairchild X, 20, 21; XI, 193, 195,
197; XXIII, 18, 19
Benjamin (June 20, 1763-June 22,
1848) m. June 16, 1785 Zada Phebe
Mead XXV, 175, 176
Burwell (July 20, 1729-Apr. 16, 1807)
m. c. 1752 Eunice Johnson X, 20;
XI, 193, 195, 197; XXIII, 18, 19
Francis (Mar. 21, 1731-Apr. 16, 1781)
m. Nov. 23, 1758 Elizabeth Fairfield XXIII, 72
Hezekiah, Sr. (July 28, 1719-Feb. 4,
1786) m. Sept. 8, 1742 Eunice Brig-
ham XIX, 157; XXVI, 214, 215
John (July 29, 1750-Sept. 22, 1834)
m. Nov. 5, 1778 Elizabeth Arms
XVIII, 142
Joseph (July 15, 1728-Mar. 8, 1795)
m. Dec. 29, 1756 Experience Drury
XXVIII, 197
Luther (1760/4-Nov. 19, 1829) m. a.
1785 Miriam Newton XXVI, 237, 238
Richard (bpt. Apr. 8, 1611-Aug. 24,
1701) m. Aug. 9, 1636 Ann Loker
MASS XIX, 157; XXIII, 72; XXV,
175, 176; XXVI, 214, 215, 237,
238; XXVIII, 197
Roger (1610-June 7, 1683) m. 1644
Mary Hooker CONN V, 70; X, 20;
XI, 193, 195, 197; XVIII, 142;
XXIII, 18, 19; XXV, 98, 99
Samuel (Dec. 7, 1737-Dec. 31, 1814)
m. May 13, 1762 Mary Camp V, 70;
XXV, 98, 99
Seth (Sept. 10, 1732-Feb. 12, 1807)
m. 1755/9 ...... Belnap XXVI,
237, 238

NICCOLLS, see NICHOLS

NICHOLLS, see NICHOLS

NICHOLS, includes NICCOLLS, NICHOLLS
Andrew (bpt. Jan. 1723/4-Jan. 29,
1795) m. Dec. 23, 1760 Abiah Plumb
XXVI, 72; XXXIII, 127, 128
Caleb (....-....) m. 1650 Ann Warde
CONN XIX, 66
David (Mar. 29, 1746-Jan. 29, 1813)
m. Aug. 11, 1768 Hannah Alvord
XXVII, 173
Ebenezer, III (Nov. 9, 1750-1800) m.
Nov. 13, 1786 Olive Bacon XXX,
151
Ephraim, II (Jan. 30, 1727-Mar. 3,
1782) m. July 5, 1741 Rebecca Gold
XVI, 76
Ephraim (Dec. 8, 1727-Nov. 22, 1805)

m. July 21, 1751 Esther Peet
XXXI, 90
Francis (c. 1595-Jan. 16, 1650) m.
1645 (2) Anna Wynes CONN XVI,
76; XXVI, 72, 73; XXVII, 98, 173;
XXXI, 90; XXXIII, 127, 128, 134,
135; XXXIV, 293
Isaac (1705-a. July 23, 1791) m.
.... Mary ...... XXXIV, 306
John (....-c. 1707) m. .... Margaret
...... MD XXXIV, 306
John (....-a. Mar. 24, 1797) m. ....
Nancy ...... XXXIV, 306
John (Sept. 21, 1736-Aug. 20, 1819)
m. June 5, 1760 Bethiah Burnap
XXXIII, 251, 252
Joseph (Jan. 16, 1749/50-Feb. 12,
1826) m. Dec. 28, 1772 Mary Winters
XXVII, 98
Nathan (Dec. 1, 1709-Feb. 3, 1789)
m. Dec. 4, 1740 Patience Hubbell
XIX, 66; XXVI, 73; XXXIV, 293
Richard (1630-Nov. 22, 1674) m. ....
Anna (Annas) ...... MASS XXX,
151; XXXIII, 251, 252
Samuel (Feb. 16, 1733-Apr. 8, 1798)
m. July 31, 1768 Freelove (Wright)
Wood XXXIII, 134, 135

NICHOLSON
Christopher (c. 1610-p. 1680) m. c.
1635 .... NC XXV, 247
Josiah (1750-p. 1830) m. 1778 Rhoda
Whitehead XXV, 247
Seth (May 28, 1734-Sept. 10, 1789)
m. c. 1753 Martha Atwood XXX, 261,
262
Seth (c. 1748-1824) m. c. 1783 .....
Luddington XXXIV, 132
William, Sr. (1604-Aug. 30, 1689) m.
c. 1630 Anne Busby MASS XXX, 261,
262; XXXIV, 132

NIEUKIRK, see NEWKIRK

NIGHTINGALE
Joseph E. (Sept. 16, 1749-Nov. 7,
1797) m. Dec. 27, 1769 Elizabeth
Waitstill Corliss XXXII, 193
William (1637-May 10, 1714) m. ....
Bethiah Deering MASS XXXII, 193

NOBLE
David (Jan. 25, 1732-Aug. 5, 1776)
m. Feb. 21, 1753 Ruth Noble XXIX,
310, 311
Matthew (July 27, 1736-Aug. 30, 1804)
m. Sept. 23, 1758 Lydia Eager XV,
67
Nathan (Feb. 4, 1722-Oct. 7, 1777)
m. May 12, 1748 Mary Gray XI, 131;

XII, 97; XV, 76
Roger (Apr. 2, 1742-Sept. 15, 1810)
m. 1772 Olive Hunt XXII, 7
Thaddeus (Jan. 9, 1734-June 14, 1809)
m. .... Sarah Peet V, 131, 132,
133; XXV, 167
Thomas (1632-Jan. 20, 1704) m. Nov.
1, 1660 Hannah Warriner MASS
V, 131, 132, 133; XI, 131; XII,
97; XV, 67, 76; XXII, 7; XXV, 167;
XXIX, 310, 311

NOE, includes NUEE
Daniel (1748-1821) m. 1769 Sealyer
Freeman XXII, 141
Lewis (c. 1753-Apr. 15, 1838) m.
Phoebe Mundy XXII, 153; XXIV, 11,
64; XXXIII, 312, 313
Pierre (....-Dec. 1709) m. 1659
Margaret Clark NY, NJ XXII, 141,
154; XXIV, 11, 64; XXXIII, 312,
313

NOLDS, see OULD

NORCROSS
Daniel (May 9, 1745-July 27, 1825)
m. .... Thankful Sawyer XI, 67
Jeremiah (c. 1600-1657) m. ....
Adrean ...... MASS XI, 67
John (1590-....) m. ....
...... MASS XXIX, 244; XXX, 55
John (c. 1748-c. 1824) m. .... Mary
Solomon XXIX, 243; XXX, 55
William (1724-a. June 5, 1777) m.
Dec. 1745 Martha Mattison XXIX,
243; XXX, 55

NORRIS
Aquila, Sr. (1739-Feb. 6, 1812) m.
1771 Priscilla Temperance Norris
XXX, 136, 137; XXXII, 285
Thomas (....-p. 1696) m. .... Eliza-
beth ...... MD XXX, 136, 137;
XXXI, 33; XXXII, 285
Thomas (1742-p. 1783) m. May 4, 1762
Hannah Norrington XXXI, 33

NORTH
John (1615-1691/2) m. .... Hannah
Bird MASS, CONN XVIII, 99;
XXXIII, 309, 310, 338, 339; XXXIV,
12
Lot (Jan. 20, 1756-Oct. 8, 1825) m.
Dec. 7, 1780 Silence Horsford
XXXIII, 309, 310, 338, 339; XXXIV,
12
Samuel, Jr. (July 17, 1740-
Aug. 11, 1806) m. Nov. 29,
1770 Lucy Deming XVIII,
99

NORTHRUP
Amos (1730-Feb. 9, 1810) m. 1758
Hannah Calkins Hatch XXXI, 194
Amos (1742-1779) m. .... Anne Grant
IV, 103
Joel (Mar. 3, 1742/3-Mar. 10, 1824)
m. 1772 Eunice Marsh XXXIV, 208
Joseph (....-Sept. 11, 1669) m. 1647
Mary Norton CONN IV, 103; XXXI,
194; XXXIV, 208

NORTHWAY
Francis, Sr. (July 26, 1756-July 17,
1829) m. Dec. 13, 1774 Susannah
Owen XXXII, 28
John (....-1690) m. Sept. 21, 1677
Susannah Briggs RI XXXII, 28

NORTON
Charles (May 11, 1742-Mar. 19, 1818)
m. 1771 Sarah Street XXI, 162
Elihu (Oct. 31, 1760-c. 1835). m. c.
1780 Sarah Beal XVIII, 88; XXVI,
44
John (c. 1622-....) m. .... (1)
Dorothy ...... CONN XXI, 162
Nicholas (1610-a. June 8, 1690) m.
1637 Elizabeth ...... MASS X,
178; XVI, 97; XVIII, 88; XIX, 95;
XXVI, 44; XXIX, 143; XXXIII, 44,
45, 330
Peter (Sept. 9, 1718-Feb. 3, 1792)
m. c. 1740 Sarah Bassett XXIX,
142; XXXIII, 44, 45, 330
Samuel (Apr. 16, 1743-Nov. 22, 1801)
m. Mar. 23, 1766 Mrs. Mary (Davis)
Norton XVI, 97; XXIX, 142
Seth (Jan. 16, 1736-Apr. 30, 1830)
m. Feb. 7, 1760 Amy Norton X, 178;
XVIII, 88; XIX, 95

NORWOOD
John Wall (Apr. 12, 1727-p. Nov. 13,
1802) m. 1765 (2) Mrs. Leah Lenoir
Whitaker XXXIV, 55
Nathaniel (c. 1704-a. Nov. 1783) m.
.... Mary ...... XXXIV, 109
William (1615-1703) m. .... Lydia
Jordan VA XXXIV, 55, 109

NOWELL
George (....-1689) m. a. 1659 Lydia
Willis MASS XXV, 198
Samuel (....-May 6, 1784) m. July
16, 1747 Elizabeth Favor XXV, 198

NOYES
James (Oct. 22, 1608-Oct. 22, 1656)
m. 1633 Sarah Brown MASS
IV, 134; X, 211; XVII,
155

NOYES, cont.
John (Aug. 28, 1745-Oct. 16, 1827)
m. .... Elizabeth Rogers IV,
134
Joseph (Oct. 9, 1727-Mar. 13, 1802)
m. July 31, 1753 Barbara Wells
XVII, 155
Joseph (Feb. 1730-p. 1788) m. Jan.
27, 1763 Prudence Denison X, 211
Nicholas (1615/6-Nov. 23, 1701) m.
c. 1640 Mary Cutting MASS VI,
105, VII, 39; XXVI, 50; XXX, 105;
XXXIII, 239, 240
Samuel, Sr. (Apr. 25, 1737-Apr. 1,
1820) m. Mar. 21, 1764 Rebekah
Wheeler XXX, 105; XXXIII, 239,
240
Samuel (Jan. 30, 1740-Dec. 10, 1777
m. 1761 Lois Whitmarsh XXVI, 50
Samuel M. (Nov. 12, 1759-June 7,
1816) m. 1791 Mary Thompson VII,
39
Simon (Nov. 10, 1717-1816) m. Dec.
10, 1754 (2) Elizabeth Eaton VI,
105

NUEE, see NOE

NUTTER
Anthony (c. 1630-Feb. 19, 1686) m.
c. 1662 Sarah Langstaff XXVII,
196
Hatevil (1603-p. Dec. 28, 1674) m.
.... Ann Ayres NH XXVII, 196
John, Sr. (Feb. 24, 1721-Sept. 19,
1776) m. Nov. 17, 1747 Anna Sims
(Symmes) XXVII, 196, 197
John, Jr. (Mar. 1, 1757-Nov. 8, 1840)
m. June 24, 1779 Elizabeth Dame
XXVII, 196, 197

NYE
Benjamin (May 4, 1620-1704) m. Oct.
19, 1640 Katherine Tupper MASS
XI, 165; XXV, 11, 213; XXVIII, 84;
XXIX, 296; XXX, 166; XXXI, 193,
202, 204; XXXII, 117; XXXIII, 138,
139; XXXIV, 274
Benjamin (May 13, 1728-Aug. 9, 1818)
m. Feb. 22, 1770 (2) Mary Crocker
XXX, 166; XXXI, 193
Ebenezer (Oct. 21, 1750-Feb. 1823)
m. Mar. 1776 Desire Sawyer XXVIII,
84
Iram (Jan. 28, 1751-June 19, 1802)
m. Oct. 29, 1772 Eleanor Ellis
XXV, 10
Jonathan (Apr. 30, 1731-July 8, 1806)
m. Mar. 18, 1756 Rebecca Freeman
XXV, 213
Nathan (Feb. 26, 1749-1826) m.

Dec. 10, 1772 Hannah Butler XXXIV,
274
Silas (1744-1812) m. Nov. 27, 1766
Patience Carpenter XXIX, 295;
XXXI, 201, 202; XXXIII, 139, 140
Silvanus (Aug. 12, 1744-p. July 8,
1820) m. Oct. 5, 1770 (1) Lydia
Freeman XI, 165; XXXI, 204; XXXII,
116, 117

NYSSEN, see DENISE

ODELL
Jacob (July 25, 1756-1846) m. ....
Ann (Devoor) Brevoort XXIII, 64
John (1739-p. May 15, 1785) m. c.
1758/9 Mary Wiltsie XXXII, 31, 32
Joshua (May 2, 1733-....) m. ....
Mary Vincent XXIX, 147
William (....-1676) m. ....
...... MASS, CONN XXIII, 64;
XXIX, 147; XXXII, 32

ODIONE
John (c. 1627-1707) m. .... Mary
Johnson MASS XIII, 92
Thomas, Sr. (Dec. 1, 1733-Apr. 29,
1819) m. Jan. 31, 1762 Joanna Gil-
man XIII, 92

ODLIN, includes AUDLIN
John (1602-Dec. 18, 1685) m. ....
Margaret ...... MASS V, 54
William (Feb. 17, 1738-Sept. 6,
1787) m. .... Judith Wilson V, 54

OGDEN
Jason, Sr. (....-1801) m. ....
Joanna Davis XXXIII, 32
John (Sept. 19, 1609-May 8, 1682) m.
May 8, 1637 Jane Bond NY, NJ VII,
41; VIII, 6; X, 62; XI, 32; XXIV,
61
John (1709-Feb. 14, 1795) m. ....
Hannah Sayre XXIV, 61
John (1750-1814) m. .... Deborah
Burrows VIII, 6
Richard (July 1, 1610-c. 1687) m.
Aug. 21, 1639 Mary Hall CONN
XXXIII, 32
Uzal (1744-Nov. 4, 1822) m. 1776
Mary Gouverneur VII, 41; X, 62;
XI, 32

OKESON
John (....-....) m. ....
...... NY XXVI, 184, 185; XXIX,
210
Nicholas Albertson (Mar. 6, 1757-Apr.

14, 1852) m. Dec. 1779 Susan
Silverthorn XXVI, 184, 185; XXIX,
210

OLCOTT
James, Jr. (Mar. 20, 1740-1818) m.
July 31, 1767 Mary Rossiter XXX,
240
Jared (July 22, 1759-July 23, 1846)
m. 1813 (2) Abigail Smith XXXIII,
135; XXXIV, 46
Joseph (1736-Mar. 29, 1823) m. 1758
Elizabeth Marsh XXXIV, 226
*Thomas (bpt. Feb. 2, 1613-p. Feb.
13, 1653/4) m. c. 1635 Abigail
Porter CONN XXVII, 195; XXX,
240; XXXIII, 135; XXXIV, 46, 226*
*Thomas, Jr. (c. 1637-p. Feb. 14,
1719) m. c. 1665 Mary Levitt CONN
XXVII, 195*
Timothy (bpt. Oct. 11, 1741-June 24,
1832) m. Feb. 11, 1766 Elizabeth
Chandler XXVII, 195

OLD, see OLDS

OLDS, includes OLD
Benjamin (a. 1738-p. 1777) m. 1758
Via Smith V, 68, 97, 98
Comfort (May 24, 1724-July 29, 1779)
m. May 23, 1745 Abigail Barns
XXIV, 37
*Robert (1645-Jan. 16, 1728) m. Dec.
31, 1669 (1) Susanna Hanford; Apr.
1, 1689 (2) Dorothy Granger CONN
V, 68, 97, 98; XXIV, 37*
Samuel (Dec. 29, 1748-July 8, 1813)
m. Feb. 11, 1777 Persis Rice
XXIV, 37

OLIVER
*David (....-....) m. .... Grace
(Parker) ME XVII, 52*
John (Jan. 15, 1756-May 6, 1806) m.
Oct. 11, 1782 Mary (Spinney) XVII,
52

OLMSTEAD, includes OLMSTED
Aaron (May 19, 1753-Sept. 9, 1806)
m. Dec. 10, 1778 Mary Langrell
Bigelow XXVII, 144
Ashbel (Dec. 18, 1750-Dec. 24, 1832)
m. 1773 Ruth Cone XXIV, 87
*James (bpt. Dec. 4, 1580-1640) m.
Oct. 26, 1605 Joice Cornish MASS,
CONN XVIII, 95; XXIV, 86; XXVII,
144; XXX, 160*
Jared (July 1, 1753-May 28, 1825) m.
Nov. 30, 1773 Hannah Betts XV,
32
Moses (bpt. Apr. 28, 1751-1776) m.

Jan. 30, 1773 Patty De Forest
XXIV, 30
*Richard (Feb. 20, 1612-p. Sept. 15,
1684) m. a. 1640 ....
CONN XV, 32; XXIV, 31; XXX, 96,
97; XXXIII, 152*
Silas (Feb. 18, 1732-Apr. 13, 1782)
m. .... (2) Lydia Sloan XXX, 96,
97; XXXIII, 152
Simeon (Sept. 21, 1748-Dec. 22, 1803)
m. Feb. 7, 1771 Roxalena Abbe
XVIII, 95; XXX, 160

OLMSTED, see OLMSTEAD

OLNEY
Stephen (Dec. 22, 1752-Dec. 12, 1841)
m. .... Martha Aldrich XXIX, 352
*Thomas (1600-1682) m. 1631 Marie
Small MASS XXIX, 352*

OOSTEROM, see OSTROM

OP DYCK, see UPDIKE

ORDWAY
*James (1618/20-p. 1702) m. Nov. 25,
1648 Ann Emery NH, MASS XXXII,
260; XXXIII, 64, 65*
John (Dec. 20, 1760-Sept. 3, 1832)
m. Jan. 5, 1786 Sally Rogers
XXXII, 260; XXXIII, 64, 65

ORTON
Azariah (Sept. 25, 1757-1835) m.
1780 Sybil Cleveland XIII, 109
John (1742-1785) m. 1762 ......
...... XVI, 36; XXXII, 280
*Thomas (1613-p. May 7, 1688) m.
June 16, 1641 Margaret Pratt
CONN XIII, 109; XVI, 36; XXXII,
280*

OSBORN, includes OSBORNE
Daniel (June 23, 1736-Mar. 18, 1818)
m. c. 1764 Hannah Ely VI, 47
Eliada (Mar. 15, 1761-Dec. 26, 1847)
m. May 31, 1794/5 Abigail Marsh
XXIII, 60
*John (1604-Oct. 27, 1686) m. May 19,
1645 Anne Oldage CONN VI, 47;
VII, 38; XXV, 122*
John (1728-1814) m. Dec. 18, 1751
Lois Peck XXIII, 60
John (1738-p. 1798) m. Jan. 22, 1761
Mary Buxton XXXIII, 83, 84
John (July 15, 1739-1778) m. ....
Anna (Nancy) Mitchell XXXIII, 306
Josiah (Apr. 22, 1761-Aug. 25, 1850)
m. Aug. 26, 1783 Hannah Scott
XXXIII, 258, 259

OSBORN, cont.
  Richard (1611/2-1685/6) m. .... (1)
  .... MASS XXXIII, 258,
  259
  Samuel Groome, Sr. (Dec. 13, 1752-
    Apr. 10, 1795) m. c. 1774 (1)
    Mary ...... VI, 99, 102
  Thomas (....-....) m. ....
  ...... NY XXIII, 60
  Thomas (Mar. 25, 1737-Mar. 14, 1813)
    m. June 1777 Lovisa Parsons XXV,
    122
  William (....-p. 1727) m. Mar. 17,
  1672/3 Hannah Burten MASS XXXIII,
  83, 84
  William (c. 1628-June 9, 1704) m.
  1694 Mrs. Margaret Walstone MD
  VI, 99, 102; XXXIII, 306
  Zebedee (Jan. 25, 1725-Jan. 4, 1796)
    m. .... (1) Abigail Osborne VII,
    38

OSBORNE, see OSBORN

OSGOOD
  Benjamin (Feb. 24, 1755-Dec. 9, 1824)
    m. Oct. 31, 1778 Tryphena Cummings
    XV, 12
  George (Dec. 1, 1758-Oct. 4, 1823)
    m. Apr. 11, 1782 Elizabeth Otis
    XXX, 207
  John (July 23, 1595-Oct. 24, 1651)
  m. June 1, 1627 Sarah Booth MASS
  V, 75; XV, 12; XXV, 24; XXX, 207
  Josiah (Nov. 20, 1732-Dec. 10, 1788)
    m. Mar. 3, 1757 Sara Stephens XXV,
    24
  Josiah (Oct. 1, 1740-Aug. 17, 1830)
    m. .... Jane Byington V, 74

OSTROM, includes OOSTEROM
  Hendrick Janse (c. 1630-....) m.
  Dec. 4, 1652 Tryntje Lubbertje
  Gysbertszen NY XXXI, 35
  Ruliff (Roelof) (bpt. May 9, 1740-
    1807) m. May 23, 1761 Elizabeth
    Yelverton XXXI, 35

O'SULLIVANT, see SULLIVAN

OTIS
  John (1581-May 31, 1657) m. ....
  Margaret ...... MASS XXV, 68
  John (Jan. 14, 1621-Jan. 16, 1684)
  m. 1653 Mary Jacob MASS XVII, 99
  John Thatcher (Oct. 31, 1758-Sept.
    18, 1842) m. Sept. 29, 1782 Lovisa
    Pomeroy XVII, 99
  Joshua (1720-1810) m. c. 1745 Jane
    Hussey XXIV, 43
  Paul (Mar. 4, 1755-July 17, 1848) m.

  1780 Elizabeth Parshley XXIV, 43
  Richard (a. 1625-June 27, 1689) m.
  1649 Rose Stoughton NH XXIV, 43
  Solomon (Oct. 13, 1696-Dec. 2, 1778)
    m. May 4, 1724 Jane Turner XXV,
    68

OULD, includes NOLDS
  Elisha (July 27, 1736-p. 1784) m.
    Sept. 13, 1760 Elizabeth Grainger
    XXXIV, 253
  Robert (1645-Jan. 16, 1728) m. Dec.
  31, 1669 (1) Susannah Hanford CONN
  XXXIV, 253

OVERTON
  David (Aug. 29, 1739-Mar. 24, 1826)
    m. .... Mary Davis XV, 66
  Isaac (....-1688) m. c. 1670 Sarah
  ...... NY XV, 67

OWEN
  Asahel (July 25, 1726-p. 1790) m.
    June 1752 Deborah Drake XXVI, 265,
    266
  David (1723-June 15, 1790) m. 1740
    Sarah Schmebger XIV, 83
  Frederick (Feb. 16, 1752-Apr. 9,
    1837) m. Sept. 10, 1778 Margaret
    Hubbard XXV, 248, 249, 250, 251
  Griffith (....-....) m. .... Sarah
  ...... PA XIV, 83
  John (Dec. 25, 1624-Feb. 1, 1699) m.
  Oct. 3, 1650 Rebecca Wade CONN
  XXV, 248, 249, 250, 251; XXVI, 204,
  205, 265, 266; XXVIII, 93
  Sylvanus (Aug. 19, 1746-Dec. 7, 1814)
    m. May 3, 1768 Eunice Roberts
    XXVIII, 92
  Timothy (Nov. 10, 1756-Aug. 24, 1837)
    m. Sept. 11, 1785 Lydia Perry
    XXVI, 204, 205

OWENS
  Isaac (May 9, 1729-Sept. 21, 1805)
    m. c. 1756 Priscilla Norman XXIX,
    116
  Richard (....-1673) m. .... (1) Mary
  ...... VA XXIX, 116

OWINGS
  Richard (....-....) m. .... Rachael
  Beale MD XV, 121; XXIV, 88
  Thomas (Oct. 18, 1740-Oct. 1822) m.
    Dec. 27, 1760 Ruth Lawrence XV,
    121; XXIV, 88

PACE
  Richard (1590-1628) m. a. 1610 Isa-
  bella Paine VA XXVIII, 19, 20;
  XXXI, 14, 233; XXXIV, 337
  Stephen (July 16, 1747-Nov. 12, 1822)
  m. 1767 Catherine Gatewood Buchanan
  XXVIII, 19, 20; XXXI, 14, 233;
  XXXIV, 337

PACKARD
  Samuel (c. 1604-a. 1684) m. ....
  Elizabeth ...... MASS XXXII, 139
  Samuel (Dec. 21, 1734-1816) m. ....
  Bethia Waters XXXII, 139, 140

PACKER
  James (1734-Aug. 24, 1803) m. ....
  Rebecca Walworth XVI, 39
  John (1626-1689) m. June 24, 1676
  (2) Mrs. Rebecca (Wells) Latham
  CONN XVI, 39; XXVIII, 70
  John, II (Feb. 7, 1753-Feb. 8, 1835)
  m. July 10, 1780 Hannah Gallup
  XXVIII, 70

PADDOCK
  David (Dec. 12, 1737-Mar. 31, 1794)
  m. Jan. 28, 1762 Marian Belden
  XV, 120
  Robert (....-....) m. c. 1634 Mary
  ...... MASS XV, 120

PAGE, includes PAIGE
  Andrew (July 30, 1751-Mar. 9, 1821)
  m. Nov. 29, 1774 Elizabeth Page
  XVIII, 53
  Asa (Jan. 25, 1756-Dec. 21, 1819) m.
  .... Lydia Stewart XII, 76
  Daniel (Apr. 17, 1724-July 4, 1779)
  m. Feb. 13, 1749 Dinah Baldwin
  XVII, 6, 7
  George (....-1689) m. .... Sarah
  Linsley CONN XVII, 6, 7
  John (....-Nov. 23, 1683) m. a. 1653
  Mary Marsh MASS XVIII, 53
  John (1627-Jan. 23, 1692) m. c. 1650
  Alice Lucken VA X, 189; XVIII,
  31
  John (1720-1780) m. 1746 Jane Byrd
  XVIII, 31
  Nathaniel (c. 1645-Apr. 12, 1692) m.
  .... Joanna Merriam MASS XII, 76
  Robert (1604-July 22, 1679) m. ....
  Lucy ...... MASS, NH XVIII, 140
  Robert (1764-Jan. 1, 1840) m. 1788
  Sarah Walker X, 189
  Stephen (Aug. 8, 1735-June 18,
  1805) m. .... Mary Dearborn XVIII,
  140

PAIGE, see PAGE

PAINE, includes PAYNE
  Abraham (May 2, 1722-Apr. 21, 1801)
  m. Mar. 8, 1743/4 Rebekah Freeman
  XXIX, 392
  Amos (Oct. 24, 1736-Oct. 25, 1790)
  m. July 12, 1764 Priscilla Lyon
  XXIX, 107
  David (Mar. 15, 1737-July 2, 1807)
  m. .... Abigail Shepard IX, 56,
  57
  Edward (Nov. 18, 1726-May 17, 1806)
  m. Feb. 27, 1749/50 Anne Holland
  Conyers XXVI, 89
  Henry (Aug. 8, 1742-c. 1822) m. Nov.
  27, 1777 Martha Blackler XX, 68
  John (1615-c. 1690) m. 1635/40 Let-
  tuce Lawson; .... (2) Margaret
  ...... VA XXVI, 89; XXXIV, 336
  John (Oct. 14, 1734-a. 1790) m. Feb.
  10, 1761 Isabella Stuart Stinson
  XIV, 32, 33; XXIX, 229
  Moses (bpt. Apr. 23, 1581-June 21,
  1643) m. Nov. 15, 1615 (1) Mary
  Bennison; c. 1618 (2) Elizabeth
  ...... MASS IX, 56, 57; X, 41;
  XXIX, 186, 222, 228, 404; XXXIII,
  175; XXXIV, 130
  Ralph (....-....) m. .... Dorothy
  ...... RI XXI, 167
  Robert (1601-1684) m. .... (2) Dor-
  cas ...... MASS XX, 69
  Roswell (Feb. 24, 1756-Mar. 7, 1806)
  m. 1782 Sarah Chamberlain XXXII,
  209
  Rufus (Apr. 8, 1750-Jan. 21, 1832)
  m. Feb. 17, 1774 Agnes Findley
  XXXII, 41
  Solomon (1745-1797) m. Aug. 13, 1768
  Mary Haskins XXI, 167
  Stephen, Sr. (....-Aug. 1679) m. ....
  Rose ...... MASS XXIX, 107;
  XXXII, 209; XXXIII, 337
  Stephen, IV (Apr. 30, 1708-1797) m.
  July 21, 1730 Deborah Weimer
  XXXII, 209
  Stephen (Aug. 17, 1716-1797) m. July
  15, 1739 Sarah Thornton XXXIII,
  337
  Stephen (Sept. 6, 1739-July 8, 1794)
  m. Jan. 14, 1787 (2) Hannah Sherman
  (Sampson) XXXIII, 175; XXXIV, 130
  Thomas (....-p. Oct. 2, 1650) m. ....
  .... MASS XXXII, 41
  Thomas (c. 1612-Aug. 16, 1706) m.....
  Mary Snow MASS XXIX, 392
  William, Sr. (Feb. 10, 1732-Mar. 2,
  1822) m. a. Jan. 24, 1768 (2) Mary
  Thomson XXXIV, 337
  William (Nov. 19, 1760-Oct. 14, 1846)
  m. Feb. 19,1787 Parmelia Parker X,
  41; XIV, 32,33; XXIX,186,222,228,404

PALFREY
  Peter (....-Sept. 15, 1663) m. ....
    Edith ...... MASS XXXII, 103;
    XXXIII, 110, 117
  William (Feb. 24, 1741-Dec. 1780) m.
    Feb. 14, 1765 Susan Cazeneau
    XXXII, 103; XXXIII, 110, 117

PALMER
  Christopher (Oct. 10, 1735-Nov. 4,
    1818) m. June 19, 1758 Deborah
    Brown XXXIII, 222
  Dudley (Mar. 5, 1752-p. 1795) m.
    Mar. 27, 1777 Rebekah Pingry XXXII,
    166
  Elias (Mar. 14, 1742-June 6, 1821)
    m. Mar. 15, 1761 (1) Phebe Palmer
    XIV, 76, 77
  Ephraim (Dec. 7, 1760-June 30, 1852)
    m. Aug. 27, 1786 Margaret Force
    XX, 14
  Gershom (Dec. 5, 1738-Feb. 9, 1815)
    m. May 8, 1760 Lucy Field XXII,
    27; XXIX, 240
  Henry (1600-1660) m. .... Kath-
    erine ...... MASS, CONN XX, 15
  Jareb (Feb. 15, 1755-1820/30) m. May
    22, 1788 (1) Esther Rice XXXIII,
    295
  John, Sr. (....-1739/42) m. July 7,
    1686 (1) Mary Southery PA XXXII,
    57
  John (June 6, 1754-1835) m. Jan. 18,
    1788 Sarah Harriman XXV, 202
  Joseph (1643-Feb. 8, 1715) m. Mar. 1,
    1664 Sarah Jackman MASS XXV,
    202; XXXII, 166
  Joseph (Jan. 22, 1736/7-1824) m. Apr.
    27, 1758 Abigail Lazel XXXII, 79,
    80, 278
  Joseph (Feb. 1, 1745-Aug. 22, 1829)
    m. 1770 Susannah Kenney XXV, 95,
    96
  Joseph (Apr. 21, 1759-July 30, 1838)
    m. May 18, 1785 Hannah Peters
    XXXII, 57
  Micah (c. 1637-p. Nov. 12, 1681) m.
    Dec. 2, 1662 Elizabeth Buckley CONN
    XXXIII, 295
  Oliver (June 25, 1763-....) m. Dec.
    28, 1786 Asenath Barnes XXII, 27
  Walter (1585/98-Nov. 1661) m. ....
    (1) ....; June 11, 1633
    (2) Rebecca Short MASS, CONN XIV,
    76; XXII, 28; XXV, 95, 96; XXIX,
    240; XXXII, 79, 278; XXXIII, 222

PALMES
  Andrew (May 6, 1755-Apr. 11, 1846)
    m. July 24, 1782 Sally Mattocks
    XIII, 69

  Edward (1638-Mar. 21, 1715) m. c.
    1678 (2) Mrs. Sarah Davis CONN
    XIII, 69

PANNILL
  Thomas (....-a. May 11, 1676) m. ....
    Katherine ...... VA XXXIV, 85
  William (Oct. 30, 1738-c. 1790) m.
    1761 Ann Morton XXXIV, 85

PARDEE
  George (bpt. Feb. 19, 1624-Aug. 4,
    1700) m. Oct. 20, 1650 Martha Miles
    CONN VI, 61; X, 162; XXI, 114, 115
  Joseph (Apr. 25, 1756-Nov. 22, 1836)
    m. Feb. 5, 1783 Sarah Fields X,
    162; XXI, 114, 115
  Noah (Jan. 12, 1757-1790) m. a. 1780
    (1) Mary Woodruff VI, 61

PARK, includes PARKE, PARKS
  Abijah (Apr. 4, 1748-Aug. 14, 1813)
    m. .... Mary Dean XII, 107
  Elijah (Sept. 25, 1756-Apr. 1, 1821)
    m. Aug. 4, 1793 Margaret Walker
    XXIX, 342
  Ezra (Jan. 8, 1759-Aug. 31, 1827) m.
    May 30, 1782 Anne Beebe XVI, 21,
    22
  Hezekiah (bpt. Apr. 15, 1740-Nov. 12,
    1776) m. .... Martha Kinney X,
    124, 138
  John (1742-1812) m. Nov. 4, 1772 (1)
    Abigail Chapman XXVI, 207, 208
  Reuben (Aug. 13, 1755-Sept. 14, 1802)
    m. July 20, 1777 Betsey Clark VI,
    55; XXXII, 221, 222; XXXIV, 135
  Robert (bpt. June 3, 1580-Feb. 4,
    1664) m. Feb. 9, 1601/2 (1) Martha
    Chaplin; .... (2) Mary Rose ......
    CONN VI, 55; X, 124, 125, 138;
    XII, 108; XVI, 21, 22; XXIX, 342;
    XXXII, 222; XXXIV, 38, 135, 317
  Rufus (Mar. 15, 1760/1-1842) m. Mar.
    25, 1779/81 Zerviah (Sophia) Lar-
    rabee XXXIV, 316
  Smith (Nov. 5, 1721-Feb. 12, 1807)
    m. July 9, 1747 Mary Davis XVI,
    21, 22; XXXIV, 38
  Thomas (....-July 30, 1709) m. a.
    1646 (1) Dorothy Thompson MASS,
    CONN VI, 55
  Thomas (c. 1628/9-Aug. 11, 1690) m.
    Dec. 1, 1653 Abigail Dix MASS
    XXVI, 207, 208

PARKE, see PARK

PARKER
  Abijah (Jan. 20, 1744/5-Dec. 4, 1811)
    m. Jan. 21, 1772 Sarah Lawrence

XXXIII, 329

Abraham (1612-Aug. 12, 1685) m.
Nov. 18, 1644 Rose Whitlock MASS
XXXII, 165; XXXIII, 70, 71

Amos (Oct. 30, 1757-May 1, 1836) m.
.... Polly Anderson XI, 49

Edward (1598-July 1662) m. c. 1646
Elizabeth Potter CONN XII, 73,
74; XXXIV, 295

Elisha (July 21, 1749-Nov. 9, 1823)
m. Sept. 24, 1771 Mehitable Hart-
shorne XXV, 197, 198

Ephraim (Oct. 20, 1738-June 26, 1811)
m. Dec. 23, 1762 Sybil Warren
XXXII, 165; XXXIII, 70, 71

George (....-a. Nov. 10, 1686) m.
.... Sarah ...... NJ XXXIV, 112

Howell, Sr. (Mar. 5, 1757-Oct. 18,
1796) m. 1780 Elizabeth Loftin
XXX, 155, 156

Isaac (July 15, 1750-Jan. 16, 1798)
m. May 16, 1770 Margery Waynard
XXXIV, 329

James (1617-1701) m. May 23, 1643
(1) Elizabeth Long MASS XI, 49;
XIII, 7, 21; XXIX, 356

John (Oct. 8, 1648-1711) m. Nov. 8,
1670 Hannah Bassett CONN XXVI,
266, 267; XXXIII, 188, 189

John (Dec. 17, 1755-p. 1801) m. 1773
Mary Rogers XIV, 104

Joseph (1614-Nov. 5, 1678) m. ....
Mary ...... MASS XXX, 218

Joseph (June 28, 1743-a. Oct. 29,
1797) m. Feb. 27, 1791 (2) Lovinia
Hastings XXIX, 355

Levi (June 18, 1757-Oct. 6, 1833) m.
July 22, 1779 Lydia Bradley XXVI,
266, 267

Linus (May 22, 1758-June 3, 1829) m.
.... Elizabeth Gunn XII, 73

Michael (Oct. 15, 1758-Sept. 15,
1815) m. c. 1778 Rachel McWithey
XXXIII, 188, 189

Nathan (June 3, 1739-1819) m. Dec.
20, 1764 Mary Wood XXX, 17

Reuben (May 4, 1733-Jan. 10, 1825)
m. June 19, 1759 Sarah Wooley
XIX, 26; XXX, 47

Richard (....-a. 1677) m. 1668 Judith
Hunt VA XXX, 155, 156

Rufus (1761-May 23, 1797) m. ....
Mercy Judd XXXIV, 295

Stephen (Mar. 8, 1738-July 4, 1814)
m. Dec. 17, 1760 (1) Mary Morse
XVIII, 142

Thomas (bpt. Mar. 31, 1609-Aug. 12,
1683) m. 1635 Amy ...... MASS
XVIII, 142; XIX, 27; XXV, 197, 198;
XXX, 47; XXXIII, 329; XXXIV, 329

Thomas (1629-1695) m. ....

Mrs. Montague VA XIV, 105

Thompson (Mar. 10, 1737-c. 1813) m.
Sept. 16, 1762 Sarah Milhous
XXXIV, 112

Titus (Feb. 23, 1728-June 25, 1811)
m. .... Martha Parker XXXIV, 295

William (Nov. 24, 1761-Jan. 9, 1833)
m. Oct. 26, 1784 Susannah Chaney
XIII, 7, 21

PARKHURST, includes PARKIS

Ebenezer (Aug. 27, 1743-Sept. 9,
1795) m. Dec. 22, 1768 Mercy Hill
XIX, 42

George (1590-....) m. .... (1) Phoebe;
....(2) Rebecca ......; .... (3)
Susanna (......) Simpson MASS XIX,42;
XXVI, 41, 229; XXIX, 154, 255;
XXX, 14; XXXIII, 218

Joel (Aug. 31, 1741-Mar. 10, 1808)
m. Oct. 19, 1762 Elizabeth Cummings XXIX, 255; XXX, 14

Josiah (1736-1832) m. 1758 (1) Elizabeth Bigelow XXVI, 41, 229; XXIX,
154

Lemuel (c. 1735-....) m. Nov. 14,
1753 Hannah Pierce XXXIII, 218

Leonard (Aug. 4, 1763-Mar. 28, 1821)
m. Dec. 2, 1790 Hannah Hills
XXIX, 255; XXX, 14

PARKIS, see PARKHURST

PARKS, see PARK

PARLIN

John (1615-....) m. ....
...... MASS XVIII, 25

John (Feb. 8, 1719-Mar. 25, 1806)
m. Apr. 12, 1745 Margaret McCollom
XVIII, 25

PARMELEE

Elias (Mar. 29, 1752-....) m. Sept.
19, 1776 Thankful Hill XX, 166

Jeremiah (Mar. 1730-Jan. 6, 1797) m.
.... Temperance Blatcaley V, 81

John (....-Nov. 8, 1659) m. .... (1)
Hannah ...... CONN V, 81; XX,
166

John (1618-Jan. 1688) m. .... (1)
Rebecca ...... CONN V, 81

PARMENTER

Caleb, Jr. (Aug. 29, 1758-1850) m.
May 18, 1780 Elizabeth Rounds
XX, 143

John (c. 1588-May 1, 1671) m. 1609
Bridget ...... MASS XX, 143;
XXV, 195; XXXIII, 253, 254

Jonas, Sr. (Jan. 23, 1744/5-Sept. 6,

PARMENTER, cont.
    1813) m. .... (1) Sarah Butrick
    XXXIII, 253, 254
    Joshua (Feb. 26, 1727/8-Oct. 19,
    1822) m. c. 1750 (1) Persis Par-
    menter XXV, 195

PARRITT, includes PARROT, PARROTT,
    PARRUCK
    John (....-Oct. 1, 1683) m. July 1663
    Sarah Smith MASS XXXIII, 266, 267
    John (May 20, 1728-1819) m. Jan. 17,
    1752 Sarah Hubbell XXXIII, 267

PARROT, see PARRITT

PARROTT, see PARRITT

PARRUCK, see PARRITT

PARSE, see PIERCE

PARSHALL
    James (....-Sept. 15, 1701) m. 1678
    Elizabeth Gardiner NY XXX, 243,
    244
    James (Sept. 1754-Apr. 24, 1834) m.
    1779 Deborah Clark XXX, 243, 244

PARSONS
    Aaron (c. 1732-p. 1810) m. ....
    ...... XXXI, 305, 306
    Abraham, Jr. (Nov. 2, 1754-Jan. 15,
    1852) m. May 30, 1781 Abigail Bur-
    leigh XXV, 100
    Benjamin (Mar. 17, 1627-Oct. 24,
    1689) m. Nov. 6, 1653 Sarah Vore
    CONN, MASS XXIX, 392
    Cornet Joseph (c. 1618-Oct. 9, 1683)
    m. Nov. 26, 1646 (2) Mary Bliss
    MASS XVI, 88; XXXI, 306
    Jeffrey (1631-Aug. 16, 1689) m. Nov.
    11, 1657 Sarah Vinson MASS XXV,
    100
    Jonathan, Sr. (Mar. 23, 1734-....)
    m. Dec. 26, 1763 Tryphene Bement
    XXIX, 391
    Joseph (c. 1617-Oct. 9, 1683) m. Nov.
    2, 1646 Mary Bliss MASS XXXI,
    221, 222
    Phillip (c. 1625-a. 1697) m. ....
    Sarah Fairfield Needham CONN IV,
    163; VIII, 11
    Thomas (Sept. 18, 1735-1811) m. c.
    1738 (1) Anne Poor XVI, 87, 88
    William (Oct. 22, 1743-Aug. 4, 1826)
    m. Feb. 19, 1769 Abigail Frost
    Blunt XXXI, 221, 222
    William (Mar. 13, 1750-May 29,
    1819) m. .... Abigail Wright IV,
    163; VIII, 11

PARTRIDGE
    Amos (Apr. 12, 1758-Jan. 3, 1844) m.
    Aug. 28, 1783 Sarah Harvey XVIII,
    30, 31
    Jesse (Feb. 28, 1748/9-Mar. 29, 1838)
    m. Sept. 9, 1770 Keziah Clapp
    XXIX, 108
    Job, Sr. (Feb. 28, 1741-Sept. 11,
    1823) m. Nov. 29, 1769 Deborah
    Fairbanks XVII, 31, 32; XXXI,
    277
    John (1620-May 28, 1706) m. Dec. 18,
    1655 Magdalen Bullard MASS XVII,
    32; XVIII, 31, 139; XXVII, 203;
    XXIX, 108; XXXI, 278
    Jonathan (Feb. 21, 1757-1818) m.
    .... Harvey XVIII, 139;
    XXVII, 203

PASLEY, includes PEASLEY
    Robert (1746-Mar. 2, 1818) m. c.
    1790 Elizabeth Crocker XXXII,
    203; XXXIV, 151
    William (c. 1603-c. 1635) m. c. 1625
    Ann Calvert VA XXXII, 203; XXXIV,
    151

PATCH
    Nicholas (bpt. June 26, 1597-Nov.
    16, 1673) m. Sept. 17, 1623 Eliza-
    beth Owley MASS XXX, 54
    Samuel (Jan. 6, 1729/30-Feb. 15,
    1817) m. Apr. 22, 1766 Lydia Wal-
    kut XXX, 54

PATCHEN
    Jacob (Dec. 27, 1764-Sept. 20, 1844)
    m. Feb. 26, 1787 Abigail Meeker
    XXXIII, 60
    Joseph (c. 1610-p. Dec. 10, 1689/90)
    m. .... Mary Morehouse CONN
    XXXIII, 60

PATE
    John (1760-1829) m. 1794 (2) Nancy
    Cowart XXIX, 63; XXX, 267
    Thomas (....-p. 1690) m. c. 1680
    Elizabeth ...... VA XXIX, 63;
    XXX, 267

PATTEN, see PATTON

PATTERSON
    Andrew (1659-Dec. 2, 1746) m. Feb.
    19, 1690 Elizabeth Peat CONN
    XVIII, 27, 107; XXXIV, 83
    Josiah (Mar. 25, 1732-Jan. 1820) m.
    May 24, 1753 Phebe Wells XXXIV,
    83
    Samuel (Feb. 1, 1743-Nov. 11, 1822)
    m. .... Esther Rowland XVIII,

27, 107

PATTISON
  Richard (1759-Nov. 13, 1823) m. Mar.
    4, 1788 Mary McKeel XVII, 105;
    XIX, 123
  Thomas (....-1701) m. .... Ann
    ...... MD XVII, 105; XIX, 123

PATTON, includes PATTEN
  John (Nov. 21, 1745-Oct. 25, 1807)
    m. 1772/3 Mary Richardson XXI, 95,
    96
  John (Nov. 26, 1747-Aug. 13, 1800)
    m. .... Hannah Johnston XXXIII,
    73, 74
  William (....-Dec. 10, 1668) m. a.
    1633 Mary ...... MASS XXI, 95,
    96; XXXIII, 73

PAXSON
  Benjamin (Oct. 11, 1761-June 27,
    1828) m. June 9, 1784 Jane Ely
    XXXIII, 170
  James (....-1722) m. .... Jane Gar-
    den PA XXXIII, 170

PAYNE, see PAINE

PAYSON
  Edward (Oct. 13, 1613-Aug. 1691) m.
    Jan. 1, 1642 Mary Eliot MASS
    XXXI, 114, 115
  Ephraim, IV (June 16, 1754-Dec. 15,
    1834) m. July 8, 1779 Hannah Went-
    worth XXXI, 114, 115

PEABODY
  Francis (1612-Feb. 19, 1697) m. a.
    1640 (1) Mary Foster MASS XXIX,
    196
  Seth (Nov. 27, 1744-1827) m. 1771
    Abigail Kimball XXIX, 196

PEACOCK
  John (1740-Aug. 1829) m. ....
    Priscilla Worrell XII, 39, 120
  John (1760-Aug. 1828) m. .... Mary
    Thomson XII, 120
  William (1648-1722) m. .... Catherine
    ...... VA XII, 39,
    121

PEAK, see PEET

PEARCE, see PIERCE

PEARSE, see PIERCE

PEARSON, see PIERSON

PEASE
  Alpheüs (Apr. 16, 1762-Apr. 1816) m.
    Apr. 1801 Dorothy Spencer XXXIV,
    154
  Israel (Jan. 24, 1726/7-Mar. 2, 1802)
    m. Mar. 15, 1753 Ann Bartlett
    XXXIV, 326
  John (bpt. Nov. 20, 1608-p. Sept.
    1677) m. c. 1630 Mary Browning
    MASS XXXIII, 87
  John (1630-July 8, 1689) m. c. 1652
    (1) Mary Goodell MASS XXXIV, 154
  Nathaniel (Feb. 21, 1731-June 5,
    1799) m. .... Lucy Page XXXIII,
    87
  Robert (1607-a. Aug. 27, 1644) m.
    .... Marie ...... MASS III, 69;
    XXXIV, 327
  Stephen (July 4, 1755-June 28, 1838)
    m. Nov. 7, 1744 (3) Roxanna Snow
    III, 69

PEASLEY, see PASLEY

PEAT, see PEET

PECK
  Abijah (1736-Feb. 5, 1804) m. 1755
    Rachel Stephens XXXII, 36
  Eliakim (1756-c. Feb. 6, 1840) m.
    Nov. 3, 1786 Polly Star XXXII, 36,
    37
  Henry (....-p. Oct. 30, 1651) m. c.
    1638 Joan Walker CONN X, 122;
    XXVI, 12; XXXII, 36
  Israel (Dec. 6, 1750-Dec. 5, 1827)
    m. Sept. 11, 1784 Sarah Marsh III,
    9
  John (Feb. 4, 1734-Mar. 4, 1812) m.
    .... Mary Drown XVI, 90
  Joseph (Apr. 30, 1587-Dec. 23, 1663)
    m. May 21, 1617 (1) Rebecca Clark
    MASS III, 9; VIII, 21, 22; X,
    247; XIV, 68, 69; XVI, 90; XXI,
    131, 132; XXII, 134
  Joseph (Aug. 23, 1623-1703) m. ....
  Mrs. Alice Burwell CONN VI, 65;
    XVI, 75
  Joseph (June 10, 1756-July 8, 1834)
    m. Dec. 21, 1780 Sarah Miller
    XVII, 130, 131
  Judson (May 27, 1749-Jan. 6, 1832)
    m. Dec. 20, 1775 Mary Blakeman
    VI, 65
  Loring (Jan. 19, 1744/5-July 29,
    1833) m. c. 1775 Jane Burk XXII,
    134
  Oliver (Feb. 5, 1736/7-June
    1796) m. .... Fear Foster VIII,
    21, 22

PECK, cont.
  Peleg (Mar. 6, 1736-June 22, 1807)
  m. 1756 Phebe Mason XXI, 131, 132
  Philip (Apr. 25, 1747-Apr. 6, 1805)
  m. July 5, 1768 Ruth Williams
  XIV, 68, 69
  Reuben (Oct. 1, 1737-1811) m. Dec.
  6, 1759 Charity French X, 122
  Richard A. (Aug. 5, 1753-Oct. 24,
  1837) m. 1775 (1) Sarah Tennant
  X, 193
  Robert (June 30, 1739-July 25, 1827)
  m. Jan. 15, 1767 Ann Reed XXIX,
  284
  Samuel (Apr. 1720-Jan. 29, 1793) m.
  Nov. 7, 1745 Mary Ferris XV, 89
  Samuel (Aug. 22, 1736-June 12, 1822)
  m. July 7, 1762 Mehitable Smith
  XVI, 75
  Samuel (1753-Aug. 9, 1796) m. 1775
  Mary Beach XXVI, 12
  Solomon (Apr. 19, 1733-Dec. 31, 1802)
  m. June 14, 1756 ...... Foster
  X, 247
  Thomas (Sept. 1, 1750-Sept. 1780) m.
  Dec. 30, 1777 Mary Johnson Ferris
  XIV, 91
  William (1601-Oct. 4, 1694) m. 1622
  Elizabeth ...... CONN X, 193;
  XIV, 91; XV, 89; XVII, 131, 132;
  XXIX, 284

PECKHAM
  Abel (Feb. 17, 1732-1825) m. Feb. 24,
  1754 Rebecca Burdick XIII, 9, 39,
  56
  George (Oct. 23, 1720-1816) m. Dec.
  19, 1754 Jerusha Bartlett
  XXXIV, 223
  John (bpt. Apr. 8, 1595-1681) m.
  .... (1) Mary Clark; .... (2)
  Eleanor Weaver RI XI, 65; XIII,
  9, 39, 56; XV, 95; XXX, 175; XXXIV,
  223
  Pardon (Aug. 12, 1763-Oct. 15, 1851)
  m. May 3, 1785 Olive Blodgett XV,
  95
  Peleg (1759-1858) m. Oct. 25, 1787
  Elizabeth Stetson XI, 65
  Philip (July 11, 1725-Apr. 19, 1819)
  m. July 28, 1753 (1) Jane Nye
  XV, 95
  Thomas (June 20, 1747-Dec. 18, 1825)
  m. June 29, 1778 Hannah Weaver
  XXX, 175

PEET, includes PEAK, PEAT
  Gideon (Dec. 24, 1742-1823) m. Apr.
  12, 1764 Bethia Burton XXIX, 79
  John (c. 1597-Sept. 1, 1684) m. June
  1635 ...... Charles MASS, CONN

XXIX, 79; XXXIV, 254
William (Jan. 24, 1743-Feb. 1786) m.
Oct. 2, 1764 Beulah Nichols
XXXIV, 254

PEIRCE, see PIERCE

PELL
  John (Feb. 3, 1643-1702) m. 1684/5
  Rachel Pinckney NY XIII, 70
  Philip, Jr. (Nov. 22, 1732-May 21,
  1811) m. 1752 Glorianna Treadwell
  XIII, 70

PELTON
  Abner, Sr. (Mar. 4, 1755-Jan. 17,
  1846) m. .... (1) Sarah Bidwell
  XII, 101
  John (c. 1616-Jan. 23, 1681) m. 1643
  Susanna ...... MASS XII, 101;
  XXIII, 34
  Samuel (Dec. 21, 1739-Dec. 20, 1801)
  m. Feb. 7, 1763 Rebecca Holmes
  XXIII, 34

PENDLETON
  Amos (June 21, 1728-Nov. 25, 1821)
  m. 1768 Anna Foster XI, 10
  Brian (1599-a. Apr. 23, 1681) m.
  ⊥Apr. 22, 1619 Eleanor Price MASS
  V, 117, 118; X, 245; XI, 10; XIV,
  65, 66, 121; XXII, 32, 33, 126;
  XXIV, 86
  Caleb (Dec. 1, 1734-Mar. 29, 1826)
  m. 1758 Hannah Closson XXII,
  126
  Henry, Jr. (1744/5-1800) m. .... Ann
  Knight XV, 136
  Henry (Dec. 4, 1762-Nov. 18, 1822)
  m. Oct. 27, 1785 (1) Alcey Anne
  Winston XVI, 88; XVII, 119
  James (June 12, 1756-Dec. 12, 1778)
  m. 1776 Sarah Lyons XXIV, 86
  John (1719-....) m. c. 1760 (2)
  Sarah Madison XVII, 12, 119
  Joshua (May 6, 1744-Apr. 9, 1824)
  m. Jan. 6, 1768 Anna (Nancy)
  Clarke XXII, 32, 33
  Peleg (July 9, 1733-July 10, 1810)
  m. Sept. 7, 1758 Ann Park V, 117,
  118; X, 244; XIV, 65, 66
  Philip (1650-Nov. 9, 1721) m. 1682
  (2) Isabella Hurt VA XV, 136;
  XVI, 88; XVII, 12, 119; XIX
  105
  Philip (Apr. 6, 1758-1842) m. ....
  Mildred Thomas XIX, 105
  William (Mar. 23, 1704-Aug. 23,
  1786) m. Mar. 10, 1725/6 (1) Lydia
  ⊥ Burrows V, 117, 118; X, 244; XIV,
  121; XXII, 32, 33

PENFIELD
Jesse (Aug. 18, 1759-Dec. 18, 1833) m. Mar. 21, 1782 (2) Mary Upson XXIX, 239, 386; XXXIV, 245
Peter (July 14, 1702-July 11, 1772) m. May 28, 1730 May Allen XXXIV, 283
Peter (Sept. 13, 1743-Jan. 12, 1812) m. Jan. 22, 1763 Hannah Lewis XXIX, 236, 387, 397
Samuel (1650-May 30, 1710) m. Nov. 30, 1675 Mary Lewis MASS XXIX, 236, 239, 386, 387, 397; XXXIV, 245, 283

PENGRY, see PINGREY

PENN
Abram (Dec. 27, 1743-June 26, 1801) m. 1767/8 Ruth Stovall XXXIII, 165, 166
William (a. 1636-....) m. .... Elizabeth ...... VA XXXIII, 165, 166

PENNIMAN
Henry (Oct. 29, 1733-Dec. 11, 1809) m. Apr. 13, 1769 Experience Wheelock XXI, 84, 85
James (1610-Dec. 26, 1664) m. .... Lydia Eliot MASS XXI, 84, 85; XXXIV, 267
Stephen (June 4, 1743-p. Apr. 11, 1823) m. Jan. 25, 1765 Sarah Holbrook XXXIV, 267

PENNINGTON
Ephraim (....-1660/1) m. .... Mary ...... CONN XIX, 50
Nathan (1758-1810) m. Jan. 7, 1783 Margaret Wescott Leonard XIX, 50

PEPPER
Joshua (Jan. 18, 1720/1-Dec. 28, 1808) m. .... Elizabeth McCaulley XXXII, 265
Robert (c. 1620-July 7, 1684) m. Mar. 14, 1642/3 Elizabeth Johnson MASS XXXII, 265

PERIN, see PERRINE

PERINE, see PERRINE

PERKINS
Abraham (c. 1619-Aug. 31, 1683) m. c. 1638 Mary Wise NH III, 25; X, 236, 259; XI, 28
Amos, Jr. (Nov. 21, 1748-p. Feb. 22, 1819) m. June 10, 1772 Abiah Downs X, 87
Daniel (June 15, 1697-Sept. 29, 1782)

m. Nov. 6, 1721 Anne Foster XXVI, 251, 252, 253
David (Mar. 3, 1739-p. Oct. 1801) m. .... Fear Canedy X, 236, 259; XI, 28
Edward (....-p. 1655) m. Mar. 20, 1649 Elizabeth Butcher CONN X, 87
Isaac (1612-Nov. 15, 1685) m. .... Susanna Wise NH XXIX, 264, 266
Israel (Jan. 10, 1757-Nov. 7, 1839) m. Nov. 20, 1781 Anna Dodge XXI, 76
Jacob (1624-1699/1700) m. 1647/8 (1) Elizabeth Lowell MASS XV, 111
Jacob (c. 1732-Oct. 6, 1821) m. Mar. 7, 1756 Elizabeth Hawlings XXIX, 264, 266
Joel (Aug. 6, 1761-Mar. 26, 1841) m. Nov. 1789 Eunice Fuller XI, 24
John (1590-1654) m. .... Judith Gates MASS XI, 24; XV, 111
John, II (1614-Dec. 14, 1686) m. 1635 Elizabeth Whipple MASS XXI, 76
Jonathan (Oct. 28, 1733-....) m. Feb. 7, 1754 Mary Trask XXI, 76
Joshua (Mar. 9, 1739/40-Nov. 13, 1832) m. May 10, 1764 Abigail Corning Bishop XV, 110
Nathaniel (June 27, 1753-1812) m. .... Polly Bryant III, 25
Richard (Mar. 2, 1730-Oct. 16, 1813) m. Oct. 9, 1760 Mary Hancock XXVI, 251, 252, 253
William (Aug. 25, 1607-May 21, 1682) m. Aug. 30, 1636 Elizabeth Wooten MASS XXVI, 251, 252, 253

PERRIN, see PERRINE

PERRINE, includes PERIN, PERINE, PERRIN, PERRYN
Daniel (1640-Sept. 6, 1719) m. Feb. 18, 1666 Marie Thorel NY V, 96; XV, 97; XVII, 110; XXXIII, 81
Henry (July 19, 1758-Mar. 9, 1812) m. 1780/1 Catherine Dey XXXIII, 81
James (Feb. 8, 1747-1830) m. May 26, 1772 Mrs. Mary Adams Smith XVII, 109, 110
James (June 20, 1752-Aug. 20, 1835) m. 1777 Isabel Clayton XV, 97
Jesse (Jan. 24, 1726-Jan. 15, 1801) m. May 11, 1749 Rachel Ide XXVIII, 202
John (c. 1614-Sept. 13, 1674) m. .... Anna ...... MASS XXVIII, 202; XXXII, 258
Lemuel (Oct. 21, 1749-July 9, 1822)

PERRINE, cont.
  m. Nov. 25, 1773 Martha Nasel
    XXXII, 258
  William (Nov. 28, 1743-1820) m. ....
    Hannah Mount V, 96

PERRY
  Anthony (1615-Mar. 1, 1682/3) m.
    .... Elizabeth ...... MASS
    XXXI, 272; XXXIV, 47
  David (Aug. 8, 1741-May 2, 1826)
    m. Jan. 12, 1764 Anna Bliss
    XXIX, 395
  Dimon (c. 1742-July 27, 1827) m.
    Apr. 28, 1763 Nabbe (Nabby) Cush-
    ing XXXIII, 118
  Edward (c. 1630-1695) m. 1653 Mary
    Freeman MASS XXIII, 56; XXXII,
    274
  Ezra (1625-Oct. 16, 1689) m. Feb.
    12, 1651 Elizabeth Burgess MASS
    XXIX, 395; XXXII, 158; XXXIV, 119
  Freeman (Feb. 4, 1795-Mar. 27, 1852)
    m. .... (1) Hannah Peckham XXXII,
    274
  Henry (May 28, 1738-Mar. 23, 1815)
    m. Dec. 25, 1760 Bethia Baker
    XXIV, 18
  Israel (Sept. 4, 1743/4-Feb. 18,
    1817) m. Oct. 15, 1769 Abigail
    Baker XXI, 55, 56
  James, Jr. (Oct. 27, 1728-a. Sept.
    10, 1778) m. Mar. 3, 1750 Mary
    Potter XXIII, 56
  John (....-Sept. 21, 1642) m. ....
    Anna ...... MASS X, 148
  John (1613-p. 1674) m. .... Johanna
    Holland MASS XV, 32; XXIX, 130;
    XXX, 148
  John (Dec. 9, 1754-Aug. 7, 1834) m.
    Nov. 2, 1781 (2) Abigail Bigelow
    XXX, 148
  Jonas, Sr. (Nov. 1, 1759-Feb. 28,
    1827) m. .... Susanna Damon XV,
    21
  Jonathan (1757-Aug. 20, 1824) m.
    June 29, 1780 Betsey Hill XXIX,
    130
  Ozias (June 20, 1757-May 10, 1837)
    m. June 5, 1785 Esther Marvin
    XXXII, 158; XXXIV, 119
  Peter (Jan. 24, 1739-Sept. 16, 1804)
    m. Nov. 6, 1763 Sarah Bradley
    XXII, 33
  Richard (....-a. Sept. 10, 1658) m.
    .... CONN XXII,
    33
  Samuel (c. 1740-Apr. 7, 1831) m.
    Aug. 14, 1766 Elizabeth Rowe X,
    147
  Samuel (Sept. 18, 1756-July 12, 1829)

  m. Jan. 9, 1784 (1) Chloe Lindley
    XXXI, 271, 272; XXXIV, 46
  Thomas (1600/15-....) m. .... Sarah
    Stedman MASS XXI, 55, 56; XXIV,
    19; XXXIII, 118

PERRYN, see PERRINE

PERS, see PIERCE

PETERS
  Andrew (1634-Dec. 1713) m. c. 1659
    Mercy (Beamsley) Wilbourn MASS XVI,
    110; XXXIII, 245
  Joseph Phelps (Nov. 7, 1761-Sept. 21,
    1843) m. Apr. 8, 1794 (2) Lydia Day
    XXXIII, 245
  William (July 17, 1746-1805) m. Apr.
    10, 1766 Deborah Strong XVI, 110,
    111

PETERSON
  John (....-Apr. 29, 1718) m. 1655
    Mary Soule MASS XXXIII, 106
  Reuben, Jr. (Apr. 10, 1749-May 22,
    1845) m. 1776 Abigail Soule
    XXXIII, 106

PETTIBONE
  Giles (Dec. 9, 1735-Mar. 17, 1810)
    m. .... Margaret Holcombe IX, 54,
    55
  John (....-July 15, 1713) m. Feb.
    16, 1664 Sarah Eggleston CONN IX,
    54, 55; XVII, 49; XXX, 120
  Jonathan (1710-Sept. 26, 1776) m.
    .... Martha Humphrey IX, 54, 55
  Samuel (Nov. 12, 1743-Dec. 3, 1816)
    m. 1763 Mrs. Martha Phelps XVII,
    48, 49; XXX, 120

PETTINGILL
  Andrew (Feb. 25, 1741-Dec. 12, 1777)
    m. Apr. 23, 1769 Abigail Greely
    XX, 69
  Richard (1620-1695) m. 1643 Joanna
    Ingersoll MASS XX, 69

PETTIT
  Thomas (1609-a. Oct. 1668) m. 1629/30
    Christian Mellows MASS, NH, NY
    XXXIII, 112
  William (Jan. 23, 1750-Mar. 22, 1832)
    m. July 4, 1773 Hannah Morell
    XXXIII, 112

PEYTON
  Ephraim (Aug. 27, 1755-1825) m. 1779
    Elizabeth Jennings XXXII, 132
  Henry (1630/1-1659) m. .... Ellen
    ...... VA XXIX, 339; XXXII, 132

PICKETT
  Ezra (July 12, 1740-a. Nov. 1, 1799)
    m. Mar. 30, 1761 Elizabeth Bene-
    dict XXXII, 273
  George (c. 1658-p. 1745) m. c. 1687
    Ida Martin VA IX, 32; X, 65
  Henry (....-c. 1702) m. ....
    ...... VA XXIX, 137
  John, Sr. (....-Apr. 11, 1684) m.
    .... Margette ...... CONN XXXII,
    273
  Martin (1740-1804) m. May 13, 1764
    Ann Blackwell IX, 32; X, 65
  William Sandford (c. 1741-p. 1809)
    m. Aug. 7, 1759 Elizabeth Metcalfe
    XXIX, 137

PIERCE, includes PARSE, PEARCE, PEARSE,
    PEIRCE, PERS
  Abiel (Sept. 10, 1733-Dec. 26, 1811)
    m. 1757 Hannah Canedy XXXII, 172
  Abner (Oct. 4, 1761-Jan. 28, 1851)
    m. Feb. 1, 1787 Hulda Wilcox X,
    127
  Abraham (Jan. 1605-1673) m. Feb.
    1650 Rebecca ...... MASS X, 69,
    127; XXXII, 172
  Anthony (1609-May 9, 1678) m. ....
    (2) Anne ...... MASS XXVII, 213
  Benjamin (May 18, 1762-May 9, 1847)
    m. Oct. 27, 1785 (1) Dorcas Love-
    joy XIX, 82, 134
  Caleb, Jr. (Aug. 31, 1733-Feb. 23,
    1815) m. May 1, 1754 Ann Menden-
    hall XXVII, 202
  Caleb (1753-1836) m. .... Mercy
    Wheeler XIX, 111
  Daniel (1611-Nov. 27, 1677) m. a.
    1638 (1) Sarah ...... MASS XV,
    11; XXXI, 240
  Ebenezer, Jr. (Sept. 11, 1711-Mar.
    2, 1805) m. Feb. 25, 1741/2 Mary
    Stowe XXVII, 217; XXXI, 307, 308
  Ebenezer (Feb. 17, 1731-1836) m.
    .... Elizabeth ...... XX, 95
  Ebenezer (June 9, 1745-Aug. 1, 1802)
    m. Oct. 10, 1770 Eunice Loomis
    XXVII, 217
  George (c. 1654-1734) m. Nov. 4,
    1679 Ann Gainor PA XXVII, 202
  Giles (1730-Apr. 11, 1793) m. ....
    Desire Case X, 208
  Isaac (Nov. 17, 1757-1804) m. Mar.
    20, 1786 Anna Sanderson XXXIII,
    20, 21
  John (1588-Aug. 19, 1661) m. ....
    Elizabeth ...... MASS XXVII, 213;
    XXXII, 204; XXXIII, 20, 21
  John (c. 1632-a. 1689) m...... Mary
    ...... RI XX, 96
  John (Jan. 26, 1743-July 7, 1812) m.

  Sept. 5, 1775 Tabitha Porter XI,
    14
  John (Apr. 20, 1754-Sept. 20, 1832)
    m. Oct. 5, 1775 Lucy Snow XXVII,
    157; XXVIII, 79, 80
  Jonathan (Sept. 17, 1757-Aug. 20,
    1808) m. Apr. 15, 1781 Lydia Bow-
    man XXXI, 307, 308
  Joseph (Mar. 13, 1752/3-Dec. 25,
    1825) m. July 25, 1780 Mary (Polly)
    Hadley XXXII, 204
  Joshua, Jr. (....-Nov. 25, 1804) m.
    May 23, 1773 Susannah Rounds XI,
    162
  Joshua (Jan. 15, 1705-Mar. 13, 1794)
    m. Nov. 20, 1729 Hopestill Hallo-
    way XXXI, 240
  Joshua (1728-p. 1785) m. Mar. 24,
    1748 Mary Norton XXV, 292
  Joshua (Nov. 8, 1730-Jan. 22, 1793)
    m. Sept. 10, 1754 Amy Johnson XXXI,
    240
  Josiah (1756-1830) m. .... Phebe
    Thompson II, 35
  Levi (Feb. 26, 1739-Jan. 1, 1826) m.
    Feb. 11, 1761 Bathsheba Babbitt
    X, 69
  Mial (Sept. 25, 1728-1810) m. Mar.
    26, 1752 Hepsibeth Mason XIII, 76
  Mial (Apr. 1, 1752-Mar. 1839) m.
    Oct. 20, 1773 Mehitable Wheeler
    XXXIV, 54
  Michael (c. 1615-Mar. 26, 1676) m. c.
    1645 (1) Persis Eames (Ames); c.
    1663 (2) Annah James MASS XI,
    162; XIII, 75; XIX, 111; XXIV,
    100; XXV, 292; XXXIV, 54
  Moses (Aug. 16, 1730-Oct. 27, 1777)
    m. Feb. 10, 1789 Mehitable Rice
    XXVII, 212, 213
  Richard (1590-....) m. .... Martha
    ...... RI X, 208
  Richard (1615-a. Oct. 28, 1678) m.
    May 5, 1642 Susannah Wright RI
    VIII, 12; XXIX, 337
  Richard (June 15, 1737-....) m. ....
    Phoebe ...... XXIX, 337
  Stephen (Dec. 17, 1753-May 14, 1843)
    m. .... Abigail Taylor VIII, 12
  Stephen (Aug. 15, 1754-Apr. 16,
    1826) m. July 30, 1778 Hannah Mar-
    shall XXXII, 45
  Thomas, Sr. (1583-Oct. 7, 1666) m.
    .... Elizabeth Pierce MASS XI,
    14; XIX, 82, 134; XXVII, 157, 217;
    XXVIII, 79, 80; XXXI, 308; XXXII,
    45
  Thomas (1608-1683) m. .... Elizabeth
    Cole MASS II, 35
  William (....-....) m. Sept. 13,
    1764 Joanna Doggett XXIV, 100

William (1735-Oct. 6, 1799) m. Jan. 28, 1766 Lydia Tilton Curtis XV, 11

PIERSON, includes PEARSON
Abraham (1608-Aug. 9, 1678) m. ....
Abigail Wheelwright MASS, NY X, 120, 151
Azel (Jan. 19, 1739-Oct. 16, 1798) m. May 20, 1760 Philothea Sayre XIII, 28; XVIII, 97
Benjamin (bpt. Jan. 15, 1758-Feb. 10, 1832) m. Dec. 22, 1779 Abigail Condict X, 151
Edward (c. 1650-Nov. 14, 1698) m. Mar. 6, 1671 Sarah Burgis PA XXIX, 84; XXXIII, 191
Ephraim (Mar. 5, 1730-Mar. 12, 1776) m. 1754 Hannah Barrett XXIX, 353; XXX, 32
Henry (1618-c. 1680) m. 1643 Mary Cooper MASS, NY XIII, 28; XVIII, 97; XXIX, 353; XXX, 32
Jesse (May 6, 1761-Jan. 10, 1837) m. Apr. 15, 1784 Lydia Stevens XXIX, 353; XXX, 32
John (Apr. 27, 1728-1784) m. 1756 Sarah ...... XXIX, 84; XXXIII, 190, 191
Samuel (July 21, 1750-Mar. 18, 1801) m. .... Rebecca Parmelee X, 120
Thomas (a. 1660-p. 1734) m. Feb. 18, 1683 Margaret Smith PA XXVIII, 40, 172, 194
William (Apr. 1, 1754-Apr. 26, 1800) m. Aug. 31, 1775 Ann Stidham XXVIII, 40, 172, 194

PIKE
Daniel (Feb. 23, 1725-Apr. 10, 1795) m. .... Sarah Kendall XVI, 108
Daniel (bpt. Aug. 9, 1747-Dec. 2, 1839) m. 1769 Lois Underwood XIII, 41
Jacob (June 1, 1737-May 7, 1805) m. .... Johanna Marshall XXIX, 169
James (....-Dec. 6, 1699) m. .... Naomi ...... MASS XIII, 41
James (Dec. 26, 1751-1820) m. Mar. 3, 1773 Ruth Ingalls XV, 7
John (1605-May 26, 1654) m. Jan. 17, 1612/3 Dorothy Day MASS XV, 7; XVI, 108
John (Oct. 2, 1729-Feb. 1, 1808) m. 1755 (2) Mary (Bennett) Davis XXVI, 75; XXXIV, 261
Joseph (June 5, 1757-c. 1802) m. .... Abigail Sawtell XVI, 108
Robert (1615-Dec. 12, 1706) m. Apr. 3, 1641 Sarah Sanders MASS XXVI, 75; XXIX, 169; XXXIV, 262

Robert (Sept. 3, 1687-p. 1776) m. Nov. 6, 1712 Hannah Gilman XXVI, 75

PILLSBURY
Caleb, Jr. (Jan. 26, 1717-Feb. 7, 1778) m. July 8, 1742 (1) Sarah Kimball XXIX, 204; XXXI, 47, 51, 160, 161
Stephen (c. 1750-Feb. 1816) m. 1773 Betsey Joy XIV, 26; XXXI, 288
William (1615-June 19, 1686) m. 1641 Dorothy Crosby MASS XIV, 26; XXIX, 204; XXXI, 47, 51, 160, 161, 288

PINGREY, includes PENGRY
John (Feb. 25, 1726-Aug. 30, 1795) m. .... Elizabeth Jenett IX, 38
Moses (1610-Jan. 2, 1696) m. 1646 Abigail Clement MASS IX, 38; XXX, 45
Nathaniel (Apr. 15, 1763-Apr. 23, 1850) m. Feb. 16, 1789 Anna Robbins XXX, 45, 46

PINKHAM
Joseph (1735-Aug. 1819) m. 1763 (2) Elizabeth Hayes XXIX, 257
Richard (....-p. 1647/8) m. .... Julia ...... NH XXIX, 257

PINNEY
Abner (1750-Nov. 23, 1804) m. 1773 Ruth Gillette XXIX, 70, 78
Abraham (Feb. 1709/10-Sept. 12, 1780) m. c. 1733 Elizabeth Butler XXIX, 195
Abraham (Dec. 23, 1735-Dec. 12, 1813) m. 1782 (3) Hester Case Higley XXIX, 195
Humphrey (....-Aug. 20, 1683) m. .... Mary Hull MASS XXIX, 70, 78, 195

PITT
Robert (c. 1600-a. Jan. 9, 1674) m. c. 1627 Martha Lear VA XXVI, 49
Robert (1738-1812) m. 1760 Mary Bridger XXVI, 49

PLACE
Enoch (1631-1695) m. Nov. 5, 1657 Sarah ...... MASS XXII, 55
Philip (Jan. 31, 1753-Feb. 18, 1835) m. Dec. 1, 1776 Mary Wightman XXII, 55

PLANT
Abraham (1727-May 5, 1793) m. May 5, 1763 Tamar Frisbie XXXIII, 145, 146

PLANT, cont.
  Benjamin (1732-Aug. 11, 1808) m. c.
  1758 Lorana Beckwith XXV, 48
  John, Sr. (....-1691) m. 1677 Betty
    Roundkettle CONN XXV, 48; XXXIII,
    145, 146

PLATT
  Jones (Oct. 9, 1727-....) m. Oct.
    17, 1747 Elizabeth Sanford X, 157
  Josiah (May 6, 1735-Jan. 5, 1804) m.
    Nov. 13, 1758 Sarah Sanford XXXI,
    299
  Moses (bpt. May 24, 1747-Sept. 18,
    1819) m. Dec. 6, 1770 Hannah Judson
    XXXIV, 83
  Nathan (Mar. 3, 1761-July 30, 1845)
    m. .... Ruby Smith XXXI, 299
  Obadiah (bpt. Mar. 23, 1745/6-Dec.
    7, 1829) m. Feb. 5, 1770 Mary Platt
    XXIV, 124; XXXI, 271
  Richard (bpt. May 6, 1604-Feb. 13,
    1684/5) m. Jan. 26, 1628/9 Mary
    Place CONN X, 157; XXIV, 124;
    XXV, 88; XXXI, 271, 299; XXXIV,
    83
  Richard, IV (Mar. 20, 1742-1799) m.
    .... (1) Sarah Camp; ....(2) Ann
    Rogers XXV, 88

PLATTS
  Abel (....-1690) m. May 8, 1672 Lydia
    Bailey MASS XV, 81
  Abel (Feb. 6, 1703/4-July 23, 1777)
    m. Apr. 21, 1725 Mary Varnum XV,
    81
  Abel, Jr. (Mar. 28, 1738-Mar. 6,
    1819) m. Apr. 26, 1759 Phebe
    Weatherbee XXXII, 136
  Samuel (....-....) m. .... (1) Sarah
    ...... MASS XXXII, 136

PLEASANTS
  John, I (bpt. Feb. 27, 1645-May 12,
    1698) m. c. 1670 Jane (Larcome)
    Tucker VA XVI, 15; XXIX, 56;
    XXXI, 168
  John (1720-p. Dec. 29, 1776) m. ....
    Susannah Woodson XVI, 15
  Samuel (Oct. 1737-Nov. 3, 1807) m.
    May 13, 1762 Mary Pemberton XXIX,
    56; XXXI, 168

PLETSOE, see BLEDSOE

PLUMB
  Benoni, Sr. (1670-Oct. 6, 1754) m.
    Jan. 8, 1715/6 Abigail (Todd) Gil-
    bert CONN XXXI, 314
  Daniel (Apr. 6, 1746-1793) m. c. 1784
    Esther ...... XXXI, 314

PLUMER, see PLUMMER

PLUMMER, includes PLUMER
  Abel (Aug. 31, 1730-c. 1820) m. Oct.
    6, 1750 Mary Early XXVIII, 161,
    162
  Francis (1598-Jan. 17, 1672/3) m.
    .... Ruth ...... MASS XIX, 154;
    XXVIII, 161; XXXII, 128, 131
  Jabez (Sept. 1757-1777/8) m. ....
    Hannah Hunt XXXII, 127, 128
  Richard (June 15, 1755-Feb. 17, 1838)
    m. Mar. 4, 1790 Susannah Moore
    XXXII, 130, 131
  Samuel (1744-Mar. 1804) m. ....
    ...... Jones XIX, 154

PLYMPTON
  Abner (May 7, 1743-May 5, 1814) m.
    Nov. 27, 1764 Esther Mann XXIX,
    17
  John (c. 1620-p. Sept. 19, 1677) m.
    Mar. 13, 1644 Jane Dammin MASS
    XXIX, 17

POILLON
  Jacques (c. 1646-1720) m. Oct. 24,
    1677 Andrianna Crocheron NY
    XXIX, 231
  Peter (Feb. 25, 1745-Oct. 22, 1780)
    m. 1768 Margaret Poillon XXIX,
    231

POINDEXTER
  George (....-....) m. .... Susanna
    ...... VA XXXI, 110
  William (....-1808) m. .... Margaret
    Daniel XXXI, 110

POLK, includes DE POLLOK, POLLOK
  Charles (Oct. 26, 1740-Aug. 28,
    1795) m. Mar. 29, 1786 Mary Man-
    love XXVII, 84, 85; XXIX, 155
  Robert Bruce (1632-June 4, 1704) m.
    1650 Magdalene (Tasker) Porter MD
    XXVII, 84, 85; XXIX, 155; XXX, 188,
    189
  Thomas (1731-1793) m. 1755 Susan
    Spratt XXX, 188, 189

POLLAY, includes POLLEY
  George, Sr. (....-Dec. 22, 1683) m.
    May 21, 1649 Elizabeth Winn MASS
    XXXII, 51
  Joseph (Sept. 3, 1728-Feb. 28, 1806)
    m. Mar. 1, 1748/9 Dorcas Colburn
    XXXII, 51

POLLEY, see POLLAY

POLLOK, see POLK

POMEROY
  Benjamin (Nov. 11, 1704-Dec. 21,
    1784) m. Oct. 23, 1734 Abigail
    Wheelock III, 50; XIII, 39;
    XIV, 55; XXVII, 176; XXIX, 13, 25;
    XXX, 128
  Daniel (Oct. 13, 1727-Jan. 23, 1785)
    m. Oct. 19, 1749 Mrs. Naomi (Kibbe)
    Phelps XIII, 89
  Ebenezer (Jan. 17, 1741-Sept. 7,
    1826) m. Sept. 3, 1766 Experience
    Clark X, 262
  Elihu (Aug. 19, 1755-Apr. 17, 1834)
    m. 1776 Lydia Barber III, 50
  Eltweed (July 4, 1585-Mar. 4, 1673)
    m. May 7, 1629 (2) Margery Rockett
    MASS, CONN III, 50; X, 123, 262;
    XI, 34; XIII, 39, 89; XIV, 55;
    XXVII, 176; XXIX 13, 25; XXX, 128
  John (Aug. 12, 1733-Sept. 21, 1810)
    m. Jan. 1, 1762 Esther Kibbee XI,
    34
  Josiah (June 18, 1745-July 1812) m.
    c. 1788/9 Mary Cook XXVII, 176;
    XXIX, 13, 25
  Seth (May 20, 1706-Feb. 19, 1777)
    m. Dec. 14, 1732 Mary Hunt X, 123

POND
  Daniel (....-Feb. 4, 1698) m. ....
    (1) Abigail Shepard; Sept. 18,
    1661 (2) Anne Edwards MASS XXVII,
    146; XXXI, 43, 131, 273
  Ebenezer (July 4, 1728-Mar. 1821) m.
    1747 Freelove Fairbanks XXXI, 131
  Elijah (Feb. 3, 1738/9-June 1830) m.
    Apr. 24, 1761 (1) Margaret Metcalf
    XXVII, 145, 146; XXXI, 43, 44
  Ezra (May 28, 1758-Dec. 16, 1843) m.
    .... Pamelia Hubbell XXXI, 273
  Jonathan (June 24, 1740-Dec. 16,
    1817) m. .... Jerusha Jerome XXXI,
    193
  Samuel (....-Mar. 14, 1654) m. Nov.
    14, 1642 Sarah ...... CONN XXXI,
    193

POOL
  John (....-1667) m. .... Margaret
    ...... MASS XXVI, 11; XXVIII, 200
  Jonathan (Jan. 14, 1719/20-Sept. 11,
    1798) m. June 4, 1741 Mary Leman
    XXVI, 11; XXVIII, 200
  Jonathan, Jr. (Apr. 21, 1747-Oct.
    25, 1807) m. Apr. 25, 1769 Ann
    Bancroft XXVIII, 200

MOORE
  Daniel (Mar. 13, 1716-Jan. 9, 1792)
    m. Nov. 23, 1739 Anna Merrill
    XXII, 72

John (c. 1615-Nov. 21, 1684) m. ....
  Sarah ...... MASS XXII, 72

POPE
  Folger (Feb. 14, 1756-Nov. 7, 1828)
    m. June 18, 1781 Theodate Holder
    XX, 118
  Henry (Jan. 1, 1748-....) m. ....
    Charity Hinton XXVI, 180, 181
  Joseph (....-a. Apr. 27, 1667) m.
    .... Gertrude ...... MASS XX, 118
  Nathaniel (....-a. Apr. 26, 1660) m.
    .... Lucy ...... MD XXVI, 180,
    181

PORTER
  Benjamin (1717-June 9, 1794) m. Dec.
    13, 1739 Eunice Nurse XVI, 37;
    XXIX, 935
  Daniel, I (....-1690) m. .... Mary
    ...... CONN XIII, 106; XVII, 57;
    XXIII, 80
  Edward (1640-c. July 5, 1705) m. a.
    1694 Mary ...... VA XXVI, 92
  Francis (Sept. 22, 1748-Mar. 7, 1815)
    m. 1779 Priscilla Hall XVI, 37;
    XXIX, 395
  Hezekiah, III (Sept. 1, 1735-1801) m.
    1757 Sarah Carver XXI, 52, 53;
    XXVI, 144, 145
  James (....-p. 1697) m. .... Junibar
    ...... MD XVI, 60; XVII, 13
  James (Nov. 19, 1737-1825) m. Nov.
    9, 1762 Lucy Bronson XIII, 106;
    XVII, 56, 57
  John (1596-Sept. 6, 1676) m. c. 1634
    Mary ...... MASS XVI, 37; XXIX,
    395; XXXIII, 331, 332
  John, Sr. (1599-1647) m. 1620 Anne
    White CONN XXI, 52, 53
  John, Jr. (1621-Aug. 2, 1688) m.
    June 1, 1650 Mary Stanley CONN
    XXVI, 144, 145
  John, Jr. (c. 1630-1691) m. ....
    Mary Sidney VA XXVI, 171; XXX,
    57, 58
  Josiah (1759-Nov. 18, 1798) m. June
    13, 1786 Mercy Brown XXXIII, 331,
    332
  Robert (June 16, 1730-1800) m. 1754
    Susannah Mercer XVI, 60; XVII,
    13; XXVI, 171, 172; XXX, 57, 58
  Thomas (May 9, 1736-Jan. 31, 1817)
    m. Dec. 12, 1758 Mehitable Hine
    XXIII, 80
  William (1754-a. Nov. 24, 1806) m.
    May 29, 1788 Mary Sandy XXVI, 92

POST, includes POSTMAEL
  Adrian (....-Feb. 28, 1677) m. ....
    Claertje ...... NY, NJ XIV, 34;

POST, cont.
XVIII, 19; XX, 61; XXI, 17, 26, 27;
XXVI, 159
Cornelius (Feb. 1, 1736-Feb. 12,
1812) m. .... Anna Maris Kough
XVIII, 19; XX, 61; XXI, 17; XXVI,
159
Garret (Aug. 18, 1739-Feb. 20, 1822)
m. .... Mary Ryerson XXI, 26, 27
Jacobus (James) (Mar. 2, 1732-....)
m. .... Mrs. Martha (Garrison) Van
Wagnen XIV, 34
Jans Jansan (....-p. 1684) m. ....
Jannetie Le Sueur NY XXXIV, 225
John (Sept. 3, 1738-Mar. 18, 1824)
m. Nov. 22, 1764 Chloe Chapman
XXIX, 263
Joseph (1720-1794) m. .... (1) Mary
Smith XII, 78, 110
Joseph (Apr. 22, 1754-Nov. 3, 1831)
m. Oct. 15, 1775 Anna Hoppin
XIII, 62
Peter (Oct. 31, 1743-Mar. 12, 1787)
m. .... Debora Schoonmaker XXXIV,
225
Phineas (Dec. 2, 1704-Mar. 21, 1787)
m. June 25, 1741 Anne Post XIV,
16
Phineas (Jan. 3, 1743-Oct. 15, 1814)
m. May 12, 1774 Sybil Barker XV,
40
Richard (Feb. 4, 1617-1689/90) m.
1640 Dorothy Johnson NY XII, 78,
110; XIII, 62
Roswell, Jr. (May 10, 1753-May 5,
1826) m. July 14, 1777 Martha Mead
XIX, 69; XXXII, 176
Stephen (c. 1596-Aug. 16, 1659) m.
(int.) Oct. 17, 1625 Eleanor Pan-
ton CONN XIV, 16; XV, 40; XIX,
69; XXIX, 263; XXXII, 176

POSTMAEL, see POST

POTTER
Anthony (1628-Jan. 22, 1690) m. ....
Elizabeth Whipple MASS V, 103
George (....-....) m. ....
...... RI XXI, 142, 143
George, Jr. (Feb. 10, 1757-Oct. 25,
1801) m. Apr. 26, 1780 Mary Still-
man XXVIII, 108
John (c. 1607-1643) m. Apr. 14, 1630
Elizabeth Wood CONN XXXII, 143
John (Apr. 28, 1736-Feb. 11, 1792)
m. .... Sarah Snipe V, 103
Matthias (Dec. 27, 1741-Aug. 25,
1819) m. .... Mary Day XXXI, 143
Nathaniel (c. 1617-a. 1644) m. ....
Dorothy ...... RI XXVIII,
108

Noel (Aug. 13, 1758-Nov. 3, 1847) m.
1784/5 Anna Roberts XIV, 98
Robert (....-1665) m. .... (2) Sarah
...... MASS, RI XIV, 98
Samuel (May 24, 1745-Oct. 1, 1777)
m. .... Lydia Matteson XXI, 142,
143

POTTINGER
John (1642-1735) m. 1687 Mary Beall
MD XXV, 254
Robert (1728/30-c. 1780) m. 1750/3
Elizabeth Willett XXV, 254
Samuel, Sr. (Apr. 29, 1754-June 20,
1831) m. c. 1782 Jane (Gray)
Withrow-Gilkey XXV, 254

POTTS
Ezekiel (Jan. 8, 1743-Jan. 16, 1809)
m. 1769 Elisabeth Mead XVII, 37
Jonas (....-p. 1737) m. .... Mary
...... PA XVII, 37

POWELL
John Peyton (Feb. 28, 1760-June 23,
1844) m. Oct. 14, 1783 Tabitha
Harris XXIX, 32
Rowland (....-....) m. .... Isabelle
...... MASS XXIV, 163
Rowland (June 9, 1730/1-1801) m. Dec.
5, 1750 Mary Richardson XXIV, 163
Rowland (Nov. 16, 1751-1789) m. c.
1773 Mary Janes XXIV, 162
Walter (....-Nov. 27, 1695) m. ....
Margaret ...... MD XXIX, 32

POWERS
Gideon (1704-May 6, 1779) m. ....
Lydia Russell XII, 70
Lemuel (1714-Dec. 11, 1792) m. Jan.
14, 1742 Thankful Leland XI, 168
Nathaniel, Jr. (c. 1740-p. 1794) m.
.... Jerusha Hart XXX, 137;
XXXIII, 124, 125
Walter (1639-Feb. 22, 1708) m. Mar.
11, 1661 Trial Shepard MASS XI,
168; XII, 70; XXX, 137; XXXIII,
124; XXXIV, 332
William (Dec. 30, 1740-Mar. 13, 1829)
m. Jan. 8, 1766 Elizabeth Gates
XII, 70; XXXIV, 332

PRATHER
Basil (a. June 1742-Oct. 7, 1822) m.
1765 Clorender Robertson XXXIII,
320, 321
James (1740-1791) m. .... Ann Turner
IV, 126
Jonathan (1630/5-1682) m. c. 1654
June Mackay (Smith) VA, MD IV,
126; XXXIII, 320, 321

PRATT

Aaron (Apr. 8, 1734-Feb. 11, 1811)
m. Apr. 6, 1758 Bridget Collier
XX, 85; XXVII, 86, 87

Abraham (....-a. Dec. 21, 1709) m.
.... Jane ...... PA XXXIII, 237;
XXXIV, 283

Daniel (June 7, 1734-May 9, 1806) m.
May 24, 1755 Abigail Bigelow XXXI,
23

Eliab (c. 1724-Aug. 15, 1809) m. c.
1748 Margaret Ely XXVII, 145

Gideon (1741-....) m. .... Sarah Butler XXVII, 205

Jacob (Oct. 3, 1735-Nov. 23, 1811)
m. Oct. 23, 1760 Lydia Eames VIII,
27; X, 279; XXXII, 239

Joel, Sr. (Feb. 1, 1752-Nov. 10,
1844) m. Dec. 22, 1785 (1) Charlotte Ball XXXIII, 291

John (bpt. Nov. 9, 1620-July 15,
1655) m. 1637 Elizabeth ......
CONN IV, 135; XXVII, 145; XXXI,
23

Jonas (....-p. Mar. 7, 1798) m. c.
1737 Ann ...... XXIX, 364; XXXI,
159

Joseph (c. 1712-Sept. 16, 1796) m.
Sept. 27, 1750 (2) Katherine Read
XVII, 156, 157; XVIII, 21, 22

Mathew (1600-Aug. 29, 1672) m. ....
Elizabeth Bates MASS XI, 57;
XXVI, 6; XXIX, 373

Mathew (Dec. 3, 1726-Oct. 5, 1799)
m. Nov. 5, 1749 Mary Lovell XXIX,
373

Mathew, Jr. (May 20, 1752-Oct. 16,
1835) m. Dec. 21, 1775 Chloe Pratt
XXIX, 373

Phineas (1590-Apr. 19, 1680) m. 1630
Mary Priest MASS XX, 85; XXVII,
87; XXXIV, 50

Samuel (July 29, 1764-Aug. 31, 1812)
m. .... Esther Wells IV, 135

Solomon (c. 1738-Nov. 6, 1776) m.
May 13, 1767 Annah White XI, 57

Thaddeus (1755-1843) m. July 23,
1774 Rachel Churchill XXVI, 6

Thomas (....-Sept. 26, 1692) m. ....
Susanna ...... MASS VIII, 27;
X, 280; XVII, 156; XVIII, 22; XXIX,
364; XXXI, 159; XXXII, 239; XXXIII,
291

Thomas (bpt. May 15, 1737-Oct. 18,
1818) m. Dec. 5, 1765 Sarah Neal
XXXIV, 50

Thomas (Jan. 13, 1764-Jan. 19, 1820)
m. Nov. 30, 1786 (1) Hannah Massey;
Mar. 29, 1813 (2) Hannah Haycock
(Heacock) XXXIII, 237; XXXIV,
283

William (....-....) m. .... Eliza-
beth Clarke CONN XXVII, 205

PRAY

John (Feb. 4, 1749-May 10, 1830) m.
.... Deborah Wade VIII, 18, 19

Quinton (1595-Apr. 17, 1677) m. ....
Joan ...... MASS VIII, 19

Richard (1630-1693) m. .... Mary
...... RI VIII, 19

PREBLE

Abraham (Jan. 23, 1603-Jan. 23, 1663)
m. June 3, 1641 Judith Tilden MASS
III, 19

Esaias (Apr. 26, 1742-Dec. 14, 1813)
m. June 30, 1776 Lydia Ingraham
III, 19

PRENTICE, includes PRENTIS, PRENTISE,
PRENTISS

Daniel (Jan. 26, 1758-Apr. 14, 1851)
m. July 18, 1779 Abigail Standley
XXXIV, 153

Henry (c. 1619-June 9, 1654) m. ....
(2) Joan Prentice MASS XIX, 81;
XXXIV, 153

John (1730-1800) m. ....
...... XXVI, 51, 52

Joseph, Jr. (Aug. 24, 1727-Mar. 20,
1791) m. Mar. 15, 1759 Abigail
Leonard XXVII, 78, 79

Reuben (Nov. 20, 1751/2-Apr. 9,
1797) m. June 9, 1778 Sarah Fowler XIX, 81

Thomas, Sr. (c. 1620-July 6, 1710)
m. c. 1643 Grace ...... MASS
XXVII, 79

Thomas (Jan. 19, 1760-1841) m. Nov.
11, 1784 Mary Spencer XVI, 96, 97

Valentine (....-1633) m. .... Alice
...... MASS XVI, 96; XXVI, 52

PRENTIS, see PRENTICE

PRENTISE, see PRENTICE

PRENTISS, see PRENTICE

PRESCOTT

David (June 28, 1728-Feb. 9, 1779)
m. Apr. 1754 Abigail Wright XVII,
18

Ebenezer (1720-Oct. 15, 1776) m.
Jan. 14, 1746 Jerusha Matthews
XXVI, 111, 112

Ebenezer (Aug. 15, 1747-Jan. 1811) m.
.... Lydia Wood XIII, 55

James (1643-Nov. 25, 1728) m. 1668
Mary Boulter NH XXV, 105, 241; XXX,
282; XXXI, 264; XXXII, 109, 187;

Peter (Mar. 26, 1735-Aug. 31, 1822)
m. Apr. 11, 1761 Mary Ball XXII,
70
Robert (....-Apr. 28, 1697) m.
Dec. 31, 1645 Jane Hildreth MASS
X, 275, XXII, 70

PROUTY
Asa (Feb. 1751-Mar. 10, 1826) m. ....
Lydia Livermore VII, 39
Isaac (Dec. 22, 1750-June 15, 1828)
m. Jan. 20, 1772 (1) Anna Dunnell
XXII, 139; XXXII, 146, 147
Richard (bpt. Sept. 30, 1652-Sept.
1, 1708) m. Dec. 12, 1676 Damaris
Torrey MASS VII, 39; XXII, 139;
XXXII, 147; XXXIII, 294, 295
Richard (Apr. 23, 1742-p. July 7,
1807) m. c. 1771/2 (2) Susanna
White XXXIII, 295

PRUDDEN
Fletcher (Aug. 30, 1737-Jan. 8, 1798)
m. June 9, 1760 Sarah Treat XI,
43
Peter (1600-July 1656) m. ....
Joanna Boyse CONN XI, 43

PRYOR, see PRIOR

PUDDINGTON, see PURINGTON

PUDNEY, see PUTNEY

PUFFER
George (c. 1600-Sept. 17, 1639) m.
.... MASS XVII,
109; XXIII, 24
James (c. 1624-July 25, 1692) m. Feb.
14, 1656 Mary Ludden MASS XXXIV,
92
Phineas (Sept. 23, 1741-1817) m. ....
Molly (Mary) Stratton XVII, 109;
XXIII, 24; XXXIV, 92

PUGSLEY
Matthew (....-p. 1730) m. Nov. 22,
1683 Mary Hunt NY XXXII, 33, 51
Samuel (c. 1758-Feb. 14, 1814) m.
c. 1782/3 Elizabeth Drake XXXII,
33, 51

PULLIAM
Edmund (1600-....) m. ....
...... VA XXXIV, 72
William P., Sr. (c. 1760-p. 1812)
m. .... (2) Mary ...... XXXIV, 72

PULSIFIER
David, Jr. (Sept. 29, 1731-1832) m.
p. Feb. 4, 1762 Hannah Pulsifer

XXXI, 286
John (c. 1663-Aug. 27, 1737) m. Dec.
31, 1684 Joanna Kent MASS XXXI,
286

PURDY
Elisha (Mar. 17, 1740-Mar. 20, 1820)
m. c. 1761 Mehitable Smith XXII,
20
Francis (1610-1658) m. c. 1642 Mary
Brandagee CONN XXII, 20

PURINGTON, includes PUDDINGTON,
PURRINGTON
Elijah (1730-....) m. .... Dolly
Green XXX, 203, 204, 272
George (....-p. July 3, 1647) m.
Feb. 5, 1630 Mary Pooke ME XXX,
203, 204, 272
Hezekiah (Jan. 10, 1752-....) m. ....
.... XXX, 203, 204, 272

PURINTON
Humphrey (Aug. 1759-Jan. 25, 1832)
m. .... Thankful Snow XIX, 44
Robert (....-....) m. .... Amy Davis
NH XIX, 44

PURNELL
Thomas (Feb. 7, 1613-Aug. 28, 1690)
m. Jan. 7, 1647 Elizabeth Darman
VA, MD XIV, 107; XV, 54
William (Aug. 10, 1745-Sept. 27,
1820) m. May 11, 1770 Ann Sylvester
XIV, 107; XV, 53

PURRINGTON, see PURINGTON

PUTNAM
Benjamin (Oct. 12, 1718-Apr. 26,
1796) m. July 28, 1741 Sarah Put-
nam XXVII, 198, 199
Benjamin (Apr. 28, 1757-July 9, 1812)
m. Apr. 15, 1775 Miriam Flint
XXVII, 198, 199
Ebenezer (Aug. 8, 1719-Feb. 2, 1782)
m. c. 1745 Mary Parker XXXII, 129
Eleazer (June 5, 1738-1806) m. ....
Mary Crosby XII, 80
Eleazer Porter (Dec. 8, 1758-1813)
m. .... Rebecca Smith XII, 62
Henry (Aug. 14, 1712-Apr. 19, 1775)
m. .... Hannah ...... XII, 80
Israel (Jan. 7, 1718-May 29, 1790)
m. July 19, 1739 Hannah Pope XVI,
77; XXX, 45; XXXII, 156
Israel (Jan. 28, 1740-Mar. 7, 1812)
m. 1764 Sarah Waldo XXX, 45
John (bpt. Jan. 17, 1579/80-Dec. 30,
1662) m. c. 1611 Priscilla ......
MASS VI, 27; XII, 62, 80; XV, 20;

PUTNAM, cont.
XVI, 77; XIX, 33; XXIV, 56; XXVII,
198; XXIX, 341; XXX, 45, 231;
XXXII, 129, 156
John (May 27, 1627-Apr. 7, 1710) m.
.... *Rebecca Prince MASS XII, 80*
Levi (1758-Apr. 10, 1830) m. May 25,
1790 Hannah Allen XXX, 231
Miles (Sept. 5, 1725-Apr. 19, 1800)
m. Sept. 23, 1747 Rachel Wilkins
XV, 20; XXIX, 341
Stephen (Feb. 22, 1742-July 8, 1809)
m. a. 1775 Susanna Herrick VI,
27
Tarrant (Sept. 2, 1733-1804) m. ....
Mary Porter XII, 62
William (Jan. 7, 1758-July 22, 1818)
m. June 25, 1778 Submit Fisk XIX,
33; XXIV, 56

PUTNEY, includes PUDNEY
David (1760-Sept. 1, 1844) m. 1790
Rebecca Sawyer XXXI, 150
John, Sr. (....-1712) m. Nov. 18,
1662 Judith Cooke MASS XXXI,
150

PYATT, includes PIAT, PYOTT
Ebenezer (1755-Jan. 30, 1835) m.
June 20, 1782 Rebecca Milburn
XXXIII, 145
Rene (c. 1650-Oct. 16, 1705) m. Dec.
13, 1677 Elizabeth Sheffield NJ
XXXIII, 144, 145

PYOTT, see PYATT

QUACKENBOS, see QUACKENBUSH

QUACKENBUSH, includes QUACKENBOS
Gozen (May 27, 1744-1830) m. a. Jan.
27, 1771 Susanna Burkheet (Borkit)
XXXIII, 298, 299
Isaac (May 19, 1760-....) m. ....
Katherine Gardinier XXXII, 226
Nicholas (Jan. 21, 1750-Apr. 21,
1830) m. Apr. 8, 1777 Madalena
Collier XXXI, 191, 192
Pieter (a. 1639-p. 1696) m. c. 1658
Maritje ...... NY IX, 6; XXXI,
191; XXXII, 226; XXXIII, 298, 299
Regnier (Jan. 30, 1730-Nov. 18, 1807)
m. .... Anetje Van Orden IX, 6

QUEEN
Joseph (1752-1802) m. Dec. 2, 1787
Ann Edwardina (Eddie) Jerningham
XXX, 152
Richard (....-a. Oct. 7, 1794) m.

.... Mary ...... XXX, 152
Samuel (....-....) m. .... Katherine
(Marsham) Brooke MD XXX, 152

QUIMBY, includes QUINBY
Jonathan (Aug. 15, 1726-p. 1790) m.
Feb. 20, 1755 Ruth Cook XXX, 85
Robert (a. 1625-July 7, 1677) m. c.
1656 Elizabeth Osgood MASS XXX,
85, 288
Samuel (July 5, 1718-1798) m. Apr.
20, 1749 Elizabeth Stevens XXX,
288
William (Apr. 7, 1767-Jan. 4, 1855)
m. Mar. 1796 Miriam Harvey XXX,
288

QUINBY, see QUIMBY

QUINCY
Edmund (....-1635) m. July 14, 1623
Judith Pares MASS XXVIII, 152
Edmund (June 13, 1703-July 4, 1788)
m. Apr. 15, 1725 Elizabeth Wendell
XXVIII, 152

RAGSDALE
Godfrey, Sr. (c. 1615-Apr. 18, 1644)
m. .... Mary ...... VA XXXIV,
144
William, Sr. (c. 1738-a. 1820) m. c.
1760 Mary Elizabeth Smith XXXIV,
144

RAIFORD
John (1730-p. 1812) m. .... Lucy
Spell XXV, 97, 98
Maurice (1755-Nov. 1824) m. 1785 (2)
Aseneath Hodges XXV, 97, 98
Philip, I (....-....) m. .... Sarah
...... VA XXV, 97, 98
William (....-1798) m. c. 1725 .....
Bryan XXV, 98

RAMBO
John (Nov. 21, 1725-Mar. 5, 1787) m.
June 8, 1757 Elizabeth Champney
XX, 165
Peter Gunnarson (....-Nov. 1698) m.
.... Bretta ...... PA XX, 165

RAND
Nehemiah (Dec. 9, 1734-July 10,
1794) m. May 27, 1774 (2) Mrs.
Mary (Prentice) Frost XVIII,
107
Robert (.....-1639/40) m.
.... Alice ...... MASS XVIII,
107

RANDALL
John (May 28, 1629-1684) m. c. 1663
Elizabeth Morton RI XXI, 42, 43;
XXIII, 58; XXXIV, 62, 63, 340
John, IV (Aug. 4, 1730-May 18, 1802)
m. Aug. 23, 1767 Thankful Swan
XXXIV, 62, 63
John, Jr. (June 24, 1758-Jan. 19,
1837) m. Apr. 20, 1780 Joanna
Phoebe Merchant XVIII, 119; XXX,
236
Nathaniel (Aug. 4, 1743-p. 1826) m.
Mar. 28, 1776 Deborah Stetson
XXV, 19
Stephen (1736-Nov. 22, 1818) m. 1763
Elizabeth Swezey XXI, 42, 43;
XXIII, 58; XXXIV, 340
William (1609-Oct. 13, 1693) m. 1640
Elizabeth Barstow MASS XVIII,
119; XXV, 19; XXX, 236

RANDOLPH
David Meade (1758-Sept. 23, 1830) m.
Apr. 1782 Mary Randolph XXVI, 53
Harrison (c. 1743-c. 1803) m. Sept.
7, 1787 Mary Jones XXXII, 92, 93,
211; XXXIII, 225, 226
Henry (1623-1673) m. .... Judith
Soane VA IX, 9, 26
Peter (c. 1750-....) m. .... Sarah
Greenhill IX, 9, 26
William (1651-Apr. 11, 1711) m. Nov.
13, 1677/8 Mary Isham VA XXVI,
53; XXXII, 92, 211; XXXIII, 225,
226

RANLET, includes RUNDLET
Charles (c. 1655-Aug. 1, 1709) m. c.
1675 Mary (Shatswell) Smith NH
XXIII, 58
Daniel (Aug. 5, 1749-Oct. 30, 1835)
m. July 23, 1771 Mehitable Lougee
XXIII, 58

RANNEY, includes RANY
Ephraim, Sr. (Apr. 10, 1725/6-June
9, 1811) m. Nov. 26, 1747 Silence
Wilcox XXXIII, 12, 13
Thomas (....-June 21, 1713) m. May
1659 Mary Hubbard CONN XXXIII,
12

RANSOM, includes RANSON
Peter (1615-a. Feb. 10, 1663) m.
....`. VA XXIX, 25;
XXXI, 182
Richard (May 13, 1740-Sept. 5, 1811)
m. Nov. 22, 1759 Mary Starlen
(Sterling) XXV, 200
Richard Payne (1752-July 22, 1827) m.
1784 Kesiah Portis XXIX, 25;

XXXI, 182
Robert (1636-Dec. 14, 1697) m. c.
1660 Susannah ...... MASS XXVI,
54; XXV, 200
Stephen (May 8, 1724-1776) m. ....
Lydia Lord XXVI, 54

RANSON, see RANSOM

RANY, see RANNEY

RAPALJE, see RAPELYEA

RAPELYEA, includes DE RAPALIE, DE
RAPALJE, RAPALJE
Jacobus (1743-Oct. 27, 1827) m. ....
Sarah Williamson XV, 78
Jeromus (c. 1718-....) m. .... Anna
...... XIV, 116
Jeronues (Dec. 10, 1756-Oct. 11,
1836) m. .... Elizabeth Bedell
XI, 146
Joris Jassan (Aug. 24, 1572-1661) m.
.... Catalyntie Frisco NY XI,
146; XIV, 116; XV, 78

RATHBONE, includes RATHBUN
Amos (Jan. 25, 1738-July 24, 1817)
m. .... Martha Robinson XI, 78
John (1634-p. Oct. 6, 1702) m. ....
Margaret Dodge RI XVII, 102;
XIX, 65; XXIX, 114
Richard (c. 1574-....) m. ....
Marion Whipple MASS XI, 78
Samuel (Apr. 16, 1705-Jan. 24, 1780)
m. Mar. 15, 1732 Elizabeth Dodge
XVII, 102, 103; XIX, 65; XXIX,
114

RATHBUN, see RATHBONE

RAVENSCROFT
Samuel (....-1692/5) m. c. 1680
Dionaysia Savage MASS, VA XXX,
270
Thomas (July 1756-May 27, 1827) m.
Sept. 7, 1786 Margaret Hinkson
XXX, 270

RAWLINGS, includes RAWLINS, ROLINGS,
ROLLINS
Aaron (1727-c. 1790) m. 1748/9
Elizabeth Ingalls XXXIII, 24
Benjamin (1734-1830) m. ....
...... XX, 91, 92
Francis (bpt. Sept. 11, 1716-Jan.
17, 1794) m. 1740 Lurana Richard-
son XVII, 105; XXI, 53, 54;
XXIV, 98; XXX, 229
James (....-a. July 25, 1691) m.
.... Hannah ...... MASS, NH XX,

RAWLINGS, cont.
91, 92; XXXIII, 24
Richard (c. 1651-1696) m. c. 1673
Jane ...... MD XVII, 105; XXI,
53, 54; XXIV, 98; XXX, 229

RAWLINS, see RAWLINGS

RAWSON
Edmund (July 1751-May 1, 1823) m.
July 10, 1770 Sarah Hull XXIX,
301
Edward (Apr. 16, 1615-Aug. 27, 1693)
m. .... Rachel Perne MASS XIII,
95; XVIII, 149; XXII, 79; XXIX, 59,
174, 301; XXX, 89, 90
Edward (Apr. 19, 1724-Apr. 16, 1785)
m. Oct. 19, 1747 Deborah Green
XXII, 79; XXIX, 174
Joseph (Sept. 21, 1756-1835) m. Apr.
1794 Lovisa Loveland XXX, 89, 90
Josiah (Jan. 31, 1727-Feb. 24, 1812)
m. Aug. 28, 1750 Hannah Bass
XIII, 95; XXIX, 59
Levi (Mar. 27, 1748-Apr. 17, 1819)
m. Oct. 26, 1775 (1) Thankful Warren XXIX, 174
Paul (Feb. 13, 1737-p. 1790) m. Mar.
6, 1760 Sarah Johnson XVIII, 149

RAY
Alexander (a. 1652-a. 1675) m. ....
Joane ...... MD XXX, 286
John (....-a. Apr. 1692) m. ....
.... MD XXXII, 160;
XXXIII, 128
John (1750-Sept. 14, 1812) m. Oct.
24, 1784 Frances ...... XXX, 286
Joseph (May 25, 1735-May 2, 1819) m.
.... Mary Sheckle XXXII, 160;
XXXIII, 128
Thomas (Dec. 23, 1720-Jan. 21, 1795)
m. Jan. 20, 1745 Sarah Edmondson
XXX, 286
William, III (1705-July 1778) m. ....
Annie ...... XXXII, 160; XXXIII,
128

RAYMENT, see RAYMOND

RAYMOND, includes RAYMENT, RAYMONT
Eliakim (Feb. 20, 1720-Dec. 29, 1801)
m. Nov. 27, 1740 Hannah Street
XXVI, 297, 298
Elisha, Sr. (Nov. 9, 1761-June 11,
1842) m. Apr. 25, 1781 Abigail
Inman XXXIV, 93, 124
Gershom (Jan. 18, 1725-....) m. Apr.
12, 1749 Abigail Taylor XXIV, 28
John (c. 1616-Jan. 18, 1703) m. ....
Rachel Scruggs MASS X, 37; XXXIV,

93, 124
John (c. 1635-c. 1695) m. Dec. 10,
1664 Mary Betts CONN XXVI, 297,
298
Jonathan (Sept. 17, 1734-1783) m.
Oct. 4, 1756 Susannah White X, 37
Lemuel (Aug. 5, 1759-May 18, 1829)
m. .... Hannah Underwood XXXIII,
289
Nathaniel (May 4, 1753-Feb. 1, 1849)
m. Aug. 3, 1772 Dolly Wood XXI,
50, 51
Richard (c. 1602-1692) m. .... Judith
...... MASS, CONN XVIII, 101;
XX, 114; XXI, 50, 51; XXIV, 28;
XXVI, 297, 298; XXXIII, 348
Samuel (1740-Mar. 19, 1821) m. c.
1765 Froena Ayers XXXIII, 348,
349
Simeon (1711-July 1795) m. ....
Hannah ...... XVIII, 101; XX, 114
William (c. 1637-....) m. .... Han-
nah Bishop NH, MASS XXXIII, 289

RAYMONT, see RAYMOND

RAYNES
Daniel (1747-Apr. 25, 1828) m. Apr.
17, 1783 Jane Gerrish XXXII, 219,
220
Francis (1610-1706) m. .... Eleanor
...... ME XXXII, 219

READ, see REED

READE, see REED

REDFIELD
Daniel (Feb. 27, 1728-Jan. 20, 1788)
m. Nov. 21, 1749 Margaret Crane
XIV, 60, 61
James (1646-c. 1723) m. May 1669
Elizabeth Howe MASS XXVI, 118
John (May 6, 1735-May 14, 1813) m.
June 8, 1758 Amanda Russell XXV,
136; XXVII, 187
Levi (Aug. 17, 1745-Sept. 15, 1838)
m. July 3, 1765 Sybil Wilcox VI,
39; XXII, 64; XXVI, 118, 119
Samuel (Sept. 18, 1762-1837) m. May
18, 1782 Nancy Fairchild XXV, 136
Seth (Jan. 17, 1757-....) m. ....
(1) Sarah Pierson XII, 102
William (1610-c. Apr. 1662) m. ....
Rebecca ...... MASS VI, 39; XII,
103; XIV, 60, 61; XXII, 64; XXV,
136; XXVII, 187

REED, includes READ, READE
Augustus (Nov. 30, 1761-p. 1789) m.
.... Rhoda Spaulding XX, 108

Bartholomew (bpt. May 14, 1727-1817)
m. Feb. 2, 1748 Mary Harris XVI,
68, 69; XXXI, 287
Daniel, Jr. (Dec. 9, 1752-Sept. 13,
1840) m. Nov. 17, 1773 (1) Sarah
Brown XXXI, 307; XXXIV, 247
David (1736-1828). m. c. 1760/1 Wait-
sill Raynsford X, 81, 92; XX,
108; XXII, 152
Ebenezer (Oct. 2, 1760-1845) m. p.
1781 Hannah Jones XXXII, 177, 178
Esdras (1595-July 27, 1680) m. ....
Elizabeth Watson MASS XXXIII,
149
George (1612-1670) m. .... Elizabeth
Martian VA XXII, 22
Israel (June 16, 1747-p. 1796) m.May
21, 1768 (1) Jemima Temple X,
300
John (1598-Sept. 1683) m. .... Sarah
...... MASS XXV, 35
John (1633-1730) m. .... (1) Mrs. Ann
Derby CONN XV, 113; XXIV, 30;
XXXII, 177
John (Nov. 11, 1751-Feb. 17, 1831)
m. Oct. 14, 1780 Hannah Simpson
XXV, 63
Joseph, Sr. (June 4, 1716-Nov. 1,
1795) m. May 30, 1737 Ruth Under-
wood XXXIII, 149
Josiah (1643-July 3, 1717) m. Nov.
1666 Grace Holloway CONN XXII,
152; XXXIV, 247
Josiah (1732-....) m. Dec. 20, 1752
Sybil Baldwin XV, 113; XXIV, 30
Nathaniel (Nov. 4, 1762-Aug. 21,
1830) m. Jan. 3, 1783 Sarah Parks
XXV, 35
Reuben (Nov. 2, 1730-May 26, 1803)
m. Nov. 1754 Tamison Meacham XIV,
17; XVI, 138
Samuel (Dec. 25, 1756-Apr. 22, 1826)
m. June 18, 1781.Betsy Smith XXX,
69, 70
Thomas (c. 1610-c. 1667) m. ....
.... MASS XXXI, 287
Thomas (Oct. 19, 1627-Sept. 13, 1701)
m. c. 1648 (1) Katherine ......
MASS XIV, 17; XVI, 138
Thomas (a. 1630-....) m. .... Mary
...... MASS XV, 63; XVI, 69
Thomas (c. 1736-June 7, 1776) m.
July 2, 1761 Rhoda Crosby XXIV, 33
William (c. 1587-Oct. 31, 1656) m.
.... Mabel Kendall MASS X, 300;
XXIV, 33
William (1605-....) m. 1635 Ivis
Deacon MASS XXV, 63; XXX, 69, 70
William (c. 1606-June 13, 1679) m.
Oct. 12, 1629 (1) Susanna Hayme
MASS X, 81, 92; XX, 109; XXXI, 307

William (1729-....) m. .... Mary
Tuttle XV, 63
William E. (1738-1815) m. .... Jean
...... XXII, 22

REEVES
Henry (June 27, 1749-Nov. 23, 1840)
m. Feb. 8, 1772 Hannah Doughty
Furness XXIX, 206
Walter (1650/57-p. 1698) m. Nov. 11,
1682 Ann Howell NJ XXIX, 206

REMBERT
Andre (....-p. Mar. 4, 1736) m. ....
Anne Bressan SC XXXII, 35
James (c. 1740-p. Sept. 7, 1810) m.
.... Mary ...... XXXII, 35, 36

REMICK
Christian (1631-1710) m. c. 1654
Hannah ...... ME XIV, 66, 67
Enock (Apr. 1, 1730-May 11, 1800)
m. 1753 Abigail Trefethen XIV,
66, 67

REMINGTON
John (1610-June 8, 1667) m. a. 1630
(1) Elizabeth ...... MASS XXIX,
105
Joshua, Sr. (Nov. 1759-Oct. 4, 1855)
m. .... Eunice ...... XXXIV, 184
Peleg (1734-1777) m. 1760 Waite
Rhodes XXIX, 105
Stephen (1695-Dec. 16, 1785) m. c.
1725 (1) Lydia Rhodes XXIX, 105
Thomas (....-....) m. Mar. 16, 1687
Remember Stowell MASS XXXIV, 185

REMSEN, see also VANDER BEECK
Abraham (Aug. 23, 1730-Oct. 12, 1807)
m. .... Mary Voorhees XIV, 38

RENALL, see REYNOLDS

RETYE, see RICHEY

REYNOLDS, includes RENALL
Benjamin (Apr. 19, 1756-Feb. 19,
1820) m. 1777 Elizabeth Reynolds
XXI, 44, 45; XXII, 66
Christopher (1611-1654) m. ....
Elizabeth ...... VA XXX, 135
George (1750-1813) m. June 12, 1779
Susannah Lansford XXX, 135
Grindall, Sr. (July 11, 1726-....)
m. Jan. 30, 1758 Sarah Searle
XXXI, 199
Grindall, Jr. (Aug. 1764-Nov. 29,
1843) m. 1789 Dorcas Landon XXXI,
199
James (....-1700) m. a. 1647 Deborah

REYNOLDS, cont.
...... *RI XXI, 44, 45; XXII, 66*
James (May 8, 1759-Mar. 2, 1833) m.
   Oct. 18, 1786 Abigail Knapp XXIV,
   57; XXIX, 51; XXX, 64, 217
John (c. 1612-p. Mar. 1651) m. ....
   Sarah ...... MASS, CONN XXIV, 57;
   XXX, 64, 217
John (....-1787) m. 1759 Rebecca
   Rundell XIX, 143
John (c. 1734-1827) m. c. 1769 Joanna
   Patterson XXXIV, 105, 106
Jonathan (c. 1635-Jan. 1673/4) m. c.
   1656 Rebecca Husted CONN XIX,
   143; XXIX, 51
Joseph (June 22, 1751-....) m. Sept.
   17, 1772 Jemima Perkins XVIII,
   122
Obediah (c. 1748-....) m. .... Ann
   ...... XXXII, 242, 243
Robert (1580/90-Apr. 27, 1659) m.
   a. 1622 Mary ...... MASS XVIII,
   122; XXXI, 199
Thomas (c. 1660-....) m. .... Mary
   ...... VA XXXII, 242
William (c. 1606-....) m. .... Mar-
   garet Exton PA XXXIV, 105, 106

RHODES
Zachariah (1603-Apr. 10, 1666) m.
   1646 Joanna Arnold MASS, RI
   VI, 49
Zachariah (Mar. 1, 1755-1834) m.
   Mar. 22, 1785 Elizabeth Rea VI,
   49

RICCAR, see RICKER

RICE, includes ROICE, ROYCE
Abner (Jan. 4, 1753-Feb. 1819) m.
   Jan. 19, 1775 Keziah Hall XX,
   135
Edmund (1594-May 3, 1663) m. a. 1615
   (1) Thomasine ...... MASS X, 78;
   XII, 41; XIII, 40, 117; XV, 25;
   XVII, 108; XXIII, 59; XXVI, 168;
   XXX, 74; XXXI, 174; XXXIII, 154,
   155
Elijah, Jr. (Sept. 11, 1749-Jan. 3,
   1827) m. Jan. 27, 1772 Relief
   Williams XXVI, 168
Gershom (1696-Sept. 24, 1781) m.
   .... Esther Haynes XXX, 73, 74
Hezekiah (Apr. 1732-Aug. 24, 1796)
   m. .... Mary Bullock XXXIV, 286
Jedediah (Apr. 22, 1755-1823) m.
   Nov. 30, 1783 Jemima Willard
   Hastings X, 78
Jehial (Aug. 23, 1758-1852) m. Mar.
   2, 1785 Pernal Sherman XVIII, 75
Joel (May 17, 1752-Dec. 16, 1834)

m. a. 1784 Lydia Farnsworth XXIV,
   7
Joel (Apr. 1762-June 25, 1833) m.
   1786 Mary Elizabeth Pryor Hickman
   XXXII, 275; XXXIII, 157
John (June 26, 1734-....) m. ....
   .... XXXIII, 154, 155
Jonas (June 30, 1731-1776) m. c.
   1750 Deborah Force XXXI, 174
Jonas (Aug. 5, 1732-Nov. 1, 1824)
   m. Dec. 3, 1751 Bathsheba Par-
   mentier XXIV, 7
Joseph (Apr. 7, 1760-Sept. 11, 1826)
   m. .... Mary Rice XII, 41
Moses (Sept. 24, 1716-Oct. 26, 1799)
   m. Jan. 6, 1740 Thankful Austin
   XVI, 134; XX, 135
Oliver (Nov. 7, 1726-Mar. 23, 1812)
   m. c. 1752 Lucy Rice XIII, 117
Robert (1594-a. Sept. 22, 1676) m.
   June 4, 1634 Mary Sims CONN XVI,
   134; XVIII, 75; XX, 135
Thomas (....-....) m. .... Marie
   ...... VA XXXII, 275; XXXIII,
   156, 157; XXXIV, 286
William (July 10, 1722-1804) m. ....
   .... XXIII, 59
William (Nov. 2, 1737-Dec. 5, 1819)
   m. July 2, 1772 Sarah Noyes XIII,
   40; XV, 25; XVII, 108

RICH
Aquila (Nov. 11, 1759-Apr. 8, 1813)
   m. Sept. 25, 1793 Hannah Thomas
   XXIV, 23
Jonathan (Nov. 1, 1737-....) m. Oct.
   17, 1760 Thankful Newcomb XXVI,
   35
Obadiah (July 15, 1707-p. 1776) m.
   Feb. 3, 1736 (2) Mary Crowell
   XXX, 114
Richard (1633-Oct. 1692) m. a. Feb.
   28, 1671 Sarah Roberts NH XXIV,
   23; XXVI, 35; XXX, 114

RICHARDS
Daniel (Sept. 8, 1750-Aug. 30, 1823)
   m. Feb. 7, 1775 Eunice Somerby
   XXVII, 211
Humphrey (....-p. 1666) m. ....
   Mehitable Ruggles MASS XXVII,
   211
Lewis (....-....) m. ....
   ...... PA XXXII, 289, 290
Lewis (1763-Jan. 3, 1846) m. May 6,
   1788 Lucy Hunton XXXII, 289, 290

RICHARDSON
Abijah (Aug. 30, 1752-May 1822) m.
   Nov. 24, 1772 Mercy Daniels XXX,
   91

Amos (p. 1618-Aug. 5, 1683) m. 1642
Mary Smith MASS, CONN XXXII, 97,
98; XXXIII, 142, 143
Bartholomew (June 19, 1735-Dec. 22,
1807) m. June 27, 1765 Abigail
Merriam XVIII, 133; XIX, 70
Caleb (1756-June 8, 1837) m. Oct. 5,
1784 Mrs. Martha (Holmes) Libby
VI, 84; IX, 29; X, 195
Ebenezer (Apr. 14, 1754-Mar. 18,
1827) m. Jan. 15, 1777 Sarah Par-
ker XIX, 152; XXIX, 24
Ezekiel (1602-Oct. 21, 1647) m. a.
Aug. 27, 1630 Susanna Richardson
MASS XVII, 53; XXXI, 250; XXXII,
207; XXXIII, 276, 277
Israel (Jan. 24, 1736-May 8, 1800)
m. 1759 Susanna Forbush V, 114;
VI, 6; X, 35
Jeremiah (....-July 2, 1826) m. ....
Ann Vansant XXVI, 30, 31
John (....-....) m. ....
...... MASS XXX, 91
John (May 26, 1748-1828) m. ....
(1) Christina Lane XII, 124
John Crowley (1754-1833) m. ....
Sarah Bainbridge Price I, 38
Joseph (Jan. 5, 1754-1796) m. 1778
Jerusha Reed XXXI, 163
Lawrence, I (c. 1606-1666) m. ....
Sarah ...... MD XXXI, 164, 239
Moses (Feb. 19, 1748-Dec. 19, 1834)
m. .... (1) Experience Fisher;
Oct. 4, 1770 (2) Miriam Merriam
XXXI, 250; XXXIII, 276
Nehemiah (June 28, 1759-1839) m.
.... (2) Kesiah ...... XXIX, 306
Richard (Sept. 23, 1751-Dec. 9, 1833)
m. .... Mehitable Smith XVII, 52,
53
Robert (1650-1682) m. .... Susanna
...... MD I, 38
Salmon Treat (bpt. May 28, 1731-1808)
m. Aug. 8, 1765 Hannah Wilkinson
XXXIII, 142, 143
Samuel (Apr. 3, 1610-Mar. 23, 1658)
m. Oct. 31, 1638 Joanna ......
MASS XVIII, 133; XIX, 70; XXVII,
165; XXIX, 306; XXXI, 163
Samuel (Dec. 1635-June 10, 1719) m.
.... Ellinor ...... PA XII, 52;
XXVI, 30, 31
Samuel (Feb. 22, 1749-July 15, 1836)
m. .... Lucy Parker V, 57
Sanford (1761-June '7, 1818) m. Mar.
1, 1780 Roxalana Burroughs XXXII,
97, 98
Thomas (July 3, 1608-Aug. 28, 1651)
m. .... (2) Mary ...... MASS
V, 114; VI, 6; X, 35, 224; XIX,
152; XX, 124; XXIX, 24

Thomas (c. 1645-a. Mar. 20, 1718/9)
m. 1668 Elizabeth ...... VA
XXVIII, 69, 70; XXXIII, 74
Thomas (June 5, 1718-....) m. 1739
Abigail Merrow XIX, 152
Vincent (1748-1777) m. Jan. 6, 1771
Martha Norris XXXI, 164, 239
Vinton (Sept. 20, 1744-Jan. 4, 1820)
m. (int.) Feb. 8, 1770 Hannah White
XXVII, 165
William (1620-Mar. 25, 1657) m. Aug.
23, 1654 Elizabeth Wiseman MASS
V, 57; VI, 84; IX, 29; X, 195
William (c. 1717-1783/8) m. a. 1741
Abigail ...... XXXII, 207
William (May 6, 1731-Dec. 30, 1814)
m. 1754 Esther Joslin X, 223; XX,
124
William (Jan. 1, 1760-c. 1826) m.
Jan. 1, 1802 Ann Sevills XXVIII,
69, 70; XXXIII, 74

RICHEY, includes RETYE
John (1655/60-1685) m. ....
...... PA XXV, 73
John (July 8, 1755-1837) m. ....
Mary Welch XXV, 73

RICHMOND
David (1748-Oct. 14, 1818) m. Dec.
1766 Nancy Davis XXXI, 263, 264
Edward (1632-Nov. 1696) m. .... (1)
Abigail Davis RI XXXIV, 328
Gideon (....-....) m. Dec. 11, 1760
Hannah Richmond XXI, 140, 141
John (1594-Mar. 20, 1664) m. c.
1626 .... MASS X, 111;
XVII, 34, 78; XXI, 140, 141; XXV,
189, 190; XXX, 213; XXXI, 264
Nathaniel, Sr. (Oct. 14, 1733-1813)
m. Oct. 14, 1756 (1) Mary Dighton
XVII, 34, 78, 79; XXV, 189, 190
Perez (Oct. 13, 1728-Nov. 23, 1800/1)
m. Feb. 3, 1754 Mercy Church
XXXIV, 328
Stephen (Jan. 7, 1754-July 11, 1831
m. .... (1) Rebecca Sisson X, 111
Zebulon (1757/8-Feb. 1832) m. Sept.
20, 1779 Susanna Beswick XXV,
189, 190; XXX, 213

RICKER, includes RICCAR
George (....-June 4, 1706) m. ....
Eleanor Evans NH XXIX, 273
Stephen (Mar. 17, 1757-Feb. 28, 1837)
m. Nov. 12, 1791 (2) Alice Goodwin
XXIX, 273

RIDDICK
James (....-1722) m. 1689 Mrs. ......
Shepherd VA XXX, 147, 148

RIDDICK, cont.
  Lemuel (Aug. 23, 1711-Dec. 2, 1775)
    m. Dec. 17, 1729 Ann Sumner XXX,
    147, 148
  Micajah (1744-Nov. 11, 1804) m. 1765
    Ruth Parker XXX, 147, 148

RIDGELY
  Charles G. (Jan. 26, 1738-Nov. 25,
    1785) m. June 2, 1774 (2) Anne
    Moore XXVII, 99
  Greenbury (July 4, 1754-Mar. 17,
    1843) m. May 1, 1774 Rachel Ryan
    XXIX, 329; XXX, 28
  Henry (....-Apr. 2, 1710) m. ....
    Sarah Warner MD XXVII, 99
  Westall, Jr. (c. 1730-1798) m. c.
    1763 Sarah ...... XXVI, 267, 268
  William, Sr. (1645-1716) m. ....
    Elizabeth ...... MD XXVI, 267,
    268; XXIX, 330; XXX, 28
  William (1703-1780) m. Apr. 14, 1726
    Mary Orrick XXIX, 330; XXX, 28

RIDGWAY
  John (Aug. 14, 1755-Apr. 12, 1845)
    m. 1774 Elizabeth Wright XXV,
    236
  Richard (c. 1650-Sept. 22, 1722/3)
    m. c. 1673 (1) Elizabeth Chamber-
    lain NJ XXV, 236

RIGGS
  Aaron, III (Mar. 18, 1749/50-Sept.
    25, 1827) m. June 22, 1775 Martha
    Adams XXXIV, 288
  Edward, I (1590-a. Sept. 2, 1670) m.
    .... (1) Elizabeth Rooke; ....
    (2) Elizabeth ..... MASS VI, 115
    XVIII, 86; XXIII, 7; XXXII, 134;
    XXXIII, 262, 263
  Edward, Jr. (c. 1614-1668) m. Apr.
    5, 1635 Elizabeth Roosa CONN, NJ
    VI, 115; XVIII, 86
  John (Apr. 10, 1742-June 18, 1814)
    m. Dec. 13, 1766 Elizabeth Hawkins
    VI, 115
  John (c. 1763-a. May 30, 1811) m.
    Feb. 5, 1780 Rachel Huskey XXXII,
    134; XXXIII, 262, 263
  Joseph (Feb. 13, 1709-Mar. 31, 1792)
    m. Feb. 20, 1740 Mabel Johnson
    XXIII, 7
  Joseph, Jr. (July 20, 1746-May 15,
    1822) m. Feb. 26, 1783 Elizabeth
    Johnson XVIII, 85; XXIII,
    7
  Thomas, Sr. (1631-Feb. 26,
    1721/2) m. June 7, 1658 (1)
    Mary Millet MASS XXXIV,
    288

RING
  Benjamin (....-Aug. 10, 1804) m. Dec.
    6, 1758 Rachel James XXVI, 146
  Issacher (Dec. 25, 1745-....) m. July
    14, 1768 Esther Barnard XXI, 32,
    33
  Nathaniel (....-1714) m. .... Eliza-
    beth ...... PA XXVI, 146
  Robert (1614-1690) m. .... Elizabeth
    ...... MASS XXI, 32, 33

RINGO
  Albertus (Feb. 25, 1763-Nov. 7,
    1855) m. Feb. 22, 1790 Hannah Rect-
    or XXV, 76
  Philip Janszen (c. 1620-1662) m.
    Aug. 11, 1647 Geertje Cornelis NY
    XXV, 76

RISLEY
  Jeremiah (Dec. 14, 1734-June 24,
    1796) m. May 4, 1758 Margaret
    Doughty X, 227
  Richard (a. 1615-Oct. 16, 1648) m.
    1640 Mary ...... CONN X, 227;
    XVI, 83, 84; XXV, 65
  Thomas (1744-1799) m. Jan. 5, 1768
    Mary Leeds XVI, 83, 84; XXV, 65

ROBBINS, includes ROBINS
  Asa (May 5, 1759-Nov. 30, 1840) m.
    Sept. 11, 1788 Olive Clark XIX,
    17
  Frederick (Sept. 12, 1756-Nov. 1,
    1821) m. Apr. 12, 1781 Mehitable
    Wolcott XXV, 103
  John (....-June 27, 1660) m. 1640
    Mary Welles CONN V, 71; XII, 118;
    XXV, 103
  John Purnell (1742-1832) m. Feb.
    17, 1770 Anna Spence XXX, 254;
    XXXI, 40, 60, 92
  Joshua (Feb. 9, 1740-1792) m. ....
    Elizabeth Hubbard V, 71; XII, 118
  Obedience (Apr. 16, 1600-1662) m.
    1634 Grace O'Neill Waters VA XXX,
    254; XXXI, 40, 60, 92
  Richard (1610-p. 1683) m. 1639
    Rebecca ...... MASS XX, 7; XXI,
    56
  Thomas (Aug. 15, 1703-June 30, 1791)
    m. May 2, 1723 Ruth Johnson XX,
    7; XXI, 56
  William (....-Aug. 18, 1725) m. Jan.
    2, 1680 Priscilla Gowing MASS
    XIX, 17

ROBERTS
  Algeron (Jan. 24, 1751-Dec. 21, 1815)
    m. Jan. 18, 1781 Tacy Warner XXIV,
    82

John (1648-June 6, 1724) m. Jan. 20,
1684 Gainor Roberts PA XXIV, 82
John (c. 1660-July 6, 1721) m. Dec.
27, 1683 Sarah Blake CONN XXVI,
215, 216, 217; XXIX, 109
John (Aug. 14, 1744-June 19, 1837)
m. Dec. 28, 1769 Sarah Merrill
XXVI, 215, 216, 217; XXIX, 109
Samuel (....-....) m. a. 1681 Sarah
Hinman CONN XXIX, 118
Samuel (Mar. 9, 1719/20-Apr. 17,
1792) m. Dec. 20, 1741 Elizabeth
...... XXIX, 118

ROBERTSON
John (....-1705) m. .... Jennelle
Coulter NJ XXXI, 321
John (Oct. 29, 1749-Mar. 2, 1823)
m. 1776 Mary Crane XXXI, 321

ROBESON, see ROBINSON

ROBIE, includes ROBY
Henry (Feb. 12, 1618-Apr. 22, 1688)
m. c. 1643 Ruth Moore MASS, NH
XXXII, 115; XXXIII, 113, 114
Walter (May 2, 1741-June 28, 1818)
m. Dec. 23, 1763 Susan Hall XXXII,
114, 115; XXXIII, 113, 114

ROBINS, see ROBBINS

ROBINSON, includes ROBESON
Andrew, Jr. (1654-Feb. 19, 1719/20)
m. c. 1685 Mary Spencer NJ
XXXII, 113, 133, 134
Andrew (1763-Sept. 5, 1845) m. Aug.
22, 1791 Rosamond Dennis XXXII,
113
Claghorn (Apr. 4, 1754-1806) m. Jan.
29, 1777 Betty Ransom XXXIV, 323
Clifford (Jan. 8, 1756-July 11, 1813)
m. Oct. 21, 1778 Lucy Morgan XIX,
115
Ebenezer (Feb. 14, 1765-Oct. 31,
1857) m. Nov. 18, 1792 Hannah Ackley XXXII, 38
George (....-Nov. 9, 1699) m. Apr.
18, 1651 Joanna Ingraham MASS
XXVII, 109
George (July 23, 1726-Aug. 19, 1812)
m. Nov. 24, 1748 Abigail Everett
XXVII, 109
Ichabod (Dec. 12, 1720-Jan. 20, 1809)
m. Jan. 16, 1752 Lydia Brown
XIX, 13
Isaac (1610-1704) m. June 27, 1636
(1) Margaret Hanford; 1650 (2)
Mary Faunce MASS XIX, 115; XXX,
89, 90; XXXIII, 142; XXXIV,
324

Isaac (1730-1814) m. Jan. 16, 1760
Mary Robinson XXX, 89, 90
James (Oct. 5, 1743-1819) m. 1769
Ann Kirkwood XXI, 63, 64
John (....-1688) m. .... Elizabeth
Potter VA XXI, 63, 64
Reuben (Jan. 15, 1725-a. Sept. 5,
1812) m. Jan. 12, 1748/9 Esther
Palmer XIX, 115
Samuel, Sr. (July 26, 1726-June 11,
1792) m. Jan. 2, 1748/9 Mary Kim-
ball XXXIII, 143; XXXIV, 323
Samuel (Apr. 15, 1738-May 3, 1813)
m. Apr. 6, 1767 (2) Esther Safford
XI, 115; XXIX, 118
Samuel (June 7, 1752-Mar. 2, 1815)
m. 1777/8 Priscilla Metcalf X,
46; XVIII, 80
Thomas, Sr. (1733/4-p. 1790) m.
1755/60 Mary ...... XXXII, 133,
134
William (....-July 6, 1668) m. ....
(1) Margaret ...... MASS X, 46;
XVIII, 80; XIX, 13
William (1640-Mar. 1693) m. 1667
Elizabeth Cutter MASS XI, 115;
XXIX, 358, 359; XXXII, 38
William (Aug. 15, 1754-Aug. 15, 1825)
m. Aug. 10, 1790 Elizabeth Norton
XIX, 13

ROBY, see ROBIE

ROCKWELL
David, Jr. (Jan. 31, 1734-July 6,
1816) m. Nov. 2, 1760 Mary Ather-
ton XXVII, 224, 225; XXXIV, 116
Enos (Oct. 16, 1763-Nov. 13, 1832)
m. .... XXVII, 224
Henry (Dec. 4, 1751-....) m. Dec.
14, 1773 Desire Cone XXXII, 242
Jabez, Jr. (July 1, 1740-1837) m.
June 30, 1759 Elizabeth Sperry
XXXIII, 220
John, Sr. (....-1676) m. .... Eliza-
beth Weed CONN XIX, 141; XXV,
261; XXVII, 224; XXXIII, 220
John, Jr. (....-a. Mar. 10, 1673/4)
m. .... CONN XXXIV,
117
John, V (May 12, 1734-Sept. 6, 1825)
m. Apr. 16, 1754 (1) Hanna Scott
XXV, 261
John (Sept. 7, 1743-Sept. 10, 1823)
m. .... Abigail Buckingham VII,
30
John, VI (Apr. 7, 1755-Sept. 1825)
m. July 22, 1777 Rebecca Ives XIX,
141; XXV, 261
Joseph (1715-July 6, 1776) m. c. 1740
Anna Dodd VII, 30

ROCKWELL, cont.
Joshua (Oct. 18, 1742-Mar. 9, 1825)
m. Jan. 1, 1772 Rhoda Doud XVIII,
47, 48
Nathaniel (Nov. 3, 1746-Aug. 22,
1822) m. .... (2) Sarah Bullen
XXXIV, 187
William (Feb. 6, 1591-May 15, 1640)
m. Apr. 14, 1624 Susannah Capen
MASS VII, 30; XVIII, 48; XXXII,
242; XXXIV, 187

ROCKWOOD
Elisha (Oct. 28, 1750-Dec. 1, 1831)
m. June 3, 1778 Eunice Clark XV,
87
Richard (....-1660) m. .... Agnes
Bicknell MASS XV, 87

ROE, see ROWE

ROGERS
Azael (July 27, 1765-Aug. 17, 1841)
m. Jan. 31, 1790 Sarah Baker
XVII, 40
Daniel (Jan. 22, 1709-Dec. 1785) m.
a. 1738 Sarah ...... XIII, 111
George (Feb. 14, 1755-Feb. 19, 1815)
m. June 15, 1779 Mrs. Mary (Tinker)
Wheeler X, 34
Giles (1643-1730) m. a. 1673 ......
Iverson VA XXXII, 206
James (c. 1615-1687) m. c. 1640
Elizabeth Rowland CONN X, 21,
34; XVII, 40; XIX, 12
James (Feb. 8, 1739/40-Sept. 28,
1820) m. c. 1762 Zilpha Hyde XIX,
12
John (....-Dec. 22, 1674) m. ....
.... MASS XXX, 243
John (Mar. 13, 1654-....) m. Nov. 7,
1679 Dinah Chiske MASS XIII, 111
Jonathan (Aug. 1750-....) m. Dec. 17,
1776 Hannah Mayo XXIX, 396
Nathaniel (1598-July 2, 1655) m. ....
Margaret Crane MASS XVI, 89;
XXVII, 131; XXXI, 122
Nathaniel (1725-1801) m. Sept. 13,
1747 (1) Theoda Miner X, 21
Nathaniel (Feb. 16, 1728/9-p. 1780)
m. Mar. 19, 1753 Abiah Ingalls
XXX, 243
Nathaniel (Nov. 11, 1754-1845) m.
Dec. 9, 1779 Abigail Lay X, 21
Nathaniel (July 25, 1755-Dec. 22,
1804) m. Aug. 14, 1783 (1) Frances
Cobbs XVI, 89; XXVII, 131; XXXI,
122
Peter (a. 1724-1785) m. c. 1760
Elizabeth Rogers XXXII, 206
Simeon (Feb. 1, 1762-June 18, 1848)

m. .... Anna ...... XXX, 243
Thomas (c. 1586/7-1621) m. ....
......`...... MASS XXIX, 396;
XXX, 164
Thomas (1725-June 23, 1804) m. Oct.
12, 1752 (2) Rebecca Hobart X,
243
William (c. 1600-1658) m. .... Anne
...... NY X, 243
William (Feb. 8, 1756-Apr. 28, 1810)
m. July 7, 1796 (2) Mary Conner
XXX, 164

ROLFE
Benjamin, Sr. (May 31, 1752-1803)
m. 1783 Mary Swett XVIII, 17;
XXIX, 207, 208; XXXI, 100
Henry (Sept. 5, 1585-Mar. 1, 1642)
m. May 28, 1621 Honor Rolfe MASS
XVIII, 17; XXIX, 207, 208; XXXI,
100

ROLINGS, see RAWLINGS

ROLLINS, see RAWLINGS

ROMEYN
Claes Jansen (....-a. Nov. 16, 1730)
m. May 2, 1680 Styntje Albertse
Terhune NY XXIV, 172
Nicholas (bpt. Nov. 13, 1728-a. 1799)
m. June 9, 1753 Margaret Minthorne
XXIV, 172

ROOD, includes RUDE
Daniel (a. 1748-a. Nov. 18, 1805)
m. .... Elizabeth Grover XXXIII,
150
Thomas (....-Oct. 18, 1672) m. ....
Sarah ...... CONN XXIX, 254;
XXXIII, 150
Thomas Park (1732-Oct. 10, 1795) m.
.... Dinah Benjamin XXIX, 254

ROOSA
Albert Heymans (....-Feb. 27, 1679)
m. .... Wyntje Allard NY XXX,
142
Jacob (Oct. 14, 1739-1807) m. ....
Jannetje Van Wagenen XXX, 142

ROOSEVELT, see ROSEVELT

ROOT, includes ROOTE, ROOTES, ROOTS
Aaron (Dec. 20, 1720-Aug. 31, 1809)
m. Sept. 8, 1748 Rhoda Ring
XXXII, 184
Benajah (May 5, 1725-Mar. 15, 1787)
m. Sept. 26, 1757 Elizabeth Guern-
sey XVIII, 99
Daniel (Sept. 27, 1764-Oct. 13, 1834)

m. .... Rhoda Coye XII, 71
Ebenezer (Dec. 1, 1760-Feb. 12, 1842)
m. Nov. 21, 1802 Cynthia Whipple
XXX, 134
Eli (Feb. 27, 1731-1804) m. .... (2)
Experience Kellog XIII, 118
Isaac (June 2, 1756-Sept. 3, 1778)
m. a. 1782 Susanna ...... XXVI,
134
Jesse (Dec. 28, 1736-Mar. 29, 1822)
m. May 18, 1758 Mary Banks XXIX,
40; XXXII, 238
John, Sr. (Feb. 26, 1608-1684) m.
1640 Mary Kilbourne CONN XII,
71; XIII, 119; XXX, 134; XXXII,
184
Jonah (Mar. 3, 1744-a. Jan. 13, 1832)
m. .... Faith Hills XXIV, 119
Josiah (....-June 1683) m. .... Sus-
anna ...... MASS XVIII, 100;
XXVI, 134
Thomas (Jan. 16, 1605-July 17, 1694)
m. a. 1637 (1) Ann Russell; ....
(2) Elizabeth ...... CONN, MASS
XXIV, 119; XXIX, 40; XXXII, 238
Timothy (Apr. 9, 1719-June 21, 1794)
m. .... Jemima Wood XII, 71

ROOTE, see ROOT

ROOTES, see ROOT

ROOTS, see ROOT

ROPER
Daniel (Oct. 2, 1730-Feb. 27, 1821)
m. Mar. 18, 1756 Sarah Greenwood
XXXI, 59
John (1588-p. 1664) m. ....
...... MASS XXXI, 59
William (1606-1670) m. 1643 Catherine
...... VA XXVIII, 65, 66
William, III (Sept. 24, 1736-1833)
m. 1779 Elizabeth Williams XXVIII,
65, 66

ROSE
Daniel (Jan. 13, 1716-June 20, 1790)
m. June 25, 1747 Achsah Ball XXXII,
121
Phineas L. (Feb. 29, 1760-p. 1803)
m. c. 1800 ...... Webb XXXIV, 90
Robert (1594-Apr. 4, 1665) m. c.
1618 (1) Margery ...... CONN
XVII, 57, 58; XXXII, 121; XXXIV,
90
Seth (July 21, 1762-....) m. Nov.
29, 1789 Sarah Bates XXXII, 120,
121
Sharon (Jan. 19, 1731-Apr. 4, 1821)
m. Mar. 1, 1758 Mercy Fowler

XVII, 57, 58

ROSENKRANS
Herman Hendrick (....-1697) m. Mar.
3, 1657 Magdelena (Dircks)
Capes NY XIV, 44; XVI, 51
John (July 6, 1724-June 15, 1786) m.
.... Margaret DeWitt XIV, 44; XVI,
51

ROSEVELT, includes ROOSEVELT, VAN
ROSENVELT
Claes Martenszen (....-....) m. ....
Jannetje Samuels-Thomas NY XXV,
49, 50
Nicholas (Feb. 16, 1715-....) m.
Nov. 23, 1754 Elizabeth Thurman
XXV, 49, 50

ROSS
George (1635-1702) m. .... Constance
Little CONN,NY XX, 25
John (Sept. 12, 1741-....) m. Apr.
7, 1773 Lois Taylor XVII, 41
Matthias (1743-1830) m. c. 1763 Mary
Halsey XX, 25
William (....-1712) m. .... Hannah
...... RI XVII, 41

ROSSITER
Edward (....-1630) m. ....
...... MASS XXV, 190, 191
Timothy (May 21, 1754-Feb. 26, 1835)
m. May 14, 1783 (1) May (Mary) Rug-
gles XXV, 190, 191

ROUNDS
Joseph, II (Mar. 7, 1753-Jan. 15,
1838) m. July 4, 1778 Susanna Mosher XXXIII, 258
Mark (....-c. 1729) m. (int.) Nov.
11, 1696 Sarah Larreford MASS, ME
XXXIII, 257, 258

ROUNDY
John (Oct. 28, 1748-Apr. 23, 1805)
m. .... Ruth Chickley XXXI, 216
Robert (1656-Nov. 16, 1715) m. July
13, 1678 Deborah Plumb MASS XXXI,
216

ROWE, includes ROE
Benjamin (Sept. 28, 1759-July 25,
1825) m. June 30, 1782 Mary Ware
XXIX, 32
Daniel (May 19, 1759-a. 1813) m.
May 25, 1780 Charlotte Griffin
XXXI, 309, 310
David (....-a. July 12, 1707) m.
.... Mary ...... NY XXIX,
32

ROWE, cont.
Hugh (c. 1618-Aug. 5, 1689) m. ....
  Abigail ...... MASS XXXI, 310
James (Apr. 9, 1744-Oct. 31, 1815)
  m. Oct. 19, 1770 (1) Elizabeth
  Eltinge XV, 22; XXII, 6
John (1628-1711) m. c. 1655 ......
  ...... NY XV, 22; XXII, 6

ROWELL
Daniel (1765-1847) m. 1788 Nancy
  Neal XXV, 279
Thomas (....-July 1662) m. .... (1)
  .... MASS XXV, 279
William (Sept. 11, 1740-Sept. 27,
  1816) m. May 5, 1763 Mary Brown
  XXV, 279

ROWLAND
David Sherman (Aug. 4, 1719-Jan. 13,
  1794) m. Feb. 20, 1754 Mary Spauld-
  ing XIV, 78
Henry (....-1691) m. .... Rebecca
  ...... CONN XIV, 78
John (1745-Mar. 18, 1858) m. ....
  Ann Mary Bainum XXI, 83, 84
Samuel (....-c. Dec. 7, 1727) m. ....
  .... PA, DE XXI, 83, 84

ROWLEY
John, Sr. (Apr. 4, 1714-May 28,
  1776) m. Jan. 4, 1743 Mary Filley
  XXIX, 94; XXXII, 188
Roger (Aug. 24, 1750-Feb. 11, 1822)
  m. May 31, 1778 (1) Anna Bunce
  XXIX, 94; XXXII, 188
Thomas (....-Aug. 4, 1708) m. May 5,
  1669 Mary Denslow CONN XXIX, 94;
  XXXII, 188

RUDD
Jonathan (....-c. 1668) m. c. 1646/7
  .... CONN XXXIV, 315
Joseph, Jr. (Mar. 26, 1740-May 25,
  1818) m. Sept. 28, 1768 Sarah
  Story XXXIV, 315

RUDE, see ROOD

RUFFIN
James (c. 1752-Sept. 11, 1802) m.
  .... Mary Roane XXXII, 130
William (....-June 1677) m. ....
  .... VA XXXII, 130

RUGG
John (a. 1634-Dec. 1696) m. May 4,
  1660 (2) Hannah Prescott MASS
  XIV, 79, 80; XXXII, 246
Joseph (Oct. 28, 1733-Dec. 27, 1825)
  m. .... Elizabeth Meacham

XIV, 79, 80
Levi, Sr. (Dec. 3, 1752-Feb. 22,
  1824) m. May 11, 1775 Relief Whitcomb XXXII, 246

RUGGLES
Edward (Aug. 20, 1723-May 21, 1778)
  m. Jan. 29, 1747 Lucy Spooner XXX,
  102, 103
John (c. 1590/1-Oct. 6, 1663) m. ....
  (1) Barbara ...... MASS XIV, 58
Samuel (1751-1795) m. June 1, 1779
  Huldah Wakelee XIV, 58
Thomas (....-Sept. 15, 1658) m. Nov.
  1, 1620 Mary Curtis MASS XXX,
  103
Timothy (Apr. 22, 1748-July 1831) m.
  .... Rachael Ward XXX, 102, 103

RUNDLET, see RANLET

RUSH
Benjamin, Jr. (Feb. 3, 1715/7-May 23,
  1801) m. Apr. 1, 1744 Alice Grigs-
  by XXX, 188, 189
William, I (....-1708) m. 1650 Ann
  Gray VA XXX, 188, 189
William (Feb. 1, 1755-Jan. 25, 1827)
  m. Feb. 9, 1774 Abigail Terrell
  XXX, 188, 189

RUSS
John, I (1611/2-Mar. 4, 1691/2) m.
  .... Margaret ...... MASS XXIX,
  140; XXXIII, 328, 329
Jonathan (May 6, 1731-1790) m. Nov.
  16, 1758 Lucy Kendall XXXIII,
  328, 329
Sempronious (July 6, 1767-Oct. 9,
  1816) m. Sept. 22, 1792 Amelia
  Potter XXIX, 140

RUSSELL
George (c. 1595-....) m. ....
  ...... MASS XXIX, 169
Jason (Jan. 25, 1716/7-Apr. 19, 1775)
  m. Jan. 28, 1739/40 Elizabeth Win-
  ship XXXI, 228
Jason (Mar. 7, 1741/2-Sept. 26, 1825)
  m. Oct. 28, 1762 Elizabeth Locke
  XXXI, 228
John (1608-Feb. 13, 1695) m. ....
  Dorothy ...... MASS XIV, 82;
  XXXIII, 343
John (Jan. 25, 1749-Nov. 3, 1826) m.
  May 28, 1778 Lovice Cooley XXII,
  84
Joshua (Feb. 20, 1710-1788) m. Mar.
  9, 1732 Lydia Spooner XXXIII, 343
Levi (Nov. 12, 1751-1833) m. c. 1772
  Hannah Simmons XXIX, 169

Nathaniel (Dec. 27, 1733-Jan. 1, 1812) m. Mar. 26, 1770 (2) Anna (Worcester) Thayer XV, 98
Nathaniel (May 5, 1741-Dec. 10, 1810) m. Dec. 25, 1766 Elizabeth Willard XXIX, 314; XXX, 237, 238
Riverus (Mar. 30, 1756-Mar. 14, 1834) m. Apr. 1776 Charity Hotchkiss XIV, 82
Robert (1630-Dec. 13, 1710) m. July 6, 1659 Mary Marshall MASS XXII, 84
William (....-Feb. 14, 1662) m. .... Martha ...... MASS XV, 99; XIX, 23; XXIV, 72; XXXI, 228; XXXIII, 160, 161
William (bpt. Oct. 11, 1612-Jan. 2, 1664/5) m. 1644 Sarah Davis CONN XXIX, 314; XXX, 237, 238
William (Mar. 4, 1737/8-Nov. 15, 1815) m. Nov. 16, 1758 Lucy Goldsmith XIX, 23; XXXIII, 160, 161
William (Dec. 23, 1760-Oct. 14, 1838) m. Aug. 30, 1785 Kezia Pierce XXIV, 71; XXXIII, 160, 161

RUST
Aloney (Feb. 19, 1766-June 29, 1857) m. 1790 Esther Doud XI, 93
George (1760-1850) m. Oct. 28, 1786 Elizabeth (Rust) Dunbar XXXIV, 207
Gershom (Mar. 1738-Oct. 8, 1823) m. .... Mary Cooley IX, 8
Henry (....-1684/5) m. .... Hannah ...... MASS IX, 8; XI, 82, 83, 93
Nathaniel Wilson (Apr. 25, 1751-Mar. 25, 1828) m. Apr. 22, 1781 Rachel Babcock XI, 82, 83
William (c. 1634-a. Nov. 22, 1699) m. a. May 17, 1662 Anne Metcalfe VA XXXIV, 207

RUTTY
Edward (....-May 1, 1714) m. May 6, 1678 Rebecca Stevens CONN XVI, 19
Ezra, Sr. (Sept. 14, 1741-1812) m. .... Mary Simons XVI, 19

RYDER
John (1732-1812) m. .... Sarah Sprague XI, 103, 104; XIII, 10
Reuben (Dec. 17, 1754-1810) m. July 23, 1778 Keziah Harding XXXII, 141
Samuel (1601-Dec. 2, 1679) m. .... Ann ...... MASS XXXII, 141
Thomas (a. 1614-Apr. 12, 1699) m. .... Elizabeth Lane MASS, NY XI, 104, 105; XIII, 10

SACKETT
Daniel (Mar. 6, 1734-1824) m. 1755 (1) ....; Sept. 22, 1768 (2) Mahitable Caldwell Dewey XXVI, 302, 303
John (c. 1628-Sept. 3, 1684) m. May 20, 1652 Agnes Tinkham CONN XXX, 269
John (Aug. 18, 1747-July 26, 1805) m. Oct. 26, 1769 Prudence Atherton XXX, 269
Samuel (Apr. 5, 1754-Feb. 13, 1833) m. Feb. 10, 1777 Sarah Manning XIII, 35
Simon (1602-p. Aug. 29, 1635) m. a. 1630 Isabel ...... MASS XIII, 35; XXVI, 303

SAFFORD
Benjamin (Dec. 1, 1734-Nov. 28, 1827) m. Feb. 1763 (3) Susan Malone XVIII, 30
Gideon (Nov. 4, 1754-Mar. 1, 1838) m. Nov. 10, 1774 Lucy Freeman XVII, 123
Jesse (Feb. 9, 1755-Aug. 2, 1834) m. Apr. 19, 1783 Abigail Damon XI, 95, 96
Joseph (bpt. Oct. 25, 1730-Jan. 19, 1798) m. Oct. 26, 1753 Martha Powers XI, 95, 96
Thomas (....-Feb. 20, 1666) m. .... Elizabeth ...... MASS XI, 95, 96; XVII, 123; XXVIII, 30

SAGE
Allen (Feb. 1, 1730-p. 1790) m. May 3, 1750 Abigail Willard XXIV, 155; XXXI, 56, 297, 298
David (1639-Mar. 31, 1703) m. Feb. 1664 (1) Elizabeth Kirby CONN XXIV, 155; XXXI, 56, 297
Selah (1752-p. Jan. 13, 1807) m. c. 1779 Mary ...... XXXI, 297, 298

ST. JOHN, includes SENSION, SENTION
John (Apr. 2, 1737-Apr. 16, 1816) m. 1761/2 Martha Northrup XI, 145
Matthias (....-1669) m. .... CONN XI, 145; XXI, 97, 98; XXXII, 119, 120
Matthias (1734-Mar. 20, 1819) m. .... (1) Naomi Weed XXI, 97, 98
Samuel (June 15, 1753-Oct. 6, 1785) m. .... Lydia (Potter) McPherson XXXII, 119, 120

SALISBURY
Jonathan (Oct. 3, 1725-Mar. 27, 1817) m. May 11, 1758 Mary Child VI, 113

SALISBURY, cont.
William, Sr. (....-June 24, 1675) m.
.... Susannah ...... MASS VI,
13

SALTONSBALL
Gurdon (Dec. 22, 1708-Sept. 19, 1785)
m. .... Rebecca Winthrop IX, 8
Richard (1586-....) m. .... Grace
Kaye MASS IX, 8

SAMBORNE, see SANBORN

SAMMIS
Alexander (Dec. 18, 1743-July 10,
1809) m. Feb. 5, 1782 Amy Gould
XXX, 30
John (c. 1648-c. Jan. 3, 1693/4) m.
1672 Abigail Corey MASS, NY XXX,
30
Jonathan (1715-May 5, 1784) m. Feb.
16, 1740 Abigail Ketcham XXIX,
259
Jonathan, Jr. (Apr. 8, 1748-Apr. 1,
1794) m. July 2, 1775 Rebeccah
Ketcham XXIX, 258
Richard (....-Oct. 23, 1650) m. ....
Esther Horsford CONN XXIX, 259

SAMS
John (c. 1630-Apr. 1727) m. ....
.... VA XXV, 186
John (1767-1790) m. 1785 Mary Bledsoe
XXV, 186

SAMSON
Benjamin (Mar. 14, 1756-Mar. 8,
1846) m. .... Anna Munro XXXIII,
352
John (1627-Jan. 27, 1711/2) m. ....
(1) .... MASS XXXIII,
352

SANBORN, includes SAMBORNE
Abraham (Feb. 28, 1735-Nov. 26, 1808)
m. July 1, 1756 Mary Choate XXXIII,
71
Abraham (Dec. 24, 1744-Oct. 5, 1820)
m. Nov. 10, 1768 Deborah Wilson
XXX, 70
Benjamin (Aug. 1, 1738-Sept. 19,
1821) m. .... Jane Mason XXX, 87
Daniel (Oct. 8, 1708-Sept. 22, 1782)
m. Sept. 2, 1731 Abigail Prescott
XXX, 70
Daniel, Jr. (June 4, 1734-Jan. 19,
1803) m. Dec. 26, 1759 Elizabeth
Sanborn XXXIV, 143
Jeremiah, Jr. (Nov. 5, 1757-Oct. 6,
1839) m. Jan. 8, 1778 Lydia Tilton
XVIII, 45

John (1620-Oct. 20, 1692) m. ....
Mary Tuck NH XI, 16; XVIII, 45;
XXX, 87; XXXII, 43, 44; XXXIII, 71
Simon (Sept. 28, 1736-July 11, 1808)
m. Dec. 10, 1760 Mary Cram XXVI,
131
Theophilus (Sept. 24, 1753-Mar. 4,
1839) m. 1799 Mary Sleeper XI, 16
Timothy (June 9, 1733-June 1813) m.
July 6, 1766 Elizabeth Leach
XXXII, 43
William (c. 1622-Nov. 18, 1692) m.
.... Mary Moulton NH XXVI, 131;
XXX, 70; XXXIV, 143

SANDERS, see SAUNDERS

SANFORD
Caleb (Aug. 23, 1761-June 9, 1822)
m. Feb. 4, 1783 Lucinda Pike
XXXIII, 63
Daniel (Jan. 6, 1729-Aug. 8, 1777)
m. Jan. 31, 1753 Thankful Toles
XXX, 108; XXXI, 31
David (Dec. 11, 1737-Apr. 7, 1810)
m. Aug. 4, 1757 Bathsheba Inger-
soll XXIII, 32, 33
Elihu (May 6, 1731-May 28, 1808) m.
June 28, 1758 Hannah Sanford XXIV,
93
James (Nov. 13, 1758-Apr. 14, 1842)
m. 1780 Sarah Beach IV, 148; XIII,
120; XX, 74; XXVI, 117, 118
Jonah (Aug. 1, 1735-Jan. 21, 1817)
m. Dec. 7, 1757 Rhoda Woodruff
XIX, 128; XXV, 260; XXVII, 68;
XXXI, 157
Jonah (July 17, 1749-Nov. 15, 1824)
m. Oct. 6, 1773 Mary Dunbar XXXI,
63
Joseph (June 20, 1736-Nov. 25,
1776) m. Nov. 2, 1762 Hepsibah
Griffith XIX, 138
Lemuel (Apr. 18, 1740-Mar. 12, 1803)
m. Sept. 20, 1768 Mary Russell
XI, 124
Philo (Sept. 7, 1761-Sept. 8, 1835)
m. Mar. 18, 1784 Lydia Whiting
XXIII, 32, 33
Robert (Nov. 11, 1615-June 1676) m.
1643 Ann ...... CONN XXIV, 119
Thomas (1607/8-1681) m. .... (1)
Dorothy Meadows; 1636/7 (2) Sarah
...... CONN IV, 148; XI, 124;
XIII, 120; XIX, 128, 138; XX, 74;
XXIII, 32, 33; XXIV, 93; XXV, 260;
XXVI, 117, 118; XXVII, 68; XXX,
108; XXXI, 31, 63, 157; XXXIII,
63; XXXIV, 82
Thomas (bpt. Apr. 13, 1736-Nov. 15,
1808) m. Oct. 8, 1768 Susannah

Palmer XXIV, 119
William (July 26, 1739-Jan. 2, 1815)
m. Dec. 12, 1763 Lydia Brockett
XXXIV, 82

SARES, see SEARS

SARGENT
David (Oct. 24, 1750-Jan. 1816) m.
May 21, 1774 Anna Evenden XIII,
27
John (1727-Nov. 14, 1797) m. Apr.
29, 1753 Susanna Harriman XXVI,
139
Orlando (Apr. 21, 1728-Apr. 3, 1803)
m. Jan. 9, 1755 Betsy Barnard
XXI, 146
Thomas (Mar. 31, 1750-Mar. 10, 1809)
m. Apr. 14, 1772 Abigail Blaisdell
XXXIII, 133, 134
*William (c. 1602-c. Mar. 1675) m. c.
1633 Elizabeth Perkins MASS XXI,
146; XXVI, 139; XXXIII, 133, 134*
*William (c. 1624-Feb. 19, 1717) m.
Sept. 10, 1651 Abigail Clark MASS
XIII, 27*

SATTERLEE
*Benedict (....-....) m. Aug. 2, 1682
Rebecca Dymond CONN XXX, 245*
Benedict (July 11, 1714-July 14,
1778) m. May 16, 1757 (2) Rachel
Parks XXX, 245

SAUNDERS, includes SANDERS
Daniel (Sept. 8, 1744-Dec. 31, 1824)
m. .... Sarah Peele IV, 91
*Edward (1625-1672) m. .... Elizabeth
Webb Hudnall VA XII, 55; XXXIII,
236*
Ephraim (Mar. 14, 1760-Nov. 1796) m.
.... Nancy McCarty XII, 54
*James (a. 1658-Feb. 9, 1717) m. Sept.
7, 1698 Sarah Shrimpshire VA
XXXIV, 286*
*John (bpt. Mar. 23, 1613-Oct. 1643)
m. .... Priscilla Grafton MASS
IV, 91*
Robert (Jan. 22, 1748-Oct. 20, 1815)
m. c. 1772 Catherine (Gannaway)
Sanders XXXIV, 286
Thomas (June 18, 1739-1808) m. 1764
Ann Turner XXXIII, 235, 236

SAVAGE
*Griffin, I (....-Feb. 1685) m. ....
Bridget ...... VA XXXII, 168*
John (June 11, 1739-Oct. 28, 1798)
m. .... Mary Greenough VIII, 14
Nathaniel Littleton (c. 1723-c. 1784)
m. c. 1759 Ann Reynolds XXVIII,

188, 189; XXXII, 18; XXXIII, 103
Richard Rogers (....-1807) m. ....
Elizabeth Sheppard XXXII, 168
*Thomas (1594-1635) m. c. 1621 Hannah
Tyng VA XXVIII, 188, 189; XXXII,
18; XXXIII, 103*
*Thomas (1606-Feb. 14, 1681) m. ....
Faith Hutchinson MASS VIII, 14*

SAWTELL
Ephraim (Jan. 18, 1734-c. 1800) m.
Dec. 22, 1757 Abigail Stone XXIX,
187; XXX, 230
Hezekiah (Feb. 26, 1761-Oct. 1, 1824)
m. Nov. 26, 1782 Sarah Russell XXX,
263
Jonathan (Jan. 31, 1753-Dec. 29,
1830) m. Oct. 9, 1777 Hannah Whit-
aker XXII, 66
*Richard (1604-Aug. 2, 1694) m. 1628
Elizabeth Post MASS XXII, 66;
XXIX, 187; XXX, 230, 263*

SAWYER
Ephraim (1719-1813) m. .... Dolly
Wilder I, 30
James (Dec. 3, 1737-1801) m. Jan. 3,
1760 Lydia Flint XXXI, 253, 254
Josiah, Jr. (Nov. 8, 1752-Feb. 9,
1817) m. Jan. 4, 1786 (3) Prudence
Johnson XXX, 163, 164
Samuel (bpt. Sept. 27, 1730-Nov. 7,
1808) m. (int.) Mar. 11, 1753
Elizabeth (Lakeman) Brown XXXII,
39, 40
*Thomas (1616/8-Sept. 12, 1706) m.
1648 Mary Prescott MASS I, 30;
XXX, 163, 164; XXXI, 253, 254*
*William (1613-1705) m. .... Ruth
Bitfield MASS XXXII, 39, 40*

SAYERS, see SAYRE

SAYLES
Daniel (Jan. 18, 1758-....) m. Jan.
4, 1778 Eunice Ballou XXIX, 139
Ezekiel, Sr. (Jan. 25, 1748-1828) m.
1774 Sarah Rice XXVI, 286, 287
*John (1633-1681) m. 1652 Mary
Williams RI X, 258, 279, 292;
XXVI, 286, 287; XXIX, 139*
William (Feb. 28, 1744-Feb. 19,
1832) m. .... Anna Mowry X, 258,
279, 292

SAYRE, includes SAYERS
Ephraim (Mar. 8, 1746-Oct. 24, 1819)
m. .... Hannah Meeker X, 152
James (Mar. 2, 1750-June 4, 1826)
m. .... Mercy Seeley X, 161
Joseph (c. 1760-....) m. c. 1788

SAYRE, cont.
  Sarah Littell (Little) XXXII,
  266
  Joshua (....-a. June 1, 1816) m.
  .... (1) Martha Halsey; .... (2)
  Elizabeth Cooper XXVI, 114, 115
  Thomas (bpt. July 20, 1597-1670) m.
  .... Margaret Aldrich NY X, 152,
  161; XXVI, 114, 115; XXXI, 166;
  XXXII, 266
  William (May 12, 1729-Sept. 16, 1796)
  m. May 25, 1762 Mary Fithian XXXI,
  166

SCENTER, see SENTER

SCHELLENGER
  Abraham (Jan. 14, 1748-Dec. 23, 1821)
  m. Nov. 12, 1769 Jane Johnson XXV,
  27, 244
  Jacobus (a. 1626-June 17, 1693) m.
  Apr. 7, 1653 Cornelia Melyn Loper
  NY XXV, 27, 244

SCHENCK
  John (Feb. 3, 1740-Oct. 10, 1794) m.
  Nov. 12, 1763 Mariah Van Dorn
  XXII, 46
  Roelof Martense (1619-1704) m. 1660
  Neeltje Geretsen Van Couwenhover
  NY XXII, 46

SCHERMERHORN
  Bernardus Freeman (Oct. 14, 1739-
  July 14, 1799) m. May 9, 1767
  Ariantje Van der Bogart XII, 121;
  XX, 105
  Jacob Janse (1622-1688) m. Feb. 20,
  1650 Jannetje Egmont NY XII, 121;
  XIX, 126; XX, 105; XXIX, 123
  Jacob R. (1761-....) m. Nov. 13,
  1780 Lucretia Covert XIX, 126
  Leonard (Oct. 12, 1758-p. Nov. 20,
  1840) m. June 12, 1780 Mary Doty
  XXIX, 123

SCHOFIELD
  Hezekiah (1723-1804) m. c. 1751 Mary
  Waterbury XX, 126
  John (bpt. May 27, 1753-c. Jan. 7,
  1805) m. Nov. 7, 1774 Hannah Turn-
  er XX, 126
  Richard (c. 1613-c. 1670) m. ....
  Mary ...... MASS XX, 126

SCHOL, see SCULL

SCHOLL, see SCULL

SCHOONMAKER
  Hendrick Joechemsen (1655-a. Nov. 6,

  1682) m. Elsie Jans Van Breestede
  NY IV, 150; V, 91, 95, 96; XXXI,
  106, 107
  Hezekiah (July 1, 1733-Jan. 6, 1793)
  m. Nov. 20, 1766 Debora Schoonmaker XXXI, 106, 107
  Martinus (May 1, 1737-May 20, 1824)
  m. .... Mary Bassett IV, 150; V,
  91, 95, 96

SCOFIELD
  Daniel (c. 1595-a. May 10, 1670) m.
  .... Mary Youngs CONN XXIX, 346;
  XXX, 13, 65, 66; XXXI, 226; XXXII,
  44, 74, 81; XXXIII, 41, 42
  David (1756-1789) m. 1784 Hannah
  Lockwood XXXII, 44, 81
  Hait (June 1, 1756-July 16, 1840)
  m. Apr. 6, 1783 Abigail Weed
  XXIX, 346
  John (Oct. 4, 1716-....) m. Mar. 4,
  1744 Hannah Mills XXX, 65, 66
  John (Sept. 4, 1746-Apr. 17, 1833)
  m. Jan. 14, 1773 (2) Sarah Nichols
  XXX, 65, 66
  Neazer (May 22, 1754-Sept. 26, 1846)
  m. Aug. 17, 1775 Thankful Scofield
  XXXI, 226; XXXII, 74; XXXIII, 41,
  42
  Peter (1743-Apr. 28, 1830) m. Nov.
  12, 1764 Hannah Bates XXX, 13
  Samuel, III (Dec. 26, 1716-p. 1788)
  m. Mar. 1, 1743/4 Elizabeth Ambler
  XXXII, 74

SCOTT
  Charles (June 17, 1763-Feb. 12, 1838)
  m. Apr. 28, 1782 Amey Briggs
  XXXII, 142
  Edmund (1625-1691) m. 1646 (1) Hannah
  Bird; .... (2) Elizabeth (Fuller)
  Upson MASS IV, 153; V, 49; XXX,
  20
  Gershom (Sept. 6, 1703-June 24, 1780)
  m. Nov. 17, 1728 Mary Fenton XXX,
  19, 20
  Richard (1605-1680) m. June 7, 1632
  Catharine Marbury MASS XXXII,
  142
  Thomas (....-a. Feb. 27, 1678/9) m.
  .... VA XXV, 233
  William (....-c. 1784) m. 1764 (1)
  Betty White; 1783 (2) Betsy Hunt
  XXV, 233
  Woolsey (Apr. 13, 1741-Dec. 1794) m.
  .... Margaret Edwards IV, 153;
  V, 49

SCOVELL
  John (1635-1696/1700) m. Mar. 29,
  1666 Sarah Barnes CONN XXI, 122

Moses (Dec. 6, 1762-July 24, 1836
m. May 5, 1785 Rachael Baker
XXI, 122

SCOVILLE
Arthur (1635/40-Feb. 7, 1706/7) m.
(1) Joanna ...... MASS, CONN
XXXI, 185
Ezekiel, Jr. (Jan. 5, 1744-Oct. 18,
1821) m. Aug. 4, 1766 Rebecca
Thompson XXXI, 184, 185

SCRANTON
John (c. 1609-Aug. 27, 1671) m.
.... (1) Joanna ...... CONN
XXXII, 32
Theophilus (Dec. 1, 1751-Feb. 16,
1827) m. .... Abigail Lee XXXII,
32

SCREVEN
James (1744-Nov. 24, 1778) m. 1764
Mary Esther Odingsell XXXI, 46
William (1629-Oct. 10, 1713) m. July
23, 1674 Bridget Cutts MASS, ME
XXXI, 46

SCRIBNER, includes SCRIVENER
Benjamin (1653-a. Oct. 15, 1704) m.
Mar. 5, 1679 Hannah Crampton NY,
CONN XXVI, 158; XXXI, 108, 137
Daniel (bpt. July 31, 1748-Oct. 1802)
m. .... Elizabeth Taylor XXXI,
16, 17
Enoch (Aug. 29, 1750-Sept. 21, 1816)
m. Mar. 22, 1781 Betty Benedict
XXVI, 158; XXXI, 108, 137
Iddo (Feb. 11, 1753-Feb. 15, 1831)
m. Dec. 30, 1773 Judith Brown
XXIV, 13
John (....-Oct. 2, 1675) m. ....
Mary ...... NH XXIV, 13; XXXI,
17

SCRIVENER, see SCRIBNER

SCROGGIN
George (c. 1660-1697) m. 1684/5 Sus-
annah ...... MD XXVII, 62, 142
Humphrey (c. 1730-c. 1821) m. 1755/8
Margaret Doggett XXVII, 142
Humphrey, Jr. (1764/5-July 1846) m.
c. 1788 Sarah Kirby XXVII, 62

SCRUGGS
Richard (....-....) m. ....
.... VA XII,
32
William (Apr. 1, 1763-July 6,
1833) m. .... Elizabeth Buford
XII, 32

SCUDDER
Amos (Feb. 14, 1739-Aug. 11, 1824)
m. Dec. 29, 1763 Phoebe Ross XIX,
139
Benjamin (June 6, 1733-Feb. 19, 1822)
m. Nov. 23, 1761 Sarah Cory XXXII,
280
Daniel (Aug. 6, 1736-1811) m. ....
Mary Snowden XII, 7
Nathaniel (May 10, 1733-Oct. 16,
1781) m. Mar. 23, 1752 Isabelle
Anderson XXIX, 151; XXXIV, 81
Robert (bpt. Feb. 10, 1751-1806) m.
1774 Esther Jennings XIX, 114,
146
Thomas, I (....-a. Sept. 30, 1657)
m. .... (2) Elizabeth ...... NY
XII, 7; XIII, 9; XIX, 114, 139,
146; XXIX, 151; XXXII, 280; XXXIV,
81
William (Apr. 6, 1739-Oct. 13, 1793)
m. .... (2) Sarah Van Dyke XIII,
9

SCULL, includes SCHOL, SCHOLL
Joseph (1731-Sept. 30, 1810) m. ....
Sarah ...... XX, 57; XXXI, 45, 46
Pieter Janson (1635-a. Dec. 31, 1697)
m. Nov. 26, 1661 Marjoritje Pro-
voost NY XX, 57; XXXI, 46

SEABURY
Gideon (Mar. 1, 1747-Oct. 29, 1827)
m. Mar. 21, 1776 Betsey Pearce
XXII, 28
John (....-a. Apr. 16, 1662) m. ....
Grace ...... MASS XXII, 29
Philip (Dec. 6, 1740-May 30, 1819)
m. Jan. 7, 1766 Sarah Pierce XIX,
97
Samuel (Oct. 10, 1640-Aug. 5, 1681)
m. Apr. 4, 1677 Martha Pabodie
MASS XIX, 97

SEALEY, see CILLEY

SEAMAN
John (1610-1695) m. 1644 (1) Eliza-
beth Strickland; .... (2) Martha
Moore MASS, NY VI, 45; XIII, 46
Micah (Dec. 1, 1748-p. 1780) m. c.
1771 Jemima Ball VI, 45
Willett (Apr. 13, 1715-a. Feb. 10,
1780) m. .... Mary Searing XIII,
45

SEAMANS, see SEAMENS

SEAMENS, includes SEAMANS
Benjamin (June 26, 1740-May 8, 1829)
m. Apr. 19, 1759 Elizabeth Hammond

SEAMENS, cont.
XXXIV, 244
John (1748/50-1838) m. 1779 Sarah
Westcott XXXIII, 56
Thomas (....-....) m. 1687 Susannah
Salisbury MASS XXXIII, 56;
XXXIV, 244

SEAMER, see SEYMOUR

SEARLE
John (....-Sept. 6, 1641) m. Mar.
19, 1639 Sarah Baldwin MASS
XXVII, 88, 89
John (May 14, 1721-July 5, 1787) m.
Sept. 7, 1761 Mehitabel Dunbar
XXVII, 88, 89

SEARS, includes SARES
Ebenezer (Dec. 15, 1754-Jan. 24,
1849) m. Oct. 21, 1779 Jane White
XVII, 22
Elkanah (Apr. 12, 1734-Nov. 24, 1816)
m. Jan. 6, 1757 Ruth White X, 294
Nathaniel (Sept. 1, 1738-Apr. 28,
1816) m. Nov. 26, 1761 Elizabeth
Winslow XXVII, 22
Richard (1590-Aug. 26, 1676) m. 1632
Dorothy Thatcher MASS V, 66; X,
294; XV, 124; XVII, 22; XIX, 90;
XXI, 132, 133; XXVI, 43; XXVII, 21,
XXX, 145
Richard (1748-Aug. 1814) m. .... (1)
Mary Lee V, 65
Seth (Oct. 31, 1736-Aug. 2, 1809) m.
.... Sarah Sears XXX, 145
Silas (Feb. 11, 1719-Feb. 29, 1780)
m. June 9, 1743 Deborah Buck V,
65
Silas (Nov. 26, 1762-Jan. 23, 1838)
m. July 11, 1782 Elizabeth West
XIX, 89; XXVI, 42, 43; XXVII, 22
Thomas (Apr. 30, 1745-Apr. 28, 1824)
m. Sept. 9, 1767 Deborah Baldwin
XV, 124; XXI, 132, 133

SEAVER
Robert (1608-Apr. 6, 1683) m. Dec.
10, 1634 Elizabeth Ballard MASS
XXVI, 113
William (May 6, 1765-Feb. 28, 1817)
m. Dec. 1, 1796 Lucy Heath XXVI,
113, 114

SEAVEY
Stephen, Sr. (Nov. 12, 1750-p. 1802)
m. Sept. 1, 1774 Elizabeth Wilde
XXXIV, 222
William (bpt. Oct. 25, 1601-c.
1688) m. .... Mary ...... NH
XXXIV, 222

SECORD, includes SICARD
Ambroise (1630/1-c. 1701) m. ....
Jennie Serot NY XX, 162
Isaac (1751-1818) m. 1771 Eleanor
Schouten XX, 162

SEDGWICK
Abraham (Apr. 27, 1721-Mar. 22, 1787)
m. Sept. 19, 1745 Elizabi (Abi)
Brace XXXIV, 234
Robert (bpt. May 6, 1600-May 24,
1656) m. c. 1628 Johanna ......
MASS VI, 43; VII, 17; X, 235;
XIV, 12, 13
Robert (bpt. May 24, 1613-May 24,
1673) m. .... Joanne Blake MASS
XXXIV, 234
Samuel, Sr. (Apr. 11, 1725-1794) m.
.... Deborah Higgins VI, 43;
VII, 17; X, 235; XIV, 12, 13
Samuel, Jr. (Mar. 14, 1754-Apr. 20,
1828) m. Oct. 20, 1774 Anna Steele
VI, 43; VII, 17

SEELEY, includes SEELY, SEELYE
Ephraim (Oct. 29, 1749-Mar. 20,
1840) m. Jan. 1, 1768 Electa
...... XVIII, 74
John (Feb. 14, 1749-Mar. 26, 1835)
m. .... Katherine Brinker XXIX,
243
Michael (1750-1823) m. 1777 Elshe
Van Campen XXIX, 98
Nathan (June 24, 1743-June 24, 1787)
m. .... Deborah Gregory XXIV, 170
Nathaniel (1726-Jan. 9, 1810) m.
Jan. 14, 1747 Rebecca Hubbell.
XVIII, 33; XXXIII, 279, 280
Obadiah (....-Aug. 25, 1657) m. 1648
Mary Miller CONN XXIX, 243
Robert (c. 1600/1-a. Oct. 19, 1668)
m. Dec. 18, 1626 Mary Mason MASS,
CONN, NY, NJ XI, 74; XVIII, 33,
74; XXIV, 170; XXIX, 98; XXXIII,
278, 279, 280
Seth (c. 1737-May 23, 1817) m. c.
1757 Joanna Odell XI, 74

SEELY, see SEELEY

SEELYE, see SEELEY

SEIMAN, see SIMON

SELDEN
Jonathan (July 15, 1740-Mar. 17,
1808) m. .... Mehitable Cady
XIII, 61; XIV, 86; XX, 157
Samuel (June 11, 1723-Oct. 11, 1776)
m. May 23, 1745 (2) Elizabeth Ely
V, 87; VI, 66

Samuel (Nov. 1, 1748-Sept. 17, 1819)
m. Oct. 2, 1783 (2) Deborah Colt
VI, 66
*Thomas (bpt. Mar. 17, 1617/8-a. Dec.
1655) m. 1643/4 Hester Wakeman
CONN V, 87; VI, 66; XIII, 61;
XIV, 86; XX, 157*

SELLECK
*David (c. 1614-1654) m. .... Sus-
annah Kibby MASS XXX, 195*
James (1742-Mar. 21, 1809) m. ....
Sarah Weed XXX, 194, 195

SELLERS
John (July 19, 1728-Feb. 2, 1804) m.
Apr. 26, 1749 Ann Gibson X, 226
*Samuel (bpt. Feb. 3, 1655-Aug. 22,
1732) m. 1684 Anna Gibbons PA
X, 226*

SELLMAN
*John (....-Oct. 19, 1707) m. ....
Elizabeth ...... MD XXX, 186,
187*
Thomas (Nov. 29, 1727-1794) m. 1754
Ruth Shipley XXX, 186, 187

SEMMES, see SIMMS

SENIX, see SINEXON

SENSION, see ST. JOHN

SENTER, includes SCENTER
Abel (Dec. 16, 1758-Nov. 14, 1835)
m. July 16, 1778 Sarah Nichols
XX, 164
*John (....-1700) m. a. Dec. 21,
1666(1) Sarah Weeden MASS XX,
164*

SERVAES, see VLEREBOME

SESSIONS
John (June 9, 1742-May 1, 1820) m.
Nov. 17, 1763 Ann Worstly XXII,
140
*Samuel (....-....) m. ....
...... MASS XXII, 140*

SETH
*Jacobus (Jacob) (1665-Dec. 22, 1697)
m. 1676 Barbara Beckwith MD XXXI,
37*
James (1750-p. Apr. 2, 1795) m. ....
(1) Hannah Martin XXXI, 37

SETTLE
*John (1654-1667) m. .... Elizabeth
...... VA XIX, 56*

Thomas (1755-1816) m. Aug. 12, 1814
Mrs. Priscilla Jefferson XIX, 56

SEWARD
Nathan (Oct. 11, 1758-Nov. 15, 1815)
m. June 3, 1779 Martha Gridley XI,
59; XII, 69
*Obadiah (....-....) m. .... Ann
Biggs NY XXXI, 26; XXXII, 30*
Samuel (Sept. 18, 1754-Apr. 22, 1828)
m. c. 1777 (1) Abigail Pitney
XXXI, 26; XXXII, 30
*William (Mar. 1627-Mar. 22, 1689) m.
Apr. 2, 1651 Grace Norton CONN
XI, 59; XII, 69*

SEXTON
Aaron (1758-Aug. 17, 1827) m. Dec.
1784 Jane Jameson XXVII, 71
*George (c. 1618-1690) m. .... Kath-
erine ...... MASS IX, 48; XXVII,
71*
Joseph (Sept. 21, 1743-Mar. 3, 1807)
m. .... Rachel Richardson IX, 48

SEYMOUR, includes SEAMER
Ashbel (Jan. 25, 1748-July 13, 1814)
m. Feb. 13, 1777 (1) Abigail Welles
XXV, 212
James (May 26, 1752-Dec. 11, 1834)
m. Feb. 13, 1775 Rebekah Keeler
III, 28
John (1710-Sept. 8, 1796) m. 1733
Ruth Belden X, 54
Jonathan (Aug. 27, 1759-July 26,
1819) m. .... Abigail Hart IX,
24
*Richard (bpt. Jan. 27, 1604/5-Nov.
25, 1655) m. Apr. 18, 1631 Mary
Muscoe CONN III, 28; IV, 76;
IX, 24; X, 55; XV, 56; XXI, 49,
50; XXIV, 12, 92; XXV, 212;
XXXIII, 193*
Samuel, Jr. (c. 1730-Apr. 11, 1818)
m. Mar. 17, 1750 Sarah Betts (Greg-
ory) XXXIII, 193, 194
Stephen (1718-Nov. 13, 1807) m.
Mar. 18, 1740 Mehitable Hicko
XV, 55
Uriah (Sept. 7, 1733-June 25, 1800)
m. .... Mary (Andrews) Hopkins
IV, 76
William (Aug. 18, 1728-Mar. 18, 1782)
m. Dec. 27, 1753 Mehitable Mer-
rill XXIV, 12, 92
William (Nov. 15, 1754-Dec. 22, 1841)
m. Mar. 20, 1783 Sarah Patrick
XXI, 49, 50

SHACKELFORD
Francis (Mar. 18, 1739-May 5, 1823)

SHACKELFORD, cont.
    m. c. 1764 Rebecca Ballard
    XXXII, 252
  Lyne, Sr. (c. 1727-p. 1782) m. ....
    Elizabeth Taliaferro XXX, 267,
    268
  Roger (bpt. Apr. 23, 1629-p. 1704)
    m. c. 1658 Mary Palmer VA XXX,
    268; XXXII, 252; XXXIII, 231;
    XXXIV, 202
  William, Sr. (1738-Nov. 23, 1777)
    m. c. 1755 Rebecca Cook XXXIII,
    231; XXXIV, 202

SHACKFORD
  Samuel (Aug. 21, 1728-Apr. 12, 1812)
    m. Nov. 3, 1747 Elizabeth Ring
    XXIV, 94
  William (c. 1640-Aug. 7, 1720) m.
    c. 1673 Deborah ...... NH XXIV,
    94

SHALER
  Ezra (Jan. 17, 1739/40-Dec. 17, 1829)
    m. Nov. 11, 1762 Jerusha Brainerd
    XXIX, 183; XXX, 36
  Rufus (May 4, 1764-Nov. 18, 1861) m.
    June 7, 1795 Hannah Cole XXIX,
    183; XXX, 36
  Thomas (....-1692) m. .... (2) Alice
    (Spencer) Brooks CONN XXIX, 183;
    XXX, 36

SHAPLEIGH
  Alexander (1585-a. July 6, 1650) m.
    .... (1) Marguerite Bloedel MASS,
    ME XXVII, 38
  Dependence (Mar. 5, 1744-Dec. 17,
    1812) m. Nov. 17, 1768 Catherine
    Leighton XXVII, 38

SHARPE
  Robert (....-1653) m. ....
    ...... MASS XIV, 23
  William (Mar. 27, 1740-Feb. 23, 1828)
    m. Feb. 9, 1764 Sarah Farrington
    XIV, 23

SHATTUCK
  Abel (1759-July 1, 1816) m. 1793 (2)
    Lydia Oak VI, 53, 98
  Jeremiah (Apr. 11, 1726-Mar. 26,
    1815) m. .... (2) Kezia Shattuck
    V, 101, 102
  William (1621/2-Aug. 14, 1672) m. c.
    1642 Susanna ...... MASS V, 101,
    102; VI, 54, 98

SHAW
  Abraham (....-Oct. 1638) m. ....
    Bridget Best MASS XII, 40; XV,129

Abraham (Aug. 10, 1757-Apr. 9, 1814)
    m. Sept. 16, 1783 Hannah Miller
    XV, 129
Caleb (July 14, 1717-Dec. 25, 1791)
    m. Oct. 16, 1747 Abigail Batchelder
    XXV, 34; XXX, 153
Joshua (May 18, 1726-Dec. 22, 1805)
    m. .... Abigail Williams XII, 40
Richard (....-p. 1671) m. c. 1659
    Temperance Garlick NY XXX, 241,
    242
Roger (1594-May 29, 1661) m. ....
    Ann ...... MASS, NH XXV, 34;
    XXX, 153
Thomas (....-Aug. 1795) m. July 5,
    1770 Hannah Goff XXX, 241, 242

SHEAFE
  Jacob, Sr. (1715-1791) m. .... Han-
    nah Seavey II, 41
  Jacob, Jr. (1745-1829) m. .... Mary
    H. Plaisted Quincy II, 41
  Sampson (1650-1724) m. .... Mehit-
    able Webb Sheafe MASS, NH II,
    41

SHED, see SHEDD

SHEDD, includes SHED
  Daniel (1620-1708) m. 1659 (2)
    Elizabeth ...... MASS XXXIII,
    125
  William (Apr. 15, 1735-....) m.
    Sept. 26, 1765 Lydia Farnsworth
    XXXIII, 125

SHELDON
  Elisha (Mar. 6, 1740/1-May 11, 1805)
    m. a. Apr. 26, 1670 Sarah Bellows
    XXXIV, 292
  Isaac (1629-July 27, 1708) m. 1653
    Mary Woodford MASS, CONN VIII,
    9, 19; XI, 46; XXXI, 221; XXXIII,
    98, 330; XXXIV, 292
  Isaac (July 3, 1752-Jan. 4, 1810)
    m. .... Mindwell Phelps XXXIII,
    98, 330
  James (Apr. 11, 1743-....) m. Oct.
    24, 1762 Hannah Beard XXIX, 83
  Joel (1746-1829) m. c. 1772 (1) Mary
    Hanchett XI, 46
  John (1630-1708) m. Mar. 23, 1660
    Joanna Vincent RI XXVI, 34
  Roger (Feb. 6, 1744-1818) m. Apr.
    30, 1765 Huldah Streeter XXVI,
    34
  Seth, Sr. (1739-Apr. 24, 1810) m.
    Aug. 9, 1770 Hannah Mary Hanchett
    XXXI, 221
  Simon (Mar. 27, 1726-Feb. 1, 1813)
    m. .... Grace Phelps VIII, 9, 19

William (1597-....) m. c. 1618 Mary
  Clarke MASS XXIX, 83

SHEPARD, see SHEPPARD

SHEPPARD, includes SHEPARD
  Abraham (1744-June 13, 1832) m.
    Sept. 9, 1769 Rhoda Ferris
    XXXI, 197
  Edward (....-a. Aug. 20, 1680) m.
    .... (1) Violet ...... MASS
    XXXI, 197
  Furman (July 6, 1756-Dec. 21, 1832)
    m. Dec. 20, 1780 Hannah Maskell
    XXX, 161
  James (1737-1791) m. 1759 Jennette
    Riddle XXVI, 192; XXX, 84, 156;
    XXXIV, 116
  John (a. 1665-c. Oct. 6, 1710) m.
    .... NJ XXX, 161
  John (1673-1756) m. Dec. 21, 1703
    Elizabeth Woodruff MASS XIV, 17
  Jonas (1722-1809) m. .... (2) Esther
    Reed II, 33, 34
  Jonathan (Feb. 6, 1757-June 22, 1838)
    m. Sept. 13, 1781 Abigail Boise
    XIV, 17, 18
  Ralph (1603-1693) m. .... Thanks
    ...... MASS II, 33, 34
  Robert (....-....) m. .... Elizabeth
    Cockerham VA XXVI, 192; XXX, 84,
    156; XXXIV, 116

SHERARD
  John (c. 1630-a. Mar. 10, 1706) m.
    c. 1651 Elizabeth ...... VA
    XXIX, 338
  Robert (....-a. June 1779) m. ....
    Lydia ...... XXIX, 338

SHERBURNE
  Henry (1612-1680) m. Nov. 13, 1637
    Rebecca Gibbons NH XXXIV, 304
  Job (May 28, 1754-May 20, 1847) m.
    .... Hannah Elliot XXXIV, 304

SHERIFF, see SHREVE

SHERMAN
  Abner (May 6, 1748-....) m. Aug. 21,
    1769 Abigail Maynard XXX, 194
  Daniel (Aug. 14, 1721-July 28, 1799)
    m. 1720 Mindwell Taylor XIII, 15
  David (Dec. 20, 1755-Oct. 30, 1826)
    m. .... Mabel Lamkin XXXII, 11
  Edmund (June 23, 1585-1641) m. ....
    Joan Makin CONN XIII, 15;
    XXXIII, 11
  John (bpt. Sept. 3, 1613-Jan. 25,
    1691) m. c. 1637 Martha Palmer MASS
    IV, 124; XXV, 252; XXX, 194

Joseph, Jr. (June 1742-Mar. 1777) m.
  Feb. 4, 1766 Abigail Muzzy IV,
  124; XXV, 252
Nathan (1736-June 18, 1806) m. Oct.
  30, 1765 Mary Wheeler XX, 80, 115
Nathan (Mar. 18, 1760-May 21, 1851)
  m. Aug. 16, 1785 Bethia Thomas
  XXVI, 202, 203, 204
Philip (bpt. Feb. 5, 1610-Mar. 1687)
  m. c. 1633 Sarah Odding RI XXXI,
  212; XXXIV, 218
Preserved, Jr. (Dec. 8, 1747-Sept.
  12, 1803) m. Dec. 14, 1775 Eunice
  Wing XXXIV, 217
Samuel (July 12, 1618-Apr. 5, 1700)
  m. 1640 Sarah Mitchell CONN XX,
  81, 115; XXXIII, 11
William (....-Oct. 25, 1679) m. Jan.
  23, 1638 Prudence Hill MASS
  XXVI, 202, 203, 204
William Bissell (Oct. 15, 1759-Mar.
  31, 1846) m. Dec. 9, 1779 Sarah
  Gardner XXXI, 212

SHERRILL
  Jacob, Sr. (1722-July 1801) m. ....
    (2) Clemens Huntting XI, 63; XXIX,
    363
  Recompense (May 11, 1741-June 9,
    1839) m. Sept. 22, 1768 Naomi Burn-
    ham XXIV, 48
  Samuel (bpt. Nov. 14, 1633-Apr. 25,
    1719) m. a. 1676 ...... Parsons
    NY XI, 63; XXIV, 48; XXIX, 363

SHERWOOD
  Albert (Nov. 18, 1733-Nov. 12, 1803)
    m. .... Anna Buckingham XIII, 29
  Daniel (Nov. 20, 1735-Apr. 5, 1819)
    m. Jan. 1760 Abigail Andrews XXI,
    170; XXII, 67
  Daniel (May 20, 1749-Mar. 18, 1838)
    m. .... Frances Linthicum XV, 37
  Hugh (1632-1710) m. .... Mary ......
    MD XV, 38
  Jehiel (Mar. 1, 1739-c. 1806) m.
    .... Eulilla Goodsell V, 77
  John (Dec. 13, 1749-1790) m. June 19,
    1775 Anne Thomas XVII, 35, 36
  Joshua (c. 1736-a. 1800) m. 1757
    Sarah Leggett XXX, 244
  Oliver (Apr. 15, 1747-Aug. 27, 1808)
    m. May 3, 1773 Glorianna (Laur-
    anna) Purdy XXX, 171, 172
  Samuel (bpt. May 28, 1732-Sept. 10,
    1802) m. .... Ann Nichols XXVI,
    147, 148
  Samuel (July 8, 1761-May 11, 1838)
    m. .... Priscilla Burr XIII, 29
  Thomas (1585/6-p. July 21, 1655) m.
    .... (1) Alice Seabrook; 1640 (2)

SHERWOOD, cont.
  Mary Fitch MASS, CONN V, 77;
  XIII, 29; XVII, 35; XXI, 170;
  XXII, 67; XXVI, 147, 148; XXX,
  172, 244

SHINN
  George (Jan. 1, 1737-Aug. 23, 1782)
    m. 1761 Rachel Wright X, 97
  John (1632-a. Feb. 20, 1712) m. ....
    Jane ...... NJ X, 97; XXXIV, 204
  Levi (1748-1807) m. 1772 Elizabeth
    Smith XXXIV, 204

SHIPPEE
  Christopher (July 22, 1747-Aug. 8,
    1833) m. Apr. 21, 1772 Hannah
    Herrington (Harrendeen) XXVIII,
    39
  David (c. 1620-c. 1718) m. Aug. 15,
    1664 Margaret Scranton RI XXVIII,
    39

SHORTRIDGE
  Richard (c. 1610-a. 1636) m. ....
    .... NH IV, 151, 152
  Richard (bpt. Oct. 20, 1734-July 8,
    1776) m. .... Mary Pitman IV, 151,
    152

SHREVE, includes SHERIFF
  Richard (Sept. 25, 1760-Sept. 12,
    1822) m. Sept. 3, 1783 Margaret
    Newbold XXXIII, 241, 242
  Samuel (June 25, 1750-1814) m. 1771
    Mira Trout XIX, 68
  Thomas (c. 1620-May 29, 1675) m. a.
    1649 Martha ...... MASS, RI XIX,
    68; XXXIII, 241, 242
  William (Aug. 4, 1737-1812) m. May
    8, 1756 Anna Ivins XXXIII, 241,
    242

SHUMWAY
  Amasa (Mar. 1, 1756-Aug. 19, 1830)
    m. .... (1) Sarah Gleason X, 175
  David, Jr. (May 12, 1742-1818) m.
    June 28, 1770 Rhoda Eddy VI, 93;
    IX, 53; XVIII, 57; XXXIII, 91
  Peter (Apr. 10, 1635-a. June 10,
    1695) m. a. 1678 Frances ......
    MASS VI, 93; IX, 53; X, 175;
    XVIII, 57; XIX, 31; XXXIII, 91,
    253
  Peter (Apr. 29, 1735-Aug. 30, 1828)
    m. June 4, 1759 Rebecca Leavens
    XIX, 31; XXXIII, 253

SIBLEY
  Elisha, Jr. (1764/5-1812) m. 1786
    Cosiah Tiffany XVII, 45

Gideon (Nov. 20, 1750-Aug. 21, 1846)
  m. .... (1) Tamar Fitts XII, 102
John (1614-June 24, 1661) m. 1639
  (2) Rachel Pickworth MASS V, 79
  XII, 102; XVII, 45, 76, 77; XXX,
  83; XXXIII, 255
John (Aug. 2, 1711-Nov. 27, 1778) m.
  Mar. 31, 1731 Hannah Marsh XVII,
  77, 78
Stephen (July 12, 1741-Aug. 25, 1828)
  m. .... Thankful Sibley XVII, 76
Timothy (Nov. 2, 1727-Dec. 6, 1818)
  m. Oct. 16, 1753 Ann Waite V, 79;
  XXX, 83; XXXIII, 255

SICARD, see SECORD

SILL
  Elisha Noyes (Jan. 15, 1761-May 24,
    1845) m. Feb. 11, 1796 Chloe Allyn
    XVII, 81
  John (....-1653) m. .... Joanna
    ...... MASS XVII, 81

SILLIMAN
  Daniel (....-1690) m. July 5, 1661
    (1) Peaceful Eggleston CONN XXXI,
    55, 86
  Daniel (June 25, 1752-Sept. 13, 1818)
    m. .... Sarah Brinsmade XXXI, 55,
    86

SILSBY
  Henry (bpt. May 20, 1613-Nov. 18,
    1700) m. .... Dorothy ...... MASS
    XXXIV, 75
  Samuel, Jr. (Nov. 4, 1755-Feb. 10,
    1825) m. Nov. 24, 1777 Hannah
    Goodell XXXIV, 75

SIMMONS
  Charles (c. 1760-1832) m. ....
    Eleanor (Nelly) Weeks XXV, 91,
    92
  George (Oct. 7, 1731-Mar. 26, 1809)
    m. 1766 Lucy Davis XXI, 22, 23
  James (1752-Mar. 1844) m. 1785
    Sarah Quinby XXXI, 87
  Moses (....-....) m. ....
    ...... MASS XXI, 22, 23
  William (1648-c. 1694) m. c. 1675
    Elizabeth ...... VA XXV, 91, 92;
    XXXI, 87

SIMMS, includes SEMMES
  James (c. 1750-1809) m. June 9, 1781
    Sarah Eleanor Ann (Lee) Key XV,
    70
  Marmaduke (....-1693) m. July
    1668 Mrs. Fostane Metford MD
    XV, 70

SIMON, includes SEIMAN
Jan (John) (c. 1650-a. 1685) m. 1679
Mercken Lucken PA XXXIV, 121
John (Aug. 14, 1744-Nov. 1798) m.
July 23, 1767 Catherine Bromery
XXXIV, 121

SIMPSON, includes SYMPSON
Ignatius (1760-Nov. 22, 1793) m.
.... Ann Semmes XXIX, 254
Thomas (c. 1640-a. 1699) m. c.
1662 Elizabeth ...... MD XXIX,
254; XXXI, 118
Thomas (c. 1755-Aug. 28, 1815) m.
1778 Mary Coleman XXXI, 118

SINCLAIR, includes SINKLER
Edward (c. Mar. 3, 1726-p. 1775) m.
Feb. 2, 1750 Martha Shaw XIV,
11; XXIX, 36, 283
George (1754-July 3, 1845) m. 1775
Elizabeth Miller XIV, 11; XXIX,
36
John (1630-1700) m. .... (1) Mary
......; a. 1660 (2) Deborah ......
NH II, 56, 57; VI, 33; XIV, 11;
XXIX, 36, 283
Joshua (Apr. 16, 1760-Nov. 1849) m.
Dec. 22, 1794 Abigail Pattee II,
56, 57; VI, 33
Richard (1730-July 27, 1813) m.
1752/3 Polly Cilley II, 56, 57;
VI, 33

SINEX, see SINEXON

SINEXON, includes SINICKA, SINEX,
SINIE, SENIX
Anders (....-....) m. .... Margaret
...... DE XXXIV, 163
Henry (May 4, 1732-p. 1790) m. Sept.
1, 1754 Anne Stalcop XXXIV, 163

SINGLETARY
Amos (Sept. 6, 1721-Oct. 30, 1806)
m. Sept. 6, 1742 Mary Dorothy
Curtis X, 277
Richard (1585-Oct. 25, 1687) m. a.
1639 Susannah Cook MASS X, 278

SINICKA, see SINEXON

SINIE, see SINEXON

SINKLER, see SINCLAIR

SIPE, see SIPES

SIPES, includes SIPE
Claas Arianse (Adraen Henrickse)
(....-May 17, 1691) m. Feb. 4,

1656/7 Grietje Warnants Van Schone-
velt NJ XXX, 99
Henry, Sr. (a. 1734-1821) m. ....
Mary ...... XXX, 99
Henry, Jr. (1762-....) m. ....
Martha ...... XXX, 99

SIPPLE
Garrett (1653-1718) m. 1674 Mary Calvert VA XXXII, 169, 197
Thomas (Sept. 8, 1760-1799) m. Jan.
25, 1785 Jemima Moleston XXXII,
168, 197

SKIFF
James (1610-p. June 9, 1687) m. ....
.... MASS XXXI, 298;
XXXII, 29
Stephen (Feb. 29, 1760-June 7, 1835)
m. Mar. 3, 1782 Adah Bates XXXI,
298; XXXII, 29

SKILLMAN
John (Jan. 10, 1753-Dec. 2, 1835)
m. Dec. 28, 1778 Mary Veghte Stry-
ker XXVI, 276, 277; XXIX, 248;
XXX, 49
Thomas (c. 1635-1698) m. 1669/70
Sarah Petit NY XXVI, 276, 277;
XXIX, 248; XXX, 49
Thomas (1727-1809) m. 1751 Mary
Beekman XXVI, 276, 277

SKINNER
Ashbel (Mar. 16, 1716-June 6, 1792)
m. .... Maria Holcombe XII, 92
Isaac (Mar. 11, 1746-Oct. 3, 1816)
m. Mar. 22, 1777 Mabel Olcott
XV, 64; XXVII, 96
John (....-Oct. 30, 1650) m. ....
Mary Loomis CONN XII, 92; XV,
64; XXVII, 96
Thomas (....-c. Feb. 10, 1675) m.
.... (1) Elizabeth ...... VA, MD
XX, 29; XXI, 133, 134
William (1741-Feb. 20, 1813) m.
1770/1 (1) Elizabeth Jones; Dec.
22, 1781 (2) Mrs. Elizabeth Fookes
XX, 29; XXI, 133, 134

SLACK
John (July 3, 1730-Apr. 15, 1788) m.
Feb. 28, 1754 Elizabeth Ruggles
XIX, 168
William (1659/60-Apr. 26, 1727) m.
.... Mary ...... MASS XIX, 168

SLADE
Peleg (Dec. 8, 1729-Dec. 28, 1813)
m. Sept. 5, 1765 Mary Mason Chase
XVIII, 37, 84, 129

SLADE, cont.
William (c. 1638-....) m. ....
...... RI, MASS XVIII, 37, 84
William (1662-Mar. 30, 1729) m. c.
1686 Sarah Holmes RI, MASS XVIII,
84, 129

SLAUGHTER
James (1751-1833) m. .... Elizabeth
Slaughter XXV, 288; XXVI, 80, 81;
XXX, 239
John (1593-1652) m. 1617 Anne Clayton
Brent VA XVI, 9; XXV, 288; XXVI,
81; XXX, 239
Robert (1724-1790) m. Dec. 11, 1750
Susannah Harrison XVI, 8, 9; XXV,
288; XXVI, 80, 81; XXX, 239

SLAWSON
David (Aug. 18, 1735-May 15, 1805)
m. 1763 Mary Ferris XXXII, 240
George (1611/7-Feb. 17, 1694/5) m.
c. 1640 .... MASS, CONN
XXXII, 240

SLEEPER
David (Nov. 16, 1721-Oct. 18, 1780)
m. Nov. 24, 1743 Margaret Scribner
XXIII, 17
Jedediah (May 17, 1753-June 28, 1833)
m. 1777 Margaret Sleeper XXXI, 229
Peter (May 28, 1746-Sept. 11, 1826)
m. c. 1770 Mary Sanborn XXIII, 17
Thomas (c. 1616-July 30, 1696) m. c.
1640 Joanna Lee NH XXIII, 17;
XXXI, 229

SLINGERLAND
Albert (bpt. May 20, 1731-1814) m.
Dec. 26, 1760 Elizabeth Moak
XXII, 151
Teunis (Mar. 4, 1722-Mar. 5, 1805)
m. c. 1746 Agnes Witbeck XXXIII,
57, 58
Teunis Cornelius (Aug. 10, 1617-
....) m. c. 1655 Engeltic Albertse
Bradt NY XXII, 151; XXXIII, 57

SLOCOMBE, see SLOCUM

SLOCUM, includes SLOCOMBE
Giles (....-1682) m. 1637/41 Joan
...... RI, NJ XXI, 54, 55
Giles (Dec. 20, 1750-Feb. 3, 1826)
m. Dec. 31, 1772 Susannah Brownell
XXI, 54, 55

SMALL
Edward (....-p. May 11, 1653) m.
.... Elizabeth ...... ME X, 163;
XXX, 210; XXXIII, 54

Edward (Aug. 12, 1751-c. 1828) m.
Sept. 9, 1773 Sarah Mitchell X,
163
Elisha (Apr. 7, 1758-Aug. 6, 1844)
m. Feb. 18, 1782 Priscilla Strout
XXX, 209, 210
Francis (Oct. 6, 1625-1713) m. 1650/1
Elizabeth ...... ME XXVIII, 129
Jeremiah (Apr. 15, 1750-p. 1845) m.
Dec. 19, 1776 Jerusha Woodbury
XXVIII, 129

SMEAD
John (Dec. 28, 1749-p. 1790) m. Sept.
28, 1773 Irena Arms XXXI, 50, 213
Joseph (Aug. 1748-Feb. 13, 1831) m.
Mar. 29, 1773 Jemima (Mindwell)
Purrington XXXIII, 54
Lemuel (July 19, 1739-Jan. 29, 1812)
m. Sept. 1764 Sarah Nims XXI, 135
William (1635-1703/4) m. Dec. 31,
1658 Elizabeth Lawrence MASS XXI,
135; XXXI, 50, 213

SMITH, includes SMYTH
Abraham, Jr. (June 6, 1733-Mar. 20,
1784) m. a. 1754 Mary Baxter II,
38; III, 7, 15, 16, 31; XIII, 42,
58
Abraham, Jr. (Aug. 15, 1754-Mar.
1808) m. Nov. 19, 1778 Sarah Crane
II, 38; III, 7, 15, 16, 31
Alexander (1635-1700) m. a. 1653
Mary Anne Coxe VA XXVI, 225;
XXXIII, 340
Amos (Oct. 23, 1747-Oct. 6, 1807) m.
July 29, 1783 (2) Christiana Phelps
XXXIV, 104, 105
Caleb (1724-1800) m. Mar. 3, 1755
Martha Smith XV, 9
Christopher (1734-Aug. 8, 1820) m.
.... Mrs. Abigail (Harger) Chat-
field XVII, 27, 28
Daniel (....-July 14, 1660) m. ....
Elizabeth Rogers MASS III, 53
David, Sr. (Apr. 25, 1736-....) m.
Apr. 11, 1761 Hannah Hibbs XXXII,
38
David (c. 1760-Mar. 27, 1833) m.
1782 Sarah Rebecca Lindley XXXII,
209
Ebenezer (Apr. 19, 1747-Aug. 13,
1832) m. Dec. 1783 Naomi Gray
XIII, 16; XVII, 51; XXX, 291
Ebenezer (Apr. 2, 1751-1825) m. ....
Mary Gould XXII, 29
Elijah (Dec. 29, 1735-....) m. Oct.
27, 1758 Elizabeth Benedict XXVI,
291
Elijah, Jr. (May 30, 1753-Dec. 31,
1824) m. July 7, 1774 Susannah Judd

XXXII, 254

Elisha E., Sr. (May 18, 1755-June 26, 1849) m. c. 1777 Rachel Hughson XXXIV, 262

Elnathan (Nov. 3, 1738-Mar. 6, 1826) m. July 9, 1767 Chloe Lee III, 4

Epenetus (Jan. 1, 1723-Aug. 8, 1803) m. .... Deborah Smith XXXII, 183; XXXIV, 115

George (....-May 17, 1662) m. c. 1642 Sarah ...... CONN XVII, 28; XVIII, 42

Giles (c. 1603-1690) m. .... (1) ....; .... (2) Eunice Porter CONN XIII, 17, XVII, 51; XXX, 291

Henry (1588-1648) m. .... Dorothy Cotton CONN XXV, 119, 120; XXX, 211; XXXIV, 15

Henry (Apr. 24, 1724-p. Nov. 20, 1797) m. c. 1750 Lucretia Moore XXVIII, 165

Hezekiah (1726-Aug. 19, 1800) m. Jan. 14, 1747 Eunice Morris XXXIII, 292; XXXIV, 144

Isaac (Mar. 18, 1734-Dec. 4, 1789) m. 1752/3 Lucy Clark XI, 180

Israel, Jr. (1781-Aug. 16, 1840) m. Feb. 15, 1809 Maria Runyan XXXIII, 287

James (....-Mar. 21, 1676) m. .... Joan ...... MASS XXXIII, 292; XXXIV, 144

James Webb (May 18, 1770-May 1856) m. 1792 Mary Downey XXXIII, 340

Jasper, Sr. (a. 1667/8-Nov. 29, 1769) m. a. 1699 .... NY XXXIII, 287

Jesse, Jr. (Feb. 1, 1736/7-Dec. 12, 1777) m. 1760 Lydia Gregory XXXI, 66

Job (Feb. 4, 1754-Dec. 1821) m. Nov. 30, 1776 Diadema Booth XIV, 56, 57

John (....-....) m. .... Isabella ...... MASS XIV, 25, 26

John (....-Nov. 1684) m. 1642 Grace Hawley CONN II, 38; III, 7, 15, 16, 31, 57; XIII, 42, 57; XV, 24; XXIII, 68; XXVI, 291

John (....-May 16, 1727) m. 1685 Mary Ellenwood MASS XIV, 56, 57

John (1595-p. 1676) m. .... (1) Alice ...... MASS, RI XV, 72; XXXII, 279

John (c. 1622-Oct. 13, 1687) m. Oct. 13, 1647 Sarah Hunt MASS XXVIII, 165

John (June 24, 1730-Feb. 28, 1779) m. Oct. 29, 1751 Clemence Mills XXIII, 68

John (Aug. 29, 1744-Feb. 22, 1796) m. c. 1762 Sarah ...... XXV, 266, 267

John (a. 1758-1835) m. 1781 Elizabeth Smith XXX, 38

Jonas, I (June 7, 1719-Nov. 4, 1802) m. Dec. 24, 1741 Thankful Fiske XIV, 25, 26

Jonas, II (Nov. 21, 1747-May 9, 1814) m. Oct. 5, 1775 Mary Parker XIV, 25, 26

Jonathan, Jr. (Mar. 4, 1741-Oct. 4, 1777) m. Apr. 25, 1765 Bethiah Doolittle XXXIV, 15

Joseph (1636-Jan. 17, 1689/90) m. Apr. 20, 1656 Lydia Huit CONN III, 10; XXVI, 59; XXXI, 177

Joseph (Mar. 15, 1730-Aug. 10, 1810) m. .... Jemima Bostwick XV, 24

Joseph (July 6, 1755-Mar. 6, 1834) m. Jan. 26, 1783 Hannah Hewitt III, 53

Joshua (Jan. 31, 1729-Oct. 4, 1798) m. Jan. 11, 1750 Elizabeth Pomeroy XVII, 159, 160; XVIII, 8

Joshua (1731-1814) m. .... Hannah Smith IV, 78

Josiah (1704-Oct. 1782) m. .... Elizabeth ...... XXIX, 62

Josiah (July 6, 1724-Jan. 18, 1784) m. Jan. 12, 1758 (2) Hannah Brown XIX, 92, 97; XXVI, 102, 103

Josiah, Jr. (1731-1826) m. Apr. 15, 1758 Mary Stevens XXIX, 62

Levi (Aug. 21, 1752-Nov. 20, 1834) m. May 18, 1790 (2) Lucy Stebbins XVI, 24, 25

Manasseh (Dec. 25, 1748-May 2, 1823) m. Feb. 17, 1774 Hannah Emerson XXI, 103

Matthew (....-....) m. July 14, 1655 Alice Loader MASS XII, 99, 100, 119

Matthew (a. 1661-a. 1715) m. 1671 Elizabeth Thomas MD XXXI, 99

Matthew (1745-1797) m. c. 1767 Elizabeth ...... XXXI, 99

Medad (1755-1831) m. .... Hannah Chandler I, 38

Moses (Dec. 10, 1733-Oct. 27, 1781) m. .... Sarah Catlin XIII, 56

Nathaniel, Jr. (1755-May 4, 1839) m. Nov. 25, 1783 Mary Barrett XXVI, 59, 60; XXXI, 177

Nehemiah (c. 1605-1686) m. Jan. 21, 1639/40 Ann Bourne MASS, CONN X, 302; XI, 19; XII, 33; XVII, 160; XVIII, 8, 66; XXVIII, 98

Nicholas Sever (....-p. 1681) m. July 12, 1666 Mary Tibbals CONN XI, 180

SMITH, cont.
Noah (July 10, 1734-p. 1790) m. Aug.
25, 1763 Keziah Man XV, 72
Oliver (Apr. 27, 1739-Aug. 1, 1811)
m. Apr. 5, 1759 Mary Denison X,
302; XI, 19; XII, 33; XVIII, 66
Othniel (c. 1732-....) m. .... Deliverance Longbothum IV, 130
Perregrine (1755-....) m. Jan. 1,
1778 Zerviah Eddy XXXII, 279
Phineas (June 5, 1717-Feb. 6, 1787)
m. 1751 (2) Elizabeth Smith XIII,
99; XVI, 24, 25
Phineas (Jan. 5, 1755-June 14, 1794)
m. May 4, 1778 Abigail Lay XXX,
210, 211
Preserved (June 25, 1759-Aug. 1834)
m. Jan. 1788 Eunice Wells XXV,
119, 120
Ralph (c. 1610-a. Oct. 27, 1685) m.
.... (1) Elizabeth Hobart; ....
(2) Grace (......) Hatch MASS
XXXI, 66; XXXII, 70; XXXIV, 104,
105, 262
Reuben (Feb. 21, 1759-Mar. 20, 1842)
m. c. 1781 Miriam Goodman III,
10
Richard (....-Mar. 7, 1692) m. ....
Sarah Folger NY IV, 78, 130; XV,
9; XXXII, 183; XXXIV, 115
Richard (Sept. 27, 1736-Dec. 19,
1819) m. c. 1760 Hannah Dunning
III, 57
Richard, Sr. (Nov. 9, 1750-Feb. 4,
1809) m. Oct. 11, 1779 Mehetable
Jaques XXXIV, 321
Robert (c. 1623-Aug. 30, 1693) m. c.
1656 Mary French MASS XIV, 19;
XXI, 103; XXXII, 157
Samuel (1602-1680)m.c.1624 Elizabeth
Chileab MASS I, 38; XIII, 56,
99; XVI, 24, 25; XVII, 127, 128;
XVIII, 34; XXII, 29, 128
Samuel (Jan. 26, 1714-Nov. 14, 1785)
m. May 27, 1734 Priscilla Gould
XIV, 19; XXXII, 157
Samuel (Dec. 3, 1729-Oct. 6, 1800)
m. May 1761 Mary Webb XXVI, 225;
XXXIII, 340
Samuel (Sept. 7, 1732-May 16, 1802)
m. Dec. 6, 1759 Mary Goodrich
XI, 72; XV, 21
Selah (Jan. 17, 1762-Mar. 23, 1830)
m. Dec. 14, 1786 Mary Taylor XXII,
128
Seth (Apr. 2, 1742-....) m. Sept.
22, 1764 Mary Talbot XXXII, 70
Silas (Nov. 30, 1754-Mar. 23, 1813)
m. Mar. 18, 1780 Aseneath Chapin
XVII, 127, 128; XVIII, 34
Stephen, III (1749-Apr. 16, 1834) m.

Nov. 17, 1774 Esther Church
XVIII, 41, 42
Thomas (\....-Apr. 1666) m. a. 1639
Rebecca Stark MASS XXXIV, 322
Thomas (1601-Mar. 10, 1692/3) m.
.... Mary Knapp MASS XIX, 92, 97;
XXVI, 102
Thomas (1648-Nov. 16, 1694) m. ....
(1) Barbara Atkins SC XXIX, 62;
XXX, 38; XXXII, 209
Thomas (Jan. 21, 1739-Sept. 17, 1821)
m. .... Mary Greene XII, 98, 99,
100, 119
Thomas (May 1753-Dec. 1, 1844) m.
Nov. 2, 1777 Thankful Bennett
XXVIII, 98
William (....-a. 1670) m. .... Mag-
dalen ...... NY XXV, 266, 267
William (....-Jan. 6, 1670) m. Aug.
16, 1644 Elizabeth Stanley CONN
III, 4; XI, 72; XV, 21; XXXII, 254
William (Feb. 2, 1655-Feb. 18,
1704/5) m. Nov. 26, 1675 Martha
Tunstall NY XXI, 5, 6
William (Jan. 22, 1669-1743) m. 1720
(2) Mercy ...... PA XXXII, 38
William (June 28, 1720-Mar. 17, 1799)
m. 1755 Mary Smith XXI, 6

SMOCK
Hendrick Matthyse (....-p. June 1708)
m. .... Geertje Harmens NY XXXII,
82, 86
John (Feb. 13, 1727-Feb. 25, 1806)
m. May 7, 1747 Elizabeth Conover
XXXII, 82, 86

SMOOT, includes SMUTE
William (1596-1670) m. .... Grace
Wood VA, MD XXXI, 38; XXXIII,
198, 199; XXXIV, 28, 62, 192
William Barton (....-1816) m. ....
Margaret Dodson XXXI, 38; XXXIII,
198, 199; XXXIV, 28, 62, 192

SMUTE, see SMOOT

SMYTH, see SMITH

SNELL
Job (c. 1743-p. 1820) m. June 8,
1769 Ruth Davenport XXXII, 200
Thomas (1625-Jan. 25, 1724/5) m. c.
1668 Martha Harris MASS XXXII,
200

SNOW
Daniel, Jr. (Apr. 2, 1756-1812) m.
Mar. 12, 1778 Dorothy Flint
XXVIII, 83
David (Mar. 22, 1739/40-1810) m.

Dec. 5, 1765 Mary Cole   XXX, 170, 171

Eleazer (Apr. 8, 1759-Aug. 11, 1838) m. Apr. 30, 1780 Hannah Dunbar XXIV, 65

Mark (Aug. 6, 1731-June 27, 1799) m. Oct. 1, 1752 Hannah Sears   X, 47; XXIV, 32

Nicholas (....-Nov. 15, 1676) m. 1627 Constance Hopkins   MASS X, 47; XXIV, 32; XXX, 170, 171

William (1624-Jan. 31, 1708) m. .... Rebecca Brown   MASS XXIV, 65; XXVIII, 83

SNOWDEN

Isaac (Apr. 14, 1732-Dec. 26, 1809) m. .... Mary (Cox) McCall   IV, 144; V, 53, 85

John (1632-May 1736) m. Feb. 13, 1682 Ann Barrett   NJ IV, 144; V, 53, 85

SNYDER

John W. (1654-p. 1681) m. .... Elizabeth ...... NY XIV, 118

Peter (Oct. 14, 1721-May 29, 1803) m. Dec. 16, 1741 Elizabeth Catherine Mann   XIV, 118

SOMERS

John (1640-1723) m. Jan. 2, 1685 Hannah Hodgkins   PA XVIII, 144

John (Oct. 14, 1727-Aug. 27, 1797) m. Jan. 1, 1784 (2) Hannah Spicer Ludlam   XVIII, 144

SOPER

Henry (....-a. Jan. 24, 1699) m. .... Sarah Wattles   NY XXXII, 269

Joseph (1720-p. 1797) m. June 3, 1746 Mary Wright   XXXII, 269

SOULE

George (c. 1590-Jan. 1680) m. 1627 Mary Beckett   MASS XXI, 150; XXIV, 48; XXX, 184, 185

James (May 25, 1761-Nov. 8, 1821) m. Dec. 6, 1789 Patience Macomber XXIV, 48

John (Mar. 12, 1740-....) m. Nov. 30, 1763 Elizabeth Mitchell   XXX, 184, 185

Josiah (1742-Aug. 12, 1806) m. 1782 Alice Soule   XXI, 150, 151

SOUPLIS, see SUPPLEE

SOUTHARD

Abraham (....-a. Mar. 31, 1778) m.

Mar. 1, 1738 Cornelia Barns   XIII, 44

Richard (1734-Nov. 6, 1787) m. Feb. 1755 Deborah Frost   XXXIV, 96, 275

Thomas, I (c. 1628-a. Oct. 7, 1690) m. .... Annica Jansen   NY XIII, 44; XXXIV, 96, 275

SOUTHERLAND, includes SUTHERLAND

Robert, I (....-....) m. .... VA XXXIV, 280

Robert, III (Aug. 30, 1747-Aug. 12, 1835) m. June 20, 1777 Patience Toullie   XXXIV, 280

SOUTHERNE

Gibson (Dec. 25, 1753-Apr. 3, 1833) m. .... Mary Peters   X, 182, 215

John (c. 1600-....) m. .... VA X, 182, 215

SOUTHMAYD

Daniel (Nov. 11, 1738-Feb. 5, 1827) m. Dec. 4, 1760 Hannah Tryon XXXIV, 134

William (1615-1648) m. Nov. 28, 1642 Millicent Addis (Addez)   MASS XXXIV, 134

SOUTHWORTH

Constant (1615-Mar. 10, 1679) m. Nov. 2, 1637 Elizabeth Collier MASS XI, 149; XXX, 32, 33

John (Jan. 4, 1743-Nov. 30, 1832) m. Dec. 6, 1762 Elizabeth Whitman XI, 149; XXX, 32, 33

SPAFFORD, see SPOFFORD

SPALDING, includes SPAULDING

Abel (July 10, 1728-Apr. 4, 1809) m. Nov. 23, 1749 Mary Anderson   XXX, 219, 220

Barzillia (Apr. 14, 1757-Apr. 21, 1838) m. .... Elizabeth Spalding XVI, 120

Eben (Mar. 27, 1750-July 1, 1808) m. Jan. 11, 1777 Amy Roundy   XXIV, 9

David (June 1740-Mar. 16, 1817) m. Dec. 20, 1764 Sarah Denison   XXV, 13

Edward (....-Feb. 26, 1670) m. a. 1633 (1) Margaret ......; 1641/2 (2) Rachel ...... MASS X, 154; XIII, 88, 93; XIV, 54; XVI, 62, 63, 120; XVII, 96; XX, 54; XXIV, 9; XXV, 13, 78; XXIX, 134; XXX, 219, 220

Edward (June 13, 1761-Feb. 25, 1813) m. May 11, 1781 Abigail Salisbury XXIX, 133

SPALDING, cont.
  Eleazer (May 26, 1733-June 1813) m.
    .... Mary Shepley XIV, 54
  Ezekiel (Mar. 18, 1734-1809) m.
    Mar. 22, 1754 Jane Mather X, 154
  Ezra (Nov. 5, 1754-Jan. 1, 1828) m.
    Mar. 11, 1781 Hannah Eaton XIII,
    88, 93
  James, Jr. (Aug. 31, 1748-June 8,
    1832) m. Sept. 26, 1769 Hannah
    Barron XX, 54
  John (Nov. 14, 1765-Feb. 19, 1828)
    m. Oct. 1, 1783 Welthy Ann Gore
    XXV, 78
  Simon (Jan. 16, 1742-Jan. 24, 1814)
    m. Apr. 15, 1761 Ruth Shepard XVI,
    62, 63; XVII, 96; XXV, 78

SPARHAWK
  John (Nov. 8, 1745-1787) m. Oct. 29,
    1767 Mary Bacon XVII, 138
  Nathaniel (1598-June 28, 1647) m.
    .... Mary ...... MASS XVII, 138

SPAULDING, see SPALDING

SPEAR, includes SPEARE, SPEERE
  George (c. 1620-Sept. 5, 1688) m.
    .... (1) Mary Heath MASS XV, 48;
    XXV, 53, 54; XXVII, 30, 31; XXIX,
    315; XXXII, 135; XXXIII, 82, 83,
    132, 133, 305, 306
  Jonathan (June 18, 1724-Oct. 10,
    1811) m. Nov. 3, 1762 (3) Margaret
    McDougle XXV, 53, 54; XXVII, 30,
    31; XXXII, 135; XXXIII, 82, 83,
    305, 306
  Lemuel (Feb. 9, 1747-Aug. 3, 1809)
    m. May 20, 1769 Ruth Hayward XV,
    47
  Moses (Jan. 5, 1735-Aug. 11, 1813)
    m. Feb. 14, 1756 Catherine Jones
    XXXIII, 132, 133
  William, Jr. (Aug. 22, 1739-Dec. 6,
    1805) m. Apr. 2, 1760 Anna Brackett
    XXIX, 315

SPEARE, see SPEAR

SPEERE, see SPEAR

SPENCER
  Caleb (Dec. 27, 1750-c. 1806) m.
    1778 Jerusha Scoville VII, 45;
    XXXIV, 168
  Calvin (Sept. 27, 1753-Jan. 19, 1801)
    m. Aug. 21, 1782 Rebecca Ford
    XXXIV, 29
  Gerard (Jared) (bpt. Apr. 25, 1614-
    Sept. 3, 1685) m. 1637 (1) Hannah
    Pratt; p. 1677 (2) Rebecca (Porter)

  Clark CONN X, 234; XI, 99, 141;
    XXI, 47, 48; XXV, 125, 126, 258;
    XXVIII, 96; XXIX, 133, 287; XXX,
    268; XXXIV, 29
  Ithamar (1733-Apr. 1, 1825) m. ....
    Rebecca ...... XXV, 258; XXVIII,
    96
  Jared Wilson (Feb. 24, 1760-May 21,
    1809) m. May 27, 1783 Margaret
    Wiggins XXI, 47, 48
  John (a. 1646-1684) m. 1664/5 Sus-
    annah Griffin RI VII, 45; XXIX,
    400; XXXIV, 168
  John (June 21, 1750-Jan. 19, 1824)
    m. Oct. 28, 1772 Susanna White
    XXV, 125, 126; XXIX, 287; XXX, 268
  Oliver (Oct. 6, 1736-Jan. 22, 1811)
    m. June 22, 1758 Ann Ogden X,
    234; XI, 99, 141
  Philip (Apr. 30, 1724-May 8, 1815) m.
    .... Abigail Moore IV, 69
  Seneca (Jan. 21, 1758-June 25, 1836)
    m. c. 1783 Rhobe Carr XXIX, 400
  Thomas (May 29, 1607-Sept. 11, 1687)
    m. .... MASS XVII,
    50
  Thomas (Feb. 27, 1725/6-a. Apr. 29,
    1801) m. Aug. 27, 1760 Thankful
    Ackley XXIX, 133
  Thomas (c. 1738-1823) m. .... Dorothy
    Hills XVII, 50
  William (....-a. Mar. 4, 1641) m.
    .... Agnes ...... MASS, CONN IV,
    69

SPERRY
  Ambrose (May 6, 1755-Sept. 23, 1817)
    m. July 15, 1780 Patience Wheeler
    XXVI, 77
  Nathan (Nov. 5, 1750-Sept. 16, 1793)
    m. 1780 Mary Johns XXXIII, 215
  Richard, Sr. (1618-1698) m. ....
    Dennise ...... CONN XXVI, 77;
    XXXIII, 215

SPOFFORD, includes SPAFFORD
  Amos (Aug. 28, 1765-Feb. 13, 1830)
    m. May 20, 1789 Mary Taggart XXVI,
    129; XXX, 210
  Bradstreet (Sept. 2, 1731-Dec. 30,
    1808) m. Oct. 16, 1752 Mary Page
    XXI, 91
  Eldad (Jan. 20, 1744/5-Jan. 6, 1809)
    m. 1768 Lucy Spalding XXXII, 178
  John, I (Sept. 6, 1612-Oct. 1678) m.
    ...... Elizabeth Scott MASS XXI,
    91; XXVI, 129; XXX, 210; XXXII,
    178

SPOONER
  Charles (Oct. 10, 1764-Nov. 14, 1846)

STANHOPE
  Jonathan (....-1681) m. Apr. 11,
  1656 Susannah Ayer　MASS　XXIX,
  71
  Peter (Nov. 24, 1759-1845) m. Nov.
  30, 1775 Elizabeth Parmenter
  XXIX, 71

STANLEY
  Marshall (bpt. 1740/1-Nov. 17, 1796)
  m. 1766 Thamor ...... XXXI, 148
  Nathaniel (Aug. 11, 1707-....) m.
  .... Mary Marshall XXVI, 52, 53
  Thomas (1634-Jan. 31, 1663) m. ....
  (2) Benett (Welltarton) CONN
  XXVI, 52, 53; XXXI, 148

STANNARD
  Elijah, Jr. (1752-Aug. 23, 1841) m.
  June 26, 1776 Peggy Divall XXIX,
  224
  Joseph (....-....) m. c. 1662 ......
  ...... CONN XXIX, 224

STANTON
  Enoch (Sept. 15, 1745-Sept. 6, 1781)
  m. .... Waity Dyer X, 298; XII,
  110; XIII, 57
  John (Nov. 16, 1746-Mar. 16, 1818)
  m. .... Hulda Freeman IX, 32, 33,
  51; XII, 28
  Phineas (Oct. 28, 1719-Feb. 3, 1790)
  m. Jan. 7, 1740 Elizabeth Stanton
  X, 298; XII, 110
  Thomas (c. 1615-Dec. 2, 1677) m.
  1637 Ann Lord CONN IX, 32, 33,
  51; X, 298; XII, 28, 111; XIII, 57

STAPLEFORT
  Edward (Sept. 30, 1745-1804) m. Oct.
  26, 1778 Sarah Tubman XIX, 124
  Raymond (....-1687) m. a. 1666 Mrs.
  Elinor (Thompson) MD XIX, 123

STAPLES
  John (Oct. 4, 1737-Aug. 10, 1813) m.
  c. 1763 (1) Elizabeth Sherwood
  XXXII, 33
  Thomas (....-a. Jan. 12, 1688) m. a.
  1646 Mary ...... CONN XXXII, 33

STARK
  Aaron (1608-1685) m. .... Mary Holt
  CONN XXIX, 100, 119; XXX, 61
  Christopher, II (Sept. 27, 1728-
  1777) m. a. 1750 ....
  XXIX, 100, 119
  Christopher, III (1750-Sept. 19,
  1807) m. c. 1772 Margaret Vineyard
  XXIX, 99, 100, 119
  William (Feb. 1745-1795) m. 1763

  Mary (Polly) Carey XXX, 61

STARKWEATHER
  Belcher (Jan. 23, 1755-Mar. 1, 1831)
  m. Dec. 30, 1784 Mary Leonard
  XXX, 219, 220
  Ezra Lorenzo (Dec. 8, 1759-Nov. 12,
  1822) m. .... Mary Cary XXXIV, 78
  Jabez (Jan. 9, 1734/5-Apr. 1, 1815)
  m. June 13, 1764 Martha Cole XVII,
  132
  John (Aug. 14, 1752-Jan. 26, 1837) m.
  May 25, 1780 Hannah Stimson Leonard
  XIII, 49; XVII, 46, 47
  Robert (....-Nov. 4, 1674) m. ....
  Jennet Roberts MASS XIII, 49;
  XVII, 47, 132; XXX, 220; XXXIV, 79

STARR
  Comfort (1589-Jan. 2, 1659) m. ....
  Elizabeth ...... MASS XIV, 45,
  46; XVIII, 100; XXI, 112; XXV, 12,
  62
  Comfort (1644-Oct. 18, 1693) m. ....
  Marah Weld MASS IX, 42, 43
  David (Dec. 7, 1724-Feb. 11, 1810)
  m. July 15, 1747 Abigail Beebe
  XXI, 112
  David (Dec. 2, 1755-Mar. 13, 1814)
  m. Oct. 8, 1778 Lucy Sanford XIV,
  45, 46
  James (May 2, 1740-Nov. 20, 1830) m.
  .... Mary Winter IX, 42, 43
  John (1711-Feb. 25, 1788) m. ....
  Sarah Taylor XVIII, 100
  Thomas (c. 1720-Apr. 27, 1806) m.
  .... Mary Sherman XXV, 62
  William (Apr. 20, 1745-Dec. 31, 1816)
  m. Nov. 1, 1770 (1) Freelove Bailey
  XXV, 12

STEADMAN
  Isaac (1605-p. Oct. 2, 1678) m. a.
  1630 Elizabeth ...... MASS XXX,
  125, 126
  John (June 1, 1735-Aug. 18, 1777) m.
  Nov. 29, 1759 Sarah Mills XXX,
  125, 126

STEARNS, includes STERNS
  Charles (....-....) m. ..... (2)
  Rebecca Gibson MASS XII, 37
  Ebenezer (Jan. 28, 1744-Jan. 26,
  1818) m. Oct. 16, 1769 Chloe Wood
  XXVII, 222
  Ebenezer (Dec. 25, 1744-1816) m.
  June 29, 1773 Rachel Ames XXVIII,
  103
  Elias (Sept. 30, 1753-Apr. 2, 1845)
  m. Dec. 12, 1776 Sarah Keyes XXV,
  94

Isaac (....-July 19, 1671) m. 1622
Mary Baker MASS XXV, 94; XXVII,
222; XXVIII, 103, 115, 211; XXXIV,
152, 327
James B. (Sept. 1, 1758-June 30,
1820) m. 1780 Elizabeth Bramhall
XXXIV, 152
John (Apr. 30, 1751-Dec. 25, 1835)
m. .... (2) Lucy Merrill XII, 37
Joseph (Oct. 7, 1751-June 2, 1829)
m. Dec. 1, 1774 Rhoda Tingley
XXVIII, 115, 211
Nathaniel (Oct. 26, 1743-Feb. 17,
1819) m. Feb. 25, 1778 Elizabeth
Stratton XXXIV, 327

STEBBINS
Davis (Apr. 20, 1741-Sept. 30, 1816)
m. Dec. 18, 1765 Rhoda Sheldon
XI, 37; XX, 15, 16
Eldad (Aug. 13, 1737-Dec. 1, 1816)
m. Apr. 21, 1763 Ann Badger XXXI,
113
Rowland (bpt. Nov. 5, 1592-Dec. 14,
1671) m. Nov. 30, 1618 Sarah Whit-
ing MASS XI, 37; XX, 15, 16
Thomas (1620-Sept. 25, 1683) m. Nov.
✦ *1645 (1) Hannah Wright MASS XXXI,*
113

STEELE
Allyn (July 21, 1757-June 17, 1802)
m. Jan. 7, 1778/9 Joanna Cadwell
XXIV, 136; XXVII, 19
Bradford (Sept. 22, 1734-Apr. 10,
1804) m. 1755 (1) Mary Perkins
XIV, 92; XVII, 125
Ebenezer (May 18, 1727-Jan. 21, 1821)
m. Aug. 10, 1749 Sarah Sage VI,
67; XXV, 80
George (....-1663) m. ....
...... CONN XIV, 75, 76, 92;
XVII, 125
Isaac (Oct. 14, 1752-Aug. 24, 1835)
m. Sept. 11, 1777 (1) Dorothy Pit-
kin XXXIII, 192
John (Dec. 12, 1591-Nov. 25, 1665)
m. Oct. 10, 1622 (1) Rachel Tal-
cott CONN VI, 67; XXIV, 137;
XXV, 80; XXVII, 19; XXXIII, 192
Josiah (bpt. June 11, 1758-Mar. 25,
1825) m. c. 1777 Susan Lewis VI,
67; XXV, 80
Zadock (Dec. 17, 1758-Mar. 23, 1845)
m. Feb. 10, 1785 'Hannah Shirtleff
XIV, 75, 76

STEELMAN
Daniel (Apr. 15, 1750-....) m. Nov.
20, 1771 Eleanor Edwards XXI,
147

James (....-....) m. ....
...... DE XV, 35
James (c. 1665-1733/4) m. a. 1690
Susannah Toy NJ XV, 35; XXI, 147
James (a. 1750-Oct. 17, 1817) m.
Dec. 23, 1772 Sophia Conover XV,
35

STEERE
John (1634-Aug. 27, 1724) m. Oct.
27, 1660 (1) Hannah Wickendon;
.... (2) Eleanor Sheringham RI
XXV, 256, 257; XXVI, 69, 70
Jonah (Jan. 1720-Apr. 14, 1798) m.
Dec. 10, 1741 Lydia Whipple XXV,
256, 257; XXVI, 69, 70

STEEVENS, see STEVENS

STEPHENS, see STEVENS

STERNS, see STEARNS

STETSON
Ezra, Sr. (Sept. 22, 1729-Apr. 7,
1805) m. Jan. 14, 1757 Sarah Ryder
XXX, 50, 71, 72, 76, 84
Robert (1613-Feb. 1, 1702/3) m. ....
Honour ...... MASS XXX, 50, 71,
72, 76, 84

STEVENS, includes STEEVENS, STEPHENS
Aaron (Apr. 29, 1762-Nov. 12, 1831)
m. Mar. 31, 1783 Phebe Post
XXXIII, 247, 248
Benjamin (Jan. 20, 1747/8-Sept. 22,
1826) m. June 10, 1784 Mehitable
Harris XXIV, 91
Cyprian (1644-1720/2) m. Jan. 22
1672 Mary Willard MASS XIII,
118; XXX, 277, 278; XXXI, 128;
XXXII, 49
Ebenezer (Apr. 4, 1713-p. July 4,
1798) m. Dec. 3, 1742 Lucy Griswold
XI, 75
Ebenezer (Aug. 12, 1751-Sept. 2,
1823) m. May 4, 1784 Lucretia
(Ledyard) Sands XXII, 80; XXV,
174, 175
Elias (Sept. 22, 1764-June 6, 1852)
m. .... Lucilla Chapman XII, 50
Elisha (Oct. 1, 1748-Mar. 8, 1813)
m. Dec. 10, 1780 Agnes Kimberly
III, 61; X, 67; XXIX, 95
Ephraim (June 29, 1758-July 4, 1837)
m. July 11, 1782 Sibbel Foster
XXVI, 125
Erasmus (....-1691) m. .... Eliza-
beth ...... MASS XXII, 80; XXV,
174, 175
Henry (c. 1611-Oct. 5, 1689) m. ....

STEVENS, cont.
   (1) Alice ...... MASS XXVI, 125
   Henry, I (1639-a. Aug. 9, 1726) m.
   1677 Elizabeth Gallup CONN IX,
   36; XXXI, 243
   Jedediah, II (May 11, 1757-Jan. 26,
   1830) m. Jan. 1, 1778 Abigail Corey
   XXXI, 243
   John (bpt. July 7, 1605-Apr. 11, 1662)
   m. Apr. 1638 Elizabeth Parker MASS
   III, 61; X, 67; XXIV, 91; XXV, 290;
   XXIX, 95; XXXIII, 58
   John (a. 1608-Sept. 11, 1670) m. ....
   Mary ...... CONN XI, 76; XII, 50,
   113; XV, 109, 112; XXXIII, 247, 248
   John (Jan. 15, 1743-c. 1790) m. May
   9, 1778 Agnes Guion XXV, 290
   John (bpt. Sept. 13, 1767-May 18,
   1838) m. Nov. 24, 1783 Elizabeth
   Deland XXXIII, 350, 351; XXXIV,
   44, 69, 70, 71
   Joseph, Sr. (June 14, 1752-1830) m.
   .... (1) Naomi Matthews IX, 36
   Josiah (Oct. 21, 1743-July 3, 1804)
   m. .... Mary Gray XII, 113
   Lemuel (Jan. 10, 1753-....) m. c.
   1772 Hannah Green XIII, 118
   Leverett (Sept. 19, 1742-Oct. 24,
   1779) m. Oct. 24, 1771 Esther
   Macumber XV, 109, 112
   Nathaniel Gove (Apr. 7, 1752-Apr.
   13, 1832) m. Nov. 10, 1774 Lois
   Stow XXX, 277, 278; XXXI, 128,
   129; XXXII, 49
   Richard (1634-p. Sept. 7, 1722) m.
   1667 Mary (Lincoln) Hacke MASS
   XXXIII, 350, 351; XXXIV, 45, 69,
   70, 71
   Simeon (1736-July 6, 1788) m. 1762
   Sarah Hadley XVI, 103
   Tristram (Oct. 8, 1751-Nov. 21, 1803)
   m. Dec. 8, 1775 Margaret Patrick
   XXXIII, 58
   William (....-....) m. ....
   ...... MASS XVI, 103

STEWARD
   Alexander (....-Apr. 6, 1731) m. Oct.
   15, 1662 (1) Hannah Templar; May
   22, 1688 (3) Deborah (Rediat)
   Forbes MASS XXXIV, 113
   Daniel, Sr. (Oct. 14, 1722-....) m.
   (int.) Apr. 13, 1747/8 Lydia Cutting XXXIV, 113

STEWART, includes STUART
   Duncan (1623-Aug. 30, 1717) m. 1654/5
   Anne Winchurst MASS XXI, 121
   Wentworth (Oct. 20, 1731-Apr. 17,
   1776) m. Feb. 7, 1753 Susanna Lom-
   bard XXI, 121

STICKNEY
   Benjamin (Mar. 5, 1739/40-Jan. 1,
   1801) m. May 15, 1765 (2) Eliza-
   beth Stickney XX, 33
   James (Aug. 6, 1742-1823) m. 1765
   Mary Belknap XXV, 129
   Richard (June 26, 1730-May 31, 1790)
   m. Oct. 24, 1751 Lydia Atkinson
   X, 61
   William (bpt. Sept. 6, 1592-Jan. 25,
   1664) m. .... Elizabeth ......
   MASS X, 61; XX, 33; XXV, 129

STILES
   Aaron (1762-June 24, 1843) m. 1778
   Catherine Conklin XIII, 79
   Ashbel (Sept. 11, 1735-Oct. 1810) m.
   1759 Hannah Stiles XXVI, 62
   Isaac (Sept. 5, 1729-Mar. 13, 1783)
   m. May 31, 1750 Mabel Clark
   XXXIII, 332
   John (bpt. Dec. 25, 1595-June 4,
   1662/3) m. c. 1631 Rachel ......
   CONN XI, 86; XIII, 79; XXXII, 96;
   XXXIII, 332
   John (c. 1632/3-Dec. 8, 1683) m. ....
   Dorcas Burt CONN XXVI, 62
   John (c. 1753-Oct. 23, 1830) m. Jan.
   1776 Mary Sandford XXXII, 96
   Martin (July 17, 1728-Dec. 9, 1808)
   m. Dec. 4, 1751 Dorcas Adams XI,
   86

STILLMAN
   Allyn (Mar. 20, 1732-July 20, 1803)
   m. Dec. 2, 1767 (2) Prudence Kings-
   bury XIII, 104; XIV, 14, 15
   Amos (Apr. 24, 1762-1807) m. 1781
   Naomi (Kanyon) Davis XIII, 48
   George (1654-Nov. 17, 1728) m. 1577
   (1) Jane Pickering; 1686 (2)
   Rebecca Smith MASS XIII, 48,
   104; XIV, 14, 15

STITES
   Benjamin (a. 1745-1804) m. 1780
   (2) Hannah Warren XIX, 5
   John (1595-1717) (age 122 years) m.
   .... NY XIX, 5

STOCKBRIDGE
   John (1608-Oct. 13, 1657) m. 1632
   (1) Anne ...... MASS XV, 6;
   XXVII, 81
   John (Aug. 17, 1757-Aug. 23,
   1820) m. Mar. 9, 1786 Mary
   Dillingham XV, 6
   William (Dec. 20, 1752-
   Feb. 20, 1841) m. Oct. 9,
   1774 Ruth Bailey XXVII, 80,
   81

STOCKING
  Abner (Apr. 1, 1726-Feb. 16, 1806)
    m. .... Ruth Higgins IX, 48, 49
  George (c. 1582-May 25, 1683) m. ....
    Anna ...... CONN IX, 48, 49

STOCKMAN
  John (c. 1653-Dec. 10, 1686) m.
    May 10, 1671 Sarah Pike Bradbury
    MASS XXIII, 50
  Roland (Sept. 26, 1716-Apr. 1783) m.
    Mar. 25, 1740 Mary Pulcifer
    XXIII, 50
  Roland (Aug. 19, 1744-Sept. 2, 1797)
    m. May 19, 1765 Bathsheba Moulton
    XXIII, 50

STOCKTON
  Richard (....-Sept. 1707) m. ....
    Abigail ...... MASS, NY XI, 133,
    135; XVII, 114; XXIX, 110
  Richard (Oct. 3, 1730-Feb. 28, 1781)
    m. .... Annis Boudinot XI, 133,
    135; XXIX, 110
  Samuel Witham (Feb. 4, 1751-June 26,
    1795) m. Dec. 12, 1785 Catherine
    Cox XVII, 113, 114

STODDARD
  John (1612-1676) m. .... Catherine
    ...... CONN V, 72; XIX, 120
  John (c. 1620-Dec. 1664) m. ....
    Mary Foot CONN XII, 94
  Mark (Oct. 10, 1743-Mar. 8, 1829) m.
    1768 Lucy Allyn V, 72; XIX, 120
  Obed (Apr. 5, 1743-Dec. 3, 1777) m.
    .... Mary Harrison XII, 94

STODDER
  Ebed (Mar. 15, 1759-Sept. 6, 1836)
    m. July 14, 1782 Deborah Marsh
    XXXI, 149
  Hosea (Aug. 16, 1756-Sept. 8, 1797)
    m. Mar. 16, 1777 Lucy Stowell
    XXIV, 138
  John (....-Dec. 19, 1661) m. ....
    Anna ...... MASS XXIV, 138;
    XXXI, 149

STOFFELSZEN, see VANSANT

STONE
  Aaron (Nov. 22, 1745-c. 1814) m. Dec.
    16, 1773 Elizabeth Ray XXX, 106,
    107
  Benjamin (1743-June 4, 1833) m. 1773
    Anna Asbury XXIX, 18
  Daniel (Apr. 11, 1727-Apr. 3, 1813)
    m. c. 1749 Persis Haynes XVI,
    121, 122
  Edmund (Apr. 24, 1743-Mar. 13, 1829)

    m. Dec. 6, 1768 Susanna Whitney
    XXXIV, 299
  Gregory (bpt. Apr. 19, 1592-Nov. 30,
    1672) m. July 20, 1617 (1) Margaret
    Garrad; 1627 (2) Lydia Cooper MASS
    IX, 50; XIII, 113; XVI, 122; XIX,
    79; XXIV, 75; XXVI, 99; XXVIII, 25,
    26; XXX, 259; XXXIII, 161, 162
  Gregory (Feb. 5, 1754-Apr. 17, 1807)
    m. Feb. 21, 1788 Lucy Jones XXXIII,
    161, 162
  Hugh (1638-....) m. 1665 Abigail
    Busecot RI XXXII, 256
  James (Aug. 7, 1722-Dec. 2, 1800) m.
    c. 1749 Hannah Holloway XIII, 112
  James (Mar. 27, 1751-Mar. 27, 1836)
    m. Feb. 15, 1776 Rebecca Sheldon
    XXXII, 256
  Jesse (Sept. 28, 1737-July 26, 1803)
    m. 1759 Elizabeth Livermore IX,
    50; XXVIII, 25, 26
  Joel (May 12, 1751-Jan. 21, 1825) m.
    1779 (2) Hannah Adams XXX, 48
  John (Oct. 13, 1745-May 23, 1790) m.
    Apr. 19, 1770 Elizabeth Crofut
    XXXIV, 190
  John (Nov. 25, 1754-July 10, 1824)
    m. Oct. 2, 1777 (1) Dolly Hoskins
    XXIV, 89; XXIX, 397; XXXI, 242
  John (Feb. 17, 1757-Aug. 18, 1844)
    m. June 25, 1778 Anne Hunt XXVI,
    99
  Jonas (Aug. 10, 1752-Sept. 23, 1846)
    m. Oct. 19, 1785 Lydia Hall XIX,
    78
  Joseph (July 12, 1750-Nov. 19,1825)
    m. Nov. 18, 1772 Lydia Rice XXX,
    259
  Josiah (1744-1825) m. Sept. 9,1777
    Mary Washington Donaldson XXII,
    26; XXIII, 29
  Levi (July 1, 1753-p. 1832) m. ....
    Bettie Clark IV, 142
  Nathan (Aug. 9, 1746-Dec. 19, 1827)
    m. Apr. 2, 1768 Freelove Phillips
    XXIV, 75
  Nathaniel (Nov. 15, 1761-Jan. 24,
    1837) m. June 16, 1793 Lucretia
    Fox XXX, 11
  Simeon (c. 1721-May 12, 1785) m.
    Jan. 16, 1744 Hannah Kendall XIX,
    78
  Simon (bpt. Feb. 9, 1585/6-Sept. 22,
    1665) m. Aug. 5, 1616 (1) Joanne
    Clark MASS XXX, 12, 48, 106, 107;
    XXXIV, 299
  Thomas (1760-1813) m. .... Sallie
    ...... XVI, 125, 126
  William (....-....) m. .... Mary
    Marvel VA XVI, 125, 126
  William (....-Nov. 1683) m. ....

STONE, cont.
    Hannah ...... CONN IV, 142; XXXI,
    242; XXXIV, 190
    William (1603-1660) m. .... Verlinda
    Cotton VA, MD XXII, 26; XXIII,
    29; XXXI, 139
    William (1650-Dec. 15, 1707) m. ....
    Sarah ...... VA XXIV, 89; XXIX,
    18, 398; XXXI, 242
    William (c. 1711-Feb. 25, 1785) m.
    c. 1731 Eleanor Westcott XXXII,
    256
    William (1750-....) m. .... Betsy
    Murray XXXI, 139
    William (May 3, 1760-Feb. 7, 1839)
    m. Mar. 9, 1780 Sarah Clark
    XXVIII, 25, 26

STOOPE, see STOOPS

STOOPS, includes STOOPE, STOPE
    Christopher (1612-1672) m. ....
    .... VA XXI, 168, 169;
    XXIV, 35, 114
    James (1754-1787) m. 1772 Jean Sherer
    XXI, 168, 169; XXIV, 114
    Robert (c. 1744-Sept. 27, 1797) m.
    1786 Rachel Milar XXIV, 35

STOPE, see STOOPS

STORER
    Amos (c. Sept. 13, 1729-....) m. Oct.
    9, 1760 (2) Susanna Bennett XXX,
    127
    Elias (c. May 5, 1765-Sept. 1824) m.
    (int.) Jan. 18, 1796 Sarah (Hamil-
    ton) Grant XXX, 127
    William (c. 1611-1658/61) m. ....
    (1) Sarah ...... NH XXVI, 292,
    293; XXX, 127
    William (May 11, 1765-May 2, 1843)
    m. c. 1795 (1) Deborah Beaman
    XXVI, 292, 293

STORM
    Dirck (1630-1716) m. c. 1655 Maria
    Peters Momfort NY XXV, 224; XXIX,
    325
    Isaac (Sept. 8, 1734-May 3, 1813) m.
    Jan. 1, 1766 Elizabeth Losee
    XXIX, 325
    Thomas (1749-Aug. 4, 1833) m. Mar.
    23, 1771 Elizabeth Graham XXV,
    224

STORRS
    Joseph (Mar. 8, 1711/2-Oct. 5, 1785)
    m. 1743 (2) Experience Gurley
    XXXI, 275
    Thomas (bpt. Apr. 25, 1605-....) m.

    .... MASS XXXI,
    275

STORY
    Andrew (....-....) m. ....
    ...... MASS XXX, 251
    Stephen, Sr. (Oct. 1760-Oct. 9, 1825)
    m. Dec. 29, 1785 Mary Boyd XXX,
    251
    Thomas (Aug. 22, 1739-July 7, 1813)
    m. Oct. 2, 1763 Alice Rouse XXVI,
    301, 302
    William (1614-Jan. 1702/3) m. ....
    Sarah Foster MASS XXVI, 302

STOUGHTON
    Oliver (May 19, 1721-Jan. 23, 1814/5)
    m. 1755 Eleanor Burbank XIV, 18
    Shem (Jan. 15, 1757-Feb. 25, 1837)
    m. 1783 Flora Gillette XXXII, 115
    Thomas (....-Mar. 25, 1661) m. ....
    (1) ....; .... (2) Margar-
    et Huntingdon CONN XIV, 18;
    XXXII, 115

STOUT
    Abel (1740-Aug. 24, 1797) m. 1767
    Williampy Wycoff XXVI, 165;
    XXXII, 121
    Benjamin (Nov. 1756-June 9, 1827)
    m. .... Mary Hutchinson XVII, 79,
    161; XIX, 14
    James (Mar. 4, 1758-1815) m. Mar. 1,
    1783 Rachel Bryant XXXII, 47
    Joseph (1752-1807) m. Oct. 28, 1771
    Sara Hancock XIV, 64, 65
    Richard (1620-a. Oct. 23, 1705) m.
    1644 Penelope Van Princes (Roth)
    NJ XIV, 64, 65; XVII, 79, 161;
    XIX, 14; XXVI, 165; XXXII, 47, 121

STOVALL
    Bartholomew (June 24, 1665-a. May 1,
    1721) m. Aug. 8, 1693 (1) Ann Bur-
    ton VA XXXI, 79
    James (1762-a. Oct. 3, 1791) m. 1784
    Mary Bradley XXXI, 79

STOW
    John (1595-Oct. 26, 1643) m. ....
    Elizabeth Bigg MASS XIV, 71
    Judeah (1757-Dec. 11, 1848) m. ....
    Sally Clark XIV, 71, 72
    Stephen (May 22, 1726-Feb. 8, 1777)
    m. .... Freelove Baldwin XIV, 71,
    72

STOWELL
    Daniel (Aug. 2, 1737-Dec. 1778) m.
    Apr. 12, 1764 Anna Bugbee XI, 84,
    85, 87; XII, 9; XIII, 14,15; XIV,21

Isaac (Oct. 6, 1739-a. June 7, 1782)
m. Feb. 9, 1758 Phoebe Root XVI,
41, 42
Samuel (....-Nov. 9, 1683) m. Oct.
25, 1649 Mary Farrow MASS XI,
85, 86, 87; XII, 9; XIII, 14, 15;
XIV, 21; XVI, 42

STRAIT
Henry (1652-June 4, 1728) m. ....
Mary Long RI XXXII, 89
Samuel (Aug. 26, 1742/3-Dec. 1838)
m. 1780 (3) Jerusha Burton XXXII,
89

STRATTON
Jonathan, Jr. (Mar. 8, 1746-1819) m.
.... Sarah Child VII, 49
Samuel (1592-Dec. 1672) m. .... (1)
Alice ...... MASS VII, 49

STREET
Nicholas (bpt. Jan. 29, 1603-Apr. 22,
1674) m. .... MASS XII,
84, 88
Nicholas (Feb. 21, 1730-Oct. 8, 1806)
m. .... (2) Hannah Austin XII, 84,
88

STREETER
Samuel (July 9, 1730-Oct. 13, 1812)
m. May 9, 1753 Joanna Morse XXV,
197
Stephen (Jan. 9, 1600-July 14, 1652)
m. Oct. 5, 1640 Ursula Adams MASS
XXV, 197

STRODE
George (....-....) m. .... Margaret
...... PA XXXIV, 265
Richard (c. 1750-a. Apr. 13, 1795)
m. 1778 (2) Ruth Shields XXXIV,
265

STRONG
Alexander (Jan. 15, 1761-Nov. 25,
1836) m. Oct. 7, 1784 Emelia Til-
lotson XVII, 93
Ambrose (Nov. 1, 1750-p. 1790) m.
Oct. 4, 1770 Mrs. Lydia Holdridge
XI, 128; XIII, 29; XV, 43; XVII,
24
Arial (Feb. 1, 1763-Dec. 13, 1813)
m. Feb. 6, 1791 Jane Dickson
XVIII, 40, 41
Benjamin (Feb. 15, 1759-c. 1818) m.
1782 Susan Trowbridge XXI, 90
Elisha (Dec. 1, 1748-Feb. 28, 1826)
m. May 1781 Mary Beebe IV, 88;
XIX, 164
George (1723-....) m. c. 1755 Sarah

Osborne XXXIII, 55
Job (Jan. 13, 1730-May 16, 1800) m.
.... Demeris Strong XXV, 217
John (1605-Apr. 14, 1699) m. Dec.
1630 (2) Abigail Ford MASS, CONN
IV, 88; V, 109, 110; VIII, 30; XI,
128; XIII, 30; XV, 43; XVII, 24,
93; XVIII, 40, 41; XIX, 164; XX,
41; XXI, 90; XXII, 61; XXV, 60,
160, 217; XXVI, 21; XXXII, 22;
XXXIII, 55
John (Feb. 7, 1739-May 6, 1821) m.
Feb. 25, 1768 Sarah Lyman XXXII,
22
John (1743-p. 1790) m. Sept. 26,
1765 Rachel Curtis V, 109, 110
John, Jr. (Aug. 11, 1743-May 8, 1822)
m. 1768 Anne Rust XXV, 60
Josiah (Sept. 18, 1729-....) m. Apr.
1, 1753 Eleanor White XXII, 61
Josiah (Jan. 28, 1740-Sept. 5, 1814)
m. Jan. 13, 1761 Mary Harris XXV,
160
Ozem, Sr. (Dec. 1, 1760-1830) m.
.... Mary (Polly) Hopkins XXVI,
21
Phineas (June 6, 1756-Mar. 1827) m.
.... Anna Filer VIII, 29
Uriel (Sept. 10, 1754-Jan. 15, 1819)
m. 1790 Phebe Miner XX, 41

STROTHER
Robert (1760-1836) m. c. 1790 Martha
Radcliff XXIX, 138, 139
William (1627-1702) m. a. 1666 Dor-
othy Savage VA XXIX, 138, 139

STRYCKER, see STRYKER

STRYKER, includes STRYCKER
Abraham (Aug. 4, 1715-Apr. 4, 1777)
m. Nov. 23, 1739 Ida Ryder XXX,
111, 112
Abraham (Jan. 10, 1752-1827) m. Dec.
9, 1775 Cornelia Beekman XXX, 111,
112
Jan (1615-1697) m .... Lambertje
Seubering NY XXVIII, 64, 65;
XXX, 112
Peter, Sr. (1761-1830) m. Mar. 5,
1784 Nelly Voorhees XXVIII, 64,
65

STUART, see STEWART

STURGES
John (1623-1700) m. .... Deborah
Barlow CONN I, 35; XVII, 87
Jonathan (Aug. 23, 1740-Oct. 4, 1819)
m. Oct. 26, 1760 Deborah Lewis
I, 35; XVII, 87, 88

STURGIS
  Anthony (....-1702) m. .... Anne
  ...... PA XXVIII, 67, 68; XXXII,
  271
  Edward (c. 1613-1695) m. c. 1640 (1)
  Elizabeth Hinckley MASS XIV, 22
  Nathan (1750-Aug. 22, 1827) m. Apr.
  17, 1773 Catherine Phillips XXVIII,
  67, 68; XXXII, 271
  Thomas (Apr. 5, 1755-Sept. 16, 1821)
  m. Mar. 25, 1786 Elizabeth Jackson
  XIV, 22

SUDLER
  Benjamin (....-a. July 31, 1784) m.
  c. 1780 (2) Elizabeth ......
  XXVIII, 168
  Joseph (....-a. May 3, 1700) m. a.
  July 9, 1682 Cecily Bright MD
  XXVIII, 168

SULLIVAN, includes O'SULLIVANT,
  SULLIVANT
  Charles (Apr. 2, 1728-Nov. 3, 1803)
  m. .... Mary Charlton Johnson
  XXV, 182, 183
  Daniel (1728-Feb. 1792) m. Jan. 1758
  Margaret Melvin XXVIII, 43
  Hewlett (Dec. 28, 1763-July 11, 1830)
  m. Dec. 19, 1787 Mary Dunklin XXV,
  182, 183
  John (1638-a. May 1698) m. ....
  ...... Hayes VA XXVIII, 43
  Thomas (1641-....) m. .... Jean
  Pleasant VA XXV, 182, 183

SULLIVANT, see SULLIVAN

SUMNER
  John, Sr. (Aug. 1, 1705-1787) m.
  Sept. 22, 1738 Jedidah Smith
  XXII, 111; XXIX, 188
  William (1605-Dec. 9, 1688) m. Oct.
  22, 1625 Mary West MASS XXII,
  111; XXIX, 188; XXXIII, 268,
  269
  William (Aug. 6, 1748-Jan. 30, 1836)
  m. June 12, 1794 (2) Mary (Polly)
  Pond XXXIII, 268, 269

SUPPLEE, includes SOUPLIS
  Andros (1634-Mar. 10, 1726) m. ....
  Gertrude Stressenger PA XI,
  102
  Isaac (Sept. 7, 1754-Dec. 18, 1789)
  m. May 13, 1777 Elizabeth Ball
  XI, 102

SUTCLIFFE, see SUTLIFF

SUTHERLAND, see SOUTHERLAND

SUTLIFF, includes SUTCLIFFE, SUTLIFFE,
  SUTTCLIFFE
  Joseph (July 27, 1712-Nov. 11, 1801)
  m. .... Sarah ...... XXIX, 128;
  XXXI, 305
  Nathaniel (....-May 19, 1676) m.
  Jan. 31, 1665 Hannah Plympton
  MASS XXIX, 128; XXXI, 305

SUTLIFFE, see SUTLIFF

SUTPHEN, includes VAN SUTPHEN
  Derrick (bpt. July 14, 1743-Jan. 27,
  1831) m. Nov. 1767 Ann Chamberlain
  XIX, 100
  Dirck Jansen (....-1702/7) m. 1680
  Elizabeth Jansen Jacobse NJ XIX,
  100

SUTTCLIFFE, see SUTLIFF

SUTTON
  John (1619-....) m. .... Juliana
  ...... MASS XXXI, 166
  Joseph (....-Oct. 5, 1814) m. ....
  Mary Riley XXXI, 165, 166

SWAIN
  Jeremiah (Mar. 1, 1643-1710) m. 1664
  Mary Smith MASS XXXIII, 30
  Joseph (Aug. 15, 1754-Mar. 4, 1831)
  m. Sept. 16, 1783 Meliscent Bar-
  rett XXXIII, 30

SWART
  Teunis (Oct. 14, 1748-Nov. 5, 1822)
  m. Nov. 17, 1770 Annatje Zielie
  XXIX, 144; XXX, 37; XXXII, 15
  Teunis Cornelisze (....-c. 1680) m.
  .... Elizabeth Van der Linde NY
  XXIX, 145; XXX, 37; XXXII, 15

SWEET
  James (1622-Apr. 4, 1695) m. a. 1654
  Mary Greene MASS, RI XIV, 73;
  XIX, 7
  Job (Dec. 1, 1734-Dec. 1806) m. 1753
  Sarah Kingsley XIX, 7
  John (1579-1637) m. 1619 Mary Periam
  RI XXI, 47; XXVIII, 85, 175; XXX
  172; XXXI, 74
  Jonathan (Apr. 15, 1755-Feb. 11,1836)
  m. 1779 Margaret Jones XXX, 172
  Lebbeus (Dec. 2, 1730-Apr. 27, 1816)
  m. Mar. 11, 1770 Catherine Collins
  XXVIII, 85
  Rufus (Sept. 3, 1753-Aug. 5, 1820)
  m. Mar. 27, 1792 Elizabeth Clarke
  XIV, 73
  Stephen (Nov. 9, 1763-1845) m. 1782
  Anna Sweet XXI, 47; XXVIII, 175;

XXXI, 74

SWEETSER, includes SWEETSTER
John (July 21, 1700-Oct. 10, 1776)
m. Nov. 16, 1738 (2) Elizabeth
Stevens XXX, 180
Nathaniel (Oct. 17, 1748-p. 1791) m.
a. 1776 Martha Mills XXXIV, 66
Seth (May 18, 1606-May 1662) m. Jan.
21, 1630 (1) Bethia Cooke; Apr.
1661 (2) Elizabeth Oakes MASS
XXX, 180; XXXIV, 66

SWEETSTER, see SWEETSER

SWETT
Enoch (Feb. 14, 1747-May 1791) m. c.
Dec. 25, 1766 Mary Perkins XVII,
110, 111
John (....-June 13, 1651) m. c. 1615
Sarah ...... MASS XII, 63; XVII,
86, 110
Stephen (Jan. 3, 1733-Jan. 6, 1807)
m. .... Sarah Adams XII, 63
Thomas Rogers (May 2, 1761-1849) m.
Nov. 17, 1791 (2) Betsy Knowlton
XVII, 85, 86

SWIFT
Asa (Dec. 30, 1742-Sept. 3, 1833) m.
Mar. 9, 1765 Lucy Briggs XX, 84
Heman (Oct. 14, 1733-....) m. Feb.
29, 1760 Mary Skiff XVIII, 121
Jireh (Aug. 20, 1738-July 28, 1776)
m. .... Sarah Delano XIII, 83
Lemuel (Oct. 31, 1752-Aug. 31, 1822)
m. Apr. 17, 1773 Betsey Briggs
XVII, 120
William (....-Jan. 1644) m. ....
Joan ...... MASS XIII, 83; XVII,
120; XVIII, 121; XX, 84

SWITS
Abraham (Dec. 1, 1730-Aug. 18, 1814)
m. Dec. 26, 1753 Elizabeth Vrooman
XIX, 71; XXVI, 234, 235
Claus Cornelius (....-1641) m. ....
.... NY XIX, 71; XXVI,
234, 235
Walter (Nov. 10, 1754-Oct. 31, 1823)
m. June 22, 1777 Sarah Peek XIX,
71; XXVI, 234, 235

SYKES
Benjamin (1762-p. Nov. 27, 1825) m.
1800 Mary Rives XV, 91
Bernard (1620-a. May 6, 1685) m. 1648
Julianna ...... VA XV, 91

SYLVESTER
Richard (....-1663) m. c. 1632

Naomi Torrey MASS IX, 52, 53;
XI, 27
William, Jr. (Apr. 25, 1737-Apr.
1780) m. Nov. 3, 1761 Mary (Spring-
er) Low IX, 52, 53; XI, 27

SYMPSON, see SIMPSON

TABER, includes TABOR
Ichabod (Mar. 11, 1755-Mar. 1, 1835)
m. May 19, 1774 Elizabeth Lawton
XXVIII, 117
Jethro (Jan. 26, 1746-....) m. Jan.
28, 1769 Anna Bennett XIX, 108
Jonathan (Aug. 12, 1712-a. May 1,
1792) m. June 29, 1735 Robe Brown
XXXIII, 237, 238, 301
Philip, Sr. (1605-1672) m. Dec. 21,
1639 Lydia Masters MASS XIX, 108;
XXVIII, 117; XXXIII, 238, 301

TABOR, see TABER

TAFT
Daniel (July 28, 1751-May 10, 1810)
m. June 3, 1779 Rhoda Ellis XXI,
175, 176
Marvel (Feb. 6, 1763/4-Nov. 30,
1832) m. Apr. 29, 1784 Ruth Mur-
dock XV, 139
Robert (c. 1640-Feb. 8, 1725) m. c.
1670 Sarah ...... MASS VIII, 7;
XV, 139; XXI, 175, 176
Silas (June 10, 1744-p. 1785) m. ....
Elizabeth Cruff VIII, 7

TAINTER
Benjamin (June 4, 1727-Aug. 1810)
m. 1748/9 Hannah Wood XXVII, 136
Jonathan (June 26, 1755-July 31,
1801) m. Sept. 21, 1776 Jemima
Root XXVII, 136
Joseph (1612/3-Feb. 20, 1690) m.
1639/40 Mary Guy MASS XXVII,
136

TAIT
James (....-....) m. a. 1688 Ann
...... VA XV, 42
James (1742-June 8, 1798) m. 1767
Rebecca Hudson XV, 42

TALBOT
David (Nov. 19, 1748-Apr. 16, 1806)
m. (int.) Apr. 16, 1781 (2) Merebe
(Margaret) Winslow XXVII, 90
Jared (....-a. Nov. 17, 1686)
m. Apr. 1, 1664 Sarah Andrews
MASS XXVII, 90

TALBOTT
  Edward (July 15, 1723-Aug. 29, 1797)
    m. .... Temperance Merryman IX,
    11
  John (July 10, 1748-1800) m. ....
    Hannah Bosley IX, 11
  Richard (....-p. Apr. 21, 1663) m.
    a. 1656 Elizabeth Ewen MD IX, 11;
    XXXIII, 86
  William (June 7, 1742-c. Apr. 1819)
    m. c. 1764 Elizabeth Magruder
    XXXIII, 86

TALCOTT
  Benjamin (June 10, 1725-Apr. 18,
    1811) m. Mar. 15, 1753 Elizabeth
    Lyman XXXII, 40
  Elizur (Dec. 31, 1709-Nov. 24, 1797)
    m. .... Ruth Wright IV, 117
  Elizur, Jr. (Apr. 19, 1759-Jan. 4,
    1835) m. Jan. 13, 1790 Sarah Bax-
    ter XIV, 40, 41
  George (Sept. 30, 1755-June 13, 1813)
    m. .... Abigail Goodrich IV, 117
  John (a. 1604-Mar. 7, 1660) m. a.
    1630 Dorothy Mott CONN IV, 117;
    V, 56; XIV, 40, 41; XXIX, 332;
    XXXII, 40
  Jonathan (May 12, 1754-July 28, 1847)
    m. Feb. 20, 1785 Sarah Hubbard
    XXIX, 332
  William (June 8, 1742-Mar. 28, 1807)
    m. .... Mary Carter V, 55

TALLMADGE, see TALMADGE

TALMADGE, includes TALLMADGE
  David (Aug. 5, 1731-May 13, 1808) m.
    Oct. 29, 1759 Lydia Pike XXXIV,
    224
  Ezra (Mar. 31, 1759-Mar. 18, 1830)
    m. 1783 Anna Polly XXII, 39
  Robert (....-1680) m. 1648 Sarah
    Nash CONN XXII, 39
  Thomas, Sr. (c. 1595-1653) m. a.
    1630 .... MASS, NY
    XXXIV, 224

TANDY
  Achilles (1758-1821) m. c. 1786 Nancy
    Ferguson XXIX, 178
  Henry (c. 1630-c. 1691) m. ....
    Rebecca ...... VA XXV, 287; XXIX,
    176, 179; XXX, 144; XXXI, 72;
    XXXII, 67
  Henry (Mar. 6, 1741-July 1, 1809) m.
    Nov. 18, 1763 Ann Mills XXV, 287;
    XXIX, 176; XXX, 114; XXXI, 72;
    XXXII, 67
  William (1727-1794) m. .... Jane
    Quarles XXIX, 179

TANEY
  Joseph (Feb. 5, 1755-Nov. 24, 1844)
    m. June 23, 1776 Dorothy Brooke
    XXII, 10
  Michael (....-May 22, 1692) m. ....
    Mary Phillips MD XXII, 10

TANNER
  Benjamin (Aug. 20, 1730-June 5, 1777)
    m. June 3, 1762 Hannah Perkins
    XXX, 93, 94
  Francis (1762-1847) m. .... Eliza-
    beth S. Peterson IV, 99, 149
  Isaac (Sept. 9, 1736-Sept. 10, 1822)
    m. .... Lydia Sherman IV, 99
  Joshua (Mar. 23, 1748-Apr. 10, 1828)
    m. a. 1774 Lois Thorpe X, 70;
    XVIII, 77
  Josias (June 10, 1734-Mar. 14, 1810)
    m. Dec. 5, 1754 Anna Blackman
    XXIV, 83
  William (1660-1740) m. .... (2) Mary
    Babcock; c. 1707 (3) Elizabeth
    Cottrell RI IV, 99, 149; X, 70;
    XVIII, 72; XXIV, 83; XXX, 93, 94

TAPPEN
  Christopher (June 2, 1742-Aug. 3,
    1826) m. May 9, 1761 Annatje Wyn-
    koop XXV, 118, 119; XXXIV, 159
  Jurian Teunisse (....-p. Mar. 3,
    1689) m. .... (1) Wybrecht Jacobse;
    June 15, 1662 (2) Aariantje Davidts
    NY XXV, 118, 119; XXXIV, 159

TARBELL
  James (Oct. 11, 1725-June 17, 1805)
    m. Oct. 25, 1755 Esther Fletcher
    XXXII, 137; XXXIII, 50, 51, 182,
    183
  Thomas (....-June 11, 1678) m. a.
    1647 Mary ...... MASS XXVIII,
    134, 135; XXXII, 137; XXXIII, 50,
    51, 182, 183
  Thomas, V (Feb. 2, 1719-Feb. 9, 1796)
    m. Jan. 19, 1741 Esther Smith
    XXVIII, 134, 135

TARBOX
  David, Sr. (Mar. 26, 1728-....) m.
    May 30, 1754 Abigail Taylor XXXII,
    29
  John (a. 1619-May 26, 1674) m. ....
    .... MASS XXXII, 29

TATE
  Henry (1720-a. 1793) m. .... Sarah
    Lynch XXX, 150
  James (1618-1727) m. a. 1688 Ann
    ...... VA XXX, 150
  Jesse (1746-c. 1805) m. Aug. 27,

1771 Margaret Miller XXX, 150

TAYLOE
John (May 8, 1721-Apr. 18, 1779) m.
July 11, 1747 Rebecca Plater XIII,
72
*William (1645-....) m. 1685 Anne
Corbin VA XIII, 72*

TAYLOR
Abel (June 9, 1730-....) m. Mar. 3,
1753 Martha Conant XXV, 56
Abraham (Apr. 3, 1763-Nov. 9, 1833)
m. July 6, 1797 Frances Blood
XXXII, 198
Benjamin (1739/40-May 28, 1814) m.
Jan. 31, 1765 Sarah Whelden XXVII,
10, 11
*Christopher (1620-Jan. 1, 1686/8) m.
.... Elizabeth ...... PA XXX,
198*
David (Nov. 6, 1750-Oct. 2, 1839) m.
Dec. 1772 Rosannah Gilbert XXX,
56, 57
Ebenezer, Jr. (Mar. 24, 1723-Jan. 3,
1809) m. .... Experience ......
XI, 183; XV, 74
Ebenezer (Sept. 18, 1737-Jan. 3,
1799) m. a. 1774 Ruth ......
XXVI, 253, 254
George (Feb. 10, 1711-Nov. 4, 1792)
m. 1738 Rachel Gibson X, 54;
XVI, 125
*James, I (....-Apr. 30, 1698) m. c.
1667 (1) Frances ...... VA X, 54;
XVI, 125; XXVI, 162; XXVII, 207;
XXIX, 262*
James, III (Mar. 20, 1703-Mar. 1,
1784) m. 1727 Alice (Thornton)
Catlett XXIX, 262
*John (....-p. Nov. 24, 1645) m. c.
1640 Rhoda ...... CONN XXXIII,
318*
*John (c. 1639-Oct. 17, 1713) m. Dec.
12, 1666 Mary Selden MASS XI,
183; XV, 74*
Jonathan Gibson (1742-1804) m. ....
Anne Berry X, 53
Levi (1765-June 1, 1832) m. ....
Sarah Smith XI, 183
*Richard (....-Dec. 13, 1673) m. Oct.
27, 1646 Ruth Wheldon MASS XXII,
124*
*Richard (Rock) (....-Aug. 1, 1703)
m. 1646 Ruth Burgess MASS XXVI,
254; XXVII, 11*
*Richard (1612-1679) m. .... Margaret
Hodges VA XXVII, 177*
Richard (Jan. 6, 1749-Aug. 30, 1825)
m. 1771 Catharine Davis XXVI,
162; XXVII, 207

Samuel, Jr. (1722-Dec. 29, 1787) m.
1743 Mehitable Ryder XXII, 124
Samuel, Jr. (1742-a. Feb. 21, 1786)
m. 1766 Sarah ...... XXX, 198
Samuel (c. 1743-Sept. 1812) m. c.
1765 Elizabeth Hughes XXVII, 177
Samuel (Sept. 21, 1744-Sept. 15,
1837) m. Nov. 28, 1769 Esther
White XXXIII, 318, 319
*Stephen (1618-Sept. 1, 1668) m. Oct.
25, 1649 Elizabeth Newell CONN
XVIII, 135*
*William (1618-Dec. 6, 1696) m. ....
Mary Merriam MASS XXV, 56; XXX,
56, 57; XXXII, 198*
William (Mar. 25, 1753-Apr. 7, 1827)
m. May 31, 1784 Priscilla Loveland
XVIII, 134

TEBBETTS, see TIBBETTS

TEFFE, see TEFFT

TEFFT, includes TEFFE, TIFT
Jeremiah (May 29, 1747-p. May 18,
1806) m. Oct. 23, 1768 Rhoda Hoxie
XXXIII, 284
*John (....-Jan. 18, 1676) m. ....
Mary Barber RI XXXIII, 284*

TEMPLE
*Abraham (c. 1600-1639) m. ....
Abigail ...... MASS XXVII, 64*
Stephen (May 15, 1731-1809) m. c.
1784 (2) Rhoda Estling XXVII, 64

TEN BROECK
Derik Wesselse (May 1, 1715-p. 1783)
m. .... Catharine Conyn XII, 112
*Wessel (....-....) m. ....
...... NY XII, 113*

TENNEY, see TENNY

TENNY, includes TENNEY
Edmund (bpt. Sept. 6, 1741-Oct. 10,
1831) m. Nov. 8, 1763 Hannah Wood
XXXIV, 257
*Thomas (c. 1614-Feb. 20, 1699/70) m.
.... Ann ...... MASS XX, 56;
XXXIV, 257 -*
William (Mar. 17, 1751-June 16, 1806)
m. Mar. 28, 1776 Phoebe Jewett XX,
56

TERRELL, includes TERRILL, TURRELL,
TURRILL, TYRELL, TYRRELL
Ebenezer (Apr. 3, 1742-July 15, 1825)
m. Feb. 26, 1766 Lois Hall XVIII,
137; XXV, 9
Henry, II (Mar. 29, 1735-Jan. 29,

Philip, Sr. (c. 1620-p. Sept. 9,
1674) m. .... Sarah Harrison MD
XXXII, 12; XXXIII, 208, 209
Richard (c. 1728-c. 1790) m. a.
Dec. 25, 1766 Sarah Coale XXXII,
12, 13; XXXIII, 208, 209
Robert (Sept. 26, 1733-1817) m.
.... Mary Sands XXVII, 85, 86;
XXVIII, 6
Thomas (....-a. Feb. 21, 1671) m.
.... Elizabeth Barton MD XXXIII,
191, 192, 206, 312
William (Jan. 31, 1741-1800) m. ....
Rachel Roe XXIV, 55; XXV, 225

THOMPSON, includes THOMSON
Amherst (May 20, 1762-Mar. 21, 1857)
m. 1787 Sarah Clark XXII, 117
Anthony (Aug. 30, 1612-Sept. 1648)
m. c. 1630 .... CONN
V, 57; X, 150; XXXIV, 315
Caleb (1712-1787) m. .... Abigail
Crossman II, 52
David, I (....-1628) m. ....
...... NH IV, 115
David, IV (July 1, 1750-1838) m.
.... Abigail White IV, 115
Elihu (Sept. 5, 1741-p. 1790) m.
Jan. 14, 1767 Desire Palmer
XV, 73
Gideon (Dec. 25, 1704-May 1759) m.
Jan. 9, 1728/9 Lydia Punderson
XXXIV, 314
James (1593-1682) m. .... (1) Eliza-
beth ......; Feb. 15, 1644/5 (2)
Susannah Blodgett MASS XXI, 143,
144; XXII, 117; XXVII, 102; XXIX,
300
James (Nov. 14, 1696-May 25, 1776)
m. .... Mary Hancock XXII, 117
Jeduthan (....-July 5, 1779) m. ....
Thankful Beardsley X, 150
John (....-Oct. 14, 1688) m. ....
.... NY XV, 73; XXX,
173, 174
John (1616-June 16, 1696) m. Dec.
26, 1645 Mary Cooke MASS II, 52;
XVIII, 149
John (1636-1710) m. 1657 Sarah .....
VA XIII, 92
John (1722-1784) m. 1748 Rachel Pea-
cock XIII, 92
John (Feb. 18, 1724/5-Jan. 18, 1777)
m. Mar. 2, 1760 Betty Fuller
XVIII, 149
Jonathan (1718-c. 1791) m. Dec. 24,
1755 Susanna (Runnells) Thompson
XVIII, 6
Jonathan (May 23, 1727-Nov. 3, 1824)
m. Oct. 16, 1750 Elizabeth Warriner
XXI, 143, 144

Joseph (Mar. 25, 1733-1795) m. Feb.
19, 1754 Abigail Sherman XXII,
117
Nathan (Feb. 14, 1726-Sept. 4, 1804)
m. Mar. 25, 1745 Hannah Dodge
XXX, 173, 174
Nathaniel (Mar. 15, 1752-Sept. 9,
1826) m. .... Anna Richardson
XXX, 173, 174
Samuel (Aug. 1, 1737-Feb. 14, 1817)
m. .... Desire Moulthrop V, 57
Thaddeus (July 2, 1751-....) m. c.
1780 Betty Whitlock XXI, 143, 144
Timothy (Jan. 14, 1750-Feb. 4, 1834)
m. Jan. 3, 1775 Mary Frothingham
XXIX, 300
William (....-1676) m. ....
...... ME, NH XVIII, 6
William (Oct. 19, 1723-May 1808) m.
Jan. 12, 1762 (2) Mary Baldwin
XXVII, 102

THOMSON, see THOMPSON

THORN, see THORNE

THORNE, includes THORN
John (May 3, 1730-Aug. 22, 1807)
m. Apr. 1753 Diadamia Ivins X,
129, 167; XXXII, 200, 201
William (a. 1617-p. 1657) m. ....
Sarah ...... MASS, NY X, 129,
167; XXXII, 200, 201

THORNTON
Dozier (Apr. 14, 1755-Sept. 1843) m.
Feb. 6, 1776 Lucy Hill XXX, 279
Luke (1650-1726) m. c. 1680 Ann
...... VA XXX, 279
Mark (1730-1809) m. 1754 Susannah
Dozier XXX, 279
Presley (1730/6-1812) m. c. 1762
Mary ...... XXIV, 161
William (....-p. 1708) m. Mar. 27,
1648 Elizabeth Rowland VA XIV,
33; XXIV, 161
William (1742-....) m. 1772 Martha
Stuart XIV, 33

THORP, includes THORPE
John (....-Sept. 18, 1799) m. Apr.
15, 1773 Abigail Penoyer XXVI,
218, 219, 220, 221; XXIX, 91
Moses (Oct. 3, 1707-Sept. 24, 1793)
m. Dec. 5, 1732 Lydia Collins
XXXII, 23
Reuben (Jan. 16, 1755-Feb. 8, 1848)
m. Aug. 23, 1778 Hannah Lobdell
XXVII, 95
Thomas (....-a. Dec. 24, 1694) m.
Mar. 27, 1656 Rebecca Milward

THORP, cont.
NY, NJ   XXVII, 95
William (c. 1605-c. 1684) m. ....
Elizabeth ...... CONN   XXVI,
218, 219; 220, 221; XXIX, 91, 92;
XXXII, 23

THORPE, see THORP

THRALL
Samuel (July 11, 1737-Dec. 3, 1821)
m. .... Lucy Winchell   XVII, 135
William (1605-Aug. 3, 1679) m. ....
...... Goode   CONN   XVII, 135

THRASHER
Christopher (....-June 3, 1679) m.
.... Catherine ...... MASS   XXX,
37, 127; XXXI, 140, 141
John (Feb. 15, 1753-Dec. 2, 1833)
m. Dec. 12, 1771 Bethania Stephens
XXX, 37, 127; XXXI, 140, 141

THROCKMORTON
James (June 20, 1754-Dec. 17, 1838)
m. .... Frances Barberie   XII, 109;
XIII, 44
John (....-a. 1687) m. .... Alice
...... RI   XII, 109; XIII, 44

THROOP, includes THROOPE
Benjamin, Sr. (1745-Jan. 17, 1842) m.
May 4, 1775 Rachel Brown   XVII, 48
William (....-Dec. 4, 1704) m. May
4, 1666 Mary Chapman   MASS   XVII,
48

THROOPE, see THROOP

THURBER
James (Aug. 26, 1660-Mar. 26, 1736)
m. June 25, 168.. Elizabeth Bliss
MASS   XIV, 84
Samuel (Feb. 15, 1757-Aug. 15, 1832)
m. Sept. 3, 1775 (1) Elizabeth
Wilson   XIV, 84

THURSTON
Daniel (....-Feb. 19, 1693) m. Oct.
20, 1655 Anna Pell   MASS   XIX,
166
John (June 20, 1737-June 25, 1814)
m. June 11, 1760 Eunice (Gott)
Stockbridge   XIX, 166

TIBBETTS, includes TEBBETTS
Henry (1596-1676) m. ....
...... MASS   XXX, 123; XXXII,
247
Jonathan (Feb. 21, 1738/9-Dec. 27,
1798) m. May 18, 1762 Sarah Emery

XXXII, 246, 247
William (Apr. 21, 1731-1807) m. 1757
Laurena Young   XXX, 123

TIBBITS
Caleb (Apr. 7, 1751-a. Mar. 4, 1828)
m. 1767 Elizabeth Power   XXXIV,
341
Henry (....-a. July 13, 1713) m. Dec.
1661 Sarah Stanton   RI   VI, 63;
VII, 33; XXXIV, 341
Jonathan (May 6, 1745-Nov. 30, 1815)
m. Aug. 21, 1763 Assa Tiffany   VI,
63; VII, 33

TIBOUT, see TIEBOUT

TICHENOR
Daniel (1742-Apr. 12, 1804) m. May
6, 1776 Anna (Byram) Condit   XIX,
110; XXI, 71, 72
Martin (....-Aug. 5, 1644) m. May
16, 1651 Mary Charles   CONN, NJ
XIX, 110; XXI, 71, 72

TICKNOR
Elisha (Dec. 26, 1736-June 18, 1822)
m. Nov. 25, 1756 Ruth Knowles
XXVII, 150, 151
William (....-p. Nov. 2, 1696) m.
Aug. 29, 1656 Hannah Stockbridge
MASS   XXVII, 151

TIDWELL, includes TYDEWELL, TYDWELL
Richard, I (....-....) m. ....
...... VA   XXXIV, 110
William (c. 1760-1781/2) m. 1779
Mary de Graffenried   XXXIV, 110

TIEBOUT, includes TIBOUT
George (June 9, 1760-Sept. 17, 1826)
m. 1790/1 Margretta Calyer   XXII,
79
Jan (a. 1656-p. 1691) m. .... Sarah
Vander Vlucht   NY   XXII, 79

TIFT, see TEFFT

TILDEN
Daniel (Nov. 5, 1743-Dec. 8, 1833)
m. Dec. 9, 1768 Esther Mason   XXIV,
166
Nathaniel (bpt. July 28, 1583-1641)
m. .... Lydia Bourne   MASS   XXIV,
166

TILLINGHAST
Charles (Apr. 5, 1729-Dec. 1776) m.
1762 Abigail Allen   XXVIII, 12;
XXXIV, 319
Pardon (1622-Jan. 29, 1718) m. Apr.

*1664 (2) Mary Masters Tabor RI
XXVIII, 12; XXXIV, 320*

TILLSON, includes TILSON
*Edmond (....-Oct. 25, 1660) m. ....
Joanne ...... MASS XXXII, 85*
Ephraim (Nov. 21, 1728-Mar. 27, 1808)
m. Dec. 25, 1752 Mercy Sears XXXII,
85

TILSON, see TILLSON

TILTON
*John (c. 1620-p. Sept. 15, 1687) m.
c. 1641 Mary ...... MASS, NY
XXXII, 48, 258*
Nathan (Feb. 2, 1755-Dec. 28, 1815)
m. Oct. 19, 1780 Susanna Gale
XXX, 121, 138, 139
Nathaniel (bpt. Feb. 3, 1745-1778)
m. p. Sept. 20, 1766 Ann Safford
V, 99; VI, 8
Silvester (c. 1740-p. May 30, 1810)
m. .... Mary ...... XXXII, 48,
258
*William (a. 1618-1653/4) m. .... (2)
Susanna Stoddard MASS V, 99;
VI, 8; XXX, 121, 138, 139*

TINGLE, see TINGLEY

TINGLEY, includes TINGLE
Benjamin (Apr. 24, 1741-Mar. 29,
1828) m. Nov. 10, 1785 Elizabeth
Philbrick XXX, 200
Elkanah (Mar. 26, 1760-Aug. 12, 1838)
m. Oct. 13, 1790 Keziah Mason
XXVII, 60
*Palmer (1614-....) m. 1635/40 Anna
Fosdick MASS XXVII, 60; XXX, 200*

TINKER
Amos (Feb. 17, 1719/20-Nov. 9, 1802)
m. Jan. 7, 1741/2 Hannah Minor
XXVI, 50, 51
*John (c. 1618-Oct. 1662) m. 1651 (2)
Alyce Smith MASS XIII, 52; XV,
85; XVI, 126; XXVI, 51*
Martin (June 26, 1739-Dec. 20, 1811)
m. Nov. 2, 1769 Mary Peck XIII,
52; XV, 85; XVI, 126, 127
Silas (Nov. 25, 1748-1840) m. Dec.
14, 1773 Lois Wade XXVI, 50, 51

TINKHAM
*Ephraim (1615-p. Jan. 17, 1685) m.
Oct. 27, 1647 Mary Brown MASS
XXII, 110*
James (May 8, 1745-July 22, 1836) m.
Nov. 21, 1777 Chloe Richard XXII,
110

TIPPETT
Erasmus Lee (c. 1758-a. Jan. 1823)
m. a. 1785 Lucy Bireling XXXIV,
49
*Philip (c. 1660-a. July 13, 1706) m.
.... Mary ...... MD XXXIV, 49*

TIPTON
*Edward (1618/20-....) m. .... (1)
Elizabeth ......; .... (2) Mar-
garet Downing MD XXXII, 171*
Jabez Murray (Nov. 17, 1754-Dec. 25,
1818) m. May 8, 1788 Elizabeth
Mitchell XXXII, 244
John (July 6, 1726-Nov. 18, 1808)
m. Feb. 8, 1747 Martha Murray
XXXII, 244
John (Aug. 15, 1730-Aug. 1813) m.
1751 Mary Butler XXXII, 170, 171
*Jonathan (1639-Jan. 21, 1757) (age
118 years) m. .... Sarah Pierce
MD XXXII, 244*

TITUS
*John (1627-Apr. 16, 1689) m. ....
Abigail Carpenter MASS XII, 119*
John (c. 1759-1827) m. .... Sarah
Mershon XXXI, 158; XXXII, 63;
XXXIV, 191
Jonah (Mar. 25, 1747-Apr. 1792) m.
.... Thankful (Bigelow) Parker
XII, 118
*Robert (1600-a. 1672) m. .... Hannah
...... MASS XII, 119; XXXI, 158;
XXXII, 63; XXXIV, 191*

TOBEY
Nathaniel (Mar. 11, 1744-p. 1795)
m. Mar. 1782 (2) Mrs. Deborah
Finney XIV, 49
Nathaniel (Aug. 17, 1747-Jan. 11,
1802) m. Sept. 26, 1772 Abigail
Burt XXXII, 50
*Thomas (....-a. Apr. 9, 1714) m.
Nov. 18, 1650 (1) Martha Knott
MASS XIV, 49; XXXII, 50*

TODD
Alexander (Sept. 7, 1736-1808) m.
.... Rachel Warfield XV, 117
*Christopher (bpt. Jan. 12, 1617-
Apr. 23, 1686) m. c. 1637 Grace
Middlebrook CONN VIII, 20;
IX, 53, 54; XI, 126; XIV, 93;
XXI, 92, 93; XXIV, 8*
Daniel (Mar. 5, 1724/5-p. Sept. 16,
1777) m. Oct. 13, 1748 Sybil Car-
rington VIII, 20; XI, 125
Daniel (Sept. 9, 1751-p. 1797) m.
Mar. 27, 1775 Eunice Hitchcock
VIII, 20; XI, 125

TODD, cont.
  George (Dec. 1, 1754-Aug. 18, 1801)
    m. Feb. 4, 1779 Lucy Bradstreet
    XX, 22
  Hezekiah (Nov. 5, 1755-May 18, 1836)
    m. Jan. 1783 Mercy Holt   XXIV, 8
  John (1621-Feb. 14, 1689) m. ....
    Susannah Hunt MASS XX, 22
  Jonah (Apr. 28, 1731-Aug. 8, 1803)
    m. Nov. 12, 1750 (1) Esther (Lowly)
    Harrison XIV, 92; IX, 53, 54·
  Thelus (May 12, 1763-Feb. 1, 1846)
    m. Oct. 15, 1794 Irene Rogers XXI,
    92, 93
  Thomas (....-a. 1671) m. ....
    ...... MD XV, 117

TOLL
  Daniel (Oct. 27, 1751-1832) m. July
    2, 1775 Susanna Swits V, 75
  Karel Hansen (1658-Mar. 1732) m.
    1683 Elizabeth Rinckhout NY V,
    75; X, 180
  Karel (Charles) Hansen (Feb. 10,
    1745-Aug. 30, 1832) m. 1767 Eliza-
    beth Ryley X, 179

TOMLINSON
  Abraham (July 20, 1738-Dec. 29, 1816)
    m. Nov. 11, 1760 Abigail Mary Gib-
    son XXIX, 336
  Henry (1606-Mar. 16, 1681) m. a.
    1638 Alice ...... CONN III, 48;
    VI, 97; VII, 5; XVI, 141; XXIX,
    336
  Isaac (Apr. 7, 1749-Jan. 15, 1817)
    m. Dec. 19, 1775 Mary Hawkins XI,
    50
  Jabez Huntington (Dec. 24, 1760-Jan.
    14, 1849) m. .... Rebecca Lewis
    VII, 5
  Jonah (Apr. 6, 1712-Oct. 2, 1796) m.
    Nov. 26, 1734 Mary Moss XVI, 141
  Joseph, Jr. (c. 1755-p. 1802) m.
    Mar. 20, 1790 Sally Curtiss III,
    48; VI, 96
  William (1643-Dec. 9, 1711) m. ....
    .... CONN XI, 50

TOMPKINS
  Gilbert (May 24, 1753-Oct. 1, 1835)
    m. July 4, 1784 (1) Lucy Brownell
    XXVI, 285, 286
  Michael (....-Nov. 1690) m. ....
    Mary ...... CONN, NJ XIX, 50
  Nathaniel (1650-1724) m. 1671
    Elizabeth Allen RI XXVI, 285,
    286
  Uzal (Oct. 26, 1747-Apr. 12, 1831)
    m. Dec. 30, 1771 Susannah Benjamin
    XIX, 49

TOPPAN
  Abraham (Sept. 10, 1606-Nov. 5, 1672)
    m. .... Susana Taylor MASS XVII,
    91
  Ebenezer (July 16, 1761-May 16, 1849)
    m. May 6, 1791 Elizabeth (Betsy)
    Forster XVII, 90, 91

TORREY
  Abner (Dec. 12, 1736-1826) m. Mar.
    9, 1758 Lydia Beal XXXIII, 259
  Caleb (Dec. 23, 1758-Mar. 16, 1808)
    m. Aug. 14, 1791 Mary Miller
    XVII, 31
  James (c. 1612/3-July 6, 1665) m.
    Nov. 2, 1643 Ann Hatch MASS
    XXXIII, 259
  William (Dec. 21, 1608-June 10,
    1690) m. 1630 Jane Haviland MASS
    XVII, 31

TOUSEY
  Richard (....-1674) m. .... (1)
    .... CONN XXIX, 85
  Thomas (Dec. 5, 1735-1783) m. ....
    Mercy Platt XXIX, 85

TOWER
  Asahel, Sr. (Oct. 9, 1760-Aug. 3,
    1833) m. May 30, 1783 Milicent
    Wyman XXXII, 75, 76
  James (Feb. 6, 1722-1796) m. Jan.
    16, 1745 Mary Day XIV, 57
  John (bpt. May 14, 1609-Feb. 13,
    1701/2) m. Feb. 13, 1638/9 Margaret
    Ibrook MASS XIV, 57; XVII, 69;
    XXXI, 144; XXXII, 75, 76
  Levi (July 25, 1756-Aug. 12, 1823)
    m. May 17, 1799 Ruth (Beal) Stod-
    dard XXXI, 144 ,
  Lynde (Dec. 11, 1749-Apr. 21, 1805)
    m. 1775 Rebecca Bowker XIV, 57
  Samuel (Mar. 17, 1728/9-Oct. 7,
    1811) m. Feb. 12, 1761 Hannah
    Collamore XVII, 69

TOWLES
  Henry (1652-a. Oct. 20, 1721) m.
    1668/9 Ann Stockley VA XIV, 24;
    XVI, 20, 21; XVII, 94, 95; XXVII,
    110
  Henry (Dec. 18, 1738-1799) m. May
    19, 1768 Judith Diggs (Haynes)
    XIV, 24
  Stockley (1740-p. 1811) m. 1773
    Elizabeth Downman XVII, 95;
    XXVII, 109, 110
  Thomas (Feb. 21, 1750-May 22,
    1800) m. 1772/3 Mary
    Smith XVI, 20, 21; XVII,
    94

TRUE
Ephraim (Dec. 21, 1756-Aug. 14, 1835)
m. 1776 Martha Eaton XXVII, 166
Henry (....-1659) m. 1644 Israel Pike
MASS XXVII, 166; XXXII, 289
William (Jan. 20, 1730/1-Mar. 3,
1825/6) m. (int.) Sept. 15, 1753
Sarah Tuttle XXXII, 289
Zebulon (May 21, 1765-Feb. 4, 1830)
m. Nov. 14, 1788 Martha Kennedy
XXXII, 288, 289

TRULL
David (June 22, 1744-Aug. 30, 1825)
m. Feb. 9, 1769 (1) Deborah Harris
XXV, 134, 135; XXVII, 44, 45
John (1633-June 15, 1704) m. Dec. 11,
1657 Sarah French MASS XXV, 134,
135; XXVII, 44, 45

TUCK
Robert (....-Oct. 4, 1664) m. ....
Joanna ...... NH XVIII, 123;
XXIX, 160; XXX, 91, 92
Samuel (Mar. 20, 1731-Dec. 19, 1789)
m. Jan. 17, 1754 Martha Blake
XVIII, 122
Samuel (Sept. 13, 1738-Nov. 12, 1777)
m. Dec. 30, 1762 Anna Moulton
XXIX, 159; XXX, 91, 92

TUCKER
Daniel (Nov. 9, 1756-Oct. 26, 1824/34)
m. Dec. 7, 1776 Rachel Noyes
XXXIII, 26
Ezra (c. 1729-Oct. 26, 1804) m. May
15, 1760 Hepzibah Pressy X, 31,
36, 72
Jacob (Sept. 22, 1717-....) m. Sept.
4, 1739 Lydia Hoyt XXX, 99, 100
John (July 8, 1719-Dec. 12, 1826) m.
Apr. 24, 1772 Rachel Thompson
XIX, 143
Morris (....-....) m. Oct. 14, 1661
(1) Elizabeth Stevens MASS X,
31, 36, 72; XXX, 99, 100.
Moses (July 11, 1743-1814) m. Jan.
12, 1768 Elizabeth Maury XXXII,
149
Robert (June 7, 1604-Mar. 11, 1681/2)
m. .... Elizabeth Allen MASS XIX,
143; XXXIII, 26
William (Jan. 7, 1589-1644) m. ....
Mary Thompson VA XXXII, 149

TUFTS
Francis (May 9, 1756-Aug. 18, 1823)
m. June 12, 1785 Hannah Greenleaf
XXXI, 251
John (Nov. 24, 1754-Sept. 10, 1839)
m. May 19, 1778 Elizabeth Perry

XVIII, 117
Peter (1617-May 13, 1700) m. 1640
Mary Pierce MASS XVIII, 117;
XXXI, 251

TULL
John (Oct. 15, 1744-Sept. 19, 1820)
m. Sept. 23, 1779 Elizabeth Cannon
XXVI, 282, 283; XXVII, 143
Thomas (c. 1640-p. Mar. 8, 1697)
m. Oct. 1666 Mary Minshall VA, MD
XXVI, 282, 283; XXVII, 143

TULLER
John (....-a. Jan. 28, 1741) m. 1684
Elizabeth (Case) Lewis CONN XVII,
153
Samuel (Feb. 2, 1745-Nov. 28, 1813)
m. 1766 Mary Jones XVII, 153

TUPPER
Thomas (Jan. 28, 1578-Mar. 28, 1676)
m. Dec. 21, 1634 (3) Ann Hodgson
MASS XXXIII, 214, 215
Zuriel (Mar. 21, 1758-c. 1800) m.
July 31, 1778 Jerusha Goodrich
XXXIII, 214, 215

TURCK, includes TURK
Benjamin (Dec. 1, 1723-....) m.
.... Eida Van Wie XXXIV, 335
Paulus Jacobse (c. 1635-....) m.
Sept. 12, 1660 Aeltje Berentse
Coell NY XXXIV, 335

TURK, see TURCK

TURNER
Edward (1633-Apr. 4, 1717) m. Oct.
25, 1656 Mary Sanford CONN
XXXIII, 164
Gurdon (Sept. 7, 1746-p. 1810) m.
.... Sarah Humiston XXIV, 44
Jedediah (May 27, 1733-Nov. 19, 1819)
m. Apr. 5, 1760 (2) Rachel Thomp-
son XXXIII, 164
John (1738-Dec. 5, 1833) m. ....
(1) Rebecca Smith XX, 139
Nathaniel (....-1646) m. ....
...... NH XXIV, 44
Thomas (Oct. 15, 1764-Nov. 17, 1847)
m. Jan. 28, 1814 (2) Annie Berry
XX, 139; XXXIII, 41
William H. (a. 1640-1696) m. ....
Katherine ...... VA, NC XX, 139;
XXXIII, 41

TURNEY
Abel (Sept. 25, 1762-Apr. 7, 1841)
m. .... Deborah Bulkley VIII,
28

Asa (Oct. 15, 1759-Apr. 5, 1833) m.
Jan. 24, 1787 Mary Downs XXXI,
180, 196
*Benjamin (a. 1690-a. Oct. 1648) m.
July 12, 1630 Mary Odell MASS,
CONN VIII, 28; XXXI, 180, 196*

TURPIN
Francis (Sept. 9, 1759-Dec. 29, 1829)
m. 1788 Nancy Smith Reid XXVIII,
107
Luzby (1730-a. Jan. 2, 1791) m. a.
1757 Sarah ...... XXX, 201;
XXXII, 184
*Michael (1635-1677) m. ....
...... VA XXX, 201; XXXII, 184*
*William (c. 1640-....) m. Jan. 16,
1668 Margaret Ivory MD XXVIII,
107*

TURRELL, see TERRELL

TURRILL, see TERRELL

TUTHILL
Daniel, Sr. (1700-Oct. 19, 1785) m.
Nov. 1727 (1) Prudence Goldsmith
XXI, 19
Daniel, Jr. (1732-1822) m. 1759
Sarah Thurston XXI, 19
Daniel (Mar. 13, 1747-July 17, 1830)
m. Feb. 1, 1770 Ruth Terry XXV,
33; XXX, 237
*Henry (June 28, 1612-a. 1650) m.
.... Bridget ...... MASS, NY
XVII, 135, 136; XXI, 19; XXV,
33; XXIX, 215; XXX, 237*
John, Sr. (1730-....) m. 1750 Abigail
Terry XXIX, 215
John (Sept. 8, 1742-Jan. 30, 1821)
m. Oct. 27, 1763 Phebe Corwin
XVII, 135, 136
John, Jr. (Jan. 7, 1757-c. 1835) m.
1785 Abigail Moger XXIX, 215

TUTTLE
Abraham (1758-May 21, 1846) m. p.
1784 (2) Clarissa Beebe XX, 9
Andrew (bpt. Mar. 25, 1739-Jan. 18,
1824) m. .... Lydia Sturgis XXIX,
241; XXXIII, 60, 61; XXXIV, 113
Andrew (June 10, 1761-1818) m. ....
Abigail Dame XXXIV, 150
Enos (c. 1755-Aug. 20, 1792) m. Jan.
16, 1776 Abigail Penoyer XV, 65,
130
Hezekiah (May 20, 1749-Feb. 19, 1834)
m. Mar. 19, 1770 Mary Turner XXXIV,
43
Ithamar (Oct. 26, 1736-Nov. 8, 1817)
m. July 28, 1762 Rhoda Barnes

XIII, 76
*John, I (....-a. 1663) m. ....
Dorothy ...... MASS XXXIV, 150*
*John (1596-Dec. 30, 1656) m. 1626/8
Joanna (Antrobus) Lawrence NH
XXXIV, 158*
John (Feb. 20, 1726-....) m. July 17,
1747 Eunice Allen XXIX, 338
Samuel (1741-May 20, 1817) m. Sept.
6, 1761 Bethia Miles V, 69; XII,
65
Simon (Dec. 19, 1733-Apr. 21, 1814)
m. Jan. 1, 1756 Rebecca Holden
XXXIV, 157
*William (1609-June 1673) m. ....
Elizabeth Southcutt CONN V, 69;
XII, 65; XIII, 76; XV, 65, 131;
XX, 9; XXIX, 241, 338; XXXIII,
60, 61; XXXIV, 43, 113*

TWIGGS, includes TRIGGS
John (1750-1816) m. .... Ruth
Emanuel II, 51
*Thomas (....-....) m. .... Mary
Southwood (Sutherd) VA II, 51*

TWINING
Thomas (July 5, 1733-Apr. 23, 1816)
m. Oct. 24, 1765 (2) Anna Cole
XXXIII, 119, 120, 141
*William (c. 1594-Apr. 15, 1659) m.
1652 (2) Anna Doane MASS XXXIII,
119, 120, 141*

TWITCHELL
*Benjamin (June 10, 1599-1675/6) m.
.... Mary Riggs MASS XXX, 264;
XXXI, 191; XXXII, 228; XXXIII, 293*
Joshua (Nov. 13, 1750-1811) m. Jan.
13, 1781 Sarah Miller XXX, 264;
XXXI, 191; XXXII, 228; XXXIII, 293

TWOMBLY
*Ralph (c. 1625-a. Aug. 7, 1686) m.
.... Elizabeth ...... NH XXI,
119*
Samuel, Jr. (Mar. 18, 1726-Mar. 12,
1794) m. .... Sarah (Roberts)
Wentworth XXI, 119

TYDEWELL, see TIDWELL

TYDWELL, see TIDWELL

TYLER
Abner (1738-Mar. 1, 1819) m. Dec. 1,
1774 Bethiah Muzzy X, 267
Benjamin (1725-p. 1785) m. 1755 (1)
.... XXVI, 177, 178
Ebenezer, II (Aug. 8, 1747-1823) m.
a. 1772 Jerusha Chapman XVI, 44

TYLER, cont.
  Elnathan (Mar. 30, 1755-Oct. 19,
    1817) m. Mar. 1786 Phoebe Atwater
    XXIII, 7, 14
  Henry (1604-c. 1672) m. a. 1640 (1)
    Mary ...... VA XXVI, 177, 178
  Job (1619-p. 1700) m. a. 1639 Mary
    ...... RI, MASS X, 267; XVI, 44;
    XVII, 9; XXVII, 27
  John Steel (Mar. 1, 1754-Oct. 1,
    1813) m. .... Sarah Whitwell
    VIII, 29
  Peter (....-Apr. 20, 1712) m. Nov.
    20, 1671 (1) Deborah Swain CONN
    V, 82; XXIII, 7, 14
  Phineas (May 17, 1738-Oct. 31, 1796)
    m. Nov. 19, 1766 Lucy Hyde XXVII,
    27
  Robert, Sr. (c. 1637-1674) m. June
    29, 1663 Joanne Ravens MD XVI,
    91
  Robert, Sr. (Aug. 19, 1751-Apr. 15,
    1815) m. 1772 Margaret Tyler XVI,
    91
  Solomon (Sept. 23, 1757-Nov. 7, 1810)
    m. Feb. 17, 1781 Mary Archer XVII,
    9, 10
  Thomas (c. 1660-1703) m. .... Miriam
    Simpkins MD VIII, 29
  Titus (bpt. Aug. 16, 1730-p. 1781)
    m. Jan. 11, 1759 Susanna Berry
    V, 82

TYRELL, see TERRELL

TYRRELL, see TERRELL

TYSON
  Jehu (1750-p. 1799) m. 1773 Mildred
    Moye XXXIII, 285
  John (1635-a. 1690) m. 1659 Sussan-
    ika ...... VA XXXIII, 284, 285

UNDERHILL
  John, Sr. (1597-July 21, 1672) m.
    Dec. 12, 1628 Helene de Hooch
    MASS XXXII, 244
  John (Jan. 25, 1729-Oct. 22, 1798)
    m. Jan. 28, 1749 Rebecca Frost
    XXXII, 244
  Thomas (Nov. 6, 1740-Jan. 29, 1815)
    m. 1764 (1) Ann Taylor VI, 55
  Thomas William (c. 1664-Aug. 1751)
    m. 1738 (2) Elizabeth Taylor VA
    VI, 55

UPDIKE, includes OP DYCK
  Lawrence (May 11, 1739-a. Apr. 14,
    1813) m. c. 1760 Alteye Lanning

  XXVII, 82; XXXIV, 139
  Louris Jansen (1600-1659) m. a. 1643
    Christina ...... NY XXVII, 82;
    XXXIV, 139

UPHAM
  Isaac (Oct. 3, 1741-Mar. 10, 1808)
    m. Oct. 10, 1769 Hepzibah Shapley
    XXXII, 269; XXXIII, 129, 130
  John (1600-Feb. 25, 1681) m. Nov.
    1626 Elizabeth Slade MASS XXIV,
    26; XXXII, 269; XXXIII, 129, 130
  Samuel (Sept. 15, 1762-Mar. 12, 1848)
    m. Feb. 10, 1790 Martha Livermore
    XXIV, 26

UPSON
  Ashbel, Sr. (Apr. 25, 1762-June 30,
    1831) m. Mar. 18, 1784 Mary Munson
    XIII, 23; XXVIII, 29; XXXIV, 57,
    219
  Benjamin (Aug. 4, 1720-Nov. 23, 1792)
    m. Nov. 17, 1743 Mary Blakelee
    XXVIII, 29
  Thomas (....-July 19, 1655) m. Jan.
    23, 1646 (2) Elizabeth Fuller CONN
    XIII, 24; XXVIII, 29; XXXIV, 57,
    220

UTLEY
  Samuel, I (1615-1662) m. Dec. 6, ✝
    1648 Hannah Hatch MASS XXXII,
    195
  William (Feb. 1724/5-Mar. 17, 1790)
    m. 1745 Sarah Peabody XXXII, 195

UTTER
  Abraham (Nov. 18, 1732-Jan. 5, 1813)
    m. Oct. 14, 1769 (2) Hannah Bur-
    dick XXV, 208; XXXIV, 185
  Nicholas (a. 1637-p. Aug. 17, 1722)
    m. .... RI XXV,
    208; XXXIV, 185

VALENTINE
  John (Apr. 25, 1643-Feb. 1, 1724) m.
    Apr. 16, 1702 Mary Lynde MASS
    X, 48
  Obadiah (1730-May 19, 1788) m. 1761
    Mary Mulford XVIII, 140
  Richard (....-c. 1684) m. ....
    ...... NY XVIII, 140
  Samuel (Dec. 7, 1745-Mar. 10,
    1834) m. Dec. 5, 1770 Elizabeth
    Jones X, 48
  Thomas (Aug. 3, 1713-Apr.
    17, 1783) m. July 17, 1735
    Elizabeth Gooch
    X, 48

VAN AACHEN, see VAN AUKEN

VAN AERTS DAALEN, see VAN ARSDALE

VAN AKEN, see VAN AUKEN

VAN AKIN, see VAN AUKEN

VAN ALSTYNE
Jans Martense (....-p. 1698) m. c.
1662 Dirckje (Dorothy) Harmenson
NY XVI, 86; XXXIV, 324
Philipus (Sept. 15, 1735-Dec. 24,
1814) m. July 8, 1761 Maritje
Van Alstyne XXXIV, 324
William (bpt. Dec. 10, 1721-May 22,
1802) m. c. 1762 Catherine Knicker-
bocker XVI, 86

VAN ANTWERP, includes ANTWERPEN
Daniel Janse (c. 1634-1717) m. 1656
Maretje Groot NY XXV, 151;
XXXIII, 325
Johannes (Feb. 13, 1732-Jan. 15,
1812) m. Mar. 4, 1755 Annatje Vee-
der XXXIII, 325
Simon (Mar. 1751-Jan. 18, 1839) m.
.... (2) Elizabeth Viele XXV, 151

VAN ARSDALE, includes ARSDALEN, VAN
AERTS DAALEN, VAN ARSDALEN
Abraham Isaac (1760-Aug. 1849) m.
1789 Mary Eoff VII, 47; XXVIII,
64, 210; XXXI, 57, 58
Cornelius Ouke (bpt. Nov. 14, 1762-
Feb. 22, 1843) m. Apr. 10, 1791
Elizabeth Van Arsdale XXVI, 183,
184
John (1722-1798) m. 1744 Deborah
Van Pelt XXIX, 227
Simon Janse (1629-Oct. 29, 1710) m.
a. 1660 Pieterje Wyckoff NY VII,
47; XXVI, 183, 184; XXVIII, 63, 64,
210; XXIX, 227; XXXI, 58

VAN ARSDALEN, see VAN ARSDALE

VAN AUKEN, includes VAN AACHEN, VAN
AKEN, VAN AKIN
Benjamin (Feb. 13, 1756-Sept. 18,
1835) m. Aug. 1782 Margaret Chesney
(Chasnor) XXXIV, 64
Daniel (bpt. Feb. 2, 1735-1815) m.
Dec. 13, 1753 Lea Kittel XVI, 133
Jacobus (James) (June 18, 1734-1812)
m. Feb. 10, 1759 Elizabeth Van
Bunschoten XXV, 108, 109
Marinus (....-p. Oct. 16, 1724) m.
a. 1685 Pieternelle DePre NY XVI,
133; XXV, 108, 109; XXXIV,
65

VAN BOSKIRK, see VAN BUSKIRK

VAN BRUNT
Albert (Nov. 14, 1720-Oct. 16, 1781)
m. Oct. 26, 1745 Jannetje Van
Brunt XXI, 111
Nicholas (Aug. 27, 1749-Sept. 5,
1802) m. Mar. 8, 1783 Mary Wyckoff
XXI, 111
Rutger Joesten (....-p. 1713) m. 1657
Tryntje Claes (Harmenson) NY XXI,
111

VAN BUSKIRK, includes VAN BOSKIRK
Laurens Andriesken (....-1694) m.
Sept. 12, 1658 Jannetje Jans
(Boreutson) NY III, 70
Martin (Oct. 18, 1755-May 18, 1828)
m. Feb. 8, 1780 Maria Van Ness
III, 70

VAN CAMPEN
Cornelius (c. 1735-Mar. 28, 1780)
m. .... Winifred DePew XXX, 289,
290
Gerritt Jansen (....-....) m. Jan.
17, 1659 Machteld (Stoffels) Lode-
wick NY XXX, 290

VAN CLEEF, includes VAN CLEAF
Isaac (Oct. 24, 1724-Jan. 30, 1804)
m. .... Dorcas Pomeroy XXXIV,
176
Jan (1628-1699) m. .... Angelica
Lawrence NY XXIX, 163; XXXIV,
176
Joseph (Feb. 6, 1760-July 20, 1843)
m. Dec. 19, 1782 Eleanor Schenck
XXIX, 163
Lawrence (Apr. 15, 1754-Jan. 15,
1830) m. 1785 Sarah Angevine
XXXIV, 176

VAN COUWENHOVEN, see CONOVER

VAN CULEN, see VAN CULIN

VAN CULIN, includes VAN CULEN, VON
KOLEN
Johan (John), I (1621-p. Dec. 24,
1704/5) m. c. 1667 Anneken (Anna)
...... PA XVII, 21
John, IV (Aug. 28, 1729-c. Apr. 1790)
m. Sept. 11, 1771 (3) Sarah Smith
XVII, 21

VANDEGRIFT
Christopher (June 8, 1732-June 8,
1816) m. .... Ruth King XXX, 207,
208
Jacob Leenderszen (bpt. 1622-1691)

VAN RENSSELAER, cont.
  Johannes (Feb. 11, 1708-1783) m.
    Jan. 3, 1734 Catherine Van Brugh
    XIV, 116

VAN REYPEN, see VAN RYPER

VAN RIPEN, see VAN RYPER

VAN ROSENVELT, see ROSEVELT

VAN RYPEN, see VAN RYPER

VAN RYPER, includes VAN REYPEN, VAN
    RIPEN, VAN RYPEN
  Daniel (June 26, 1736-July 1818) m.
    Oct. 13, 1761 Elizabeth Terhune
    IX, 46, 47; XXX, 154
  Juriaen Tomassen (....-Sept. 12,
    1695) m. May 12, 1667 Pryntje
    Hermans NJ IX, 46, 47; XXX, 154

VANSANT
  Garret Stoffelszen (....-a. June
    1706) m. .... Lysbet Gerrits NY,
    PA V, 78
  Garrett (1743-Apr. 13, 1797) m. ....
    Elizabeth Larue V, 78

VAN SCHAICK, see VAN SCHOICK

VAN SCHOICK, includes VAN SCHAICK, VAN
    SCOYOC, VAN SKIHAWK
  Cornelis Aertsen (c. 1610-c. 1669)
    m. a. 1641 (1) Belitje Hendrickse
    NY XXIX, 399; XXXIII, 162, 163,
    334
  David (Apr. 14, 1730-p. 1782) m. May
    23, 1757 Hannah Holmes XXIX, ʾ398
  Stephen (c. 1718-a. 1805) m. c. 1772
    Rachel Bales XXXIII, 162, 163,
    334

VAN SCOYOC, see VAN SCHOICK

VAN SICKELEN, see VAN SICKLE

VAN SICKLE, includes VAN SICKELEN,
    VAN SYCKLIN
  Ferdinandus (c. 1635-1712) m. 1660
    Eva Antonis Jansen NY XXIX,
    136
  Reinier (bpt. Nov. 17, 1723-Dec. 12,
    1803) m. May 29, 1746 Mayke (Mercy)
    Longstreet XXIX, 136

VAN SKIHAWK, see VAN SCHOICK

VAN SUTPHEN, see SUTPHEN

VAN SYCLIN, see VAN SICKLE

VAN TINE, includes FONTEYNE, FUNTINE
  Charles (....-p. Aug. 1, 1687) m.
    a. May 1658 Katrina Baaly NY
    XXXIII, 80, 81
  Ephraim (Feb. 7, 1762-Dec. 28, 1831)
    m. Nov. 26, 1782 Anne Pumme
    XXXIII, 80, 81

VAN VALKENBURG, see VAN VALKENBURGH

VAN VALKENBURGH, includes VAN VALENBURG
  Bartholomew Thomas (Oct. 21, 1753-p.
    July 18, 1790) m. Nov. 25, 1774
    Engeltie Van Slyck XXXIV, 330
  John Jost (Jan. 20, 1745-Mar. 28,
    1815) m. Apr. 2, 1765 Magdalena
    Brown XXXII, 251
  Lambert (c. 1616-a. 1697) m. c. 1642
    Annetje Beekman NY XXII, 101;
    XXXII, 251; XXXIV, 331
  Lambert (bpt. May 1731-a. 1782) m.
    1752 Catarina Van Veghten XXII,
    101

VAN VEGHTEN
  Dirck (July 15, 1699-Nov. 24, 1781)
    m. .... (3) Sarah Middagh III,
    49
  Teunise Dircksen (....-....) m. ....
    .... NY III, 49

VAN VOORHEES, see VOORHEES

VAN VRANCKEN, see VAN VRANKEN

VAN VRANKEN, includes VAN VRANCKEN
  Claas Geritse (....-....) m. ....
    .... NY XI, 56
  Nickolas (May 24, 1763-May 20, 1804)
    m. Feb. 11, 1787 Ruth Comstock
    XI, 55

VAN WIE
  Garett (Feb. 20, 1739-....) m. Sept.
    10, 1762 Catherine Lansing XXII,
    85
  Hendrick Gerritse (....-1691) m. ....
    .... NY XXII, 85

VAN WINKLE
  Jacob (Wallingen) (....-1657) m. c.
    1647 Tryntje Jacobe NY, NJ
    XIII, 59; XXXIV, 158
  Jacob (July 26, 1727-Dec. 17, 1778)
    m. .... Rachel Commugear XIII, 59
  Michael (Apr. 6, 1736-May 22, 1803)
    m. July 13, 1758 Phoebe Carter
    XXXIV, 158

VAN ZANDT, includes VANZANDT
  Geret Stoffelse (1620-1705) m. ....

VAN ZANDT, cont.
*(2) Lysbeth Geritse NY, PA XXIX,
58*
Jacobus (James) (Aug. 18, 1727-Jan.
31, 1798) m. Aug. 23, 1756 Jannetje
Bennet XXIX, 58
*Johannes (Jan) (....-1729) m. ....
Jannetje ...... NY V, 125*
John (Apr. 30, 1762-Apr. 11, 1841)
m. Aug. 30, 1787 Lentje (Helen)
Lansing XVII, 152
*Joseph Janse (....-a. Oct. 16, 1753)
m. July 5, 1688 Seytje Marcelis
NY XVII, 152*
Peter Praa (1708-Aug. 12, 1812) m.
.... Sarah Marschalk V, 125

VANZANDT, see VAN ZANDT

VARNUM
*George (....-1649) m. .... Hannah
...... MASS XXXI, 272; XXXIV,
155*
Joseph Bradley (Jan. 29, 1750- Sept.
11, 1821) m. Jan. 26, 1773 Molly
(Mary) Butler XXXI, 272; XXXIV,
154
*Samuel (c. 1619-p. 1702) m. ....
Sarah Langton MASS XXII, 136*
Thomas (May 5, 1748-July 1, 1805)
m. Aug. 11, 1781 Polly Atkinson
XXII, 136

VAUGHAN
Daniel (1721-Nov. 15, 1786) m.
June 6, 1744 Abigail Hanson XXV,
20
*George (1621-Oct. 8, 1694) m. 1652
Elizabeth Hincksman MASS XXV,
20*

VAUGHN
*John (....-1687) m. 1638 Gillian
...... RI XV, 136, 138*
Jonathan (....-p. 1778) m. Jan. 1,
1756 Elizabeth Gould XV, 136,
138

VAWTER
David (1720-....) m. .... Mary Rucker
XIV, 48, 49
*John (1665-....) m. ....
...... VA XIV, 48, 49*

VEACH, includes VEICH, VEITCH
Elias (May 5, 1759-Sept. 13, 1839)
m. Feb. 18, 1790 Jean Brown XXXII,
196
*James (July 15, 1628-May 1685) m.
Aug. 17, 1657 Mary Gakerlin MD
XXXII, 196*

VEASEY
*George (c. 1635-a. Jan. 2, 1673) m.
Jan. 23, 1664 Mary Wiggin NH, ME
XXIX, 376*
Thomas (1750-Sept. 23, 1829) m. Oct.
1, 1778 (2) Lydia Wiggin XXIX,
376

VEAZEY
Edward (Nov. 12, 1730-Apr. 24, 1784)
m. June 19, 1755 Elizabeth DeCour-
sey XXIX, 383
*John (....-c. 1701) m. .... Martha
...... MD XXIX, 383*

VEDDER
Albert Alexander (bpt. Mar. 17, 1737-
June 21, 1800) m. May 30, 1761
Neeltje Bancker VI, 106, 107
*Harmen Albertse (....-c. 1713) m.
.... NY VI, 106,
107*

VEEDER
Gerrit Symouse (July 4, 1751-Feb.
18, 1836) m. Jan. 12, 1782 Jammeke
Ten Eyck XXIX, 197
Johannes (1734-1793) m. July 6,
1759 Lena Vrooman XIX, 142
*Symon Volkertse (1624-p. Jan. 8,
1697) m. .... Engeltie ...... NY
XIX, 142; XXIX, 197*

VEELEN, see VER VALIN

VEICH, see VEACH

VEILE
*Cornelis Volkertszen (....-a. 1650)
m. .... Marie du Trieux NY XXV,
84*
Cornelise (1718-....) m. .... (1)
Rachel Swartwout XXV, 84
Myndert (....-....) m. Sept. 26,
1777 Johanna Palmatier XXV, 84

VEITCH, see VEACH

VENABLE
*Abraham (....-....) m. c. 1700
Elizabeth Lewis VA XII, 67, 71,
91*
John (1740-1811) m. .... Agnes Moor-
man XII, 67, 71, 91

VER VALIN, includes VEELEN, VIELEN
*Daniel (....-p. 1712) m. .... Aeltie
Schaets NY XXXIII, 271*
Gideon (Feb. 10, 1742-p. 1791) m.
Jan. 24, 1786 (1) Jane Low XXXIII,
271

VER VALIN, cont.
Johannes (c. 1616-1700) m. 1637
Anna Jaarsvelt NY XXXIII, 271

VIA
Amer (?) William (1650-....) m. ....
.... VA XXV, 234, 245,
246
William (1761-June 27, 1836) m.
Mar. 17, 1784 (1) Mary Craig XXV,
234, 245, 246

VICKERY
George (....-Apr. 20, 1679) m. 1635
Rebecca Phippeny (Phippin) MASS
XXIX, 271
Matthias (Sept. 20, 1741-Nov. 12,
1812) m. Nov. 9, 1767 (1) Ruth
Horton XXIX, 271

VIELE, includes VIELEN
Cornelis Volkertzen (1622-1649) m.
.... Marie de Trieux NY VII, 31
Ludovicus (Oct. 27, 1742-Dec. 27,
1800) m. .... Effie (Eva) Toll
VII, 31

VIELEN, see VER VALIN, VIELE

VINAL
Israel (1725-1804) m. Sept. 25,
1760 Marcy Cushing XI, 122;
XII, 95
John (1632/3-Aug. 21, 1698) m. 1664
Elizabeth Baker MASS XI, 122;
XII, 95

VINCENT
Adriaen (....-....) m. a. 1646 ·....
...... NY XXIX, 357
Gilbert (Feb. 21, 1756-Mar. 26, 1842)
m. 1780 Phoeba Vail XXIX, 357

VINING
David (Sept. 25, 1740-July 1, 1830)
m. Dec. 23, 1762 Lydia Torrey
XXXIV, 173
John (bpt. Apr. 17, 1636-Feb. 1685)
m. Jan. 22, 1660 Mary Read MASS
XXXIV, 173

VINTON
Benoni (Sept. 2, 1756-Jan. 24, 1837)
m. Apr. 27, 1779 Rebecca Dix XIV,
70
David, Jr. (Mar. 18, 1759-1830) m.
Mar. 10, 1778 Persis Newton XXXIII,
24
John (c. 1620-p. 1662) m. .... Ann
...... MASS XIV, 69, 70; XXXIII,
24

VISSCHER
Frederick (Feb. 21, 1741-June 9,
1809) m. May 22, 1768 Gazena De
Graff XV, 29
Harmon B. (1619-1693) m. .... Hester
Tjerkse NY XV, 29

VLEREBOME, includes SERVAES, VLIEREBOOM
Serevas (Selvester) (Mar. 24, 1743-
Apr. 7, 1818) m. a. 1765 Femmetje
(Phebe) Schamp XXXIII, 179, 180
Tys (Mathew) (c. 1632-a. May 19,
1700) m. c. 1661 Maria (Maritie)
Jacobze NY XXXIII, 179, 180

VLIEREBOOM, see VLEREBOME

VON KOLEN, see VAN CULIN

VOORHEES, includes VAN VOORHEES
Abraham (June 8, 1725-Nov. 15, 1807)
m. May 9, 1747 Adrianna Lefferts
V, 47
Abraham (Sept. 16, 1730-1812) m.
1751 Maria Van Doren XXXI, 81,
82, 302; XXXII, 110
Garret (Mar. 15, 1739-Nov. 16, 1816)
m. .... Ann Beekman XXX, 247
Hendrick (Van) (May 12, 1740-Nov.
12, 1827) m. Mar. 25, 1763 Jane
Lesley XXII, 62
Isaac (Oct. 8, 1758-Oct. 4, 1844) m.
Apr. 19, 1781 Sarah Nevius XXXI,
287
John C. (Dec. 1731-1805/7) m. Jan.
28, 1776 Margaret Van Zant XI,
151
Lucas Stevanse (1650-1713) m. ....
(1) Catherine Hanson Van Noort-
strand NY V, 47
Steven Coerte (1600-Feb. 16, 1684)
m. .... NY V, 47;
XI, 151; XXII, 62; XXX, 247; XXXI,
81, 82, 287, 302; XXXII, 110

VOSE
Jeremiah (Apr. 8, 1747-May 31, 1823)
m. Jan. 11, 1769 Hannah Holmes
XVII, 20, 21; XXVI, 45
John (May 21, 1756-Sept. 30, 1825)
m. Oct. 16, 1777 Militiah Daven-
port XXX, 76, 77
Oliver (Feb. 10, 1734/5-Aug. 31,
1810) m. July 12, 1755 Elizabeth
Badcock XXX, 77
Robert (c. 1599-Oct. 11, 1683) m.
July 25, 1629 Jane Moss MASS
XVII, 21; XXVI, 45; XXX,
77

VROMAN, see VROOMAN

VROOMAN, includes VROMAN
  Adam (1649-Feb. 25, 1730) m. 1678
  Engeltie (Angelica) Bloom NY
  XXVI, 123
  Hendrick Meese (1618-Feb. 1690) m.
  1648 Geertruy Johannis NY XXXIII,
  34; XXXIV, 156
  Martynus (Dec. 6, 1745-Mar. 6, 1821)
  m. Jan. 15, 1769 Santje (Santis)
  Swart XXVI, 123
  Samuel (Oct. 14, 1735-Dec. 6, 1805)
  m. Mar. 6, 1760 Catherine Zeile
  XXXIII, 34, 35
  Walter Jacob (Nov. 4, 1744-Feb. 17,
  1817) m. 1767 Jacomytje Barheyt
  XXXIV, 156

WADE
  Amos (1707-....) m. 1728 (1) Phoebe
  Williams XXV, 146
  Benjamin (1646-1699) m. c. 1670 Ann
  Looker NY, NJ VI, 13
  Ichabod (1742-1812) m. Aug. 29, 1762
  Mary Peck XX, 156
  John (Nov. 16, 1735-a. 1781) m. ....
  Abigail Brawner XXVII, 194
  Nehemiah (1736-Oct. 19, 1776) m.
  1758/9 Abigail Mulford VI, 13
  Nicholas (1616-Feb. 7, 1683) m. 1638
  Elizabeth Ensign MASS XX, 156;
  XXV, 146
  Zachary (....-a. May 25, 1677) m.
  .... Mary Henson MD XXVII, 194

WADHAMS
  John (....-Dec. 19, 1676) m. ....
  Susanna ...... CONN XXXIV, 289
  Seth (Nov. 3, 1743-Apr. 18, 1817) m.
  June 11, 1767 Anne Gatlin XXXIV,
  289

WADSWORTH
  Christopher (....-1679) m. .... Grace
  Cole MASS V, 123, 124; XXI, 11;
  XXV, 187; XXXII, 189, 207
  John (Dec. 12, 1735-Mar. 21, 1776)
  m. Oct. 18, 1759 Jerusha White
  XXV, 187; XXXII, 189, 207
  Peleg (May 6, 1748-1829) m. ....
  Elizabeth Bartlett V, 123, 124
  Recompence (1729-1798) m. 1760 (2)
  Abigail Lyon XXI, 11, 12
  William (....-1675) m. .... Sarah
  ...... MASS XXX, 122
  William (1742-1816) m. .... Mercy
  Clark XXX, 122

WAIT, includes WAITE
  Benjamin (Feb. 13, 1736-June 28,

  1822) m. Jan. 11, 1767 Lois Gil-
  bert XXX, 27
  John (1618-Sept. 26, 1693) m. ....
  Mary Hills MASS XXIX, 122; XXXII,
  211
  John (Nov. 20, 1730-c. 1815) m. 1752
  Martha Wolcott XVIII, 76
  Joseph (Mar. 1, 1754-July 26, 1819)
  m. 1779 Hepzibah Sherman XXXIII,
  234, 235, 238
  Peleg (Oct. 22, 1761-Oct. 17, 1847)
  m. Dec. 25, 1783 Mary Greene X,
  95
  Richard (1608-Jan. 16, 1668/9) m.
  .... Mary ...... MASS II, 32, 33;
  XVIII, 76; XXX, 27; XXXIII, 234,
  235, 238
  Richard (1711-1790) m. .... Rebecca
  Higgins II, 32, 33
  Thomas (1601-c. Apr. 1677) m. ....
  Eleanor Wardwell RI X, 95; XII,
  59; XIII, 57; XXI, 107, 108; XXXI,
  70; XXXIII, 36, 37
  Thomas (Oct. 6, 1749-Aug. 13, 1828)
  m. Oct. 10, 1771 Lydia Hitchings
  XXIX, 121; XXXII, 211
  William (Jan. 9, 1730-Mar. 20, 1826)
  m. 1751 Mary Nichols XII, 59;
  XIII, 57; XXI, 107, 108
  Yelverton (Sept. 14, 1743-Feb. 29,
  1816) m. Dec. 20, 1761 Margaret
  Whitford XXXI, 70; XXXIII, 36, 37

WAITE, see WAIT

WAKEFIELD
  John, Sr. (1614/5-June 18, 1667) m.
  a. 1638 Ann ...... VA, MASS XXV,
  166; XXVI, 170, 171; XXXI, 315;
  XXXII, 295; XXXIV, 103
  Joseph (May 9, 1752-June 1827) m.
  Nov. 5, 1777 Relief Kendall XXXI,
  315; XXXII, 295; XXXIV, 102
  William, Sr. (c. 1726-p. 1815) m.
  Nov. 15, 1751 (2) Dorcas Hayward
  XXV, 166; XXVI, 170, 171

WAKEMAN
  John (bpt. Mar. 29, 1601-1661) m.
  Jan. 1628/9 Elizabeth Hopkins CONN
  XXXIV, 194
  John (Jan. 29, 1730-July 24, 1809)
  m. Oct. 3, 1754 Esther Bradley
  XXXIV, 194

WALDERNE, see WALDRON

WALDO
  Cornelius (c. 1624-Jan. 3, 1700/1)
  m. Jan. 2, 1651 Hannah Cogswell
  MASS XXII, 130; XXIV, 132; XXV,

WALDO, cont.
216; XXVI, 257; XXX, 129, 130;
XXXI, 65, 218; XXXIII, 15
Edward (May 14, 1742-....) m. Nov.
17, 1763 Jerusha Thompson XXXIII,
15
Jesse, Sr. (Sept. 6, 1736-Feb. 28,
1823) m. Apr. 2, 1760 Bridget
Thompson XXXI, 65, 218
Jonathan (Mar. 22, 1728-Dec. 21,
1788) m. Apr. 7, 1773 Joanna Mighill XXII, 130; XXIV, 132; XXV,
216
Jonathan (Aug. 17, 1738-July 17,
1821) m. May 25, 1762 Ann Palmer
XXVI, 257; XXX, 129, 130

WALDRON, includes WALDERNE
Resolved (May 10, 1610-a. May 17,
1690) m. May 10, 1654 (2) Tanneke
Nagel NY XII, 7
Richard (1609-June 28, 1689) m. 1636
(1) .... NH XXXII, 213
Samuel (May 10, 1723-1806) m. 1781
Lydia Salisbury XII, 7
Thomas Westbrook (July 26, 1721-Apr.
3, 1785) m. .... Constance Davis
XXXII, 213

WALE, see WHALEY

WALES
Nathaniel (Feb. 26, 1586-Dec. 4,
1661) m. .... (2) Susan Greenway
MASS XXVI, 108
Oliver (Feb. 23, 1744-Mar. 23, 1816)
m. c. 1767 (1) Elizabeth Lawrence
XXVI, 108

WALKER
Bezaliel (May 7, 1724-June 16, 1810)
m. Apr. 3, 1755 Deborah Barns
XXX, 212
Bruce (May 17, 1760-July 27, 1840)
m. Oct. 12, 1780 Mehetabel Currier
XXX, 166, 167
Christopher (1757-May 6, 1841) m.
June 8, 1782 Patience Foster X,
79, 102, 115
Daniel (....-p. 1702) m. .... Alice
...... MD X, 79, 103, 115
Daniel (July 1, 1764-Aug. 9, 1847)
m. .... Patience Newton XXX, 212
James (June 12, 1603-a. 1660) m. May
1, 1627 Ellen Maybole MD XXXIV,
312
James (1619/20-Feb. 15, 1691) m. ....
Elizabeth Phillips MASS XXIV,
152; XXVI, 105
James (Aug. 4, 1739-Nov. 20, 1797) m.
June 1, 1769 Ellen Clayborn

XXXIV, 312
Joseph (Feb. 13, 1731-June 1816) m.
.... Abigail ...... XXXIII, 250
Joseph (May 25, 1731-Nov. 1, 1818)
m. 1752 Sarah Thomas XXIV, 157
Lewis (....-Dec. 23, 1728) m. Apr.
22, 1693 Mary Morris PA XXIV,
157
Lewis (Dec. 13, 1745-May 21, 1813)
m. .... Hannah Cooper V, 103, 104
Peter (Dec. 19, 1747-Sept. 26, 1824)
m. Aug. 1, 1769 Deborah Gooding
XXIV, 152; XXVI, 105
Philip (c. 1627-1702) m. ....
...... MASS V, 103, 104
Richard (c. 1593-May 17, 1687) m.
.... (2) Jane Talmadge MASS XXIX,
66, 85, 225
Robert (1606-May 29, 1687) m. c.
1635 Sarah ...... MASS XXXIII,
250
Samuel (Oct. 1, 1642-Jan. 18, 1704)
m. Sept. 10, 1662 Sarah Read MASS
XXX, 166, 167
Samuel, Jr. (Aug. 30, 1721-Dec. 15,
1817) m. Dec. 20, 1750 (1) Mary
Stratton XXIX, 84, 225
Solomon (bpt. July 19, 1722-July 21,
1789) m. a. Dec. 1741 Miriam ......
XXIX, 66
Thomas (....-c. 1697) m. a. 1661
Mary ...... MASS XXX, 212
Thomas (....-1724) m. a. 1685 Eliza-
beth Parris RI III, 42
William (July 25, 1748-1825) m. ....
Marie Von Siegfried III, 42

WALLACE, see WALLIS

WALLBRIDGE
Henry (....-July 25, 1729) m. Dec.
25, 1688 Anna Amos MASS, CONN
XIII, 22; XXIX, 280; XXXII, 11
Henry (Jan. 23, 1727-Sept. 17, 1809)
m. Dec. 25, 1750 Anna Safford
XIII, 22
John (Apr. 1740-1823) m. .... Mary
...... XXIX, 280; XXXII, 11

WALLER
George, II (Feb. 8, 1731-Mar. 18,
1814) m. Apr. 6, 1760 Ann Winston
Carr XXXII, 229; XXXIV, 330
John (....-1667) m. .... Alice Major
MD XXXIV, 18, 285
John (1617-....) m. .... Mary Key
VA X, 280, 281
Joseph (Nov. 21, 1751-1818) m. a.
1777 Elizabeth Flint XXXIV, 17,
18, 285
Thomas (July 9, 1732-1787) m. c.

1770 Sarah Dabney X, 280, 281
William, I (c. 1635-a. Nov. 24, 1694)
m. .... Mary Allen VA XXXII, 229;
XXXIV, 330

WALLING
Ladis (....-a. Nov. 18, 1787) m. p.
Sept. 25, 1775 Ruth Brewster XXXI,
98, 99, 186
Thomas (c. 1630-a. July 19, 1674) m.
.... Mary Abbott RI XXXI, 99,
186

WALLIS, includes WALLACE
David (c. 1730-1811) m. c. 1754
Mary Williston XXV, 150, 176,
177
Francis (Oct. 5, 1749-1787) m. 1774
Sophia Brooks XII, 89; XIV, 39,
40; XVI, 54; XVII, 104; XXVII, 170
Henry (....-p. 1699) m. ....
...... MD XII, 89; XIV, 39, 40;
XVI, 54; XVII, 104; XXVII, 170
Robert (c. 1618-c. 1643) m. ....
Rebecca ...... VA XXV, 150, 176
177

WALTON
Edward (c. 1656-Apr. 27, 1720) m. c.
1697 Elizabeth ...... VA XXVIII,
41, 42
George (Nov. 1725-p. 1783) m. Sept.
3, 1749 Jean Black XVIII, 71
Mark (1754-May 14, 1808) m. 1781
Ann Delaplaine XXIX, 38
Robert (Sept. 25, 1749-July 24, 1837)
m. Nov. 20, 1769 Mary Hobson
XXVIII, 41, 42
Thomas (....-1689) m. Dec. 16, 1671
Esther Lawrence NY XXIX, 38
William (....-a. 1686) m. ....
...... MD XVIII, 70

WANDEL, includes DE WANDELAER
Daniel (c. 1749-....) m. ....
...... XIX, 48
Johannes (c. 1652/4-p. 1720) m. 1675
Sara Schepmoes NY XIX, 48
John (1709-p. 1798) m. 1744 ......
Thurston XIX, 48

WARD, includes WARDE
Abraham (....-1802) m. 1776 Hannah
Riggs XVI, 80
Andrew (....-p. June 8, 1659) m.
.... Hester Sherman MASS, CONN
XII, 75; XXX, 225, 266; XXXII, 117;
XXXIII, 197
Artemus (Nov. 27, 1722-Oct. 27, 1800)
m. July 31, 1750 Sarah Trowbridge
XIV, 86

Caleb (Nov. 22, 1748-June 20, 1813)
m. Jan. 22, 1772 Rebecca Foster
XXVI, 188
Daniel (Jan. 30, 1764-Aug. 19, 1841)
m. June 30, 1795 Bridget French
XVIII, 35
George (....-a. 1666) m. ....
...... CONN XXV, 114
Humphrey (Nov. 16, 1764-....) m.
.... Martha Grice XXV, 41
John (1619-1698) m. ....
...... RI II, 55
John (1620-Nov. 2, 1694) m. ....
Sarah Lyman CONN, NJ XVI, 80
John (Aug. 12, 1720-1805) m. 1745
Mariah Torrey X, 49, 50, 51, 52
Jonathan (Feb. 3, 1727-July 7, 1791)
m. .... Susannah Stone V, 110,
111
Joseph, Jr. (Aug. 15, 1760-Sept. 2,
1834) m. Feb. 1, 1785 Elizabeth
Treadway X, 89; XVII, 72
Josiah (Sept. 4, 1741-Feb. 27, 1795)
m. Dec. 3, 1761 Sarah Goodale X,
35; XXIX, 164
Josiah (Jan. 20, 1748-Sept. 5, 1780)
m. Apr. 12, 1770 Mary (Polly) Trott
Wiswall X, 49, 50, 51, 52
Josiah (1756-Apr. 20, 1824) m. ....
Hannah Morse IX, 47
Nathan (1721-June 15, 1804) m. Sept.
25, 1746 Tamasin Neland XVI, 129,
130
Peter (1755/6-Mar. 15, 1812) m. May
27, 1781 Nancy Mead XXV, 114
Samuel (1725-1776) m. .... Anne Ray
II, 55
Samuel (July 20, 1739-Aug. 19, 1828)
m. .... Hannah Lee XII, 75
Samuel, Jr. (1756-1832) m. ....
Phebe Green II, 55
Stephen (Sept. 17, 1757-....) m.
Nov. 4, 1780 (1) Patience Cook
XVIII, 52, 53
William (....-Aug. 10, 1687) m. ....
(2) Elizabeth ...... MASS V, 110,
111; IX, 47; X, 36, 49, 50, 51, 52;
XIV, 86; XVI, 130; XVIII, 35, 52;
XXV, 41; XXVI, 188; XXIX, 164
William (Aug. 16, 1632-Mar. 28, 1690)
m. Mar. 26, 1660 (2) Phoebe ......
CONN X, 89; XVII, 72
William (Dec. 18, 1736-Nov. 6, 1829)
m. Nov. 25, 1766 Anne Palmer XXX,
225, 266; XXXII, 117; XXXIII, 197

WARDE, see WARD

WARDWELL
Jacob (Aug. 1744-....) m. Oct. 1,
1769 Hannah Whitney XXI, 9, 10

WARDWELL, cont.
  Jonathan (bpt. Dec. 16, 1711-Jan.
  31, 1788) m. Apr. 5, 1748 Rachel
  Pevey XXII, 36
  Thomas (....-Dec. 10, 1646) m. ....
  Elizabeth ...... MASS XXII, 36
  William (Apr. 1604-....) m. ....
  Alice ...... MASS XXI, 9, 10

WARE, includes WEARE
  Ebenezer (Apr. 22, 1726-June 26,
  1795) m. Nov. 7, 1751 Esther Hunt-
  ing XVII, 23, 24
  Elias (May 26, 1755-Feb. 7, 1819) m.
  c. 1783/4 Chloe ...... XXXII, 114
  Nicholas (a. 1648-1662) m. a. July
  1655 Ann Vassall VA XXXIV, 81
  Peter (c. 1618-Apr. 18, 1692) m. Feb.
  5, 1665 Mary Purrington ME XXXII,
  114
  Reuben (....-a. May 1803) m. ....
  Susanna ...... XXXIV, 81
  Robert (....-Apr. 19, 1699) m. Jan.
  24, 1645 Margaret Huntinge MASS
  XVII, 24

WARFIELD
  Charles (Aug. 30, 1738-June 23, 1790)
  m. Apr. 15, 1762 Elizabeth Warfield
  XIX, 129
  Elisha (1741-1818) m. Aug. 22, 1778
  Ruth Burgess XXV, 181
  Richard (....-1703) m. 1670 Elinor
  Browne MD XIX, 129; XXV, 181;
  XXXI, 32, 176
  Seth (Jan. 15, 1723-a. May 14, 1805)
  m. .... Mary Gaither XXXI, 32,
  176

WARING
  Ephraim (May 4, 1754-Dec. 18, 1804)
  m. Jan. 7, 1778 Huldah Hickox
  XXIV, 63
  Jonathan, Jr. (Aug. 15, 1740-....)
  m. .... Rachel Webb XXXI, 238,
  239
  Richard (c. 1643-1688) m. .... Lydia
  Akerly NY XXIV, 63; XXXI, 238
  Samson (1617-1668) m. 1648 Sarah
  Leigh MD XVI, 66
  Thomas Trumen Greenfield (1752-Jan.
  1818) m. 1780 Lydia Walton XVI,
  66

WARNE
  George (Apr. 23, 1713-Oct. 23, 1789)
  m. .... Abigail Warford XI,
  45
  Thomas (c. 1632-May 15, 1722) m.
  c. 1698 Mary (Lord) Carhart NJ
  XI, 45

WARNER
  Andrew (c. 1595-Dec. 18, 1684) m.
  .... (1) Mary ,.....; .... (2)
  Hester Seldon CONN, MASS II, 32;
  XI, 98; XXIX, 331, 406; XXXI, 276,
  298; XXXIV, 272
  Consider (May 19, 1762-p. 1803) m.
  c. 1784 Peggy Thorne XXVI, 189,
  190; XXIX, 41, 324
  Daniel (1717-Dec. 11, 1804) m. 1746
  Jemima Wright XVII, 17; XIX, 156
  Daniel (June 30, 1729-Sept. 1, 1814)
  m. 1756/7 (2) Martha Case XXVII,
  106, 107; XXIX, 106, 107
  Daniel (Dec. 22, 1734-1823) m. May
  31, 1758 Mary Wright XXIX, 331
  Eleazer (Feb. 8, 1738-June 2, 1821)
  m. Apr. 29, 1762 (1) Johanna Hale
  XI, 98
  Jabez Ichabod (May 17, 1761-Jan. 14,
  1849) m. Apr. 5, 1784 (1) Ann
  Wakeley XXXI, 276, 298
  Jesse, Sr. (May 6, 1718-May 10, 1793)
  m. Oct. 30, 1739 Miriam Smith
  XXXIV, 272
  Jesse, Jr. (Feb. 1, 1747-Aug. 14,
  1834) m. May 11, 1769 Sarah War-
  riner XXXIV, 272
  John (1615-1679) m. 1649 (1) Ann
  Norton; .... (2) Margaret ......
  CONN XXVI, 56, 190; XXVII, 106;
  XXIX, 41, 106, 107, 324
  Jonathan (1728-1810) m. .... Eliza-
  beth Selden II, 32
  Martin (Jan. 11, 1735-July 15, 1807)
  m. 1762 Mary Ruggles XXIX, 406
  Samuel, Sr. (Oct. 3, 1708-Sept. 10,
  1783) m. July 17, 1732 Mary Gilling
  XXIX, 149
  Samuel, Jr. (Jan. 1, 1733-Dec. 1823)
  m. Apr. 20, 1758 Ann Steele XXIX,
  149
  Samuel (c. 1759-Sept. 3, 1840) m.
  Sept. 25, 1788 Lydia Hitchcock
  XXVI, 56
  Seth (Dec. 2, 1760-July 5, 1845) m.
  Sept. 10, 1797 Polly Painter XXIX,
  149
  William (....-a. 1648) m. ....
  ...... MASS XIII, 27; XVII, 17;
  XIX, 156; XXIX, 150
  William (June 13, 1756-Sept. 13,
  1827) m. Nov. 21, 1780 Susannah
  Palmer XIII, 27

WARREN
  Abijah (Aug. 8, 1754-Sept. 24, 1824)
  m. Feb. 28, 1793 (2) Ann Hayward
  XXV, 218, 219, 220
  Arthur (....-p. July 6, 1658) m.
  1638 Mary ...... MASS XXIV, 19;

Mar. 25, 1790 Mary (Polly) Morse
XXIV, 27

Peter (1720-1802/3) m. May 31, 1754
(2) Lydia Davis   XXIX, 184

Richard (May 18, 1751-June 5, 1842)
m. c. 1778 Judith Ann Reynolds
XXX, 59, 60

Samuel, Sr. (1604-Jan. 25, 1709) m.
.... Elizabeth ...... VA XXX,
236

WEBB

Alexander (Aug. 20, 1559-....) m.
.... Mary Wilson MASS XV, 134

Azariah (Oct. 11, 1748-Apr. 10,
1846) m. c. 1770 Lucy Andrews
XV, 27

Charles (1755-1806) m. .... Mary
(Polly) Todd Ware   XXVI, 236, 237

Christopher (c. 1599-1689/90) m.
.... Humility ...... MASS XVII,
128, 133; XX, 130; XXV, 28; XXVI,
65; XXVIII, 162

Christopher (1630-May 30, 1694) m.
Jan. 18, 1654/5 Hannah Scott MASS
XV, 28; XXXIII, 13

Ebenezer (Jan. 12, 1718/9-Feb. 11,
1803) m. Dec. 3, 1740 Ruth Crane
XXXIII, 13

Ebenezer (May 29, 1757-Aug. 14, 1845)
m. Aug. 28, 1777 Abigail Rude   XXV,
28

Epenetus, Jr. (Aug. 6, 1740-a. Jan.
2, 1797) m. May 30, 1762 (1) Sarah
Judson   XI, 88

James (1755-Sept. 1, 1825) m. Nov.
7, 1782 Nancy Conney   XXVIII, 162,
163

John (....-....) m. July 14, 1673
Mary Sanford VA XXVI, 236, 237

Joshua (Feb. 9, 1721/2-Apr. 17, 1808)
m. May 28, 1744 Hannah Abbe   XXVI,
65

Richard (1611-Mar. 15, 1675/6) m.
.... (1) Elizabeth ...... MASS,
CONN XI, 88

Stephen (Oct. 4, 1742-Dec. 10, 1819)
m. May 22, 1766 Content Hewitt
XVII, 128, 133; XX, 130

William (Apr. 26, 1758-Apr. 6, 1824)
m. May 16, 1782 Lois Brewster
Strong   XV, 134

WEBBER

John (1735-1816) m. Nov. 20, 1766
Alice Harty (Hartier)   XXIII,
16

Josiah (....-....) m. ....
...... MASS XIII, 120

Thomas (c. 1630-May 1690) m. 1655
Mary Parker MASS XXIII, 16

WEBSTER

Abel (July 2, 1726-Feb. 14, 1801)
m. Mar. 12, 1746 Hannah Emerson
XVII, 62, 63; XX, 137; XXII, 5

Abijah (1762-Sept. 8, 1832) m. 1788
(2) Sarah Warren   XXV, 188, 189;
XXX, 42

Caleb (July 12, 1752-Nov. 13, 1796)
m. May 20, 1777 (2) Joanna Smith
XVIII, 91

Cyprean (July 25, 1733-Apr. 12, 1809)
m. Feb. 25, 1768 Sarah Hayden
XIII, 73

David (Aug. 12, 1758-Sept. 1, 1847)
m. 1787 Sarah Carr   XXIX, 371

Gideon (bpt. June 16, 1751-June 6,
1820) m. Dec. 30, 1779 Sarah Cadwell   XXIX, 111

Jacob (Feb. 12, 1748-Oct. 3, 1776)
m. May 13, 1770 Abigal Goodrich
XIX, 147

Jesse, Sr. (Apr. 18, 1748-Sept. 14,
1830) m. Apr. 29, 1773 Abigail
Eaton   XXXIII, 351

John (1590-Apr. 5, 1661) m. Nov. 7,
1609 Agnes Smith CONN XIII, 73;
XIV, 37; XVI, 64; XIX, 147; XXI,
158; XXV, 188, 189; XXIX, 111, 350;
XXX, 42; XXXII, 152, 179; XXXIII,
57

John (c. 1605-a. Sept. 4, 1646) m.
.... Mary Shotswell MASS XII,
44; XVII, 62, 63; XX, 138; XXII,
5; XXXII, 84; XXXIII, 351; XXXIV,
167

John (Oct. 14, 1730-1827) m. Apr.
19, 1757 Phebe Haseltine   XXXIV,
167

Jonathan, II (May 4, 1764-Sept. 24,
1817) m. Jan. 4, 1787 Huldah
Orvis   XXXII, 178, 179

Joshua (Apr. 16, 1750-1830) m. July
14, 1790 (2) Prudence Smith   XIV,
37, 38

Joshua (Nov. 24, 1754-Nov. 9, 1840)
m. Nov. 3, 1778 Susanna Bailey
XXXII, 84

Nathaniel (Nov. 23, 1753-Apr. 29,
1836) m. Mar. 11, 1777 Mehitable
Smith   XX, 137; XVII, 62, 63;
XXII, 5

Oliver (May 6, 1735-1816) m. Mar.
25, 1760 Patience Wright   XXI,
158; XXXII, 152

Samuel (Feb. 21, 1744/5-p. 1817)
m. Nov. 15, 1770 Jerusha Smith
XXIX, 350

Samuel (Oct. 11, 1748-May 9, 1813)
m. Mar. 2, 1786 Mary King Seymour
XXXIII, 57

Thomas (bpt. Nov. 29, 1631-Jan. 5,

WEBSTER, cont.
  1715) m. Nov. 2, 1657 Sarah Brewer
  MASS XVIII, 91; XXIX, 371
  Thomas (Feb. 10, 1711/2-Dec. 31,
    1781) m. .... Abigail (Webster)
    Emery XII, 44
  William (July 24, 1738-1815) m. 1765
    Edee Drake XVI, 64

WEDGE
  Isaac (1751-Aug. 16, 1812) m. Oct.
    10, 1774 Ruth Parmalee XXXIV,
    296
  Thomas (c. 1640-Sept. 6, 1685) m. c.
    1666 Deborah Stevens MASS XXXIV,
    296

WEEKS, see also WICKES
  John (1749-1818) m. Dec. 25, 1770
    Deborah Brackett XIX, 145
  John (Sept. 8, 1762-Sept. 17, 1852)
    m. Oct. 10, 1786 Hannah Moody
    XXXIV, 48
  Leonard (bpt. Aug. 7, 1639-a. Nov.
    24, 1707) m. 1667 Mary Haines NH
    XIX, 145; XXXIV, 48

WELCH
  John (c. 1625-....) m. .... (2) Mary
    ...... MD XXXIV, 86
  John (1745-May 1831) m. 1764 Deborah
    Monroe XXVI, 191, 192
  Philip (1643-....) m. Feb. 20, 1666
    Hannah Haggett MASS XXVI, 191,
    192
  Robert (....-c. 1811) m. Nov. 1777
    Eleanor Carr XXXIV, 86

WELD
  Eleazar (Feb. 20, 1737/8-Aug. 5, 1800)
    m. Apr. 23, 1761 Mary Hatch XXX,
    196
  Ezra (June 13, 1736-Jan. 13, 1816)
    m. .... Anna Weld V, 90
  Joseph (c. 1598-Oct. 7, 1646) m. ....
    Elizabeth Wyse MASS XXX, 196
  Thomas (1590-Mar. 23, 1661) m. ....
    Margaret Doreslye MASS V, 90
  Thomas (1626-Jan. 17, 1682) m. ....
    Dorothy Whiting MASS V, 90

WELLES, see WELLS

WELLINGTON
  Elisha (July 20, 1758-Jan. 12, 1799)
    m. Apr. 9, 1780 Lucy Cutler
    XVIII, 83
  George (Oct. 21, 1749-....) m. Dec.
    24, 1772 .... XVIII, 63
  Roger (1609/10-Mar. 11, 1697/8) m.
    1638 Mary Palgrave MASS XVIII,

  63, 83

WELLS, includes WELLES
  Abner (Nov. 13, 1737-Sept. 21, 1797)
    m. Dec. 10, 1758 Mary Case XXV,
    23
  Barker, Sr. (May 16, 1750-1780) m.
    1769 Rebecca Clark XXXIII, 166
  Bayzie (Aug. 16, 1744-Oct. 24, 1814)
    m. Feb. 9, 1769 Ruth Gaylord XXI,
    69, 70
  Edward (Feb. 26, 1726-1798) m. Dec.
    25, 1749 Elizabeth Sheffield XXI,
    173
  Ezekiel, Sr. (July 22, 1745-Dec. 7,
    1818) m. Nov. 25, 1779 Phoebe
    Meacham XXV, 89
  Hezekiah (Dec. 9, 1725-....) m. Dec.
    17, 1747 Mary Boardman XXI, 77,
    78
  Hezekiah (June 25, 1736-Mar. 8, 1817)
    m. 1770 Sarah Trumbull XXI, 80,
    81
  Hugh (c. 1590-c. 1645) m. c. 1619
    Frances ...... CONN, MASS XXI,
    69, 70; XXV, 89
  James (Jan. 12, 1748-Mar. 25, 1825)
    m. Sept. 4, 1785 Abigail Gaylord
    Peck XXXIV, 20
  John Calvin (June 1761-Apr. 19,
    1810) m. 1782 Amy Homan XXV, 23
  Jonathan (Apr. 13, 1718-Apr. 29,
    1780) m. c. 1741/2 Abigail Dickin-
    son XXIX, 361
  Joshua (....-....) m. ....
    ...... CONN XXI, 80, 81
  Joshua (1742-p. 1776) m. ....
    ...... XIII, 87
  Joshua (Jan. 18, 1763-Oct. 20, 1855)
    m. 1785 Hannah Finch XIII, 87
  Josiah (July 25, 1756-....) m.
    Apr. 30, 1780 (2) Ruth Rich XXI,
    77, 78
  Matthew (Feb. 17, 1735/6-July 28,
    1818) m. Jan. 5, 1758 Bridget Bur-
    dick XXX, 216
  Nathaniel (Aug. 21, 1705-July 1776)
    m. c. 1736 Dorothy Light X, 28;
    XI, 123
  Peter, Sr. (....-p. 1715) m. ....
    .... RI XXXIII, 166
  Richard Duckett (Mar. 22, 1752-Apr.
    13, 1833) m. Jan. 22, 1774 Sarah
    Lakin XXXIII, 302
  Robert (Feb. 6, 1743-Feb. 17, 1820)
    m. Apr. 25, 1769 Abigail Jefferds
    XXXIII, 17
  Robert (1756-1849) m. Dec. 9, 1779
    Ann Wheeler XXXII, 184, 185
  Roger (Dec. 29, 1753-May 27, 1795)
    m. .... Jemima Kellogg XII, 36

Samuel (c. 1728-Dec. 29, 1800) m.
Aug. 1752 Lucy Kilbourn XXXII,
249
Stephen (Apr. 4, 1754-June 14, 1838)
m. .... Love Ford XXI, 173
Thomas (c. 1560-....) m. ....
...... CONN XXIX, 361
Thomas (1598-Jan. 14, 1660) m. 1618
(1) Elizabeth Hunt CONN XII, 36,
37; XXI, 77, 78; XXXII, 185, 249;
XXXIII, 17; XXXIV, 20
Thomas (c. 1620-1676) m. Mar. 1651
Mary Beardsley CONN, MASS XXI,
69, 70
Thomas (1626-Feb. 12, 1700) m. Feb.
12, 1655 Naomi Marshall MASS, RI
XXI, 173; XXX, 216
Thomas, Sr. (c. 1637-1718) m. c.
1684 Frances ...... MD XXXIII,
302
William (1608-Nov. 13, 1671) m. c.
1656 Mary (Marie) Youngs NY XIII,
87; XXV, 23

WELTON
John (a. 1667-June 18, 1726) m. ....
Mary Upson CONN XX, 64
Nathaniel (Apr. 4, 1742-Apr. 23, 1777)
m. Feb. 6, 1764 Martha Tuttle XX,
63
Samuel (Nov. 2, 1744-1777) m. Nov.
23, 1770 Jerusha Hill XX, 64

WENDELL
Evert Janse (1615-1709) m. .... (1)
Sesannah Du Grienx NY XII, 90
Jacob Abram (May 6, 1753-....) m.
.... Mary Swart XII, 90

WENTWORTH
Amaziah (Mar. 30, 1760-1813) m. ....
Sally Davis V, 48
Benjamin (May 24, 1732-Apr. 19, 1818)
m. .... Rachel Wentworth XXXII,
249, 250
Timothy (Jan. 22, 1747-Nov. 29, 1842)
m. Nov. 29, 1770 Amy Hodgdon XX,
88
William (Mar 15, 1615/6-1696/7) m.
.... Elizabeth (Kenny) ME, NH
V, 48; XX, 88; XXXII, 250

WESSELL, see also EVERTSZEN
Lucas (1754-a. Nov. 4, 1825) m. Apr.
5, 1779 Jannetje Hugenor XXXII, 34

WESSON, see WESTON

WEST
Ebenezer (Nov. 11, 1757-....) m.
1779 Mehitable Nye X, 12, 19, 27

Francis (....-....) m. a. 1660 Sus-
anna Soule MASS XXXIII, 50
Francis (1616-Jan. 2, 1692) m. Feb.
27, 1639 Margery Reeves MASS X,
12, 19, 27; XIX, 6; XXI, 7, 8
George (....-a. Nov. 1707) m. ......
Susannah ...... VA, DE XXXI, 61,
62, 93, 103, 140; XXXIV, 300
Hezekiah (1754-Jan. 15, 1805) m.
Nov. 20, 1777 Experience Davis
XXXIII, 50
Isaac (....-1814) m. 1769 Susannah
Anderson XXXI, 20
John (Dec. 14, 1590-1659) m. ....
Anne ...... VA XXXI, 20
Joseph, Jr. (Nov. 2, 1728-Sept. 25,
1805) m. Mar. 10, 1752 (2) Lois
Strong XXI, 8
Matthew (....-p. 1655) m. ....
...... MASS, RI XXIV, 117
Oliver (Oct. 2, 1733-Apr. 23, 1816)
m. 1757 Thankful Nye X, 12, 19,
27; XIX, 5
Osborne (1749-1819) m. .... Dorcas
Trail XX, 127; XXI, 23, 24
Thomas (July 9, 1577-1618) m. Nov.
25, 1596 Ceciley Shirley VA
XX, 127; XXI, 23, 24
Thomas, Jr. (c. 1740-a. Apr. 1, 1802)
m. .... Rachel Burton XXXI, 61,
62, 93, 103, 140; XXXIV, 300
William (1732-c. 1790) m. a. 1767
Hannah Coates XXIV, 217

WESTBROOK
Anthony Janz (Jansen) (....-....) m.
c. 1659/60 Osseltjie Dircksz (Rich-
ards) NY XXIX, 88
Jacob (bpt. July 1, 1722-Sept. 19,
1784) m. Apr. 11, 1746 Lydia West-
fall XXIX, 88

WESTCOTT
Daniel (Aug. 4, 1751-Mar. 9, 1823)
m. Apr. 24, 1774 Marcy (Mercy)
Warner XXX, 78, 79
John (Mar. 26, 1745/6-Dec. 26, 1831)
m. Oct. 21, 1770 Amey Clarke XXV,
237, 238; XXVII, 120
John (Dec. 1758-1813) m. Feb. 2,
1775 Sarah Diament XXI, 64, 65
Richard (1612-1651) m. 1634 Joanna
Baldwin CONN XXI, 64, 65
Stukely (1592-Jan. 12, 1677) m. Oct.
5, 1619 Juliana Marchante MASS,
RI XXV, 237, 238; XXVII, 120;
XXX, 78, 79

WESTON, includes WESSON
Ebenezer, Jr. (Feb. 10, 1731-Dec.
22, 1805) m. Nov. 16, 1758

WESTON, cont.
Esther Taylor XIX, 27
John (1631-1723) m. Apr. 18, 1653
  Sarah Fitch   MASS II, 44; IV,
  157; IX, 16; X, 229; XIX, 27;
  XXXI, 209
John (Dec. 1, 1711-Sept. 30, 1786)
  m. July 22, 1740 (1) Ruth Death
  IV, 157; IX, 16; X, 229
Joseph (Mar. 7, 1732-Oct. 16, 1775)
  m. 1756 Eunice Farnsworth XXXI,
  209
Levi (May 27, 1753-June 9, 1852) m.
  .... Olive Locke IV, 157; IX, 16
Sutherick (1751-1831) m. .... Mary
  DeLancey II, 44

WESTOVER
Jonas, Sr. (c. 1642-Jan. 15, 1708)
  m. Nov. 19, 1663 Hannah Griswold
  CONN XXVII, 16
Moses (Mar. 24, 1744-p. 1790) m.
  Dec. 2, 1767 Elizabeth Holmes
  XXVII, 16

WETHERBEE, includes WITHERBEE
John (1650-1711) m. Sept. 16, 1684
  (2) Lydia Moore MASS XXIV, 146;
  XXIX, 205; XXXI, 282
Joseph (1725-Apr. 14, 1809) m. Apr.
  16, 1748 (1) Elizabeth Whitney
  XXXI, 282
Oliver (Apr. 9, 1743-1820) m. Mar.
  11, 1762 Rachel Willard XXIV, 146
Paul (Aug. 12, 1749-Apr. 24, 1834)
  m. Feb. 12, 1775 Dorcas Hovey
  XXIX, 205

WETHERILL
Christopher (c. 1646-Jan. 26, 1711)
  m. .... Mary Hornby NJ IV, 85
Samuel (Apr. 12, 1736-Sept. 24, 1816)
  m. .... Sarah Yarnall IV, 85

WETMORE
Joseph (Feb. 3, 1760-July 6, 1836)
  m. c. 1790 Rhoda Webster XXIX, 68
Thomas (1615-Dec. 11, 1681) m. Dec.
  11, 1645 (1) Sarah Hall CONN
  XXIX, 68

WHALEY, includes WALE, WHALLEY
Edward (1615-Apr. 21, 1718) m. Jan.
  29, 1668/9 Elizabeth Middleton MD
  XXX, 182
Seth (1753-Sept. 19, 1825) m.
  Hester (Ester) Baker XXX,
  182

WHALLEY, see WHALEY

WHARTON
Thomas (Oct. 16, 1664-July 31, 1718)
  m. Jan. 20, 1686/9 Rachel Thomas
  (Friend) PA XXV, 159, 160
Thomas, Jr. (c. 1735-May 22, 1778)
  m. Dec. 7, 1774 (2) Elizabeth Fish-
  bourne XXV, 159, 160

WHEATON
Christopher (....-Mar. 20, 1683/4)
  m. 1674 Martha Prince MASS XXXIV,
  276
Christopher (Mar. 16, 1749-May 30,
  1798) m. July 26, 1770 Abigail
  Brewer XXXIV, 276
Jonathan, Jr. (May 28, 1758-Sept.
  30, 1841) m. Nov. 13, 1792 (2)
  Serepta Martin XVIII, 28
Robert (c. 1606-1696) m. 1636 Alice
  Bowen MASS XVIII, 28

WHEELER
David (June 22, 1730-Nov. 10, 1803)
  m. Mar. 15, 1757 Rebecca Jones
  XX, 66; XXVII, 70
David, Jr. (June 30, 1758-Oct. 5,
  1806) m. May 22, 1783 Martha Brooks
  XXVII, 70
Elnathan (May 20, 1740-Feb. 14, 1809)
  m. Jan. 26, 1765 Charity Frost
  XVII, 6
Ephriam (....-c. 1669) m. .... Ann
  ...... MASS, CONN XVII, 55
George (Aug. 1600-June 2, 1687) m.
  .... Katherine ...... MASS XXVII,
  225; XXXII, 59
Ignatius (1744-Aug. 1793) m. ....
  Henrietta Maria (Neale) Smith
  XXXIII, 205
Jacob (1755-a. July 9, 1799) m. 1770
  Ann ...... XXVIII, 186
John (....-Aug. 29, 1670) m. ....
  Ann ...... MASS XXX, 33, 34
John (1630-a. Jan. 9, 1694) m. ....
  Mary ...... MD XXVIII, 186;
  XXXIII, 205
John (1738-....) m. Jan. 26, 1761
  Esther Mallett XVII, 55
John (Feb. 28, 1743-Nov. 20, 1788)
  m. Mar. 8, 1766 Elizabeth (Part-
  ridge) Richardson XXVII, 160
John (June 2, 1756-....) m. ....
  Sybil Todd XIX, 108
Jonathan (Aug. 8, 1735-....) m. Jan.
  8, 1753 Patience Cole XXX, 33, 34
Joseph, Sr. (Jan. 23, 1747-Nov. 7,
  1836) m. Sept. 18, 1774 Prudence
  Palmer X, 299; XVII, 101
Lester (July 24, 1757-May 15, 1835)
  m. Feb. 9, 1774 Eunice Bailey

XXI, 159

Moses, I (1598-Mar. 1, 1698) m. c.
1642 Miriam Hawley CONN XVII,
6; XIX, 108

Nathan (Feb. 9, 1726-1823) m. May 25,
1749 Mary Hunt XXX, 171

Richard (....-Feb. 9, 1675/6) m.
June 2, 1658 (2) Sarah Prescott
MASS XXVII, 160

Samuel (1744-Jan. 13, 1832) m. ....
Ruth ...... XXVII, 225

Shepard, Jr. (Dec. 5, 1756-Dec. 9,
1798) m. Feb. 22, 1780 Lucy Wheeler
XXXI, 57

Thaddeus (Dec. 16, 1742-....) m. Oct.
17, 1769 Elizabeth Farmer XXXII,
59

Thomas (1602-Mar. 6, 1686) m. 1645
Mary Noyes MASS, CONN X, 299;
XVII, 101; XXI, 159; XXXI, 57

Thomas (1620-Dec. 24, 1704) m. ....
(1) Sarah Meriam MASS XX, 66;
XXVII, 70; XXX, 171

WHEELOCK

Eleazar (Apr. 23, 1711-Apr. 24, 1779)
m. Nov. 21, 1747 (2) Mary Brinsmead
XXX, 95, 96

Eleazar (Aug. 17, 1756-Dec. 7, 1811)
m. 1792 Thankful Pennock XXX, 95,
96; XXXI, 123

Joseph (Jan. 20, 1765-c. 1809) m.
Mar. 9, 1786 Sally Slater XXXIII,
116, 117

Ralph (c. 1600-Jan. 11, 1684) m. c.
1634 Rebecca ...... MASS XXX, 95,
96; XXXI, 123; XXXIII, 116, 117

WHILLDEN

Gabriel (....-p. Feb. 11, 1654) m.
.... Margaret ...... MASS X, 126,
136, 141, 142

James (1714-Nov. 5, 1780) m. ....
(1) Jane Hand X, 126, 136, 141,
142

WHIPPLE

Benajah (June 17, 1734-Mar. 17, 1816)
m. .... Tabitha ...... X, 110

Eleazer (Jan. 20, 1733-p. 1781) m.
1757 Anna Brown XXXIV, 174

Ichabod, Sr. (Apr. 2, 1738-p. 1791)
m. Feb. 16, 1762 Catherine Browne
XIX, 101; XXXI, 138

John (c. 1617-May 16, 1685) m.
1639 Sarah Darling MASS X, 110,
XIX, 101; XXXI, 138; XXXIV,
174

Nathaniel (Nov. 12, 1713-Sept. 1792)
m. Apr. 22, 1736 Bethiah Slack
XIX, 101; XXXI, 138

WHITAKER

Hudson (Oct. 23, 1757-July 5, 1817)
m. 1777 Susannah Thomas XXXIII,
323

Jabez (Dec. 6, 1595-p. 1628) m. p.
Nov. 19, 1624 Mary Bourchier VA
XXXII, 133; XXXIII, 225, 228, 323

John (May 21, 1745-Nov. 1823) m. Apr.
18, 1786 (2) Ferebee Pearson
XXXII, 133; XXXIII, 225, 228

John (May 12, 1747-July 20, 1816)
m. Aug. 9, 1770 Christian Benton
XXIX, 125, 382; XXX, 122

Richard (1645-1696) m. .... Eliza-
beth ...... VA XXIX, 125, 381;
XXX, 122

WHITCOMB

Anthony (July 17, 1766-a. 1809) m.
a. 1795 Lucy Right XXIX, 214

Asa (Feb. 29, 1735/6-Mar. 31, 1812)
m. Feb. 18, 1759 Joanna Raymond
XXIX, 214

Elisha (Oct. 18, 1742-Sept. 17,
1814) m. Oct. 7, 1764 Joanna Whitcomb XXXII, 264

John (c. 1588-Sept. 24, 1662) m. a.
1635 Frances ...... MASS XV, 79,
XVIII, 72; XXIX, 214; XXXII, 264

Joseph (1743-Apr. 21, 1832) m. Oct.
25, 1770 Hannah Nicholas XV, 79

Oliver (Nov. 26, 1732-Mar. 1776) m.
Dec. 17, 1754 Sarah Whitney
XVIII, 72

WHITE

Cornelius, III (1721-Nov. 18, 1787)
m. .... Susannah Howell XIV, 45

Cornelius, IV (1755-Dec. 11, 1806)
m. 1778 Abigail Leonard XIV, 45

Daniel (1632-c. 1699) m. a. 1670
Magdelin ...... VA XXXI, 157,
200

Daniel (1749-1815) m. .... Sarah
Hale II, 45

Ebenezer (1737-Oct. 11, 1817) m. a.
1770 Sarah Church III, 67

Elihu (1734-Dec. 23, 1793) m. ....
Zeriah Cole XV, 14

Enoch (Feb. 1747-Jan. 10, 1813) m.
.... Susanna Goodman XII, 46

Ezekiel (June 8, 1746-Jan. 10, 1821)
m. June 30, 1766 Sarah Vinton
X, 130

George (1722-p. Oct. 8, 1790) m.
1748 Susannah Read XXXI, 157,
158, 200

George (Mar. 6, 1746-Jan. 17, 1777)
m. .... Mary Benton XXI, 8, 9

Isaac (1752-1822) m. .... Thankful
Clark V, 46

WHITE, cont.
  Joel (Apr. 6, 1705-June 28, 1789) m.
    Jan. 22, 1736 Ruth Dart II, 45;
    IV, 155; VI, 83; XI, 157; XV, 98
  John (....-June 3, 1685) m. ....
    Sarah Stevens MD XVII, 61
  John (....-p. May 30, 1697) m. ....
    .... VA XXX, 84
  John (c. 1600-Jan. 1, 1684) m. 1622
    Mary Levit MASS, CONN II, 45;
    III, 67; IV, 155; V, 46; VI, 83;
    XI, 157; XII, 46, 116; XIII, 18,
    63; XV, 14, 98; XXI, 8, 9
  John (Mar. 3, 1601/2-p. Mar. 28,
    1673) m. May 28, 1627 Joan West
    MASS XXI, 33, 123, 124
  Joseph (June 25, 1738-Feb. 5, 1805)
    m. Mar. 15, 1759 Deborah Fish
    XXVI, 100, 101; XXVIII, 89, 90
  Josiah (Jan. 3, 1714-Sept. 1, 1806)
    m. Mar. 14, 1739 Deborah House
    XXI, 33, 123, 124
  Lemuel (Nov. 6, 1736-May 4, 1780) m.
    June 12, 1760 Martha Loomis IV,
    155; VI, 83
  Lemuel (Nov. 1, 1762-Dec. 8, 1843)
    m. June 25, 1793 (2) Mary Welles
    IV, 155; VI, 83
  Luther (Sept. 11, 1749-July 4, 1838)
    m. June 1797 (2) Mary Weldon XII,
    116; XIII, 18, 63
  Moses (1749-Aug. 1794) m. .... Sarah
    Elizabeth Poindexter XXX, 84
  Moses (June 29, 1756-May 28, 1833)
    m. .... Elizabeth Amelia Atlee
    XII, 64
  Nathan (June 10, 1755-Jan. 27, 1829)
    m. Jan. 14, 1779 Eunice Chapin
    XX, 35
  Nathaniel (1629-1711) m. .... (1)
    Elizabeth ...... CONN V, 46
  Nicholas (May 22, 1759-May 8, 1815)
    m. .... Deborah Ford X, 174
  Noah (Feb. 15, 1728-Mar. 2, 1788) m.
    Sept. 18, 1751 Sarah Swett X, 174
  Peter (Dec. 6, 1714-May 8, 1782) m.
    May 20, 1736 Jemima Taft XX, 35
  Resolved (c. 1614-1680) m. Apr. 8,
    1640 Judith Vassail MASS XVII,
    38
  Seth (Apr. 18, 1756-Feb. 5, 1837) m.
    May 22, 1779 Jemima Keith XI,
    97, 118, 132; XIV, 125
  Thomas (1599-Aug. 1679) m. ....
    ...... MASS X, 130; XI, 97, 118,
    132; XIV, 125; XX, 36; XXVI, 101;
    XXVIII, 90
  William (....-....) m. July 1, 1612
    Susanna Fuller MASS XVII, 38, 39
  William (1610-Sept. 28, 1690) m.
    .... (1) Mary ...... MASS X,

  174; XII, 64
  William (c. 1620-1673) m. .... Eliza-
    beth ...... MASS XIV, 45
  William, Sr. (1723-1787) m. 1742 Ann
    ...... XXX, 84
  William A. (1756-Aug. 24, 1802) m.
    .... Eunice White XVII, 38, 39
  William Stevens (May 10, 1756-Feb.
    20, 1821) m. .... Eliza Scott Wag-
    gaman XVII, 61

WHITEHURST
  James (....-c. 1719/20) m. ....
    .... VA XXIX, 29
  Jonathan (1720-1790/1) m. .... Eliza-
    beth ...... XXIX, 29

WHITFIELD
  Matthew (....-p. 1708) m. .... Pris-
    cilla Lawrence VA XXIX, 187, 233;
    XXX, 59; XXXIII, 275
  William, II (May 20, 1715-Mar. 31,
    1795) m. Nov. 6, 1741 Rachel Bryan
    XXIX, 187, 234; XXX, 59; XXXIII,
    275
  William, III (June 1, 1743-Mar. 1817)
    m. 1795 Sarah Bryan Hatch XXIX,
    187, 234

WHITFORD
  Joshua (June 23, 1731-Sept. 1813)
    m. 1754 Prudence Burdick XXIX,
    81
  Pasco (c. 1640-1700) m. ....
    ...... RI XXIX, 81

WHITING
  Allyn (1740-1818) m. .... Elizabeth
    Merry XXIX, 282
  John (Feb. 24, 1760-Sept. 3, 1810)
    m. May 24, 1785 Orphia Danforth
    XXV, 273, 274
  Jonathan (May 25, 1726-....) m. ....
    Elioenai Thurston IX, 33, 34
  Nathaniel (c. 1617-Jan. 15, 1682)
    m. Sept. 4, 1643 Hannah Dwight
    MASS IX, 33, 34; XII, 26; XIII,
    97; XXI, 106, 107
  Samuel (Nov. 20, 1597-Dec. 11, 1679)
    m. Aug. 1629 (2) Elizabeth St.
    John MASS XXV, 273, 274
  Samuel (May 15, 1720-Feb. 15, 1803)
    m. .... Elizabeth Judson VIII,
    18; XIX, 10
  Timothy (Feb. 24, 1732-July 12, 1799)
    m. .... Sarah Osgood XXV, 273,
    274
  William (a. 1613-July 1647) m. ....
    Susannah ...... CONN VIII, 18;
    XII, 15; XIX, 10; XXIX, 282, 369
  William Bradford (Apr. 15, 1731-

WHITTIER, cont.
  1646 Ruth (Rolfe) Green   MASS
  XXIII, 48; XXIV, 95; XXXIII, 76;
  XXXIV, 214

WHITTINGTON
  Cornelius (Apr. 24, 1749-1835) m.
  1774 Rebecca Gilliam XXXIII,
  230, 231
  William, I (1616-....) m. .... (3)
  Elizabeth Weston VA XXXIII, 230,
  231

WHITTLESEY
  David (Aug. 18, 1750-Jan. 31, 1825)
  m. May 19, 1793 (2) Martha Pomeroy
  IV, 154; XI, 41; XVI, 56
  John (July 4, 1623-Apr. 15, 1704) m.
  June 20, 1664 Ruth Dudley   CONN
  IV, 154; XI, 41; XVI, 56; XXX, 256
  Roger Newton (Feb. 24, 1754-Mar. 15,
  1835) m. Apr. 20, 1775 Ann Wood-
  ruff XXX, 256

WIATT, see WYATT

WICKER
  Thomas (....-Apr. 4, 1704) m. ....
  .... VA XXVIII, 109;
  XXXIII, 108, 109
  Thomas (1754-a. Aug. 1, 1832) m.
  1780 Sally Talley XXVIII, 109;
  XXXIII, 108, 109

WICKES, or WEEKS
  Silas (Sept. 10, 1758-June 21, 1838)
  m. Feb. 22, 1784 Elizabeth Ruscoe
  XXIV, 118
  Thomas (c. 1612-1671) m. ....
  ...... CONN XXIV, 118

WIGGIN
  Andrew (May 5, 1737-Sept. 16, 1778)
  m. Oct. 15, 1760 Mary (Jewett)
  Weeks XX, 146
  Issachar (June 10, 1740-June 1815)
  m. Nov. 11, 1773 Elizabeth Peavey
  XXXII, 191, 192
  Thomas (....-1666/7) m. 1632/3
  Katherine ...... NH XX, 146;
  XXXII, 192

WIGHT
  Daniel (Mar. 22, 1756-....) ·m. Apr.
  10, 1777 Hannah Lyon XXXIII, 43
  Henry (May 26, 1752-Aug. 12, 1837)
  m. June 21, 1789 Alice Burrington
  XVI, 85; XXIX, 63
  Joseph (Dec. 29, 1729-Oct. 20, 1804)
  m. June 9, 1763 Abigail Ware
  XXIV, 24

  Thomas (c. 1600-Mar. 17, 1673) m.
  Oct. 1626 (1) Alice ...... MASS
  XVI, 85; XXIV, 24; XXIX, 63;
  XXXIII, 43

WIKOFF, includes WYCKOFF, WYKOFF
  Peter Claesen (1625-June 30, 1694)
  m. 1649 Grietje Van Ness NY
  XXIX, 368; XXXI, 78; XXXIII, 18
  Samuel (Oct. 12, 1732-Apr. 24, 1826)
  m. Nov. 1, 1759 Gertrude Shipman
  XXIX, 368; XXXI, 78
  Samuel, Jr. (June 10, 1760-Mar. 4,
  1842) m. Feb. 11, 1780 Maria Bur-
  ger XXXIII, 18

WILBER, includes WILDBORE
  George (Sept. 23, 1718-Oct. 1777)
  m. Oct. 26, 1738 Rachel Sherman
  XXII, 82
  William (c. 1630-1710) m. 1653 Mar-
  tha ...... MASS XXII, 82

WILCOCKSON, see WILCOX

WILCOX, includes WILCOCKSON, WILCOXSON,
  WILLCOCKS
  Abel, Jr. (Mar. 3, 1731/2-Jan. 2,
  1807) m. Nov. 25, 1756 Mary Hull
  XXXII, 177
  Edward (....-....) m. ....
  ...... RI XXI, 109
  Isaiah (1738-Mar. 3, 1793) m. Oct.
  15, 1761 Sara Lewis XXI, 109
  James (Feb. 18, 1764-Jan. 23, 1838)
  m. Feb. 18, 1787 Elizabeth Bradley
  Augur XVIII, 10
  John (....-Oct. 11, 1651) m. ....
  (2) Mary ...... CONN XVII, 53
  Jonathan (July 13, 1752-Oct. 19,
  1818) m. .... Elizabeth Todd
  XVII, 53, 54
  Joseph (1763-Nov. 2, 1826) m. 1783
  Olive Dowd XXII, 76
  Robert (c. 1753-Oct. 11, 1808) m.
  Apr. 9, 1777 Sarah Wilbur XXVII,
  182
  Stephen (c. 1633-a. Feb. 6, 1690)
  m. 1658 Hannah Hazard RI XXVII,
  102
  William (1601-Nov. 1652/3) m. c.
  1633 Margaret Birdseye CONN XVI,
  11; XVIII, 10; XXII, 76; XXXII,177
  William (Apr. 1, 1727-Nov. 1775) m.
  .... Lucy Case XVI, 11

WILCOXSON, see WILCOX

WILD, see WILDES

WILDBORE, see WILBER

WINGFIELD
  John (Feb. 13, 1742-1814) m. 1764
  Robina Langford XXXII, 154
  Thomas (....-....) m. ....
  ...... VA XXXII, 154

WINKLEY
  Francis (bpt. Oct. 28, 1733-Oct. 9,
  1818) m. 1763 Martha Hunking
  XXI, 166, 167
  Samuel (c. 1666-c. 1736) m. 1684
  Sara Trickey NH XXI, 166, 167

WINN, includes WINNE, WYNN, WYNNE
  Benjamin (Oct. 22, 1759-Jan. 28,
  1840) m. May 9, 1786 Sarah Allen
  XVIII, 123; XIX, 29
  Edward (....-Sept. 5, 1682) m. ....
  .... MASS XVIII, 123
  John (....-1793/5) m. .... (2) Ann
  Stone XXXII, 214
  Joseph (....-Feb. 22, 1715) m. ....
  Rebecca Reed MASS XIX, 30
  Joshua (c. 1740-1805/6) m. ....
  Elizabeth Apling XV, 78, 134
  Pieter (....-1684) m. .... Tannatie
  Adams NY XXI, 118
  Pieter, Jr. (bpt. Sept. 9, 1753-....)
  m. May 13, 1775 Maria Oesterhaut
  XXI, 118
  Robert (c. 1630-1675/8) m. .... Mrs.
  Mary Poythress VA XV, 78, 134;
  XXIX, 200; XXXII, 214
  Robert (1742-Nov. 25, 1811) m. 1766
  Elizabeth ...... XXIX, 199
  Thomas (1620-a. 1692) m. 1643 Eliza-
  beth ...... MD XXI, 72, 73
  Thomas (1757-1797) m. 1775 Phila-
  delphia Winn XXI, 72, 73

WINNE, see WINN

WINSHIP
  Edward, I (Nov. 2, 1613-Dec. 2, 1688)
  m. .... (2) Elizabeth Parke MASS
  XXXII, 73
  Richard, II (Nov. 30, 1762-1838/9)
  m. 1787 Catherine Hannah Terrell
  XXXII, 73

WINSLOW
  Abner (May 17, 1732-Apr. 13, 1803)
  m. Aug. 16, 1759 Rebecca Hathaway
  XV, 86
  Benjamin (June 19, 1717-Apr. 26,
  1796) m. Aug. 11, 1738 Hope Cobb
  XXIV, 54
  John (Apr. 15, 1597-Oct. 1674) m.
  Oct. 12, 1624 Mary Chilton MASS
  XXVI, 217, 218
  John (1749-Nov. 1778) m. ....

  Rebecca Hathaway XI, 25
  John (Sept. 29, 1753-Nov. 29, 1819)
  m. May 18, 1782 Ann Gardner XXVI,
  217, 218
  Kenelm (Apr. 29, 1599-Sept. 13, 1672)
  m. June 1634 Eleanor (Newton)
  Adams MASS V, 89; X, 194; XI, 25;
  XV, 86; XXII, 73; XXIV, 54
  Nathan (Mar. 14, 1736-Dec. 31, 1820)
  m. Sept. 12, 1760 Eunice Mayo X,
  194; XXII, 73
  Stephen (Aug. 21, 1747-Feb. 14, 1838)
  m. .... Elizabeth West V, 89

WINSOR
  John (Mar. 22, 1723-Mar. 30, 1808)
  m. .... (1) Mary Smith XVI, 52,
  53
  Joshua (....-1679) m. ....
  ...... RI XVI, 52, 53

WINSTEAD
  Manley (Oct. 29, 1760-Dec. 26, 1846)
  m. c. 1777 ...... Trapp XXXI, 231,
  232
  Samuel (....-a. Nov. 16, 1726) m.
  .... VA XXXI, 231,
  232

WINSTON
  Anthony, II (Nov. 25, 1750-Dec. 20,
  1828) m. Mar. 11, 1776 Keziah Jones
  XXXI, 39; XXXIII, 324
  William (....-1702) m. ....
  ...... VA XXXI, 39; XXXIII, 324

WINTER
  John (1552-Apr. 1662) m. ....
  ...... MASS XXVII, 197
  Moses (Mar. 22, 1724-Apr. 22, 1799)
  m. Nov. 22, 1749 Keziah Cady
  XXVII, 197, 198

WISWALL, includes WISWELL
  Amasa (Apr. 3, 1762-....) m. Sept.
  28, 1787 Polly Heath XXXIII, 212,
  213; XXXIV, 11
  Ebenezer (Feb. 25, 1682-....) m.
  Nov. 30, 1721 Anna Capen MASS
  XXXIII, 212, 213
  Noah (Nov. 27, 1727-Aug. 10, 1813)
  m. Nov. 8, 1753 Hannah Hodges
  XXXIII, 212, 213; XXXIV, 11
  Thomas (....-Dec. 6, 1683) m. a.
  1633 Elizabeth ...... MASS
  XXXIV, 11

WISWELL, see WISWALL

WITBECK
  Jan Tomasse (....-p. 1696) m. ....

WOODBRIDGE, cont.
  XI, 7, 15; XIII, 49; XXXII, 21
  John (1613-Mar. 17, 1695) m. 1639
    Mercy Dudley MASS VI, 14; X,
    107, 286, 287, 288, 289; XI, 7, 15;
    XIII, 49; XV, 100; XXXII, 21
  Russell (May 8, 1719-Nov. 5, 1782)
    m. Jan. 14, 1741 Anna Olmstead
    XV, 100

WOODBURY
  John (1579-1641) m. .... (2) Agnes
    ...... MASS XVII, 80, 81; XVIII,
    114, 117; XXX, 78
  John (Sept. 26, 1749-Dec. 12, 1831)
    m. Oct. 17, 1770 (1) Mary Chase
    XVII, 80, 81
  Peter (May 20, 1736-Feb. 24, 1806)
    m. Jan. 18, 1759 ....
    XVIII, 117; XXX, 78
  Peter (May 28, 1738-Oct. 11, 1817)
    m. June 23, 1761 Elizabeth (Dodge)
    Rea XVIII, 114

WOODCOCK
  John (c. 1615-Jan. 20, 1700) m. ....
    (1) Sarah ...... MASS IV, 139,
    140
  Nathan (Jan. 9, 1737-May 17, 1817)
    m. .... Lavina Goodenow IV, 139,
    140

WOODFORD
  Joseph (1636-1701/10) m. .... Rebecca
    Newell CONN XVI, 73
  Joseph (Mar. 12, 1731/2-1822) m. 1738
    Eunice (Hart) Cowles XVI, 13, 14
  Thomas (....-Mar. 6, 1667) m. Mar.
    4, 1635 Mary Blott CONN XVI, 14
  William (Mar. 13, 1722-Mar. 26, 1803)
    m. Oct. 31, 1745 Susanna Garrett
    XVI, 73

WOODHULL
  John (Jan. 15, 1719-Jan. 3, 1794) m.
    Nov. 27, 1740 Elizabeth T. Smith
    XIII, 45; XXXIII, 188
  Josiah, Jr. (1733-Nov. 9, 1787) m.
    1759 Hannah Terry XXXII, 232, 233
  Richard (Sept. 13, 1620-Oct. 17,
    1691) m. .... Deborah Crewe NY
    XIII, 45; XXXII, 232, 233; XXXIII,
    188

WOODMAN
  Edward (Dec. 27, 1606-July 3, 1692)
    m. a. 1628 Joanna Bartlett MASS
    III, 5; XXXI, 97; XXXIII, 55, 56
  Joseph (Aug. 22, 1748-Sept. 28, 1807)
    m. Mar. 8, 1771 Esther (Whittemore)
    Hall III, 5

Joshua (Oct. 25, 1703-Nov. 4, 1778)
    m. c. 1735 Elizabeth Doe · XXXI, 97
  Joshua (Jan. 22, 1720-1800) m. May
    25, 1749 Alice Stimson XXXIII, 55,
    56

WOODRUFF
  Enos (1749/50-Dec. 5, 1821) m.
    1770/1 Charity Ogden XXII, 9,
    XXV, 82; XXX, 101
  John (1604-May 9, 1670) m. 1636 Ann
    Gosmer NJ XXII, 10; XXV, 82;
    XXVII, 74; XXX, 101
  John (Dec. 28, 1729-Sept. 22, 1799)
    m. Mar. 13, 1757 Hannah Lambert
    XXXIV, 111
  Mathew (c. 1633-Sept. 1682) m. ....
    Hannah ...... CONN XXXIV, 111
  Thomas (1734-Apr. 23, 1805) m. 1780
    Mary Tyson XXVII, 74
  Timothy (1716-Apr. 26, 1798) m. 1736
    Elizabeth Parsons XXV, 82; XXX,
    101

WOODS
  Ebenezer (Dec. 19, 1728-p. 1781) m.
    June 25, 1752 Eunice Boyden XX,
    77
  Henry (Sept. 4, 1733-Mar. 5, 1804)
    m. Apr. 13, 1756 Deborah Parker
    XI, 22
  Samuel (c. 1636-Jan. 1717/8) m.
    Sept. 28, 1659 Alice Rushton
    MASS XI, 22; XX, 77

WOODSON
  John (1586-Apr. 18, 1644) m. a.
    1619 Sara ...... VA XXIX, 267;
    XXX, 204, 245, 251
  John, Sr. (1696-....) m. Aug. 1731
    Mary Miller XXX, 204, 245, 251
  John, Jr. (1747-....) m. .... Joanna
    Booker XXX, 204, 245, 251
  Tucker (c. 1720-a. 1795) m. Oct. 14,
    1760 (2) Mary Netherland XXIX,
    267
  Wade Netherland (Jan. 16, 1763-Apr.
    8, 1847) m. Feb. 28, 1792 (1)
    Mary Harris XXIX, 267

WOODWARD
  Abel (Apr. 1, 1736-Dec. 31, 1820) m.
    Mar. 20, 1765 Lucy Atwood XI, 28
  Abner (Jan. 10, 1762-Jan. 28, 1840)
    m. May 19, 1795 Eunice Fuller XXI,
    28, 29
  Ambrose (Sept. 9, 1743-Mar. 25, 1828)
    m. Dec. 24, 1772 Rachel Lincoln
    XXXI, 41, 42
  Beza (July 16, 1745-Aug. 23, 1804) m.
    Feb. 5, 1772 Mary Wheelock XIV, 74

Elisha (Nov. 1, 1754-May 2, 1841) m. Feb. 22, 1778 Lucy Manson XXVI, 133

Henry (Mar. 22, 1607-Apr. 7, 1685) m. .... Elizabeth ...... MASS XI, 21; XIV, 74

Isaac, Jr. (Mar. 20, 1762-Mar. 24, 1855) m. .... Eunice ...... XXXIV, 242

Jason (July 19, 1753-July 15, 1821) m. June 20, 1782 Sarah Sumner XXI, 14, 15

John (July 11, 1712-May 25, 1791) m. Sept. 3, 1741 Mary Denison XXVI, 153, 154

Joseph (Jan. 21, 1725-July 8, 1814) m. May 19, 1748 Elizabeth Perkins XXI, 28, 29

Joseph (Nov. 4, 1737-May 31, 1812) m. Nov. 1760 Rebecca Martin XXX, 53

Nathaniel, Sr. (1589-p. 1673) m. .... (1) Margaret ...... MASS XXVI, 133; XXXI, 41

Peter (....-May 9, 1685) m. .... MASS XXVI, 153

Richard (Jan. 25, 1588/9-Feb. 16, 1665) m. c. 1618 Rose ...... MASS XXI, 14, 15, 28, 29; XXIX, 113; XXXIV, 242

Richard (1636-Jan. 8, 1706) m. .... Jane ...... PA XXX, 53

Samuel (Sept. 25, 1742-Dec. 2, 1824) m. Apr. 11, 1786 (2) Priscilla Jackson XXIX, 113

Stephen (June 16, 1758-Apr. 27, 1819) m. Jan. 20, 1780 Elizabeth Morris XXVI, 153, 154

WOODWORTH

Asa (Jan. 17, 1743/4-Mar. 16, 1817) m. Jan. 12, 1769 Sarah Ford XXII, 115

Ephraim (Sept. 22, 1732-July 25, 1825) m. 1754 Anna Moore XXXIII, 228

Gershom (Sept. 16, 1728-May 16, 1810) m. Nov. 24, 1749 Rosanna Evarts XIII, 25; XXXII, 91

Walter (....-1685) m. .... MASS XIII, 25; XXII, 115; XXXII, 91; XXXIII, 228

WOOLARD

John (c. 1712-Sept. 13, 1800) m. .... (1) Elizabeth Vines XXIX, 97

Richard (c. 1645-Feb. 4, 1707) m. .... (1) Ann ...... NC XXIX, 97

WOOLFOLK

John (Nov. 6, 1727-Jan. 18, 1816) m.

1750 Elizabeth Wigglesworth XXIV, 165

Richard (....-....) m. .... Elizabeth ...... VA XXIV, 165

WOOLFORD

Roger (....-1701) m. Mar. 1660/1 Mary Denwood MD XXXII, 173

Stevens (a. 1729-May 6, 1800) m. a. 1766 Elizabeth Whitely XXXII, 173

WOOLVERTON, see WOLVERTON

WOOSTER

Edward (1622-July 6, 1689) m. 1669 Tabitha Tomlinson CONN XX, 45, 46

Walter (July 7, 1745-July 21, 1829) m. Nov. 15, 1780 Ursula Beebe XX, 45, 46

WOOTEN

Shadrach (1739-Apr. 1812) m. c. 1762 (2) Elizabeth Allen XXXI, 265

Thomas (a. 1624-p. Mar. 15, 1669) m. .... Sarah (Jennings) Wood VA XXXI, 265

WORCHESTER

Jesse (Apr. 30, 1761-Jan. 20, 1834) m. .... Sarah Parker V, 93, 94, 100

Noah (Oct. 4, 1735-Aug. 13, 1817) m. Feb. 22, 1757 Lydia Taylor V, 93, 94, 100; XVI, 82, 83

Samuel (1635-Feb. 22, 1681) m. .... Elizabeth Parrot MASS V, 93, 94, 100

Thomas (1756-Mar. 18, 1822) m. c. 1783 Susannah ...... XXVIII, 145

William (Oct. 5, 1595-Oct. 28, 1662) m. .... Sarah ...... MASS V, 93, 94, 100; XVI, 83; XXVIII, 145

WORTHINGTON

Elias (Oct. 31, 1722-Sept. 23, 1811) m. Sept. 30, 1744 Rhoda Chamberlain XVI, 120, 121

Nicholas (....-Sept. 6, 1683) m. c. 1666 (1) Sara (Bunch) White CONN XVI, 121

WRIGHT

Daniel (Sept. 27, 1759-May 24, 1838) m. Jan. 24, 1782 Nancy Young XXVIII, 44, 47, 48; XXX, 235

Ebenezer (Apr. 11, 1756-Oct. 28, 1798) m. .... Martha Wellman IV, 136

Edward (....-Aug. 28, 1691) m. .... Elizabeth ...... MASS XXVI, 13

WRIGHT, cont.
  Henry (1732-Oct. 12, 1806) m. Jan.
    1753 Sarah Spalding XX, 153
  Jesse (1753-1827) m. .... Lydia
    Parker II, 54
  John (....-a. May 4, 1695) m. ....
    Elizabeth Lewger (Lugar) MD
    XXXI, 73
  John (c. 1601-June 21, 1688) m.
    .... Priscilla ...... MASS II,
    54; XX, 153; XXIII, 61
  John (1728-Oct. 30, 1789) m. c. 1750
    Ann Williams XXVIII, 44, 47, 48;
    XXIX, 381; XXX, 165
  John Lugar (....-a. Aug. 7, 1794) m.
    .... Margaret ...... XXXI, 73
  Joseph (Apr. 10, 1707-....) m. ....
    Ruth Sawyer XXIII, 61
  Joseph, Jr. (Nov. 2, 1746-Dec. 17,
    1803) m. May 25, 1774 Martha
    Eveleth XXIII, 61
  Josiah (Apr. 9, 1752-Jan. 2, 1817)
    m. 1785 Susannah Pratt XXX, 213,
    214; XXXII, 61, 74
  Moses (Jan. 10, 1727-p. 1783) m.
    .... Hannah Knight IV, 136
  Obediah (bpt. Feb. 24, 1740-Nov. 27,
    1815) m. .... Sarah Adams XXIII,
    22
  Peter (....-p. Dec. 13, 1660) m.
    .... Alice ...... MASS, NY XXIII,
    22
  Richard (1633-p. Aug. 16, 1663) m.
    c. Mar. 1656/7 Ann Mottrom VA
    XXVIII, 44, 47, 48; XXIX, 381;
    XXX, 165, 235
  Samuel (1614-Oct. 17, 1665) m. ....
    Margaret ...... MASS IV, 136;
    XXX, 213, 214; XXXII, 61, 74
  Stephen (May 24, 1764-Feb. 16, 1857)
    m. Apr. 5, 1787 Sarah Prescott
    XXVI, 13

WYATT, includes WIATT
  Edward (1619-1690) m. 1644 Jane
    Conquest VA XV, 127; XVI, 95, 96
  Thomas (....-Apr. 3, 1704) m. ....
    Judith ...... MD XXX, 111
  Thomas (May 6, 1755-....) m. Sept.
    30, 1778 Ann North XXX, 111
  William (1742-1815) m. 1766 Frances
    Newton XV, 127; XVI, 95, 96

WYCKOFF, see WIKOFF

WYETH
  Ebenezer, Jr. (Apr. 8, 1727-Aug. 4,
    1789) m. Nov. 5, 1751 Mary Winship
    XXXI, 314
  Nicholas (1595-July 19, 1680) m. Jan.
    1647 Rebecca Parks MASS XXXI, 314

WYKOFF, see WIKOFF

WYMAN
  Francis (Feb. 24, 1619-Nov. 30,
    1699) m. Oct. 20, 1650 (2) Abigail
    Reed MASS XXXII, 151
  Hezekiah (Aug. 5, 1720-July 1779) m.
    Feb. 20, 1745 Sarah Reed XXV, 228
  John (Feb. 3, 1621-May 9, 1684) m.
    Nov. 5, 1644 Sarah Nutt MASS XXV,
    228
  Samuel, III (June 13, 1731-May 17,
    1782) m. Feb. 1, 1759 (2) Mary
    (Hosmer) Merriam XXXII, 151

WYNES, see WINES

WYNKOOP
  Cornelius (....-c. 1676) m. ....
    Maria Janse Langendyck NY XXII,
    77
  Evert (Sept. 8, 1743-Apr. 6, 1830)
    m. May 30, 1765 Aeltje Meyer XXII,
    77

WYNN, see WINN

WYNNE, see WINN

YALE
  Elisha (Aug. 29, 1742-Apr. 1, 1825)
    m. Sept. 16, 1761 Rebecca North
    XVII, 147, 148
  Josiah (June 19, 1752-May 13, 1822)
    m. Sept. 26, 1776 Ruth Tracy IX,
    26; XXII, 144
  Nathaniel (Jan. 5, 1720-c. 1800) m.
    .... Abigail G. Pratt XVI, 66, 67
  Thomas (1616-Mar. 27, 1683) m. 1645
    Mary Turner CONN IX, 26; XVI, 66;
    XVII, 147, 148; XXII, 144

YANCEY
  James (....-....) m. 1800 Zelpah
    Johnson XV, 49
  John (....-....) m. .... Abigail
    Hicks VA XV, 49

YARD
  Benjamin (July 23, 1714-1808) m.
    .... Ann Pierson XVI, 8
  William (a. 1687-Dec. 8, 1744) m.
    .... Mary Peace PA, NJ XVI, 8

YARNALL
  John (Feb. 8, 1739-Sept. 24, 1799)
    m. Feb. 3, 1774 Elizabeth Newlin
    XXVII, 55
  Philip (....-c. 1734) m. 1694

Dorothy Baker   PA   XXVII, 55

YATES, includes YEATES
  George, I (....-a. Nov. 11, 1691) m.
    p. May 4, 1671 Mary Wells Stockett
    MD   XXVII, 216, 218, 220; XXXII,
    268; XXXIII, 81, 82, 182; XXXIV,
    171
  George, IV (1728-a. Dec. 11, 1777)
    m. c. 1750 Frances Lewis XXVII,
    218, 220; XXXII, 268; XXXIII, 81,
    82, 182; XXXIV, 171
  Joshua (Jan. 28, 1741-May 6, 1831)
    m. c. 1762 Nancy Boilston XXVII,
    216

YEATES, see YATES

YE DUITCHER, see DUTCHER

YEOMANS
  Edward (bpt. Feb. 23, 1634-....) m.
    Dec. 6, 1652 Mary Button MASS
    XX, 134; XXIX, 259
  Edward (1758-Aug. 5, 1840) m. Feb.
    11, 1790 Marcy Clark XX, 134
  Elijah (Sept. 20, 1751-Apr. 7, 1801)
    m. Dec. 2, 1778 Lydia Simonds
    XXIX, 259

YONGE, see YOUNG

YOUNG, includes YONGE
  John (1731/2-July 11, 1798) m. ....
    (2) Sarah Martin XXXIII, 45, 72

Jonas (1745-c. 1800) m. .... Prudence
  Riggs XII, 90
Laurence (....-p. Apr. 1687) m. ....
  .... VA XXXIII, 45, 72
Robert (1663-Nov. 7, 1726) m. ....
  Sara Baldwin NJ XII, 90
Thomas (Aug. 10, 1579-p. 1642) m.
  1619 Mary Strachey VA XIX, 62;
  XXXII, 283
Thomas (1712-1780) m. 1734 Ann
  Potter XIX, 62
Thomas Kent (a. 1746-p. Mar. 10,
  1813) m. 1765 Anne Potter XXXII,
  283

YOUNGS, includes YONGES
  Eli (Oct. 1, 1752-Aug. 15, 1843) m.
    Dec. 5, 1776 Cleopatra Topping
    XXVII, 166, 167; XXX, 39
  James (Jan. 22, 1752/3-Sept. 20,
    1783) m. .... (1) Elizabeth Low-
    rain XIV, 35
  John (1598-Feb. 1671/2) m. .... (1)
    Joan Harrington; .... (3) Mary
    (Warren) Gardiner NY III, 62;
    XII, 18, 19; XIV, 35
  John (bpt. Apr. 10, 1623-Apr. 12,
    1697) m. c. 1653 (1) Mary Gardi-
    ner NY III, 62
  Joseph (c. 1605-p. Nov. 1656) m.
    Feb. 5, 1632 Margaret Warren MASS
    XXVII, 167; XXX, 39
  Thomas (1719-Feb. 19, 1793) m. June
    1, 1746 Rhoda Budd III, 62; XII,
    18